*Protestant Poems and*
*Seventeenth-Century Religious Lyric*

BARBARA KIEFER LEWALSKI

# Protestant Poetics
## and the
## Seventeenth-Century
## Religious Lyric

Princeton University Press

*Princeton, New Jersey*

Copyright © 1979 by Princeton University Press

Published by Princeton University Press, Princeton, New Jersey
In the United Kingdom: Princeton University Press, Guildford, Surrey

All Rights Reserved

Library of Congress Cataloging in Publication Data will be
found on the last printed page of this book

Publication of this book has been aided by a grant from The
Andrew W. Mellon Foundation

This book has been composed in Linotype Janson
Clothbound editions of Princeton University Press books
are printed on acid-free paper, and binding materials are
chosen for strength and durability.

Printed in the United States of America by
Princeton University Press, Princeton, New Jersey

ISBN 0-691-06395-8
ISBN 0-691-01415-9 (pbk.)

First Princeton Paperback printing, 1984

TO MY MOTHER

IN MEMORY OF MY FATHER

# Table of Contents

# Foreword

This study explores the thesis that the spectacular flowering of English religious lyric poetry in the seventeenth century occurred in response to a new and powerful stimulus to the imagination—the pervasive Protestant emphasis upon the Bible as a book, as God's Word encapsulated in human words and in the linguistic features of a variety of texts. Viewed in this light, as a book requiring philological and literary analysis, the Bible became normative for poetic art as well as for spiritual truth. The argument proceeds by extrapolating from contemporary Protestant materials a substantial and complex poetics of the religious lyric, and examining in some detail the precepts it holds forth—regarding religious lyric genres, figurative language, symbolism, modes of meditation and self-analysis, ways of perceiving and portraying the vacillations of the spiritual life, ways of conceiving the poetic persona, and theories about rendering divine truth in human art. These contexts and concepts have some importance for intellectual history, but I survey them for a literary purpose, to define the Protestant poetics variously reflected in the major religious lyric poets of the century— Donne, Herbert, Vaughan, Traherne, and Edward Taylor. Combining literary history and criticism, this book undertakes to describe the course taken throughout the century by the distinctive literary current this poetics produced, and also to illuminate the individual poets work by considering what and how each one drew from the common stream.

The argument is revisionist in proposing that the major seventeenth-century religious lyrists owe more to contemporary, English, and Protestant influences than to Counter Reformation, continental, and medieval Catholic resources. It is revisionist also in asserting that these poets and most of their contemporaries shared a broad Protestant consensus in regard to doctrine and the spiritual life, grounded upon belief in the absolute priority and centrality of scripture and upon paradigms afforded by the Pauline epistles, a consensus overarching the Anglican-Puritan divide and having great significance for religious poetry. I do not wish to propose a new "school" or a new terminology for seventeenth-century poetry to replace the familiar labels—metaphysical, meditative, baroque, Augustinian. But this study does look beyond those familiar and very elastic categories to a more precise definition of aesthetic principles and practices, and in so doing recognizes a new configuration in seventeenth-century lyric poetry.

(ix)

*A book long in the making incurs many debts, some of which will inevitably be overlooked in any attempted enumeration. Of first importance are long-standing intellectual debts to seminal studies by Ernst R. Curtius, Erich Auerbach, Lily B. Campbell, Louis L. Martz, Joseph A. Mazzeo, Rosemond Tuve, and Rosalie Colie, among others. In its evolution this book has profited immensely from the incisive questions and comments of audiences who have heard some part of its argument—at MLA, the Academy of Literary Studies, the International Association of University Professors of English, the Clark Library, Cornell University, Bryn Mawr College, the Universities of Wisconsin, Oslo, and Trondheim, and at Renaissance Colloquia sponsored by the New England Renaissance Society, Brown University, and the University of Massachusetts. It has also benefited greatly from the criticism and contributions of my fellow participants in the Princeton seminar on literary uses of typology (1974) organized by Earl Miner, and from lively discussions with participants and my co-director, Mason I. Lowance, Jr., in an NEH summer seminar at Brown on the Puritan imagination (1976). Occasional references in the notes cannot properly record the stimulation and insights I owe to several former doctoral students whose published and unpublished research has explored related issues—Heather Asals, Elizabeth Jefferis Bartlett, Clark Chalifour, Jeannie De Brun Duffy, Ellen Goodman, Alan Kimbrough, Mary Ann Cale McGuire, Jason Rosenblatt, James Scanlon, Winfried and Louise Schleiner, David Watters, Steven Zwicker. Elizabeth Kirk, Mason Lowance, Ellen Goodman, and Susanne Woods saw the manuscript in one or another of its versions and raised dozens of helpful issues and questions. Joseph A. Wittreich and Mary Ann Radzinowicz read the book for the Press with meticulous care, offering penetrating criticism, invaluable suggestions for improvement, and much-too-generous praise. Obviously, blame for what faults remain should fall squarely upon my own head.*

*Research for this study was partially supported by a National Endowment for the Humanities Senior Fellowship in 1974-75, and by special research funds from Brown together with a research leave in 1978. The librarians and staff of the British Library, the Bodleian Library, the Folger Shakespeare Library, the Houghton and Widener Libraries of Harvard University, the Beinecke Library, and the John Hay, John Carter Brown, and Rockefeller Libraries of Brown University were most helpful with research materials. Some portions of chapter four, in an earlier formulation, were incorporated in essay contributions to* Illustrious Evidence, *ed. Earl Miner (University of California Press, 1975), and* Literary Uses of Typology from the Late

Middle Ages to the Present, *ed. Earl Miner (Princeton University Press, 1977); some portions of chapter six were incorporated in "Emblems and the Religious Lyric: George Herbert and Protestant Emblematics," HSL, 6 (1978).* I want to thank the British Library for supplying and permitting reproduction of all the emblems in this volume with the exception of Figures 8 and 10, kindly supplied to me by the Bibliothèque Nationale. Meg Lota Teagarden, Rebecca Fullerton, and Deborah Courville helped at various times as research assistants; Deborah Courville and Shirley Rodrigues typed the manuscript. Toni Oliviero brought her unique combination of research and editorial skills to bear upon the manuscript in its final stages and also prepared the index. Mrs. Arthur Sherwood of Princeton University Press gave the book her intelligent and painstaking editorial attention throughout, and its author her constant support.

My deepest thanks, as always, go to my husband, Kenneth F. Lewalski, for intellectual stimulation and comradeship in all the offices of life, to my son David for his infectious good humor and unfailing good nature, and to both for bearing with the book's constant presence and its author's occasional absence during the years of its writing. The book is dedicated to my mother, Vivo K. Delo, and to the memory of my father, John P. Kiefer.

*Barbara Kiefer Lewalski*
*Brown University*

# List of Abbreviations

| | |
|---|---|
| *AL* | *American Literature* |
| ANCL | Ante-Nicene Christian Library, ed. Alexander Roberts and James Donaldson, 24 vols. (Edinburgh, 1867-1872) |
| *AQ* | *American Quarterly* |
| *ArlQ* | *Arlington Quarterly* |
| *AUMLA* | *Journal of the Australasian Universities Language and Literature Association* |
| *EAL* | *Early American Literature* |
| *EIC* | *Essays in Criticism* (Oxford) |
| *ELH* | *Journal of English Literary History* |
| *ELR* | *English Literary Renaissance* |
| *ES* | *English Studies* |
| *HLQ* | *Huntington Library Quarterly* |
| *JEGP* | *Journal of English and Germanic Philology* |
| *JWCI* | *Journal of the Warburg and Courtauld Institute* |
| *MLR* | *Modern Language Review* |
| *MP* | *Modern Philology* |
| *NEQ* | *New England Quarterly* |
| Pat. Lat. | *Patrologiae Cursus Completus . . . Series Latina*, ed. J.-P. Migne, 221 vols. (Paris, 1844-1864) |
| Pat. Graec. | *Patrologiae Cursus Completus . . . Series Graeca*, ed. J.-P. Migne, 162 vols. (Paris, 1857-1912) |
| *PBSA* | *Papers of the Bibliographical Society of America* |
| *PMLA* | *Publications of the Modern Language Association of America* |
| *PQ* | *Philological Quarterly* (Iowa City) |
| *RES* | *Review of English Studies* |
| *RN* | *Renaissance News* (*Renaissance Quarterly*) |
| *SEL* | *Studies in English Literature, 1500-1900* |
| *SP* | *Studies in Philology* |
| *SRen* | *Studies in the Renaissance* |
| *TLS* | *Times Literary Supplement* |

# List of Emblems

Figures may be found following page 210.

*Protestant Poetics and the*
*Seventeenth-Century Religious Lyric*

## "Is there in truth no beautie?": Protestant Poetics and the Protestant Paradigm of Salvation

M ost sixteenth- and seventeenth-century poets and theorists of poetry would have met Herbert's rhetorical question from "Jordan I" by affirming as positively as he could wish that truth is indeed the proper subject of poetry, that beauty and truth are finally one. But the key terms of that question may carry diverse meanings, reflecting quite different assumptions as to just how poetry conveys truth. One prominent strain of Renaissance theory and poetic practice, described in recent studies of Renaissance poetics by John M. Steadman, Michael Murrin, Don Cameron Allen, and S. K. Heninger, presents the poet as maker of fictions which allegorically conceal and reveal profoundest philosophic truths; or as the inspired shaper of myths and symbols which shadow forth cosmic truth and divine revelation; or, in Sidney's terms, as the creator of a golden world which embodies and mediates a truer vision of the real than can nature's brazen world.[1] But it is just these notions of poetry as pointing by means of fictions to philosophical truth, or shadowy revelation, or the platonic ideas, that Herbert eschews in "Jordan I":

> Who sayes that fictions onely and false hair
> Become a verse? Is there in truth no beautie?
> Is all good structure in a winding stair?
> May no lines passe, except they do their dutie
>     Not to a true, but painted chair?
>
> Is it no verse, except enchanted groves
> And sudden arbours shadow course-spunne lines?
> Must purling streams refresh a lovers loves?
> Must all be vail'd, while he that reades, divines,
>     Catching the sense at two removes?

> Shepherds are honest people; let them sing:
> Riddle who list, for me, and pull for Prime:
> I envie no mans nightingale or spring;
> Nor let them punish me with losse of rime,
>    Who plainly say, *My God, My King*.[2]

The poetics implied in the final line of Herbert's poem proposes instead a direct recourse to the Bible as repository of truth: the speaker calls upon biblical models and biblical poetic resources (the quotation from Psalm 145:1), and associates himself straightforwardly with the Psalmist in heartfelt and uncontrived (plain) utterance.

The biblical poetics which Herbert here partly articulates and which (I shall argue) several other notable Protestant poets of his period follow, is parallel to, but at the same time distinct from, another kind of "true" poetry, the biblical prophetic mode various critics (M. H. Abrams, Angus Fletcher, Joseph A. Wittreich, William Kerrigan, Northrop Frye, Murray Roston) have found relevant to the major poetry of Spenser, Milton, and a number of the Romantics.[3] Prophecy, though often directed to the mind and heart, is a public mode, concerned to mediate through testimony, archetypal symbol, and story the prophet's inspired visions of transcendent reality or of apocalyptic transformations, present or future. The great biblical models are the Old Testament prophets (Isaiah, Daniel, Ezekiel), and especially the Book of Revelation, which is said to subsume them all. Religious lyric, though often didactic in intention or effect, is a private mode, concerned to discover and express the various and vacillating spiritual conditions and emotions the soul experiences in meditation, prayer, and praise. The great biblical model is the Psalmist with his anguished cries *de profundis*, and his soaring *te deums* of praise.

I do not intend to maintain, with Northrop Frye, that the Bible is in fact the comprehensive storehouse and source of western literary genres, archetypes, and forms,[4] but will only observe that some such assumption seems to inform a good deal of the major poetry, epic and lyric, of the sixteenth and seventeenth centuries. I do assert that, despite the impact of biblical language upon the eighteenth-century sublime, and of the discovery of the true principles of Hebrew versification upon the Romantic poets' perception and use of the Bible as poetic model, the articulation and practice of a fully-developed theory of biblical aesthetics is not a pre-Romantic or Romantic but a Renaissance/seventeenth-century phenomenon.[5] Specifically, my concern here is with the biblical, Protestant poetics informing a. major strain of English seventeenth-century religious lyric: the chief characteristics of that poetics can, I suggest, be clearly discerned, and the history of its literary impact traced with some precision—from the quickening response of Donne to the developing theory, to the exhaustion of this particular tradition in the American colonial poet Edward Taylor.

This study, then, will argue two propositions. First, that an extensive and widely accessible body of literary theory, chiefly pertaining to the Bible and to fundamental Protestant assumptions about the spiritual life and about art, can be extrapolated from such sixteenth- and seventeenth-century materials as biblical commentaries, rhetorical handbooks, poetic paraphrases of scripture, emblem books, manuals on meditation and preaching. Second, that such theory, and the biblical models it identified, helped to shape contemporary attitudes about religious poetry, contributing directly to the remarkable flowering of the religious lyric in the seventeenth century, and especially to that major strain represented by Donne, Herbert, Vaughan, Traherne, and Taylor. The argument should begin with some justification for studying these particular materials and poets in terms of a biblical and Protestant aesthetics.

My contention that the poetics of much seventeenth-century religious lyric derives primarily from Protestant assumptions about the poetry of the Bible and the nature of the spiritual life calls for some adjustment of scholarly directions. Several basic studies have pressed claims for medieval and Counter Reformation influences upon these poets: Louis L. Martz has located the dominant influence in Ignatian and Augustinian meditative traditions; Patrick Grant has specified the Augustinianism of the medieval Franciscans (modified by certain countervailing Renaissance concepts) as the primary intellectual context.[6] By contrast, Malcolm M. Ross finds this poetry to be Protestant and aesthetically the worse for it, in that Protestantism undermined incarnational eucharistic symbolism, fragmented the medieval analogical universe, and so brought about the attenuation of analogical poetic symbolism—flattening symbol into metaphor or simile.[7] But this is surely a curiously blinkered approach to some of the finest religious lyric in the literature.

I suggest rather that the primary poetic influences upon the major devotional poets of the century—Donne, Herbert, Vaughan, Traherne, Taylor—are contemporary, English, and Protestant, and that the energy and power we respond to in much of this poetry has its basis in the resources of biblical genre, language, and symbolism, the analysis of spiritual states, and the tensions over the relation of art and truth which were brought into new prominence by the Reformation. Of course Roman Catholic theology, spirituality, and aesthetics were far from monolithic, even after Trent, and we can find precedents and analogues for some elements of Protestant biblicism, theology, spirituality, and aesthetics in the Augustinian tradition, the nominalists, Erasmus, the *Devotio Moderna* movement, the Jansenists, and even in the scholastic and Tridentine mainstream. Nevertheless, these common Christian elements took on distinctive form within the total frame of English Protestantism, and that contemporary milieu is the immediate source of a new Protestant poetics. The poets described here do not derive their principal strength from the tag-ends of medieval or Counter Reformation spirituality and symbolism which they sometimes exhibit, but rather from their active engagement with new modes of religious thought and their eager experimentation with new resources for religious poetry.

Some modification is in order also in regard to theories relating this poetry to an "Augustinian" poetics derived primarily from the *De Doctrina Christiana*.[8] According to J. A. Mazzeo's illuminating essay, Augustinian poetics presupposes a symbolic universe in which the movement of thought is Platonic—"through the words to the realities themselves, from the temporal realities to the eternal realities, from talk to silence, and from discourse to vision."[9] Though Mazzeo does not draw the inference, it seems clear that the Augustinian position must finally depress the significance of poetry along with all arts of human discourse, since, though words are important as signs, truth is conveyed not by words but by revelation and intuition. In describing Herbert's poetics, both Joseph H. Summers and Arnold S. Stein have appealed to Augustine's directive that the preacher seek wisdom and truth rather than eloquence, and Stanley E. Fish has pressed hard the implications of the Augustinian poetics in relation to Donne's sermons, Herbert's poetry, and various prose works of the seventeenth century.[10] Fish argues that the seventeenth-century writers in the Augustinian tradition ultimately renounce human art, and enact this renunciation by undermining the expected logical and rhetorical development of their works—a strategy calculated to demonstrate the incapacity of human art to present divine truth, and to display the need for utter dependence upon God to gain an intuition of truth.

We should, however, approach Augustinian aesthetics not in medieval but in Reformation terms, taking account of the important new factor introduced by the Reformation—an overwhelming emphasis on the written word as the embodiment of divine truth. In this milieu the Christian poet is led to relate his work not to ineffable and intuited divine revelation, but rather to its written formulation in scripture. The Bible affords him a literary model which he can imitate in such literary matters as genre, language, and symbolism, confident that in this model at least the difficult problems of art and truth are perfectly resolved. My proposition is, then, that far from eschewing aesthetics for a rhetoric of silence or a deliberate anti-aesthetic strategy, these poets committed themselves to forging and employing a Protestant poetics, grounded upon scripture, for the making of Protestant devotional lyrics.

## A. BIBLICAL POETICS AND THE EMERGENCE OF A PROTESTANT AESTHETICS

Ernst Curtius has provided both the term "biblical poetics" and some consideration of the early history of the concept in the Patristic period and the Middle Ages.[11] In essence the concept affirms the poetry of the Bible to be analogous to, and usually prior and superior to, pagan poetry. Over the centuries this concept was invoked, variously, to defend the literary quality of the Bible as against pagan literature, to defend the practice of poetry among Christians by appeal to biblical authority, and to propose the Bible as (in certain respects) a model for Christian poets. In this vein the patristic Christian poet Sedulius identified David the Psalmist as the true model for Christian poets, and the mid-seventeenth-century Protestant commentator Edward Leigh asserted that "The Book of the *Psalms, Job*, and the *Songs of Moses*, are the only patern of true Poesie."[12] Early and late, the chief categories for describing the poetic nature of scripture were genre, figurative language, and symbolic mode (typology).

The *loci classici* for discussions of genre in the Bible are provided by Jerome and Isidore of Seville. Basing his comparisons chiefly upon the supposed metrical similarities of biblical and classical poetry, Jerome declared that the Book of Job was written in hexameter (epic) verse, and that the Psalms, in various lyric meters, invite comparison with the great classical lyrics.[13] Isidore greatly expanded the list of literary and non-literary kinds to be found in the Bible, and indeed asserted their biblical origin: Moses first wrote hexameter verse in Deuteronomy 32, "long before Pherecydes and Homer"; hymns in praise of God were first composed by David; the first epithalamium was Solomon's; the inventor of threnody was Jeremiah and only later Simonides among the Greeks; Isaiah first wrote rhetorical prose; the first historian was Moses.[14]

The poetic nature of the Bible, or at least of certain portions of it, was also urged on the basis of figurative language—the presence of the recognized rhetorical and poetic figures and tropes. Cassiodorus discovered over one hundred and twenty rhetorical figures in the Psalms alone, and both he and the Venerable Bede claimed the prior appearance in scripture of all the figures of language and thought.[15] The claim that the Bible is "strewn with figures of speech" was reaffirmed by Charlemagne in outlining his program for the reform of studies, and much later by Petrarch in arguing the harmony of poetry and theology: "When Christ is called now a 'lion,' and now a 'lamb,' and now a 'worm'—what is that if not poetic?"[16]

Perhaps the most important feature identifying the Bible as poetry was its presumed symbolic mode. The basic medieval formula, enunciated by Augustine and repeated constantly, recognized a literal or historical meaning of scripture residing in the signification of the words, and, in addition, a spiritual meaning whereby the things or events signified by the words point beyond themselves to other things or events.[17] Aquinas' classic account of the so-called four-fold method of exegesis recognized in addition to the literal meaning three spiritual senses: allegorical or typological, tropological or moral, and anagogical.[18] The method is illustrated by Dante's famous reading of Psalm 114, on the Exodus theme:

> If we consider the letter alone, the thing signified to us is the going out of the children of Israel from Egypt in the time of Moses; if the allegory, our redemption through Christ is signified; if the moral sense, the conversion of the soul from the sorrow and misery of sin to a state of grace is signified; if the anagogical, the passing of the sanctified soul from the bondage of the corruption of this world to the liberty of everlasting glory.[19]

Dante's discussion of the *Commedia* in these terms provides the most notable medieval example of a poet taking the symbolic mode of scripture as a model for his own religious poetry.

My contention is that the new focus on scripture occasioned by the Protestant Reformation promoted in sixteenth- and seventeenth-century England a specifically biblical poetics, which revived and further developed these ancient assumptions under the impetus of Protestant theology and the new literary and philological interests of the period. I suggest further that this biblical poetics is itself the most important component of an emerging Protestant aesthetics.

A pioneering study by Lily B. Campbell has pointed to the multiplication in sixteenth-century England of verse translations, metaphrases, and poetic versions of the so-called poetic parts of the Bible— Psalms, the Song of Songs, Isaiah, Lamentations, Proverbs, the Book of Job—and also the widespread use of the stories of Abraham, Moses,

Noah, David, Judith, and Job as subject matter for narrative or "epic" poems and for religious drama.[20] On the theoretical side, Protestant Englishmen of the period testified in some numbers to the need to create a biblically inspired substitute for the supposedly licentious or scandalous or worldly poetry of their contemporaries, rallying to the standard of Guillaume de Salluste Du Bartas' new muse for Christian poetry—the erstwhile muse of Astronomy, Urania.[21] In a dream-vision poem, Du Bartas recounted Urania's visit to him, urging him to re-claim for God the noble gift of poetry which had originated in the Bible, but was then perverted to idolatrous and immoral uses. The poem was translated into English by King James I (1585) and Joshua Sylvester (1605); and Urania's arguments, or dream-visions modeled upon that of Du Bartas, are recounted in the prefaces to several con-temporary religious poems.[22] Urania's arguments for the writing of Christian poetry draw upon the ancient precepts of biblical poetics, and these precepts were marshalled for similar purposes by Sidney, Puttenham, Lodge, Quarles, Vaughan, Milton, and many others.

In a series of ground-breaking articles Israel Baroway has investi-gated the patristic sources and Renaissance development of certain of these concepts—the notion of the "Hebrew hexameter" for example, and of the metrics of the Psalms.[23] Other literary scholars have ex-plored the impact of biblical poetics theories upon specific poets and genres in the period—e.g., the effect of Protestant attitudes toward the Old Testament upon the choice and treatment of biblical materials in the drama, or the influence of Hebraic biblical rhythms and dialogic modes upon the Metaphysical poets, several prose writers, and espe-cially Milton.[24] In particular, several Miltonists have explored Milton's major poems with reference to the Exodus "epic," the Mosaic prophetic voice, the Jobean brief epic, and the model of tragedy or prophecy in the Apocalypse.[25] It is not at all surprising that Milton's poetry has given rise to some of the most extended and suggestive inquiries into biblical poetics, since he was himself a forthright exponent of the the-ory, making frequent comparisons between biblical and classical forms and implying, if not overtly maintaining, the influence of biblical models upon his own poetry. The most explicit passage is the familiar one from *The Reason of Church Government*:

Time servs not now, and perhaps I might seem too profuse to give any certain account of what the mind at home in the spacious cir-cuits of her musing hath liberty to propose to her self, though of highest hope, and hardest attempting, whether that Epick form whereof the two poems of *Homer*, and those other two of *Virgil* and *Tasso* are a diffuse, and the book of *Job* a brief model: . . . Or whether those Dramatick constitutions, wherein *Sophocles* and *Euripides* raigne shall be found more doctrinal and exemplary to a Nation, the Scripture also affords us a divine pastoral Drama in the Song of *Salomon* consisting of two persons and a double *Chorus*, as *Origen* rightly judges. And the Apocalyps of Saint *John* is the majestick image of a high and stately Tragedy, shutting up and intermingling her solemn Scenes and Acts with a sevenfold *Chorus* of halleluja's and harping symphonies: and this my opinion the grave autority of *Pareus* commenting that booke is sufficient to confirm. Or if occasion shall lead to imitat those magnifick Odes and Hymns wherein *Pindarus* and *Callimachus* are in most things worthy, some others in their frame judicious, in their matter most an end faulty: But those frequent songs throughout the law and prophets beyond all these, not in their divine argument alone, but in the very critical art of composition may be easily made appear over all the kinds of Lyrick poesy, to be incomparable.[26]

Interestingly enough, despite Milton's large claims for the lyric poetry of scripture, the contribution of biblical poetics theory to seventeenth-century devotional poetry has not been much explored. To be sure, the presence of biblical allusion, structure, and style in some of these poems has been noted, as well as the special influence of the Psalms and Psalm commentary upon them.[27] But we need to know much more about assumptions current in the Renaissance regarding the genres, figurative language, symbolism, and other poetic elements in scripture, to determine the full impact of such assumptions upon Protestant poets attempting a serious but subtle and artful use of the biblical tradition in their own religious lyric.

In addition to the theory of biblical poetics, several popular genres of religious writing also contributed to the development of a Protestant aesthetics of the religious lyric. These genres—meditation, emblem literature, arts of preaching, and minor devotional poetry—were transformed in the sixteenth and seventeenth centuries by the emergence of characteristically Protestant forms reflecting the new biblical emphasis, the Protestant paradigm of the Christian life, and Protestant ideas regarding the use of art in the presentation of sacred truth.

The very extensive contemporary literature on meditation is clearly important for the poets studied here: three of them (Donne, Vaughan, Traherne) produced their own manuals of meditation, and a fourth, Edward Taylor, labelled his poems "Preparatory Meditations."[28] I shall argue, however, that the primary influence comes not from the

Ignatian and Augustinian modes so thoroughly studied by Martz, but rather from the several emerging Protestant kinds—deliberate meditation on scripture texts, meditation on the creatures, occasional meditation, meditation on personal experience, heavenly meditation.

Emblem books also contributed to contemporary theories about poetic language and symbolism in the seventeenth century. As several pioneering studies have shown,[29] the emblem manner generally, as well as individual emblems, influenced the structure and imagery of particular poems and collections of poems. But, although religious emblem books have been regarded as virtually a Jesuit preserve, I shall urge the special significance for the poets here studied of the numerous Protestant books of moral and sacred emblems, both revisions of Jesuit originals and new collections. These emblem sequences often provide close and suggestive analogues for the ways in which the Protestant poets render biblical tropes, allegorical images, nature symbols, and the course of the Christian life.

Contemporary Protestant *ars praedicandi*, and also certain poetic precedents, afford other relevant contexts. The questions, posed most insistently by George Herbert but important to all the major Protestant poets, as to what kind of art may be used in presenting sacred subject matter and as to how sinful, fallen man may write of divine truth, were explored in greater depth in sixteenth- and seventeenth-century Protestant debates about the framing of sermons than anywhere else. Moreover, these treatises often addressed such specifically literary issues as levels of style in relation to subject, plainness or ornateness of language, and the uses of simile and metaphor. Finally, major seventeenth-century poets writing out of an emerging Protestant aesthetics had to engage the question of how a poet using biblical materials and models can find his own artistic stance and release his own poetic voice through these materials. For this issue, other poets provide a useful context: the poets of the Bible, about whom some theory had evolved concerning the relation of their own experiences, conceptions, and artistry to divine inspiration; and the experiments with poetic personae undertaken by predecessors and contemporaries, upon which better poets could build.

I have not attempted to treat the liturgy as an independent context for this poetry, because it is often not possible or profitable to distinguish between general biblical influences conveyed through private reading, study, sermons, and the like, and biblical influence conveyed through the liturgy.[30] Cranmer's preface to the Book of Common Prayer proclaims that the basic principle of that liturgy is the restoration of the Word of God to the central place in Christian worship:

"vayne and superstytious" extra-biblical material from the inherited liturgy is deleted, and scripture readings are expanded from selected verses to entire chapters and passages. The order of services calls for the Psalter to be read through once each month, the Old Testament once a year (except for portions of certain books thought not to be edifying), and the New Testament three times a year (except for the Apocalypse, from which only chapters 1 and 22 were assigned).[31] Moreover, the fact that most parishes celebrated Holy Communion only a few times a year meant that the liturgical experience for most worshipers most of the time centered upon the extensive scripture readings which chiefly comprise the services for Morning Prayer, the Ante-Communion, and Evening Prayer, together with a sermon or homily.[32] Puritan worship focused even more exclusively upon the Bible for readings and sermon texts. Such constant communal reading and hearing was surely a major means by which poets became conscious of the poetic elements of scripture, and of the models it might present for Christian lyric poetry.

A word is now in order about the selection of these five poets—Donne, Herbert, Vaughan, Traherne, and Taylor—as the primary exemplars of a Protestant aesthetics of the religious lyric, constituting a distinct strain or "school." Readers may find something odd in the inclusion of Donne or Traherne among the exponents of a Protestant aesthetics, and may well protest certain omissions. I hasten to confess that of course Milton and Marvell belong in this company: they were excluded only because they have written very few (though very great) poems specifically in the genre of the devotional lyric,[33] and I am concerned here with poets for whom this form is a major vehicle of poetic expression. Herrick, despite some influences from biblical and Protestant materials, does not seem to belong here, for he does not scrutinize his soul and his art in the serious terms the Protestant aesthetics demands. Crashaw writes out of a very different aesthetics emanating from Trent and the continental Counter Reformation, which stresses sensory stimulation and church ritual (rather than scripture) as means to devotion and to mystical transcendence.

The five poets of my argument, despite large differences among themselves in style and in thought, all wrote major devotional poetry calling variously upon biblical poetics, and upon the other Protestant traditions discussed here. This Protestant poetics links them together, as forming a clearly recognizable major strain in the religious lyric of the period, and their poetic production, spanning the century as it does, unfolds diverse possibilities within a common aesthetics. Donne presents a fascinating example of beginnings, of a conscious alignment with, and creative development of, the new poetics, together with some admixture of older patterns. And the poetry of Edward Taylor in America provides an eminently satisfying sense of an ending, since it seems at once to exhaust many of the poetic conventions for the religious lyric produced by this biblical, Protestant aesthetics, and at the same time to open out to new ways with language and imagery.

## B. The Protestant Paradigm of Salvation

Besides looking to the Bible as source and model for the presentation of sacred truth as art, Protestant poetics also calls for the treatment of another kind of truth in religious lyric poetry—the painstaking analysis of the personal religious life. Working in these terms, the Protestant lyric poet must explore such questions as his relationship to God, the state of his soul, and his hopes of salvation with direct reference to his own theological assumptions, whereas the dramatic or epic poet may, if he wishes, treat the biblical stories in themselves. For this reason, a fundamental ground for the poetics I am describing, and a major influence, thematic and structural, upon the poetry of its chief exponents, is the classic Protestant paradigm of sin and salvation. The poets of this study reflect some spread of theological opinion, and their poems highlight different aspects of the spiritual life, but all plot the experience treated in their lyric sequences in relation to this widely accepted schema.

It is hardly necessary now to argue that the theological tenor of the English Church in the late sixteenth and early seventeenth centuries was firmly Protestant, even Calvinist, though literary critics have been in some danger of forgetting that fact as they stress Roman Catholic influences upon Donne or the medieval literary heritage of Herbert, or the contribution of both to the emerging spirit of Anglicanism.[34] As H. R. McAdoo has noted,

> Calvinism . . . was in the ascendant in England until the middle of the [17th] century. The disagreement between Anglican and Puritan began with questions of church order and not of teaching, and it has been said that there was hardly one of the Elizabethan bishops who was not a Calvinist. . . . The fall of Laud and the convening of the Westminster Assembly [1642] mark the summit of its development in England.[35]

Or as Norman Pettit well states, " 'Anglicanism' in a normative sense did not become a reality until after the Restoration"; Lancelot Andrewes and George Herbert preached within the same tradition of reformed theology as did such Puritans as Richard Greenham, Richard Rogers, Arthur Hildersam, and William Perkins.[36]

The influence of this theological milieu upon the so-called Metaphysical poets has begun to be recognized. In *The Protestant Mind of the English Reformation* Charles H. and Katherine George assimilate Donne to the dominant Calvinist doctrinal consensus, concluding that he was "in a general sense unqualifiedly Protestant" and that "his revolt from the Church of Aquinas is in some ways the most absolute of that of any English divine."[37] Substantiating this view, I have elsewhere argued that Reformation theology and Protestant modes of meditation are of primary importance for several of Donne's poems.[38] Similarly, William H. Halewood argues that the pervasive Augustinianism of the period—Augustine as interpreted by the Reformation—led Donne, Herbert, Vaughan, Marvell, and Milton to develop a poetic mode exploring man's radical sinfulness and God's overpowering grace.[39]

In stressing the Calvinist theological milieu I do not of course deny the importance or the divisiveness of the major theological disputes which raged throughout the century—predestination versus Arminianism; total versus less-than-total depravity; the sole authority of scripture versus some appeal to reason and tradition; unconditioned free grace versus human cooperation with or preparation for grace. Nor do I suggest that the somewhat different stances on these and other issues taken by various Protestant poets—those here studied and others such as Herrick, Marvell, and Milton—are without significant impact upon their poetics. My point here is simply that Calvinism provided a detailed chart of the spiritual life for Elizabethan and seventeenth-century English Protestants, and that this map also afforded fundamental direction to the major religious lyric poets.

The theological ideas that chiefly influenced the way in which these poets portrayed their own (and everyman's) spiritual condition were for the most part derived from the Pauline epistles. Both Luther and Calvin wrote influential commentaries on Romans and Galatians which achieved early translation into English, and William Perkins' advice to preachers to begin their study of scripture with the Epistle to the Romans seems to have been widely followed.[40] Thomas Draxe is typical in finding Romans to contain "the *Quintessence* and perfection of saving *Doctrine*," and the eighth chapter to be a conduit conveying the waters of life to the Church.[41] The crucial verses from Romans are the following:

There is none righteous, no not one (3:10).

Therefore by the deedes of the Law, there shall no flesh be justi-
fied in his sight (3:20).

For all have sinned, and come short of the glory of God,
Being justified freely by his grace, through the redemption that is
in Jesus Christ (3:23-24).

For whom he did foreknow, he also did predestinate to be con-
formed to the image of his sonne. . . .
Moreover, whom he did predestinate, them he also called: and
whom he called, them he also justified: and whom he justified, them
he also glorified (8:29-30).[42]

From Paul's epistles, the Protestant extrapolated a paradigm against
which to plot the spiritual drama of his own life. In the first place, he
understood that his very nature, as originally created in integrity and
holiness, had been marred almost beyond recognition by original sin,
and that the image of God according to which Adam had been formed
was in him obliterated. In the Thomistic formula the effects of the
Fall chiefly involved the disordering of the faculties and the rebellion
of the senses against reason, resulting from the removal of the super-
natural perfection and harmony man enjoyed in innocence.[43] For the
Protestant however, the Fall meant the depravity of all his natural
faculties—the blinding of the intellect and the bondage of the will in
Luther's formulation. For Calvin also "nothing remains after the ruin
except what is confused, mutilated, and disease-ridden"; "the mind is
given over to blindness and the heart to depravity."[44] Donne also spoke
in these terms: man in the condition of original sin "hath no interest
in his own natural faculties; He cannot think, he cannot wish, he can-
not do any thing of himself" toward supernatural ends; original sin
is "that indeleble foulnesse, and uncleanesse which God discovers in
us all," and the death attendant upon it "hath invaded every part and
faculty of man, understanding, and will, and all."[45] Because man's
natural state is so desperate, there can be no question (as in some
Roman Catholic formulations) of a man's preparing himself through
moral virtue for the reception of grace, or of performing works good
and meritorious in themselves; everything that he does of himself is
necessarily evil and corrupt. As the tenth of the Thirty-nine Articles
of the established church put it, "The condition of man, after the fall
of Adam is such that he cannot turne, and prepare himselfe by his owne
naturall strength, and good workes, to faith, and calling upon God,
wherefore we have no power to doe good workes pleasant, and ac-
ceptable to God, without the grace of God preventing us, that we may

have a good will, and working with us when we have that good will."[46] The drama of man's spiritual restoration, his regeneration, must then be understood wholly as God's work, effected by the merits of Christ and apprehended by a faith which is itself the gift of God; failure to recognize one's utter dependence upon grace, or laying claim to any kind of merit or desert for any of one's own works is a dangerous sign of reprobation.

The Pauline terms—election, calling, justification, adoption, sanctification, glorification—mark the important stages (some of them concomitant rather than sequential) in the spiritual life of any Protestant Christian, who was urged by dozens of manuals to seek constantly for the evidence of those stages in his own life. Inaugurating the whole process is God's *Election* from all eternity of certain persons to salvation and eternal life. Reformation theology gave rise to various views as to whether God's predestinating decrees of election and reprobation are in any way conditional, and as to whether God laid down those decrees before or after the Fall; some—Donne among them—took exception to the so-called "double predestination," denying that the decree of reprobation can be wholly unconditional, and a matter of God's first intention.[47] Yet English Protestants of the period were in general agreement as to what election is. In Perkins' words, "Election, is Gods decree, whereby on his owne free-will, he hath ordained certaine men to salvation, to the praise of the glorie of his grace."[48] Englishmen were, however, constantly warned (for the peace of the state and that of their souls) not to dwell upon abstruse theological questions concerning when, how, and why the elect are chosen, but rather, as Perkins put it, to gather "by signes and testimonies in our selves . . . what was the eternall counsell of God concerning our salvation."[49]

The *Calling* of the elect Christian involves God's awakening in him at whatever time God has appointed and by whatever means (extraordinary, as when he struck Paul off his horse on the way to Damascus, or ordinary, by the voice of the minister preaching the gospel) such a sense of his desperate sinfulness but also of the gospel promises that he is prepared to receive the accompanying gifts of effective repentance and saving faith.[50] This process is wholly of God's causation; the Christian will be aware of the effects within himself, and some theologians assign him duties in preparing his heart to receive the call,[51] but neither the preparation of the heart nor the effectual calling is achieved by his own efforts.

*Justification*, which alone makes possible the sinner's salvation, is also God's gift; for the Protestant it involves forgiveness of his sins by

Christ's satisfaction for them, and the imputing of Christ's righteous-
ness to him as a cloak or covering to hide his true filthiness and wicked-
ness. As Calvin explained, when God regards the justified man he does
not see that sinner but the merits and righteousness of his own perfect
image, Christ: "He does not justify in part but liberally, so that they
may appear in heaven as if endowed with the purity of Christ."[52] The
Reformers were adamant in their insistence that this justification is
only imputed to the sinner, not infused into him as the Roman Cath-
olics held, so as actually to restore God's image in him; however, the
imputed righteousness is really his because he is joined to Christ as
body to head. Accordingly, the Protestant apprehended his spiritual
condition in terms of a radical paradox, whereby he is perfectly holy
in Christ in heaven even while he remains radically sinful in his earthly
state. This paradox is nowhere better stated than in Luther: "A Chris-
tian man is both righteous and a sinner, holy and profane, an enemy of
God and yet a childe of God. . . . These two things are quite contrarie:
to wit, that a Christian is righteous and beloved of God, and yet not-
withstanding he is a sinner . . . most worthy of Gods wrath and in-
dignation."[53]

Because the Christian remains radically sinful in himself, this justi-
fication and imputed righteousness alone can give him peace of mind,
assurance of forgiveness and salvation, and finally an awareness of his
*Adoption* as a son of God and heir of heaven with Christ. As justifica-
tion defines the Christian's new legal relation to God the law-giver, so
adoption defines his new personal relation to a loving father. This
adoption is based upon several Pauline texts, notably Romans 8:15-17:

> For ye have not received the spirit of bondage againe to feare; but
> ye have received the spirit of adoption, whereby we cry, Abba,
> father.
> The spirit it selfe beareth witnes with our spirit, that we are the
> children of God:
> And if children, then heires; heires of God, and joynt heires with
> Christ; if so be that we suffer with him, that wee may bee also
> glorified together.

Explaining the term further, William Ames declared:

> All the faithfull doe expect Heaven as it were by a double title,
> namely by the title of redemption which they have by justification,
> and by the title as it were of Son-ship, which they have by Adop-
> tion . . . The faithfull are taken as it were into Gods Family, and

are of his household. Gal. 6.10. That is, they may be alwayes under the fatherly tuition of God, depending upon him, for nourishment, education, and perpetuall conservation. . . .

Together with the dignity of sons there is joyned also the condition of heires, *Rom.* 8.17 . . . this inheritance to which the faithfull are adopted, is blessednesse eternall.[54]

Reformation Protestants also held that at the time of justification the process of *Sanctification* is also begun, for God's graces come not singly but together. Sanctification involves the actual but gradual repairing of the defaced image of God in the soul, whereby it enjoys a "new life." Luther declared that this sanctification "has merely its beginning in this life, and it cannot attain perfection in this flesh."[55] Calvin, defining the restored image in terms of Ephesians 4:24 as "righteousness and true holiness," held that the elect cooperate in the gradual development of these qualities by keeping the commandments and practicing the Christian virtues, but the process itself must nevertheless be seen as wholly God's work: "This restoration does not take place in one moment or one day or one year; but through continual and sometimes even slow advances God wipes out in his elect the corruptions of the flesh, cleanses them of guilt, consecrates them to himself as temples . . . this warfare will end only at death."[56] Moreover, because the godly are still sinners, and their good works are always incomplete and redolent of the vices of the flesh, there can be absolutely no question of human merit attaching to any good works which they do; performance of the works of righteousness (the Commandments) are the evidences of election, and the natural fruits of conversion and faith, but are not in any degree meritorious for salvation.[57] The final stage, *Glorification*, or the perfect restoration of the image of God in man and the enjoyment of eternal blessedness, may begin in this life but is fully attained only after death.

This paradigm of regeneration was widely accepted by English Protestants of whatever persuasion regarding church order and discipline; it was in no sense peculiar to Puritans. Even Richard Hooker, that eloquent defender of church establishment, liturgy, sacraments, and the natural law's comprehensibility to fallen reason, distinguished these essential doctrines of Protestantism sharply and with admirable clarity from those of Rome. On the question of justification he observed:

This grace [of justification, the Roman Catholics] . . . will have to be applied by infusion . . . so the soule might be righteous by the inherent grace: which grace they make capable of increase . . . the augmentation whereof is merited by good workes, as good works are made meritorious by it. . . . But the righteousnesse wherein we must be found if we wilbe justified, is not our owne: therefore we cannot be justified by any inherent quality. Christ hath merited righteousnesse for as many as are found in him. In him God findeth us, if we be faithfull, for by faith we are incorporated into Christ. Then although in our selves we be altogither sinnefull, and unrighteous, yet even the man which is impious in him selfe . . . him God upholdeth with a gracious eie; putteth away his sinne by not imputing . . . and accepteth him in Jesus Christ, as perfectly righteous, as if he had fulfilled all that was commanded him in the lawe: shall I say more perfectly righteous, then if him selfe had fulfilled the whole law?[58]

With regard to sanctification Hooker insists that it is necessarily incomplete in this world, and that the works it promotes are in no way meritorious for salvation:

Now concerning the righteousnesse of sanctification, we deny it not to be inherent; wee graunt that unlesse we worke, we have it not: . . . [But] God giveth us both the one justice and the other . . . The proper and most immediate efficient cause in us of this later, is the spirit of adoption we have received into our hearts. . . .

The best things which we doe, have somewhat in them to be pardoned. How then can wee doe any thing meritorious, or worthy to be rewarded? . . . We acknowledge a dutifull necessity of doing well; but the meritorious dignity of doing well, wee utterly renounce.[59]

Donne also describes Christian salvation in terms of the familiar Calvinist paradigm, with the same emphasis upon man's depravity, the imputation of Christ's righteousness, the slow process of sanctification, and the inability of any to perform meritorious works:

No man hath any such righteousness of his own, as can save him; for howsoever it be made his, by that Application, or Imputation, yet the righteousness that saves him, is the very righteousness of Christ himself.

*David* does not say, Do thou wash me, and I will perfect thy worke. . . . Let him that is holy be more holy, but accept his Sanctification from him, of whom he had his Justification; and except he can think to glorifie himself because he is sanctified, Let him not think to sanctifie himself because he is justified; God does all.[60]

For many English Calvinists, including most Puritans and Separatists, these Protestant doctrines received clear, rigorous, and sanctioned formulation in the five points of the Synod of Dort (1618-1619): total depravity, unmerited election, limited atonement (for the elect only), irresistible grace (admitting no element of human cooperation or free response), final perseverance of the saints. Among the poets here studied, the Puritan Edward Taylor held firmly to the principles of Dort. On the other hand, as J.F.H. New points out,[61] many English Calvinists who remained within the established church inclined to moderation and ambiguity in regard to certain of these points: they tended to find some value (and therefore less than total depravity) in the natural faculties of man and the goods of the natural order; to see (with Richard Hooker) the realms of nature and grace as hierarchically ordered rather than dialectically opposed; and to reserve some role, however ambiguously stated, for human response to divine grace. Such attitudes are evident in Donne's comments on man's responsiveness to grace: though grace is always God's free gift and must always preempt and enable any human response, yet man "can answer the inspiration of God, when his grace comes, and exhibit acceptable service to him, and cooperate with him."[62] Donne discusses in the same way, and with the same reservation of God's entire freedom, causality, and initiative, the proper use of our natural faculties in preparation for grace, so that "that *free will* which we have in *Morall* and *Civill* actions, [may] be bent upon the *externall duties* of *Religion*, (as every naturall man may, out of the use of that *free will, come to Church, heare the Word preached, and believe it to be true*)."[63] Many of the same assumptions seem to underlie the moral discipline of Herbert's "The Church-porch," which is presented as an appropriate preparation for, though not the cause or sure guarantee of, the elect youth's entry into "The Church." As we shall see, such differences of theological emphases are not unimportant for the attitudes of Protestant poets toward the role of grace in the creation of religious poetry.

Of particular interest to this study are the feelings which sixteenth- and seventeenth-century Protestants understood to accompany the working out of this paradigm of the spiritual life in the elect Christian's soul. These feelings involve well-defined emotional, psychological, and spiritual states or conditions which the Christian was urged to try to discern in himself and his own experience. This emphasis upon the constant scrutiny of personal emotions and feelings is a primary cause of that introspective intensity and keen psychological awareness so characteristic of seventeenth-century religious lyrics. The conventional descriptions of the affective states of the elect provide an illuminating perspective upon the subject matter and manner of treatment in such lyrics.

Responding to God's calling, the Christian first undergoes a conversion experience, which is the great crisis or turning point of his spiritual life. As an essentially passive instrument acted upon by God's grace, he experiences a purging, or mollifying, or breaking of the heart which readies it for the gifts of repentance and saving faith. The understandings and sensations attendant upon this mollifying of the heart are well-described by William Perkins, with reference to the usual proof-text on the subject from Ezekiel:

> The heart . . . must be bruised in peeces, that it may be fit to receive Gods saving grace offered unto it. Ezech. 11. 19. *I will give them one heart, and I will put a new spirit within their bowels: and I will take the stonie heart out of their bodies, and I will give them an heart of flesh.*
>
> There are for the bruising of this stony heart, foure principall hammers. The first, is the knowledge of the Law of God. The second, is the knowledge of sinne, both original and actuall, and what punishment is due unto them. The third, is compunction, or pricking of the heart, namely, a sense and feeling of the wrath of God for the same sinnes. The fourth, is an holy desperation of a mans own power, in the obtaining of eternall life.[64]

Recognizing that this bruising and preparation of the heart is in essence God's work, some Protestants also point to a role for the Christian in the process of afflicting, pricking, and purging his own heart by meditating intently upon his own sins and God's Law. On this point Richard Sibbes declared that we must "join with God in bruising ourselves," and "lay seige to the hardness of our own hearts and aggravate sin all we can,"[65] though all power of accomplishment of this work is understood to rest in God only.

The next experiential state is that of repentance. Concomitant with, or precedent to, repentance is the beginning of saving faith in the elect, but the repentance shows itself visibly first. Perkins waxes eloquent on the sorrow the elect experience as God makes them aware of their desperate sinfulness and their imminent danger of damnation:

> When the spirit hath made a man see his sinnes, he seeth further the curse of the Law, and so he findes himselfe to be in bondage under Satan, hell, death, and damnation: at which most terrible sight his heart is smitten with feare and trembling, through the consideration of his hellish and damnable estate.

This sorrow if it continue and increase to some great measure, hath certen symptomes in the body, *as burning heat, rouling of the intralls, a pining and fainting of the solide parts.*

Repentance is a worke of grace, arising of a godly sorrow; whereby a man turnes from all his sins unto God, and bringeth forth fruites worthie amendment of life.[66]

This sorrow and repentance usually show themselves with special force at the time of conversion and again on the deathbed, but they continue throughout life. Calvin notes that "the more earnestly any man measures his life by the standard of God's law, the surer are the signs of repentance that he shows."[67]

God's gift of saving faith may now be experienced by the broken and humbled sinner, whereby he understands that the Gospel promises of salvation pertain to him, and that Christ's grace and merits may be applied specifically to himself. Explaining much of this out of David's Psalms, and especially Psalm 51, Perkins provides a suggestive analysis of the psychological states involved:

In the next place it is to be considered how the Lord causeth faith to spring and to breed in the humbled heart. . . . First, when a man is seriously humbled under the burden of his sinne, the Lord by his spirit makes him lift up himselfe to consider and to ponder most diligently the great mercie of God offered unto him in Christ Jesus. . . . He comes in the second place to see, feele, and from his heart to acknowledge himselfe to stand in neede of Christ, and . . . of every droppe of his most precious blood. Thirdly, the Lord stirreth up in his heart a vehement desire and longing after Christ and his merits: this desire is compared to a thirst. . . . Lastly, after this desire he begins to pray, not for any worldly benefit, but onely for the forgivenes of his sinnes. . . . Now this prayer, it is made, not for one day onely, but continually from day to day: not with lips, but with greater sighes and groanes of the heart then that they can be expressed with the tongue. . . . After this, Christ Jesus will temper him a plaister of his owne heart blood; which beeing applied, he shall find himselfe revived, and shall come to a lively assurance of the forgivenes of all his sinnes.[68]

Richard Rogers observes that this faith grows throughout the elect Christian's life. At the time of his conversion it may be only a "little faith," whereby he understands his sins to be pardonable but is not sure that they are forgiven; subsequently, he may attain to some weak assurance but will often lose it and need to strive hard to recover it. At length he attains to a ripe and strong faith, so that most of the time he has a full persuasion of the mercy of God effecting his own salvation, unless God remove that assurance for a season, to try him.[69] This faith is the vehicle for justification and adoption, which conditions manifest themselves also by certain emotional states, according to Perkins: a sense of reconciliation with God; a consciousness that affliction is not punishment but only fatherly chastisement; peace and quietness of conscience; a sense of God's favor; an awareness of spiritual joy in the heart; and an expectation that all the good things God has begun in the elect will be accomplished.[70]

As regards sanctification, Protestants could find in Richard Rogers' *Seven Treatises* a detailed account of the mental and psychological states attending the gradual restoration of the image of God in the elect.[71] The work is addressed to those already converted and embarked upon the Christian life, and in a prefatory epistle Ezechial Culverwell terms it "the Anatomie of the soule, wherein . . . we may as it were, with the eye behold . . . the right constitution of the whole and every part of a true Christian."[72] Rogers finds the emotions attendant upon sanctification to be uneven and fluctuating, like the process itself, though over the long term the Christian experiences growth in holiness and perfection. He invokes the metaphor of a plant to explain this growth: "They being *the Lords plants*, take not their full perfection at once: but according to the nature of a plant, require a daily watering and dressing, whereby in the end they attaine to a full growth in Christ."[73] At the beginning of sanctification, "at the first conversion of a sinner," the purging and cleansing of the heart occurs, renewing our good will and causing hatred of sin and amendment of life, but thereafter the Christian must watch and examine and keep his heart with diligence throughout his life, "seeing no man can watch so carefully, but that much evill will creepe in."[74]

The Christian is warned by Rogers to expect great vacillations in his emotional temper. As he is sensible of God's great gifts, he will often feel an outpouring of love and joy in his heart, moving him to praise God and giving "matter and occasion *of singing and making melodie to the Lord*"—a stimulus the Christian poet must feel with special urgency.[75] On the other hand God sometimes removes the sense of his presence from the Christian, stirring him to quite other responses: "God doth, as it were, hide himselfe sometime for a season . . . that they may with more earnest desire mourne for Gods wonted grace; and that when they have obtained it againe, they may with more joyfulnesse of heart praise him."[76] This state is poignantly portrayed in such Herbert poems as "Deniall," "Grace," "The Glimpse," "The Flower."

Rogers designates three principal stages of the Christian's life, which are relevant to the poetic sequences we shall be examining. Those who are as yet little children in the spiritual life will often be sad, anxious, and distrustful when their comforts cease and their sense of assurance departs: "As in all trades or sciences, the beginnings are hardest and fullest of discouragements; so it fareth with Christians, namely, that their first entrings are most doubtfull, and fullest of weakenes."[77] Those who are in the middle age of the Christian life experience that life as a "combate and a conflict" against sinful lusts, unruly desires, and all manner of temptation, as well as a pilgrimage in the course of which they experience many lets and hindrances. This is the period in which the Christian is especially aware of himself as a wayfarer or as a *miles Christi*, and in which he undergoes constant emotional vacillations "betwixt feare and hope, sorrow and joy"[78]—such as Donne, for example, records vividly in Sonnet XIX. The final stage is that of mature, experienced Christians upheld by many proofs of God's saving grace and constant help which "kept many of them from sore falles, holden them from manifold and great afflictions."[79] Such Christians have the sense of steady progress toward the final perfection to be achieved at their glorification in heaven.

Perkins' somewhat different terms for the psychological states evoked by the process of sanctification are also relevant to this poetry. He describes four "sanctified affections"—zeal for God's glory, fear and awe from the sense of being in God's presence, hatred and detestation of sin and especially of a man's own corruptions, joy of heart in contemplating the day of judgment.[80] He also distinguishes three principal temptations and trials of a Christian life and the emotions attendant upon them: (1) A constant "fight and battell betwixt the flesh and the spirit," the course of which he illustrates out of Paul's Epistles. (2) A disquieted and troubled heart and mind because of a distant relationship with Christ, or because Christ seems to be departed for a time, or because he himself seems to forego the relation by seeking the vanities of the world (illustrated out of Canticles). (3) Heavy and bitter outward afflictions, driving him sometimes to impatience or a fear of God's wrath and displeasure, but at length to a settled consciousness of peace and righteousness.[81] This spectrum of feeling has close consonance with the emotions portrayed in Herbert's five poems entitled "Affliction," and indeed in "The Church" as a whole.

The Protestant-Pauline paradigm of salvation and the emotional states supposed to accompany it influenced variously but profoundly the religious lyrics of Donne, Herbert, Vaughan, Traherne, and

Taylor, in regard to subject matter, structure, and range of feelings portrayed. In one way or another, all these collections concern themselves centrally with the progress of the speaker's soul in terms related to this paradigm.

John Donne's "Holy Sonnets" focus especially upon the beginnings of the process, dramatizing the speaker's pleas for justification and regeneration in language often remarkably precise: "Impute me righteous," "make me new."[82] The sonnets explore the spectrum of emotional states associated with conviction of sin, conversion, repentance, faith, and spiritual struggle; and the emotions portrayed run the gamut from anguish, terror, dread, fear of God's rejection, anxiety about election, and near despair, to grief for sin, love of Christ, and dismay that the vacillations of mind and heart persist throughout life. The sonnet sequence as a whole reflects the Calvinist sense of man's utter helplessness in his corruption, and total dependence upon God in every phase of his spiritual life.

George Herbert's *The Temple*, and especially the collection of lyrics, "The Church," has as its primary subject the whole, lifelong process of sanctification, presented under the metaphor of building the Temple in the Heart. The speaker is devoted to the visible church—its ritual, architecture, sacraments—but his theology is Calvinist: he affirms the double predestination (in "The Water-course") and he struggles hard throughout the volume to relinquish any claim to any good thing as emanating from himself: all is from God. After an analysis of the externals of the Christian life in "The Church-porch," the speaker presents himself in "The Church," where the major motifs are: 1) the struggle to understand, accept, and respond to justification through Christ's sacrifice—beginning with the broken heart of "The Altar" and culminating in "Repentance" and "Faith"; 2) an extended portrayal of the joys and griefs, pleasures and trials, victories and backslidings attendant upon the slow process of sanctification; and 3) the attainment of something like a plateau of assurance. The speaker's frequent distresses and anxieties are not directed to the issue of his election (which he takes largely for granted) but are rather elicited by his persistent sins and afflictions, and especially by the condition of spiritual barrenness he often experiences.

Henry Vaughan[83] also focuses upon the process of sanctification, explored through the motif of the wandering pilgrim or exile. The opening poem, "Regeneration," presents the effectual calling: the speaker turns from the primrose path of sin, attempts to live by the Law (the scales), is called into the Garden of the Church and there confronts the mystery of election: the Spirit blows *"Where I please,"* awakening some souls and leaving others dormant. The two parts of *Silex Scintillans* display two stages in the spiritual life—an initial, more troubled stage in which the new life struggles to maintain and augment itself in an atmosphere of death, dimness of vision, and distance from God; and a higher plane, a plateau of assurance in which the dominant mood is the speaker's longing for transcendance.

Thomas Traherne,[84] with his ecstatic celebration of infant innocence which all but denies hereditary original sin, his Neoplatonic conception of man's dignity and unlimited potential for spiritual growth, his insistence upon the freedom of the will and the uses of good works, and his celebration of vision as the means by which the Christian can even now experience eternity, seems to diverge very far from the Protestant paradigm. Indeed, on some of these points Traherne occupies a unique position well beyond the Anglican pole of Reformed Protestantism. Yet the contours of the speaker's spiritual life as exhibited in the poems conform to the paradigmatic spiritual history of the human race— initial innocence, fall into sin and grief, and a process of restoration through Christ. And the turning point for the speaker's restoration is the thoroughly Protestant experience of discovering the Bible to be a full commentary on his own life and spiritual condition. We may see Traherne's poems as developing (in an admittedly singular way) a late stage in the Pauline paradigm, in that they analyze the privileges of adoption, exploring just what it means to be the son of God and heir to all things. This focus encourages Traherne's remarkable near-fusion of the states of sanctification and glorification, for the Christian who knows himself adopted by God has claim even now to his full inheritance, if he can but see and enjoy it.

Edward Taylor[85] occupies the Puritan pole. His poems everywhere reflect the theology of Dort in their dominant theme of the unfathomable gulf between God's greatness and goodness and the speaker's abject depravity, a gulf which can be bridged only by irresistible grace. The occasion of most of Taylor's poems is the reception of the Sacrament, seen in Calvinist terms as a "Seal" of regeneration and so also as the sign of full membership in the gathered church of elect saints. Though fairly confident of his election, the speaker is led by the occasion of the Sacrament days to consider over and over again whether, and how certainly, he wears the "wedden garment" of justification and sanctification required of all who partake of the sacrament. Though Taylor's *Second Series* suggests some development in the spiritual life, conforming in very general terms to the familiar Protestant pattern of recurring conflicts, distresses, and struggles which culminate in something like a plateau of assurance, all the poems essentially repeat the same experience. Every time the speaker considers any topic relating to the spiritual life the same question must be confronted: has the speaker the right to apply to himself the spiritual promises and goods described? The posing of this question is seldom agonized, since the speaker has grounds for assurance, but his resolution is almost always tentative, conditional, petitionary; and he can seldom move beyond this fundamental, overwhelming question to reach some higher spiritual state.

The Pauline paradigm informs these collections of poems in various ways. It may make a more or less direct contribution, as in Donne's "Holy Sonnets"; it may undergird sequences related to other parts of the Bible—the Psalms in Herbert, Canticles in Vaughan and Taylor; and it may serve as a norm against which a significantly different range of spiritual emotions and experiences may be set for contrast, as in Traherne. Calvin, Perkins, and many others illustrated the emotional states attendant upon conversion from David's Psalms, with special focus upon Psalm 51 (Herbert's starting point as well); many also explicated Canticles (so constantly a reference point for Vaughan and Taylor) as a portrait of the fluctuations of mind and spirit the elect experience as Christ by turns approaches and departs from them. This disposition to relate the lyric sections of the Bible to the fundamental Protestant paradigm of salvation influenced the ways in which poets used certain biblical books as generic and stylistic models for Christian lyric poetry. To that resource we now turn.

# PART I

*Biblical Poetics*

# Biblical Genre Theory: Precepts and Models
## for the Religious Lyric

Protestant poets of the sixteenth and seventeenth centuries looked to the Bible and its commentators both for genre theory and for generic models for the religious lyric. For most other kinds of poems, classical genre theory and classical exemplars provided direction, but the poets had not that resource for their religious lyrics. Though classical hymns to the gods were constantly cited in Renaissance defenses of poetry as evidence of the seriousness, the antiquity, and the didactic function of poetry,[1] Christian poets felt some compunction about writing praises of the Christian God in the forms used to praise Venus or Apollo. And there were no classical models for the introspective, soul-searching, analytical religious lyrics which are among the era's most impressive poetic achievements. But the Bible was a potential model, in that several parts of it had been identified as poetry in the Hebrew tradition, and in Christian commentary from patristic times onward. From such sources we can deduce some basic assumptions about Biblical lyric kinds which influenced the major poets of this study.

As Wellek and Warren note, genre may be examined in terms of broad categories based on manner of imitation—narrative, dramatic, lyric—and also in terms of such historically recognized kinds as comedy, tragedy, elegy, ode, and epigram. Classical definitions of the historical genres were based on the meter used, whereas modern (and Renaissance) definitions regard both outward form (specific meter and structure) and inner form (attitude, tone, subject, audience, purpose).[2] Both broad and specific approaches to biblical genres emerge from Renaissance biblical commentary. General discussions differentiating the poetic parts of the Bible from the prose parts identify a rather large corpus of biblical verse, of considerable range and variety, from which poets might learn. More specific comments, pointing to biblical examples of particular lyric genres or dividing that compendium of religious lyric, the Book of Psalms, into lyric categories, may suggest how Renaissance theorists conceived of the biblical lyric kinds.

## A. Compendiums of Biblical Lyric

The corpus of Biblical lyric poetry was identified to the Renaissance reader or poet in several ways. One was through the tradition of labeling, and sometimes giving separate publication to, the so-called poetical part of scripture. This tradition originated in the Hebrew Bible's specification of three principal parts of sacred scripture, the Law, the Prophets, and the Hagiographia—which includes three poetical books (Psalms, Proverbs, Job), the five Megillôth (rolls) associated with various festivals (Song of Songs, Ruth, Lamentations, Ecclesiastes, Esther), and three late narrative books (Daniel, Ezra-Nehemiah, and Chronicles).[3] In the Christian tradition five books—Job, the Psalms, Proverbs, Ecclesiastes, and the Song of Solomon—were often identified as the poetical "third part" of scripture, a classification used in Coverdale's Bible, and the influential Protestant Latin Bible of Junius and Tremellius.[4] These five books were often published separately in duodecimo or smaller format for use in private devotions—in the Geneva version in 1580, 1583, 1614, and 1616, and in the Authorized Version in 1632 and 1642.

A concomitant English Protestant tradition beginning with the Matthew Bible (1537) and its revisions—the Great Bible of 1539 and the Bishops' Bible of 1568—provided the basis for regarding this third or poetical part of scripture as a compendium of lyric poetry. Perhaps responding to the tradition identifying the Book of Job as an epic poem in hexameter verse,[5] these bibles assimilated Job to the historical part of scripture, leaving the third "poetical" part comprised of Psalms, Proverbs, Ecclesiastes, and Canticles. This third part received separate publication in Taverner's version in 1550.[6] Also, though it does not number or label the parts of the Bible, the Authorized Version of 1611 reflects this conception in that it sets the Book of Psalms off from the preceding book, Job, and makes another such division after the Song of Songs.

The lyric poetry of the Bible received further display, encouraging its use as model for Christian poetry, in several collections of verse which brought together metrical selections from the "poetic" books of the Bible, songs and hymns from other biblical books, traditional medieval liturgical hymns in vernacular translation, and original compositions presented as analogous in some respects to the above. The early German hymn books were broadly inclusive, randomly organized collections of this kind,[7] and Luther's contributions to them were various: close metrical paraphrases of psalms (e.g., of Psalms 12, 14, 124); free vernacular descants on other biblical lyrics such as the

Angels' song to the Shepherds (Luke 2:10-14); vernacular versions of traditional hymns such as Sedulius' *Herodes hostis impii* and the Gregorian hymn, *O lux beata Trinitas*; several original hymns; and most interesting of all for our purposes, hymns grounded upon the Psalms but developed so freely in regard to New Testament and contemporary reference as to be virtually new poems on the same themes—for example, *Ein' feste Burg* (from Psalm 46).[8] In his preface to a 1525 hymn book, Luther cites the Old Testament prophets and early Christian poets as models he has endeavored to follow, so that "we may boast, as Moses doth in his song (Exodus xv) that Christ is become our praise and our song."[9]

Miles Coverdale's *Goostly Psalmes and Spirituall Songes drawen out of the Holy Scripture* (published sometime before 1539 and greatly influenced by Luther)[10] includes metrical selections from scripture— both close paraphrases and free elaborations—offering these as a substitute for licentious popular ballads and secular songs and sonnets:

> Would God that our minstrels had none other thing to play upon, neither our carters and ploughmen other thing to whistle upon, save psalms, hymns, and such godly songs as David is occupied withal! And if women, sitting at their rocks, or spinning at the wheels, had none other songs to pass their time withal, than such as Moses' sister, Glehana's wife, Debora, and Mary the mother of Christ, have sung before them, they should be better occupied than with *hey nony nony, hey troly loly,* and such like phantasies.[11]

He obviously hopes to stimulate original composition in the biblical mode: "Why should not we then make our songs and mirth of God, as well as they?"[12] John Hall's collection, *The Courte of Virtue* (1565), intensifies the *paragone* with secular verse by offering "Many holy or Spretuall Songes, Sonnettes, psalms, & shorte sentences, as well of holy Scripture as others" specifically as a counter to the popular miscellany of love poetry, *The Court of Venus* (1549-1550?); he also invites other "godly men" to add to his compilation.[13] Hall includes a long dream-vision poem modeled on the prefatory poem of *The Court of Venus*, poems on various virtues chiefly paraphrasing Pauline definitions and exhortations, metrical versions of Psalms 51-92, an *omnium gatherum* of other poems or poem-like passages of scripture, and even some sacred parody of secular lyrics—notably by Wyatt.

Other compendiums, often conceived as song-books for the Church, were predominently or exclusively biblical.[14] These restrictive collections might seem to discourage the writing of original poems in this mode and certainly did exclude such from church services, but they had the effect of focusing yet more sharply upon the corpus of biblical lyric available as models for private religious poems. In the more liberal tradition, the vernacular metrical psalters by Sternhold-Hopkins, Matthew Parker, and Thomas Ravenscroft, among others, also included the New Testament canticles which had been used traditionally in the medieval offices (the *Magnificat*, Luke 1:48-55; the *Benedictus*, Luke 1:68-79; the *Nunc Dimittis*, Luke 2:29-31), together with vernacular poetic versions of other biblical passages, liturgical hymns, and chants—the Song of the Three Children, the Ten Commandments, the Creed, the *Pater Noster*, the *Gloria Patri*, the *Veni Creator*, the *Te Deum*.[15] On the other hand, several reflected the Calvinist belief that *only* biblical songs are appropriate to Christian worship lest God's Word be contaminated by human invention, and so presented a selection of biblical poems to supplement the central corpus of songs for Christian worship, the metrical psalms. In this tradition, Michael Drayton subtitled his *Harmonie of the Church* (1591) "The Spirituall Songes and holy Hymnes, of godly men, Patriarkes and Prophetes . . . ," and his preface disclaimed original composition for the better way of strict biblical paraphrase:

> Gentle Reader, my meaning is not with the varietie of verse to feede any vaine humour, neither to trouble thee with devises of mine owne invention, as careing an overweening of mine own wit: but here I present thee with these Psalmes or Songes of praise, so exactly translated as the prose would permit, or sense would any way suffer me.[16]

George Sandys' *Paraphrase upon the Divine Poems* (1638) is among the most complete and most instructive of these compilations.[17] It contains the whole of Job; the Psalms as set by Henry Lawes; Ecclesiastes; Lamentations; and the usual additions—Moses' two songs (Exod. 15 and Deut. 32); the song of Deborah and Baruch (Judges 5); the song of Hannah at the birth of Samuel (1 Sam. 2:1-10); the lamentation of David over Saul and Jonathan (2 Sam. 1:19-27); three songs from Isaiah (Isa. 5, 26, and 28); the song of Jonah (Jon. 2); 2 Samuel 7:18-29; Habbakkuk 3; and the three New Testament Canticles from Luke. Of special interest is the intimation in several commendatory verses that the poems in Sandys' collection (including Job) share common lyric features, in that together they express the full range of human passions. Henry Rainsford's dedicatory poem describes this range:

> Afflicted Job a Veile of Sorrow shrouds;
> But heavenly Beams dispell those envious Clouds.

The Royall Psalmist, borne on Angels wings,
Now weepes in Verse, now Halelu-jahs sings.
Converted Salomon to our eyes presents
Deluding Joyes, and curelesse Discontents.
That good Josiah's Name may never dye,
Thy Muse revives his Mournfull Elegy.
With the same Zeale, doth to our Numbers fit
All the Poeticke Parts of Holy Writ.
And thus Salvation thou maiest bring to those
Who never would have sought for it in Prose.[18]

The New England *Bay Psalm Book* (1680) stands in this same tradition, bringing together metrical versions of the Psalms, the Song of Songs, Lamentations, and the usual Old Testament and New Testament lyrics—expanded to include five poems from Isaiah and nine from the Book of Revelation.[19]

A few of these inclusive biblical collections hark back somewhat to earlier models in that they include some non-biblical material. George Wither, who perhaps contributed more than any other single person to the theory of biblical lyric poetry in England, supplemented his remarkable *Preparation to the Psalter* (1619) and his metrical version of the Psalms (discussed below) with collections intended to provide a large corpus of biblical lyrics and related poems. The most complete such collection was *The Hymnes and Songs of the Church* (1623), set forth with the claim that James I had approved it as a supplement to the Psalter for liturgical use.[20] Wither presented the poems approximately in their biblical order, adding a few to those found in Sandys: The Song of Songs, 1 Chronicles 39:10, Nehemiah 1:5, Proverbs 31:10, Isaiah 12, 37:15-20, and 38:10-20, The Angels' nativity hymn (Luke 2:10-14), and a song from Revelation (15:3-4). He also included metrical versions of the Ten Commandments and the Lord's Prayer, ancient liturgical hymns such as the *Veni Creator* and the *Te Deum*—and, as Part II of his collection, original "spiritual songs" for feast-days and other public ceremonials, an addition which stirred up a storm of controversy. Moreover, Wither directly encouraged contemporary writing in the biblical mode by suggesting adaptations to contemporary occasions of certain biblical songs (such as Nehemiah's prayer), and by directing poets to David's lamentation over Jonathan "as a Patterne for our Funerall Poemes."[21] A somewhat similar project was undertaken for the Church of Scotland by Zachary Boyd, who offered a supplement to his metrical version of the Psalms with much the same content as Wither's; significantly, Boyd's inclusion of George

Buchanan's nativity hymn, "A Morning Hymn for Christ," just after the New Testament songs from Luke intimates that the modern poem is in the biblical mode.[22]

On the theoretical side, influential literary and exegetical formulations helped to articulate and extend the assumptions underlying such collections, and thereby to further the development of a theory of biblical lyric genres. Sidney's *Defence of Poesie* emphasized the analogy between biblical songs and classical hymns:

> The chiefe [poets] both in antiquitie and excellencie, were they that did imitate the unconceiveable excellencies of God. Such were *David* in his Psalmes, *Salomon* in his song of songs, in his *Ecclesiastes* and *Proverbes*. *Moses* and *Debora*, in their Hymnes, and the wryter of Jobe: Which beside other, the learned *Emanuell Tremelius*, and *F. Junius*, doo entitle the Poeticall part of the scripture. . . . In this kinde, though in a full wrong divinitie, were *Orpheus, Amphion, Homer* in his himnes, and manie other both *Greeke* and *Romanes*: and this *Poesie* must be used by whosoever will follow S. *Paules* counsaile, in singing Psalmes when they are mery.[23]

From another vantage point, John Donne, preaching on a text from Deborah's song (Judges 5:20), waxed eloquent about the range, variety, excellence, and emotional power of the lyric poetry of scripture, claiming that God's revelation is,

> sweetest of all, where the *Holy Ghost* hath been pleased to set the word of *God* to Musique, and to convay it into a Song; . . . God himselfe made *Moses* a Song [Deut. xxxii], and expressed his reason why; The children of *Israel*, sayes *God*, will forget my Law; but this song they will not forget; . . . This world begun with a Song, if the *Chalde Paraphrasts*, upon *Salomons Song of Songs*, have taken a true tradition, That assoone as *Adams* sinne was forgiven him, he expressed . . . his peace of conscience, in a Song; of which, we have the entrance in that *Paraphrase*. This world begun so; and so did the next world too, if wee count the beginning of that (as it is a good computation to doe so) from the comming of *Christ Jesus*: for that was expressed on Earth, in divers Songs; in the blessed *Virgins* Magnificat; *My soule doth magnifie the Lord*; In *Zacharies* Benedictus; *Blessed be the Lord God of Israel*; and in *Simeons*, Nunc dimittis, *Lord now lettest thou thy servant depart in peace*. This world began so, and the other; and when both shall joyne, and make up one world without end, it shall continue so in heaven, in that Song of the *Lamb*,

*Great and marveillous are thy workes, Lord God Almighty, just and true are thy wayes, thou King of Saints.* And, to Tune us, to Compose and give us a Harmonie and Concord of affections, in all perturbations and passions, and discords in the passages of this life, if we had no more of the same *Musique* in the *Scriptures* (as we have the Song of *Moses* at the *Red Sea*, and many *Psalmes* of *David* to the same purpose) this Song of *Deborah* were enough, abundantly enough, to slumber any storme, to becalme any tempest, to rectifie any scruple of Gods slacknesse in the defence of his cause.[24]

Looking to the Bible itself for theoretical principles, many Protestants found in two Pauline verses the starting point both for a biblically sanctioned poetics of the religious lyric, and for the theory of biblical genres. Colossians 3:16 urges, "Let the word of Christ dwell in you richly in all wisdome, teaching and admonishing one another in Psalmes, and Hymnes, and Spirituall songs, singing with grace in your hearts to the Lord." Ephesians 5:19 employs the same terms, "Speaking to your selves, in Psalmes, and Hymnes, and Spirituall songs, singing and making melodie in your heart to the Lord." There was constant controversy throughout the period as to whether extra-biblical songs are allowable in congregational worship, and whether instrumental accompaniment is permitted. But English Protestants generally agreed that these Pauline stipulations about the origin of such songs in the hearts of the faithful and their function in teaching and admonishing must forbid the use of Latin hymns not understood by the congregation, as well as any highly artful music more noteworthy for the art than the substance. As Robert Rollock's comment on Colossians suggests, these precepts would also seem to govern imitations of the biblical models for private use, which all sides were promoting:

All the matter of Psalmes, Hymnes, and Canticles, should be spirituall. For why? they come from the riches of the word in the heart. If thou have this substance within thee, all thy songs will be of Scripture, of heavenly things, and all to glorifie thy God, and to edifie thy brother. . . . The forme of singing . . . should *be gracious*, that is, it should have such gratiousnes, and gravitie, as might convey grace to the heart of the hearer. . . . This word *grace* condemnes all, [that] . . . feede not the heart with the words and sentences of the Scripture, but feed the eare with a vaine tune. . . . The chiefe Organ, that is, the instrument wherewith they should sing . . . is not with the Organs of the Papists, no not with thy tongue; but it is with the heart, and with the affection of a well ruled heart. . . . Even so before thou sing, temper thou thy heart; and let thy song rise, not from thy throte, but from the depth of thine heart, that is, from thine affections set upon God.[25]

The Pauline verses were seen to urge a poetics for the religious lyric in which artfulness of expression is not pursued for its own sake, but in which the goodness of the (biblical) matter and of the speaker's heart give rise to appropriate forms of expression.

Moreover, though it is misleading to suggest agreement on the matter, there was some disposition to regard the three "kinds" identified in the Pauline verses—psalms, hymns, and spiritual songs—as the basic categories under which the corpus of biblical lyric could be distributed, and also as the categories for original compositions in the biblical mode. Definitions of these three categories sometimes focused upon manner of presentation (psalms were intended to be accompanied upon the psaltery whereas songs were for vocal presentation only),[26] but the more usual definitions called attention to distinctions in subject matter as well. The annotation to Colossians 3:16 in the Geneva Bible reads, "By Psalmes hee meaneth all godly songs which were written upon divers occasions, and by Hymnes, all such as conteine the praise of God, and by spirituall songs, other more peculiar and artificious songs which were also in praise of God, but they were made fuller of Musicke."[27] Nehemiah Rogers provides a more ample definition of the three kinds in his exposition of Isaiah 5:1-17, which he terms Isaiah's "Parabolical Song of the Beloved":

Three kindes of Songs were in use especially amongst the Jewes: Some they called *Psalmes*; othersome *Hymnes*; and another sort they had which they called *Songs* or *Odes*: . . . The first of these were such as were artifically framed in a certaine full number of words and measure . . . and containeth in it holy matter, of what argument soever: whether *Precatorie*; Praiers for benefits to be received: or *Deprecatorie*; Petitions against adversities: or *Consolatorie*; Matter of comfort and consolation. These were wont to be sung both with *Instrument* and *voice*.

The second sort, were speciall songs of praise and thanksgiving, and come of a word which signifieth the lifting up or exaltation of the voice . . . and these are properly those that set forth the Almighties praise: therefore saith *Chrysostome; A Hymne is more divine than a Psalme*. These were wont to be sung either with the *Instrument*, or without.

The third kinde contained in them doctrine of the chiefe good, or mans eternall felicitie, with other such like Spirituall matter, and

were artificially made, and after a more majesticall forme than ordi-
nary. These were sung only with the *voice*, without any Instrument.
. . . As for this Song of our Prophet, it is of this latter kinde, and
was most artifically composed, and set out with the most exquisite
skill that might be. It is of the like nature and kinde with that of
*Solomons*, which is called the Song of Songs.[28]

We find, then, in general, three chief kinds of biblical lyrics identi-
fied on the basis of the Pauline texts. The first kind are prayer-like or
meditative poems called psalms, evidently lending themselves especially
to self-probing and petitionary postures. The second are hymns—
praises of and thanksgivings to God in a particularly sublime and ex-
alted style; this generic conception is in line with the classical and
neoclassical location of the hymn to the gods at the apex of the epi-
deictic kinds—the "highest and stateliest" of all poetry, as Puttenham
declared.[29] The third kind are "spiritual songs," evidently artful, ele-
gant, ode-like poems celebrating special occasions and lofty matters.
All these kinds, and several sub-genres, were understood to be repre-
sented in the Book of Psalms, the most often translated, heavily an-
notated, and widely imitated of all the biblical books. Contemporary
discussion of this book is accordingly the most fruitful source of in-
sights into the biblical lyric genres and their would-be imitators.

## B. The Book of Psalms

The Book of Psalms was widely recognized as the compendium *par
excellence* of lyric poetry—a view reinforced by the avalanche of
metrical versions of the Psalms in the sixteenth and seventeenth cen-
turies.[30] Beginning with Coverdale's imitations of Luther's psalm trans-
lations, major and minor poets of the period and dozens of hack writers
included metrical versions of some psalms (often some or all of the
seven penitential psalms) in their poetic *œuvre*.[31] By 1640 there were
well over three hundred editions (in several versions) of the complete
psalter in English verse.[32] Among the most significant were: Robert
Crowley's, the first complete metrical psalter in English (1549); the
Sternhold-Hopkins Old Version (1562), in simple common meter and
often doggerel rhyme, which became the standard version for congre-
gational singing and achieved well over two hundred editions by 1640;
versions by Archbishop Parker, King James I, Thomas Ravenscroft,
George Sandys, George Wither, and Henry King, many of which
claimed greater accuracy or poetic elegance than Sternhold-Hopkins
but did not replace it for general congregational use; the French

Marot-Bèze psalter (completed in 1562) impressive for its metrical diversity and adaptation of contemporary love tunes to the psalm texts; the Sir Phillip Sidney-Countess of Pembroke psalter (written and widely circulated between 1589-1599) which was particularly striking for its stanzaic and metrical variety; and the *Bay Psalm Book*, the authorized text for congregational singing in New England (1640).[33]

The several reasons advanced for turning the Psalms into English meter highlight the importance and the difficulty of the undertaking. In the tradition of Luther and Coverdale, the Sternhold-Hopkins title page presents the Psalms as a wholesome substitute for licentious secular lyric—"Very mete to be used of all sortes of people privately for their solace and comfort: laying apart all ungodly Songes and Ballades, which tende only to the norishing of vyce, and corrupting of youth."[34] The psalm-books would also make available to the Congregation scripturally sanctioned songs for public worship. The *Bay Psalm Book* urged this point in a prefatory essay, "declaring not onely the lawfulnesse, but also the necessity of the heavenly Ordinance of singing Scripture Psalmes in the Church of God."[35] Attempting to meet these needs, many psalm versifiers felt a special challenge to find an appropriate poetic garb for works which were in themselves superlative poetry in the Hebrew originals. In this regard, Wither observed that the Psalms had long been deprived of their "naturall ornaments of *Poesy*" in English, whereas the Holy Ghost had presented them in that form partly because of the "extraordinary majesty and pleasingnes which is in *Numbers*."[36]

The prefaces to these metrical versions, together with countless commentaries and sermons upon the Psalms, developed several grounds for considering them to be superlative religious lyrics in themselves and particularly suitable models for Christian poets. In the first place, the Hebrew Psalms were thought to be in meter—indeed in something closely resembling if not identical to the classical lyric meters. The *loci classici* on the topic from the patristic era were well known. They include Josephus' declaration that "David . . . composed songes and hymnes to God of divers Metres, some trimetres and some quinquemetres"; Eusebius' comment that Exodus 15 and Psalm 119 are in "Heroicall Metre" and that "They have also . . . other, as well *trimetres* and *tetrametres*"; Jerome's often reprinted observation in his "Preface" to Paulinus that "David [is] our Simonides, Pindar and Alcaeus, Flaccus and also Catullus and Serenus"; and Jerome's rhetorical question to Eusebius—"What can be more musical than the Psalter! Like the writing of our own Flaccus [Horace] and the Grecian Pindar, it now runs along in sonorous Alcaics, now swells in Sapphics, now marches in half-foot meter."[37] In the Renaissance such texts were quoted and expanded upon by the famous Hebrew scholar Franciscus Gomarus, by Thomas Lodge and Thomas Churchyard, and perhaps most succinctly by Henry Hammond: *"Simonides, Pindar,* and *Alcaeus* among the *Greeks,* and *Horace,* and *Catullus,* and *Serenus* among the *Latines,* were famous for their *Odes* or *Poetick* songs, but *David* to us supplies abundantly the place of all them."[38] Even those more sophisticated writers and exegetes—e.g., Philip Sidney, Henry Ainsworth, George Wither— who discarded the theory of Hebrew metrical equivalents to the classical meters nevertheless stated that the Psalms were metrical, though their rules "be not yet fully found."[39]

The significance of the Psalms as a compendium of lyric poetry was enhanced by the well-nigh universal agreement as to the range and inclusiveness of its subject matter. The book was described as the epitome of the entire scripture, the compendium of all theological, doctrinal, and moral knowledge in lyric form. The Douay Bible summarized the Fathers' agreement "that it is the abridgement, summe, and substance of al holie Scriptures, both old and new Testament."[40] Both Matthew Parker's *Psalter* (1567) and the ubiquitous Sternhold-Hopkins psalter reprinted an extract from Athanasius, declaring that "whatsoever was conteyned abroade in the whole Scripture, was fullye reported in the Psalter booke: . . . The bokes of the Psalmes (beyng wel resembled to a pleasant garden of all deliciousnes) did universally by Metre expresse them all, by playing them as it were sweetely upon musicall instrumentes."[41] Basil expanded at length upon the universal knowledge of religion and virtue comprehended in this epitome:

> The booke of the psalmes comprehende in it selfe, the whole commoditie of all their doctrines aforesaid, for it prophecieth of thinges to come, it reciteth the histories, it sheweth lawe for the governaunce of life, it teacheth what ought to be done, and to be shorte, it is a common storehouse of al good doctrine. . . . The Psalme is an introduction to beginners, it is a furtherer to them which go forwarde to vertue, it is to the perfect man a stable foundation to rest on, it is the swete voyce, the onely mouth of the spouse of Christ the church. . . . Now as for the matter and content of the Psalme, what is there, but that a man maye learne it there? Is not there to be learned the valiauntnes of fortitude? The righteousnes of justice? The sobernes of temperance? The perfection of prudence? The forme of penaunce? The measure of patience? Yea and whatsoever soundeth to vertue or perfection is it not there taught?

In the Psalme is conteined absolute divinitie, both prophecy of christes comming in the flesh. The thretfull warninges of the judgement. The hope of our rising agayne. The feare of Gods punishmentes. The promises of everlasting joye. The revelation of all mysteries, all these be laide and couched up in the Psalter booke, as in a great treasure house common to al men.[42]

Writing in this tradition, Luther termed the Book of Psalms "a little Bible; for in it all things that are contained in the whole Bible are . . . condensed into a most beautiful manual"; the Junius-Tremellius introduction virtually paraphrases Basil in declaring the Book of Psalms to be a most elegant epitome of the Law and the Prophets and the sum of all theology; and the "Argument" to the *Dutch Annotations* terms it "the compleat Summary or compendious rehearsal of the whole Bible, Law and Gospel."[43]

Of still more importance in intimating the significance of the Psalms as lyric models was the idea that they present an epitome of human emotions, a searching analysis or anatomy of the soul of each and every Christian. This view was also firmly rooted in the patristic tradition. Basil emphasized particularly the comprehensive emotional range of the Psalms, able to work, as Plato thought the Greek modes did, upon all men's passions and temperaments: "The psalme is the rest of the soule, the rodde of peace, it stilleth and pacifieth the ragyng bellowes of the minde, for it doth asswage and mollifie that irefull power and passion of the soule, it induceth chastity, where reigned wantonnes, it maketh amitie, where was discorde, it knitteth frendes together, it returneth enemies to an unitie againe."[44] Athanasius laid the groundwork for seeing the Psalms as an anatomy of the soul—"it conteyneth the motions, the mutations, the alterations of every mans hart and conscience described and lively paynted to his owne sight."[45]

Protestants found this view especially sympathetic, and drew out all its implications. Luther declared that the Psalms record the emotional history of all the faithful:

We have . . . the feelings and experiences of all the faithful, both under their sorrows and under their joys, both in their adversity and their prosperity: . . . The Holy Spirit . . . himself has drawn up this manual for his disciples; having collected together, as it were, the lives, groans, and experiences of many thousands, whose hearts he alone sees and knows. . . . You have therein, not only the works and acts of the saints, but their very words and expressions, nay, their sighs and groans to God, and the utterance in which they conversed with him during their temptations; . . . the very hidden treasure of their hearts' feelings—the very inmost sensations and motions of their soul.[46]

Calvin made the same point:

> Not without cause am I woont to terme this book the Anatomy of all the partes of the Soule, inasmuch as a man shal not find any affection in himselfe, wherof the Image appeereth not in this glasse. Yea rather, the holy Ghost hath heere lyvely set out before our eyes, all the greefes, sorowes, feares, doutes, hopes, cares, anguishes, and finally all the trubblesome motions wherewith mennes mindes are woont to be turmoyled.[47]

Among English Protestants also we find this notion and this language everywhere. John Bate termed the Penitential Psalms "The Anatomy of the spirit and the heart, as it were, of the new man."[48] John Donne, preaching on one of the Penitential Psalms (51) declared, "So doth *Davids* history concerne and embrace all . . . wee need no other Example to discover to us the slippery wayes into sin, or the penitentiall wayes out of sin, then the Author of that Booke, *David*."[49] And the *English Annotations* conclude:

> This Book is by some called, *The Anatomy of the Soul*: And that not unfitly, for herein we see all the affections of Gods servants lively expressed in excellent paterns. We finde them sometimes grieving for sin, and troubles: otherwhiles, rejoycing in deliverances: Now praying to God, then praising of God: Putting forth one while their desire of God, and dependance on him: another while, their joy in God, and care to please him. . . . This varietie of Hymns is left us upon record, that we might in Gods publike service, and in private singing, make use of them, according to severall occasions.[50]

The various systems of classifying the Psalms open up a very wide range of possibilities for the religious lyric, and point to specific psalmic models for imitation in the various kinds. One classification is by rhetorical forms and uses: Athanasius identified ninety-nine distinct uses for specific psalms, according to the applicability of their subject matter to various states of soul and personal occasions.[51] Luther contracted this proliferation of forms and uses into five principal ones—prophecy, doctrine, consolation, supplication or prayer, and thanksgiving—a system retained by Theodore Beza with the addition of one category, victories or triumphs, and the qualification that certain psalms are mixtures of two basic kinds.[52] Invoking somewhat different rhetorical terms, John Diodati (1643) analyzed the subject matter of the Psalms according to speaker and forms of address:

In some Psalmes God speaketh to his Church and to his elect, and in other some to his enemies; to the first by instructions, exhortations, corrections, consolations, promises, and prophecies, especially of the *Messias* and of his spirituall and everlasting kingdome. . . . To his enemies he speaks by threatnings and reproofs. . . . In other places the Psalmists speak, or cause the Church to speak unto God, in confessions, complaints, prayers, prayses and thanksgivings; or to the faithfull, in instructions, exhortations, corrections, and reprehensions.[53]

Other classifications are based primarily upon the emotions exhibited in and evoked by the various psalms. Luther offers such a scheme, declaring that the Psalms render with special intensity the spectrum of human emotions, because of their special dramatic circumstance of portraying the human soul speaking to God:

Wherever the feelings of joy are described, you will never find the sensations of a heart, filled with gladness and exultation, more significantly and expressively described, than in the Psalms of thanksgiving, or the Psalms of praise. . . . On the other hand, you will never find the straits, the sorrows, and the pains of a distressed mind any where described in a more expressive manner than in the Psalms of temptations, or of complaints; as in Psalm vi. and the like; where you see all dark and gloomy, all full of anguish and distress, under a sight and sense of divine wrath, and the working of despair.

And so again, where the Psalms are speaking of hope or fear, they so describe those feelings in their true and native colours, that no Demosthenes or Cicero could ever equal them in liveliness, or descriptiveness of expression. For, as I have before observed, the Psalms have this peculiarity of excellence above all other books of description . . . this that above all things gives a seriousness, and reality to the feelings,—it is this that affects, as it were, the very bones and the marrow,—when a creature feels itself speaking in the very sight and presence of its God![54]

Matthew Parker presents another version of such a classification: he sets forth eight psalm settings as variations upon the basic Doric, Lydian, and Phrygian modes, distributing the Psalms among them in accordance with the primary emotion conveyed:

> The first is meeke: devout to see,
> The second sad: in majesty.
> The third doth rage: and roughly brayth.
> The fourth doth fawne: and flattry playth.

> The fyfth delighth: and laugheth the more,
> The sixt bewayleth: it weepeth full sore,
> The seventh tredeth stoute: in froward race,
> The eyghte goeth milde: in modest pace.[55]

Even more directly relevant to the perception of the Psalms as models for religious lyric were materials focusing upon the generic forms the Psalms were thought to exhibit, and representing the Book of Psalms, quite explicitly, as a compendium of lyric kinds. No doubt the metrical version of the Psalms by Sir Philip Sidney and his sister was influential in promulgating this view; though not published for two centuries, these poems circulated extensively in manuscript and were known to, among others, Donne, Fulke Greville, Samuel Daniel, Ben Jonson, Joseph Hall, Sir John Harington, and probably to Herbert. Unfortunately, the Sidneys do not supply a theoretical preface to their psalter, but their assumptions are clear from the amazing diversity of stanzaic patterns and rhyme schemes displayed in the collection. In marked contrast to the monotonous repetition of the ballad stanza or "fourteener" in the Sternhold-Hopkins psalms, there are only four instances in the entire Sidney collection of an exact repetition of any one combination of rhyme scheme and stanza form.[56] Sidney and the Countess have evidently undertaken to devise appropriate English lyric forms to reflect the sheer diversity of kinds they found in the Psalms themselves.

Contemporary theoretical statements proposed generic classifications of the Psalms according to various systems. As might be expected, the Pauline categories—psalms, hymns, spiritual songs—were most often invoked to provide a basic classification. Henry Ainsworth explains, "There be three kinds of songs mentioned in this booke [of Psalms]; 1 *Mizmor*, in Greeke *Psalmos*, a *Psalme*; 2 *Tehillah*, in Greeke *hymnos*, a *hymne* or *praise*; 3 and *Shir*, in Greeke *Odé*, a *song* or *Laie*."[57] George Wither's *Preparation to the Psalter*, an important summary of received views of the Psalms, refined and subdivided the Pauline categories, finding them analogous in some respects to the familiar lyric forms: sonnets, songs, and hymns. He also identifies several other kinds (which are perhaps to be assimilated to the three Pauline classes) from the titles or headings in the scripture text:

> The Names of the *Psalmes* are many: such as these, *A Psalme: A Song: A Hymne: A Prayer: Instructions: Remembrances: Of Degrees: Halleluiah, or Praises. A Psalme a Song; and a Song a Psalme.* By a *Psalme*, the Auncient Expositors understood such verses as being composed in the honour or prayse of some Subject, were indifferent-

ly intended, to be either read or sung; as are our ordinary English Sonnets, consisting of foureteene lines. A *Song* was made of *Measures*, composed purposely to be Sung. *Hymnes* were Songs, in which were the praises of God onely, and that with joy and triumph; and therefore the Songs of *Jeremy* cannot be properly called *Hymnes*, but rather Tragedies, or Lamentations: those that are intituled *Halleluiah*, are *Hymns* also, mentioning particularly the praises of God for benefits received. Now of what nature they are which be called *Prayers, Psalms of Instruction*, or such like; the very names of some of them doe plainely enough declare. . . . Those that are Inscribed, *A Psalme a Song*; and those that have the words transposed, *A Song a Psalme*, are such as were both sung and playd together.[58]

Some particular psalms or groups of psalms were regularly identified with particular genres. The so-called Penitential Psalms (6, 32, 38, 51, 102, 130, 143) had been appointed to persons in the medieval church who were reunited to the church after satisfying open, canonical penance for sin; among Protestants they were generally regarded as meditations. Victorinus Strigelius declared that David in these psalms sought "to mollify his miseries with meditating of God's mercies," and Beza used them as framework and model for his own meditations on sin, affliction, and repentance.[59] Psalm 104 was often identified as another kind of meditation—on the creatures: Henry Hammond termed it "a most elegant pious meditation on the power and wisdome of God, in framing and preserving all the creatures in the world."[60]

Several psalms were regularly designated as hymns of praise—notably Psalms 8, 19, 66, 103, 104; the Alleluia Psalms (113-118); and most of the final fifteen, especially those which begin, "Praise ye the Lord." The fifteen Gradual Psalms or Songs of Degree (120-135) were identified as a special group of praises and thanksgivings for favors received—in this case the return of the Israelites out of Babylon and their ascent to the Temple.[61] And many observed that the final fifty psalms were chiefly praises and thanksgivings, looking forward to our blessed occupation in heaven.

Some other specific kinds were also identified. Thomas Gataker described Psalms 25, 34, 37, and 119 as artful acrostics—"composed according to the order of the *Hebrew Alphabet*, the verses of them beginning, as in *Acrosticall Poems*, with the letters thereof in their vulgar and usuall order."[62] (There is biblical warrant here for witty Herbertian hieroglyphics, it would seem.) And Psalm 45 was regularly identified as an epithalamium—"An excellent prophetical Ephithalamium or wedding-song, by occasion of Solomon his marriage with Pharo's daughter, endited for the spiritual marriage of the bride-groom Jesus Christ, with his dear spouse, the Catholick Church of Jewes and Gentiles."[63] Donne, citing St. Jerome with approval, indi-cates the presence of still other small kinds, though without identifying particular examples—eclogues, pastorals, ballads.[64]

In his *Preparation to the Psalter* Wither considered the question of genre in broad as well as particular terms. In doing so he found both lyric and dramatic forms, and all the fundamental literary modes—tragic, pastoral, satiric, heroic—in the Psalms:

> Note also, that these holy *Hymnes* are not written all in one kinde of *Poesie*, but the Prophet hath made use almost of all sorts. Sometime he bringeth in severall persons speaking together, according to the manner of *Dramaticke Poems*; . . . Sometimes his *Odes* are heroicall, sometime tragicall, sometime pastorall, sometime satyricall: and this is by reason of the necessity of the matter. For one while he in-troduceth *Adam* and his posteritie bewayling their miserable condi-tion, under Sinne and the Law; or else he brings in Christ or his Church, lamenting the unjust persecutions of the *Jewes* and *Gentiles*, and then his *Odes* are tragicall. Other while he takes occasion to set forth the malicious conditions of the enemies of the *Messias*, and his kingdome: then he is Satyricall. Another while he sings the sweet contentments of that shepheard with his flocke: there he maketh Pastorals. But when he intends either to set forth the wondrous works of the eternall God, or the glorious magnificence of our Redeemers Empire, then his divine *Muse* mounts the height of Heroi-call *Poesie*.[65]

In his own version of the Psalms, Wither justified his metrical variety on the ground of this diversity of kinds: "I have used some, varietie of Verse; Because, *Prayers*, *Praises*, *Lamentations*, *Tryumphs*, and subjects which are *Pastoral*, *Heroical*, *Elegiacall*, and *mixt* (all which are found in the *Psalmes*) are not properly exprest in one sort of *Measure*."[66] Frances Quarles also identified in the Psalms all the literary modes, from epic to elegiac, under the patronage of the various muses:

> Who ever sung so high, so rapt an *Io*
> As *David* prompted by heroick *Clio*?
> But when thy more divine *Urania* sung,
> What glorious Angell had so sweet a tongue?
> But when *Melpomene* began to sing,
> Each word's a *Rapture*, or some *higher thing*:
> Sweet were thy *triumphs*; sweet those *joyes* of thine;
> O, but thy *Teares* were more then most *Divine*.[67]

Donne's sermons provide perhaps the most coherent "literary" view of the basic kinds of lyric in the Psalms: he delighted in them and turned to them again and again for sermon texts. His description of the "external form" of the Psalms as organic, intricately contrived lyrics would delight a New Critic: "God gives us . . . *Psalms*, which is also a limited, and a restrained form; . . . such a form as is both curious, and requires diligence in the making, and then when it is made, can have nothing, no syllable taken from it, nor added to it."[68] His categories (as with Wither) are suggested by the titles of the Psalms, but are justified by a sophisticated analysis of what those titles imply in terms of "inner form." In the first place, Donne recognized the most fundamental distinction among the Psalms to be that of prayer and praise: he divides "all the Psalmes in our service" into "those of Praise, and those of Prayer."[69] He specified as praises the Alleluia Psalms, recalling a tradition "that that *Hymne*, which Christ and his Apostles are said to have sung after the Institution and celebration of the Sacrament, was a *Hymne* composed of those six Psalms, which we call the *Allelujah Psalmes*, immediatly preceding the hundred and nineteenth." He analyzes the Penitential Psalms as prayers and also Psalms 90-100, noting that these "and divers others besides these, (which made up a faire limme of this body, and a considerable part of the Book) are called Prayers."[70]

Analyzing the category of prayer further he distinguishes two kinds—deprecatory (begging release or relief from divine wrath and affliction) and postulatory (asking for benefits)—both of which may be present in a single psalm.[71] At a somewhat less fundamental level he recognizes two other kinds. Noting that one of the Penitential Psalms (32) is entitled "*Davidis Eruditio, Davids* Institution, *Davids* Catechisme," he observes that David often "delivers himselfe, by way of Catechising, of fundamentall and easie teaching," and finds "eleven Psalmes that have that Title, *Psalmes of Instruction*."[72] Again, he recognizes some psalms as meditations: he treats Psalm 38 as, in part, a "Remembrance" or "Contemplation" of our human condition, and notes that the Penitential Psalms generally are "the Churches Topicks for mortification and humiliation."[73]

Yet at the same time he indicates that these distinctions are in some ways arbitrary, that all the Psalms might be subsumed under any one of them. Accordingly, he cites with approval the tradition labeling the Book of Psalms, meditations: "Our Countreyman *Bede* found another Title, in some Copies of this booke, *Liber Soliloquiorum de Christo*, The Booke of Meditations upon Christ."[74] In another place he treats them all as prayers: "Prayer is our whole service to God. . . . This

Prophet [David] here executes before, what the Apostle counsailes after, *Pray incessantly*; Even in his singing he prayes; . . . *Davids Songs are Prayers*."[75]

Most fundamentally, all the Psalms are praise. Again and again Donne comments on the Hebrew title of the book, *Sepher Tehillim*, the Book of Praises, and insists that all the categories are appropriately subsumed under that title. Commenting on those termed prayers, he declares, "The Book is Praise, the parts are Prayer. The name changes not the nature; Prayer and Praise is the same thing . . . the duties agree in the heart and mouth of a man. . . . Gods house in this world is called the house of Prayer; but in heaven it is the house of Praise."[76] So also with the group entitled Instructions; they also are songs, and praises:

> The whole booke is *Sepher Tehillim, The booke of prayses*; and it is a good way of praysing God, to receive Instruction, Instruction how to praise him. Therefore doth the holy Ghost returne so often to this Catechisticall way. . . . The manner how Instruction should be given, is expressed also; It must be in a loving manner, for the Title is *Canticum Amorum*, a song of love for Instruction. For . . . True Instruction is a making love to the Congregation, and to every soule in it.[77]

Donne recognizes the Book of Psalms as a compendium of lyric kinds, but at the same time perceives a fundamental unity in the book, arising from the fact that all the Psalms display certain basic devotional impulses which are, in the final analysis, one.

A word remains to be said about the structural patterns sometimes discovered in the Book of Psalms, as ordering the one hundred fifty lyrics. Some commentators, following a Hebrew tradition, divide the book into five parts on the basis of a double "Amen" or "Amen Hallelujah" occurring after Psalms 41, 72, 89, and 106, but few sixteenth- and seventeenth-century exegetes took this to be a meaningful structural division.[78] George Wither describes various suggested topical organizations, but he is suspicious of such attempts, observing that the disjunctions in chronological order and history evident in the Psalms is appropriate to collections of lyrics: "there is no reason wherefore any man should expect the same order, in Subjects of this nature, which is observed in Histories; since it was never used, nor required as necessary in *Lyricke Poems*."[79]

Notwithstanding such justifications of randomness, the very general structural pattern discerned by St. Augustine received considerable acceptance. Augustine identified three groups of fifty psalms each as representing distinct stages of the spiritual life: "For it seems to me not without significance, that the fiftieth is of penitence, the hundredth of mercy and judgment, the hundred and fiftieth of the praise of God in His saints. For thus do we advance to an everlasting life of happiness, first by condemning our own sins, then by living aright, that . . . we may attain to everlasting life."[80] Archbishop Parker's psalter arranged the Psalms in just such "Quinquagenes," with collects after each group relating to the general plane of spiritual life treated therein. The prayer after the first fifty is that we may be "discharged of the burden of sinne"; after the second fifty, "that we maye feele in our hartes the delectable comfortes of thy true promises"; and after the third set, "that . . . wee may at last bee associated to that heavenly quire above."[81] Wither's summary indicates that these divisions were sometimes assimilated to the medieval pattern of the three stages of the mystical life, but were more commonly understood as general stages of spiritual progress:

> Some there be, who say, that in those three fifties, are expressed the three degrees of blessednesse: the first discovering the estate of penitence, the second of progression, and the third of perfection. Or thus: the first fiftie are of repentance and correction, the second of righteousnesse and mercy, the last of praises & thankesgivings, which shall be the employment of the righteous, in the perfection of their blessednesse.[82]

In these terms, a very general structural and narrative pattern in regard to spiritual progress may be seen to undergird and give coherence to these disparate lyrics.

Clearly, theoretical observations about the poetic parts of scripture and about the Psalms in particular yield very suggestive insights about the generic kinds appropriate to divine lyric, and available in its primary model. On all sides the Book of Psalms is seen as a compendium (of all theological, doctrinal, and moral knowledge; of all the modes of God's revelation—law, prophecy, history, proverbs; of all the emotions and passions of the human soul; and, apparently, of all the lyric genres and styles appropriate to divine poetry. The major kinds supposed to be included were psalms, hymns, and spiritual songs: the first comprehended divers matters and emotions but evidently were primarily argumentative or meditative or prayer-like in manner; the second included exalted and sublime praises and thanksgivings to God; and the third, artful, majestic, ode-like poems which were lyrical in character. Within these broad categories, the range of forms identified in the Book of Psalms is staggering: meditations, soliloquies, complaints, laments for tribulations, prayers for benefits, petitions against adversities, psalms of instruction, consolations, rejoicings, praises of God for his glory and goodness, thanksgivings to God for benefits received, triumphs celebrating God's victories over his enemies, artful acrostic poems, ballads, pastoral eclogues, pastoral songs, satires, elegies, love songs, an epithalamium, dramatic poems, tragical odes, heroic odes. In addition, there is some theory accommodating all the Psalms to the two major categories of address to God, prayer and praise, or sometimes to the primary category of praise. Also there is some suggestion of a loose narrative and thematic structure in the book, relating to the progress of the soul.

Such theory seems to encourage just such a collection of lyric poetry as we find in Herbert's *The Temple* (specifically, "The Church")— and to a lesser extent in Vaughan's *Silex Scintillans*. In both, but especially in Herbert, lyric poems in a variety of kinds explore a very wide range of emotions and spiritual states, and in both, such poems are at once deeply personal self-probings, an "anatomy of the soul," and at the same time presentations of everyman's spiritual autobiography. Both collections eschew a precise structural pattern of thematic or narrative development, but yet portray in general terms a movement from penitence and conversion to some higher plane of spiritual life. And both, moreover, incorporate a few psalm paraphrases or descants on particular psalms (for Herbert Psalms 23, 51, 57:7-11, 104, and for Vaughan Psalms 65, 104, 121) in evidence that the poets are relating themselves to David, and undertaking some version of his task.

Herbert's debt, of course, is the more profound: he seems to have attempted to provide in "The Church" just such a compendium of lyric kinds as the Book of Psalms was thought to contain: sonnets and sonnet-like poetic arguments, melodious songs, meditations, instructions, petitions, penitential poems echoing the Psalms (for instance, "The Altar" echoes Psalm 51), acrostic and hieroglyphic poems, hymnic praises of God, and many more. Also, as we shall see, he relates his poems in a host of subtle ways to the Psalms, as if presenting them as new creations in the psalmic mode. Moreover, Herbert's speaker is centrally concerned throughout the volume with contriving worthy praise: like the Psalms, all his poems, whatever their kind, contribute to the construction of a "Temple" of praise.

The other poets drew more selectively upon the genre theory associated with the Psalms, though all of them found here a primary reference point for defining their own work. Donne's verse letter "Upon the translation of the Psalmes by Sir Philip Sydney, and the Countesse of Pembroke his Sister" praises the inspiration and the art of those translations as virtually on a par with the Psalmist's originals—not so much translations as "re-revelations" of God's Spirit. They are also an appropriate model: "They tell us *why*, and teach us *how* to sing."[83] Yet for all this, and despite the pervasive presence of quotations from the Psalms in his sermons, Donne's poems make little overt use of the genre theory of the Psalms. He does make covert use of it: certain of the "Holy Sonnets" (especially Sonnet XIV) are imaginative "re-revelations" of the Penitential Psalms; and in the "Hymne to God my God, in my sicknesse" the speaker's postponement of hymn-singing until he arrives in heaven plays wittily with the theory of the hymn as sublime, exalted praise. Beyond this, Donne developed in the sermons an impressive theoretical basis for regarding the Book of Psalms as the central model for the religious lyric poet and the preacher. But he left it to others—most strikingly, Herbert—to make that theory the governing principle of an entire *corpus* of poetry.

Vaughan's collection does not approach *The Temple* in range of kinds and forms, nor does Vaughan find his chief model for religious lyric in the Book of Psalms. Yet his collection is also a compendium of kinds—chiefly, kinds of meditation—and he does employ psalm paraphrases at significant junctures to help define its nature. His version of Psalm 104 is a close rendering of the Psalmist's eloquent celebration of all God's works, and serves as a centerpiece and reference point for Vaughan's most distinctive genre—meditations on the creatures. And his version of Psalm 65 transforms that rather eclectic psalm into a unified, exalted hymn. Placed among his final poems and spoken as by one welcomed to the heavenly mansions and joining with the saints in exalted praise, it represents the speaker's achievement at last of appropriate praise—derived from the saints' common store, the Psalter, but yet individual. Like Donne he locates this generic accomplishment in heaven but, unlike him, renders it in verse, in the present.

Traherne relied directly and massively upon genre theory deriving from psalm commentary, though not, interestingly enough, for his short religious lyrics. He appears to regard the Psalms as presenting two major generic models, meditation and praise, and he makes each of these the basis of a long, major work. His prose *Centuries of Meditation* contains at its center a long sequence of paraphrase-cum-meditations upon a series of psalms; the speaker first amalgamates his own meditations thoroughly with the Psalmist's, and at the end of the series devises original meditations as New Testament continuations of, or perfections of, the Davidic works. And his hymnic *Thanksgivings* are long, rhapsodic, majestic praises and thanksgivings to God, interweaving passages from various psalms, e.g., 8, 65, 104 (without identifying them as such), among the poet's own original lines written in the same exalted mode. Unlike any of the previous poets and no doubt as a direct result of a theology based upon present enjoyment of the divine inheritance, Traherne shows his speaker creating—on earth and without much anxiety—hymnic praises of the most exalted kind. But the Psalms are the vehicle and the measure of that achievement: the speaker is imagined to succeed *because* his own voice is indistinguishable from that of the Psalmist.

For Taylor the Psalms are not a generic or conceptual model, but they serve nonetheless a vital role in the negative definition of the poet and his poems. Taylor's speaker refers constantly to the instruments and tunes of the Psalms as mediums he wishes to, but cannot, employ in the present; he thereby declares his inevitable and unequivocal failures in praise and his utter inability to imitate the biblical generic models directly. By invoking and then relinquishing biblical models (especially Canticles and the Book of Psalms), Taylor defines what his poems (and he himself) can attain, and what they cannot—until he is glorified. Yet, over and over again he promises that he will sing true, artful, exalted praises in glory, taking the Psalms as a primary model.

## C. Proverbs, Ecclesiastes, Canticles

A second major source of theoretical discussion about biblical poetry is to be found in poetic versions of and commentary upon the three canonical books of Solomon. The Song of Songs was second only to the Book of Psalms in the frequency with which it was rendered in verse,[84] and Proverbs and Ecclesiastes also invited several verse paraphrases.[85] The three books were usually understood to have been written in distinct and progressively more complex genres and styles—the adage or *sententia*; the sermon; and the lofty, artful, allegorical song.

The progression applied to subject matter as well. Origen found in these books a natural, developmental progression from ethics to natural philosophy to contemplative wisdom:

First, in Proverbs he [Solomon] taught the moral science, putting rules for living into the form of short and pithy maxims, as was fitting. Secondly, he covered the science known as natural in Ecclesiastes; in this, by discussing at length the things of nature . . . he counsels us to forsake vanity and cultivate things useful and upright. . . . In this [Song of Songs] he instils into the soul the love of things divine and heavenly, using for his purpose the figure of the Bride and Bridegroom.[86]

Origen also discerned a progression of the three books in terms of the stages of the spiritual life—not unlike the pattern found in the three principal divisions of the Psalms: the soul is "as a beginner, in Proverbs; then as advancing, in Ecclesiastes; and lastly as more perfect in the Song of Songs."[87] Altering this pattern slightly, the Douay Bible associated the three books with the stages of the mystical way.[88] But Protestants, with their characteristically greater attention to the historical situation of the Old Testament writers, related the progression in matter and style to Solomon's own development and experience—which led him, as Henoch Clapham put it, to the deliberate choice of various modes of teaching:

> His owne three books evince his repentance: first the booke of Proverbs specially the Preface lying in the first nine chapters: wherin. he specially admonisheth his people to beware of the strange woman: . . . as speaking from experience. In which booke he laboreth therfore to settle his Puple (of what degre or calling soever) in the rudiments and grounds of religion.
>
> Secondly, his booke termed Preacher, wherein . . . he preacheth worldly vanitie from selfe same experience, admonishing others to beware by his evill. . . .
>
> Thirdly, this most divine Song penned (as before is proved) in his olde age: vaine lustes then turned to contemplative loves passing betwene Messiah and his Church.[89]

Some Protestants tended to conflate the matter and manner of Proverbs and Ecclesiastes, regarding both as didactic poems presenting precepts for moral and political behavior and denouncing worldly vanities. Several Commonplace Books compiled from the maxims of the two books reinforce this view—examples are Joseph Hall's *Salomons Divine Arts, of 1. Ethicks, 2. Politicks, 3. Oeconomicks*, and Thomas Rogers' *Pretious Pearles of King Salomon*.[90] Protestants also often compared the spiritual progression in Solomon's three books to the three parts of the Hebrew Temple—in terms suggestive for Herbert's "The Church-porch" and "The Church." Beza worked out such an equation, pointing first to,

> the utter common court for the people, unto which *the booke of the Proverbs* may be compared: after that was the inner place, provided for the Priestes: and lastly the Sanctuarie called the holy of Holies. Even so we may say, that the Church is as it were lead to enter into the Holy place by *the booke of Ecclesiastes, called the Preacher*, and from thence by this Canticle or Song, brought even to the entery of the Sanctuary, or Holy of Holies.[91]

When they discussed the Book of Proverbs alone, Renaissance commentators were in general agreement as to its genre: it is a handbook of manners, or ethics, or of moral and civil duties pertaining to God and our neighbor. William Perkins described it as "a treatise of Christian manners, teaching pietie towards God, and justice towardes our Neighbour."[92] The Junius-Tremellius Bible maintained that it presents "sacred Christian ethics, that is, moral precepts concerning the sacred duties owed to God and men," as defined by both the Law of Nature and the Word of God; and the English annotators included as well, "household offices and affairs."[93] Most commentators noted a structural division in Proverbs conforming to its two distinct subjects: the first nine chapters concern matters of faith and piety owing to God and general precepts referring to true wisdom and fear of the Lord; and the remaining chapters (10-25) set forth more particular precepts relating to vices and virtues of the Second Table, and pertaining to specific circumstances of life.[94]

In an interpretive tradition dating back to Jerome, Gregory Nazianzen, and Augustine, the Book of Proverbs was said to be addressed in a special way to the young, or to beginners in the religious life, with the author assuming the stance of father or teacher.[95] The Bishops' Bible notes that the Book treats of the "instruction and nurture of such as begin to serve God"; and the Geneva Bible extends the father-children relation to include the preacher and his flock—an identification linking Proverbs yet more closely with Ecclesiastes, the Book of the Preacher: "[Solomon] speaketh . . . in the Name of God, which is the universal Father of all creatures, or in the Name of the pastor of the Churche, who is as a father."[96] Seeking to clarify these terms, Miles Mosse warned against interpreting too literally the commonplace assigning of the Book of Proverbs to the young and to civil manners, noting that it contains much instruction for old men as well, and that the definition of manners applicable here must include "our mannerly and holy cariage of our selves outwardly and inwardly towards the majesty of God."[97]

As regards formal characteristics, the Renaissance commentators concerned themselves most with the definition of the rhetorical and poetic figure, "proverb." It was usually glossed as *sententia* (or maxim), and as a synonym for "parable." The Geneva Bible uses the three terms interchangeably: "This worde Proverbe, or Parable signifieth a grave and notable sentence, worthy to be kept in memorie." The Junius-Tremellius Bible observes that Proverbs are "sentences, maxims, or sayings rendered gravely and with brevity." John Trapp terms them "*Mastersentences*, Axioms, Speeches of special precellency and predominancy: Received Rules that must over-rule matters, and mightily prevail in the minds of men"; he concludes that "Solomon . . . better (a deal) deserves to be stiled *Master of the Sentences*, than Peter Lombard."[98] Alternatively, the term "proverb" or "parable" was often equated with "similitude" or with various "dark" tropes. Conrad Pellican speaks of "Proverbs or Similitudes, which are called Parables in Greek."[99] Thomas Wilcox understood by the term the many "figurative and darke kinde of speeches" in the work, including similes, allegories, metaphors, and especially the "sentences, words, or speaches . . . gravelie and shortlie uttered, [which] containe in them plentie of good matter."[100] Donne also emphasized the obscurity of these tropes: "There was an Order of Doctors amongst the Jews that professed that way, To teach the people by Parables and darke sayings; . . . And this was the way of *Solomon*, for that very word is the Title of his booke of Proverbs."[101]

Others resolved the apparent discrepancy by distinguishing more than one variety of parable or proverb in the work. The Douay Bible identified two: "*Proverbes*, that is, *common & usual pithie sentences*, shorte in wordes, ample in sense, and *Parables*, signifying likenes or *similitudes*, wherby more important thinges are understood then expressed."[102] Robert Cleaver found three varieties: "sometimes . . . darke, and mystical sayings, not easie to be understood . . . sometimes a borrowed speech, a similitude, or comparison . . . and sometimes short, and sweete proverbiall sentences, full of weight, and wisedome."[103]

Moreover, noting the sharp structural division after chapter nine, commentators often explained the first segment as a prologue, a continued or flowing discourse by Solomon, or Wisdom, or both, whereas the Proverbs proper begin, as the chapter heading indicates, at chapter ten.[104] Cleaver explained this mix of genres in the following terms:

> The [first] . . . nine Chapters being prefixed as a preface to these, contained a continued discourse, wherein the commendation of Wisedome, and the exhortations to many good duties were prosecuted with variety of arguments: whereas in these that follow, for the most part, are set downe briefe sayings, every verse almost comprehending a whole point in it selfe, not growing upon dependance of that which went before, nor ministring the occasion of that which commeth after.[105]

Some also identified the final chapter (31)—the praise of good women —as yet another genre, a "Song" of King Lemuel.[106]

The poetic quality of the Book of Proverbs was often emphasized. It is clearly exhibited in Melancthon's Latin poetic version, in which the first nine chapters are presented in verse paragraphs; chapters ten to thirty as epigrams in short, pithy, rhymed couplets; and the final chapter in a more flowing, discursive form.[107] Cornelius à Lapide described the first part as Solomon's exhortation or discourse on Wisdom, culminating (in chapter 9) in a dialogue between Solomon and Sapientia which was the model for Plato's *Symposium*; he described the second part as a collection of gnomes, adages, and sentences which are poetic and rhythmic in Hebrew, and which are rendered still more elegant by much use of antithesis, paronomasia, schemes, reversals of parts in the hemistich, metonymy, metalepsis, similitudes, and other such figures.[108] Francis Bacon had high praise for the book as a unique example of "allusive or parabolical poetry" concerned with *negotium*—private business and civic duties—and commended its aphoristic style: "*In this kinde* nothing is extant which may any way be compar'd with those Aphorismes which *Solomon the King* set forth."[109]

Ecclesiastes was thought to be a sermon, a related didactic form. Though certain of the Fathers had spoken of it as a treatise on natural philosophy containing knowledge of all things in nature,[110] Renaissance commentators were virtually unanimous in describing it as moral philosophy—a description which related it closely to Proverbs. Its chief subject, all agreed, was the true happiness or highest good of man. Serranus called the book "a most weighty piece of true moral philosophy, concerning the cheefe and soveraign good, and of the way to attaine it"; Donne agreed that Solomon's "principal scope [is] . . . moral and practique wisdom"—though not without an admixture of prophecy and theology; Thomas Granger urged the same point: the book "is *Solomons Ethiks*, his treatise *de summo bono*, of the chiefe and compleat felicity."[111]

There was considerable agreement also in recognizing a two-part division in Solomon's subject, reflected in the structure of the book—the discrediting of all the goods (wealth, pleasure, honor, human wisdom) from which men seek happiness (the first six chapters); and then the demonstration that happiness is to be found only in the fear of God and concern with heavenly things (the last six chapters).[112] The Geneva Bible described the two topics broadly: "the deceiveable vanities of this worlde: that man shulde not be addicted to any thing under the sunne, but rather inflamed with the desire of the heavenly life."[113] Other kinds of knowledge, including various aspects of the natural and social sciences, were also found in the book: Luther, for example, termed it "the politikes, or Oeconomickes of Salomon," inasmuch as it gives counsel on the kinds of misfortune which many times fall out in all affairs of the public and private life.[114]

The title of the book—whether in Hebrew (Coheleth) or in Greek (Ecclesiastes)—defined the stance of the speaker: a king who has on an extraordinary occasion or in an extraordinary fashion assumed the role of preacher to the congregation. As Beza put it, "yee shall heare a Preacher, not of the common sort, but even a King, making a Sermon unto you."[115] Protestants especially portrayed him as a repentant sinner preaching of worldly vanities out of his own life's experience. As a corollary to this, they often agreed with the Hebrew exegetes that he composed the work in his old age: Serranus observed that "he writeth in such sort as if he had learned this doctrine by verie great experience of things and long use."[116] The Dutch annotators described the supposed scene in some detail:

> Many among the learned are of opinion, that *Salomon* wrote this Book in his old age, after that he . . . was now again converted unto God. . . . Wherein he by inspiration of the Holy Ghost, before the whole Congregation of God, testifieth his earnest sorrow and repentance for the former part of his life, loathing and abhorring it, as being vanity of vanities. . . . His intent and purpose is, by his own example and pattern to lead all men to vertue and piety. To this end and purpose he doth in the first place make a short recital of the whole course of his life.[117]

Donne regarded Solomon's sermon as a model for other preachers in this use of personal experience: "To call up the Congregation, to heare what God hath done for my soule, is a blessed preaching of my selfe. And therefore *Salomon* . . . poures out his owne soule to the Congregation, in letting them know, how long the Lord let him run on in vanities, and vexation of spirit, and how powerfully and effectually he reclaimed him at last."[118]

Ecclesiastes, then, is understood to be an ordered sermon or public oration on a set topic, drawing heavily upon the preacher's own experience—and the verse paraphrases of Thomas Surrey and Henry Lok so render it, with personal application to themselves of Solomon's experience.[119] Some Protestants, loath to suggest a biblical precedent for the confusion of the offices of magistrate and minister, argued that Ecclesiastes was set forth as a sermon though Solomon may not have preached it himself to the congregation. Luther, drawing perhaps upon his own practice, speculated that it might have been written down by others from Solomon's Table Talk, so that the book, though not the man, "maketh as it were a publicke sermon."[120] Another generic interpretation was advanced by Donne, who specified the rhetorical form of Solomon's sermon as an "Anatomy" (thereby finding an interesting precedent for one of his own favorite poetic forms): in it, *"Solomon shakes the world in peeces, he dissects it, and cuts it up before thee, that so thou mayest the better see, how poor a thing, that particular is, whatsoever it be, that thou sets thy love upon in this world."*[121] Others made the point that it is a poetic sermon: Lok remarked on the many paradoxes and the matter "couched well by art, / Adorned with words, and figures," while Luther found Solomon's language in this book to be more elegant and courtly than David's, "as having his communication more beutified with flowers and figures."[122]

The Song of Songs, or Canticles, was second only to the Psalms as a work of biblical poetry inviting literary analysis. Christian exegetes—patristic, Roman Catholic, and Protestant alike—agreed that the work is in some sense an allegory, portraying under the images of the Bridegroom and Bride the relation of Christ and the Church, or of Christ and the individual soul as part of the Church, or both.[123] In Hebrew exegesis Canticles had been approached in similar terms—as an allegory of the interaction of Yahweh with his chosen people. But though exegetes agreed in regarding it as some kind of allegorical narrative, only partial agreement obtained as to just what allegory that narrative projects, and just what generic form serves as vehicle for the allegory.

The central Christian tradition of interpretation viewed the work as a literary allegory grounded upon a fiction: that is, the fictional narrative of the love between Bride and Bridegroom is used to convey the true meaning, the love between Christ and the Church, or Christ and the faithful soul. In Augustine's words, the Song of Songs treats of "the marriage of that King and Queen-city, that is, Christ and the Church . . . in allegorical veils."[124] So also the Geneva Bible: "In this Song, Salomon by most sweete and comfortable allegories and parables describeth the perfite love of Jesus Christ, the true Salomon and King of peace, and the faithfull soule or his Church, which hee hath sanctified and appointed to be his spouse."[125] Because the work is so intensely symbolic and prophetical, discussions of Solomon's artistic role often emphasized his situation as instrument of the Holy Ghost, contriving his allegorical fiction after receiving prophetic visions concerning the state of the Church in all ages. Accordingly, exegetes seldom interpreted the work typologically, with Solomon and Pharaoh's daughter as types of Christ and the Church. Origen invoked the typological perspective only when explaining Solomon's name, "Peaceable," and when explaining Canticles 1:5, "I am blacke, but comely," as having reference to the visit of the Queen of Sheba to Solomon: "This Queen came, then, and, in fulfilment of her type, the Church comes also from the

Gentiles to hear the wisdom of the true Solomon."[126] Some exegetes flatly denied typological significance to the work, Beza on the ground that the condemnation of the marriage of Solomon and Pharaoh's daughter prevents its functioning as a type of the holy marriage of Christ and the Church, and Lapide on the ground that Solomon intended literal and direct reference to Christ and the Church.[127] However, some Protestant commentaries—with their characteristic attention to the experiential basis of the biblical poems—suggest that the work may be read typologically, as grounded very generally upon Solomon's experience: thus, the *Dutch Annotations* describe the work as "A Dialogue between Christ, as the Bridegroom, and his Church, as his Spouse or Bride, under the type and figure of Salomon and his Spouse or Bride."[128] Occasionally, the exegetes postulate that Solomon was aware of himself as type, that he wrote the poem about his own experience and designed it to carry typological significance: in this vein the headnote in Taverner's edition of the Matthew Bible (1539) explains that "Salomon made this Balade or songe by him selfe and his wyfe the doughter of Pharao, under the shadowe of him selfe fyguryinge Christ, and under the person of his wyfe the Church."[129]

Addressing the question of the nature of the allegory, patristic, Roman Catholic, and Protestant exegetes agreed that the work refers in the first instance to the Church, and secondarily to the faithful soul, though in fact the two meanings were taken to be inextricably linked in that the Church is itself the entire company of the faithful. Within these broad limits, however, Catholics and Protestants diverged rather sharply. For Origen, and for many of the medieval exegetes, the ecclesiastical dimension of the work was seen as pertaining to the situation of the whole church at all times and places: as the Douay Bible put it, summarizing these views, "By the *Spouse* or *Bride*, the ancient fathers understand . . . the whole Church of the old and new Testaments; of al that are, and shal be perfect, making one mystical bodie, free from sinne, without spotte, or wrinkle, sanctified in Christ."[130] There is little sequence or historical development in these readings—save for some consensus in identifying the opening verses with the Synagogue's longing for Christ's coming, and the verses celebrating the coming of spring after "the winter is past" (ii:11-12) with the Incarnation or public manifestation of Christ. Otherwise, particular verses were interpreted eclectically, on the basis of their specific thematic import, as pertaining variously to the Synagogue, to the Church of the Gentiles, to the Church of the New Testament, or to the Heavenly Jerusalem in its perfected condition. Indeed, Origen declared that the events in this book "do [not] maintain any continuous narrative, such as we find in other Scripture stories."[131]

By contrast, Protestant exegetes tended to find the semblance of a coherent plot in the work, presenting either the situation of the Church in history as it developed progressively from the first ages of the world to the last, or else a general paradigm of spiritual life lived by the Church in every age—or both. Dudley Fenner invoked both explanations: the first six chapters of the Song treat the universal condition of the Church, beginning at peace, then undergoing various temptations to impatience and worldly drowsiness, and at length finding the remedies for these failings; the last two chapters present the Church in history—her longing for Christ before the Incarnation (chapter 7) and then her duties after his coming, which include labor among the Gentiles, and prayers for his constant presence (chapter 8).[132] Henoch Clapham conflated the two patterns, understanding the first two chapters of the work to present the spiritual condition of the church in three ages: before the Incarnation, in the winter state (1); after the Incarnation when she is brought forth into the springtime (2:1-7) and there enacts the paradigm of her New Testament condition, "sometimes praying, sometimes straying, sometimes in a love-traunce, sometimes revived"; and finally her close union with the Bridegroom (2:8-17) as she longs for and anticipates the Second Coming.[133] George Wither also understood that in the Song "the *Church* is diversely spoken of, according to the diversity of her estate and Ages": the Old Testament estate (1-2); the Incarnation and life of Christ (3-6); the Church Militant after the Ascension (6:9-7:13); and finally (8:5) the millennial state, wherein the Bride is at rest, leaning upon the Bridegroom's bosom.[134]

Those exegetes who emphasized the Church's relation to Christ in all ages, without regard to history, define the paradigm for that relationship as one of initial union, fall, and recovery. The Junius-Tremellius annotations suggest that the first verses of Canticles show the mutual love of the Church and Christ; subsequent passages show the Church's frequent imprudences and offences, together with her efforts to recover from these; and the final passages display a more mature state of habitual union with the Bridegroom.[135] William Gouge specifies the parts more precisely: the first four chapters present Christ and the Church as friends, enjoying mutual benefits and pleasures; then their estrangement due to the Church's weakness is shown, followed by her repentance and a renewal of their loves.[136] Richard Sibbes traces a similar paradigm, in five states: the Church's strong desire for nearer communion with Christ; then some declining in her affection; then her recovery and regaining of Christ's love; then again some declining and a sense of Christ's aloofness; and finally, her perception of the Bridegroom's constant affection to her despite her failings, so that she recovers and cleaves to him more firmly than ever before.[137]

In interpreting the allegory pertaining to the individual soul, Protestant exegetes diverge more sharply than in their ecclesiastical allegory from the patristic and Roman Catholic tradition. In that tradition the Bride usually figures the soul in an exalted condition of spiritual perfection, at times enjoying the mystical experience. Origen defined the Bride as one far advanced in the spiritual life, whereas her maidens are faithful souls not yet so exalted. The invitation to the Bride to "awake" after the winter is a calling of the soul forth from the winter of disorders and vices to a cultivation of the flowers of virtue; her later progress into the fields is a departure from the house (fleshly vices) and the city (worldly things) into a life contemplating unseen and eternal things.[138] The idea of ascent to higher and higher stages of perfection, attaining at length to mystical union through contemplation, is the core of St. Bernard's reading also. He pictures the soul constantly yearning for and sometimes enjoying such union, "rapt in ecstasy":

> The soul . . . clothed . . . in that beauty of holiness . . . ventures to think of union with the WORD. Why should she not do so, when she sees that the more she resembles Him, the more fitted she is for that spiritual marriage? . . . It sometimes happens that the soul is so transported out of itself, and entirely detached from the bodily senses, that, though conscious of the WORD, it has no consciousness of itself . . . it is rapt out of itself to enjoy the Presence of the WORD. . . . Sweet is that communion; but how seldom does it occur, and for how brief a time does it last![139]

In François de Sales the same emphasis is present: the Bride is the soul already married to Christ and progressing to the highest order of union with him through meditation and contemplation. The kisses at the beginning of the Song signify "spiritual consolations; faintings, happiness and joys; sleeps and inebrieties, raptures and ecstasies." The soul advances along the three stages of the mystical way—purgative, illuminative, and unitive—first purging vices, then becoming a garden of virtues, then through meditations on the Passion developing an overwhelming desire of the Bridegroom; finally, perfected, she escapes into the fields (chapter 5) to consider God in himself, and in this highest stage of contemplation she is "united to God and absorbed in him by a perfect devotion."[140] Less explicitly mystical in its formulations, the Douay Bible yet identifies the Bride as the perfected soul: the Song treats "the fervant spiritual love, of the inward man, reformed in soule, and perfected in spirite," and therefore it is "not for sinners, nor for beginners, nor for such as are yet in the way towards perfection, but only for the perfect."[141]

In sharp contrast, Protestants did not explain the allegory of the Song in terms of the pinnacle of spiritual perfection or the raptures of mystical union, but rather as a rendering of the common stages of the Christian life, the pilgrimage of all elect Christian souls from tentative beginnings to an assured condition of hope and expectation of glory. These stages were commonly identified in accordance with the Protestant-Pauline paradigm. For George Gifford the kisses in Canticles 1:2 ("Let him kisse me with the kisses of his mouth") refer to the doctrine and preaching which calls the Christian soul to repentance and regeneration. The winter and night of Canticles 2:10-12 refer to the soul before its calling, while the spring—"Rise up, my Love, my faire one, and come away. / For loe, the winter is past"—is the state of the regenerate soul bringing forth flowers and fruits by the dew of grace. The soul is made into a garden enclosed (chapter 4) by Christ (the fountain which waters it with the scriptures) and by the Holy Spirit (the north and south winds). The remaining chapters portray Christ's manner of dwelling with the elect soul—seeming at times to withdraw from it but in fact always present.[142]

John Dove found a somewhat more dramatic plot in the Song, analogous to the fall-and-restoration paradigm that also characterized Protestant interpretations of the ecclesiastical allegory. At the outset the elect soul is recovering from the sickness of sin and coming forth into the springtime of grace; she is then exercised by temptations of diffidence, distraction, and infidelity, and she suffers the sense of spiritual desolation, but Christ makes her a garden, set off by election and purged by the wind of the Spirit (chapter 4). Then she succumbs to the temptation of carnal security, and fails to admit the bridegroom when he comes to her (chapter 5); she repents, goes forth to seek him, and at length is reunited with him.[143] John Robotham traces the stages of the Christian progress in the Song in the same terms but in fuller detail: the initial kisses are the calling of the soul through preaching; the cry of the Bride, "Draw me, we will runne after thee" (Cant. 1:4) signals the opening of the heart by grace, which alone makes progress possible; the Bride's description of herself as "blacke, but comely" testifies to her own sinful condition but withal the inward justification she has by grace; the winter refers to her bondage in sin before her calling, and the spring to her regeneration. She is given power to be a garden, watered by a fountain (Christ), and purged by the winds (the Spirit); she sleeps in the weakness of the flesh but the heart or spirit remains awake to the voice of the Bridegroom (chapter 5). After his withdrawal she goes forth to seek him, and is accepted by him as one of the lillies among which he feeds. Chapters 7 and 8 show her so overcome with the desire for heavenly things that she goes out of the world into the villages where "she will now lodge in a continuall meditation and delight of divine things," waiting for the Spouse to come on his throne of glory (the mountain of spices).[144]

It is evident that Protestant readings of both the ecclesiastical and the personal allegory of Canticles emphasize a progressive, historical development whereby the narrative of Bridegroom and Bride is often carried forward to the millennium or at least to a state of millennial expectation. In New England, as David Watters has noted,[145] this tendency is much strengthened: the two allegorical applications are drawn together into a comprehensive prophetic interpretation correlating historical and millennial events figured in the Song of Songs with those prophesied in the Revelation of St. John. Exegetes such as Thomas Brightman and John Cotton read the Song as a prophecy of Christ's working in human history, and his glorious, personal return at the end of time to enjoy the Bride—that is, the Church composed of all elect souls as they will be in millennial glory.[146]

Even as almost all commentators regarded the Song of Songs as some kind of allegorical narrative, so did they largely agree in the generic description of it as some species of love song or epithalamium, though with interesting variations within that large classification. Jerome's observation that in this work Solomon "sweetly sang the epithalamion of the sacred nuptials" of Christ and the Church was widely echoed— by, among others, Samuel Slater who termed the work an epithalamium or "mysterious Marriage-song"; by Robotham; by John Donne; and by John Dove, who described the book as a three-part epithalamium (the Bride met at the door of the Bridegroom's house; her entrance with her maidens; and her entertainment within).[147] Some others emphasized a pastoral element: John Hall termed it a "Pastoral-mariage Song" and Matthew Henry, "a Pastoral and an Epithalamium."[148]

Still others invoked more general lyric categories for the work. Though William Baldwin refers approvingly to Origen's account of it as a "spousal song," he himself sees it as a group of ballads, "the principall Balades of holy Scripture"; the Matthew Bible also refers to it as a "Balade or songe" and entitles it "The Ballet of Balettes of Salomon."[149]

Alternatively, Francis Quarles entitles his paraphrase, "Sion's Sonets," and he develops that generic conception by breaking up the eight chapters into twenty-five short, sonnet-like poems, so that the Bride and the Bridegroom and their companies of friends are envisaged as singing love sonnets back and forth to each other. The work's meditative aspects are emphasized by John Dove, who compares these "holy meditations" of Solomon to those of Isaac awaiting his bride Rebecca in the fields—a classic Protestant type of the meditator.[150] And Henoch Clapham justifies this habit of identifying the Song of Songs with various lyric kinds, stating that it merits its title in part because it partakes of and excels all the other modes of lyric expression in scripture:

> Touching the [work] . . . it self, it is a *Song*. A *Song* hath divers names according to the manner and matters diversitie. If they containe matter of Gods praise, they are termed *Hymnes*: if it be soong by turnes of two *Chorusses* it is called *Antiphona*. . . . A *Psalme* containeth any sort of matter indifferently, and it is thought of som to derive that name from the instrument termed *Psaltery* . . . : as also specially to containe morall doctrine. For the title *Spirituall song*, it is either the generall to all divine songs; or rather *A Song* of exultation and spirituall rejoycing, specially respecting *Hope of eternal blessednes*. Touching this Song of *Salomon*, it containeth matter of divine laud, for the which it may be called an *Hymne*: it containeth matter of Exultation in the hope of a better life, for the which it may be called a *Spirituall Song*: it containeth morall doctrine, & doctrine of all natures, for the which it may be hight a *Psalme*. As for the forme, we find sundry parties singing, and the one side answering to the other: for which it may be nominated an *Antiphonie* or *Responsorie*. And for these (and like) considerations, it is of the holy ghost called . . . the *Song of Songs*.[151]

Some others emphasized a dramatic or dialogic element in this epithalamium. Origen inaugurated a long tradition of interpreting Canticles as a dramatic epithalamium in which the characters come and go as upon a stage:

> I seem to find four characters—the Husband and the Bride; along with the Bride, her maidens; and with the Bridegroom, a band of intimate companions. Some things are spoken by the Bride, others by the Bridegroom; sometimes too the maidens speak; so also do the Bridegroom's friends. . . . We have thus four groups: the two individuals, the Bridegroom and the Bride; two choirs answering

each other—the Bride singing with her maidens, and the Bridegroom with his companions. . . .

These are the characters in this book, which is at once a drama and a marriage song. And it is from this book that the heathens appropriated the epithalamium, and here is the source of this type of poem; for it is obviously a marriage-song that we have in the Song of Songs.[152]

The dramatic or dialogic element is emphasized by the Douay Bible, which describes it as a "*sacred Dialogue* between Christ and his spouse: or . . . an *Enterlude*, in respect of divers speakers and actors, and of divers persons, to whom the speaches are directed, and of whom they are uttered"; by the Matthew Bible which apportions the text among various characters as in a playbook; by Beza who declares that Canticles is "in the manner of a dialogue, many persons being introduced in a most wonderfull and artificiall maner, speaking and answering one the other"; by David Paraeus, who summarizes and supports Origen's description of it as a wedding song in the manner of a drama.[153] Some observed that the mode of the dramatic poem was pastoral: Cornelius à Lapide explicated it as a five-act poetic pastoral drama in a style "Comic and Bucolick," with the Spouse presented as a pastoral virgin and the Bridegroom as a shepherd; and Milton described it as a divine pastoral drama "consisting of two persons and a double *Chorus*, as *Origen* rightly judges."[154]

Gervaise Markham produced the most imaginative poetic rendering of the work in the Renaissance,[155] uniting the lyric, dramatic, and pastoral impulses. This very free poetic paraphrase is in eight pastoral eclogues, each with a different stanzaic form, and it has three interlocutors, Ecclesia, Thaumastos, and Judea (the daughter of Jerusalem). Something of the Spenserian verbal texture and stanzaic variety may be sampled from the opening stanza of the first eclogue, and the concluding stanzas of the eighth:

> Imprint upon my lips pure livorie
> The hony pleasure of thy mouthes deere kisse,
> For why thy love, bounded in no degree,
> Exceedes the sence-inchaunting sugred blisse
> Which from the taste of wine attracted is.
> . . . . . . . . . . . . . . .

THAU. O thou which in the garden dwelst for ever,
> Unto thy voyce all thy familiars tend:
> Exhale it then, let thy sweet tunes persever,
> Teach me to heare, which taught'st me to commend.

ECCL. O my deere Love, my soules desired friend,
If thou depart, or list away to flie,
Be like to Roes, or lustie harts that wend
And play upon the Mountaines cheerefully,
Where spices grow, sweet fumes, and all to please the eye.[156]

Discussing the style of the work, commentators emphasized its lyric and pastoral rather than dramatic qualities. Partly because of its matter (being, as Origen noted, the Song of the Bridegroom himself) but also because of its lofty and highly figurative language, the work was declared the most excellent of all the thousand and five songs supposedly written by Solomon but not now extant, and indeed the most exquisite of all the songs and hymns in the scriptures.[157] Beza pronounced it "the most heavenliest and excellentest ditty, concluded in terms and phrases of speach altogether enigmaticall and allegoricall"; Gouge remarked its obscurity of style, having "manie Rhetoricall allegories, and hyperbolicall metaphors"; and Aylett proclaimed categorically, "No Men nor Angel ever yet did hear / Diviner Musick from a mortal tongue."[158] Lapide surmised that its pastoral style afforded the precedent to Theocritus and Virgil, and that its meter approximated the elegiac, while Simon Patrick (1710) underscored the presence of "such Phrases, as are becoming a *Pastoral*; borrowed from Flowers and Trees (under which Shepherds delight to sit and eat the Fruit) and from such Creatures as frequent the Fields and Woods, etc."[159] And John Cotton found it stocked more largely than any other biblical lyric "with more store of sweet and precious, exquisite and admirable Resemblances, taken from the richest Jewels, the Sweetest Spices, Gardens, Orchards, Vineyards, Winecellars, and the chiefest beauties of all the workes of God and Man."[160]

The three poetic books of Solomon had an importance second only to the psalms as a source of generic precepts, ideas, and models for seventeenth-century religious lyric. Most obviously, these books greatly extend the variety of lyric kinds which biblical precedent seemed to recommend to the Christian poet. The Proverbs of Solomon were adages or epigrams concerned with ethics or Christian manners. Ecclesiastes was a sermon in verse based upon personal experience and pertaining to moral philosophy—the pursuit of the highest good. The Song of Songs was a sequence of love songs or ballads, or, more often, an exalted epithalamium in dramatic form and pastoral mode, presenting an allegory of spiritual pilgrimage pertaining to the Church and to every elect soul.

It seems eminently clear that Herbert's "The Church-porch" and

Vaughan's "Rules and Lessons" draw heavily upon the generic assumptions relating to Proverbs and Ecclesiastes. The generic features identified with Proverbs—that it is a book of Christian ethics and manners; that it is addressed to young persons at the beginning of their Christian pilgrimage; that the speaker adopts the role of father, preacher, or teacher; that it is in the form of maxims, adages, and epigrams—are also the primary generic features of these Herbert and Vaughan poems. The dramatized location of Herbert's poem on the church porch, and its dry sermonic tone of steady exhortation, relates it also to the Ecclesiastes tradition as a sermon in verse based upon the speaker's own life. Proverbs and Ecclesiastes were thought to be closely related in subject matter (moral philosophy) and stance of speaker, and their maxims were often amalgamated in handbooks relating to Christian manners and morals. They were, moreover, linked with specific architectural elements of the Old Testament Temple—the Outer Court and the Holy Place respectively—through which one must pass to approach the Holy of Holies. Herbert had in this tradition of commentary a clear rationale for constructing the preparatory poem within his *Temple*, through which one passes to enter his lyrical "Church," in the generic terms afforded by these two books of Solomon.

More significant still were the generic terms provided by the Song of Songs. For Herbert, Vaughan, and Taylor they were a shaping influence upon the entire corpus of religious lyric. This influence is most subtle and complex in Herbert, whose poems portray a personal relationship between Christ and the speaker, but usually a relationship of friend and friend rather than of lovers or spouses. Nonetheless, the dialogic/dramatic element in Solomon's epithalamium seems to provide points of reference for tracing the development of the intricate, ever-shifting relationship between the speaker and his sometimes present, sometimes absent Friend. Canticles perceived as a sequence of love songs also provides some warrant for Herbert's extensive use and transmutation of conventions from the secular love-sonnet sequences.

For Vaughan and Taylor, Canticles is a more direct and even more central resource. The conception of Canticles as a collection of exalted, highly figurative lyrics pertaining to a spiritual pilgrimage no doubt goes far to explain Vaughan's extensive use of quotations from and allusions to the Song of Songs in the text and epigraphs of his own highly figurative lyrics. Through such references he associates his own portrayal of the soul's spiritual pilgrimage and its constant longing for transcendence with the chief biblical model for that subject in that form. Edward Taylor's poems are saturated with Canticles' language:

almost one-third of his *Preparatory Meditations* are on texts from Canticles, including a long sequence of poems on consecutive Canticles verses (5:10-7:6). These poems are chiefly meditative descants upon Canticles texts, through which the speaker explores his own claims to participate in the spousal relation with the Bridegroom and to be an elect member of the Church, his Bride. Only very occasionally —at the end of his *Second Series of Meditations*—does Taylor attempt a closer generic imitation of Canticles in a few love songs praising the Bridegroom. But this generic self-denial is deliberate: the poet discovers in Canticles the most exalted, indeed divine, model for praise in the Bridegroom's praises of the Bride—but his fallenness and his human insignificance make direct imitation of that model utterly impossible. However, he looks forward in poem after poem to the time when he will meet this standard and will praise the Bridegroom in the Bride's own terms—though he can do this only when he achieves the glorious estate of the Bride. Canticles defines for Taylor what the religious lyric ideally should be, what it cannot now be (and thereby sanctions his invention of other modes), and what in fact it will be in the millennium and in heaven.

Genre theory relating to other parts of the Bible was generally of lesser significance for the poems here studied. The New Testament Canticles from Luke (the *Magnificat*, the *Benedictus*, the *Nunc Dimittis*) were of course recognized as biblical lyrics long established in Church liturgy and, as we have seen, they were included in many of the Reformed biblical song-books, but no independent genre theory concerning them emerged. The New Testament parables were also discussed as a literary genre, though usually with reference to sermon theory: nevertheless, the parable manner is adopted in certain Herbert poems which present and then interpret a simple fable or story— "Redemption," "Peace," "The Bag." A few other recognized biblical lyric kinds warrant brief examination, since they extended somewhat the range of models and precepts available to and at times followed by the seventeenth-century religious lyrists.

The Lamentations of Jeremiah was usually regarded as a complaint, or more specifically, a funeral elegy mourning the death of Josiah and foreshadowing in that death and that mourning the Babylonian Captivity and the destruction of Jerusalem.[161] Donne wrote a fairly close verse paraphrase of this work which has considerable literary merit, but its most significant influence is upon Donne's *Anniversaries*— which are not religious lyrics in any strict sense, and so not properly part of this study. In these poems, as in Lamentations, a particular death

(Elizabeth Drury's) is made an augury of greater misery to come, with the speaker adopting the stance of one already experiencing the full range of such miseries. In quite another vein, Herbert's long poem "The Sacrifice" is modeled upon Lamentations seen in medieval typological terms as a complaint: Christ is heard from the cross voicing elaborate variations upon themes from Lamentations as he himself suffers the desolation which that poem predicts for the Jews, and which all mankind deserve for their betrayal of him.

Both Deuteronomy 32 and Isaiah's "Song of the Vineyard" (5:1-7) were identified as a generic mix of denunciation and praise, of invective and heroic hymn.[162] Donne's *First Anniversary* is explicitly related to the Mosaic song in Deuteronomy: its speaker claims to usurp Moses' role in denouncing the utter corruption and death of the sinful world, while also praising God in and through Elizabeth Drury.[163] Herbert's "The Church Militant" is also of the kind represented by these scriptural prophetic songs: it combines satiric denunciation of the ravages wrought by sin, idolatry, and the Roman Babylon against the Church of God, together with praises of God's greatness in establishing his Church and overseeing its earthly course until the Judgment.

Finally, some other lyrics—the Songs in Exodus 15 and in Isaiah, and the choruses of Angels and Saints in Revelation—provide models for the sublime, public, heroic hymn. The hymns most often found in the Book of Psalms are thanksgivings for benefits received; the higher kinds—triumphs celebrating the victories of God and the Saints, and praises of God's glory—occur very occasionally among the Psalms, and are especially prominent in Revelation.[164] Herbert attempts the higher kind once, in "Antiphon (II)," as he imagines an earthly human choir joining with a choir of Angels in a hymn of praise. But it is Traherne who most fully explores the range of the biblical hymnic mode. As we have seen, he relies centrally on the Psalms to define that mode. But he also incorporates passages from Canticles, Isaiah, and Revelation in his *Thanksgivings*, and these references are multiplied as he reaches toward the highest hymnic mode, praises of God's great glory, in his "Thanksgivings for the Beauty of his Providence," and "Thanksgivings for God's Attributes."

One point perhaps warrants further emphasis. As we have seen, biblical poetics theory invited poets to regard the Book of Psalms, the Books of Solomon, and indeed the Bible as a whole not only as collections of assorted genres and kinds, but also as totalities whose completeness and whose truth is in part manifested by exhausting the possibilities of expression. The Book of Psalms is said to contain the full range of human feeling and emotion, of prayer and praise, of styles and lyric genres, and to provide an epitome of the whole Bible (Law, Prophets, Gospel). The Song of Songs is so named because it surpasses, and supplies the quintessence of, all the biblical lyrics—all those supposedly lost as well as those preserved. Solomon's three books, taken together, are precise analogues to the three areas which constitute the total structure of Solomon's Temple—designed by God himself. The Bible contains all literary kinds—epic, dramatic, and lyric—and is accordingly the supreme example of *genera mista* contained within a comprehensive whole rendering the course of history from Genesis to Apocalypse.

The divine model offered to poets is accordingly one of richest variety within an all-encompassing order. An epic poet like Milton might imitate this model by creating a cosmic, encyclopedic, mixed-genre poem; a lyric poet might do so by incorporating a great multiplicity of lyric genres within a volume which makes of them a comprehensive order, the mimesis of the total Christian life. Herbert obviously attempted and brilliantly achieved such a mimesis of multiplicity within unity in *The Temple*. Vaughan's *Silex Scintillans* contains a somewhat narrower range of genres and a looser ordering principle, but it is also an eminently successful endeavor of this kind. Traherne's generic range is much narrower still, and the ordering principles informing his two collections of meditative lyrics are somewhat obscure and are imperfectly realized. Donne, at the beginning of the poetic development here traced, wrote magnificently in several religious lyric kinds but made no attempt to comprehend them within some inclusive design. Edward Taylor, who supplies our terminus, eschewed both generic variety and unity: all his *Preparatory Meditations* are poems of the same kind; and, though a very loose thematic order may inform his *First Series*, the *Second Series* contains virtually discrete poems and sequences of poems which only very generally, and in part fortuitously, reflect the shape of a life.

# The Poetic Texture of Scripture:
# Tropes and Figures for the Religious Lyric

When John Donne exclaimed, "My *God*, my *God*, Thou art . . . a *figurative*, a *metaphoricall God*,"[1] he was voicing an intense concern with biblical imagery and biblical tropes entirely characteristic of his age. Although attention to the rhetorical figures in the biblical text had characterized Christian exegesis from the patristic ages onward, the Reformation brought in its wake both a greater emphasis upon, and a more systematic analysis of, the tropes and schemes that made biblical language radically poetic. Theoretical grounds for this new emphasis are to be found in the Protestant view that the literal meaning of scripture is often conveyed through figurative language and so can be properly apprehended through rhetorical and poetic analysis, and in the Protestant habit of referring to biblical figures and tropes to interpret and authenticate the signs and emblems presented by nature and our individual lives. Manifestations of and reinforcements for this intensified concern with biblical tropes may be found in numerous contemporary *Rhetoricae Sacrae*, as well as in countless sermons.

Malcolm Ross has rightly emphasized the influence of Calvinist theology and of the controversy over the Real Presence in the Sacrament upon religious poets' ways with figurative language in the seventeenth century, though I find somewhat perverse his equation of true poetic symbolism with Catholic sacramentalism and his conclusion that religious poetry necessarily declined as Protestantism replaced this kind of symbolism with a "metaphorical relationship . . . between the sign and that which it signifies."[2] A more useful point of departure is Horton Davies' observation that the Puritans "rejected the ecclesiastical 'scenery' of the medieval Church for the symbolism and imagery of the Bible."[3] I suggest that the Bible became the treasury of images and symbols for English Protestants generally in the sixteenth and seventeenth centuries, and that ecclesiastical ceremonies and sacraments, nature itself, and personal experiences of all sorts came to be interpreted through the language of scripture, recognized as radically figurative.

This process offered biblical imagery and poetic figures to the Christian poets as vehicles of charged significance, presenting universal religious meanings against which particular observations and experiences might be measured and analyzed. The universe of discourse created by this new attention to the metaphorical power of biblical language degenerated into tasteless jargon when biblical language ceased to mediate in some vital way between general spiritual concepts and personal experience. But in the seventeenth century the Bible's images and tropes could and did fire the imagination of the major devotional poets, making no small contribution to their remarkable achievements.

## A. THE BIBLE AS *Ars Rhetoricae*

We may measure shifts in attitude in regard to the poetic texture of scripture by comparing some characteristic Protestant statements with the formulations of Augustine and Aquinas. Augustine's *De Doctrina Christiana* was still the point of departure for such discussion in the sixteenth and seventeenth centuries, constantly cited both in exegetical manuals and arts of preaching. Central to Augustine's system of interpreting scripture is the idea that words and signs point (literally and figuratively) to things, and that those things may themselves be signs of a higher spiritual meaning. This distinction is the ground for Augustine's concept of multiple senses in scripture, whereby both the words and the things they signify may point to spiritual or allegorical meanings.[4] As Stanley Fish has noted, however, the distinction between words and things breaks down in Augustine's argument, for words and signs are also things, "for that which is not a thing is nothing at all." Moreover, all things, not only in scripture but throughout the natural world, are also signs—specifically, signs of God's presence: "to the healthy and pure internal eye He is everywhere."[5] All signs then, words and things, point to God, as Augustine demonstrates in *De Trinitate* by ingenious enumeration of all the signs of the Trinity throughout the created universe. And such signs may be properly read only by the mind infused with faith, hope, and charity.[6]

Yet Augustine gave careful attention to the words of scripture, the literal sense, as the ground for the spiritual significances, and this concern especially endeared him to Protestants. His practical recommendations for recovery of the literal meaning became commonplace in virtually all subsequent *ars praedicandi*: they include attention to the meanings of words and to the circumstances in which they were spoken, collation with related passages, and interpretation according to the sum of revealed doctrine (the analogy of faith). Attention to the words involves knowledge of the original languages, of logic (rules of valid inference), of history, and especially of the rhetorical figures—a precept leading directly to the conception that the Bible's texture is poetic:

> Lettered men should know, moreover, that all those modes of expression which the grammarians designate with the Greek word *tropes* were used by our [Scriptural] authors, and more abundantly and copiously than those who do not know them . . . are able to suppose or believe. Those who know these tropes, however, will recognize them in the sacred letters, and this knowledge will be of considerable assistance in understanding them. . . . And not only examples of all of these tropes are found in reading the sacred books, but also the names of some of them, like *allegoria, aenigma, parabola*.[7]

Though he eschews a full review of such tropes as tedious and in the province of the grammarians, Augustine points to a few examples of catachresis, irony, and antiphrasis as keys to certain scriptural ambiguities, concluding that when the sense is absurd if it is taken verbally, "it is to be inquired whether or not what is said is expressed in this or that trope."[8]

As J. A. Mazzeo has noted, Augustine's usual classifications for exegesis are *signa propria* and *signa translata*, the first the object of a philological study of the text, the second involving everything else— both the figures and tropes of scripture and the higher spiritual or allegorical senses. These signs are partly clarified by the sciences of *things*, which explain what it means to be as wise as a serpent, or why the phases of the moon might be taken as an allegory of the soul. But the deepest meanings of the scripture tropes—as also of the things and events of scripture, of the sacramental signs, and of the things of the created world—must finally be perceived intuitively, since God has invested them with meaning as signs of ultimate spiritual reality. As Mazzeo cogently puts it, "Not only was Scripture itself an endless allegory but the world that Scripture described was itself a further silent, wordless allegory of the eternal."[9]

In line with all this, Augustine does not in the last analysis attach profound significance to the biblical words themselves. Similitudes (and, we assume, the other poetic figures in scripture) are not really necessary to convey meaning since "hardly anything may be found in these obscure places which is not found plainly said elsewhere." They exist rather to give pleasure and a profitable challenge to the wit of men: "it seems sweeter to me than if no . . . similitude were offered in the divine books, since . . . no one doubts that things are perceived more readily through similitudes and that what is sought with difficulty is discovered with more pleasure."[10] Moreover, all canons of precise interpretation relax and become unimportant in relation to an over-arching concern with spiritual reality, and those who clearly perceive that reality may dispense with scripture altogether:

> Whatever appears in the divine Word that does not literally pertain to virtuous behavior or to the truth of faith you must take to be figurative. . . . Scripture teaches nothing but charity, nor condemns anything except cupidity, and in this way shapes the minds of men.

> A man supported by faith, hope, and charity, with an unshaken hold upon them, does not need the Scriptures, except for the instruction of others.[11]

Also, Augustine's profound sense of the inadequacy of words to render divine mysteries and ineffable realities leads him to justify multiple and highly personal interpretations of scripture, literally false but spiritually true, as properly accommodated to a text and sanctioned by the mind of God:

> When . . . from a single passage in the Scripture not one but two or more meanings are elicited . . . there is no danger if any of the meanings may be seen to be congruous with the truth taught in other passages of the Holy Scriptures. . . . Certainly the Spirit of God, who worked through that [scriptural] author, undoubtedly foresaw that this meaning would occur to the reader or listener. Rather, He provided that it might occur to him, since that meaning is dependent upon truth. For what could God have more generously and abundantly provided in the divine writings than that the same words might be understood in various ways.[12]

Augustinian allegorical exegesis is based firmly upon a Platonic conception of mimesis in which all things and all linguistic forms are symbols of a reality which transcends them but to which they may help to elevate the soul. The movement is *through* the words to a silent, intuitive grasp of divine reality.[13] Augustine's is obviously a radically symbolic universe, one whose divine significances cannot be directly represented in or conveyed by language—even the language of scripture.

Aquinas' discussion of the senses of scripture in the *Summa Theologica* rationalized the sweeping Augustinian account of figurative meaning into the classic Roman Catholic formula: a literal sense, and a spiritual or allegorical sense having three levels—allegorical or typological,

tropological or moral, and anagogical.[14] Thomas also articulated what
came to be the accepted Catholic formulation of the distinction be-
tween the literal and spiritual senses: the literal sense is the significa-
tion of the words (i.e., the things pointed to by them) and the spiritual
sense in its three levels comprises the further significances those things
themselves convey, by reason of God's providential design.[15] In regard
to the literal sense, Thomas declares that it necessarily includes not
merely the obvious meaning of the words but also the whole range of
rhetorical figures—the so-called figurative-literal sense:

> By words things are signified properly and figuratively. Nor is the
> figure itself, but that which is figured, the literal sense. When Scrip-
> ture speaks of God's arm, the literal sense is not that God has such
> a member, but only what is signified by this member, namely,
> operative power.[16]

As William G. Madsen perceived, there is some literary problem with
this Catholic position, in that it involves deriving metaphorical meaning
only from the significance of the thing (the tenor), bypassing any real
interplay between vehicle and tenor, God's arm and operative power.[17]
This disposition to move immediately to "true" meaning rather than
regarding metaphorical language as itself constituting such meaning,
is evident in Thomas's justification of the presence of poetic language
in scripture. Since poetry deals with matters unable to be grasped by
reason, poetic language "leads the reason aside"; it is appropriate to
scripture, which is above reason, and it is necessary to aid the simple
to grasp intellectual things through sensible objects.[18]

Thomas's formulation suggests that the poetic language of scripture
does not convey truth directly. He holds rather that similitudes often
obscure truth, leading the reader to look beyond the figures and in
doing so to form within himself truer conceptions than they present.
This comment reflects, in more restricted and essentially negative terms,
Augustine's view of scriptural language as a stimulus to intuition. For
Thomas, the figures in scripture serve chiefly to intimate the dispro-
portion between these formulations and the divine reality:

> The ray of Divine Revelation is not extinguished by the sensible
> imagery wherewith it is veiled . . . it does not allow the minds . . .
> to rest in the likenesses, but raises them to the knowledge of intel-
> ligible truths; . . . The very hiding of truth in figures is useful for
> the exercise of thoughtful minds, and as a defense against the ridicule
> of the unbelievers. . . . Similitudes drawn from things farthest away
> from God form within us a truer estimate that God is above whatso-
> ever we may say or think of Him.[19]

Neither Augustine or Aquinas places great value upon the poetic language of scripture as such. Certainly, neither assumes that the particular verbal formulations and figures are to be seen as the precisely appropriate vehicles for conveying truth, whether of natural things or of God. But something very like such a poetics developed from the new valuation of the literal text of scripture in the Reformation. As everyone knows, the rallying cry of the Reformation was "the one sense of scripture," the sole authority of the literal meaning. But it is evident from the studies of Preus on Luther, and Forstman and Wallace on Calvin, as well as the investigations of various literary historians, that this precept by no means led to prosaic literalism.[20] As we shall see in more detail later, the tirades against medieval allegorizing leveled by Luther, Tyndale, Calvin, Perkins, and many others were accompanied by clear recognition of the prevalence of typological symbolism in scripture, and even by some justification for restrained allegorical interpretation as an "accommodated" meaning useful for illustration and teaching. Moreover, the Reformation focus upon the literal text led Calvin and his English followers to pay the closest attention to the tropes and figures of scripture as the very vehicle of the Holy Ghost. Tropes are now perceived as God's chosen formulations of his revealed truth which man must strive to understand rightly, in themselves, and not as a stimulus to a higher vision.

This attention to figurative language was dictated also by Calvin's doctrine of the sacraments, especially of the Lord's Supper. In controversy with the Catholics over the doctrine of the Real Presence, Calvin insists over and over again that *they* are the literalists, unable to recognize Christ's phrase, "This is my Body," as a figurative statement —a metonymy conforming to the common scriptural usage of such figures:

[Those who state that] the bread is the body . . . truly prove themselves literalists. . . . I say that this expression is a metonymy, a figure of speech commonly used in Scripture when mysteries are under discussion. . . . For though the symbol differs in essence from the thing signified (in that the latter is spiritual and heavenly, while the former is physical and visible), still, because it not only symbolizes the thing that it has been consecrated to represent as a bare and empty token, but also truly exhibits it, why may its name not rightly belong to the thing? Humanly devised symbols, being images of things absent rather than marks of things present . . . are still sometimes graced with the titles of those things. Similarly, with much greater reason, those things ordained by God borrow the names of those things of which they always bear a definite and not misleading signification, and have the reality joined with them. . . . Let our adversaries, therefore, cease to heap unsavory witticisms upon us by calling us "tropists" because we have explained the sacramental phraseology according to the common usage of Scripture.[21]

Calvin's explanation of the Eucharist grounds it in a real correspondence whereby "physical signs . . . represent to us, according to our feeble capacity, things invisible; and spiritual truth, which is at the same time represented and displayed through the symbols themselves."[22] In the case of the Eucharist, the real correspondence and analogy is that "our souls are fed by the flesh and blood of Christ in the same way that bread and wine keep and sustain physical life"; in this way and by God's appointment, "by the showing of the symbol the thing itself is also shown."[23]

Working from such assumptions about the centrality of figurative language to theological truth, sixteenth- and seventeenth-century Protestants intensified and systematized the study of the rhetorical tropes and schemes in scripture. Pronouncements regarding the importance of understanding the poetic figures and the stylistic features of scripture, and directives as to how to accomplish that aim came from all sides—reformers, biblical exegetes, writers of *ars praedicandi*, literary men. This emphasis urged the skills of the literary critic upon the reader of the Bible and, in so doing, obviously promoted the sense of it as a poetic work.

Among the earlier reformers, Wiclif's preface to the first English translation of the Bible (reprinted in 1550) took note of the "manye figuratife speachis" in the Bible—"moe than grammarians moune gesse."[24] Erasmus' manual for preachers provided a detailed analysis of the tropes and figures of word and sentence available for the preachers' own discourse and exemplified in scripture—hyperbole, synecdoche, metaphor, apostrophe, epithet, catechresis, simile, allegoria, image.[25] Luther declared, "the Scriptures are full of . . . metaphores and similitudes borrowed of nature, so that he that should take them out of the holy Bible, shoulde take therewith much light from it also."[26] And Tyndale recommended, "Cleave unto the texte and playne storie, and endeavour thy selfe to searche out the meanyny of all that is described therein, and the true sence of all maner of speakinges of the Scripture, of proverbes, similitudes, & borowed speach."[27]

Seventeenth-century English Protestants showed considerably more awareness of figurative language in the Bible, and embraced the skills of literary and rhetorical analysis with much more earnestness. Richard

Bernard's survey of the knowledge needed by ministers includes wide learning in the various natural sciences specifically for the purpose of interpreting scriptural similitudes, which "are fetcht from almost all things in Heaven above, in earth below, from Sun, Moon, Stars, fire, haile, snow, windes, lightning, and thunders."[28] He also urges competence in languages, in logic, in the skills of the grammarian (to understand such figures as ellipsis, pleonasmus, enallage, zeugma), but especially in the knowledge of rhetoric,

> Because everie where a Divine shall meet with figurative speeches in holy Scripture, which without Rhetoricke hee cannot explaine. (1) This Art sheweth him all the tropes wheresoever hee meeteth with them, as these foure, *Metaphora, Metonymia, Synechdoche, Ironia,* with their three common affections, *Allegoria, Catechresis, and Hyperbole,* both in the figure *Auxesis* increasing, or *Meiosis* in diminishing. . . . (2) By Rhetorick, he knowes the figures of a word, and the use of them. . . . (3) By Rhethoricke, hee acquainteth himself with figures of a sentence. . . . With these a Divine shall meet with every where in the booke of *Job,* Psalmes, Prophets, Epistles of the Apostles, and in other places of Scripture.[29]

John Weemse's rules for interpretation outline various means to arrive at the literal sense of scripture—knowledge of Hebrew, of various translations, of Jewish history and customs; and especially the collation of related texts, so as to draw together clusters of images, figures, and passages which illustrate each other.[30] Such a procedure encourages attention to certain pervasive and richly allusive unifying tropes and terms in the Bible.

William Perkins also urges the analysis of scripture, "Using a grammaticall, rhetoricall, and logicall analysis, and the helpe of the reste of the arts,"[31] and he exemplifies this method by discussing several scripture texts in terms of various figures—e.g., ellipsis, pleonasm, irony. More remarkably, he finds certain fundamental theological concepts presented as "sacred tropes" in scripture: *anthropopathia* is a "sacred Metaphor, whereby those things, that are properly spoken of man, are by a similitude attributed unto God"; and the communication of properties is "a *Synecdoche,* by the which . . . that is spoken of the whole person of Christ, which doth properly belong to one of his two natures." Again, following Calvin, he discusses the words of institution of the Lord's Supper as a "sacramentall Metonymie," a figure "whereby the name of the adjunct, as also of the helping cause is put for the thing represented in the Sacrament."[32] In discussing the Sacrament elsewhere, he argues that the very nature of the sacramental signs given by God account for and necessitate the abundance of figurative language in scripture:

> There is a certaine agreement and proportion of the externall things with the internall, and of the actions of one with the actions of the other: wherby it commeth to passe, that the signes, as it were certaine visible words incurring into the externall senses, do by a certaine proportionable resemblance draw a Christian minde to the consideration of the things signified, and to be applyed.
>
> This mutuall, and as I may say, sacramentall relation, is the cause of so many figurative speeches and Metonymies which are used.[33]

Those who addressed the question of biblical style from a literary rather than a specifically exegetical viewpoint came to similar conclusions about the prevalence and significance of the poetic figures. Sir Philip Sidney extols the excellence of David's rhetorical strategies and poetic language in the Psalms:

> For what else is the awaking his musical Instruments, the often and free chaunging of persons, his notable *Prosopopeias*, when he maketh you as it were see God comming in his majestie, his telling of the beasts joyfulnesse, and hils leaping, but a heavenly poesie, wherin almost he sheweth himselfe a passionate lover of that unspeakable and everlasting bewtie, to be seene by the eyes of the mind.[34]

George Wither found the Psalter the "most excellent Lyricke *Poesy* that ever was invented," remarking both upon the decorous and appropriate use of the figures, and upon their quality:

> If you have respect to those things which are the ordinary ornaments of other mens *Poesy*, as Similies, Metaphors, Hyperboles, Comparisons, and such like . . . I dare maintain that no volume of the same bignesse, hath so many as this. . . . Were I pleased to enter into such a taske, I dare both promise and performe, even from hence to bring examples of every Rhetoricall figure, which may be found in any learned *Poet* among the *Greekes* or *Latines*.[35]

He does not attempt such a catalogue, but he does offer notable examples of various kinds of rhetorical speech: synecdoche and metonymy in a variety of forms; hyperbole; and the various figures of sentence including parable, enigma, and allegory.

A further manifestation of this concern with and analytic attention to the poetic language of scripture is provided by the many treatises and manuals setting out the biblical tropes and figures, either as an aid to exegetes and preachers, or in the format of an *ars rhetoricae*. These works are usually structured according to the basic rhetorical distinction between tropes (figures in which the meaning of a word or phrase is altered from its proper signification) and schemes (figures of grammar or rhetoric pertaining to words, sentences, or the amplification of longer speeches, which do not involve transfer of meaning). The earliest was that of Cassiodorus (sixth century), which provided an alphabetical list of the kinds of schemes and tropes found in the Psalms—about one hundred thirty-five kinds, from *aenigma* to *zeugma*.[36] Bede's treatise, "De Schematis et Tropis Sacrae Scripturae Liber"[37] vastly simplifies the list, treating in detail only the most eminent scriptural figures and arranging them by basic categories—seventeen schemes and thirteen tropes, some with subspecies; he illustrates each figure from the whole range of scripture though chiefly from the Psalms, the Epistles, and Isaiah.

After the Reformation such handbooks greatly multiplied in number, size, and complexity. Philip Melancthon's *Institutiones Rhetoricae* (1521) describes and illustrates by scriptural examples some fifty rhetorical schemes and twenty-five tropes of words and speech: metaphor, synecdoche, metonymy, catachresis, and allegory in its several varieties—enigma, adage, allusion, irony, paradigm, parable.[38] Much longer and more elaborate is Henry Peacham's *Garden of Eloquence* (1577), a Ramist rhetoric treating only the topic of ornament, not invention or disposition, and including about two hundred figures in six categories: tropes of words in four chief species (metonymy, synecdoche, catachresis, and metaphor), tropes of sentence, grammatical schemes, syntactical schemes, rhetorical schemes, and schemes of amplification. Peacham asserts that knowledge of the rhetorical figures is "so necessary, that no man can read profytably, or understand perfectlye, eyther Poets, Oratours, or the holy Scriptures, without them."[39] The highly influential *Clavis Scripturae* of Flacius Illyricus (1617) is much more comprehensive than these rhetorics, addressing at great length the various kinds of language and meaning in scripture. Part I is an alphabetical listing of single words and names, with references identifying their occurrences and with definitions of the proper and figurative meanings each word bears in each of its occurrences. (The résumé provided for the word "*Cor*," for example, might well prove suggestive to a poet like Herbert, concerned to explore the ramifications of the "heart" image).[40] Part II offers, under various rubrics, rules for analyzing scripture distilled from many authorities. One tract addresses the issue of multiple senses; another considers varieties of style in scripture—*stylus Paulinis, stylus Joannis*, etc.[41] Tract 4, "De Tropis et Schematibus Sacrarum Literarum," is a rhetoric,

offering elaborate rules for interpreting each category of figure—
tropes of sentence such as periphrasis, icon, emphasis, allusion, meiosis;
grammatical and rhetorical schemes such as *anaphora, tautologia*, cli-
max, gnome, image, mimesis; tropes of words whose large categories
are metonymy, synecdoche, and simile, each with several varieties.
Among the species of simile he includes, interestingly, not only such
figures as metaphor, allegory, and parable, but also image or prophetic
picture and vision, prophetic deed or act, and sacramental sign.

Salomon Glass undertook a still more comprehensive and schematic
analysis of the language of scripture. His *Philologia Sacra* (1623) is
in five books.[42] The first justifies the integrity of both testaments and
analyzes biblical style as a whole and in its several parts—the prophetic,
the Pauline, the Joannine, etc. The second analyzes the senses of scrip-
ture, identifying two senses, literal and mystical, and distinguishing the
latter into three modes of discourse—allegory, type, and parable. Books
III and IV are concerned with the schemes and figures of grammar in
scripture. Book V is a *Rhetorica Sacra*,[43] discussing four basic species
of tropes in Ramist terms, with reference to the logical places govern-
ing them—metonymy, irony, synecdoche, and (very extensively)
metaphor, which includes the sacred tropes of *anthropopathia* and
*prosopopeia*. Glass also treats the so-called "affections" of the met-
aphorical tropes—catechresis which hardens them, hyperbole which
makes them more audacious, and allegory (with its subspecies proverb
and enigma) which extends or continues them. His second tract ana-
lyzes the schemes of words, of sentence (in continued speech and in
dialogue), and of amplification.

Later works attempt some simplification of these materials in hand-
books for more popular use. Henry Lukin's *Introduction to the Holy
Scripture* (1669) offers a greatly simplified, layman's version of such
philological and rhetorical theory. Lukin states that his book is designed
to promote a "right understanding of the *Genuine sense*, meaning, and
intendment of the expressions and propositions of truth in Scriptures
. . . in *Tropes, Figures*, and other such *Schemes* of Speech as the Scrip-
ture abound with."[44] He insists, moreover, that scriptural metaphors
not only are vehicles for divine revelation but also illuminate the true
emblematic character of nature: "the Scriptures . . . [show] the
Analogy which is between *Natural* things, and *Spiritual*; and *how the
invisible things of God are clearly seen, and understood, from the
things that are made*, Rom i.20."[45] Thomas Hall's *Centuria Sacra*
(1654) presents "About one hundred Rules for the Expounding, and
clearer understanding of the Holy Scriptures"; appended to this is
a *Rhetorica Sacra*, which likens scripture to "a fruitfull field, full of

precious Treasures" and proposes to "dig into those Sacred Minerals, for the better finding out of those Metaphors, Metonymies, Synecdoches, etc. which lye hid there," since "ignorance of Rhetorick is one ground of many errours" of interpretation.[46] John Smith's *Mysterie of Rhetorique Unveil'd* (1656) proposes definition and illustration of "above 130 The Tropes and Figures" with Latin, English, and scriptural examples of each, as an aid "to the right understanding of the Sense of the Letter of the Scripture";[47] it also states that "ignorance of Rhetorique is one ground (yea, and a great one) of many dangerous Errors this day."[48] Benjamin Keach's *Tropologia: A Key to Open Scripture Metaphors* (1682) is derived in part from Glass, but transforms his more comprehensive work into a rhetoric-*cum*-analysis of scripture metaphors.[49] The first book essentially presents Glass's analysis of tropes of words and their particular affections, including the elaborate treatment of "theological" metaphors like *anthropopathy*. Book II collects and analyzes the metaphors and similes in scripture for each of the persons of the Trinity (e.g., Christ the corner-stone, Christ the sun of righteousness, Christ a lamb), and Book III, the figures for the scriptures themselves—as a light, as a hammer, as the sword of the Spirit.

Other such books examine only one variety of figurative language. Joachim Zehner compiled an exhaustive and descriptive list of the adages of scripture;[50] and Robert Cawdrey's remarkable *Treasurie or Store-House of Similies* locates biblical similes, or constructs similes based on biblical texts, for such topics as adversity, Church, envy, Original Sin, Virtue, Word of God—alphabetically arranged in the style of a commonplace book.[51] Cawdrey's collection is offered to preachers and men of all estates to illumine "many grounds and principles of Christian Religion" and also to display the vast knowledge of the scriptural authors in natural as well as divine things, manifested in their similes "fetched off, and from the very secrets and bowels of nature: as namely, from wilde and tame beastes, foules, wormes . . . fire, water, earth, ayre, rivers, brookes, welles, Cesternes, Seas, stars, pearles . . . bloud, milke, women in travaile, in child birth, drosse, Iron, Gold, Silver. . . ."[52]

This pervasive theoretical concern among the Protestants with scripture tropes and figures was not primarily directed to them as ornament, but was in the interest of the most precise apprehension of divine truth. The governing assumption—important for poetry—was that the poetic language of scripture in itself, and not only as something to be transcended by higher spiritual insight, is a vehicle of truth, validated by God himself who chose such forms for his revelation. This assumption promoted the closest attention to biblical images and figures in countless sermons, exegeses, and divine poems, as a specially charged, significant language having the deepest, most personal, and most immediate relevance to the human world and human experience as well as to heavenly things. As we might expect, Donne's sermons and other religious prose articulate these common premises with particular cogency and literary sensitivity; indeed his sermons contribute centrally (more so than his poems, which are not so markedly biblical in their diction) to the evolution of a Protestant biblical poetics.

In the first place, Donne was fully persuaded of the plenitude and elegance of the rhetorical tropes and figures in the scriptures:

> There are not so eloquent books in the world, as the Scriptures: Accept those names of Tropes and Figures, which the Grammarians and Rhetoricians put upon us, and we may be bold to say, that in all their Authors, Greek and Latin, we cannot finde so high, and so lively examples, of those Tropes, and those Figures, as we may in the Scriptures: whatsoever hath justly delighted any man in any mans writings, is exceeded in the Scriptures. The style of the Scriptures is a diligent, and an artificial style; and a great part thereof in a musical, in a metrical, in a measured composition, in verse.[53]

He also identifies particular features of the rhetoric of scripture, attributing some of them to the individual writers, others to the Holy Spirit. The human writers created their figures for the spiritual life by drawing directly upon their own experiences (even as Donne himself so notoriously did in framing his own *Divine Poems*):

> The Prophets, and the other Secretaries of the holy Ghost in penning the books of Scriptures, do for the most part retain, and express in their writings some impressions, and some air of their former professions; those that had been bred in Courts and Cities, those that had been Shepheards and Heardsmen, those that had been Fishers, and so of the rest; ever inserting into their writings some phrases, some metaphors, some allusions, taken from that profession which they had exercised before.[54]

But in addition, the Holy Spirit, as the ultimate source of biblical style as well as content, has certain characteristic linguistic habits: when he would "express a *superlative*, the highest degree of any thing" he does so "by adding the name of God to it," for example, "*sopor Domini*, *The sleep of the Lord*." He also has characteristic metaphors—"*Idiotismus Spiritus sancti*"—such as "God's Arrows."[55] Donne's sermons everywhere abound with remarks upon such features of the divine style: "To pursue then the *Holy Ghosts* two *Metaphors*, of *selling away*, and *putting away*"; or, "It is a blessed Metaphore, that the Holy Ghost hath put into the mouth of the Apostle, *Pondus Gloriae*."[56] Or again,

> As God hath spangled the firmament with starres, so hath he his Scriptures with names, and Metaphors, and denotations of power. Sometimes he shines out in the name of a *Sword*, and of a *Target*, and of a *Wall*, and of a *Tower*, and of a *Rocke*, and of a *Hill*; And sometimes in that glorious and manifold constellation of all together, *Dominus exercituum, The Lord of Hosts*. God, as God, is never represented to us, with Defensive Armes; He needs them not . . . yet God is to us a Helmet, a Breastplate, a strong tower, a rocke, every thing that may give us assurance and defence.[57]

Indeed, as Donne sees it, the clearest evidence that the Holy Spirit is a magnificent poet is the glorious excess of figurative language, the proliferation of metaphor and figure that pervades the texture of God's literal Word:

> My *God*, my *God*, Thou are a *direct God*, may I not say a *literall God*, a *God* that wouldest bee understood *literally*, and according to the *plaine sense* of all that thou saiest? But thou art also . . . a *figurative*, a *metaphoricall God* too; A *God* in whose words there is such a height of *figures*, such *voyages*, such *peregrinations* to fetch remote and precious *metaphors*, such *extentions*, such *spreadings*, such *Curtaines* of *Allegories*, such *third Heavens* of *Hyperboles*, so *harmonious eloquutions* . . . as all *prophane Authors*, seeme of the seed of the *Serpent*, that *creepes*; thou art the *dove*, that flies. O, what words but thine, can expresse the inexpressible *texture*, and *composition* of thy *word*.[58]

This poetic texture—metaphors expanded to allegories and hyperboles—does not constitute a special "level" or sense, but is the very character of the literal text in many places, and is the Holy Spirit's chosen instrument to convey truth:

> The literall sense is not alwayes that, which the very Letter and Grammar of the place presents, as where it is literally said, *That Christ is a Vine*, and literally, *That his flesh is bread*, and literally, *That the new Jerusalem is thus situated, thus built, thus furnished*: But the literall sense of every place, is the principall intention of the Holy Ghost, in that place: And his principall intention in many places, is to expresse things by allegories, by figures; so that in many places of Scripture, a figurative sense is the literall sense.[59]

The Holy Spirit chooses this method in order to represent divine things with a complexity and majesty appropriate to the subject—with, one might say, a fitting decorum: "God in the Old, and Christ in the New Testament, hath conditioned his Doctrine, and his Religion . . . so, as that evermore there should be preserved a Majesty, and a reverentiall feare, and an awfull discrimination of Divine things from Civill, and evermore something reserved to be inquired after."[60] Indeed, Donne argues, and his sermon method demonstrates, that each individual word and trope in scripture is profoundly significant, inviting the most careful analysis and probing: "We must . . . crack a shell, to tast the kernell, cleare the words, to gaine the Doctrine. I am ever willing to assist that observation, That the books of Scripture are the eloquentest books in the world, that every word in them hath his waight and value, his taste and verdure."[61] Or again, "There is an infinite sweetnesse, and infinite latitude in every Metaphor, in every elegancy of the Scripture."[62] Such theoretical justifications of every element of poetic texture in scripture proved suggestive in a variety of ways, as we shall see, to Protestant poets developing a poetics for the religious lyric.

## B. BIBLICAL TROPES FOR THE CHRISTIAN LIFE

The figurative language of the Bible[63] influenced seventeenth-century religious lyric not only in regard to theory, but also substance. Not surprisingly, certain common and pervasive metaphors from scripture which shaped, and were shaped by, the seventeenth-century imagination as reflected in hundreds of sermons, tracts, and assorted documents attracted the poets as well. Such metaphors were understood to be grounded upon true analogies between natural and spiritual things, with the Word itself giving apt and authoritative formulation to the similitudes. Also, though they were used in the service of doctrinal exposition, such tropes were not transformed into simple doctrinal statements, but rather provide an imaginative rendering of the experience of living the Christian life.[64] This kind of attention to metaphor breaks down the distinction between *mythos* and *logos* which U. Milo Kaufmann associates with Puritan writing,[65] since the metaphors make a *mythos* of personal experience, relating it to biblical paradigms through the figures used. Though these key metaphors were sometimes developed in isolation with rather straightforward logical exposition of their terms, the more imaginative of the preachers, prose writers, and poets released their poetic suggestiveness by exploring the tensions arising from the various connotations carried by a given metaphor in different scripture texts. And often (like the biblical verses themselves) they fused these figures into complex networks and interconnected webs of reference.

For clarity, I shall isolate certain key tropes, examining how they are built up by collation of the several scripture texts in which the trope appears, and how they are developed—through elaboration of the various terms, or through extension into an allegory. The tropes examined here are not of course the only ones important for seventeenth-century religious lyric, nor are they peculiar to the lyric genres or to Protestants. Nevertheless, they constitute an especially rich and important resource for the major Protestant religious lyrists. The biblical metaphors most often invoked to describe spiritual experience are of two kinds: those relating to the contrasting conditions of the soul under sin and under grace; and those relating to the enduring experience of living the Christian life. Both kinds admit of considerable complexity and tension, owing to the Protestant sense of the radical imperfection of the elect in this life: the soul in the state of grace still bears the marks (and the metaphorical associations) of its sinful state; and the Christian life can never be experienced as a steady, straightforward advance toward perfection.

One prominent metaphor for the state of sin is sickness—in which context Christ is a physician and his grace or redemption is the balm or medicine which cures us. The metaphor is grounded upon the numerous miracles in the New Testament in which Christ cures physical illness, such as leprosy (Luke 5:12) and palsy (Matt. 9:1-12, Luke 5:18-31), with direct reference to the ills of the soul—"Thy sinnes be forgiven thee." With primary reference to Matthew's version of the story of the palsied man, William Perkins explores the metaphor to exhibit the process of spiritual cure:

> A sinner is compared [Luke 5:18, Matt. 9:11, 12] to a *sicke man* oft in the Scriptures. And therefore the curing of a disease fittely resembleth the curing of sinne. A man that hath a disease or sore in his body, before he can be cured of it, he must see it, and bee in a feare least it bring him into danger of death: after this he shall see himselfe to stand in neede of Physicke, and he longeth till he be with the Physitian: . . . he will not spare for any cost: then he yeelds himselfe into the Physitians hands . . . after this he comes to his former health againe. On the same manner, every man is wounded with the deadly wound of sinne at the very heart: and he that would be saved . . . must see his sinne, be sorrowfull for it . . . must see himselfe to stand

in neede of Christ, the good Physitian of his soule, and long after him . . . after this, Christ Jesus will temper him a plaister of his owne heart blood.[66]

Other biblical texts could easily be assimilated to the terms of this basic metaphor. Thomas Adams derived two sermons from the text he cites from Jeremiah 8:22, "Is there no Balme at Gilead? Is there no Physician there? why then is not the health of the daughter of my people recovered?" He justifies an allegorical elaboration of this text on the ground that the sin-sickness metaphor has clear biblical sanction: "The Allegory is Tripartite. . . . The *Balme* is the *Word*. The *Physitians* are the *Ministers*. The *Sicke* are the *Sinners*. . . . The un-erring Wisedome of Heaven hath giyen this comparison."[67] The metaphor of sin as sickness was also a favorite one in Donne's sermons, as Winfried Schleiner has shown, and it is the core of the *Devotions upon Emergent Occasions*, which explores the correspondences between the "occasions" or stages of Donne's own physical illness, and the stages of the sickness of soul due to sin.[68]

A related metaphor for the state of sin is death, deadness—with the contrasting representation of Christ's redemption as a restoration to life, a regeneration. Among the many biblical texts with this burden is Romans 6:23, "For the wages of sinne is death; but the gift of God is eternall life"; or Ephesians 2:1, "And you hath hee quickned, who were dead in trespasses, and sinnes." Richard Sibbes' sermon, "The Dead-Man, or, the State of Every Man by Nature," is based upon the Ephesians' text, and develops by analysis the metaphors of deadness and quickness. Spiritual deadness is graphically depicted, in itself and as it inheres in some degree even in the elect who are quickened:

And what doth death worke upon the body? unactivenesse, stiffnesse; so when the Spirit of God is severed from the soule, it is cold, and unactive, and stiffe. . . . Let any naturall man be as witty, and as learned, and as great, and as rich as you will . . . yet hee is but a carrion. . . .

The best of us all, though we be not wholly dead, yet there are some relicks of spirituall death hanging upon us, there be corruptions which in themselves are noysome. . . . For there bee usually three degrees of persons in the Church of God. Some open rotten persons that are as graves, open sepulchres, that their stincke comes foorth and they are the profane ones. There are some that have a forme of godliness that are meerely ghosts, that act things outwardly but they have not a spirit of their owne. . . . But the godly have this death in part; . . . spirituall life is in us by little and little wrought in the meanes, the Spirit of life joynes with the Word of life and quickens us daily more and more.[69]

Extending this metaphor are several texts presenting the body as dead (in its corruption and infirmities and mortality) even while it is physically alive, and finding life only in the regenerate Spirit—e.g., Romans 8:10, 1 Corinthians 15:22, and Romans 7:24 ("O wretched man that I am: who shall deliver me from the body of this death?"). Though the theme was popular, no one has matched Donne's eloquent treatment of this metaphor throughout *Deaths Duell*, as he elaborates upon the ubiquity of death:

> Wee have a winding sheete in our Mothers wombe, which growes with us from our conception, and wee come into the world, wound up in that *winding sheet*, for wee come to *seeke a grave*. . . . This whole *world* is but an *universall church-yard*, but our *common grave*; and the life and motion that the greatest persons have in it, is but as the shaking of buried bodies in their graves by an *earth-quake*. That which we call life, is but *Hebdomada mortium, a week of deaths*, seaven dayes, seaven periods of our life spent in dying.[70]

Donne's text is Psalm 68:20, "And unto God the Lord belong the issues of Death. i.e., From Death," and it affords him a typical paradoxical resolution: through Christ's death we attain deliverance from death, both by the regeneration and eternal life of the soul and by the resurrection of the body. The metaphor gains further complexity and tension through several texts from Romans 6-8 and Colossians 3:3, the latter of which—"For yee are dead, and your life is hid with Christ in God"—affords the title and theme of one of Herbert's acrostic poems. These texts assign death a positive value in that the death of the carnal nature is a requisite to the growth and final perfecting of the regenerate life in Christ.[71]

Another metaphor is that of sin as darkness or blindness, and Christ, his Word, and the regenerate state as light. A key text is John 1:4-5, 9: "In him was life, and the life was the light of men. / And the light shineth in darkenesse; and the darkenesse comprehended it not. / . . . That was the true light, which lighteth every man that commeth into the world." Other passages include Ephesians 5:8, "For yee were sometimes darkenesse, but now are yee light in the Lord: walke as children of light"; 2 Corinthians 4:6, "For God who commaunded the light to shine out of darkenes, hath shined in our hearts"; 1 Thessalonians 5:5, "Yee are all the children of light, and the children of the day: we are not of the night, nor of darkenesse"; or again Matthew 5:14-15, "Yee are

the light of the world . . . / Neither doe men light a candle, and put it
under a bushell, but on a candlesticke, and it giveth light unto all that
are in the house." Drawing upon all these texts Thomas Goodwin's
treatise, *A Childe of Light Walking in Darknesse*, analyzes the dark-
ness characterizing the state of sin:

> Since the fall, our hearts of themselves are nothing but *darknesse*.
> . . . The Apostle compareth this native darknesse of our hearts unto
> that *Chaos*, and lumpe of *darknesse* which at the first creation
> *covered the face of the deepe*: when he sayes, that *God who com-
> manded light to shine out of darknes* (hee referreth to the first crea-
> tion, *Gen.* 1.1,2.) *hath shined into our hearts*. . . . And if at any time
> he withhold *that light*. . . . Then so farre doe our hearts presently
> returne to their former darkenesse: . . . Darknesse *covereth not the
> face of this deepe only*, but it is darknes to the bottome, throughout
> darknesse. No wonder then, if when the *Spirit* ceaseth to *move upon*
> this *deepe* with beames of light, it cast us into such *deepes* and *dark-
> nesse*.[72]

Goodwin's sermon reveals the complexity of this metaphor, for he is
primarily concerned with the ways in which this darkness may yet
engulf a child of light when God, temporarily and for his own reasons,
"drawes but the curtaines, and shuts up the light from us."[73]

The metaphor is also explored with reference to the light of God's
Word, in regard to which the Old Law is presented under the metaphor
of Moses' veil as contrasted with the clear glass of the Gospel. A central
text is 2 Corinthians 3:13-18, expounded in the Geneva Bible as an
allegory contrasting the Law, unable to dispel the darkness of sin, with
the Gospel which could transmit and focus the light powerfully.[74] But
complicating this opposition were other texts such as 1 Corinthians
13:12, "For now we see through a glasse, darkely; but then face to
face," which indicate the dimness of the Gospel light itself in this life.
Further tension is introduced through texts wherein veils and obscure
vision are given a positive value—Christ's flesh as a veil hiding the
majesty of the godhead lest we be blinded (Heb. 10:20); and the as-
sociation of faith with blindness in 2 Corinthians 5:7, "For we walke
by faith, not by sight," and in Hebrews 11:1, "Now faith is the sub-
stance of things hoped for, the evidence of things not seen." Milton's
association of corporal blindness and spiritual sight in the "Invocation
to Light" in *Paradise Lost* embodies this significance, as does Herbert's
striking phrase in "Submission"—"Thou hast both my eyes."[75]

Again, the sinful state is often seen as a debtor's servitude, a state of
bondage, the slavish bearing of heavy burdens, while the regenerate

condition is that of release from debts and bondage and liberation from slavery. Romans 7:14, "I am carnall, sold under sinne," presents the sinner as one sold into servitude. The condition of bondage under sin and the Law is exposed in several verses from Galatians: "We, when wee were children, were in bondage under the Elements of the world" (4:3); "Stand fast therefore in the libertie wherewith Christ hath made us free, and bee not intangled againe with the yoke of bondage" (5:1). William Cowper develops this metaphor graphically:

> Without Christ we lived in a vile servitude and bondage, of all servants those are in worst case who are sould . . . who must doe service in prison, and . . . most lamentable is their estate who are chayned and bound in prison, yet such servants were we by nature before Christ made us free. . . . Our oppressors in this bondage, are Sathan and Sinne. . . . A Tyranny lawlesse, and most intollerable: for where as any other oppressor will sometime give rest to such as are under his bondage . . . this spirituall oppressor gives no rest to his miserable captives.[76]

Yet even the elect liberated from bondage continue to experience something of this bondage to sin and corruption. Another biblical text, especially significant for Vaughan's treatment of the tensions and complexities of this metaphorical cluster, is the passage from Romans 8:10-23 representing the entire creation in bondage, groaning in hope and expectation of future liberation:

> For the earnest expectation of the creature, waiteth for the mani-
> festation of the sonnes of God.
>
> . . . . . . . . . . . . . . . . . . . . . . . . . . . .
>
> Because the creature it selfe also shall bee delivered from the bondage
> of corruption, into the glorious libertie of the children of God.
> For wee know that the whole creation groaneth and travaileth in
> paine together untill now.
> And not only they, but our selves also which have the first fruites of
> the spirit, even we our selves groane within our selves, waiting for
> the adoption, to wit, the redemption of our body.
>
> (vv. 19, 21-23)

Summarizing a wide range of commentary on this passage in his *Hexapla on Romans*, Andrew Willet calls attention to the figure *prosopopeia*, which ascribes to the unreasonable creatures "a kind of sense and feeling of their miserie, and longing desire to be losed" from the bondage they suffer because of man's sin; it highlights the greater longing of the regenerate for the complete liberation from the bondage of corruption which their glorified bodies will enjoy.[77]

Several other metaphors represent the Christian life as a continuous process which can be imagined in stages, and thus they encourage narrative or thematic development. Some of these—e.g., the Christian life as a warfare or as a pilgrimage—have long invited allegorical treatment in epic or romance-like forms, but they also have importance for the devotional lyric. Some other tropes have particular affinity for the lyric forms: The Christian as little child who is heir to a kingdom, the Christian as sufferer undergoing chastisement and purification, the Christian as sheep of God's pasture (inviting to pastoral development), as plant or tree in God's garden (inviting to georgic), and as building or temple constructed by God's architecture.

The metaphor of the Christian warfare derives from several texts: 2 Timothy 4:7-8, "I have fought a good fight, I have finished my course . . . : / Hencefoorth there is layde up for me a crowne of righteousnesse"; Romans 7:23, "I see another Lawe in my members, warring against the lawe of my minde, and bringing me into captivity"; the several passages of symbolic warfare in the Book of Revelation; and perhaps most notably Ephesians 6:11: "Put on the whole armour of God, that ye may be able to stand against the wiles of the devill." Subsequent verses indicate what that armor consists of: the loins girt with truth, the breastplate of righteousness, the feet shod with the gospel of peace, the shield of faith, the helmet of salvation, the sword of the Spirit. Such passages stand behind Prudentius' elaborate allegory in the *Psychomachia*, Spenser's *Faerie Queene*, Book I, Bunyan's *Holy War* and parts of *Pilgrim's Progress*, and literally hundreds of spiritual biographies, sermons, and guides to the Christian life;[78] they also extend the significance of the battle scenes in Renaissance epics such as Tasso's *Gerusalemme Liberata* and Milton's *Paradise Lost*, and resonate throughout Milton's brief epic of spiritual combat, *Paradise Regained*. Samuel Hieron's sermon, "The Good Fight," on the Timothy text offers a graphic account of the pressures of such warfare on the psyche, in terms not irrelevant to lyric treatments of emotional states:

> He is but a titular Christian, and hath but a *shew of godlinesse*, who hath not had personall experience of the Stratagems of Satan, now puffing up to presumption, now pulling downe to despaire, one while working to security, another while pressing to dismayednes: sometimes extenuating, and hiding, and painting sinne, that before it is committed it may beguile; sometimes opening and aggravating it,

that when it is performed it may affright: turning himselfe into many shapes, sometimes like an industrious agent to advance our profit, sometimes like a pleasant companion, to further our delight, sometimes like a true-hearted friend, to respect our good name, but alwaies a venomous adversarie to empoyson our soule. . . . How requisite is it, that Christian souldiers should be daily practising the feats of spirituall armes.[79]

Perhaps the most pervasive of the metaphors for the Christian life is that of pilgrimage. The chief biblical texts are Hebrews 11:13-16, "These . . . confessed that they were strangers and pilgrims on the earth / . . . . They desire a better countrey, that is, an heavenly"; Hebrews 12:1, "let us runne with patience unto the race that is set before us"; Hebrews 13:14, "here have we no continuing citie, but we seeke one to come"; and 1 Peter 2:11, "as strangers and pilgrimes, abstaine from fleshly lusts." Associated with this metaphor of wayfaring and journeying are the images of the strait gate and the narrow way (Matt. 7:13-14) as characteristics of the pilgrim's path; John's identification (14:6) of the way with Christ, "I am the Way"; and various Old Testament stories of wandering—Adam's expulsion from paradise, the storm-tossed ark of Noah, the Israelites' wandering in the wilderness, the setting forth of Jacob for Laban's country with only his pilgrim's staff—as types of our earthly condition. Literary developments of the pilgrimage metaphor in long narrative include Dante's *Commedia*, Langland's *Piers Plowman*, Guillaume de Deguileville's *Le Pélerinage de l'Âme* and *Le Pélerinage de Vie Humaine*, and of course Bunyan's *Pilgrim's Progress*, but the trope could be adapted to lyric, introspective analysis (as in Vaughan's *Silex Scintillans*).[80] Some of the possibilities inherent in the metaphor for representation of various psychological stages and phases of the Christian life are suggested in William Cowper's comment:

Our progresse in this journey is not made, *pedibus, sed affectibus*, by motion of our feete, but of our affections. . . . We have not attained to the end of our journey . . . but must walke forward through this valley of teares. . . . We are not yet past the red sea, nor the vaste wildernesse, nor the fierie Serpents, what shal we do, but . . . with feare and trembling walk on the rest of the way which yet is before us? . . . There should be a continuall progresse in godlinesse . . . yet I would not so be understood as if the Christian had not his owne fainting and falling in the way of godlinesse; yet . . . we so faint that we may revive, we so fall that wee rise againe.[81]

A funeral sermon by Thomas Taylor also describes very vividly the pilgrim's path as interior landscape:

> In this way be content if sometimes thou art weary, as one that goeth up a steepe hill, if sometimes thou sighest and pantest in thy painfull travell, through a foule way, and stormie weather; Let the tedious-nesse of the way make thee desire the wayes end, and to covet to be at home with Christ. . . . But be sure in thy wearinesse thou sit not downe . . . but *presse hard forward to the marke* [Phil. 3:13], as one resolved to goe through and persevere to the end; considering that after an hill commeth a valley; after foule way commeth fayre; and after a storme a faire shine and gleame againe; *heavinesse may endure for a night, but joy returneth in the morning.*[82]

Another metaphor for the Christian life is childlikeness—attaining to the consciousness of a child and thereby becoming a son of God and heir of a kingdom. In some texts this implies a kind of reverse pilgrim-age, as in Matthew 18:3, "Except yee be converted, and become as little children, yee shall not enter into the kingdome of heaven"; or Mark 10:14-15, "Suffer the little children to come unto mee, and forbid them not; for of such is the kingdome of God. . . . Whosoever shall not receive the kingdome of God as a little childe, he shall not enter there-in." According to Diodati, such texts refer to our "putting on the true humility, docility, simplicity, and such innocency as is in little chil-dren."[83] Other texts, as, for example, Romans 8:15-17, emphasize es-pecially the status of the child of God as the kingdom's heir: "Ye have received the spirit of adoption, whereby we cry, Abba, Father. / The spirit it selfe beareth witnes with our spirit, that we are the children of God. / And if children, then heires; heires of God, and joynt heires with Christ." Richard Baxter points out, with allusion to the parable of the prodigal son, that our growing apprehension of our status as children and heirs should lead to a present participation in the heavenly joy and gladness that is our inheritance:

> There is no man so highly honoreth God, as he who hath his con-versation in Heaven; and without this we deeply dishonor him. Is it not a disgrace to the Father, when the Children do feed on Husks, and are cloathed in rags, and accompany with none but Rogues and Beggers? Is it not so to our Father, when we who call our selves his Children, shall feed on Earth, and the garb of our souls be but like that of the naked World? . . . Sure we live below the rates of the Gospel, and not as becometh the Children of a King, even of the great King of all the World. We live not according to the height of

our Hopes, nor according to the plenty that is in the Promises, nor according to the provision of our Fathers house, and the great preparations made for his Saints.[84]

In this development of the metaphor we have some faint intimation of Traherne's striking and well-nigh unique exploration of what it means to understand oneself as child of God and heir of his kingdom. Yet the metaphor is made more complex by the texts in Galatians 4:1-7, which liken the child (though an heir) to a servant in that he is "under tutors and governours" until, in the fullness of time, he "grows up" to enter upon his inheritance. Accordingly, most exegetes deferred full enjoyment of the status of children and heirs to the time of entrance into the heavenly inheritance.

The Christian life is also represented as chastisement, purgation, trial through afflictions. This trope is often related to the former in that the chastisement may be that of a father correcting and punishing his children: as Calvin put it, "whoever desireth to bee exempted from the crosse, such a one renounceth therewithall his childs part among the children of God, and . . . esteeme[s] not the benefit of Adoption."[85] The basic text is Hebrews 12:5-8:

> My sonne, despise not thou the chastening of the Lord, not faint when thou art rebuked of him.
> For whome the Lord loveth hee chasteneth, and scourgeth every sonne whom he receiveth.
> If yee endure chastening, God dealeth with you as with sonnes; for what sonne is he whom the father chasteneth not?
> But if ye be without chastisement, whereof all are partakers, then are ye bastards, and not sonnes.

Other texts readily invoked to develop this metaphor are from Job, Isaiah, Lamentations, and especially the Psalms of affliction and complaint. Henry Ainsworth elaborates the trope by such association, linking together several Old and New Testament texts on the afflictions of the people of God:

> He [God] awakeneth us somtime . . . by corrections & punishments for our misdeedes inflicted upon our bodies; sometime by striking our consciences with dread dismay and terrour for our syns. . . . For he withdraweth his face and favour from us, [Job 19:11], kindleth his anger against us, & counteth us as his enemies, the horror of his wrath is as fyre sent from above into our bones; the curse written in the law, is powred upon us [Dan. 9.11], and is as the arrowes of the Almightie, the venim wherof drinketh up our spirit. . . . Ther is

nothing sound in our flesh because of his anger [Psal. 38.3, 5, 7];
neither is ther rest in our bones because of our sin: our wounds stink
and ar corrupt, our reynes ar ful of burning, our hart is as waxe
[Psal. 22.14], it melteth in the mids of our bowels; our bones are
parched like an hearth [Psal. 102:3], and our moysture is turned to a
summers drowth [Psal. 32:4], so heavy is his hand upon us night and
day. . . . Also when we crie & shout, he shutteth out our prayer, and
is even angrie against it [Psal. 80:4] . . . that he will not hear. . . . We
are layd in the lowest pit, in darknes, in the deep . . . [But] when we
shal confesse our iniquities, and in faith ask mercy at his hands . . .
the Lord wil repent towards his servants [Deut. 32:36]. . . . Thus
God which had wounded us, bindeth us up; after two dayes [trou-
bles] he reviveth us, in the third day he raiseth us up & we live in his
sight; he healeth our broken harts [Psal. 147.3], and bindeth up our
sores. . . . And though our bark hath been tossed in the sea of afflic-
tions . . . yet now his gracious voyce doth comfort us, and his pres-
ence ceaseth al winde & tempest [Matt. 14:24-32].[86]

In a most interesting passage, Cowper links the chastisement trope with
a number of others, all of which are of primary importance in the de-
votional poetry of the period:

> The prodigall sonne concluded not to returne home to his Father
> till he was brought low by affliction. . . . The earth which is not
> tilled and broken up, beares nothing but thornes and bryers; the
> Vines waxe wilde in time, unlesse they be pruned and cut: so would
> our wilde hearts overgrow with the noysome weedes of unruly af-
> fections, if the Lord by sanctified trouble did not continually manure
> them. . . .
>     No worke can be made of gold and silver without fire, stones are
> not meet for pallace worke unlesse they be pollished and squared by
> hammering, no more is it possible that we can be vessels of honor in
> the house of our God, except first we be fined and melted in the fire
> of affliction: neyther can we be as living stones to be placed in the
> wall of the heavenly Jerusalem, except the hand of God first beat
> from us our proud lumps, by the hammer of affliction.[87]

The Christian is also a sheep in a flock of which God or Christ (or
the Christian minister by deputation) is a shepherd. The metaphor
draws its force from the pastoral ethos of biblical peoples, so promi-
nently concerned with sheep-tending activities, and it encouraged the
development of pastoral imagery in some seventeenth-century religious
lyric. The Old Testament *locus classicus* is Psalm 23:1-3, "The LORD

is my shepheard; I shall not want. / He maketh me to lie downe in greene pastures: he leadeth mee beside the still waters. / He restoreth my soule: he leadeth me in the pathes of righteousnes, for his names sake." The New Testament texts are Matthew 18:12-14, the shepherd who leaves the ninety-nine to rescue one lost sheep, and John 10:1-16, in which Jesus contrasts the good shepherd and the hireling, identifies the dangers to the flock from thieves and wolves, and sets forth his own pastoral claims: "I am the good shepheard: the good shepheard giveth his life for the sheepe" (v. 11). Further resources for elaboration of the pastoral metaphor were found in the role of the shepherds at Christ's nativity; the characterization of David the Psalmist as shepherd before he was called to fight Goliath, serve Saul, and become king; and the identification of Christ as sacrificial lamb, "Lambe of God" (John 1:36, Rev. 14:1-4). Lancelot Andrewes' sermon on Psalm 77:20: "Thou diddest leade thy People like Sheepe, by the hand of *Moses* and *Aaron*," explores the connotations of the similitude, *sicut oves*:

> There is no terme, that the HOLY GHOST more often sendeth for (then this of His *flocke*) to express his people by. . . . When they are . . . taught to submit themselves to government; [they] . . . become gentle and easie to be *led*, *Sicut oves*, *led* to *feeding*, *led* to *shearing*, to feede those that feed them; tractable of nature, and profitable of yeeld: . . . But now againe, when they be brought thus farre, to be *like sheepe*; they are but *like sheepe*, though: that is, a *weake* and *unwise* cattell, farre unable to guide themselves. . . . For, a feeble poore beast (we all know) a *sheepe* is; of little or no strength for resistance in the world, and therefore in danger to be preyed on by every Woolfe.[88]

Of central importance in the poetry of Herbert, Vaughan, and Edward Taylor, is the metaphor of the Christian as "God's husbandry" (1 Cor. 3:9), and of the Christian life as the growth and fruition of a seed, plant, vine, or tree in God's garden, planted and tended by his hand, and required to bring forth a good harvest or good fruit. Fundamental to the metaphor is the biblical story of the garden God planted in Eden which Adam was to dress and keep but of which he was also a part; and also the garden of Canticles, long allegorized as the Christian soul or the Church, the garden of Christian souls.[89] These texts establish a complex metaphor whereby the Christian is himself the object of God's husbandry and also a sharer in it, affording a basis for the important use of georgic motifs in seventeenth-century religious lyric.

The metaphor may be couched chiefly in agricultural terms, according to which God's Word or God's regenerating grace is the seed and we are the soil upon which it is cast. The basic text is Christ's parable of the sower who sowed good seed in a variety of soils—the wayside, stony places, thorns, good ground—and reaped a corresponding variety of harvests (Matt. 13:3-8, 19:23, Mark 4:3-20, Luke 8:4-8). It is supplemented by verses in Mark 4:26-29, likening the Christian life to the seed which grows and bears fruit in mysterious ways until the harvest is come. The human share in this husbandry—the further tilling of the soil (ourselves) and the further cultivation of the seed sown in us—is the burden of Galatians 6:7-8: "Be not deceived; God is not mocked: for whatsoever a man soweth, that shall he also reape. / For hee that soweth to his flesh, shall of the flesh reape corruption: but he that soweth to the spirit, shall of the spirit reape life everlasting." The Christian's share in and sense of the life lived under this husbandry is the burden of Samuel Hieron's sermon entitled "The Spiritual Tillage," on Proverbs 11:18, "He that soweth Righteousnesse, shall receive a reward":

> The curse which God for mans sinne laid upon the earth, (*thornes, and thistles shall it bring forth* [Gen. 6:5]) lieth upon every uncoverted heart. . . . When will any good seed grow in this soyle, if it be never well manured? To breake up this flinty and craggie hart, the Lord hath appointed the preaching of the Law. That is as *fier* to burne out the weedes, and as a *hammer* [Jer. 23:29] to breake the clods in peeces. . . . Great is the care that the seede put into the ground may thrive and prosper; the fields be hedged, the cattell be shut out, the birds driven away, the stones pickt out, it is ever and anone looked upon to see how it goeth on. . . . Sowing and reaping come not at once. . . . In spirituall things . . . it is the pleasure of God to exercise us with delaies: to give us the *first fruits* only, and the *earnest of our inheritance* in this life [Rom. 8:23, Eph. 1:14] and to make us looke long for the fulnesse of happinesse.[90]

Alternatively, the garden-husbandry metaphor often presents God as keeper of a vineyard or orchard, the Christian as branch or tree, and the Christian life as the growth and bearing of appropriate fruits of virtues and good works in evidence of a regenerate nature. A key text is Matthew 7:16-17, "Yee shall knowe them by their fruits: Doe men gather grapes of thornes, or figges of thistles? / Even so, every good tree bringeth forth good fruit: but a corrupt tree bringeth forth evill fruit." A related text is the parable of the barren fig tree (Luke 13:6-9) upon which the vineyard keeper sought for fruit for three years, then gave over to the dresser for further cultivation, after which, not bearing, it would be cut down. Another is John 15:1-5, in which Christ identifies himself as the vine and Christians as the branches, growing and bearing fruit in him: "I am the true vine, and my Father is the husbandman. / Every branch in me that beareth not fruit, hee taketh away: and every branch that beareth fruit, he purgeth it, that it may bring foorth more fruit" (vv. 1-2). Bunyan's tract, *The Barren Fig-Tree*, works out a full-scale allegory from this parable. First he identifies the figures: the certain man is God, the vineyard is the Church, the fig-tree is the barren professor, the dresser is Jesus, the three years defines the limits of God's patience, digging and dunging are efforts to make the tree fruitful, cutting down the fruitless tree is damnation. The meaning inhering in these figures is graphically rendered in a series of exhortations:

> Barren *Fig-tree*, dost thou hear? God expecteth Fruit, God calls for Fruit; yea, God will shortly come *seeking* Fruit on this Barren *Fig-tree*. . . . There is a Fruit among Professors that withers, and so never comes to be ripe. . . . There is an *hasty* Fruit . . . that runs up *suddenly*, violently, with *great stalks* and *big shew*, and yet at *last* proves *empty* of Kernel. . . . There is a Fruit that is *vile and ill-tasted*. . . . There is a Fruit that is *Wild*. . . . There is also untimely Fruit. . . . God expecteth Fruits, *according to the Seasons* of Grace thou art under. . . . Perhaps thou art planted in a good Soil, by great Waters, that thou mightest bring forth Branches, and bear Fruit. . . . How many showers of Grace, how many dews from Heaven, how many times have the Silver Streams of the City of God, *run gliding by thy Roots, to cause thee to bring forth Fruit*.[91]

The marriage trope—the Christian soul as Bride engaged in a love-relationship with Christ the Bridegroom—was also a central one for describing the Christian life; its principal terms are drawn from the Song of Songs. As has been noted above, the characteristic Protestant interpretation of that work did not exploit the sexual aspects of the marriage metaphor to render mystical experience, but read it instead as presenting a betrothal or a marriage solemnized but not yet consummated.[92] Christian life is portrayed thereby as the preparation, trials, and longings of the Bride. Donne expatiates upon the gracious prevalence of the marriage metaphor in scripture: "God is *Love*, and the *Holy Ghost* is amorous in his *Metaphors*; everie where his *Scriptures* abound with the notions of *Love*, or *Spouse*, and *Husband*, and *Marriadge Songs*, and *Marriadge-Supper*, and *Marriadge-Bedde*"—and this is in the context of affording reassurance to fearful Christians that the contract is sure, that Christ will not "divorce" them.[93] Donne put it succinctly in the *Second Anniversarie* (ll. 461-462): Elizabeth Drury was "here / Bethrothed to God, and now is married there." Richard Sibbes also read the metaphor in these terms: we "shall have a glorious Communion in heaven, when the marriage shall be consummated; but now the time of this life is but as the time of the contract, during which there are yet many mutuall passages of love between him and his Spouse, a desire of mutuall Communion of either side."[94] The marriage metaphor is closely related to the husbandry metaphor through those verses identifying the Bride as a fruitful garden or as a lily in the garden which the Bridegroom tends and nurtures and in which he delights—"A garden inclosed is my sister, my spouse" (Cant. 4:12-5:1, 6:2-3).

The metaphor of the Christian as building or temple, and the Christian life as the process of being built up, furnished, and inhabited by the divine architect is of obvious importance to Herbert's *The Temple*. This metaphor is linked with that of husbandry in a key text from 1 Corinthians 3:9, 16-17:

> Ye are Gods husbandry, yee are Gods building.
> . . . . . . . . . . . . . . . . . . . . . . . . . .
> Knowe yee not that yee are the Temple of God, and that the
>    Spirit of God dwelleth in you?
> If any man defile the Temple of God, him shall God destroy:
>    for the Temple of God is holy, which Temple ye are.

The metaphor obtains some of its power by reference to the Old Testament houses for God's worship—the tabernacle for the Ark (Exod. 25-27) and the Temple built by Solomon (2 Chron. 1-6), interpreted typologically in accordance with Acts 7:48, "Howbeit the most high dwelleth not in temples made with hands." It is further elaborated through various texts in which Christ identifies himself as a temple (John 2:19-21) or as the foundation stone or corner stone of his Church (Matt. 21:42, 1 Cor. 3:11, 1 Pet. 2:6), and by the text identifying the Christian as a living stone in Christ's Church: "Ye also, as lively stones, are built up a spirituall house, an holy priesthood to offer up spirituall sacrifice" (1 Pet. 2:5). With such verses in mind, Donne concluded, "The Holy Ghost seems to have delighted in the Metaphore of *Building*."[95] Thomas Adams, preaching on 2 Corinthians 6:6, probed the metaphor to exhibit the immense worth of the individual Christian as temple:

> What are the most polished corners of the Temple, to the spirituall
> and living stones of the Church? . . . what is a glorious edifice, when

the whole world is not worth one Soule? . . . As the Church is his great Temple, so his little temple is every man. We are not onely through his grace, living stones in his Temple, but living temples in his *Sion*: each one bearing about him a little shrine of that infinite Majestie. Wheresoever God dwels, there is his Temple: therefore the beleeving heart is his Temple, for there he dwels.[96]

Daniel Featley's sermon, "The Arke under the Curtaines," on 2 Samuel 7:2, derived elaborate analogies from the metaphor of the Christian as temple, built by God's architecture:

This spirituall and inward temple farre surpasseth . . . the outward or materiall. For that is holy only by denomination and relation, this by inhesion and infusion of the graces of sanctification: that is adorned with lights and tapers, this with the Word of God: that with rich vestments and ornaments, this with heavenly habits and divine virtues: that when it is once built needs only to be repaired, and when it is sufficiently repaired, needs no more cost or labour to bee bestowed upon it for a good space; this needeth continually to be built, repaired, enlarged, and adorned: for to *build* it in the ignorant, to *repaire* it in the relapsed, to *enlarge* it in the proficient, and *beautifie* and adorne it in those that are perfect, is the . . . whole duty of the *man of God*.[97]

One other biblical trope should be recognized here: the heart as synecdoche for the Christian himself, the stage for the whole of his spiritual experience. The basis for taking the heart as a synecdoche is succinctly stated by John Weemse: "In naturall generation the *heart* is first framed; and in supernaturall regeneration, it is first reformed. . . . The life of Grace begins in the *heart* first, and is last left there."[98] Accordingly, as we have seen, other biblical metaphors for the Christian life are often couched in terms of actions upon or actions of the heart: the light of God shines upon the darkness of the heart; the battlefield of the Christian warfare is primarily the heart of man (when the godly are tempted, declares William Perkins, "there is a fight betweene the heart and the heart; that is, betweene the heart and it selfe");[99] the Christian pilgrimage is a "moving of the heart from one thing to another"; our hearts need to be purged and chastised by the afflictions sent from God; our hearts are earth to be weeded and vines to be pruned by God's husbandry; but especially our hearts are temples (or the altars or arks within the temples) framed by God. The heart synecdoche is a primary trope in Herbert's *The Temple*, and in other seventeenth-century religious lyric as well.

The synecdoche is often employed to explore the action of God in renovating and regenerating man. Key texts are Jeremiah 31:33, "I will put my law in their inward parts, and write it in their hearts"; and Ezekiel 36:26, "A new heart also will I give you, and a new spirit will I put within you, and I will take away the stonie heart out of your flesh, and I will give you an heart of flesh." Calvin argued the crucial doctrinal point of utter depravity from this metaphor: "By this comparison the Lord wished to show that nothing good can ever be wrung from our own heart, unless it become wholly other. . . . When his Spirit is taken away, our hearts harden into stones."[100] William Perkins also invoked this trope to discuss regeneration—hardness of heart, the action of God in mollifying the heart, the new covenant of faith located in the heart:

> The heart . . . must be bruised in peeces, that it may be fit to receive Gods saving grace offered unto it. . . . There are for the bruising of this stony heart, four principall hammers. The first, is the knowledge of the Law of God. The second, is the knowledge of sinne, both original and actuall, and what punishment is due unto them. The third, is compunction, or pricking of the heart. . . . The fourth, is an holy desperation of a mans owne power, in the obtaining of eternall life. . . . The highest degree of faith, is . . . a *full perswasion* of the heart, whereby a Christian . . . maketh full and resolute account that God loveth him, and that he will give him by name, Christ and all his graces pertaining to eternall life.[101]

Various stages or aspects of the Christian life are also presented in terms of the heart synecdoche, usually with reference to Psalm texts: "Create in mee a cleane heart, O God" (Psalm 51:10); "My heart is fixed, O God, my heart is fixed: I will sing, and give praise" (Psalm 57:7); and especially Psalm 51:15-17:

> O Lord open thou my lips, and my mouth shall shew forth thy praise.
> For thou desirest not sacrifice: else would I give it: thou delightest not in burnt offering.
> The sacrifices of God are a broken spirit: a broken and a contrite heart, O God, thou wilt not despise.

These last verses contrast the sacrifice of the broken and contrite heart to the Old Testament sacrifice of sheep and oxen upon altars of unhewn stone (Exod. 20:25), and stand behind the common Christian representation of the heart as the altar of the New Covenant temple, and the locus of its praise. Joseph Hall develops the figure in terms which explicate Herbert's poem "The Altar" most vividly, and illuminate all the lyrics of his volume, "The Church":

> In every renewed man, the individuall temple of God, the outward parts are allowed common to God and the world; the inwardest and secretest, which is the heart, is reserved onely for the God that made it. . . . What is the Altar whereon our sacrifices of prayer and praises are offered to the Almightie, but a contrite heart? . . . O God, doe we finde our unworthy hearts so honoured by thee, that they are made thy very Arke, wherein thy Royall law, and the pot of thy heavenly Manna is kept for ever. . . . Behold, if *Salomon* built a Temple unto thee, thou hast built a Temple unto thy selfe in us! We are not onely through thy grace living stones in thy Temple, but living Temples in thy Sion: . . . Let the Altars of our cleane hearts send up ever to thee the sweetest perfumed smoakes of our holy meditations and faithfull prayers, and cheereful thanks-givings.[102]

In a different kind of development Donne in a sermon on Matthew 6:21, "For, where your Treasure is, there will your Heart be also," explores the way the Holy Spirit has exploited the heart synecdoche in numerous scripture texts to exhibit the vacillations of our lives:

> No word in the Scriptures [is] so often added to the heart, as that of intireness; *Toto Corde, Omni Corde, Pleno Corde*: Do this with *all thine heart*, with a *whole heart*, with a *full heart*: for whatsoever is indivisible, is therefore immoveable. . . . When God says, *Fili, da mihi Cor; My Son, give me thy heart*; God means, the whole man. . . . The heart is the man; the heart is all. . . . And yet, even against this, though it be natural, there are many impediments: . . . First, there is *Cor nullum*, a meer Heartlesness, no Heart at all, Incogitancy, Inconsideration: and then there is *Cor & Cor, Cor duplex*, a double Heart, a doubtful, a distracted Heart . . . Perplexity and Irresolution: and lastly, *Cor vagum*, a wandring, a wayfaring, a weary Heart; which is neither Inconsideration, nor Irresolution, but Inconstancie.[103]

As these passages indicate, the fact that these metaphors originated in scripture did not rob them of their experiential ground for the seventeenth-century Protestant preachers and poets; rather, such metaphors provided a nexus between the biblical paradigms and the individual Christian life. Of course these basic Christian tropes, especially the marriage and pilgrimage metaphors and the light-darkness antithesis, had considerable currency in medieval religious lyrics and in

Southwell, Crashaw, and other contemporary Roman Catholic poets. But the Protestant poets in this kind exploited biblical metaphor even more intensively, and in the characteristic Protestant ways sketched here. The superb religious lyrics of the seventeenth century reflect in various ways the heightened Protestant regard for biblical figurative language as a principal vehicle for uniting divine truth and the truths of human experience.

Donne's *Divine Poems* use biblical language somewhat sparingly but with great wit and subtlety; as poet no less than as exegete Donne's method is to probe particular biblical words and figures from many points of view, drawing out even their bizarre ramifications, on the assumption that the language so analyzed must yield not only wit but significant meaning. Accordingly, he examines the various ways the little world of man might suffer the burning the great world expects on the last day ("Holy Sonnet V"); he proves his need of re-creation as a new Adam from his embodiment of the qualities that name signifies, "red earth" ("A Litanie" #1); he demonstrates by tortuous logic that he is both first and second Adam ("Hymne to God my God, in my Sicknesse").

Moreover, Donne uses several of the major tropes with impressive effect. Although the *Divine Poems* are essentially discrete works, a distinctive Donnean characteristic is evident in the "Holy Sonnets" especially—the framing of the tropes so as to show the Christian speaker subject to various kinds of holy violence and force. Some sonnets ring changes upon the sinful state as a living death—"my feebled flesh doth waste / By sinne in it" ("Holy Sonnet I")—and several reflect terror of the death to come. Others present sin as bondage: the speaker has been ravished or captured or stolen by Satan (II, XIV, XV) and Christ must unbind him, or, paradoxically, "enthrall" him in order to free him (XIV). A related trope is that of chastisement or purgation. "Goodfriday, 1613. Riding Westward" finds its resolution through the metaphor of God wielding instruments of chastisement upon the speaker's bared back: "I turne my backe to thee, but to receive / Corrections, . . . / O thinke mee worth thine anger, punish mee, / Burne off my rusts, and my deformity (ll. 37-40)." "Batter my Heart" (XIV) extends this metaphor yet further, as the speaker prays that the whole of God's force be bent upon his heart (taken as synecdoche for himself) to batter-break-blow-burn him. Even the marriage trope is couched in terms of violence. In the same "Sonnet XIV," Christ the Bridegroom of the soul is urged to become its ravisher or rapist, since the speaker cannot be "chast, except you ravish mee." And in

"Sonnet XVIII" Christ the Bridegroom of the Church is urged to become a pander to his Spouse, exposing her to many lovers, since she best pleases him "When she'is embrac'd and open to most men." In "Holy Sonnet II" the speaker sets forth several of the familiar tropes as metaphoric "titles" by which God could and should claim him— son, sheep, image, temple; then, recognizing Satan's challenge to these titles, he employs and recasts the Christian warfare trope, asserting that not his own warfare but God's is necessary to support and defend these metaphoric claims.

George Herbert's way with biblical language and figure is indicated in "The H. Scriptures (II)," as he alludes to the recommended exegetical procedures of collating related texts and applying all of them to the self:

> This verse marks that, and both do make a motion
>     Unto a third, that ten leaves off doth lie:
>     Then as dispersed herbs do watch a potion,
> These three make up some Christians destinie:
> Such are thy secrets, which my life makes good,
>     And comments on thee: for in ev'ry thing
>     Thy words do finde me out, & parallels bring,
> And in another make me understood.
>
>                   (ll. 5-12)

These procedures are everywhere apparent in *The Temple*. Herbert builds up out of a rich complex of biblical allusions and images certain governing figures, which recur in poem after poem—the temple in the heart, the stony heart-altar, the Christian as flower or plant. Or, alternatively, allusions and figures from many biblical texts are brought together to define or explore an aspect of the Christian life—to make up the series of epithets in "Prayer (I)" for example, or to amalgamate in a few lines images and tropes from Luke, Exodus, Genesis, and Revelation: "what account can thy ill steward make? / . . . O do not blinde me! / I have deserv'd that an Egyptian night / Should thicken all my powers; because my lust / Hath still sow'd fig-leaves to exclude thy light: / . . . O do not fill me / With the turn'd viall of thy bitter wrath!"[104]

The governing trope of Herbert's collection of lyrics, "The Church" is that of the speaker as temple of God. The heart is designated as the site of this architecture, and all the biblical texts relating to the stony heart, the Old Testament altars of unhewn stone, and the designations of the Christian as God's building and temple are laid under contribution in the complex development of this trope. Several poems use it explicitly and centrally—"The Altar," "The Sinner," "Sepulchre," "Nature," "Discipline," "The Church-floore"—and it affects to some degree all the poems in the volume. A subordinate but extremely important metaphor is that of the speaker as God's husbandry—a tree or plant or flower seeking for and often complaining of the lack of fruition, or conscious of the nurturing dew and rain and sun of grace, or experiencing the Lord's pruning ("Affliction (I)," "Employment (I)," "Employment (II)," "Grace," "Paradise," "The Flower"). Other tropes figure less centrally. The speaker is a sheep in Herbert's version of Psalm 23, and a shepherd with a flock of thoughts in "Christmas." He complains of but at length accepts God's chastisement and discipline in the five "Affliction" poems, "Discipline," "The Temper (I)," "The Temper (II)," "Josephs Coat," and "Sighs and Grones," among others. In "The Collar" he invokes the childhood metaphor to striking effect: the Lord's call, "*Child*," dispels the speaker's rebellion by redefining his condition from that of servant to a strict master to that of child to a loving Father. Throughout the sequence the speaker sees himself in several metaphoric conditions: sometimes as child, sometimes as servant of a great and powerful Lord ("Love unknown," "Redemption"), often as friend conversing with and aided by his Friend, and finally, in "Love (III)," as guest of a gracious host who serves him a heavenly banquet.

Henry Vaughan incorporates biblical language into his poetry more extensively and more directly than Herbert: indeed, he often does what he prays to be able to do in his poem, "H. Scriptures"—"plead in groans / Of my Lords penning." The very frequent use of biblical quotations (often from Canticles and Revelation) as epigraphs at the beginning or end of the poems charges the imagery of those poems with multiple meaning. An example is the epigraph of "Regeneration" (Cant. 4:16), which attaches significance from a mass of biblical commentary to the poem's key images—the primrose path, the winter followed by spring, the fountain of life, the lively stones, the sunflowers, the rushing wind. Again, the pervasive biblical allusions and imagery create a poetic universe for the speaker in which biblical and actual landscape are wholly interfused: he walks in the Old Testament groves where prophets talked with God; he searches for his Savior in New Testament places; he confronts Isaac in the field awaiting his bride and praying; he sees the British Church enacting the role of the Bride of Canticles; he takes the Mount of Olives as his poet's mount (in place of Parnassus, or the Cotswold hills, or Cooper's Hill); he seeks to travel back to his innocent infancy; he is suddenly surprised to hear an angel cry, "*Arise! Thrust in thy sickle.*"[105] Or, in a single poem such as

"The Morning-watch," he can fuse several biblical images—the manna falling by night, the water-blood-spirit imagery from 1 John 5:6-8; the praises of the Psalmist and all creation from Psalms 57 and 148—applying them all to the inner landscape of the soul.

Several major biblical tropes are important for Vaughan's poems but the pilgrimage trope unifies the entire collection. The speaker as pilgrim often travels through a quasi-biblical landscape ("Regeneration," "The Search," "Religion," "The Pilgrimage," "The Ass"); elsewhere, his life's journey is envisioned (with reference also to the childhood trope) as a return to childhood nearness to God and heaven ("The Retreate," "Childe-hood"). The pilgrimage often takes place through a dark, cloudy land, thereby assimilating to the pilgrimage trope what is perhaps the most characteristic combination of metaphors in Vaughan—the representation of life on earth in terms of darkness, deadness, clouded or veiled vision; and the life to come (or the life of grace) as true light, unclouded vision, and "Quickness."[106] Occasionally, the light-darkness metaphor is reversed ("The Night," "The Morning-watch") so that the time of natural darkness is presented as peculiarly the season of spiritual illumination, a treatment made possible by the paradox of light and darkness united in God: "There is in God (some say) / A deep, but dazling darkness."[107]

Vaughan's speaker also sees himself as God's husbandry. He is sometimes aware of a seed of grace planted in him and nurtured by God's dews and sun ("unprofitablenes," "Disorder *and* frailty," "The Proffer," "The Seed growing secretly"); sometimes he laments his failure to bear fruit; and sometimes (invoking also the chastisement trope) he experiences frosts nipping his ill weeds. He is in bondage to sin in "Day of Judgement," and at the beginning of "Regeneration"; in "And do they so?" he sees the entire creation in bondage, longing for the liberty promised the Sons of God. More broadly, the frequent Canticles allusions and quotations evoke the marriage trope, which Vaughan explores in terms of election: in "The World" the bright ring of eternity glimpsed above the darksome world is finally recognized by the speaker as the spousal ring intended for the elect, "*This Ring the Bride-groome did for none provide / But for his bride* (ll. 59-60)."

Traherne formally eschews "curling Metaphors," "painted Eloquence," "Poëtick Strains and Shadows" in favor of a presentation of "naked Truth" by means of "transparent Words."[108] Though he does not find the Bible plain—nothing could be "For Beauty more excellent, / For manner more Gorgeous, / For Materials more Rich"[109]— this beauty is not so much of language as of essence, the revelation of things in their true glory: "real Crowns and Thrones and Diadems."[110] Accordingly, his poems use biblical language extensively, but in a comparatively straightforward manner: the technique is often that of listing and repeating in somewhat incantatory fashion biblical terms which evoke rather than describe the essence they name—words and phrases relating to the jewels, thrones, and glories of God's Kingdom.[111] Or again, he evokes the metaphorical complexities associated with common biblical tropes simply by naming and listing them: "I am his Image, and his Friend. / His Son, Bride, Glory, Temple, End."[112]

Two biblical tropes dominate Traherne's lyrics. In a unique development of the childhood trope the speaker presents himself in the process of enacting the injunction to become a child again in order to enjoy God's kingdom. At times the speaker remembers most vividly his innocent infancy and strives to reclaim it: "I felt no Stain, nor Spot of Sin / . . . I was an Adam there, / A little Adam in a Sphere / Of Joys! . . . / I must becom a Child again."[113] More often, he emphasizes his present status as child of God and thereby heir to his Kingdom, identifying that inheritance with this world and all its glory: "The Earth, the Seas, the Light, the Day, the Skies, / The Sun and Stars are mine; if those I prize. / . . . Into this Eden so Divine and fair, / So Wide and Bright, I com his Son and Heir."[114] Traherne's remarkable evocations of feasts, jewels, lights, rich and lustrous objects of all sorts are related to this child-heir trope.

A second controlling metaphor is that of spiritual light-sight-vision set against the darkness, blindness, and corruption of custom or of the ordinary world. In Traherne's unusual formulation of this trope, the source of the light suffusing all things with glory is not God directly but the image of God in the speaker. This metaphor is linked with the childhood trope in that the source of the light is often identified as the speaker's "Infant-Ey" which sees things "Ev'n like unto the Deity."[115] In "The Preparative" the soul is "A Living, Endless Ey, / Far wider then the Skie"; and the speaker is "an Inward *Sphere of Light*, / Or an Interminable Orb of *Sight*, / *A vital Sun* that round about did *ray* / All life and Sence" (ll. 12-19). And in "My Spirit," the eye is Traherne's emblem or synecdoche for the redeemed Christian self: the eye, not the heart as for Herbert, is the "Temple of his Whole Infinitie!" (l. 109).

Edward Taylor everywhere praises the metaphors of scripture as the vehicle of God's communication to man and as an ultimate standard of eloquence—"What Golden words drop from thy gracious lips, / Adorning of thy Speech with Holy paint."[116] Yet he finds himself better able to meditate upon such tropes, than to adopt them as his own.

His poems most often explore the central term or metaphor from the biblical texts which serve as titles: for example, the Lord as ointment, as lily, as apple tree, as morning star, as vine. The method is sometimes (I.4) an analysis of a particular figure in all its aspects: Christ as Rose of Sharon is praised according to the various permutations of the rose—perfume, syrup of the rose, rose oil as balm, sugar of roses as medicine, rose water as cordial, mangled roses as physic, and finally the rose as a crown of triumph. But normally the tropes are diverse, thickly sown, and much less unified.

The poems are studded with metaphors suggested by the biblical verses he takes as subjects, prominent among which are eucharistic images such as banquets, feasts, vessels of wine. Almost all the tropes we have examined are here. The speaker in some poems explores the sin-as-sickness trope, finding in his soul leprosy, ulcers, wheezings, tumors, dropsy, gout, scurvy, and a host of other diseases which can be cured only by Christ, the Son of Righteousness with healing in his wings.[117] Elsewhere the speaker is in bondage to sin and a debtor to the law, looking to his advocate, Christ, to free him.[118] Calling upon the heart synecdoche, the speaker finds that his is variously a rocky heart, an icy heart bedded in snow, a frozen or congealed heart needing to be warmed by Christ's flames of love, a filthy heart full of corruptions, an altar-heart upon which prayers and praises are offered.[119] Other poems employ the light-darkness metaphor: God is the pole-star shining into the world's darkness, a shine reflected in and through the biblical types, and the source of the speaker's own light— "Lord ting my Candle at thy Burning Rayes."[120]

The two most important biblical tropes for Taylor derive from Canticles texts, his most frequent subjects. Though the speaker cannot adopt the stance of the Bride directly, he reviews her praises of the Bridegroom (under such titles as Rose of Sharon and Lily of the Valley) for his beauty, his sweetness, his lips dropping the myrrh of forgiveness, his hands showering graces.[121] And though the marriage trope is usually referred to the wonder of Christ marrying our manhood, Taylor sometimes exploits its amatory connotations—with reference, however, to future bliss or else to a declaration of the scantiness and insufficiency of his own love compared to Christ's. The Canticles' imagery of the Spouse as garden leads Taylor also to the husbandry metaphor. The speaker presents himself as garden or vineyard from which the Bridegroom seeks fruits or nuts or spices. Or else, taking the Church as garden or vineyard, he prays to be set as a pomegranate or lily in that garden, a vine in that vineyard, a spice-tree in that olive grove. Elsewhere he focuses upon the Bridegroom as gardener, cultivating or weeding his garden and using his pruning hook on fruitless branches.[122] And, independently of Canticles, the speaker is sometimes a withered tree grafted into Christ the Tree of Life, a branch grafted into the True Vine, a marigold facing the sun, a fruit tree failing to bear good fruit.[123]

For Donne the common storehouse of biblical tropes provides, especially in the "Holy Sonnets," imaginative norms which can receive characteristically Donnean formulations and often witty extensions, forcing them to carry a singular vision of the Christian life as subjection to divine force and violence. Herbert's entire sequence is dominated by the single, central trope of the Christian as temple of God, supplemented by the related metaphoric clusters of stony hearts, stone altars, and the Christian as God's husbandry. Four or five pervasive and complexly interrelated tropes provide Vaughan's poems with their primary poetic strategy—pilgrimage, light-darkness, bondage and exile, childhood, husbandry. Disclaiming metaphor, Traherne yet uses two interlinked tropes to define his speaker: the childhood-heir-of-God trope, and the light-sight-vision-eye cluster. Edward Taylor uses more biblical tropes than any of his predecessors, but derives and explores them in more direct and conventional ways; his most successful poems develop a strategy of meiosis whereby the biblical tropes are recast in homely, colloquial terms, or else are opposed to base, antithetical figures which render the speaker's vileness and worthlessness. The end of an era seems to be signalled by Taylor's inability to appropriate the biblical tropes to his own use as the great shaping forms of religious lyric poetry.

# The Biblical Symbolic Mode: Typology and the Religious Lyric

That the ancient mode of Christian symbolism we call typology was alive and well after the Reformation and prominent in six-teenth- and seventeenth-century theology—and literature—is not now a matter of much controversy.[1] What is not sufficiently recognized is the fact that the medieval exegetical principles which created typology as a hermeneutical system underwent during the Protestant Reformation some significant changes in emphasis, and that these changes profoundly affect the uses of typology throughout this period. These changes contribute directly to the importance of typological symbolism for the religious lyrics of the period, as a means for probing and exploring the personal spiritual life with profundity and com-plexity.

As Erich Auerbach has shown, many medieval exegetes asserted the primacy of the literal sense of scripture, and in addition made a gen-erally consistent conceptual, though not linguistic, distinction between typological symbolism and various kinds of allegorical meaning.[2] Alle-gory was understood to involve the invention of fictions, or the contrivance of other systems of symbols, to represent underlying spir-itual truth or reality. Typology by contrast was recognized as a mode of signification in which both type and antitype are historically real entities with independent meaning and validity, forming patterns of prefiguration, recapitulation, and fulfillment by reason of God's provi-dential control of history. In precise terms, typology pertains to Old Testament events, personages, ceremonies, and objects seen to fore-shadow and to be fulfilled, *forma perfectior*, in Christ and the New Dispensation. Typological exegesis found biblical warrant from several places in the Gospels—Matthew 2:14-15, 5:17, 12:41; Luke 11:30-31, 17:26-30, 24:27; John 3:14-15 and 6:31-35—wherein Christ refers to himself as the fulfillment of various Old Testament signs and prophe-cies. The Pauline epistles provide other typological texts wherein Christ or the New Law are set forth as the fulfillment of personages or events or dispensations in the Old Testament—e.g., Romans 5:14; 1 Corinthians 5:7, 10:1-4, 11, 15:20-23; Galatians 4:22-26; 2 Corinthians 3:13-14; Hebrews 9:8-12. In addition, the Epistles supply the classic texts for the definition of typology: Hebrews 10:1 refers to the Law as "having a shadow of good things to come, and not the very Image of the things," and Colossians 2:17 refers to the laws and ceremonies of the Old Testament as "a shadow of things to come, but the body is of Christ." The nature of the type as a historical event that adumbrates another event to come is suggested in such passages, but the terminology is not consistent: Galatians 4:22-24 describes Abraham's two wives as an *allegoroumena* of the two covenants; Hebrews 10:1 refers to events in the Old Testament as *skia* or "shadows" of the reality to come in Christ; 1 Corinthians 10:11 uses the term *typos* in the same context, as does Romans 5:14, "Nevertheles, death reigned from Adam to Moses . . . who is the figure [*typos*] of him that was to come"; the Epistle to the Hebrews, typological in its very essence, uses *skia*, *hypodeigma* (pattern), *parabole*, as well as *typos* to describe the foreshadowing event.[3] Moreover, the distinction between allegory and typology, clear enough in theory, was blurred by widespread patristic and medieval use of the general term "allegory" for both kinds of signification. Early to late, it is the sense afforded by the context rather than the particular term used that must determine whether, and how, a typological symbolic mode is being used.

Early patristic exegetes identified several kinds of spiritual and allegorical meanings in scripture without distinguishing very sharply between modes and without defining very clearly the status of the literal text in relation to those meanings. As Jean Daniélou has noted, some emphasized Old Testament prefigurations of the life of Christ; others such as Justin Martyr regarded Old Testament figures as referring principally to the sacraments of the Church; Iranaeus, drawing heavily upon Jewish tradition, stressed figures of eschatological prophecy; Clement of Alexandria pointed up allegories of the spiritual life.[4] Origen called upon all these senses, linking with them Philo's conception that the three meanings of scripture (literal, moral, mystical) correspond allegorically to the three parts of man (body, soul, spirit); he also employed esoteric systems of numerology, etymology, and Platonic allegory. Origen's conception that everything in scripture has a figurative meaning, and his readiness to discard the literal sense as frequently gross and absurd[5] made him a byword among the Reformers for irresponsible exegetical methods. Such attitudes, carried on through the School of Alexandria, encouraged the medieval practice of intermixing a plethora of allegorical interpretations with stricter typological readings as equivalent levels of meaning, and so promoted the interpretation of the Bible in the Middle Ages as a multi-level allegorical work.

Augustine's famous formula invested both literal and spiritual interpretations of scripture with value and significance, and served as a point of departure for most subsequent medieval discussion of hermeneutics. As we have seen, Augustine defined the literal meaning of scripture as residing not in the words themselves but in the things signified by the words.[6] He defined the figurative or spiritual sense as that whereby the things or events signified by the words point beyond themselves to other things or events: "Figurative signs occur when that thing which we designate by a literal sign is used to signify something else; thus we say 'ox' and by that syllable understand the animal which is ordinarily designated by that word, but again by that animal we understand an evangelist, as is signified in the Scripture, according to the interpretation of the Apostle, when it says, 'Thou shalt not muzzle the ox that treadeth out the corn.' "[7] For Augustine the figurative or allegorical sense includes the covert or obscure meanings conveyed by metaphors or parables or other such tropes, the symbolic meanings embodied in nature or in number, and also Old Testament foreshadowings or types. This broad inclusiveness rests upon Augustine's conviction that God as creator has invested the things of Creation with rich emblematic significance (as with the ox) and as designer of providential history has invested the persons, things, and events recorded in scripture with figurative (typological) significance, whereby they foreshadow what is to come. His own universal history, the *City of God*, writes God's typology large: the six days of creation foreshadow the six ages of human history; the conflict of Cain and Abel foreshadows the conflict of the City of God on earth with the City of Man in all ages; and the Old Testament patriarchs, prophets, and ceremonies of the Law prefigure Christ and the Christian dispensation.[8]

Though of cardinal importance to the development of Christian notions of symbolism, Augustine's distinction between the literal and the figurative senses (words signifying things and those things signifying other things) was far from unambiguous. Under the pressure of Augustine's Platonism the distinction itself tended to collapse, since all signs (words and things) ultimately point to the ineffable God. Also, besides claiming a vast domain for the figurative or spiritual sense, Augustine often gave it such clear priority that the literal meaning is quite abandoned—as in his arbitrary allegorization of Genesis 1, and his reading of the Psalms with such entire reference to the antitype, Christ and the Church, that the Psalmist's voice and experience is all but obliterated.[9] Augustine could even embrace as a divine boon the idea—anathema to Protestants—of multiple spiritual meanings elaborated freely according to the law of charity: he takes the phrase, "be fruitful and multiply" (Gen. 1:22), as a kind of allegory of allegory, a God-given blessing whereby we are able "to express in many ways what we understand but in one; and to understand in many ways what we read as obscurely delivered but in one."[10]

Overlaying the literal-figurative distinction is the further distinction between Law and Grace introduced in *De Spiritu et littera* as another sense.[11] Here Augustine comes close to isolating a distinct "typological" sense, identifying the "letter" with the Old Testament Law which kills by demanding righteousness and manifesting sin, and the Spirit with the Christian Gospel which proclaims the grace that fulfills the letter and overcomes sin. As J. S. Preus and Karlfried Froehlich have noted, this sharp division between Old Testament and New is followed in much medieval typological exegesis, wherein the "meer letter," or "the carnal sense," is frequently equated with the "sense of the Jews," now wholly abrogated by Christ.[12] This view encouraged the medieval devaluation of the historical and spiritual signification of the Old Testament in itself, as affording mere shadowy types of the spiritual substance we enjoy through Christ the antitype.

The usual medieval formulation of the four senses of scripture expands but also simplifies and systematizes the literal-spiritual division of Augustine by naming three specific modes of the spiritual—allegory or typology (*credenda*); tropology or *moralitas* (*agenda*); anagogy or eschatology (*speranda*); this formula, illustrated by the familiar example of the literal Israel foreshadowing allegorically the Church on earth, tropologically the soul of man, and anagogically the heavenly Jerusalem, seems to have appeared first in John Cassian.[13] A similar scheme based upon three senses (anagogy being subsumed under allegory) was enunciated by Hugh of Saint Victor:

> Now of this subject matter Divine Scripture treats according to a threefold sense: that is, according to history, allegory, and tropology. History is the narration of events, which is contained in the first meaning of the letter; we have allegory when, through what is said to have been done, something else is signified as done either in the past or in the present or in the future; we have tropology when through what is said to have been done, it is signified that something ought to be done.[14]

But the classic definition of the literal and the three spiritual senses, based upon and clarifying Augustine's description of the literal level as the things signified by the words, and the spiritual senses as the things further signified by those things, is the well-known passage from Aquinas:

> The author of Holy Scripture is God, in Whose power it is to signify His meaning, not by words only (as man also can do), but also by things themselves. So, whereas in every other science things are signified by words, this science has the property that the things signified by the words have themselves also a signification. Therefore that first signification whereby words signify things belongs to the first sense, the historical or literal. That signification whereby things signified by words have themselves also a signification is called the spiritual sense, which is based on the literal, and presupposes it. Now this spiritual sense has a threefold division. For as the Apostle says (Heb. x. 1) the Old Law is a figure of the New Law, and Dionysius says *the New Law itself is a figure of future glory*. Again, in the New Law, whatever our Head has done is a type of what we ought to do. Therefore, so far as the things of the Old Law signify the things of the New Law, there is the allegorical sense; so far as the things done in Christ, or so far as the things which signify Christ, are signs of what we ought to do, there is the moral sense. But so far as they signify what relates to eternal glory, there is the anagogical sense.[15]

In this and related passages Aquinas locates all figurative language squarely in the realm of the literal sense: arguing that words may signify either properly or figuratively, he explains that in the case of figures the literal sense is not "the figure itself, but that which is figured."[16] If Christ is designated as a stone cut out of a rock without hands (Dan. 2:34) this usage remains within the realm of the literal since the thing pointed to by the words is not the stone, but Christ. All poetic fictions such as metaphoric and parabolic modes also remain within the literal sense because they are "not ordered to anything but signifying." All this also locates the three symbolic senses squarely within the spiritual realm, in which things themselves signify other things.[17] As F. E. Cranz has argued, Thomas seems to take both the realm of words and the realm of things as totalities.[18] Ultimately, Thomas defines the literal sense as "that which the author intends," observing that "the author of Holy Scripture is God";[19] the literal meaning hereby comes to mean all that can be derived from a text while remaining within the realm of the meaning of *words*. But the realm of *things* is also a totality and the spiritual senses are located within this realm, where God and God alone can determine meaning. Poets can contrive the use of "other words or feigned likenesses to signify something" whereas God can use "the very course of things themselves for signifying other things."[20] Among the spiritual senses the "allegorical" now receives a definition that limits it rather strictly to typology—Old Testament foreshadowings of Christ or the Church —and the moral or tropological meaning achieves the dignity of a distinct and separate "sense."

Though Aquinas insists that God alone can make things signify other things, Dante supplies an example of poetic use of the realm of typological meaning. In his *Convivio* Dante differentiates the "allegory of the poets," "a truth hidden under a beautiful fiction,"[21] from the allegory of the theologians. But he subsequently describes his *Commedia* in terms of the allegory of the theologians:

> The meaning of this work is not of one kind only; rather the work may be described as "polysemous," that is, having several meanings; for the first meaning is that which is conveyed by the letter, and the next is that which is conveyed by what the letter signifies; the former of which is called literal, while the latter is called allegorical, or mystical. And for the better illustration of this method of exposition we may apply it to the following verses: "When Israel went out of Egypt, the house of Jacob from a people of strange language; Judah was his sanctuary, and Israel his dominion." For if we consider the letter alone, the thing signified to us is the going out of the children of Israel from Egypt in the time of Moses; if the allegory, our redemption through Christ is signified; if the moral sense, the conversion of the soul from the sorrow and misery of sin to a state of grace is signified; if the anagogical, the passing of the sanctified soul from the bondage of the corruption of this world to the liberty of everlasting glory is signified. . . . The subject, then, of the whole work, taken in the literal sense only, is the state of souls after death, pure and simple. For on and about that the argument of the whole work turns. If, however, the work be regarded from the allegorical point of view, the subject is man according as by his merits or demerits in the exercise of his free will he is deserving of reward or punishment by justice.[22]

Dante can explain the *Commedia* in terms of theological allegory because in this poem, unlike the *Convivio*, he is presenting significations which have their ground in the nature of things, in the relationships God has contrived between acts in time and their future fulfillments. These meanings may be discovered by the poet, but are not made by him; he merely displays the significances God has produced.

Holding high the banner of the "one sense of scripture, the literal sense," the reformers loudly denounced the profusion of allegories and the doctrine of the four senses. Tyndale declares, "there is not a more handsome or apte thyng to beguile withall, then an allegory, nor a more subtle and pestilente thyng in the world to perswade to a false matter."[23] In his *Table Talk* Luther laments his days as a friar when he "allegorized everything, even a chamber pot," and in the *Commentarie ...upon ...Galathians* he censures the "idle and unlearned Monks and the Schooledoctors . . . which taught that the Scripture hath foure senses. . . . With these trifeling and foolish fables, they rent the Scriptures into so many and divers senses, that seely poore consciences could receave no certaine doctrine of any thing."[24] But the Reformers accepted, and indeed exalted, typological symbolism, endeavoring by more and more rigorous means to distinguish this divinely sanctioned symbolic method from arbitrary allegorizing. In doing so they revised medieval concepts in several ways—perhaps most fundamentally in their recognition of typological meanings as a part or dimension of the literal text rather than as one of several distinct senses. This may seem to be a distinction without a difference, but, from a literary point of view, at least, it is not. Though the terminology used to define this conception of typology is not consistent, the new Protestant emphasis is clear: it makes for a different sense of the Bible as a unified poetic text, and for a much closer fusion of sign and thing signified, type and antitype. The characteristic Protestant approach takes the Bible not as a multi-level allegory, but as a complex literary work whose full literal meaning is revealed only by careful attention to its poetic texture and to its pervasive symbolic mode—typology.

Luther refers constantly to Old Testament foreshadowings or types of Christ: Adam and Eve wedded are types of Christ and the Church; the flight of the dove from the Ark foreshadows New Testament redemption; the story of the Passover adumbrates Christ's redemption of us; the Levitical law and ceremonies type Christ's sacrifice; the story of Joseph's sale into bondage and his later restoration and forgiveness of his brothers figures the crucifixion and resurrection of Christ; all the prophets and the promises direct themselves upon Christ and his kingdom.[25] Yet such examples, and Luther's more sweeping assertions that the entire Bible in the spiritual sense speaks only of Christ,[26] need to be seen in reference to the shift which takes place in the course of Luther's commentary on the Psalms. Appealing at first to the traditional four senses, he interprets the Psalms in medieval typological terms as the very words of Christ and the Church; later however he emphasizes the literal, Old Testament situation of David the Psalmist and the Hebrew people, seen as responding in their own terms to the promises and expectation of Christ whose coming fulfills and clarifies these promises.[27] Seen in this way, the prophetic dimension, which pertains to Christ, is integrally a part of the literal meaning—what Wilhelm Pauck terms the spiritual-literal sense[28]—but it is also typological, in that the New Testament events clarify and demonstrate more fully the meaning of these foreshadowings and promises of the Messiah. As Preus notes, Luther came to describe the whole of scripture, New Testament as well as Old, as "Testimonies" of Christ which look toward the future for their fulfillment.[29] Developing this perception, Luther set forth a new typological structure based upon the three advents of Christ:

> Just as the advent of Christ in the flesh has been given out of the sheer mercy of the promising God . . . nevertheless it is still necessary that there be preparation and a disposition to receive him, as was done in the whole old testament through the line of Christ. . . . So also the spiritual advent comes through grace, and the future [advent] through glory. . . . Hence, just as the law was a figure and preparation of the people for receiving Christ, so our doing what is in us (*factio quantum in nobis est*) disposes us to grace. And the whole time of grace is preparation for future glory and the second advent.[30]

In these terms, the single *res* toward which all the signs in scripture point is Christ: he is "the goal of all things and the thing signified through all other things."[31] But the mode of that signifying is no longer a separable spiritual or prophetic sense; rather it is an integral part of the literal-historical meaning of the text, which contains as its prophetic dimension figures and promises referred to the future for their clarification and fulfillment.

Typology occupied a more central and more precisely defined place in Calvin's exegesis than in Luther's, and his highly influential hermeneutical recommendations and practice in these matters provided a model for later exegetes—and for Christian poets. Passage after passage in scripture Calvin treats typologically: the Jews' deliverance from Egypt and from Babylon foreshadows Christ's deliverance of his people from sin; Joseph's imprisonment and restoration figure the death and resurrection of Christ and all believers; David's life often adumbrates the gospel story and especially the passion; David's kingdom figures Christ's; the sacrifices of the Law are a type of Christ's sacrifice; Christ is "the archetype of [all] the figures."[32] Characteristically, Calvin found in many passages a threefold reference—actually and literally to some historical situation in Israel, typologically to Christ, and (again typologically) to the state of the contemporary Church. In consonance with the principle of the one sense of scripture Calvin, like Luther, flatly denied the Catholic formulation of multiple senses—words signifying things at the literal level and these things signifying other things at the spiritual level. But he did not therefore resort—or lead his followers to resort—to the "desperate expedient" indicated by Madsen, of either taking typological significance to be simply an accommodated meaning, or else asserting that the typological passages refer only and literally to Christ and not to the ostensible Old Testament subjects.[33] Calvin's exegesis of Psalm 22 provides a good example of his usual method of relating historical reference and typological meaning: he explains that David in describing his own sufferings and expressing his own genuine feelings is at the same time describing Christ, for "it was the wil of the heavenly Father, that in the person of His Sonne, there should appeere a visible accomplishment of the thinges that were shadowed in David." Moreover, in writing this Psalm David was dimly conscious that he was also describing another, for he speaks of himself in hyperbolic language, to lead us to recognize "by excesse of speech . . . the dreadfull encounter of Christ ageinst death," which "he knew by the spirit of Profesie."[34] What is significant here is that the text itself, the literal level, is taken as a sign which present both a more restricted meaning (David's sufferings) and a more adequate, complete, and total meaning (Christ's sufferings)—the language of the text being formulated by David, and the Spirit guiding him, to convey this dual significance. So also with the events and ceremonies of the Law seen as types: Calvin explains that the Old Testament Jews learned of Christ through such types, obscurely at first but then with progressive clarity, and that their prophets, imperfectly but yet with some degree of consciousness, understood and taught these Christic significances. The Gospel antitypes then point out "with the finger what the law foreshadowed under types."[35] The spiritual meaning of the types (Christ) is thus contained within and revealed by the literal or historical signs, though by reference to the New Testament antitypes we read the signs more fully and completely than did the Jews. Calvin's analogy is that of a painter's rough charcoal sketch as compared to his finished painting:

> For painters are wont to drawe that which they purpose to counterfeit or represent with a cole, before they set on the lively colours with the pensill. The Apostle then puts this difference betweene the law and the Gospell: to wit, that that which at this time is drawne and painted with fresh and lively colours, was onely shadowed out under the law by a rude or grosse draught.[36]

Following this lead, Calvinists customarily distinguished typological meaning from allegory and all other figurative modes in scripture, identifying it as part of the full or entire or perfect literal sense—the symbolic dimension of the literal sense which, in the course of time, is uncovered and fulfilled. A favorite biblical text for making the necessary distinctions was Galatians 4:22:

> For it is written, that Abraham had two sonnes, the one by a bond-maid, the other by a freewoman.
> But he who was of the bondwoman was borne after the flesh: but hee of the freewoman, was by promise.
> Which things are an Allegorie: for these are the two Covenants; the one from Mount Sinai, which gendereth to bondage, which is Agar.
> For this Agar is mount Sinai in Arabia, and answereth to Jerusalem, which now is, and is in bondage with her children.
> But Jerusalem which is above is free, which is the mother of us all.

William Whitaker's comment on this text, in his tract directed against the Jesuit Robert Bellarmine,[37] supplies perhaps the most cogent formulation of the conception towards which many of the reformers seemed to be groping—the identification of the typological-anagogical meaning as the symbolic dimension of the literal text. In explaining the operation of this symbolism, Whitaker avoids the medieval formula of things signifying other things, appealing instead to the symbolic reach of language itself, which forces the conjunction in our minds between the symbol (type) and the later revelation of meanings (antitype) obscurely pointed to by the symbol.[38] Whitaker declares:

> The apostle . . . interprets the history of Abraham's two wives allegorically, or rather typically, of the two Testaments; for he says in express words, ἅτινά ἐστιν ἀλληγορούμενα, &c. [which things are an allegory]. . . . Indeed, there is a certain catechresis in the word ἀλληγορούμενα, for that history is not accommodated by Paul in that place allegorically, but typically; and a type is a different thing from an allegory. The sense, therefore, of that scripture is one only, namely, the literal or grammatical. However, the whole entire sense is not in the words taken strictly, but part in the type, part in the transaction itself. In either of these considered separately and by itself, part only of the meaning is contained; and by both taken together the full and perfect meaning is completed. . . . When we proceed from the sign to the thing signified, we bring no new sense, but only bring out into the light what was before concealed in the

sign. . . . For although this sense be spiritual, yet it is not a different one, but really literal; since the letter itself affords it to us in the way of similitude or argument. . . . By expounding a similitude, we compare the sign with the thing signified, and so bring out the true and entire sense of the words.[39]

William Perkins, also expounding Galatians 4:22, offers a similar formula:

> There is but one full and intire sense of every place of scripture, and that is also the literal sense. . . . To make many senses of scripture is to overturne all sense, and to make nothing certen. . . . It may be said, that the historie of Abrahams familie here propounded, hath beside his proper and literall sense, a spiritual or mysticall sense. I answer, they are not two senses, but two parts of one full and intire sense. For not onely the bare historie, but also that which is therby signified, is the full sense of the h[oly] G[host].[40]

Similarly, John Weemse discusses typological meanings in terms of a "compound sense," which phrase is "not taken here to make two Senses out of one scripture (for that were contradictory:) but onely . . . two parts, literall and figurative, to make up one sense, which is fulfilled two manner of wayes, *Historicê* and *Propheticê* in the type, and literally in the thing signified."[41] He clarifies the point elsewhere, discussing the Old Testament types and prophecies as intending both an immediate and partial, and also a future and more complete, signification:

> The Spirit of God intendeth *propinquius* & *remotius*, something nearer and something farther off; yet these two make up not two divers senses, but one full and intire sense. . . . Example, 2 *Sam.* 7.12. The Lord maketh a promise to *David, I will set up thy seede after thee which shall proceede out of thy bowels.* This promise looked both *ad propius & remotius*, yet it made up but one sense, *propius* to *Salomon*, and *remotius* to Christ.[42]

Though this conception of typology as the symbolic dimension of the literal text is the usual Protestant formula, the older medieval distinction between the things signified by the words and the further signification of the things themselves is sometimes invoked. In such cases, however, the writers are usually at pains to deny that this kind of signification constitutes a special spiritual sense.[43] They are also at pains to make clear distinctions between typology and allegory, accounting for the latter in terms of the Augustinian precept that passages patently absurd or contradictory to the analogy of faith had to be understood figuratively and allegorically. Some Protestants, among them Flacius Illyricus, Salomon Glass, and Henry Lukin, retained the old language of the multiple senses to explain such allegory.[44] However, Protestant theory generally eschewed the concept of a pervasive allegorical and spiritual sense, and sought rather to define allegory as a literary mode invoked at particular times for special reasons.

The basis for discrimination was sometimes generic. As we have seen, the Song of Songs was usually described as an allegorical fiction composed by Solomon, and this designation allowed James Durham to distinguish quite precisely between typological and allegorical modes as well as between medieval and Protestant approaches to allegory:

> We say, that this Song is not Typical, as being made up of two Histories, to wit, *Solomon's* Marriage, and Christ's, nor doth it any way intend the comparing of these two together in the events, as to their facts or deeds: But it is Allegorick, not respecting *Solomon*, or his Marriage, but aiming to let out spiritual Mysteries in figurative expressions. . . . The Divine Mystery intended, and set forth here, is the mutual Love, and spiritual Union, and Communion that is betwixt Christ and his Church, and their mutual carriage towards one another, in several conditions and dispensations.
>
> . . . . . . . . . . . . . . . . . . . . . . . . .
>
> There is a great difference betwixt an Allegorick Exposition of Scripture, and an Exposition of Allegorick Scripture: The first is that, which many Fathers, and School-men fail in, that is, when they Allegorize plain Scriptures and Histories, seeking to draw out some secret meaning, other than appeareth in the words; and so will fasten many senses upon one Scripture. This is indeed unsafe, and is justly reprovable; . . . An Exposition of an Allegorick Scripture, is, the opening and expounding of some dark Scripture (wherein the mind of the Spirit is couched and hid under Figures and Allegories) making it plain and edifying, by bringing out the sense according to the meaning of the Spirit in the place. . . . This way of expounding such dark Scriptures, is both useful and necessary.[45]

Similarly, the parables of Christ were often characterized as a fictional form related to allegory.

At other times, allegorical exegesis was understood to be invited by the presence of certain rhetorical figures: *allegoria*, *parabola*, and the like. John Diodati's definition of "Parable" affords an illustration of this limited and literary approach:

> [Parable] was a kinde of teaching used amongst the Jews, and followed by our Saviour, as very usefull to make the truth known . . .

by a well appropriated similitude of some framed narration. Wherein a parable differeth from an allegory, which takes the figure of a true history, but in a various sense to represent morall or spirituall things; and from an enigma, which hath more obscurity, and brevity, then a parable; and from a plain similitude inserted in the naturall and proper extent of the discourse, and is therefore clear and plain to be understood.[46]

In addition, scriptural precedents such as Christ's explanation of the parable of the seed sowed in various kinds of ground were often seen to justify the elaboration of allegories from suggestive scripture passages—not as inherent meanings, but as defensible "applied" meanings useful for teaching. As William Whitaker put it, "we contend that allegories, tropologies, and anagoges are not various senses, but various collections from one sense, or various applications and accommodations of that one meaning."[47]

The Protestant theory of typology was clearly formulated and widely accepted: the types constitute the symbolic dimension of the literal text. The Protestant conception of allegory was less clearly formulated, but in this area also the exegetes endeavored to tie the spiritual meanings of scripture firmly to the literal text and to refine the literary and linguistic analyses through which they might be sought. Indeed, the Calvinist commentators in particular place enormous pressure upon the forms and modes of language in the literal text, as the key to all the other signs in history or nature or ritual through which spiritual truth may be manifested. My reading of the evidence on this point does not support William Madsen's conclusion that "by the middle of the seventeenth century the distinction between the Catholic theory of manifold senses and the Protestant theory of the one literal sense had, for all practical purposes, become meaningless."[48] Rather, as the century progressed handbooks of typology appeared in ever increasing numbers—by, among others, William Guild, Thomas Taylor, Henry Vertue, Benjamin Keach, Samuel Mather[49]—which reinforced the importance of typology to Protestants, schematized the types chronologically or by categories, paired the types with their New Testament antitypes noting similarities and dissimilarities, and crystallized the new Protestant directions in typological thought. All these works assume that typological symbolism is a part or dimension of the literal text rather than a separate spiritual sense, and that the meaning of the types was clarified by degrees under the old dispensation and exhibited openly under the Gospel. As Samuel Mather explains, "You will find many Treasures of divine Wisdom and Gospel-light in the Scriptures, by . . . accommodating typical Scriptures both to *Type* and *Antitype*, not excluding either, they being really meant of both, and most fully of Christ the *Antitype*, who is the scope and center of all the Counsels and Dispositions of God."[50] Moreover, all these works distinguish typology sharply from allegory by their method of treatment: Guild and Taylor deal only with the types; Vertue gives one book to the Old Testament types of Christ and a second to metaphors and similes used to describe him, while the third book presents first the types, then the metaphors, for the Church; and Benjamin Keach appends a separate treatise to his exhaustive collection of scripture tropes to treat of the types.[51]

Samuel Mather's massive compendium, very influential on both sides of the Atlantic, schematizes mid- and late seventeenth-century typological theory. Working from the text in Hebrews 10:1 referring to the type as "a shadow of good things to come," Mather proceeds by a series of carefully framed definitions to distinguish the types from other figures in scripture with which they are sometimes confused. Types differ from arbitrary similes and comparisons (such as the comparison of the union of Christ and the Church to marriage) by reason of their divine institution to foreshadow Christ and his benefits, and from parables and allegories by reason of their historical reality:

> There is an historical Verity in all those typical Histories of the Old Testament. They are not bare Allegories, or parabolical Poems, such as the Song of *Solomon*, or *Jothams* Parable, *Judg.* 9.7. or *Nathans* Parable to *David*. 2 *Sam.* 12. but they are a true Narrative of things really existent and acted in the world, and are literally and historically to be understood.[52]

He discusses the types in two large categories: persons, including individuals (such as Adam, Noah, Joseph, David) and entire classes (such as the nation of the Israelites, or the prophets, or priests); and things, including those which are occasional and extraordinary (such as the manna and the brazen serpent) and those which are instituted (such as the ritual elements of the ceremonial Law). Moreover, Mather provides an especially interesting testimony to contemporary trends in his broad definition of antitype, which allows for the assimilation of contemporary history, and sometimes individual spiritual and providential experience, to the divine typological scheme:

> The types relate not only to the Person of Christ; but to his Benefits, and to all Gospel Truths and Mysteries, even to all New Testament Dispensations.
>
> I mention this the rather, because I have observed that it doth

much darken the thoughts of many, that they study to accommodate every *Type* directly to the Person of Christ; because we commonly call them Types of Christ. But that expression is not meant of his Person exclusively to his Benefits; but of both together, Christ and the good things of Christ: the *Types* shadowed forth Christ and all the good that comes by him.[53]

Closely related to this understanding of the types as an integral part of the literal text whose meanings are progressively clarified in history is a second important Protestant revision of medieval theory, involving a new sense of the essential spiritual identity of the two Testaments. In the usual medieval conception, Old Testament personages and typical things are merely literal signs, shadows, or corporal figures, important only as they point to the substance, the body, the true spiritual reality found solely in Christ and the New Testament. This view, recurring in Augustine, Hugh of St. Victor, Peter Lombard, and Aquinas,[54] is cogently restated in the Rheims New Testament, in a comment on Hebrews 10:1:

> The sacrifices and ceremonies of the old law, were so far from the truth of Christs Sacraments, and from giving spirit, grace, remission, redemption, and justification, and thereupon the entrance into heaven & joyes celestial, that they were but shadowes, unperfectly and obscurely representing the graces of the New Testament and of Christes death: whereas al the holy Churches rites and actions instituted by Christ . . . conteine and give grace, justification, and life everlasting to the faithful.[55]

According to this understanding, the Israelites under the Old Covenant lived a carnal life without knowledge of the Law's intention, acting out without knowing it a typological history which led them nowhere. This history has spiritual value only for Christians who understand it as pertaining to Christ, and for a few chosen patriarchs and prophets who understood the Law and the types to pertain to Christ and so enjoyed a kind of proleptic membership in the New Covenant.[56] By contrast, the Protestant formulations emphasized the continuities between the two covenants in regard to the spiritual condition of the faithful. Of course, the Protestant exegetes declared that Christ has fulfilled the types, and they insisted, none more vigorously, that Old Testament ceremonies and practices have been abrogated. Yet, partly because of their doctrine of the sacraments as signs rather than conduits of special grace, Protestants saw the spiritual situation of Christians to be notably advantaged by the New Covenant but not different in es-

sence from that of the Old Testament people, since both alike depend
on signs which will be fulfilled in Christ at the end of time. The Old
Testament is still *figura*, but in the sense of a real historical time of
preparation for and expectation of the future. And the Christ of the
*eschaton* rather than the incarnate Christ of the Gospel is the ultimate
antitype for all the types.

Preus has traced the long process of development whereby Luther
arrived at the perception that for the Old Testament Jews—the "Faith-
ful Synagogue"—the types were not merely carnal promises but dis-
played true spiritual realities. The Israelites therefore are not merely
figures for Christians (the true Israel), but both peoples stand on much
the same spiritual plane, saved by faith and waiting in hope. In a com-
ment on Psalm 111:2, Luther insists that the situation of the Old Testa-
ment people is very like (*simul*) that of Christians:

> Therefore it is *simul* true that they were "upright" and yet not yet
> (*tamen nondum*) illuminated; *simul* upright . . . and yet not righteous
> with the perfect righteousness of faith. So *also are we now* [up-
> right] in relation to those things which we have; and yet, in regard
> to those things which we do not yet have, we are in shadows. . . .
> For just as it has not yet appeared to us what we shall be, so also it
> had not yet appeared to them what the future deeds were to be.
> Hence it is clear that they are called "upright" because their hearts
> were directed to the future, awaiting what was invisible, not con-
> tent with present, visible things.[57]

Calvin is yet more explicit on this point, and his terms are more
directly relevant to the English scene. Though Calvin recognized the
New Covenant as more perfect than the Old, offering a more liberal
dispensation of grace, he insisted that the Old Testament Fathers "had
and knew Christ the Mediator," and that faith in Christ is the mode
of salvation in both covenants. He concludes therefore that "The
covenant made with all the patriarchs is so much like ours in substance
and reality that the two are actually one and the same."[58] He draws
the same conclusion with reference to worship under the two cove-
nants:

> That God is to bee worshipped spiritually belonged aswell to the
> Jewes, as to us, even from the beginning . . . (God is a spirit, Johan
> 4.24). But he began not then first to be a spirit, when he abrogated
> the ceremonies of the Law. It foloweth therfore, that he ment to be
> woorshipped of the fathers after the same maner that he is wor-
> shipped now. And wheras he loded them with ceremonies, he did

it in consideracion of the tyme, like as he provided for us, in putting
the same away. Neverthelater the worshipping is all one, as touching
the substance, and differeth only in outward appeerance.[59]

Again, with special reference to the sacraments Calvin flatly rejected
the medieval dichotomy of shadow and substance. Commenting on 1
Corinthians 10:3, he observes:

> That opinion of the scholemen is commonly knowne, how that the
> Sacramentes of the old Lawe figured grace, and ours give grace.
> Thys place is very apt to confute that error. For he testifieth that
> the matter of the Sacrament was no lesse exhibited unto the ancient
> people than unto us ... in degree onely there is a difference betweene
> us and them: bycause we have a more plentifull taste of them geven
> unto us: but they lesse: and not that they had bare figures, and we
> the very thing....

> For that people was a figure of the Christian Church in such wyse,
> that it was also the true Church: their condition did so delineat and
> represent ours, that nevertheles it was even then the proper state of
> the Church: those promises that were geven unto them, did so
> shadow and prefigure the Gospell, that they did include the same
> within them selves: their sacraments served in such way to prefig-
> urate ours, that yet nevertheles according to that tyme also they were
> true sacraments of present efficacie: to conclude, they had the same
> spirit of fayth that we have, who used at that tyme rightly, both
> doctrine and signes.[60]

Calvin's own exegesis of the Pauline term "shadow" has already been
noted. Borrowing the terminology of painting, he compares the differ-
ence between the two covenants to that between a rough draft (the
shadow or type) and the lively image provided by a colored portrait.
Both the rough draft and the colored portrait may be said to be the
same in substance (though differing markedly in brightness and com-
pleteness), and both represent imperfectly the reality which the Divine
Creator will ultimately reveal:

> For although it had not the perfect image of heavenly things, as if the
> workman had put his last indeavour to it, yet even this rough draught
> was greatly profitable to the Auncient Fathers: albeit our condition
> be now much better. And let us observe, that even those things which
> are now set before our eyes, were shewed to them a farre off. And
> therefore both we, and they have the same Christ, the same right-
> eousnesse, the same sanctification, and the same salvation: there is
> no difference or diversitie, but in the manner of setting them forth.

I thinke by these words *of good things to come*, he meanes eternall good things. I confesse indeede that the kingdome of Christ which we now enjoy, was long agoe foretold to come: but the words of the Apostle signifie that we have the lively portraiture of good things to come. He meanes then that sample and spirituall patterne, the full enjoying whereof is deferred untill the day of the resurrection, and to the world to come. And yet I doe againe confesse that these good things begin to be revealed from the beginning of Christ his kingdome: but the question is now, that the *good things to come* in this place are not onely so called in regard of the old Testament, but because we also doe yet hope and waite for them.[61]

Calvin's revision of conventional typology presents both Old Testament types and New Covenant antitypes as alike referred to the supreme antitype to come at the end of time, thereby permitting Protestants to identify their spiritual experiences much more closely with those of the "typical" Israel than medieval exegetes customarily did, and to regard history as a continuum rather than as two eras of time divided by the Incarnation of Christ. Calvin's language of the rough draft and the lively image—with the same implications regarding the essential unity of the two covenants—recurs in the Bishops' Bible, in John Diodati's *Annotations*, in Taylor's *Christ Revealed*, and in a host of other texts.[62] The dedicatory epistle (by William Jemmat) to Taylor's handbook is characteristic:

> The same Testator made both Testaments, and these differ not really, but *accidentally*; the Old *infolding* the New with some darknesse, and the New *unfolding* the Old with joyous perspicuitie. . . . [Yet] Even now, in this marvellous light of the Gospell, we have our divine ceremonies and sacraments, see him afarre off, know but in part, darkly as in a glasse, and receive our best contentment by the acts of faith, while the Word and Spirit make us know the things freely given us of God in Christ Jesus. But time shall bee when (to say nothing of the estate of the Church after the ruine of Antichrist, and calling of the Jewes) we shall in heaven see him whom we beleeved, face to face, clearly, perfectly, immediately, without Sacraments or Types.[63]

And Samuel Mather restates with his customary clarity the grounds for this identity of essential spiritual experience:

> We see they had the same Gospel blessings preached unto them of old, that we have at this day . . . God never had but one way only to save men by, but it had divers fashions and forms, divers outward

discoveries and manifestations; in those times in a more legal manner, but afterwards more like it self, in a more evangelical manner. . . .

As we say of our Sacraments, *Sacramentum est verbum visibile* . . . so it was with the Types of old. The *Types* were visible Promises, and not only Signs, but Pledges and Assurances of the good they represented. They did represent those great Mysteries not only by way of resemblance to the understandings, but by way of assurance to the Faith of Gods People.[64]

In general, the Protestant exegetes held that Christians are greatly blessed by the abrogation of the Old Covenant, since it was more burdensome, more obscure, and more terrifying than the New Covenant, but for all that, Christians are at one with the Israelites of old in regard to the essence of their spiritual lives.

A third major modification in Protestant typological exegesis, stemming in part from this narrowing of the divide between the two Covenants, involves the assimilation of the events and circumstances of contemporary history—and even the lives and experiences of individual Christians—to the providential scheme of typological recapitulations and fulfillments throughout history.[65] One ground for this exegetical practice is the traditional understanding that the types find their antitypes not only in Christ himself but also in his mystical body, the Church. In the Middle Ages such antitypes were found chiefly in the sacramental and institutional life of the Church, whereas the Reformers and especially the Puritans found them (often with the support of ingenious contemporary applications of the prophecies of Daniel, the Song of Songs, and the Book of Revelation)[66] in the continuing historical experience of God's elect—most notably in the Reformation, the English Civil War, and the great Puritan adventure in the New World.

The public or political dimension of typological exegesis, according to which sixteenth- and seventeenth-century Englishmen understood that church and state in England or New England recapitulated or fulfilled the historical experience of Israel, has been explored by William Haller, Steven Zwicker, Sacvan Bercovitch, and William M. Lamont, among others,[67] and need not be treated in detail here. It is worth noting, however, that two formulas were used to interpret contemporary history typologically. On the one hand, Protestants could view their church and nation as antitypes of the Old Testament Israel, in that their inclusion within Christ's mystical body, the Church, enables them to participate in his fulfillment of the types *forma perfectior*. William Perkins employs these terms in presenting the English Reformation as an escape from spiritual Egypt (Rome), fulfilling the Jews' escape from the Egypt of the pharaohs:

> Gods children wonder at the excellencies of Gods *mercies* unto them, so also at their owne *basenesse* and unworthinesse. . . . If any Nation have cause to say thus, it is *England*. God hath delivered us out of the thraldome of *spirituall Egypt*, and led us out: not by a *Moses*, but first by a childe, then by a woman . . . and did not God in our late deliverance, overthrowe our enemies, not so much by the power of man, as by his owne hand? Did not hee fight from heaven? *Did not the starres and the windes in their courses fight against that Sisera of Spaine?*[68]

Samuel Mather's identification of the Church of Rome as the antitype figured in the Old Testament types of Sodom, Egypt, Jericho, Edom, and Babylon is also grounded upon this formula:

> There were typical Mercies, Deliverances, Preservations of his People of old *which happened to them in Types, and are written for our Instruction, upon whom the ends of the World are come.*
> The Lord intended those ancient Dispensations to be Types and Patterns, and Pledges of what he intended to do for his People in the latter days. . . .
>
> The *Jews* were a typical people, and did prefigure and represent the whole Church of God under the Gospel: So the neighbour Nations with whom they had to do, were also Typical of Gospel Enemies to the Church; and their Sins and Judgments, did prefigure and shadow forth something Analogous under the New Testament.[69]

Seventeenth-century Englishmen and New England Puritans were likely to see themselves and their institutions as antitypes of the biblical Israel when the emphasis was upon the greater perfection which the New Covenant of Grace exhibits over the Old, or when, as Bercovitch has noted,[70] a strong millenarian impulse led them to view their own contemporary history as the last age spoken of in the millennial prophecies. From this perspective they see themselves fulfilling the types.

When, on the other hand, the millennium does not seem imminent, and when Protestants are conscious of themselves in more general terms as recipients of special divine providences, they are more likely to view themselves according to another formula—as correlative types, recapitulating the situation of Israel of old on much the same basis, in that they await afar off the millennial antitypical fulfillment of all the types.[71] As Thomas Adams put it, "*Israel* and *England*, though they lye in a divers climat, may be said right *Parallels*."[72] These parallels, however, are more than analogies: in the charged polemic of the period they are felt as genuine recapitulations in the domain of God's Providence, wherein he deals with his new Israel as he did with the old. The pamphlet literature and the political poetry of the seventeenth century is studded with correlative types: Queen Elizabeth is a new Judith, Deborah, Joshua; King James is a new Solomon; Prince Henry is a new Josiah (full of promise in reforming the Church and dying young); Oliver Cromwell is a new Moses or Gideon or David; Charles II restored is a new David reuniting the tribes after a long warfare.[73] The Puritans in the throes of civil war are a new Israel delivered from Pharaoh, called out of Egypt, embattled in the wilderness, and en route to the Promised Land of a reformed church and state.[74] And the Puritans in the New World are a new Israel, called forth into a wilderness and enroute to a new Canaan or a new Eden.[75]

Of more interest for religious lyric poetry is the use of typology in the private or devotional, rather than the political, sphere. Here also, remarkably enough, Protestant exegetes assimilate the lives and experiences of contemporary Christians to the typological paradigm of recapitulations and fulfillments throughout history. One ground for this was the Reformation emphasis upon the application of all scripture to the self, the discovery of scriptural paradigms and of the workings of Divine Providence in one's own life. Medieval four-level exegesis had of course provided for the personal application of the scripture text as the third or tropological level of meaning—*quid agas*, moral allegory, in the familiar formula. Such tropological analysis was normally pursued in terms of the *imitatio Christi*, the Christian's conformation of himself to Christ through participation in the sacramental life of the Church—"So far as the things done in Christ, or so far as the things which signify Christ, are signs of what we ought to do."[76] But this formula was discredited by the Reformation insistence upon the "one sense of Scripture" and also by Reformation theology: the Protestant sense of the desperate condition of fallen men dictated a shift in emphasis from *quid agas* to God's activity in us. And this in turn led to some effort to assimilate the pattern of individual lives to the pervasive typological patterns discerned in Old and New Testament history. Christians were invited to perceive the events and personages of Old and New Testament salvation history not merely as exemplary to them but as actually recapitulated in their lives, in accordance with God's vast typological plan of recapitulations and fulfillments. This new, primary focus upon the individual Christian does not of course replace the traditional recognition of Christ as the antitype who fulfills all the types *forma perfectior*, though ultimate fulfillment is usually referred to Christ's Second Coming rather than to his Incarnation.

In the private sphere the same two formulas were available for relating the contemporary Christian to the biblical type. When the emphasis is upon the great benefits and advantages the Christian enjoys in his religious life, the ease and comfort of the Gospel in comparison to the Law, the Christian may see himself (through Christ) as an antitype of the Israelite of old. But when on the other hand he concentrates upon his essential spiritual life and situation, his dependence upon faith and his imperfect spiritual vision in this life, he is more likely to view himself as a correlative type with the Old Testament Israelites, located on the same spiritual plane and waiting like them for the fulfillment of all the signs in Christ at the end of time. The two approaches were not incompatible, and both contributed importantly to the power, profundity, and psychological complexity with which the great seventeenth-century religious lyric poets probed the personal spiritual life.

Such assimilation of the individual Christian to the typological pattern is evident in Luther. Preus has noted[77] that Luther's revision of the tropological formula from *quid agas* (what you do) to *opus Dei* (what God does) transformed the so-called "tropological" sense beyond recognition. In addition, Luther's growing empathy with the Psalmist, evident as he proceeds in his commentaries on the Psalms, causes him to shift the emphasis from the Christian's identification with or conformation to Christ as pattern and model to his identification with the faith of the Old Testament people—the "Faithful Synagogue." The Christian, it would seem, recapitulates the spiritual essence of the Old Testament experiences in himself, thereby bringing his own life close to the province of typology. Commenting on Psalm 121:2, Luther urges this point:

> For they stand who wait expectantly, that it might be opened to them, and they might enter . . . the person of the synagogue is speaking. Not only the synagogue, however (as I have often said), but everyone who is progressing ought to feel and speak like this, *as if he were in the synagogue.* For as long as we do not receive the promises, we have not entered Jerusalem, but we stand and await our entrance.[78]

Luther still terms such recognitions of relatedness as the "moral sense," but they prepare directly for Calvinist formulations suggesting the Christian's actual recapitulation of Old Testament situations.

Calvin incorporates the individual Christian within the typological relation, using both the approaches outlined above. In the Psalm commentaries he often emphasizes our recapitulation of David's experience by reason of our fusion with Christ—in which terms we "fulfill" the Davidic type, as a kind of antitype:

> And truly it is to be knowen, that although David speak of himself in this Psalme: yit he speaketh not as a common person, but as one that beareth the person of Christ, bicause he was the universall pattern of the whole Churche: and the same is a thing worth the marking, too the intent eche one of us may frame himselfe too susteine like lotte. For like as it behoved the thing too bee substauncially fulfilled in Christ, which was begun in David: so must it of necessitie come to passe in every of his members.[79]

At other times Calvin uses the language of correlative types, suggesting that the Christian recapitulates more or less precisely the spiritual experience of his Old Testament counterpart. Speaking of Joseph's resurrection to glory and honor after his trial in prison, Calvin observed that this pattern is recapitulated in all believers in Christ: "We, also, who have received the gratuitous adoption of God amid many sorrows experience the same thing."[80] But David's experience especially is recapitulated in the Christian—and Calvin insists that his own life testifies to that recapitulation:

> To thintent I might the fuller understand his [David's] complaints concerning the inward mischeeves of the Church, it availed mee not a litle that I had abiden the same things that he bewaileth or much like, at the handes of the housholde enemies of the Churche. . . . Yit did it greatly availe mee to beholde as it were in a Glasse, bothe the beginnings of my vocation, and also the continuall race of my ministerie. . . . Like as hee was advaunced from the sheepfolde too the high estate of a kingdome: even so God drawing mee from base and slender beginnings, hathe vowtsaved me this honorable office, to make me a preacher and minister of his Gospel. . . . [And] like as that holy King was sore bayted with continewall warres by the *Philistines* and other forreine foes, but more sorer wounded by the inward malice and wickednesse of faithlesse persons at home: so I also beeing assaulted on all sides have scarcely had one Minutes rest, eyther from outwarde or from inward fightings.[81]

Later, he generalizes: "For too the asswagement of greef, greatly avayleth this comparison, that nothinge befalleth us at this day, which

Gods church hath not had experience of in old time: but rather that wee are exercysed in the same listes with David and the other holy fathers."[82]

The typological focus upon the individual is everywhere evident in characteristic seventeenth-century treatments of the conventional types. Israel saved from the Red Sea and led through the wilderness to Canaan was traditionally identified as a type of Christ's deliverance of mankind from Satan through Baptism, bringing them to the true Canaan, heaven; tropologically, the episodes represent the release from sin.[83] Now, however, the emphasis falls upon the Israelites' experiences, trials and enemies as direct correlatives of the Christian's experience in this world and of the contours of his spiritual life. In William Perkins' commentary on Hebrews 11, which names various Old Testament heroes of faith as a "cloud of faithful witnesses," the metaphor is taken as an allusion to the pillar of cloud that led the Israelites through the desert. Christ was the traditional antitype for the pillar of cloud and of fire, but in Perkins the whole event finds its antitype in these Old Testament faithful leading *us* through the wilderness:

> Now, these things beeing *ensamples* unto us, and evident types of our estate who live under the Gospel, shewe apparently, that howsoever Beleevers be greatly cheered in their spirituall travell, by the gratious promises which God in Christ had made unto them; yet this their joy is much encreased, by the view of those that have gone before them in the way of faith; who are unto them as a *Cloud of Witnesses*, or a *cloudie Pillar*. . . .

> Now, looke as that cloud guided the Israelites from the bondage of Egypt, to the Land of Canaan: so doth this companie of famous beleevers, direct all the true members of Gods Church in the new Testament, the right way from the Kingdome of darkenesse, to the spirituall Canaan the kingdome of heaven.[84]

Jacob wrestling with the Angel—traditionally a figure of Christ's suffering or of the Church prevailing with and winning grace from Christ—is discussed by William Cowper in terms of the recapitulation of this experience in the lives of all Christians:

> The Lord when hee appeareth most familiarly to *Jacob*, hee exercises him with a wearisome wrestling . . . hee tosses and shakes him too and fro, and exercises him with fighting and strugling all the night long! . . . And in this is shadowed unto us, the manner of that victory, which the children of God obtain in their wrestlings, to wit, that it was such a victory as is not without a wound. . . . As it was with

*Jacob*, so it is with all the true Israelites of God; wrestling abides them, and in wrestling they must be exercised.[85]

The shift from Christic antitype to a focus upon the individual Christian is evident in commentary on the Old Testament Temple—and especially illumines Herbert's treatment of this symbolism in his lyrics. Traditionally the Old Testament Temple was in the first instance a type of Christ whose death fulfilled and abrogated the sacrifices of the Old Dispensation; and secondly of the Christian Church, antitype to the synagogue and its typical ceremonies. The parts of the Old Testament Temple typified elements of the Church: the Outer Court or the Porch, the external and visible church from which none are excluded; the Holy Place, the communion of the invisible church on earth; and the Holy of Holies, the heaven of the Saints. Alternatively, in Daniel Featley's terms, the three parts typify the states of nature, grace, and glory.[86] These significations are continued in most Protestant commentary, but often with changed emphasis: on the strength of Paul's description of the elect as "the Temple of the living God" (2 Cor. 6:16) the individual Christian is presented as—through Christ—the antitype of the Old Testament Temple. Thomas Adams, after developing the expected Temple-Church typology, works out in as great detail the terms by which every Christian is the antitype.[87] But the most striking evidence of the shift is Joseph Hall's argument that the temple in the heart of the Christian is the *primary* antitype and that the Church and the Kingdom of Heaven are only extensions founded upon and derived from that:

> Where ever God dwels, there is his Temple; Oh God, thou vouchsafest to dwell in the beleeving heart . . . thou the Creator of heaven and earth hast thy dwelling in us. . . . The most generall division of the Saints is in their place and estate; some strugling, and toyling in this earthly warfare; others triumphing in heavenly glory; therefore hath God two other, more universall Temples; One the Church of his Saints on earth; the other, the highest heaven of his Saints glorified. . . . In every renewed man, the individuall temple of God; the outward parts are allowed common to God and the world; the inwardest and secretest, which is the heart, is reserved onely for the God that made it. . . . What is the Altar whereon our Sacrifices of prayer and praises are offered to the Almightie but a contrite heart? What the golden Candlestickes but the illumined understanding. . . . Behold, if *Salomon* built a Temple unto thee, thou hast built a Temple unto thy selfe in us! We are not onely through thy grace living stones in thy Temple, but living Temples in thy Sion: . . . Let the

Altars of our cleane hearts send up ever to thee the sweetly perfumed smoakes of our holy meditations and faithfull prayers, and cheerfull thanks-givings.[88]

As Luther and Calvin had done, so also later Protestants saw themselves as correlative types or as antitypes of David the Psalmist. Perkins stresses the correlative aspect, proclaming that David's spiritual experiences precisely conform to our own:

The Booke of the Psalmes was penned by *David*, *Asaph*, *Moses*, and others . . . for the present state of the Church in those dayes. . . . Why then do we sing them now in our Churches? The answer is: The Church in all ages consists of a number of beleevers, and the *faith is* alwaies one, and makes all that apprehend Gods promises, to be alike to one another in grace, in meditations, in dispositions, in affections, in desires, in spirituall wants, in the feeling and use of afflictions, in course and conversation of life, and in performance of duties to God and man: and therefore the same *Psalmes*, *Prayers*, and *Meditations*, are now as fit for the Church in these dayes, and are saide and sung with the same use and profit.[89]

Henry Hammond's formulation puts the Christian rather in the position of antitype fulfilling and completing and perfecting the Davidic type through his own recapitulation of the experience:

*It is necessary that we say the Psalms with the same spirit with which they were composed, and accommodate them unto our selves in the same manner as if every one of us had composed them . . . not satisfying our selves that they had their whole completion in or by the Prophet, but discerning every of us our own parts still to be performed and acted over in the Psalmists words, by exciting in our selves the same affections which we discern to have been in David . . . loving when he loves, fearing when he fears, hoping when he hopes, praising God when he praises, weeping for our own or others sins when he weeps . . . admiring and glorifying God as he stands amazed and glorifies him.*[90]

Donne's sermons illustrate all these kinds of typological exegesis, for his is perhaps the most creative use of typology by any seventeenth-century English Protestant. Especially in the early sermons he uses the conventional four-fold medieval scheme—noting (for example) that the matters treated in Psalm 38:4 are "*literally* spoken of *David*; By *application*, of us; and by *figure*, of Christ. *Historically*, *David*; *morally*, we, *Typically*, Christ is the subject of this text."[91] He can also call upon the simpler formula of the reformers, recognizing in Christ the antitype who completes the full literal sense "of all that was shadowed in the Types, and figur'd in the Ceremonies, and prepared in the preventions of the Law, of all that was foretold by the Prophets, of all that the Soule of man rejoyced in."[92] However, Donne also constantly relates the individual Christian to the typological scheme of history; at one point he articulates quite precisely both formulas we have noted, in considering whether his text (Psalm 2:12) presents the Christian as a correlative type or as (through Christ) an antitype— whether it tells of "a repeating againe in us, of that which God had done before to Israel, or . . . a performing of that in us, which God promised by way of Prophesie to Israel."[93]

Donne invokes correlative typology for his sermon on Ezekiel 34:19, describing the Babylonian Captivity. His interpretation takes in the continuing recapitulations of the experiences of the Babylonian Captivity in several ages of the Church, including the contemporary age:

> The literall sense is plainly that, that amongst the manifold oppressions, under which the Children of *Israel* languished in *Babylon*, this was the heaviest, that their own *Priests* joyned with the *State* against them. . . . And then the *figurative* and *Mysticall* sense is of the same oppressions, and the same deliverance over againe in the times of *Christ*, and of the *Christian Church*; for that's more than figurative, fully literall. . . . This prophecy then comprehending the kingdome of Christ, it comprehends the *whole* kingdome of Christ, not onely the oppressions and deliverances of *our forefathers*, from the *Heathen*, and the *Heretiques* in the *Primitive Church*, but that also which touches *us* more nearly, the oppressions and deliverance of *our Fathers*, in the *Reformation of Religion*, and the shaking *off* of the yoak of *Rome*, that *Italian Babylon*, as heavy as the *Chaldaean*.[94]

More often, perhaps, and especially when explicating the Psalms, Donne invites his hearers to consider themselves (through Christ) as direct antitypes of the Psalmist, enjoying all the privileges of the New Dispensation: "*David* was not onely a cleare Prophet of Christ himselfe, but a Prophet of every particular Christian; He foretels what I, what any shall doe, and suffer, and say."[95] Or again, he locates the entire nexus of typological relationships pointed to in his text in the particular Christian audience he addresses, so that David's experiences in themselves are recapitulated in us as we are incorporated in the type, but are also recapitulated *forma perfectior*, as we are incorporated in the antitype. David's Psalms must, he declares, be considered, historically, and literally . . . of *David*. And secondly, in their *retrospect*, as they look back upon the first *Adam*, and so concern *Mankind collectively*, and so *you*, and *I*, and all have our portion in these calamities; And thirdly, we shall consider them in their *prospect*, in their future relation to the *second Adam*, in *Christ Jesus*, in whom also all mankinde was collected.

. . . . . . . . . . . . . . . . . . . . . . . . . . . .

In all *Davids* confessions and lamentations, that though that be always literally true of himself . . . yet *David* speaks *prophetically*, as well as *personally*, and to us. . . . That which *David* relates to have been his own case, he foresees will be ours too, in a higher degree.[96]

Even more remarkably, Donne intensified the Protestant focus upon the individual Christian as correlative type or antitype, so as to incarnate the whole process of providential history in the particular Christian audience he addresses or in the individual he celebrates. He can declare to his congregation, "All Gods *Prophecies*, are thy *Histories*: whatsoever he hath promised to others, he hath done in his purpose for thee: And all Gods *Histories* are thy *Prophesies*; all that he hath done for others, he owes thee."[97] Or again, he finds all scripture and also the Church located in, incarnated in, the individual Christian: "As every man is *a world* in himself, so every man hath *a Church* in himselfe; and as Christ referred the Church for hearing to the Scriptures, so every man hath Scriptures in his own heart, to hearken to."[98]

At times, though with no real consistency of terminology, Donne also assimilates things and events of the natural order to the typological scheme. His assumption seems to be that God's Word and his World are to be explicated in much the same fashion:[99] typology and anagogy together constitute the figural dimension of scripture, and God's mode of working in biblical history is at one with his continuing work in nature, so that the two make up a common symbolical mode. Accordingly, the English government can be described as "a Type and Representation of the Kingdom of heaven."[100] Or again, "*Peace* in this world, is a pretious *Earnest*, and a faire and lovely *Type* of the everlasting peace of the world to come: And *warre* in this world, is a shrewd and fearefull *Embleme* of the everlasting discord and tumult, and torment of the world to come."[101] These examples indicate, however, that Donne has not simply confused or amalgamated the various figurative modes or reverted to the pervasive Platonic symbolism of Augustine. His "types" from the natural world are few; they are not arbitrary metaphors but are understood to be specifically designated and instituted by God; and most important, they are understood to be

analogous to the Old Testament types in that they usually adumbrate
something in the future—heavenly glory to come—rather than simply
serving as a shadow of a higher realm of being. Donne does not relin-
quish the historical ground of typological symbolism.

Indeed, he seems to formulate in terms pertaining to the individual
Luther's future-oriented typological system based upon Christ's three
advents—in nature, grace, and glory:[102] these are the categories with
which Donne constantly works, and he understands these orders to be
related typologically, with the Christian's state in glory as the ultimate
fulfillment. The point is best illustrated from Donne's sermons on
special occasions, notably weddings. In his sermon for Margaret Wash-
ington on a text from Hosea 2:19, "And I will mary thee unto me for
ever," Donne presents the occasion of her marriage as type of all the
figural relationships between the marriages of Adam and Eve, of Christ
and the Soul, and of the Lamb and his Bride:

> The first mariage that was made, God made, and he made it in
> Paradise. . . . The last mariage which shall be made, God shall make
> too, and in Paradise too; in the Kingdome of heaven. . . . The mariage
> in this Text hath relation to both those mariages: It is it self the
> spirituall and mysticall mariage of Christ Jesus to the Church, and to
> every mariageable soule in the Church: And it hath a retrospect, it
> looks back to the first mariage; . . . And then it hath a prospect to the
> last mariage. . . . Bless these thy servants, with making this secular
> mariage a type of the spirituall, and the spirituall an earnest of that
> eternall, which they and we, by thy mercy, shall have in the King-
> dome which thy Son our Saviour hath purchased.[103]

Similarly, Donne discovers certain actual events in the course of his
own life to be divinely designated types adumbrating fulfillments to
come. In the *Devotions upon Emergent Occasions* he recognizes his
long and serious physical illness and subsequent recovery in the order
of nature as types of the sickness of soul and regeneration he sustains in
the order of grace. Moreover, both these experiences adumbrate his
hope of escape from eternal suffering and death through a resurrection
to eternal life.[104]

More than a century later the American Puritan Jonathan Edwards
attempted to systematize and defend types from the natural world as
an extension of biblical typology.[105] But in doing this, as Mason I.
Lowance, Jr., has argued, he extended typological symbolism beyond
recognition by using its terminology to describe a Platonic *allegoresis*
based upon correspondences between things in nature and higher,
spiritual realities.[106] Thus, Edwards declares that "The silk-worm is a

remarkable type of Christ"; or that "The flame of a candle or lamp . . . seems designed by providence to represent the life of man"; or that "The rising and setting of the sun is a type of the death and resurrection of Christ."[107] In a methodological statement in his *Miscellanies* Edwards states explicitly that biblical types and natural symbols are precisely analogous:

> This may be observed concerning types in general, that not only the things of the Old Testament are typical; for this is but one part of the typical world; the system of created beings may be divided into two parts, the typical world, and the antitypical world. . . . The material and natural world is typical of the moral, spiritual, and intelligent world, or the city of God . . . as things belonging to the state of the church under the Old Testament were typical of things belonging to the church and kingdom of God under the New Testament.[108]

Edwards does not, however, extend the concept of typology to embrace arbitrary allegory: he insists that "types" from the natural order are divinely designated to symbolize the higher spiritual orders, and he usually argues such designation on the evidence of biblical metaphors.[109] The fundamental change in typological theory carried forward by Edwards can be indicated by comparison with Donne, who, for all his creative uses of typology, made very limited use of natural types and usually retained the historical dimension, whereby the types in the natural order even as those in the Old Law adumbrate a perfection to come in the course of history. It is specifically the loss of the historical dimension that divides Edwards' symbolism sharply from the imaginative and personal extensions of typology discussed above, which are yet based upon classical Protestant theory.

Typological symbolism, understood in terms of these special Protestant emphases, is employed variously but always centrally by the major seventeenth-century religious lyric poets.

Conventional typological references are not pervasive in Donne's *Divine Poems* as a whole, but the recapitulation of biblical events and experiences within the self is of major importance to several poems. As in his sermons, Donne's poetic practice is to embody in the self, or in a particular individual, the entire network of typological relationships pointed to in God's Word, and through that symbolism to explore our human condition. Often, he presents the individual experiencing a particular event in the order of nature, which is designated in God's providence as a type with antitypes in the orders of grace and glory: the individual thereby embodies in himself all these states. In the *Anni-*

*versary* poems the untimely/religious death of Elizabeth Drury (like Donne's own illness in the *Devotions*) is ordered in God's providence to incorporate and manifest the course of salvation history: she recapitulates in some sense the image of God in the order of nature which we had in the created perfection of our first innocence; she bears that image robed with Christ's perfections in the order of grace; and both these conditions prefigure what the image of God in us will be in the condition of glory.[110] In some of his *Divine Poems* Donne embodies that web of typological relationships in the same daring manner in his own persona, the speaker. In "A Litanie" the speaker finds (or seeks to find) certain divine actions recapitulated in himself—the creation of Adam from red earth, Christ's crucifixion (stanzas 1, 2). His "Holy Sonnets" reenact Paul's version of the Christian predicament, and in some of them he inserts himself into Christ's place, attempting to take on the role of antitype—he would be crucified instead of Christ (XI); he would conquer Death (X). In the "Hymne to Christ" he is a new Noah about to encounter a new Flood. And in the "Hymne to God my God, in my sicknesse" he finds himself in his death throes encompassing at one moment the First and the Second Adam as well as the three states of nature, grace, and glory—"Looke Lord, and finde both *Adams* met in me."

George Herbert also locates typological paradigms in a particular individual—the poetic speaker of the volume entitled *The Temple*. But whereas Donne invokes typological symbolism only in certain poems, Herbert finds it absolutely central to his poetic vision, and couches it in somewhat more traditional terms. Moreover, the two poets employ quite different typological symbols to embody their different perceptions of the spiritual life. Donne, locating the two Adams and the three states of nature, grace, and glory in a single individual, probes the vast dislocations and disjunctions between those states. Herbert, in his book of lyrics from *The Temple*, "The Church," characteristically presents his speaker's uneven, anxious, vicissitude-filled progress from an identification with the various Old Testament types he finds himself recapitulating (the Old Testament altar, the Israelites in the wilderness, the Old Testament high priest, Aaron) to a recognition within himself of the Christic fulfillment of those types. He makes himself thereby the stage for the enactment of the typological movement from type to antitype.[111] The drama is sometimes worked out within the compass of an individual poem, as in "The Altar," "The Bunch of Grapes," "Aaron," and "Josephs coat." But it is also carried on throughout the volume, as motifs relating to the speaker's self-definition as regenerate man, Christian poet, and Christian priest are explored in several poems by the progressive clarification of the typological terms, and are brought to full resolution in the last poem of "The Church," "Love (III)." Moreover, *The Temple* as a whole is unified by typological symbolism, its three parts related in terms of a radically personalized and somewhat altered version of the traditional symbolism of the Old Testament Temple: the Church Porch is the antitype of the Outer Court (the traditional equation); the Church is the antitype of the Temple itself, but in the special sense that the true New Covenant Church is built in the hearts of the elect; and the Church Militant is the antitype of the wandering Ark (so prominently mentioned in the poem) figuring the fluctuations and conflicts of the corporate Church in the world, until the Judgment. As has been suggested above, Herbert also called upon the established links between the typology of the Temple and the three books of Solomon—relating "The Church-porch" to Proverbs and Ecclesiastes, and "The Church" to Canticles.

Typology is not the dominant symbolic mode for Vaughan that it is for Herbert. Nevertheless, Vaughan's speaker in *Silex Scintillans* sometimes finds himself in a quasi-biblical landscape recapitulating the experience of the Old Testament types. At times the speaker emphasizes his spiritual advantages through the New Covenant, so that he fulfills the types *forma perfectior* ("Mans fall, and Recovery," "The Law, and the Gospel"); but usually he does not stress Christ's redemption or assert his own privilege as an antitype by reason of that redemption. This is so largely because his sense of the progressive decay and corruption of religion from the time of the patriarchs introduces considerable ambiguity into the usual reading of the typological equation. Most often, as in "The Mutinie," "The Timber," "Begging [II]," "Providence," "The Pilgrimage," "White Sunday," and "The Night," Vaughan perceives himself standing on much the same plane of spiritual experience with certain Old (and New) Testament figures—Jacob, Israel wandering in the desert, Ishmael, Nicodemus. He is a correlative type with them: his posture, like theirs, is one of anticipation and expectation rather than fulfillment—though he expects to share in the great antitypical fulfillment of all the promises and types at the end of time or in the next world. Typology also affords a loose unity to the volume, helping to distinguish and relate the two parts in terms of the level of spiritual experience rendered in each. Part I, inaugurated by the poem "Regeneration," treats spiritual beginnings; in "Ascension-day," the opening poem of Part II, the speaker takes Christ's ascension as a figure of his own spiritual ascension to a higher plane of spiritual assurance and a heightened longing for the Apocalypse. This longing steadily increases throughout Part II until it culminates in an intensely vivid and dramatic imagination of Judgment Day in the final poem, "L'Envoy."

Thomas Traherne also found in typology an important symbolic framework for exploring the human condition in his *Centuries of Meditation, Poems*, and *Thanksgivings*. Unlike most Christian philosophers who see eternity as apart from and outside our time, Traherne perceived it (as Richard Jordan has noted)[112] as the infinite duration and succession of ages. Therefore, since life is lived in eternity, even as we live our lives we can experience all the ages before us as well as eternity itself. Progress toward such understanding is grounded upon typology. In his various sequences Traherne finds the course of human history recapitulated in himself: Adam in Eden, Adam fallen, Christ incarnate, Christ in glory are all figures for the stages of human existence—innocence, misery, grace, glory. These figures and these states are not merely moral exemplars or analogies for Traherne, but are said to be actually repeated in him: notably, he sees himself as correlative type with Adam repeating the Edenic experience ("The Salutation," "Eden," "Innocence"), and as antitype and fulfillment of David the Psalmist (*Centuries of Meditation*, III.66-100). Typology also serves in some degree as a unifying element. In the loosely-knit poetic sequence from Philip Traherne's manuscript, the speaker's spiritual development is plotted very generally in terms of typology: the speaker sees his infant innocence as a recapitulation of Adam's state; associates his new birth after his fall from innocence with the celebration of Christ's birth ("On Christmas-Day," "Bells"); and finally undertakes by his right thoughts about God and Man to replicate David's "Temple in the Mind" ("The Inference, II"). The states of human goodness and the progress of the soul Donne locates in the dead Elizabeth Drury and occasionally and partially in the speaker of the *Divine Poems*, Traherne places radically and completely in the self of his speaker as a present possession in this life.

Throughout his poems, and especially in the so-called "typological series" (*Preparatory Meditations* II.1-30), Edward Taylor scatters typological symbols broadcast. Unlike Herbert and Vaughan he does not associate himself with some one or some few, but rather with the types inclusively. Nor does he place himself in the course of typological history as a correlative with the Old Testament types, but rather as one insistently claiming relation to Christ the antitype. His treatment of typology is essentially conservative: in categories seemingly drawn directly from Samuel Mather, he relates various personal and ritual Old Testament types to their antitype in the Incarnate Christ. Like the other poets he also refers the typological process to himself in the Protestant way. However, he cannot confidently locate that process in himself, as they often do, but instead seeks some place for himself in God's vast typological design. Sometimes he does this by discerning the antitype in the types and praying to enjoy the Christian salvation figured there: he would be another Joseph with "brightsome Colours," an Israel freed from bondage and celebrating the passover, an Isaac rather than an Ishmael.[113] Again, he sometimes associates himself directly with Christ the antitype by writing a humble role for himself in Christ's salvific actions—he would be an altar upon which Christ's sacrifices are offered, a vessel or "drippen pan" to catch the redeeming blood, a golden pot for the Manna.[114] At other times he asserts something of an antitypical role for himself—seeking a better Canaan, finding a new Ark in the Church, and enjoying the Garden of the Church which is the antitype of Solomon's garden and Isaiah's vineyard.[115] Also, for Taylor as for Traherne, typology provides a loose structure for a sequence of poems (*Preparatory Meditations, Second Series*) which renders in very general terms the speaker's spiritual development: he first works through the panorama of Old Testament types of Christ; then he focuses directly upon Christ the redeemer; at last he identifies himself in some measure with the Bride of Canticles, and thereby claims some share in that redemption.

Typological symbolism is one of the most important components of Taylor's poetry, though he did not use it with the imaginative daring and constant personal reference exhibited by his English predecessors in the religious lyric. His poetry presents the late, limited flowering of this symbolic mode as it developed under the aegis of a distinctively Protestant aesthetic. Typology is not unimportant in later poetry, American and English, but given the changes in consciousness and religious attitudes, good poets necessarily used it obliquely and ambiguously.[116] Taylor was perhaps the last important religious lyric poet who could use biblical typology directly, pervasively, and personally, as a primary way to explore the inner spiritual life.

# PART II

*Ancillary Genres*

# Protestant Meditation: Kinds, Structures, and Strategies of Development for the Meditative Lyric

S upplementing the influence of biblical poetics upon the major reli-
gious lyric poems of the seventeenth century were certain popular
literary and sub-literary genres which explore the spiritual life. Promi-
nent among these ancillary genres was meditation, as Louis Martz's
seminal studies have demonstrated. It is important not to overstate the
influence: to label and to approach all or most of this poetry as poetry
of meditation[1] does some violence to the variety of religious lyric
kinds provided for in contemporary genre theory and evident in the
lyric collections. Yet meditation—especially Protestant meditation in
its various modes—is clearly important for these Protestant poets:
Donne, Vaughan, and Traherne contributed directly through their
own prose meditations to an emerging Protestant meditative theory,
and Taylor signalled his generic intent by calling his poems, *Prepara-
tory Meditations*. The broad range of contemporary Protestant
theory and practice of meditation had significant impact upon the
kinds, structures, and strategies of development of many seventeenth-
century meditative poems.

Martz has forged numerous links connecting major seventeenth-
century poets with Counter Reformation and medieval meditative tracts
and traditions, but without much consideration of this developing in-
digenous Protestant tradition. Martz relates many of Donne's *Divine
Poems* to the Ignatian *Spiritual Exercises* in terms of subject matter
(events in the life of Christ and the Virgin, the Passion, the four last
things, and the state of the sinful soul), and especially in terms of
structure (*compositio loci*, or vivid imagination of a scene by means
of the memory and the senses; methodical analysis of the subject
by the reason; and colloquy with God, engaging the will and
pouring forth the affections). He finds that Herbert's poetry reflects
the gentle tone of St. François de Sales' *Introduction à la Vie dévote*,
with its emphasis upon maintaining a constant, lively apprehension of
the presence of Christ, its focus on the Passion, and its recommenda-

tion of ejaculatory prayer. He associates Vaughan's and Traherne's writings with the looser, more intuitive Augustinian method of groping back through the memory to an apprehension of God and original blessedness. This method was especially influenced by Bonaventure's *Itinerarium Mentis in Deum*, which calls for an ascent to God in three stages—meditation on the traces of God in the creatures, on God's image in the mind of man, and on God's essential attributes.[2]

Though these and other Catholic manuals were undoubtedly well-known in England, their influence was being undermined by a developing Protestant tradition which had some remote roots in the biblical focus and devotional practices of the pre-Reformation *Devotio Moderna* movement, with its links to Thomas à Kempis, Erasmus, and Luther.[3] By the final decades of the sixteenth century, a self-consciously Protestant concept of meditation was taking shape, as writers such as Thomas Rogers and Edward Bunny produced bowdlerized versions of some of the famous Catholic treatises (*The Imitation of Christ*, the pseudo-Augustinian *Soliloquia animae ad Deum*, and Robert Parson's *Christian Directory*),[4] deleting all reference to suspect Roman doctrine and adding a heavy overlay of biblical language and citations. In such works the Catholic materials were given so distinctive a Protestant dress that the Jesuit Parsons complained of being made to sound throughout like an English Protestant.[5] More important, as Norman S. Grabo has pointed out, by the end of the sixteenth century Protestants were already producing devotional and meditative tracts of their own in some numbers—"collections of prayers and meditations, instructions in meditation, treatises, guides to the good life and instructions for rectifying crooked and fallen souls, road maps to heaven."[6] U. Milo Kaufmann has traced the origins of Puritan meditative traditions at least as far back as Joseph Hall (1606), and I have argued elsewhere the relevance of a distinctively Protestant theory of meditation for Donne's *Anniversaries*.[7]

Though Catholic and Protestant meditation are understandably similar in their profound concern with the interior life, and their emphasis upon the conversion experience,[8] seventeenth-century English Protestants were themselves aware of important differences. Two elements especially characterize Protestant meditation, whatever the subject or the formal structure: a focus upon the Bible, the Word, as guiding the interpretation of the subject and providing meditative models; and a particular kind of application to the self, analogous to the "application" so prominent in Protestant sermons of the period. The first important Protestant treatise on meditation, included in Richard

Rogers' *Seven Treatises, Containing . . . the practice of Christianity* (1603), displays both of these Protestant emphases.[9] Challenging Parsons' assertion that Protestants had produced no materials for the daily direction of the Christian life, Rogers pointed to many Protestant "catechismes, sermons, and other treatises . . . which may cleerely direct Christians, and stir up godly devotion in them." Offering his own massive work as a Protestant counterpart to the two Jesuit manuals, Parsons' *Christian Directory* and Gaspar Loarte's *Exercise of a Christian Life*, he denounced their mechanical methods of meditation and devotion as a "ridiculous tying men to a daily taske of reading some part of the storie of Christs passion, and saying certaine prayers throughout the weeke."[10] By contrast, he proposed to encourage purification of the heart by means of meditation upon a great variety of topics grounded upon the scripture, and the application of these topics to the self so as to produce experiential knowledge of them.

The biblical emphasis is everywhere evident. Thomas Rogers, defending his addition of biblical language and citations to the *Imitatio*, declared, "I have studied, as nigh as I could, to expresse [the sense of the author] by the phrase of the holie Scripture, supposing it to be a commendation as to Ciceronians to use the phrase of Cicero: so to Christians most familiarly, to have the wordes of the holy Scripture in their mouthes and bookes."[11] Richard Greenham urged his readers to "let the word be the object" of meditation; Ezechiel Culverwell insisted that we should always have "our meditation tyed to the word"; and Thomas Gataker held David forth as a model for meditation in that "He maketh *Gods Law his daily*, yea and *his nightly meditation*."[12] Many Protestant treatises also identified Isaac as a meditative model on the strength of Genesis 24:63, which records that he "went out, to meditate in the field, at the eventide"; the text was taken as a precedent for ambulatory and solitary meditation, out of doors, on the evidences of God in nature and on the day's experiences.[13]

The manner of application to the self in Protestant meditation also distinguishes it from Ignatian or Salesian meditation. In these continental kinds, the meditator typically seeks to apply himself to the subject, so that he participates in it; he imagines a scene vividly, as if it were taking place in his presence, analyzes the subject, and stirs up emotions appropriate to the scene or event or personal spiritual condition. The typical Protestant procedure is very nearly the reverse: instead of the application of the self to the subject, it calls for the application of the subject to the self—indeed for the subject's location in the self, as William Haller's comment on Puritan symbolism suggests:

. . . the symbolism of the nativity and the passion came to mean little to the Puritan. . . . The Puritan saga did not cherish the memory of Christ in the manger or on the cross, that is, of the lamb of God sacrificed in vicarious atonement for the sins of man. The mystic birth was the birth of the new man in men. The mystic passion was the crucifixion of the new man by the old, and the true propitiation was the sacrifice of the old to the new.[14]

In this vein William Tyndale advised, "As thou readest therefore thinke that every sillabe pertayneth to thine own selfe, & sucke out the pithe of the scripture." Bishop John Jewel made the same point: "There is no sentence, no clause, no syllable, no letter, but it is written for thy instruction. . . . The word of God teacheth . . . us to know our selves."[15] And Donne's sermons urged endlessly that the Christian is to trace salvation history in his own soul: "This is *Scrutari Scripturas, to search the Scriptures*, not as thou wouldest make a *concordance*, but an *application*; as thou wouldest search a *wardrobe*, not to make an *Inventory* of it, but to finde in it something fit for thy wearing."[16]

Appreciation of what is involved in this Protestant manner of application forces a modification of Kaufmann's view that Calvinist emphasis upon doctrine (Logos) in meditation was a force making for abstraction and against poetic imagination.[17] To be sure, Protestant meditation did not stimulate the senses to recreate and imagine biblical scenes in vivid detail; it would not therefore give rise to poetry based upon visual imagery and sensuous immediacy. But Protestant meditation did engage the mind in an effort to penetrate deeply into the motives and motions of the psyche, and also to understand the self as the very embodiment of the subject meditated upon. The Word was still to be made flesh, though now in the self of the meditator (or of the preacher and his audience). This emphasis contributed to the creation of poetry with a new depth and sophistication of psychological insight, and a new focus upon the symbolic significance of the individual.

Protestant manuals of meditation in general recognized two basic categories or kinds of meditation, neither of them employing the methods recommended in the Counter Reformation manuals. Joseph Hall's influential *Arte of Divine Meditation* (1606)—taken over in substance and elaborated upon in treatises by Isaac Ambrose (1659) and Edmund Calamy (1680)[18]—established a characteristically broad definition of meditation, distinguishing these two fundamental kinds:

Divine Meditation is nothing else but a bending of the minde upon some spirituall object, through divers formes of discourse, untill our thoughts come to an issue; and this must needs be either Extemporall, and occasioned by outward occurences offred to the mind, or Deliberate, and wrought out of our owne heart.[19]

"Extemporall" or, as they were often called, "Occasional" meditations drew subjects from the ancient tradition of meditation upon the creatures or the Book of Nature, adding to them all the usual or unusual occurrences or events, and sometimes also the doctrinal or moral topics or scripture texts, which might be presented to the mind in the course of the daily round. As Hall put it, "There is no creature, event, action, speech which may not afford us new matter of Meditation. . . . Wherefore as travellers in a forraine countrey make everie sight a lesson; so ought wee in this our pilgrimage."[20] Hall observed that there is "no rule" for this kind of meditation, since "our conceits herein varie according to the infinite multitude of objects, and their divers manner of profering themselves to the minde; as also for the suddennesse of this acte."[21] Robert Boyle found this kind of meditation of great usefulness to the Christian, as a way to "make the World vocal, by furnishing every Creature, and almost every occurence, with a Tongue to . . . read him Lectures of Ethicks or Divinity"; its subjects are "the works of Nature, and of Art . . . the Revolutions of Governments . . . and on the other side, the most slight and trivial Occurences."[22] Isaac Ambrose found biblical models for occasional meditations in Isaac in the fields, and David (Psalm 8:3) exclaiming over the glories of "thy heavens, the work of thy fingers, the moon, and the stars."[23]

Protestants who wrote about, or compiled handbooks of, occasional meditation typically drew together diverse topics from scripture, nature, and experience, presenting each very briefly, in a few sentences or a paragraph or two. Such "Considerations" or "Reflections" or "Observations" are set forth as brief essays, usually with reference to scripture passages and often intermixed with or culminating in apostrophes or ejaculatory prayers to God.[24] Some early Protestant books in this vein—by Henry Bull, Lewis Bayly, and I. Alliston—mix brief spiritual reflections and daily devotions on such topics as awakening, dressing, the lighting of candles, taking meals, retiring, Christ's passion, God's providences, the last things, walking in the fields and observing the creatures, the various circumstances developing in the course of an illness.[25]

Others relate occasional meditation closely to the brief familiar essay. Bacon himself provides a model for this kind of exercise in his Latin *Meditationes Sacrae*, first published in 1597 with his *Essayes*; they were translated under the title *Religious Meditations* when this volume was reissued the following year.[26] The twelve meditations are on various aspects of doctrine and religious practice; typically they state an appropriate biblical text, begin with an aphorism, and then in a few sentences or paragraphs analyze the topic in the light of the scripture text cited. Examples are: "Of the miracles of Our Saviour" with the text, "He hath done all things well"; "Of the moderation of cares" with the text, "Sufficient for the day is the evill thereof"; and "Of Heresies," with the text, "Ye erre not knowing the Scriptures nor the power of God." Joseph Hall in his *Meditations and Vows* and *Holy Observances* typically begins (like Bacon) with an aphorism from common knowledge or natural observation or scripture, and proceeds in a few sentences to analyze its meaning or suggest its implications.[27] His *Occasionall Meditations* are somewhat longer essays (a substantial paragraph or two with a concluding prayer) on such topics as: "Upon the sight of a Raine in the Sun-shine," "Upon the sight of a darke Lanthorne," "Upon the singing of Birds in a Spring-morning," "Upon the tolling of a passing-Bell," "Upon the Crowing of a Cocke," "Upon the beginning of a sicknesse," "Upon a quartan ague."[28] Isaac Ambrose's examples of occasional meditation are brief essays, often soliloquies or addresses to the self, on similar topics—"Upon sight of the morning sky," "Upon occasion of lights brought in."[29] Robert Boyle recommended stylistic diversity and shifts in subject matter in a given occasional meditation to accommodate those "emergent thoughts which fortuitous Occasions . . . awaken or suggest to us"; such "emergent thoughts" dictate the development of his own meditative sequences, "Upon the Accidents of an Ague," and "Angling Improv'd to Spiritual Uses."[30]

Hall's second category, "Deliberate Meditation," also admits a wide variety of topics, chiefly supplied from biblical texts, doctrinal formulations, or personal spiritual experience. Deliberate meditation is characterized by the formal choice and methodical development of a topic in a period of time specifically set aside for meditation. The structural model for deliberate meditation was the sermon: English Protestants constantly identified the two basic parts and purposes of meditation in terms long familiar from sermon theory—the exposition and analysis of a text or doctrine in order to instruct the understanding, and the forceful application of these matters to the self in order to stimulate the affections and the heart.[31] Given this identity of elements and purposes, the terms *sermon* and *meditation* become well-nigh interchangeable in Protestant theory. The sermon was frequently described as the fruit of the preacher's meditation shared with the congregation. Richard Bernard in his *Faithfull Shepherd* advises that the minister "seriously meditate" upon the matter he proposes to speak about, and to realize that "to make Application to his hearers, to doe it profitably, he must *First*, preach to them from knowledge out of himselfe."[32] Similarly, Donne declares that, "as a hearty entertainer offers to others, the meat which he loves best himself, so doe I oftnest present to Gods people, in these Congregations, the meditations which I feed upon at home." Donne also reversed this proposition, urging his listeners to "preach over the Sermons which you heare, to your owne soules in your meditation."[33] This way of linking sermon and meditation was also a commonplace. According to Richard Greenham, the chief difference between the two forms lay in the greater rigor with which the meditator could apply the preacher's text or doctrine in the sermon to himself: "For by the Spirit of God wee shall be taught to applie it more particularly to our selves, than hee did or could doe, because wee are most privie to our owne estate."[34]

Joseph Hall's *Arte of Divine Meditation* formally adapted the two-part structure of the Protestant sermon to the meditation. After a preparatory prayer, Hall begins directly with an analysis of the topic, in accordance with a method outlined by the monk Joannes Mauburnus, who had borrowed it from the crypto-Protestant Johan Wessel Gansfort. But Hall replaces Mauburnus' rather complex directions for the analytic stage with a simple method of considering the topic according to some of the places of logic (causes, effects, qualities, contraries, similitudes, titles and names, testimonies from scripture); moreover, he permits great flexibility in the analytic stage, asking only for a "deep and firme *Consideration* of the thing propounded." Indeed, he declares any manner of analysis acceptable which can achieve the primary end of meditation—as also of the Protestant sermon—the stirring of the heart: "That . . . is the verie soule of Meditation, whereto all that is past [of analysis] serveth but as an instrument."[35] Hall's means for stirring the affections involve such devotional and literary postures as: relish of what we have thought on, complaints of and wishes for what we lack, humble confessions, earnest petitions, cheerful confidence of obtaining our desires. Isaac Ambrose proposes a similar two-part structure for deliberate meditation, taking over the places of analysis from Hall but even more firmly subordinating logical analysis to application, since "the end of this *Duty* is not to practise Logick, but to exercise Religion, and to kindle Piety and Devotion."[36] Edmund Calamy's manual, in some respects a revision of Hall's, reiterates yet more forcefully the primacy accorded in Protestant meditative literature to the stirring of the affections through close application to the self: this is "the very life and soul of Meditation . . . to get your affections warmed and heated by the things you meditate upon; for the work of the under-

standing is nothing else but to be as a Divine *pair of bellows*, to kindle
and inflame the heart and affections."[37] This emphasis has clear im-
portance for the intense probing of the psyche, and the power and
range of emotional expression in poetry influenced by this tradition.

Richard Baxter states explicitly that the sermon affords the most use-
ful methodological model for both parts of the meditation, termed by
him cogitation and soliloquy:

> Because meer Cogitation if it be not prest home, will not so pierce
> and affect the heart, Therefore we must here proceed to a second
> step, which is called Soliloquy, which is nothing but a pleading the
> case with our own souls. . . . As every good Master and Father of a
> Family, is a good Preacher to his own Family; so every good Chris-
> tian, is a good Preacher to his own soul. Soliloquy is a Preaching to
> ones self. Therefore the very same Method which a Minister should
> use in his Preaching to others, should a Christian use in speaking to
> himself. . . . Dost thou know the right parts and order of a Sermon?
> and which is the most effectual way of application? why then I need
> to lay it open no further: thou understandest the Method and partes
> of this soliloquy. Mark the most affecting, heart-melting Minister;
> observe his course both for matter and manner; set him as a patern
> before thee for thy imitation; and the same way that he takes with
> the hearts of his people, do thou also take with thy own heart.[38]

In this fusion of meditative and sermon method it seems clear that
Baxter makes no new departure, but merely elaborates at considerable
length upon what had been, for half a century at least, a Protestant
commonplace.[39] Some years later, Baxter's *Christian Directory*, a sum-
mary of Protestant meditative theory and subject matter, urges the in-
corporation of sermon and also prayer methods in meditation:

> Turn your cogitations often into soliloquies; methodically and ear-
> nestly preaching to your own hearts, as you would do on that subject
> to others if it were to save their souls. . . . Turn your meditations
> often into ejaculatory prayers and addresses unto God: for that
> will keep you reverent, serious and awake.[40]

Essentially, the Protestant concern in both categories of meditation,
occasional and deliberate (as in the sermon) is to trace the interrela-
tion between the biblical text and the Christian's own experience, so
that the one is seen to be the reflection or manifestation of the other.
In occasional meditation the starting point is some occasion or event or
observation in the meditator's personal experience, and his purpose is
to interpret that in terms of God's providential plan and Word; in

deliberate meditation the starting point is usually a biblical text or event or theological doctrine, and here the emphasis is upon "application to the self." The Christian's experience is to comment upon the biblical text, and the text upon his experience.

Protestant meditative theory recognized three large categories of meditation beginning, respectively, from the Word, from the self, and from the creatures—with each category incorporating several specific kinds. Much the most common was meditation on the Word, the scriptures. Advice to meditate on the Word was repeated on all sides. Richard Rogers cites Psalm 119:97 and Joshua 1:8 as directives to such meditation: "the Prophet calleth meditation . . . where he saith, *All the day long doe I meditate on thy word*: and in *Josua; Thou shalt meditate day and night on the booke of the law.*"[41] Richard Greenham urges such meditation, explaining that "a man then meditateth on the word, when he so remembreth it and museth on it, that he goeth from poynt to poynt, applying generally some things unto himselfe."[42] Thomas Goodwin's advice for meditating upon texts of scripture envisions a soliloquy turning into a dialogue with the Word (a program enacted in some of Herbert's poems—"The Collar," "A true Hymne" —and most graphically in Bunyan's *Grace Abounding*):

> Laying up the Word in the heart, and being much conversant in it, and getting knowledge out of it, is an effectuall meanes to keepe our thoughts well exercised when wee are alone: . . . when a man is *riding*, or *walking*, or *lying downe*, and rising up, (which are often and usually our most retired times for thoughts) . . . then . . . thou shalt . . . *talke of it* to thy selfe. . . . By thy thinking of it, it will talke with thee when thou and it art alone: So as thou shalt not need a better companion, it will bee putting in and suggesting some thing.[43]

Not surprisingly, Protestants were often urged to find their direction for the topics of such meditation on the Word in the texts and doctrines of the sermons they heard. Samuel Hieron directed his congregation, "When you are departed from the Sermon, forget not to finde a time as soone as possible . . . to *commune with your own heart*, and to ponder, and scanne, and *search diligently* those things which were delivered. This is that which we call meditation."[44] Archbishop Ussher declares that "every Sermon is but a preparation for meditation," and advises his hearers to "Set a part some time for Meditation, that the word may be engrafted in thy heart. The Minister indeed he breaks the bread of life, that is it which must beget Grace, yet if it be not digested, it will doe thee no good . . . You see the necessity of labour to retaine the word, to digest it, to make it thine own."[45] Edmund Calamy agreed that only by such meditation can the sermon bear proper spiritual fruit in the individual life: "It is with Sermons as it is with meat, it is not the having of meat upon your table will feed you, but you must eat it; and not only eat it, but concoct it, and digest it. . . . And *one* Sermon well digested, well meditated upon, is better than *twenty* Sermons without meditation."[46] John Donne urges the same point, meditation upon and application of sermon doctrine with particular reference to the soul's own needs:

> They that come to heare Sermons, and would make benefit by them, by a subsequent meditation, must not think themselves frustrated of their purposes, if they do not understand all, or not remember all the Sermon. . . . If thou remember that which concerned thy sin, and thy soul, if thou meditate upon that, apply that, thou hast brought away all the Sermon, all that was intended by the Holy Ghost to be preached to thee.[47]

For English Protestants, especially those of Calvinist inclination, the topics especially favored in meditation based upon the Word are doctrines relating to the paradigm of salvation. Richard Rogers proposes meditation upon those things especially "which may make thee sound in the matter of thy salvation"; and his enumeration of topics emphasizes man's condition, God's gifts, and the process of regeneration:

> The matter of this our meditation, may be of any part of Gods word: on God himselfe, his wisedome, power; his mercie, or of the infinite varietie of good things which wee receive of his free bountie; also of his workes and judgements: or on our estate, as our sinnes, and the vilenes of our corruption, that wee yet carrie about us, our mortalitie, of the changes in this world, or of our deliverance from sinne, and death: of the manifold afflictions of this life, and how wee may in best manner beare and goe through them, and the benefit thereof, and the manifold and great priviledges which wee injoy daily through the inestimable kindnes of God toward us: but specially of those things which we have most speciall neede of.[48]

He devised a long list of doctrines drawn from the scriptures as meditative topics, always insisting that "thou must apply that which is set downe generally to all Christians, to thy selfe, as if it were spoken onely to thee."[49] Richard Baxter also emphasized such topics:

> *Search the holy Scriptures, and acquaint your selves well with the Oracles of God, which are able to make you wise unto salvation.* . . . What mysterious Doctrines! How sublime and heavenly, are there

for you to *meditate* on as long as you live? What a perfect Law! a system of precepts most spiritual and pure! What terrible threatnings against offenders, are there to be matter of your meditations? What wonderful histories of Love and Mercy! What holy examples! What a treasury of *precious promises*, on which lyeth our hope of life eternal! What full and free expressions of grace! What a joyful act of pardon and oblivion to penitent believing sinners! In a word, the *character* of our inheritance.[50]

Some of the common medieval and Counter Reformation topics for meditation are also recommended in the English Protestant manuals— for example, on events in the life of Christ, on the four last things— but the meditator is usually not urged to consider these topics in them- selves, or to imagine them in elaborate sensuous detail. Rather, such meditation was tied firmly to the Word, and to the apprehension of and enactment of the paradigm of salvation in the self. Joseph Hall included such topics among the large number pertaining chiefly to the meditator's own spiritual state, as being topics "which can most of all worke compunction in the hart, & most stirre us up to devotion."[51] By the same token Isaac Ambrose concluded his manual with several vividly imagined meditations on the last things, but they are set forth like sermons on specific scripture texts—e.g., "Deaths Arrest, Luke 12:20"; "Doomes day, Matt. 16:27"; "Hells Horrour, Matt. 13:30"; "Heavens happiness, Luke 23:43"—and are organized like sermons in terms of division, doctrines, and uses (application).

Sacramental meditations in connection with taking communion ap- proach more closely some traditional methods of meditating on Christ's passion, though the focus remains the effect of his sacrifice for us. Since Protestants generally viewed the sacrament as a representation of Christ's passion, they licensed imaginative recreation of the passion scenes in sensory detail, in order to stir up repentance and promote proper affective responses.[52] Christopher Sutton advises the commu- nicant to "exercise thy minde . . . some time thinking of his ineffable love, some time of his extreme suffering," and he supplied several short meditations on the events of the Passion from the Last Supper to the Crucifixion, to be used before or after receiving communion.[53] Arthur Hildersam links meditation upon "the unspeakable and infinite torments which the Son of God in his passion indured for us aswel in his soule as in his body" directly to the realization of the salvific effects on us— "without which we could never have been redeemed from the least of all our sins, nor from the intollerable wrath of God."[54] Though some would limit sacramental meditation to the Passion,[55] others were more flexible. Edmund Calamy declares that "the Sacrament is a meditating

Ordinance . . . an Ordinance for *Meditation*: and the great work that
we have to do at the Sacrament, is to meditate upon Christ crucified,"[56]
but he also supplies additional topics drawn from the love of God and
Christ; the sacramental elements, actions, and promises; and our own
spiritual condition. Richard Sibbes would have meditation proceed
from a focus on Christ's passion to a recognition of him in glory, in
order that we may feel more directly how that event promotes our
own salvation:

> In the Sacrament, our thoughts must especially have recourse, in the
> first place, to *Christs* Body broken, and his blood shed, as the Bread
> is broken, and the Wine poured out; that we have benefit by *Christs*
> abasement and suffering, by satisfying his Fathers wrath, and rec-
> onciling us to God. Then thinke of *Christ* in Heaven, appearing
> there for us, keeping that happinesse that he hath purchased . . . and
> applying the benefit of his death to our soules by his Spirit.[57]

Meditation might also begin from the self. As Culverwel put it:

> Christians must often meditate and consider what blessings and what
> afflictions they have in private and in common, and how they under-
> goe both, and what use they make of them, likewise, to what cor-
> ruptions they be most carryed, and what meanes they use against
> them, and what profit they finde by them, also how constant or un-
> setled they be in a good course, and what be causes of either.[58]

Protestants practiced three varieties of such meditation: meditation
upon one's own sins and upon the evidences of one's regeneration, un-
dertaken as a regular duty of watchfulness and repentance or as a
preparation for communion; meditations on the radical sinfulness and
corruption of the heart as a preparation for conversion; and meditation
upon experience—God's providences, afflictions, and graces inpinging
upon one's own life.

Meditation upon one's own sins and evidences of election was widely
proclaimed as a necessary duty to be undertaken at regular intervals—
daily, monthly, and especially before sacrament days—to promote
humiliation, repentance, and constant watchfulness over the deceitful
heart. Many spoke of this procedure as a formal audit or accounting
or judicial trial: Thomas Taylor recommends, "In thy selfe, for the
helping forward of Repentance, keep a continuall audit, and take ac-
count of thy selfe and estate," getting thereby a clear sight of sins
and weighing them by the Law of God.[59] Thomas Gataker discusses
such meditation as a necessary aid to the spiritual watchfulness de-
manded of all Christians:

A . . . helpe to this watchfulnesse is to be oft sifting and examining our selves, viewing and surveying our heartes and our lives, taking account of our selves how wee watch and how wee walke, how the case standeth betweene us and God, how wee goe backward or forward in the good wayes of God, and how we thrive or pare in the gifts and graces of his spirit. . . . And were wee as carefull for the state of our soules, as the *children of this world* are for their worldly estates, wee would bee as carefull of keeping and oft casting up our accounts . . . as they.[60]

Isaac Ambrose recommends the careful keeping of a diary or day-book of actions, and daily and monthly meditation upon it as "a kinde of judiciary proceeding, in which a man keepeth private Sessions at home, passing a Sentence on his Thoughts, Words, and Actions."[61] He outlines three stages of such meditation: the discussion or sifting of our lives and dealings; the application or laying of these acts to the rule of God's Law; and judgment upon the acts according to that Law. As a method he especially urges the soliloquy or dramatic questioning of the heart: "Heart, how dost thou? how is it with thee for thy Spiritual state? . . . Heart, what wilt thou do? or, Heart, what doest thou think will become of thee and mee?"[62] Ussher's manual of meditation focuses almost entirely upon such self-examination: "Examine thy selfe which way thou art going, to heaven, or hell; to cast up thy accounts, and see whether thou thrivest in Grace."[63]

One particular occasion for such meditative stock-taking with the self was in preparation for the sacrament. The Protestant manuals agreed that the Christian must find in himself the evidences of regeneration—faith, repentance, charity, and amendment of life—before he could approach the table. To stir up repentance the Christian is advised, in Hildersam's words, to "labour and take paines with his own heart; both to find out and know his speciall sinnes, and to bring his heart to this unfained repentance for them, especially at that time, when hee prepareth himselfe to come to the Lords Table."[64] If he is regenerate, declares Bradshaw, the Christian will also find the signs of regeneration in himself by searching meditation: "What an incouragement then ought this to be unto everyone of us to rifle and ransacke our own soules, searching every corner of them, as one would search for a Mine of gold seeing wee are sure before hand to finde . . . a setled pardon of the forgivenesse of our sinnes; Yea, some evidences and Indentures of a firme title to the Kingdome of Heaven."[65]

A special variety of meditation upon the self, directed especially to those not yet regenerate, was recommended by Calvinist "preparationists" who stressed intense and continual and detailed meditation upon sin.[66] Such meditation, promoting fear and self-loathing, is to prepare the heart for God's breaking and softening action upon it, leading to conviction of sin and repentance. Though such preparation in no way merits or insures saving grace, upon which alone salvation depends, yet it was recognized by many as the divinely ordained first stage of the conversion process. This kind of meditation upon sin is most thoroughly discussed by Thomas Hooker in *The Application of Redemption*: the guide for the exercise is Psalm 51, the standard is the Mosaic Law, and the effect sought is to render the burden of sin unsupportable:

> A serious thought and right apprehension and application of a sin, toucheth and troubleth the sinner; but daily meditation flings in one terror after another, and followes the soul with fresh consideration of yet more sin, and yet more evil, and that more hainious and yet more dangerous . . . so that the sinner is stoned to death as it were and breaks under the burthen of it. . . . Meditation . . . observes the woof and web of wickedness, the ful frame of it, the very utmost Selvage and out-side of it, takes into consideration all the secret conveyances, cunning contrivements, all bordering circumstances. . . . It draws out the venom, and quintessence of the evil of a corruption, and lets in that upon the heart and conscience of a sinner, which stings and torments him in greatest extremity: makes him see more in his distemper than ever he suspected, makes him feel it far worse than ever he could have imagined.[67]

Hooker proposes for such meditation the usual two stages: intellectual analysis of the inward springs and outward fruits of sin, and then application to the heart through the will and affections of the full weight of the sins so enumerated, promoting conviction: "Meditation . . . before . . . played the part of an Accomptant, brought in al Bils; now takes the place of a Serjeant, laies them to the charge, and attacheth the sinner."[68] This drives the soul to seek deliverance by Christ, and, if God proffers saving grace, conversion follows.

Yet another variety of meditation beginning from the self was meditation upon experience—God's providences, graces, afflictions, and threatenings visited upon the community or upon oneself. Experience is viewed as the proving-ground of the Word, a second scripture which reveals God's will and provides a basis for determining our spiritual state. In these terms Richard Sibbes recommends grounding our faith upon former experiences: "If we were well read in the story of our own lives, wee might have a divinity of our own, drawne out

of the observations of God's particular dealing toward us."[69] John
Bartlet urges a careful cataloguing of such experiences and providences:

> Meditate on the Experience you have had of God's faithfulness,
> and goodness you have had in all his Providences. . . . To help you
> herein, you shall do well to make a Catalogue, and keep a Diary of
> God's special providences; to take a Book, and write down the most
> remarkablest Providences of God, over you, and yours: often read
> them over, and ponder them well in your minds. . . . The sight of
> such a Catalogue of gracious Providences, will so much the more
> affect our hearts with love to so good a God, and quicken us to a
> holy dependance on him.[70]

Isaac Ambrose offers a particularly detailed account of meditation on
experience, which he regards as a reprise and verification of the Word
in personal terms. In such exercises he urges Christians to take note
of what happens to them, under such heads as Promises, Threatenings,
Deceits of the Heart; then to consider what scripture texts are verified
thereby; and finally to sanctify the experiences by seeking appropriate
responses from the heart.[71] His several pages of examples, each analyzed
under these three heads, include such experiences as: a Canticles-like
ravishment of the soul in a spiritual love-trance; the battle of Preston
and the resultant deaths; the torment of fearful dreams produced by
Satan; the sense of Christ's withdrawing from the soul; the sense of the
Spirit's presence during prayer. To safeguard against "misprison of
Gods Providences," Ambrose insists upon interpreting them by the
standard of the Word: "It is our best and onely course, for our secur-
ity, to interpret all Gods works out of his Word: We must make the
Scriptures . . . a construing book to the book of Gods Providences."[72]
    One popular topic for such meditation upon experience, long popular
in manuals of devotion, was illness, with its attendant circumstances.
Calling upon the ancient *topos* of sin as sickness, and considering illness
both as the effect of sin and as a providential affliction sent by God,
such books provide the Christian who falls ill with general meditations
for the course of the illness from its inception to its termination in
recovery or death.[73] Others begin ostensibly from personal experience.
Joseph Hall's brief occasional meditation "Upon the beginning of a
sicknesse" takes his own physical illness as an analogue of his spiritual
state, and thereby the instrument of God's Providence correcting and
instructing him: "Since I have interspersed my obedience with many
sinfull faylings, and enormities, why doe I thinke much, to interchange
health with sickenesse? . . . I have sinned and must smart. It is the glory
of thy mercy to beat my body for the safety of my soule."[74] Robert

Boyle also includes among his *Occasional Reflections* a long sequence "Upon the Accidents of an Ague," in which the physical circumstances of each stage of his illness suggest immediately their spiritual parallels.[75] A death or funeral might similarly be seen as a providential warning and as an occasion for vicarious experience of one's own death. Richard Rogers urges "That we observe the departure of men out of this life. . . . And that we meditate and muse often of our own death, and going out of this life, how we must lie in the grave, all our glory put off."[76] Hall explores the experience or occasion of hearing the tolling of a passing bell: "This sound is not for our eares, but for our hearts; it calls us not onely to our prayers, but to our preparation . . . for our own departing. . . . And for me, let no man dye without mee, as I dye dayly, so teach me to dye once; acquaint mee before hand with that Messenger, which I must trust too."[77] And of course, though the matter is not relevant to our immediate concerns, Christians in both England and New England were constantly directed to meditate upon God's public providential acts in the nation and the church.[78]

Protestant meditations might also begin from the creatures. Accepting the commonplace that the Book of Nature or Book of the Creatures is a second divine revelation, Protestants developed this ancient meditative kind in distinctive ways, eschewing both the fantastic allegorizations of the creatures characteristic of the medieval bestiaries, and also the notion of a meditative scale of ascent from the creatures, to man, to God himself.[79] Protestants approached the creatures as objects of meditation in two ways: emblematically, as a rich source of moral lessons and *exempla* which the meditator should derive and apply to his own life; and symbolically, as sacramental objects invested by God with significances which may reveal something about God to the meditator.[80] The guide and standard for both is scripture: the nature similes, metaphors, and parables in the Bible provide the key to the lessons or the significances which the creatures present, and several biblical passages (for instance, the Creation account in Genesis; Psalms 8:3, 19:1, 104; Job 38; and Romans 8:19-22) are persistently identified as models of nature meditation or else as indices of appropriate topics for such meditation.

The natural creatures (as well as artifacts such as the lamp or the wheel) were favorite topics for occasional meditation, and usually regarded as emblems presenting moral lessons. Pointing to the Psalmist's meditative consideration of the heavens, the moon, and the stars in Psalm 8:3, Joseph Hall declares, "The creatures are halfe lost if wee only imploy them, not learne somthing of them: God is wronged if his creatures bee unregarded; our selves most of all, if wee read this great volume of the creatures, and take out no lesson for our instruction."[81] In his book, *Occasionall Meditations*, Hall took out many such lessons: he identifies the ivy tree as "a true Embleme of false love" whose embracements are kind but deadly; "the sight of a Raine in Sun-shine" teaches him to expect afflictions and vicissitudes amidst the joys of this life; "the singing of the Birds in a Spring morning" at sunrise teaches of the joy the penitent soul finds in the true Son of Righteousness; the marigold ever following the Sun in its motions presents the good heart wholly dependent upon God; and "the Crowing of a Cocke" calls him, as it did Peter, to repentance.[82] In the same didactic spirit, Robert Boyle urges the meditator to become an Aesop, able to turn "all kinds of Creatures in the world, as well mute and inanimate, as irrational, not onely into Teachers of Ethicks, but oftentimes into Doctors of Divinity," thereby making "the whole World . . . a Pulpit, every Creature turn a Preacher, and almost every Accident suggest a Use of Instruction, Reproof, or Exhortation."[83]

Other creature-meditations took their rise from the Bible rather than from nature directly. In his *Spiritual Chymist* William Spurstow looks to the similes and metaphors of the Bible to identify both the creatures to be contemplated, and their biblically authorized meanings. So, in a meditation upon the dew he observes that the meaning "is soon come by, because God hath brought it to my hand, having often in his Word resembled the *Dew* (which makes the earth fruitful) *to his Grace*, that maketh the hearts of men, naturally barren, to bring forth fruits of righteousness." And when Spurstow chooses an object of meditation directly from nature (as the balsam tree) he infers its significance from analogous scripture similes and texts.[84] Some other creature meditations are derived from the account of the creation: these are deliberate rather than occasional meditations, and proceed according to the sequence of the days, with an orderly consideration of the creatures named. In his *Heptameron* Archibald Symson first analyzes and praises the excellence of each creature, and then either points to its traditional spiritual significance (e.g., Christ is our Sun, the Sun of Righteousness) or else considers that creature in other biblical contexts in order to derive a spiritual lesson. So, in meditation upon the fish, fowls, and birds of the Fifth Day, he finds his lesson in Christ's allegory of the fishers: "The Sea is the World . . . the Boate is the Church: the Fishers are the Apostles and Ministers, who should be Fishers of Men." Often, also, the creatures teach man by example: for instance, the birds teach him to praise God.[85]

In addition to these didactic readings, the Book of Nature or Book of the Creatures was also read symbolically, as a true manifestation or revelation of God (*vestigia Dei*), invested with spiritual significance which the meditator does not piously devise but rather discovers. An important stimulus to such meditation was Calvin's argument that we can best know the attributes of the invisible God through his works, rather than through metaphysical speculations: "This skillful ordering of the universe is for us a sort of mirror in which we can contemplate God, who is otherwise invisible. . . . The most perfect way of seeking God, and the most suitable order, is . . . to contemplate him in his works whereby he renders himself near and familiar to us, and in some manner communicates himself."[86] Calvin observes, however, that we cannot now comprehend God's symbolism directly, because the Fall has virtually destroyed man's capacity to discern the spiritual significances in nature (and has thereby made impossible the scale of meditative ascent described by Bonaventure and Bellarmine):

> But although the Lord represents both himself and his everlasting Kingdom in the mirror of his works with very great clarity, such is our stupidity that we grow increasingly dull toward so manifest testimonies. . . . It is therefore in vain that so many burning lamps shine for us in the workmanship of the universe to show forth the glory of its Author. . . . Although they bathe us wholly in their radiance, yet they can of themselves in no way lead us into the right path. Surely they strike some sparks, but before their fuller light shines forth these are smothered.[87]

Accordingly, we must turn to scripture, and be illumined by faith, to know God with any clarity.[88] But after we have put on the "spectacles" of the scriptures, Calvin urges a return to meditation on the creatures as our best way of understanding something of God's attributes:

> Let us not be ashamed to take pious delight in the works of God open and manifest in this most beautiful theater. . . . There is no doubt that the Lord would have us uninterruptedly occupied in this holy meditation; that, while we contemplate in all creatures, as in mirrors, those immense riches of his wisdom, justice, goodness, and power, we should not merely run over them cursorily, and so to speak, with a fleeting glance; but we should ponder them at length.[89]

Such concern with the divine symbolism of the creatures dominates several Protestant discussions of or examples of creature meditation. Edward Topsell's latter-day bestiary drawn from Conrad Gesner emphasizes the "divine knowledge . . . imprinted in them [the creatures] by nature, as a tipe or spark of that great wisedome whereby they were created."[90] Thomas Taylor approaches the creatures identi-

fied in Psalm 8:3—"thine Heavene, even the workes of thy fingers, the
Moone and the Starres which thou hast ordained"—with Calvin's scrip-
tural spectacles: "Wee will not discourse of this voice [of the crea-
tures], as if we were in the School of *Plato*, or *Aristotle* or *Tully de
natura deorum*: but as in the Schoole of Christ, taught by the Scrip-
tures, and the Spirit speaking in them." He finds that all the creatures,
so considered, teach us by example to love and serve God, and to
await our deliverance from sin (Rom. 8:17); that they also reveal
the Divine attributes—God's eternity, wisdom, power, bountifulness;
and that they are conduits of divine revelation: "Thus the creation of
the world is a Scripture of God, and the voice of God in all the
creatures, and by them all speaketh unto us alwayes and every where."[91]
Richard Baxter also urges the regenerate to study the creatures for
revelations of God, and especially his divine attributes:

> The World is Gods book, which he set man at first to read; and
> every Creature is a Letter, or Syllable, or Word, or Sentence, more
> or less, declaring the name and will of God. There you may behold
> his wonderful Almightiness, his unsearchable Wisdom, his unmeasur-
> able Goodness, mercy and compassions; and his singular regard of the
> sons of men! . . . Those that with holy and illuminated minds come
> thither to behold the footsteps of the Great and Wise and bountiful
> Creator, may find not only matter to *employ*, but to *profit* and *de-
> light* their *thoughts*.[92]

Yet another approach to meditation on the creatures is found in God-
frey Goodman's amazing treatise, *The Creatures praysing God*, which
argues from Psalm 148:7-9 that the creatures have and display all the
elements of a natural religion—a creed, a praise and service to God, a
vocal prayer or liturgy, a law, and a sacramental system—and that con-
templation of these things reveals to us what our spiritual religion
should be.[93]

As the century progressed, considerable Protestant interest was di-
rected to "Heavenly Meditation," whereby the Christian was urged to
call forth, by a meditative process emphasizing the senses and the imagi-
nation, some foretaste of heavenly joys.[94] Its proponents considered
heavenly meditation not so much a distinct meditative kind as the
development of "heavenly-mindedness," whereby other kinds of medi-
tation—on scripture texts, on the creatures, on providential experiences
—would be redirected to focus on heavenly joys. To this end, Richard
Baxter advises the meditator to choose scripture texts relating to the
Gospel promises or the glory of the saints, and encourages him also to
learn "to open the creatures, and to open the several passages of provi-

dence, and to read of God and glory there. Certainly by such a skilful industrious improvement, we might have a fuller tast of Christ and Heaven, in every bit of bread that we eat, and in every draught of Beer that we drink, then most men have in the use of the Sacrament."[95]

Baxter's *Saints Everlasting Rest* (1650) was a central document in systematizing and disseminating this method, though its principles had been set forth earlier by Joseph Hall and Richard Sibbes. Hall in his *Arte* had illustrated his method of deliberate meditation with an exercise in heavenly meditation, asking "Whereon shouldest thou rather meditate than of the life and glory of Gods Saints?"[96] And in a later treatise he advised that a meditation on Christ's redemptive act should culminate in a consideration of his (and our) glorious exaltation in Heaven: "With what intention and fervour of spirit shouldst thou fix thine eyes upon that heaven where he lives, and raigns? How canst thou be but wholly taken up with the sight and thought of that place of blessedness."[97] All these writers agreed that heavenly meditation should not displace other forms of meditation for many purposes and persons, and that it pertains to regenerate Christians already well advanced in their Christian pilgrimage. As Baxter declares, "Its the work of the Living, and not of the dead. Its a work of all others most spiritual and sublime, and therefore not to be well performed by a heart that's meerly carnal and terrene."[98]

One common method for such meditation was an imaginative visualization and apprehension of the glories of heaven, directed, as Sibbes suggests, by the similes and figures of scripture: "Seeing God hath condescended to represent *heavenly* things to us under *earthly* termes, we should follow Gods dealing herein: God represents *heaven* to us, under the term of a *banquet*, and of a *kingdome*. &c. our *union* with Christ under the term of a *mariage*."[99] Baxter recommends the same method: "When thou settest thy self to meditate on the joyes above, think on them boldly as Scripture hath expressed them. . . . Think of Christ as our own nature glorified; think of our fellow Saints as men there perfected; think of the City and State, as the Spirit hath expressed."[100] Alternatively, in contemplating the creatures or God's providences, meditators might imaginatively develop and savor the analogy between earthly and heavenly things. Sibbes also commends this method:

For the things of the life to come, there are few of them, but God's children have some experimentall taste of them in this world: . . . He gives a grape of *Canaan* in this wildernesse. . . . If peace of conscience bee so sweet here; what is eternall peace? If a litle joy bee so pleasant and comfortable . . . what will bee that eternall joy there? If the delights of a kingdome bee such, that they fill mens hearts so full of contentment . . . what shall we think of that excellent kingdom? So by way of taste and rellish, we may rise from these pettie things, to those excellent things.[101]

Baxter also urges an analogical method, whereby the delights of the senses, the creatures, and the experience of God's special providences would be regarded as foretastes of heavenly joys:

Think with thy self, how sweet is food to my taste when I am hungry? . . . O what delight then must my soul needs have in feeding upon Christ the living bread? . . . How delightful are . . . Gardens stored with variety of beateous and odoriferous flowers; or pleasant Medows which are natural gardens? O then think every time thou seest or remembrest these, what a fragrant smell hath the pretious ointment . . . which must be poured on the heads of all his Saints?

What glory is in the least of yonder stars? what a vast, what a bright resplendent body hath yonder Moon, and every Planet? O what an inconceivable glory hath the Sun? Why, all this is nothing to the glory of Heaven [when] . . . I shall be as glorious as that Sun.

How sweet was it to thee, when God resolved thy last doubts? . . . healed thy sickness, and raised thee up as from the very grave and death? How sweet, then, will the Glory of his presence be?[102]

Though all who promoted heavenly meditation recognized the vast discrepancy between the heavenly goods themselves and the earthly analogues or biblical similitudes, they differed somewhat as to how freely the imagination might range in conceiving the joys of heaven, and how substantial our earthly vision or experience of those joys might be. Sibbes finds no danger in any imaginative use of analogy, guided by revelation, precisely because the discrepancy between earth and heaven is so great:

After God hath revealed spiritual truths, and *faith* hath apprehended them, then *imagination* hath use while the soule is joyned with the body, to *colour* divine truths and make lightsome what *faith* beleeves; for instance, it does not *devise* either *heaven* or *hell*, but when God hath revealed them to us, our *fancie* hath a fitnes of inlarging our conceits of them, even by resemblance from things in nature, and that without danger; because the joyes of heaven and the torments of hell are so great that all representations which nature affords us fall short of them.[103]

But Joseph Hall in *The Invisible World* ties heavenly meditation more closely to true perception. God's grace must remove our spiritual blindness, thereby enabling us to approach natural things as transparent glasses through which to see heavenly glories rather than simply as remote analogies for those glories:

> O God, if thou please to wash off my clay with the waters of thy Siloam, I shall have eyes; and if thou annoint them with thy precious eye-salve, those eyes shal be clear, and enabled to behold those glories which shall ravish my soul. . . . Every action, every occurance shall remind me of those hidden and better things: and I shal so admit of all material objects, as if they were so altogether transparent, that through them I might see the wonderfull prospects of another world. And certainly, if we shall be able to withdraw our selves from our senses, we shall see, not what we see, but what we thinke . . . and shall make earthly things, not as Lunets, to shut up our sight, but Spectacles to transmit it to spiritual objects.[104]

The five poets upon whom this study centers were influenced variously by Protestant meditation. Three of them—Donne, Vaughan, and Traherne—produced prose meditations which contributed to the development of these Protestant modes. And all of them wrote at least some religious lyrics related by title, form, or central concerns to these meditative traditions.

Donne's prose classic, *Devotions upon Emergent Occasions*, has often been discussed in terms of the Ignatian meditative tradition,[105] but is more obviously related to contemporary Protestant meditation upon experience. Its topic—a personal illness and its circumstances—was a common one, often presented in the format of an occasional meditation. Donne's *Devotions* is associated with this occasional kind by its basis in a particular experience—Donne's serious illness of November and December, 1623,[106] regarded as a providential occasion fraught with spiritual significance to be discerned by the speaker. This classification is also supported by the work's organization according to the progressive stages and circumstances of the illness, labeled "emergent occasions." Yet, somewhat exceptionally, Donne also calls upon the methods of deliberate meditation, in that the speaker undertakes an extended, ordered, sequential exploration of the complex relationship between sin and sickness much as a preacher might develop that topic in a sermon.[107] Indeed, as Janel M. Mueller has persuasively argued, Donne's *Devotions* fuse homiletic and devotional methods (as deliberate meditation customarily did), exploring the vicissitudes of the speaker's condition by an exegesis of several apt biblical texts.[108]

The structure Donne has devised examines the experience of the illness in terms of twenty-three "emergent occasions," each of which is explored in three stages—meditation, expostulation, and prayer. The "Meditations" are all grounded in particular physical circumstances, as, "3. The Patient takes his bed"; "5. The Physician comes"; "15. I sleepe not day nor night"; "17. Now, this Bell tolling softly for another, saies to me, Thou must die." They explore, with almost exclusive reference to the natural order,[109] what such circumstances reveal about the speaker's physical state, the human condition generally, and the universal malaise affecting all aspects of the fallen natural world. The "Expostulations" are a tissue of biblical texts and analogues which illuminate or reinterpret the terms and issues identified in the "Meditations," and which generally present the particular phase of the illness considered in each "Meditation" as an image and effect of the sickness of soul caused by sin. In the "Expostulations" the speaker debates with God or his own soul, seeking to understand his case by the evidence of God's word. In the "Prayers" the speaker strives to experience the affections and emotions appropriate to each clarification of his condition, thereby obtaining some assurance that God will restore him spiritually, that he has a place in the Register of the elect.[110] The conclusion to the "Prayer" of Section 7, entitled "The Physician desires to have others joyned with him," demonstrates this effort clearly, and also voices the challenge widely recognized by Protestant meditators—to discern and apply the significance of his experience rightly:

When therfore in this particular circumstance, *O Lord* . . . that he, whom thou hast sent to assist me, desires *assistants* to him, thou hast let mee see, in how few houres thou canst throw me beyond the helpe of man, let me by the same light see, that no vehemence of sicknes, no tentation of Satan, no guiltines of sin, no prison of death, not this first, this *sicke bed*, not the other prison, the close and dark *grave*, can remoove me from the determined, and good purpose, which thou hast sealed concerning mee. Let me think no degree of this thy correction, *casuall*, or without *signification*; but yet when I have read it in that language, as it is a *correction*, let me translate it into another, and read it as a *mercy*; and which of these is the *Originall*, and which is the *Translation*, whether thy *Mercy*, or thy *Correction*, were thy primary, and original intention in this sicknes, I cannot conclude, though death conclude me; for as it must necessarily appeare to bee a *correction*, so I can have no greater argument of thy *mercy*, then to die in *thee*, and by that death, to bee united to him, who died for me.[111]

Several of Donne's religious poems display the influence of various meditative traditions. The interlinked "La Corona" sonnets no doubt find one important source, as Louis Martz has argued, in the Corona rosary meditations developed for a special set of six decades; even more relevant is the English transformation of this Marian devotion into a "Corona of our Lord."[112] The nineteen "Holy Sonnets" have some affinities with Protestant exercises analyzing the meditator's spiritual condition, in that they set forth and probe certain states of soul and a wide range of emotions the speaker experiences as he regards his own sins and searches for evidences of his election.[113] But the closest affinities are those between certain of Donne's occasional poems and hymns, and the genre of occasional meditation upon a providential experience. "Goodfriday, 1613. Riding Westward," though often approached as a classic Ignatian meditation upon the crucifixion, is in fact an occasional meditation on the specific experience of being kept by pleasure or business from conducting the expected meditation, and the conclusion of the poem finds in this unlikely circumstance a potential spiritual boon. "A Hymne to Christ, at the Authors last going into Germany" is an occasional meditation on Donne's imminent departure with the Earl of Doncaster's diplomatic mission, in which the foreseen uncertainties and tribulations of the sea voyage become the speaker's opportunity to relinquish the world totally and seek God alone. The "Hymne to God my God, in my Sicknesse" is, quite obviously, an occasional meditation upon an illness expected to be terminal (probably the illness of 1623). Here, as in the *Devotions*, the actions of the physicians, the sick man's state, the fever itself are analyzed for their spiritual significance; at length the speaker derives from the occasion a confident expectation of his imminent salvation.

We have no prose meditations from Herbert's hand, and he seems to have conceived of his poems as a collection of lyrics whose primary concern is divine praise, rather than specifically as meditations. But he is vitally concerned with certain exercises and activities closely related to meditation in the Protestant view. Herbert's manual on the country parson's duties, *The Priest to the Temple*, devised for his own guidance at Bemerton and that of other parsons similarly situated, discusses various dialogic and hortatory methods to be used with the congregation in catechizing and in sermons. The preparation for both these pastoral exercises is the parson's use of the same methods upon himself: the catechist's Socratic questioning "exceedingly delights him as by way of exercise upon himself."[114] The country parson will also preach to himself "for the advancing of his own mortification," and the account of his temptations and victories become sermons when recounted to others.[115] Whether or not Herbert thought of these private exercises as forms of meditation, they are as closely related to sermon method as Protestant meditations customarily were. They also reflect the Protestant meditative emphasis upon soliloquy, expostulation with the self and with God, self-examination, and self-questioning.

The sequence of poems in "The Church" from "The Sacrifice" to "Easter" ostensibly constitutes a meditative series upon the Passiontide events. But, as Ilona Bell has persuasively argued, the ironies informing "The Sacrifice" and especially "The Thanksgiving" transform this sequence into a conscious Protestant critique of Ignatian meditation on the Passion with its emphasis upon imaginative identification with and imitation of the crucified Christ.[116] In fact Herbert's speaker is forced, painfully, to recognize and admit that he cannot in any meaningful way either apprehend Christ's sufferings or imitate his sacrifice—and that his attempt to do so is near-blasphemous folly. Chastened, he takes up an appropriate Protestant meditative stance toward these events—focusing upon his own response to them and upon their significance for his salvation. Some other Herbert poems resemble, in certain respects, Protestant meditations upon scripture texts—"The Altar," "Aaron," "The Odour," "Coloss. 3:3," "A true Hymne"; their method, like that recommended by Thomas Goodwin, is to engage in a dialogue with the text in question. A very few might be called meditations upon the creatures, deriving lessons from them: "The Starre," "Life," "The Storm." Many more resemble meditations upon experience, especially afflictions, trials, or graces sent by God at particular moments: the five "Affliction" poems, "The Temper (I)" and "The Temper (II)," "Deniall," "Artillerie," "The Glimpse," "Grief," "Josephs Coat," "The Flower." Still others have some affinity with those meditations upon one's spiritual state intended to promote repentance and the consideration of one's evidences: "Conscience," "Assurance," "Nature," "The Bunch of Grapes," "The Familie," "Longing." Moreover, in a special sense all the poems of "The Church" are records of and meditations upon experience—the speaker's varied experiences in living the Christian life within the Church, and in building the spiritual temple within himself. But this is to stretch a point, for the poems of "The Church" ask to be considered in terms of several genres and modes.

Henry Vaughan's prose manual, *The Mount of Olives: or, Solitary Devotions*, resembles many Protestant meditative handbooks in its conjunction of admonitions, meditations, and prayers. Vaughan thinks of these exercises primarily as devotions; he has, he says, omitted "the ordinary Instructions for a regular life . . . lest instead of Devotion, I should trouble thee with a peece of Ethics."[117] In this work he illustrates or recommends a large variety of Protestant meditative kinds: occasional (on taking a journey, at the setting of the sun, on the passing seasons, on a sickness); deliberate (meditations before and after the Lord's Supper, to be drawn chiefly from Christ's life and passion); meditations on death; meditations on the creatures; meditations on the glories of heaven. These kinds are not categorized and classified schematically, but are casually intermixed with prayers for various times and occasions, as if to suggest that such a mix and variety of meditative and devotional helps best suits the devout Christian's life. Vaughan's poem "Rules *and* Lessons" recommends a similar range of meditations—on the creatures, on experience, and on death: "Observe God in his works"; "When night comes, list thy deeds; make plain the way / Twixt Heaven, and thee"; "Spend in the grave one houre / Before thy time."[118]

The poems present an even more comprehensive collection of Protestant meditative kinds. Interestingly enough, Vaughan also includes among the first poems in *Silex* a sequence in which Catholic modes of meditation on the events of Christ's life ("The Search") and upon the creatures as an ordered scale of ascent to God ("Vanity of Spirit") are tested and found wanting. The corrective is supplied in "*Isaacs* Marriage," through an analysis of the Protestant meditative exemplar, Isaac in the fields. Vaughan's poems include a few meditations upon biblical events—"The Passion," "Christs Nativity," "Easterday," "Jesus Weeping [I]" and "Jesus Weeping [II]"—but they focus in the Protestant way upon the significance of these events for the speaker's spiritual life. A few others are rather conventional communion poems on the nature, benefits, and proper preparation for the sacrament: "Dressing," "The Holy Communion," "The Sap." Several are meditations upon experience in a Herbertian vein, probing God's dealings with the soul and its responses—"Distraction," "The Relapse," "Unprofitableness." Particularly interesting is a sequence of occasional meditations on the very painful experience of the death of a loved one, probably Henry's brother William; these are dispersed throughout the volume but linked together by the same typographical symbol, and they present the changing responses of the speaker to this experience as he learns to derive spiritual profit from it.

Some of the finest and most distinctive of Vaughan's poems are meditations on the creatures. *Mount of Olives* gives particular attention to this kind of meditation. Some creatures are identified as genuinely symbolic, invested by God with significances the meditator must discover (for instance, those that fall into a dead sleep in winter and

revive in the Spring are a "*Symboll* of the resurrection"); others are
regarded as sources of moral lessons which, taught by scripture exam-
ple, we should derive and apply.[119] Vaughan's poems also propose both
approaches to the creatures. "Rules *and* Lessons" urges meditation
upon them as symbols of God's attributes: "Each *tree, herb, flowre* /
Are shadows of his *wisedome*, and his Pow'r" (ll. 95-96). "I walkt the
other day" contains a prayer to understand nature's symbolism prop-
erly, as a means to ascend to God:

> That in these Masques and shadows I may see
> Thy sacred way,
> And by those hid ascents climb to that day
> Which breaks from thee
> Who art all things, though invisibly.
>
> (ll. 50-54)

"The Starre," however, proposes didactic application: "Yet, seeing all
things that subsist and be, / Have their Commissions from Divinitie, /
And teach us duty, I will see / What man may learn from thee" (ll.
9-12). In addition, several poems approach the creatures as emblems,
which either offer lessons to man ("The Showre," "The Constellation,"
"The Storme," "The Tempest"), or else serve as divinely ordered
symbols of God's truths or of man's condition ("Cock-crowing," "The
Bird," "The Timber," "The Rain-bow," "The Water-fall"). Finally,
several poems are of that classic Protestant kind, meditations upon a
biblical text. Often the speaker encounters and engages with the text
dramatically, analyzing and applying it to illuminate a personal ex-
perience, as in "And do they so?" "The World," "The Seed growing
secretly," "The Night." Though Vaughan's poems are responsive to
several influences besides meditation, they yield more readily than the
*œuvre* of any other poet here studied to a classification by meditative
kinds.

   Thomas Traherne left in manuscript prose works relating to diverse
meditative traditions. Two are largely derivative, incorporating long
passages almost verbatim from influential sources. *The Church's Year-
Book*, a collection of devotions, prayers, brief essays, and liturgical
passages in the eclectic manner of Henry Bull, Daniel Featley, and
Henry Vaughan, is organized according to the principal days in the
Church calendar from Easter to All Saints.[120] The *Meditations on the
Six Days of the Creation* relies very extensively, as Lynn Sauls has
shown, upon the structure, ideas, and phraseology of the Jesuit Luis de
la Puente's nine meditations on the creation,[121] but Traherne gave his
text a more Protestant flavor by adding extensive biblical extracts, and

he ended each "day" with his own poem of praise. Much more interesting is the recently discovered manuscript, "Select Meditations,"[122] whose themes and topics are closely related to those of the published *Centuries of Meditation*—felicity as the end of man; man as God's image and thereby possessor of divine glory and of all the world; love as the current conjoining God, man, and the world; man as the end of all things, even of God himself. Essentially these are directives to or examples of a transformed "heavenly meditation": Traherne's central concern is to reveal how the regenerate may learn to enjoy not merely the foretaste of heaven but the divine glories and joys themselves. The mode is primarily expository: the entries, arranged in centuries,[123] are for the most part brief essays, interspersed with occasional prayers, expostulations, and poems.

The magnificent *Centuries of Meditation*, four books of one hundred numbered passages each, and a fifth apparently unfinished,[124] display the impress of the Protestant meditative tradition in their mixture of hortatory, meditative, and expository modes, though the mixture is uniquely Traherne's. Addressed to his friend Susanna Hopton, the work proclaims as its central purpose to make her "Heir of the World" —defining that state as the present possession and enjoyment of God, of herself, and of all created beings and things through properly knowing, valuing, and loving them.[125] The *Centuries* have been related variously to Bonaventuran and Neoplatonic meditative paradigms,[126] but all such ordered patterns of progression are tenuous, since the three categories through which Traherne proposes to explore felicity— God, the World, Yourself—are interconnected in each of the books. What we find rather is that all the books are transformed heavenly meditations, undertaking to lead Susanna by different meditative means to a constant focus upon divine glories and heavenly joys. But whereas heavenly meditation characteristically cultivates spiritual perception ("heavenly-mindedness") by regarding earthly things as foretastes and similitudes of heaven, Traherne finds that the saints' eternal joys and blessedness are even now present to spiritual vision and able to be enjoyed in this life.

The *First Century* is primarily exposition of fundamental principles: its entries, in the manner of the Baconian short essay, often elaborate upon an initial aphorism or principle concerning God, the glorious self as image of God redeemed by Christ, Christ's sufferings as the root of felicity, or the world as temple of eternity. In this *Century*, meditation is defined as thinking rightly about such things: "To think well is to serv God in the Interior Court; To hav a Mind composed of Divine Thoughts, and set in frame, to be Like Him within."[127] The *Second*

*Century* is a meditation on the creatures turned to the purposes of Traherne's special kind of heavenly meditation. The topic is the services the creatures render to man: these analytic entries begin with the works of God and proceed to derive the other interlocking principles —God, Christ, Yourself—from them. The *Third Century* proposes to teach the same things "by Experience": it is formally a meditation on experience turned into a heavenly meditation in Traherne's special terms. The speaker sets forth in brief prose passages and short poems his infant perception of himself as possessor of the glorious world, his fall from this perception, and his restoration to it, in order to show his reader "by what Steps and Degrees I proceeded to that Enjoyment of all Eternity which now I possess."[128] This is the familiar Protestant examination of personal spiritual experience to find a replication of the classic conversion paradigm. Moreover, Traherne's assimilation of his personal experience to that of the Psalmist David, as he discovers in amazement that the Psalms enact his own spiritual condition, is also a familiar Protestant meditative motif; it is developed in the final portion of this *Century* by a sequence of meditations on the Psalms fusing David's voice and the speaker's own.[129] In the *Fourth Century* the speaker declares, in the third person and in abstract terms, the principles pertaining to virtue or "Active Happiness" he has derived from his meditations upon experience and upon the true ideas of things. The ten extant sections of the *Fifth Century*, analytic and celebratory at once, focus upon God's attributes and especially his eternity and infinity as the means and end of our enjoyment—"perfecting and compleating our Bliss and Happiness."[130]

Traherne's two sequences of devotional lyrics bear some relation to Protestant meditative practices. The *Poems of Felicity* (excluding the poems which also appear in the Dobell manuscript) may have been intended as a separate, unified sequence:[131] their mode is primarily meditation upon personal spiritual experience, correlated (as in the *Third Century*) with the conversion paradigm. The poems trace the speaker's spiritual life in several basic stages: the glorious vision and felicity of innocent childhood; the Fall from innocent bliss and the resultant grief, poverty, solitude, and sense of loss; the desire for and then reception of a book from heaven (the Bible, as in the *Third Century*); the experience of regeneration, appropriately correlated with the feast of Christmas; and finally the adult experience of felicity wherein childhood "sense" is improved by clearer Reason, the evidence of the Word, true experience, and right thoughts.[132] The Dobell poems were more certainly intended as a unified meditative sequence, as John M. Wallace has perceived[133]—though not, I think, as an Ignatian meditation. The subject is the attainment and exercise of true spiritual vision, regarded as an extension and perfection of the innocent vision of childhood. This sequence begins from personal experience, but proceeds to general principles, universal truths: it is a transformed heavenly meditation in Traherne's particular terms, in that his own spiritual vision in childhood serves as the foretaste, the earnest, the evidence of the heavenly joys and divine blessedness the regenerate may enjoy even now as they regain and perfect (through grace) their spiritual vision.

Most of Edward Taylor's shorter poems are related to specific Protestant meditative kinds. Several often-anthologized miscellaneous poems are occasional meditations on providential experiences ("When Let by Rain," "Upon Wedlock, and Death of Children," "Upon the Sweeping Flood Aug: 13.14"), or else on the creatures regarded emblematically ("Upon a Wasp Child with Cold," "Upon a Spider Catching a Fly," on a spinning wheel ["Huswifery"]). On the other hand, the two numbered sequences of devotional poems—I, 1-49 and II, 1-165—composed over a period of more than forty years (1682-1724) are presented as deliberate meditations preparatory to receiving the sacrament: the general title Taylor supplied for these poems is *Preparatory Meditations before my Approach to the Lords Supper. Chiefly upon the Doctrin preached upon the Day of administration.*[134] This authorial designation indicates that Taylor wished to identify his poems with the genre of preparatory meditations before taking the sacrament, and to indicate their close relation to sermons—even though the issue of just how closely and in what ways these poems were related to sacrament-days and the sermons Taylor preached may remain in dispute.[135] The poems in the *Christographia* series (a sequence in which we have, exceptionally, fourteen sermons and their companion poems) take the form Protestant theorists on meditation constantly urged: they are personal applications of the sermons' necessarily broader concerns, bringing home to the meditator's own soul and condition some aspect of the sermon perceived to pertain especially to him.[136] Indeed, in II.138 Taylor specified such application as the primary function of meditation—distributing the nourishment gained from chewing and digesting the Word by faith.

Taylor's own recommendations regarding preparatory meditation for the sacrament are set forth in his *Treatise Concerning the Lord's Supper*.[137] He calls in the first place for meditative self-examination or trial to determine whether the soul is possessed of the "wedden garment" of God's gracious election and regeneration; even the clearly regenerate Christian is to "look into this matter afresh, and to make it out to thy soul," recalling and repenting his sins and reviewing his evidences of conviction and conversion.[138] He proposes also a second kind of meditation or "contemplation" upon the sacramental feast itself, as an epitome of the covenant of redemption: "Meditate upon the feast: its causes, its nature, its guests, its dainties, its reason and ends, and its benefits, etc. For it carries in its nature and circumstances an umbrage, or epitomized draught of the whole grace of the gospel. For here our Saviour is set out in lively colors."[139] Explaining this directive, Taylor specifies such topics as: man's ruin by sin, Christ's death accepted in payment for sin, the covenant of redemption, Christ's fulfilling the law, the sacrament as image of the covenant in Christ's blood, the properties of that redeeming blood.[140] Taylor also recommends developing such a train of meditations with special reference to the metaphor of the sacrament as a "wedden-feast":

> The wedden will set thy contemplations going upon the glory of the wedden, the glory of the King, the glory of the Prince the Bridesgroom, Oh! the King of Glory. How doth it shine forth here? The beauty of the bride, the happiness of the bride, and her honorable preferment. The dowry laid down for her, that the Bridesgroom covenanted to lay down: as His estate to redeem her, to pay her debt, to purchase her her freedom, her furniture and her felicity; and that He came to her out of His Father's bosom, from His Father's palace, on His Father's errand, and here in this dirty world was attached on her account, imprisoned, arraigned, condemned, executed, and put to death, held a prisoner in the grave till the third day; then he broke the bands of death asunder, threw the prison door off of its hinges, came out a valiant conqueror, ascended up into glory, sits at the Father's right hand, set up ordinances, sent out suitors His spokesmen, sent down gifts to bestow on His bespoken for, contracts them to Himself and celebrates the contract now in this wedden feast.[141]

Most of Taylor's *Preparatory Meditations* reflect in some way, though not in accordance with a rigid scheme,[142] the self-examination in regard to worthiness recommended in the *Treatise*. Moreover, whenever originally conceived or written, Taylor's "First Series" (1-49) seems at some juncture to have been accommodated to a conceptual design like that of the passage cited.[143] The poems address in sequence the topics enumerated, displaying the sacrament as an epitome of the covenant of redemption: Christ's love for mankind; the beauty, excellence, and glory of the Bridgegroom and the feast; Christ's mediatorial role (his offices, his passion, his exaltation and enthronement in heaven); the benefits the soul enjoys through the covenant of grace (it is espoused by Christ, granted forgiveness of sins and fullness of grace, adopted by God, made a new creature, and made heir to all things present and to come); the joys of the heavenly kingdom as the final benefit of the covenant. The "Second Series" (1-165) does not exhibit such a unified design but does contain several tightly knit sequences: the typological sequence (1-30), the *Christographia* sequence (42-56), the sequence on the words of institution of the sacrament (102-111) the sequence on consecutive verses from Canticles 5:10-7:6 (115-153). Beyond this, in very general terms the "Second Series" presents something of a developmental pattern intimating the speaker's own growth: he progresses from meditation upon the Old Testament types of the covenant, to Christ the Redeemer, to the benefits of the covenant, to the Bridegroom-Bride relation of Canticles, to a hesitant identification with the Bride. It would be misleading, however, to suggest that this pattern is more than the broadest outline, or to attempt to fit all the poems in the series to it, or to assume that it necessarily conforms to Taylor's own spiritual development. What does seem clear is that the Protestant meditative emphasis upon the analysis of spiritual experience in relation to some version of the classic paradigm of the spiritual life acts as a shaping force upon apparently amorphous collections of devotional poetry, as surely as it does upon individual poems.

## CHAPTER 6

## Protestant Emblematics: Sacred Emblems and Religious Lyrics

Emblems—curious amalgams of picture, motto, and poem—are a minor literary kind which contributed significantly to theories about, and particular formulations of, poetic language and symbolism in the seventeenth-century religious lyric. Knowledge of the ways in which Renaissance emblem books influenced sixteenth- and seventeenth-century literature has been notably advanced by the comprehensive theoretical and bibliographical work of Mario Praz, W. S. Heckscher, and the Henkel and Schöne *Handbuch*, as well as by specialized studies of particular aspects of this tradition and its effect upon particular poets.[1] My concern here is with sacred and moral emblem books, especially those composed or revised by Protestants, since Protestant emblem theory and characteristic emblematic representation of biblical tropes, religious symbols, and natural objects influenced in some important ways both the poetics and the poetry of Donne, Herbert, Vaughan, Traherne, and Taylor.

### A. Emblem Theory

Renaissance emblem books have their origins both in rhetorical and Neoplatonic traditions—a derivation clearly evident in the earliest of them, Alciati's *Emblematum liber* (1531), with its debts both to the *Greek Anthology* and to the *Hieroglyphics* of Horapollo. Emblems on secular and moral subjects were developed long before sacred emblems on Christian religious themes, but Neoplatonic theory attached to emblems generally something of the mystical religious significance associated with their supposed source—the Egyptian hieroglyphs.[2] Randomly organized and inconsistent in philosophy, Horapollo's book (supposedly written by an ancient Egyptian and rediscovered in 1419)[3] promoted delight in secret meanings and certain hermetic ideas, including the mistaken notion that the hieroglyphs of the Egyptians were ideographs, direct symbols of things or ideas. Contributing to this theory were Francisco Colonna's *Hypernerotomachia* (1499), which spread the fashion for hieroglyphs, and Pierio Valeriano's *Hierogly-phica* (1556), a Latin commentary upon Horapollo which established the Renaissance habit of using the term *hieroglyph* as a synonym for *symbol* and also the practice of deriving specific Christian meanings from Horapollo's figures.[4] The Florentine Neoplatonists Ficino and Pico della Mirandola assimilated the hieroglyphs along with other ancient wisdom to the true philosophy, believing that these mystic ideographs present images of "the very nature of the universe" and of the Divine Ideas.[5] As Ficino explained, "When the Egyptian priests wished to signify divine mysteries, they did not use the small char-acters of script, but the whole images of plants, trees or animals; for God has knowledge of things not by way of multiple thought but like the pure and firm shape of the thing itself."[6]

Alciati took over several of Horapollo's plates, but he approached emblem-making rather as a charming hobby than as a mystic exercise; he did not use the term "hieroglyph" for his emblems, nor did he set forth philosophical or religious theories about them. However, his most exhaustive and influential editor and commentator, Claude Mignault (Minos) made the connection between hieroglyph and emblem all but explicit. Defining Egyptian hieroglyphs as symbols which use things themselves (rather than words) to signify other things and which, like Platonic myths, hide profound truths, he attributed to Alciati's emblems the two most important features of hieroglyphs: esoteric significances evident only to the initiate, and the representation of ideas by picture rather than words.[7] Later, vague references to the hieroglyphic ancestry of the emblem became commonplace in the theoretical literature, but they were most often divested of mystical or consistent Neoplatonic assumptions.

Indeed, the primary tradition behind most Renaissance emblem books was probably rhetorical, finding the essence of the emblem not in a natural, mysterious, divine correspondence but in a contrived rhetorical similitude or conceit, with close affinities to epigram. Epigrams origi-nated as inscriptions on tombs or statues; the term *emblem* was traced to *emblematura*, mosaic work or inlay. Praz argues a close connection between emblem and epigram, in that emblems are things (representa-tions of objects) used to illustrate a conceit, and epigrams are words (a conceit) used to illustrate objects, such as works of art or tombs; he observes further that many epigrams in the *Greek Anthology* written for statues are emblems in all but name.[8] Alciati based over fifty of his emblems, especially on love, upon the *Greek Anthology*, and emblema-tists also used and illustrated Petrarchan conceits. Moreover, the emblem tradition received a special impetus from the crystallization of ancient

ethics into collections of adages, proverbs, and mottoes—often sources
of the mottoes for emblems. In line with all this, Scipione Bargagli
flatly denied the association of *imprese* or emblems with hieroglyphs
or other mystical symbols, defining them simply as illustrated conceits
or metaphors. Almost a century later Emanuale Tesauro argued the
same rhetorical point: "The perfect *impresa* is a metaphor."[9]

Renaissance theorists recognized two large divisions of their subject
—the emblem and the *impresa* or device—both composed of a figure in
conjunction with words. The parts of the emblem were defined as the
drawing, the inscription, and the epigrammatic poem; the *impresa* had
two parts, drawing and motto. Some early theorists tended to press
the distinction between the two forms, finding the *impresa* to be more
obscure, esoteric, mysterious, witty, symbolic, more closely related to
the hieroglyph or ideograph, and more rigidly controlled by strict
rules governing its composition. Emblems, by contrast, had general
moral application to all mankind and were more open in method and
more didactic in intention. Capaccio states the distinction as follows:

> The emblem has only to feed the eyes, the device the mind. The for-
> mer aims only at a moral; the latter has for its purpose the concept of
> things. The one is more delightful the more it is adorned with ob-
> jects, and, although such things do not pertain to the essence of the
> emblem, it needs other images, great or small, or grotesques and
> arabesques, to adorn it. The other sometimes has more loveliness to
> the eye when it is simple and bare, with no other ornament but a
> scroll. In a word, the emblem has its title as a text, to be in the spirit
> of the image, and the *imprese* contains the motto which gives spirit
> only to the creator, who with a secret conception brought forth the
> picture.[10]

Capaccio believed, however, that the device might serve as an emblem
when deprived of its motto and enriched with an inscription, and an
emblem as a device when provided with a motto.[11] But Ercole Tasso
disagreed, on the ground that the essential distinction between the two
forms is not a matter of the words used: "neither does the device derive
its essence from the motto alone, nor is the emblem what it is because
of the inscription. For if the latter contains a moral and has a universal
application, it will be an emblem as much without an inscription as with
one."[12] Defining symbol as the figure synecdoche, Abraham Fraunce
used that term as a synonym for "device" as he contrasted the ways
significance is conveyed in the two kinds, and their diverse audiences:
"In emblems the speech explains the figure, while in the symbol this
practice is accounted to be the greatest possible fault, in which not the

speech explains the figure, nor the figure the speech, but the figure with the speech explains the idea. The emblem therefore is made so that the precept and doctrine will be for the common people; the symbol however is private and its purpose is revealed and accommodated to one or another man."[13] In similar terms, Henry Hawkins provided both a theoretical statement about, and in his *Parthenia Sacra* an illustration of, the ways of turning symbolic devices into emblems—by enhancing the detail of the picture to appeal to the senses, and making its meaning more explicit through a poem.[14]

Working from such distinctions, Henri Estienne set forth as criteria for the emblem that it be intended for instruction, comprehensible to many but not too common or obvious, and conversant about three main sorts of subject matter—nature, history, morals:

> For the Embleme is properly a sweet and morall Symbole, which consists of picture and words, by which some weighty sentence is declared. . . . Emblems are reduced into three principall kinds, *vis.* of Manners, of Nature, of History or Fable. The chiefe aime of the Embleme is, to instruct us, by subjecting the figure to our view, and the sense to our understanding: therefore they must be somewhat covert, subtile, pleasant, and significative. So that, if the pictures of it be too common, it ought to have a mysticall sense; if they be something obscure, they must clearly informe us by the words, provided they be analogick and correspondent.[15]

On the other hand, many discussions of the *impresa* or device began from the much more rigorous and complex specifications laid down by Paolo Giovio (whose tract was translated into English by Samuel Daniel):

> An invention or *Impresa*, (if it be to be accounted currant) ought to have these five properties, First just proportion of body and soule. Secondly, that it be not so obscure, that it need a *Sibilla* to enterprete it, nor so apparant that every rusticke may understand it. Thirdly, that it have especially a beautifull shewe, which makes it become more gallant to the vew, interserting it with Starres, Sunnes, Moones, Fire, Water, greene trees, Mechanicall instruments, fantasticall birds. Fourthly, that it have no humane forme. Fifthly, it must have a posie which is the soule of the body, which ought to differ in language from the *Idioma* of him that beareth the *Impresa*, to the ende the sence may bee the more covert. It is requisite also it bee briefe, yet so that it may not breede scrupulous doubts, but that two or three words may fit the matter well, unlesse it bee in the forme of a verse, either whole, or maymed.[16]

There was, in short, some disposition to associate the *impresa* or device with symbol, the emblem with metaphor or allegory. Yet at the same time many theorists blurred this distinction, implying that the method of signifying is essentially the same in both kinds. Scipione Bargagli assumed that both forms are grounded upon the metaphor or conceit, and his prescription for contriving *imprese* was applied by later theorists to both forms: figure and words should be "so strictly united together that being considered apart, they cannot explicate themselves distinctly the one without the other."[17] Henri Estienne also assumed that both *imprese* and emblems are witty, contrived forms carrying imposed authorial meaning rather than mystic significance; accordingly, whereas Mignault and Paolo Giovio discuss the figure as the body of the device and the motto as its interpreting soul, he argues rather that the two parts together by their conjunction must lead the reader to apprehend the author's meaning.[18] The English theorists from their more pragmatic point of view also seemed to find the distinction between emblem and *impresa* not worth belaboring. Geoffrey Whitney and Henry Peacham do not deny differences, but formally eschew the attempt to work them out, referring their readers to the earlier theorists.[19] And Puttenham, in a chapter entitled "Of the device or embleme," presents the various terms as strictly interchangeable synonyms:

> These be the short, quicke, and sententious propositions . . . [which] commonly containe but two or three words of wittie sentence or secrete conceit till they [are] unfolded or explained by some interpretation. For which cause they be commonly accompanied by a figure or purtraict of ocular representation, the words so aptly corresponding to the subtiltie of the figure, that aswel the eye is therwith recreated as the eare or the mind. The Greekes call it *Emblema*, the Italiens *Impresa*, and we, a Device. . . . For though the termes be divers, the use and intent is but one whether they rest in colour or figure or both, or in word or in muet shew, and that is to insinuat some secret, wittie morall and brave purpose presented to the beholder, either to recreate his eye, or please his phantasie, or examine his judgement or occupie his braine or to manage his will either by hope or by dread, every of which respectes be of no litle moment to the interest and ornament of the civill life.[20]

An early French book of religious emblems, entitled *Emblemes, ou Devises Chrestiennes*, also treats these terms as synonyms.[21]

Under this pressure the name "emblem book" came to be used of quite different kinds of subject matter and figures, and a particular book might include a wide variety of kinds. Moral emblems constituted one of the three common subject-matter categories for emblems—natural, historical, moral—as in Whitney's *Choice of Emblems* and Estienne's treatise. Whitney declared that the moral emblem "pertaining to vertue and instruction of life . . . is the chiefe of the three"[22] and, as emblem practice developed, figures and plates borrowed from other contexts were often applied to moral ends through changes in the motto or poem. Divine or sacred emblems were a new kind which flourished especially in the seventeenth century; they were often produced by simple transformation of characteristic figures from the love-emblem books. Thus Eros and Anteros from Otto van Veen's book *Amorum Emblemata* (1608) became, by the expedient of added haloes and wings, Divine Love and Anima in the same author's *Amoris divini emblemata* (1615).

Emblem-making in general, and especially the creation of sacred emblems, is often regarded as a Jesuit enterprise, and certainly that art's basic method of rendering divine truth by means of and in ways delightful to the senses is in line with Tridentine aesthetics.[23] Yet for all that, a French Protestant woman, Georgette de Montenay, produced what is usually taken to be the first book of sacred emblems, the *Emblemes, ou Devises Chrestiennes* (1571). Associated with the staunchly Protestant court of Navarre, Montenay consciously undertook to create emblems quite different in nature from those of Alciati:

> Alciat feit des Emblémes exquis,
> Lesquels voyant de plusiers requis,
> Desir me prit de commencer les miens,
> Lesquels je croy estre premier chrestiens.[24]

We might also consider *A Theatre for Worldlings* (1568, 1569) by the Dutch Protestant John Van der Noot—with poems translated by Spenser—to be the first sacred and first English emblem book, although the plates are not supplied with mottoes.[25] Intending "to sette the vanitie and inconstancie of worldly and transitorie thyngs"[26] before the reader's eye, the twenty plates of *A Theatre* present, in turn, emblematic scenes with accompanying epigrams based on Petrarch's *Rime* #323, to exhibit the mortality of earthly love and beauty; and emblematic scenes with sonnets from Du Bellay's *Songe* to display the transience of (Roman) worldly wealth and pomp. Finally, four original plates and sonnets setting forth notable emblematic images from the Book of Revelation (the seven-headed Beast, the Whore of Babylon, the Man on a white horse, the New Jerusalem) subsume the whole argument to the scriptural and apocalyptic terms of the conflict between Anti-

christ and Christ, this world and the New Jerusalem. Protestants re-
mained active in the field—sometimes revising Catholic collections,
sometimes devising new plates and books along somewhat different lines.

The sacred-emblem books, especially books by Protestants, moved
resolutely away from Neoplatonic esotericism. These theorists did,
however, reinforce the view of emblems as grounded in the divine order
of things rather than simply in the conceits of human wit—that is, as
symbols or allegories found, not made. They did this, however, on a
biblical ground, reinforcing from the story of the creation the con-
ception of nature as God's emblematics. Calvin's idea, discussed above,
that nature can serve as a mirror revealing something about God's at-
tributes only if we put on the spectacles of the scriptures[27] provides a
basis for this approach. Estienne labors this point in asserting that
hieroglyphic writing must have emanated from the Hebrews rather
than the Egyptians since the Hebrews were encouraged to contemplate
God's own emblematic practice in nature:

> God framing this world with such varieties of living creatures, set
> before the eyes of our first Parents some draughts and resemblances,
> whence men might perceive, as through the traverse of a Cloud, the
> insupportable rayes of his Divine Majesty. . . . So many objects which
> presented themselves to the view of *Adam, Enoch, Moses*, and the
> other Patriarchs, were as so many Characters illuminated by the
> Divine splendour, by means whereof the Eternall Wisdome did con-
> signe his name into the heart of man.[28]

Francis Quarles prefaced his *Emblemes* with a statement of the same
doctrine: "Before the knowledge of letters, GOD was knowne by
*Hieroglyphicks*; And, indeed, what are the Heavens, the Earth, nay
every Creature, *Hieroglyphick*s and *Emblemes* of his Glory?"[29] Things
in nature could accordingly be taken as emblem subjects, and regarded
as God's hieroglyphics exhibiting divine truth to our senses, but any
disposition toward the esoteric was controlled by the biblical frame of
reference.

On the other hand, a sacred emblem might begin with the rhetorical
element—the witty conceit or maxim constituting the emblem's motto or
inscription. Among Protestants such conceits, metaphors, proverbs and
maxims were drawn overwhelmingly and directly from scripture, there-
by relating the wit of the emblems not to human ingenuity but to the
true wit of God's Word. Francis Quarles justified his own procedure
on just this ground: "An Embleme is but a silent Parable. Let not the
tender Eye checke, to see the allusion to our blessed SAVIOUR fig-
ured, in these Types. In holy Scripture, He is sometimes called a Sower;

sometimes, a Fisher; sometimes, a Physitian: And why not presented so, as well to the eye, as to the eare?"[30]

Protestants also looked upon several of the symbolic objects in the Bible as divinely constituted emblems with figure and motto and explanation. Sacred-emblem-makers might copy or imitate these scriptural emblems, or study them for their theoretical implications. From this perspective, Andrew Willet altered Whitney's tripartite classification of subject matter so as to substitute for the "moral" kind a category of "Emblemata Typica sive Allegorica," consisting mainly of biblical symbols such as Noah's Ark.[31] Joseph Hall's remarkable sermons entitled "The Imprese of God" develop a theoretical basis for the use of symbolic objects and metaphors from the Bible as sources for emblems. Using as text Zechariah 14:20, "In that day shall be written upon the bridles (or bells) of the Horses, Holinesse unto the Lord," Hall explains the *impresa* in terms suggestive for Herbert's poem, "Aaron":

> As in all Impreses, there is a bodie, and a soule, as they are termed; So both are here without any affectation: The Soule of it is the *Motte*, or Word, *Holinesse to the Lord*: The bodie, is the subject it selfe . . . *Bells of the horses*. . . . The Israelites were charged to make their Embleme the Law of God; for their posts, for their garments. But these things must not be written upon our walls, or shields only; They must be written upon our hearts; else we are as very painted walls. . . . Happy is it for us, though we write no new Emblems of our owne, if we can have this holy *Imprese of God*, written not in our foreheads, but in our hearts, *Holinesse to the Lord*.[32]

Moreover, Calvinist sacramental theology identifies several scripture passages as emblems, not only in the general sense in which physical elements are seen as invested with spiritual significance, but also in the rather more specific literary sense of the emblem books, wherein image, motto, and (verse) explication all set forth a theme in their different modes, mutually interpreting and reinforcing each other. Calvin's discourses on the interplay of word and sign in the sacraments have broad reference to "all those signs [circumcision, the passage through the Red Sea, the manna, and much else in the Old Testament and the New] which God has ever injoined upon men to render them more certain and confident of the truth of his promises."[33] Calvin's comments discuss these physical signs as emblem figures; they are seals of God's promises, representing those promises "as pointed in a picture . . .

portrayed graphically and in the manner of images." The word of the promises is like the motto—in Calvin's view prior to the sign in importance so that "the sign serves the word," and the preaching or explication of the word makes us understand "what the visible sign means." For Calvin, then, in the sacrament as in the emblem, "the outward sign so cleaves to the word . . . that it cannot be separated from it," and both set forth the same truth, Christ, in different ways,[34] but in this case the word of the biblical text is clearly the dominant element in the emblem configuration, the medium through which Truth is primarily apprehended.

Indeed, the book with seven seals described in the Apocalypse as supplying the matter of John's visions was conceived of by Joseph Mede as something like an emblem book. In an epistolary exchange with one Haydock prefaced to his *Key of the Revelation*, Mede adopted enthusiastically Haydock's idea that the "book" must have been a scroll containing several sheets of parchment, each of them sealed "with a Seal, and severall impression of Emblimaticall signiture" which could be successively opened.[35] Mede proceeded to outline his notion that the "book" so opened must have portrayed in some graphic fashion the several visions displayed to John scenically—serving rather like a prompt-book in the hands of the angelic stage-manager who opened the seals:

> It seemed too unseemly a thing to affirme, that the thing was performed by a meere outward representation, the book conferring nothing thereunto; I fell into the opinion, that both were to be joyned together, and that we must say, that indeed the Prophecies were described and pourtrayed in the Volume, whether by signes and shapes, or letters; but that these were no otherwise exhibited to *John* and other beholders of this coelestiall Theater, then by a forraigne [i.e., scenic] representation, supplying the roome of a rehersall, not much unlike to our Academicall interludes, where the prompters stand neere the Actors, with their books in their hands.[36]

From such theory, then, the seventeenth-century Protestant found encouragement to look to emblems in nature, in scripture, and in emblem books to enhance his knowledge of spiritual matters, and to assist his meditations. The Protestant emblem-maker found a directive to produce sacred emblems which present and explore the resonances of God's own emblems, or which provide visual counterparts or representations for the metaphors, conceits, and maxims in God's Word that invite such treatment. And the Protestant lyric poet found a basis for his own witty exploitation of images drawn from, or resembling those found in, contemporary books of sacred emblems, and for highlighting the visual, emblematic qualities of those images, since they have their ultimate origin in the true wit of God's creation and God's Word.

## B. Kinds of Sacred Emblem Books

In the several kinds of moral and sacred emblem books, poets could discover models and examples of various ways to represent and exploit biblical conceits and images from nature, ways closely related to the forms of God's own wit. On theoretical and historical grounds the name "emblem book" was applied to works containing very different kinds of figures, and, more important for our purposes here, to collections which mixed the various kinds indiscriminately and haphazardly —abstract symbols and designs of the sort associated with devices and *imprese*; personifications in the manner of Cesare Ripa; creatures of nature set forth as bearers of a divine symbolism; allegorical scenes from fable or imaginary story. All these modes of visualization have their analogues in, and could contribute to, poetic imagery in the period. In general, we can identify five kinds of emblem books dealing with moral and spiritual matter, whose subjects and methods of presentation proved suggestive to the seventeenth-century lyric poets, both in regard to particular images and figures and also in the representation of the whole course of the spiritual life.

( 1 ) One large category contains those general collections of discrete emblems on diverse subjects, which were given pervasive moral or Christian significance.[37] Works of particular importance in this kind include the compendium of nature emblems in four "Centuries"— plants, animals, birds, fish and reptiles—compiled by the German Protestant Joachim Camerarius; collections of the devices of kings, ecclesiastics, and nobles as in Claude Paradin's *Devises Heroiques*; and iconographical manuals such as that of Ripa, crystallizing the allegorical representation of the attributes and properties of various virtues, vices, and abstractions.[38] The first English emblem book, by conventional definition Whitney's *Choice of Emblemes* (1586), included continental plates from a number of sources ostensibly representing three classes of subjects—natural, historical, and moral—but Whitney's method is more accurately indicated by his title-page promise that all these borrowed plates have been "Englished and Moralized."[39] Henry Peacham's *Minerva Brittanna* declares its moral purpose explicitly—"to feede at once both the minde, and eie, by expressing mistically and doubtfully, our disposition, either to *Love, Hatred, Clemencie, Justice, Pietie, our Victories, Misfortunes, Griefes* and the like";[40] the poems also include some biblical allusions and specifically religious associations. A variation on this format was developed in Jacob Cats' *Silenus Alcibiadis*, which presents an entire set of plates three times (in the same order), applying them first to love, then to civic and public virtue, and finally to the spiritual life. The figures remain constant but the mottoes, quotations, and poems are altered from section to section, and usually derive from the Bible or the Fathers in the final part; the suggestion is that levels of perception are related to levels of perfection.[41] Zacharias Heyns' collection, *Emblemata Moralia*, contains a large number of animal figures and is distinctive in using scripture quotations as inscriptions for these "moral" emblems—which often relate to overtly Christian themes.[42] George Wither took over plates without verses from the German emblem book of Gabriel Rollenhagen, undertaking to "quicken" them with poems "both Morall and Divine";[43] and indeed he often gives the figures a moral signification very different from the meanings they originally carried in Alciati or Camerarius, or Cats, or Rollenhagen. All these are Protestant collections, and this kind of emblem book proved especially attractive to Protestants.

(2) Closely related to these books, and also a favorite mode for Protestants, are collections of discrete emblems labeled sacred or Christian—and often claiming that name from the use of biblical quotation or allusion in motto or inscription. These emblems are often presented as literal renderings of biblical metaphors rather than of significant natural or imagined objects. An example is the familiar figure of the marigold following the sun and responding to its beams: in Camerarius the emblem bears the motto "*Non Inferiora Secutus*," suggesting general aspiration to higher things and enjoyment of God's blessings, while in Hulsius' and Heyns' sacred emblems an inscription from John 8:12, "I am the Light of the World," presents marigold and sun as embodying the Johannine metaphor; Heyns also adds the motto, "*Christi actio imitatio nostra*."[44] Georgette de Montenay's emblems are of this kind; the plates are chiefly allegorical scenes, the mottoes often allude to but do not directly quote scripture, and the collection imposes a slight pattern upon the discrete plates by beginning with the image of a young Christian soldier arising from sleep (the motto is "*Surge*"), and ending with two emblems of last things—an angel blowing the Last Judgment trumpet, and a coffin with thorns in it bearing the motto *Patientia Vincit Omnia*.[45] Other works in which the significance of the emblem figure is interpreted by a scripture quotation beneath the plate

are Zacharias Heyns' *Emblemes Chrestienes* (not sharply distinguished in kind or manner of presentation from his *Emblemata Moralia*), Bartholomaeus Hulsius' *Emblemata Sacra*, and Johann Mannich's *Sacra Emblemata* LXXVI.[46]

(3) Closely related to this category is another kind of sacred emblem book using discrete plates ordered around a central theme and highlighting that theme by presenting some constant element in every emblem of the collection. This method also found favor with English Protestants. Robert Farley presents a sequence in which the common element is the candle (usually representing the Christian) striving toward heaven, consuming itself by its own burning, sheltered from storms in a lantern; there is no ordered thematic progress, save that the first plate shows the candle flame rising upward under the motto *"Sursum"* and the final plate shows the candle extinguished. Francis Quarles' *Hieroglyphikes of the Life of Man* also uses the candle motif, but in a more structured fashion and with biblical inscriptions as keys to each of the plates: the candle is first unlit, then lit by God's hand, then subjected to various vicissitudes as it steadily declines in size until it is almost extinguished (old age). John Saltmarsh's *Holy Discoveries and Flames* uses the same two emblems throughout—an eye cast upward with beams directed from it or to it prefacing meditations titled "Discovery," and a heart on fire within and surrounded by flames prefacing prayer-like passages entitled "The Flame."[47]

(4) Another variety of sacred emblem books—especially associated with the Jesuits—transfers Eros and Anteros from the secular love emblems and presents them as characters in a series of exploits, adventures or stages of a pilgrimage rendering aspects of the spiritual life. The plates are allegorical scenes representing such episodes—sometimes discrete, sometimes related in a loose narrative sequence. The child figures who are the actors in these scenes—appropriately termed by Praz "dolls for the spirit"—perhaps intend to suggest what it is to become a child again to attain the Kingdom of Heaven, but inadvertently associate a quality of playfulness with the Christian life.

The most direct appropriation of the Eros-Anteros motif is in *Typus Mundi*, attributed to Phillippe de Mallery;[48] this work transforms the little figures of Eros and Anteros into Earthly Love and Heavenly Love, setting them in playful opposition to each other in a series of discrete plates whose common feature is a globe or globes (*typus mundi*). After introductory plates presenting Adam picking globe-apples, and the changes in the world after the fall, the rest of the plates portray the attractions and dangers of the world, which the Earthly Love succumbs to and the Heavenly Love resists: the little figures play at bowls or croquet with globes; Earthly Love seeks honey in a globe and is stung by wasps; the globe shows hell scenes within; it is the perch of the peacock of pride and of the motley fool, vanity. The final plate displays Earthly Love trying unsuccessfully to push the globe into Heavenly Love's heart.

The more usual transformation of the Eros-Anteros figures, however, is that which Otto van Veen inaugurated in the first example of this kind of sacred emblem book, the *Amoris Divini Emblemata*.[49] In Veen and most of his followers the figures are Anima and Divine Love: they are not antagonists but rather loving companions enjoying a sure and steady and comforting relationship through all the trials and tribulations of the Christian life. The relationship itself, and often many specific plates or entire sequences, builds upon the allegory of the Song of Songs in celebrating the love between Christ and the Christian soul. Veen's book presents the little figures in a series of essentially playful engagements, with very little that suggests the difficult or painful in the Christian experience; there is also little narrative progress, though the sequence begins with Divine Love awakening Anima by paraphrasing Canticles 2:10, "Arise my Love, my dove, my fair one, and come away," and it ends with two emblems suggestive of their achievement of closer union: they are enthroned together on a pedestal, and then seated peacefully at table, conversing. In this vein also are the emblems of Michael Hoyer, which chiefly illustrate quotations from Saint Augustine by presenting a Divine Love figure calling, aiding, and leading an Anima figure who is often attacked or hampered by a worldly Eros.[50] A much more sequential narrative is developed in Benedict van Haeften's *Regia Via Crucis*, whose theme is the imitation of Christ through carrying the cross.[51] The characters are now somewhat older—an adolescent Anima and Divine Love; and the tone is more somber, in keeping with the "cross" motif, which appears in every plate. The three books present, respectively, the introduction to the way of the cross; the best way of bearing the cross (showing Anima carrying hers along various paths and in various difficulties as Divine Love offers aid and consolation, until at length both are crucified together on the same cross); and the fruits or benefits of the cross—it is variously a paddle to row Anima's boat over the sea of life, a square for building the Temple, a hammer to beat out the crown of victory, a ladder upon which to climb to heaven, and, in the last plate, a knocker with which to knock at Heaven's gate.

The *Pia Desideria* of Hermannus Hugo is the most elaborate and carefully organized of the Anima-Divine Love sequences.[52] The emblems present an unfolding narrative of the progress of the soul en route to salvation according to the traditional three stages of the mystic way—purgative, illuminative, unitive. The first book, "Sighs of the Penitent Soul," shows such emblems as: Anima dressed in motley with fool's cap and bells while Divine Love hides his face; Anima grinding at a mill, in bonds, lashed by Divine Love; Anima adrift in stormy seas reaching out to Divine Love on shore for help; Anima with an optic glass viewing Death far off as a skeleton with sword and palm branch, and with a heavenly scene displayed above him. The motto texts are chiefly from the Penitential Psalms and Job. Book II, "The Vows of the Holy Soul," displays Anima advancing more confidently: she makes her way across a labyrinth by holding the end of a thread while Divine Love, standing on a high tower, holds the other; she goes forth into the fields hand in hand with Divine Love, dressed as shepherd and shepherdess—interpreted as an invitation to contemplation; she seeks him unsuccessfully in her bedchamber but he is by the side of the bed on a cross. The texts are from the Psalms and especially Canticles. Book III, the "Exstasies of the Enamour'd Soul" also draws texts from Canticles and Psalms. Anima, sick of love, languishes and pines; she sits with Divine Love in a garden among lilies, each crowning the other; she is encased within a skeleton of bones and begs release; she grows vast wings and attempts to fly to heaven but is chained by one foot to earth; she enjoys a vision of Divine Love enthroned in heaven.[53]

Francis Quarles undertook a thoroughgoing Protestant reworking of Hugo (and of *Typus Mundi*) in 1635; his *Emblemes* went into numerous editions and was probably the chief vehicle for presenting and interpreting these plates to his countrymen.[54] Quarles' changes—the combination of the two books, the many alterations in the order of the plates in both, the omission of several of the original plates and the addition of some new ones—create a new Protestant narrative sequence on the spiritual life which deliberately undermines the orderly progressions of the Jesuit devotional books. Quarles' version has an analogue in the somewhat random arrangement of poems in Herbert's and Vaughan's poetic versions of the spiritual life: for Protestants that life is to be viewed not as an orderly progress from penitence to contemplative ecstasy, but as a much more uneven, uneasy, and essentially episodic sequence of trials, temptations, failures, successes, backslidings, until the end of life crowns all. Reworking *Typus Mundi* plates for his Books I and II, Quarles recasts the Earthly Love figure as an Anima being taught the errors of her ways and loves by Divine Love; he adds plates presenting more serious aspects of worldly wickedness in heavier and more somber pictures than those of *Typus Mundi*; and he alters the final plate so that the globe is being removed from the child-Anima's heart, which is then offered to God by Divine Love (the conversion experience). The following three books reproduce most of Hugo's plates from *Pia Desideria*, but eliminate the titles suggestive of clearly-defined stages of spiritual progress. The introductory emblem (the arrows of prayer from the heart aimed at God's disembodied eye and ears) is treated as a transition to the soul's new life; occasionally, a new plate is substituted for a theologically suspect one; and the several figures rendering contemplative and mystical ecstasy (IV.7 and the final plates of Book V) are reinterpreted as the enjoyment of meditative solitude and the desire for Christ's presence, rather than achieved union. A new concluding emblem is supplied on a text from Revelation 2:10— "Be thou faithfull unto death, and I will give thee the crowne of life," a tentative ending in harmony with the final poem of Herbert's *The Temple* ("Church Militant" rather than "Love [III]"), and with Vaughan's final poem, "L'Envoy," which presents the soul's eager desire for the Second Coming but its acceptance of a life of waiting and longing.

(5) The final kind of sacred emblem book—of special importance for the religious lyric poets—comprises the so-called schools of the heart, in which a heart figure is represented undergoing progressive purgation from sin and spiritual renovation. Again there are marked differences between Roman Catholic and Protestant sequences. The first such book, *Schola Cordis* by the Jesuit Benedict van Haeften, takes over the characters of Anima and Divine Love from the other sequences, and shows them in every plate engaged in some activity with or upon the heart of Anima—disembodied and usually held between them.[55] The plates are embedded in prose meditations organized according to the traditional stages of the mystical way and introduced by an argument (in Book I) concerning the centrality of the heart in the religious life. In Book II (The Purgative Way) we find such plates as: Anima holding her heart from which all manner of vanities fly out as a small fiend blows a bellows into it (*"Cordis Vanitas"*); Divine Love hammering a heart held on an anvil by a fiend (*"Cordis Durities"*); Anima grinding the heart with mortar and pestle as Divine Love watches (*"Cordis Contritio"*); Divine Love melting the heart held by Anima with fiery beams from his face (*"Cordis Emollitio"*); Divine Love tossing the heart into a fiery furnace as Anima watches (*"Cordis Probatio"*). Book III, Part 1 (The Illuminative Way) contains such plates as: Divine Love lighting a candle in the heart (*"Cordis Illumi-*

*natio*"); Divine Love writing on the heart held by Anima ("*Cordis Tabula Legis*"); Divine Love and Anima ploughing the heart ("*Aratio Cordis*"), sowing seeds in it ("*Seminatio in Cor*"), watering it ("*Cordis Irrigatio*"), and at length viewing flowers growing from it ("*Cordis Flores*"); the last plate shows Divine Love playing upon a harp in Anima's heart ("*Cordis Dilatatio*"). Book III, Part 2 (The Unitive Way) shows the heart with the Dove in it ("*Cordis Inhabitatio*"); the heart wounded by arrows shot from Divine Love's bow ("*Cordis Vulneratio*"); Divine Love plunging a torch into the heart ("*Cordis Inflammatio*"); the heart winged, flying from Anima to Divine Love in heaven ("*Cordis Volatus*"); and, finally, the heart held firmly by Divine Love above, while Anima watches from earth ("*Cordis Quies*"). Book IV shows Anima and Divine Love taking the heart stage by stage along the way of the cross—it weeps blood in the Garden of Olives, is chained to a pillar for scourging, is crowned with thorns, is stretched and nailed to a cross, has a cross planted within it, is pierced by a lance, and at last buried (with Anima) in a sepulchre.

Christopher Harvey produced an English Protestant *Schola Cordis* (1647)[56] with forty-seven emblems, most of which were taken from among van Haeften's fifty-five, though there are new, more somber, plates at the beginning, representing the fall of man, the taking away of the heart by devils, and the darkness of the heart. Harvey also excised all the prose meditations, substituting devotional poems, and often supplied also new biblical texts as mottoes for the plates. Moreover, although for the most part he retains van Haeften's order, he wholly omits any division according to stages or planes of the spiritual life, so that, though there is clearly some progress shown in the renovation of the heart, there is no finality of achievement. The most remarkable changes to this end occur in the plates from van Haeften's "Unitive Way," which Harvey interprets as signifying simply the firm love of God and desire for rest in him; also, the final plates no longer represent the heart enduring Christ's passion in union with him, but merely record its further tests and trials by God in various afflictions.

Another variety of Jesuit heart book is that in which the heart becomes the stage for exploits by the Child Jesus. A series of plates executed by Anton Wiericx, "Cor Jesu Amanti Sacrum," was used to illustrate various Jesuit emblem books, appearing in different order in the various editions. In a collection put together by Jean Messager, *Vis Amoris Jesu in Hominum corda singularis*,[57] the plates trace Christ's actions and their progressive effects in the heart: the Christ-child knocks at a large wooden door in the heart; Christ with a lantern searches the corners of the heart and finds them full of beasts and vipers;

he sweeps them out with a broom; he places the instruments of the passion in the heart; he teaches it to sing as he sits within it with a songbook (with the dove above); he strums a harp within the heart; he sets fires and flames within it which exude smoke. The final figure displays the heart crowned with palm leaves by the Christ-child.

The original Protestant heart emblems are markedly different. There are a number of them among the discrete emblems of Wither and especially Mannich,[58] but the only complete Protestant heart sequence is that of the Lutheran Daniel Cramer.[59] The special feature of all these plates, and of Cramer's sequence, is that God acts powerfully *upon* the heart—not located within it as the Christ child, and not in conjunction with an Anima figure. The implication is (in accordance with Protestant doctrine) that the renovation of the heart is entirely the work of grace and not a cooperative venture.[60] Cramer's fifty plates, all but five of which display the heart figure, present no steady narrative progress, although the first and last plates provide a frame. The sequence begins with the disembodied hand of God softening a stony heart by striking it with a hammer on an altar-like stone; the motto is "*Mollesco*," interpreting the biblical inscription from Jeremiah 23:29, "Is not my word . . . like a hammer that breaketh the rocke in pieces?" And the sequence ends with a *Memento Mori*—the heart and a death's-head resting together on a table. All the plates have biblical texts as inscriptions, and present the metaphors in those texts visually and through their brief mottoes. The plates clearly present the episodic nature of the Christian life, in that the renovation of the heart is seen to involve a number of characteristic actions wrought upon it at God's hands, though in no fixed order or sequence: When it is warmed by the sun the heart sprouts a few grains of wheat despite the thorns around it ("*Cresco*"—Luke 8:15). The heart placed in a bonfire is perfumed by the hand of God and blown upon by the wind ("*Amo*"—Cant. 4:16). The heart fixed on an altar burns in flames and is blown upon by many winds ("*Sum Constans*"—Psalm 39:4). The heart is wounded by a sword but God's hand above squeezes balm into the wound ("*Sanor*"—Hos. 6:1, "he hath smitten, and he will binde us up"). The heart is weighed in a scales held by God's hand against the tables of the Law and proves too light ("*Nil Sum*"—Rom. 7:14), but in the next plate with the symbols of Christ's passion added to it the heart outweighs the Law ("*Praepondero*"—Rom. 6:14). The hand of God writes the name *Jesu* in the heart with a pen ("*Praedestinor*"—Isa. 44:5). The hands of God shovel the heart into a flaming furnace ("*Probor*"—Isa. 48:10). The winged heart seeks to fly to heaven away from an earthly city ("*Emigrandum*"—Heb. 13:14). An angel bearing

wreath and crown prepares to crown the winged heart (*"Per Augusta"*
—Acts 14:22).

The emblem tradition, and especially the Protestant moral and re-
ligious emblems, are an important resource which, as we shall see, the
major religious lyric poets utilized variously but extensively. The em-
blems provide, for one thing, striking visualization and pictorial analyses
of prominent biblical metaphors or natural objects, which can be
wittily evoked in verse. Larger structural features of the emblem
books are also suggestive: Herbert's book of lyrics has close thematic
and structural affinities to the *Schola Cordis* emblem books; and
the Protestant revisions of the Jesuit sequences in the direction of
randomness provide one model for the comparable portrayal—in
Donne's "Holy Sonnets," in Herbert's *The Temple*, in Vaughan's
*Silex Scintillans*, in Traherne's poems, in Taylor's *Preparatory Medita-
tions*—of the Christian life as an irregular, episodic sequence of graces
and temptations, successes and failures, rather than an ordered progress
by set stages to spiritual perfection. Most important, the emblem ma-
terials made available to the seventeenth-century poet a visual symbolic
mode whose established significances could be evoked to enrich par-
ticular lines, complete poems, or entire lyric collections.

## C. EMBLEMS AND RELIGIOUS LYRICS: SOME AFFINITIES

Although it is not often possible to prove that particular emblem
sources determined particular poetic usages, certain remarkable af-
finities between emblems and poems are at least presumptive evidence
of these poets' awareness of certain emblematic traditions. Some em-
blems seem to be pervasive, evoked by the different poets in distinctive
ways. But there is also an emblematics characteristic of each poet here
studied—evident in the particular emblems, the kinds of emblems, and
the basic emblem strategies he most often places under contribution.

In this connection, a brief glance at Crashaw's *Carmen Deo Nostro*
(1652), arranged, published, and in part written after his conversion to
Rome, affords an instructive contrast to the seventeenth-century Protes-
tant poets' emblematics.[61] Crashaw's use of Christian iconography is
altogether more direct and pervasive. This collection, unlike his earlier
*Steps to the Temple* (1646, 1648) containing several of the same poems,
is supplied with illustrations, though most of them are holy pictures
rather then emblems—a nativity and an epiphany scene, a pieta, a cruci-
fix, a monstrance, a portrait of Saint Teresa. The poem "The Flaming
Heart" is about a picture, the familiar baroque representation of Teresa
ecstatically swooning as she receives a seraph's dart of love. Two illus-

trations probably executed by Crashaw himself are heart emblems—the wounded, winged, flaming heart in the breast of the weeping Magdalen prefixed to "The Weeper," and the padlocked heart prefixed to the poem "To the . . . Countesse of Denbigh." This last emblem, its motto "Non Vi," its epigram, and the poem itself reflect the theology of the Jesuit heart books in insisting that the heart is not to be taken by force, but willingly surrendered to divine love. Crashaw's Saint Teresa poems, "Prayer: an Ode," the "Denbigh" poem and many others recall the motifs and atmosphere of the *Pia Desideria*, the *Schola Cordis*, and the *Cardiomorphoseos*: the heart bathed in Christ's blood or in a fountain of grace; the heart burning in flames of love, besieged by grace, filled with flowers and perfumes; the Anima-Soul dissolving before the glances and graces shed from Divine Love. In addition, Crashaw's poems often allude to medieval emblems such as the Pelican (Christ) drawing forth its own heart's blood, and Crashaw's expanded versions of several liturgical hymns to the Virgin constantly recall the Jesuit Henry Hawkins' elaborate emblem book on the symbols for the Virgin.[62] As compared to the Protestant religious poets of the period, Crashaw clearly calls upon different emblematic resources and exploits them in characteristically different ways. Whereas Crashaw renders an atmosphere by evoking a myriad of fleeting images from baroque sacred art and Jesuit emblem books, the Protestant poets often interpret biblical and sacred metaphors in images which are, like the Protestant discrete emblems, strongly visual, logically precise, and elaborately detailed.

An emblem which has structural as well as thematic importance for a number of the Protestant religious lyric poets is the wreath, signifying the fitting tribute of praise accorded notable achievement; it is often positioned among the final plates in collections of discrete emblems. Examples are Camerarius' three intersecting crowns of laurel, olive, and oak, with the motto *"His Ornari aut Mori,"* and Paradin's individual emblems of laurel, grass, and oak crowns, referring to distinct kinds of Roman honors; the motif was Christianized in Wither's collection, which has as its final plate the hand of God holding forth a wreath to the Christian who perseveres to his goal—*"Dabitur Perseveranti."*[63] Donne's "La Corona" sonnets call upon these significances: the crown of prayer and praise the speaker seeks to offer God is set over against the crown of glory he hopes at last to obtain from him. Moreover, the work is itself an emblematic wreath, created by subtle uses of repetition, ploce, and antithesis which weave lines and half-lines together within individual poems and in the sequence as a whole. Both Herbert and Vaughan include a "Wreath" poem among their final poems, and these poems, with their interweaving and interlinking of words and lines, are themselves emblematic wreaths of praise for God— wreaths which, if they could be worthy, would thereby crown the poets' efforts as well. Taylor also concludes his first series of *Preparatory Meditations* with three poems on the Crowns of Life, Righteousness, and Glory, respectively, which the Christian will at last wear.[64]

Several emblems from the Anima-Divine Love narrative sequences resound throughout these poems. Hugo's first plate, reproduced in Quarles' *Emblemes*, in which Anima sends forth from her breast arrows of prayers directed to the disembodied divine eye and ears in the heavens, find analogues in some very visual metaphors for prayer [Figure 1]. Donne in "A Litanie" cries out to God, "Heare us . . . O Thou Eare. . . ." Herbert in "Prayer (I)" defines prayer as an "Engine against th'Almightie"; in "Deniall" his devotions seek to "pierce / Thy silent eares"; in "Prayer (II)" his requests "invade" those ears; in "The Search" his sighs seek God "Wing'd like an arrow" but are not received.[65] Another emblem which reverberates widely is Hugo's picture (reproduced in Quarles) of Anima finding her way across a Labyrinth by holding onto a thread whose other end is held by Divine Love on a High Tower [Figure 2]. In Herbert's "The Pearl" the speaker, feeling the attractions of the ways of learning, honor, and pleasure, gives thanks that "thy silk twist let down from heav'n to me, / Did both conduct and teach me, how by it / To climbe to thee." In Vaughan's poem "Retirement" God tells the speaker that "at the very brink / And edge of all / When thou wouldst fall / My *love-twist* held thee up, my *unseen link*." In Edward Taylor's Meditation II.113 the speaker begs for "thy Sweet Clew" to lead him through the labyrinth of the doctrine of the Incarnation.[66] Again, Hugo's emblem of the winged Anima striving to fly away to Divine Love in Heaven but chained by one foot to earth is also recalled in several poetic images: Vaughan's speaker, temporarily associating himself with Christ in "Ascension-day," feels himself able to "soar and rise / Up to the skies"; Taylor's speaker in Meditation I.20 begs his ascended Lord to "Lend mee thy Wings" to "fly up to thy glorious Throne"; and Herbert's "Home" sets forth all the elements of the emblem:

> Oh loose this frame, this knot of man untie!
> That my free soul may use her wing,
> Which now is pinion'd with mortalitie,
> As an intangled, hamper'd thing.
> O show thy self to me,
> Or take me up to thee![67]

Of particular importance for both Herbert and Vaughan are a number of emblems which variously embody a biblical metaphor central to both—God as gardener and man as plant or tree. Several plates present flowers growing under beneficent heavenly influences. Camerarius sets forth an image of flowers revived and made to flourish by the rains of heaven ("*Coeli Benedictio Ditat*"); Wither has two emblems of flowers and fruits basking in the sun, presenting the dependence of all growth upon God's grace, with the mottoes "*Solum a Sole*" and "*Florebo Prospiciente Deo.*"[68] Similarly, in "Grace," Herbert's speaker sees himself as a dead stock and begs for dews from above, and in "Vanitie (I)" he sees God mellowing his ground "With showres and frosts, with love & aw." In "The Showre," Vaughan's speaker prays for a shower to soften the earth of his hard heart and hopes that "(Some such showres past,) / My God would give a Sun-shine after raine," and in "The Sap" the speaker finds himself straining to heaven for dew. Taylor's speaker also sees himself as God's garden, as a lily seeking "sweet Spice Showers of Precious grace," as a branch requiring dew from Christ the well of living waters.[69] A related emblem personalizes God's role as gardener by presenting a single plant set out carefully among others in a garden, watered from above by an urn held in a disembodied hand and refreshed as well by the sun and wind: Wither's motto is "*Poco a Poco*" [Figure 3] and Peacham's is derived from 1 Corinthians 3:6, "*Qui Plantavi irrigabo.*" We may think especially of the sun and wind directed to the carefully tended flowers in Vaughan's "Regeneration," and of the passage in Taylor's *God's Determinations* presenting the elect as a knot of flowers growing and flowering at different rates as God's showers fall upon them.[70]

Most important of all these images of cultivation is that which shows a bed of flowers scorched by the sun of affliction (on one side of the plate) and then revived by the rain of God's favor and grace on the other: Wither's motto is "*Post Tentationem Consolatio*" [Figure 4]. Mannich uses the image of wheat growing forth from the heart, and the motto "*Post Tristia Laeta Vicissim.*"[71] Herbert's "The Flower" develops a similar emblematic program: the speaker is the flower experiencing the return of spring showers after winter frosts, querying in surprise, "Who would have thought my shrivel'd heart / Could have recover'd greennesse?" and hardly believing "That I am he / On whom thy tempests fell all night." Vaughan's "Unprofitablenes" shows the speaker recently subjected to "snarling" blasts and "Cold showres" but now revived by dew and sun; "Mount of Olives[II]" presents him as formerly bleak and bare and tempest-tossed but now enjoying soft dews and sun: "My wither'd leafs again look green and flourish."

Similarly, Vaughan's "Affliction" and "Love, and Discipline" defend the alternation of tempests and dews as a means to disperse "weeds, and thistles" and to produce continuous fruition: "So thrive I best, 'twixt joyes, and tears, / And all the year have some grean Ears."[72]

Another emblem of cultivation is that of pruning or training a vine or tree to control or enhance its growth. Montenay portrays a husband-man pruning a grapevine by cutting away the dead branches; Heyns transfers the motif to the training of the branches of a young tree, with reference to the education of children; Peacham presents a tree with branches lopped off, signifying needful pruning. Perhaps most striking of all is Hulsius' tree from which the hand of God holding a pruning knife is lopping branches, interpreting John 15:1-2, "I am the true vine, and my Father is the husbandman. / Every branch in me that beareth not fruit, hee taketh away: and every branch that beareth fruit, he purgeth it, that it may bring foorth more fruit" [Figure 5].[73] Edward Taylor may recall some version of this emblem when he presents himself so graphically as a branch of the true vine and begs for fruit, "Lest fruitless I suffer thy prooning Hook."[74] But the most remarkable poetic embodiment of it is Herbert's "Paradise," in which letters are lopped off from the poem's rhyming words in each succeeding line, in emblem-like representation of God's pruning, to produce in the speaker better fruit:

> I blesse thee, Lord, because I G R O W
>   Among thy trees, which in a R O W
> To thee both fruit and order O W.
> . . . . . . . . . . . . . . .
>
> When thou dost greater judgements S P A R E,
> And with thy knife but prune and P A R E,
> Ev'n fruitfull trees more fruitfull A R E.
>
> Such sharpnes shows the sweetest F R E N D:
> Such cuttings rather heal then R E N D:
> And such beginnings touch their E N D.

The primary emblematic resources for Donne were abstract, *imprese*-like figures with fixed, conventional symbolic meaning, which Donne characteristically utilized and extended in significant structural as well as thematic ways. This emblematic habit of mind extended to his life as well as his poetry, and continued throughout his life. His Latin poem to George Herbert, "With my Seal, of the Anchor and Christ," refers to his choice of a new seal after his ordination, which Isaak Walton describes as follows: "He caused to be drawn a figure of the

Body of Christ extended upon an Anchor, like those which Painters draw when they would present us with the picture of Christ crucified on the Cross: his, varying no otherwise then to affix him to an Anchor (the Emblem of hope)."[75] According to Donne's poem, his former "sheafe of snakes" seal (interpreted symbolically as the nature shed in baptism like a snakeskin), has been replaced by a new seal depicting the cross gained in baptism and now extended at his ordination into an anchor of hope. But also, the new seal (with typological reference to Christ as brazen serpent) redeems the old, and the two may now be used in conjunction to represent the crucifying of nature in him. We find the cross alone, the cross with the brazen serpent twined about it, and the anchor with cross-shaped handle (defined as an emblem of the hope deriving from our salvation through Christ's cross) among Paradin's *Devises*, a collection which may well have aided Donne in the selection of his own device and its interpretation.[76] Walton reports that shortly before his death Donne sent a number of these anchor-seals, made of heliotrope stones and set in gold, to his friends to use as seals or rings in memory of him.[77]

An even more remarkable manifestation of this emblematic imagination is Donne's making of a *memento mori*—a death's-head or rather death's-body—out of himself in his own shroud. Walton describes its preparation:

> He brought with him into that place [the study] his winding-sheet in his hand; and having put off all his cloaths, had this sheet put on him, and so tyed with knots at his head and feet, and his hands so placed, as dead bodies are usually fitted to be shrowded and put into the grave. Upon this *Urn* he thus stood with his eyes shut, and with so much of the sheet turned aside as might shew his lean, pale, and death-like face; which was purposely turned toward the East, from whence he expected the second coming of his and our Saviour. . . . When the picture was fully finished, he caused it to be set by his bed-side, where it continued, and became his hourly object till his death.[78]

This portrait—as a bust with a motto affixed—was prefaced to the first publication of *Deaths Duell*, presenting an emblem of hope in death through Christ's grace. The motto is, "*Corporis haec Animae sit Syndon, Syndon Jesu*"[79]—a prayer that his own white shroud might typify the white shroud (Christ's shroud) covering his sinful soul. Donne's last action was thus to make of himself in his burial weeds an emblem for his own and others' contemplation.

Donne has used conventional emblems centrally in a few poems.

"The Crosse" might almost stand as an emblem poem beneath a fascinating plate in Justus Lipsius' *De Cruce*, representing emblematically a variety of "crosses" in nature [Figure 6]. Though Donne's enumeration of such natural crosses is accompanied by his usual witty pyrotechnics, he describes most of the same figures—a globe with meridians crossing parallels, the mast of a ship, a bird flying with outstretched wings, a man swimming, a man praying with arms in cruciform shape.[80] In quite another way, the circle as emblem of God and eternity—defined as such by Valeriano and Beza—is introduced in Donne's "Upon the Annunciation and Passion" to suggest the similarity of God and man: "of them both a circle embleme is."[81] The circle has also more fundamental structural significance for this poem, in that the coincidence of these feasts upon the same day serves as emblem of the perfect circularity and unity of the Christian vision. In the "Hymne to Christ," written upon the occasion of Donne's voyage to Germany as chaplain to Doncaster's diplomatic mission, he adapts the conventional ship-tempest emblem to his own situation as he interprets allegorically the tempests and storms awaiting his passage: "In what torne ship soever I embarke, / That ship shall be my embleme of thy Arke." Hulsius has an emblem plate of a ship on a tempest-tossed sea (likened in the accompanying poem to the Ark) exemplifying the Psalm text 107:23, 28: "They that goe downe to the sea in shippes, that doe businesse in great waters: / . . . They cry unto the LORD in their trouble: and hee bringeth them out of their distresses."[82] And, as has been indicated, the wreath emblem is even more directly at the center, structurally and thematically, of the "La Corona" sonnets.

Some other emblems are less central, but yet illuminate particular lines in Donne. One example is Valeriano's presentation, in sequence, of the lamb and the ram as emblems, respectively, of *Mansuetudo* and *Ferocitas*—Christ's mercy and innocence, and Christ's cross as our redemption; these figures explicate Donne's apostrophe (in "La Corona"), "O strong Ramme, which hast batter'd heaven for mee, / Mild lambe, which with thy blood, hast mark'd the path."[83] Another example is Montenay's emblem of the heart drawn like iron to heaven by a huge adamantine rock (*"Non tuis Viribus"*) which seems directly recalled in a line from one of Donne's "Holy Sonnets": "And thou like Adamant draw mine iron heart" [Figure 7].[84] Interestingly enough, Donne's "Holy Sonnet XIV" has close affinities with some of Cramer's emblems, indicating (since the respective dates of the works put influence out of the question) a common emblematic way of visualizing biblical metaphor:

> Batter my heart, three person'd God; for, you
> As yet but knocke, breathe, shine, and seeke to mend;
> That I may rise, and stand, o'erthrow mee, 'and bend
> Your force, to breake, blowe, burn and make me new.
>
> (ll. 1-4)

We recall Cramer's first emblem of God's hand with a hammer, striking a flintlike heart on a stone ("*Mollesco*"), and his fourth emblem ("*Amo*") of the heart in a bonfire, itself in flames and with the wind blowing on it vigorously; also Mannich's emblem of God's hand working a bellows, fanning the flames of the heart.[85]

Herbert's use of the emblem tradition is more extensive and more profound than that of the other poets here studied. For one thing, several of his poems develop in terms of the significances conventionally attached to certain emblematic figures. The emblematic beasts in the short allegory, "Humilitie," have the respective properties that were assigned in Valeriano and Camerarius to the peacock (pride), the lion (ire), the hare (fear), and the turkey (jealousy).[86] In the poem "Hope," as Rosalie Colie has noted,[87] the gifts exchanged between the speaker and the personified Hope derive their meaning from established emblematic significances. The speaker gives his watch (time), and receives in return an anchor (hope); he then gives an old prayer-book (his long-continued devotion) and receives an "optick" glass (with which to see, like Anima, heaven afar off). He responds with a "viall full of tears" (his repentance), and is given a few "green eares" (recalling the Camerarius plate, often reprinted, of a few ears of wheat sprouting from skeletal bones).[88] Disappointed, he then breaks off the exchanges with the "Loyterer" Hope, declaring "I did expect a ring"—the emblem of the accomplished wedding with the Bridegroom. The point, which the reader should infer by interpreting the emblems better than the speaker, is that the business of Hope is with expectation, not fruition: the speaker must patiently wait to receive his ring hereafter. More generally, as we have seen, several of Herbert's poems use the husbandry metaphor, drawing upon various emblematic visualizations of God as gardener and man as plant or tree in his garden.

Some poems—"The Church-floore," "Jesu," "Love-joy," "The Bunch of Grapes," "The Pulley"—by reason of their description and explication of a central visual image sometimes not mentioned by name, are highly sophisticated and artful versions of the kind of poem we might find accompanying a visual emblem in a moral or sacred emblem book. Several other poems ("The Altar," "Paradise," "Easter-wings," "Deniall") are themselves complete emblems—or in Joseph Summers' term, hieroglyphs[89]—for they not only develop a verbal argument but also present a visual embodiment for that theme in the shape and structure of the poem itself.

Finally, Herbert's entire collection of religious lyrics, "The Church," invites analysis as a kind of "heart book." The governing biblical metaphor, the temple in the heart of man, is perhaps given clearest expression in the poem "Sion," which contrasts the glory of Solomon's temple, "Where most things were of purest gold; / The wood was all embellished / With flowers and carvings, mysticall and rare" to its New Testament antitype in the Christian heart: "now thy Architecture meets with sinne; / For all thy frame and fabrick is within. / There thou art struggling with a peevish heart." The most suggestive emblematic visualization of this metaphor in Herbert is Zacharias Heyns' plate showing the risen Christ inhabiting a large heart, behind which the Old Testament Temple is shown: the motto is *Templum Christi cor hominis*," interpreting 1 Corinthians 3:16 [Figure 8].[90] Like the Christ of the Heyns' plate, the Divine Friend Herbert sometimes addresses as occupant of his heart is always conceived as adult and mature, not a childlike Divine Love playing with a child-Anima, and this governing conception controls the way in which several Herbert poems use but also modify emblematic imagery reminiscent of van Haeften or the *Vis Amoris*.

Making the appropriate substitutions, we can recognize affinities between the complaint of the speaker in "The Sinner" that his heart contains "quarries of pil'd vanities" and the van Haeften plate in which vanities of all sorts are blown out of Anima's heart by a bellows [Figure 9].[91] In "The Familie" the speaker envisions Christ resident in the heart but disturbed by "loud complaints and puling fears." In "Decay" he finds that Christ immures himself "In some one corner of a feeble heart: / Where yet both Sinne and Satan, thy old foes, / Do pinch and straiten thee"—recalling plates in the *Vis Amoris* in which the Christ-child with a lantern searches out the dark corners of the heart, finding beasts and vipers all about, and in the following emblem sweeps them out with a broom.[92] The speaker's plea in "Whitsunday," imploring the Dove to "spread thy golden wings in me; / Hatching my tender heart," recalls the van Haeften plate of the Dove with wings outspread in Anima's heart ("*Cordis Inhabitatio*").[93]

There are emblematic analogues also for Herbert's "Easter," which identifies the three elements requisite to the creation of true praise as the heart, the lute attuned to Christ's cross, and the Spirit; two emblems from the *Vis Amoris* present the Christ-child singing from a song-book and then playing upon a harp within the heart, with the Dove hovering above [Figure 10].[94]

But the discrete emblems of Cramer, Wither, and Mannich afford nearer and more numerous analogues. The opening lines of "The Altar" recall several such plates:

> A broken ALTAR, Lord, thy servant reares,
> Made of a heart, and cemented with teares:
>   Whose parts are as thy hand did frame;
>   No workmans tool hath touch'd the same.
>       A   HEART   alone
>       Is   such   a   stone,
>       As   nothing   but
>       Thy pow'r doth cut.
>
>                     (ll. 1-8)

These lines allude to Psalm 51:17, "The sacrifices of God are a broken spirit: a broken and a contrite heart, O God, thou wilt not despise," even as does the plate and motto of Wither's emblem of the burning heart resting upon an altar; we think also of Cramer's plate "*Mollesco*" in which God's hammer strikes and shapes a hard heart on an altar-like stone [Figure 11].[95] The opening lines of Herbert's poem "JESU"— "JESU is in my heart, his sacred name / Is deeply carved there"— conform closely to Cramer's emblem of the hand of God stretching forth from a cloud, carving the name JESU upon a heart resting upon a book [Figure 12].[96] Herbert's witty sonnet "Redemption"—in which the speaker in the role of tenant seeks to have his old lease replaced by a new one and discovers this already accomplished by the crucified Christ—might almost serve as emblem poem for Cramer's plate "*Absolvor*," which shows the hand of God with a stylus crossing out the writing on a scroll nailed to a cross. The emblem interprets the metaphor in Colossians 2:14 of Christ "blotting out the handwriting of ordinances, that was against us . . . nayling it to his Crosse" [Figure 13]. Mannich has a similar plate showing a scroll written in Hebrew letters and hung about with symbols of Jewish worship, indicating that it is the Old Law being expunged by the brush in God's hand.[97]

Several poetic images of God's "arrows" of affliction shot into the heart—the speaker's prayer in "Longing" that God will "Pluck out thy dart" and his portrait of God in "Discipline" as a "man of warre" with a bow, who "can shoot, / And can hit from farre" recall Cramer's emblem of God's hand with a bow, shooting arrows from heaven, several of which are transfixed in the heart ("*Vulneror*," Psalm 38:3).[98]

In another vein, Herbert's "An Offering" catechises the heart as to its purity and wholeness, advising it to search for "a balsome, or indeed a bloud, / Dropping from heav'n, which dóth both cleanse and close / All sorts of wounds." Cramer has two *"Sanor"* emblems relating to this imagery: in one of them a heart cloven by a sword receives balm poured out from an urn by God's hand; in the other, God's hand from above squeezes wine-blood from a bunch of grapes over a heart pierced by arrows [Figure 14].[99]

Easily the most emblem-like of Herbert's heart poems is "Love unknown." Because there is some interplay between the speaker and the divine power in relation to the heart, we are led at first to think of some of van Haeften's plates presentiñg Anima and Divine Love in somewhat similar situations.[100] But the tone is very different: Herbert's speaker does not cooperate actively in what happens to his heart but is surprised and shocked by the treatment it receives, not from a childlike Divine Love but from a lord whose actions seem bizarre and strange. We are in the world of the discrete heart emblems again, with God's hands acting powerfully and arbitrarily upon the heart. The speaker first reports that he offered the lord his heart in a dish of fruit, but the lord's servant cast it into a font where it was bathed with blood from a rock; the friend interprets, *"Your heart was foul, I fear"* (l. 18). Montenay has an emblem of a man offering his heart toward heaven in a dish, and God's arm pouring liquid (Christ's blood) over it from a vase—with the motto, *"Beati Mundo Cor."* Herbert's speaker then recounts seeing a huge furnace labeled "AFFLICTION" and offering sacrifice from his fold to the lord who owns it, but the lord threw his heart into the furnace; the friend declares, *"Your heart was hard, I fear"* (l. 37). For this scene a near analogue is Cramer's *"Probor"* showing God's two hands out of the clouds shoveling a heart into the door of an open furnace [Figure 15]. Finally the speaker records that his bed has turned into a bed of thorns (pricking thoughts) and the friend observes, *"Your heart was dull, I fear"* (l. 56). Analogues are Mannich's heart encased within piercing thorns while the divine arm extends the cross above, and Cramer's plate of the heart pierced by thorns yet sprouting flowers, indicating that the heart is rather aided than hindered in its fruition by tribulation.[101]

Henry Vaughan indicated his concern with emblematics in the title emblem prefaced to the 1650 edition of his book of religious lyrics, *Silex Scintillans*. The figure shows the speaker's heart as a flint from which God's weaponry (lightning bolts) strikes fire; the accompanying Latin emblem poem describes the heart so attacked as flashing spiritual and poetic fire—the poems themselves being flashes struck off from that

flint. The emblem is clearly in the tradition of the Protestant heart em-
blems, in which God's disembodied hands act powerfully on the heart.
In the same tradition, Cramer's scales emblem—the heart weighed
against the Tables of the Law in a balance held in God's hands [Figure
16]—comments upon an image in Vaughan's "Regeneration," in which
the speaker's "late paines" in climbing Sinai are weighed against
"smoake, and pleasures" and found too light.[102] Similarly, the speaker's
desire for the engraving of the Holy Scriptures in his heart—"O that
I had deep Cut in my hard heart / Each line in thee!"—recalls van
Haeften's figure of Divine Love inscribing the Tables of the Law in
the heart held by Anima.[103] But the heart metaphor with its emblematic
representations is not central to *Silex Scintillans*, and Vaughan showed
his awareness of that fact by dropping the prefatory emblem and poem
in the completed 1655 edition. Without this distraction it is easier to
perceive that Vaughan's poetry is indebted to the emblem tradition
primarily for emblematic representations of the creatures.

Such emblematic representations and their conventional interpreta-
tions—from the repositories of abstract emblems of the creatures in
Valeriano, Camerarius, Cats, Peacham, and others—contribute signifi-
cantly to passages and entire poems. The emblem of the marigold fol-
lowing the sun signifies aspiration to heavenly things in Camerarius, in
Wither, and in Paradin, where it is designated as the device of Margue-
rite of Navarre; in Hulsius and Heyns it presents our response to Christ
as Light of the World and our imitation of Christ [Figure 17].[104]
Vaughan's poem, "Sure, there's a tye of Bodyes!" reverses this emblem,
complaining that man is "such a Marygold . . . / That shuts, and hangs
the head." But some of the flower-souls in his "Regeneration"—"broad
eyed / And taking in the Ray"—are like the marigold in responding to
the light of God.[105] The emblematic silkworm shedding its cocoon,
which is the central figure of Vaughan's "Resurrection and Immortal-
ity," is reminiscent of Cats' final image of the butterfly emerging from
its cocoon, with the motto, "Ecce! Nova Omnia" [Figure 18].[106]

Several of Vaughan's numerous creature meditations—on the handi-
work of man as well as of God—could be seen as complex and sophisti-
cated versions of emblem poems, "blind" emblems, analyzing the title-
figure. "The Lampe" is such a poem: the speaker finds that the lamp
shining in darkness surpasses him in their common duty of shining
virtuously before men—a reversal of Quarles' emblem figure of the
candle hidden in a dark lantern, but yet an embodiment of its motto
drawn from Matthew 5:16, "Let your light so shine that men [see] . . .
your good workes." The poem concludes by contrasting the lamp's
extinction when its oil is consumed with the escape of the human flame

to heaven at life's end; this is the burden also of Farley's last plate, and the implication of Quarles' long series of candle-human life emblems in *Hieroglyphikes*.[107] "The Palm-tree" is also an emblem poem, likening the speaker to the emblem-figure. Originating with Alciati and often republished, the figure portrays the palm tree pressed down by a board but flourishing all the more as it thrusts against the pressure; Alciati's motto is *"Obdurandum adversus Urgentia"* while Wither interprets the figure as signifying patient endurance.[108] Other poems, ostensibly treating scenes or objects in nature, explore those objects as emblems from which didactic lessons are to be derived, or symbolic meanings infused by God are to be understood. Such poems—"The Bird," "The Timber," "The Rain-bow," "The Water-fall"—are creature meditations with strong affinities to the emblem poem. In other poems a familiar nature emblem may have contributed to the thematic development. Vaughan's meditation on the root enduring through the winter to flower again in the spring ("I walkt the other day") finds a suggestive analogue in Camerarius' emblem, reproduced in Paradin, of a few ears of wheat shedding seeds into the earth among skeletal bones, with the motto, *"Spes altera Vitae"* [Figure 19].[109]

Some of Vaughan's poems also call upon emblematic traditions in the elaboration of biblical metaphor: as we have seen, the husbandry metaphor as visualized in several emblems is primary among these. In another vein is "The World," a meditation on John 2:16-17. Opposing to eternity the full range of transitory worldly goods ("The lust of the flesh, the lust of the eys, and the pride of life") the speaker interprets that text in terms of four very clearly delineated icons. These are devised emblem-fashion on the model of several plates in Quarles, Ripa, Peacham and others.[110] Eternity is a "great *Ring* of pure and endless light" (conflating the rainbow with the wedding ring of Christ's spouse). The three lusts are, respectively, "the doting Lover" with his lute, his gloves, his love-knots, and his gaze fixed upon a flower; the "darksome States-man hung with weights and woe"; and the "fearfull miser on a heap of rust," hugging his gold.

The emblem tradition impinges in much more limited ways upon Traherne, and we can seldom point to a particular emblem as a close analogue to a poem or a passage. To be sure, Wither's presentation of Ganymede on his eagle as the soul desiring God—"Take wing, my *Soule*, and mount up higher; / For, Earth, fulfills not my *Desire*"— closely resembles Traherne's interpretation of the Ganymede figure in "Love," one of his very rare uses of classical myth.[111] In "Misapprehension," Traherne evokes a familiar emblem in the lines, "The World set in Man's Heart . . . / It doth entire in me appear / As well as I in it," but he reverses the usual *significatio*. Heyns portrays the globe inside the heart as an emblem of the radical corruption of the heart by original sin, but Traherne glories in his possession of it as his spiritual treasure and delight.[112] Most important, however, are several eye emblems which provide a basis for the speaker's view of himself as a disembodied "Infant-ey." Saltmarsh's several plates present an eye with beams shining from or into it, raised steadily to heaven. Horapollo has a figure in which a large eye floats alone, disembodied, above the landscape, and Wither presents a heart with an eye at its center as an emblem of vision focused on heavenly things [Figure 20].[113] Traherne's speaker views his infant self as "a Living Endless Ey"; "An Infant-Ey / Abov the Sky," an eye whose spherical contours relate it to and enable it to reflect and thereby encompass those other globes, the world and the universe. Traherne's eye-self is a unique creation, but one element in the definition is emblematic: the speaker is a "Sphere of Light," a "Living Orb of Sight," able to encompass God himself—"The hev'nly Ey, / Much wider than the Sky, / Wherin they All included were."[114]

More generally, several of the Anima-Divine Love emblems seem to explicate and give substance to the child-self speaker in Traherne. The playful qualities of these figures in Veen, and the serenity of the Hugo-Arwaker plate in which Divine Love and Anima go forth into the fields hand in hand as shepherd and shepherdess [Figure 21] illuminate Traherne's remarkable view of infant innocence: "He in our Childhood with us walks, / And with our Thoughts Mysteriously He talks."[115] In generic terms, Traherne has three especially interesting poems which combine the emblem with the occasional meditation upon a specific providential experience. These poems—"Shadows in the Water," "On Leaping over the Moon," and an untitled third—turn a remembered childhood episode into an emblem which is visualized and described in sharp detail and then "read" by the mature speaker for its spiritual significance, in accordance with the usual method of the emblem poem.

Edward Taylor is more self-consciously and overtly emblematic than the other poets here studied. One reason for this is that he considers many biblical metaphors and types, as well as certain objects in nature, to be emblems not only in their substance and significance but in their very form. God has made them emblems, in that their spiritual significance is conveyed by various visual details of physical appearance and circumstances. A passage in the *Christographia* (the title itself indicates that the fourteen sermons so labeled will present an engraving or portrait of Christ)[116] goes far to illuminate such thinking, identifying several metaphors from Canticles 5 as emblems:

And should I here introduce that Allegorical Song made of him [Christ] by Solomon Can. 5, wherein the Severall parts of his Body are Set out by rich, and weighty Metaphors, that cannot bee well understood of anything so fitly, as to emblemize the eminency of the Operations of those [parts] . . . As that of his Head, v. 11, its said to be as most fine Gold, as a note of the Surpassing excellency of Counsills, and Determinations.[117]

In his *Preparatory Meditations* Taylor identifies several "real" and ceremonial types as emblems. The poems which make these identifications are not structured precisely as emblem poems, but they do describe the objects with the visual detail and in the analytic manner characteristic of such poems, and they also articulate the *significatio*. The rainbow is a type of Christ's mediatorship and it is also an emblem of that office, visually displaying it: "Thy Mediatoriall glory [is] in the shine / . . . Emblemiz'd in Noahs pollisht shrine" (II.3, ll. 8-10). The burnt offerings of heifers and doves, used for sin offerings in the Old Testament and thereby types of Christ's sacrifice, are also (calcined and added to water for washing) emblems of spiritual cleansing: "They Emblemize the Fountain Spring / Thy Blood, my Lord, set ope to wash off Sin" (II.26, ll. 23-24). And yet again, the manna, type of the Eucharist, is in the physical circumstances of its delivery an emblem of the way Christ is conveyed (by types) in his word:

> This Bread came down from heaven in a Dew
>   In which it bedded was, untill the Sun
> Remoov'd its Cover lid: and did it shew
>   Disht dayly food, while fourty years do run.
>   For Isr'ls Camp to feast upon their fill
>   Thy Emblem, Lord, in print by perfect Skill.
>
> Thou in thy word as in a bed of Dewes
>   Like Manna on thy Camp dost fall and light
> Hid Manna, till the Sun Shine bright removes
>   The Rug, and doth display its beauty bright
>   Like pearly Bdellium White and Cleare to set
>   The Sight, and Appetite the same to get.
>                                        (II.60[A], ll. 13-24)

The nut garden (Cant. 6:11) offers various kinds of nuts "as meate, and med'cine, emblems choice / Of Spirituall Food, and Physike" (II.63, ll. 43-44). The vine which produced the wine of Canticles 1.2 "Did Emblemize thy selfe the True Vine" (II.98, l. 9). Christ as lily, residing in the lowly valley "doth Emblemize / Thy Fitness for the Mediatoriall Guise" (II.160).

Figure 1   Hugo, *Pia Desideria*

Figure 2   Hugo, *Pia Desideria*

Figure 3   Wither, *Emblemes*

Figure 4   Wither, *Emblèmes*          Figure 5   Hulsius, *Emblemata Sacra*

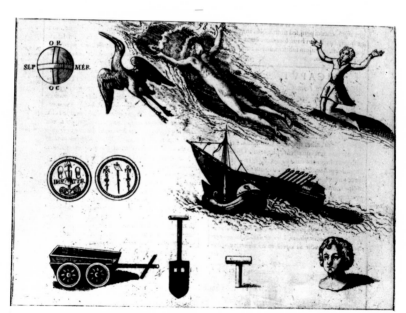

Figure 6   Lipsius, *De Cruce*

Figure 7    Montenay, *Emblemes, ou Devises Chrestiennes*

Figure 8    Heyns, *Emblemes Chrestienes*

**CORDIS VANITAS.**

Qui minoratur CORDE, cogitat inania.

Ambitio follis, vento distendit honorum

Figure 9   van Haeften, *Schola Cordis*

Pulsa chordas, sonet chelys,    Dulce melos intonabunt,
Dum nos recreas de cælis    Nouum nobis excitabunt
IESV cordis gaudium;    Angeli tripudium.

Io. Gallo incud.    C. de Mallery sculp.

Figure 10   Messager, *Vis Amoris*

E M B L E M A  I.

Nunquid non verba mea, funt quaſi malleus conte-
rens petram?

*Ierem.* 23.29.

Iſt mein Wort nicht wie ein Hammer der Felſen zer-
ſchmeiſt?

Cor mihi ſaxoſum eſt, mollit me malleus, ictus
Suſtineo: quid tum, dummodo ſim melior?

B

E M B L E M A  XXIII.

Ille vocabit in nomine Iacob, & hic ſcribet manu ſua
Domino.

*Eſa.* 44.5.

Jener wird genennet werden mit dem Namen Jacob.
Und dieſer wird ſich mit ſeiner Hand dem HErren
zuſchreiben.

Annumeror Chriſto, cui ſum de nomine notus,
Rubrica is vitæ eſt penna liberque meæ.

G 5　　PRO.

Figure 11　Cramer, *Emblemata Sacra*

Figure 12　Cramer, *Emblemata Sacra*

### EMBLEMA XXI.

Chriſtus donavit vobis omnia delicta , delens quod
aduerſus nos erat chirographum decreti, quod erat
contrarium nobis.

*Coloſſ. 2. 14.*

Chriſtus hat vns geſchenckt alle Sünde / vnd außgetilget
die Handſchrifft ſo wider vns war.

*Scripta ſuit dica magna mihi : Crux aurea Chriſti
Sola ſatiſfecit , ſola ſatiſfaciet.*

G          NON

### EMBLEMA XLI.

Erunt ubera tua ſicut botri vineæ, & odor oris tui ſicu
odor malorum.

*Cant. 7. 8.*

Laß deine Brüſte ſeyn wie Trauben am Weinſtock / vnn
deiner Naſen Ruch wie Epffel.

*Lædit me modicè , medicè me curat, ita uvæ
Sunt mihi ſtillantes ubera, Chriſte, tuæ.*

M          ALTA

Figure 13   Cramer, *Emblemata Sacra*          Figure 14   Cramer, *Emblemata Sacra*

EMBLEMA XXIV.
Elegi te in camino paupertatis.
*Efa.* 48.10.
Jch wil dich außerwehlet machen im Ofen des Elendes.

Figure 15   Cramer, *Emblemata Sacra*

---

EMBLEMA XVIII.
Scimus quia lex est spiritualis, ego autem carnalis sum.
*Rom.* 7. 14.
Wir wissen daß das Gesetz Geistlich ist / ich bin aber fleisch-
lich.

Figure 16   Cramer, *Emblemata Sacra*

LI.

Claud.

*Asperius nihil est humili, cum surgit in altum.*

Seneca.

*Fortuna nimis quem fovit, stultum facit.*

O KINDER-

Figure 18  Cats, *Silenus Alcibiadis*

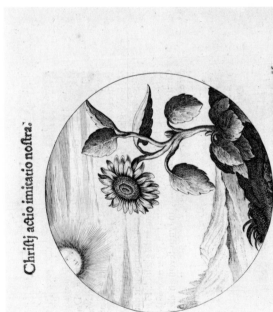

Christi actio imitatio nostra.

Ick ben het licht der werelt, die my navolgt
sal in duysternisse niet wandelen : Maer sal
het licht des levens hebben.

*Jesus la lumiere du monde : qui me suit, il ne che-*
*minera point en tenebres, ains il aura la lumiere de*
*vie.*

Ioh. 8,12.

D 2                De

Figure 17  Heyns, *Emblemes Chrestiennes*

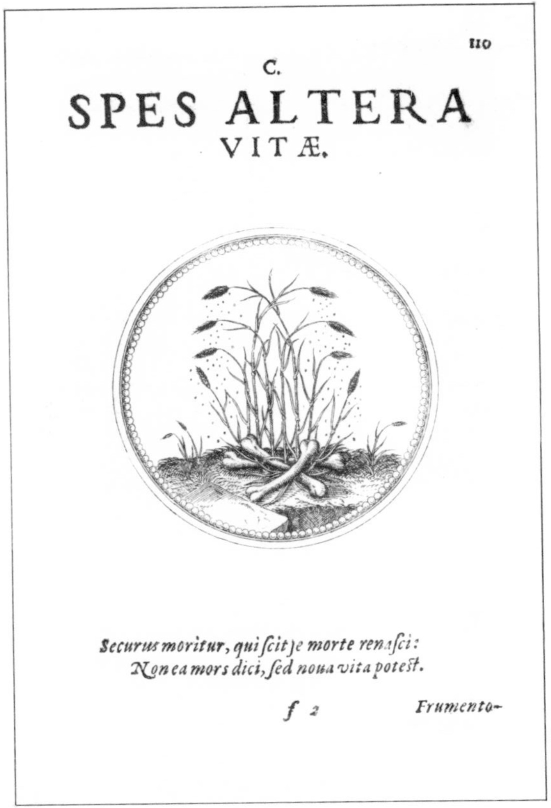

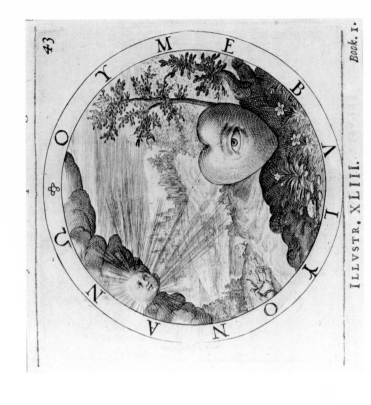

110
C.
SPES ALTERA
VITÆ.
Securus moritur, qui ſcit ſe morte renaſci:
Non ea mors dici, ſed noua vita poteſt.
f 2
Frumento-

Figure 19 Camerarius, *Centuriae*

43
ILLVSTR. XLIII.
Book. I.

Figure 20 Wither, *Emblemes*

Come my Beloved, let us go
forth into the Fields, let
us lodge in the Villages
Cant. 7. 11.          P. 108.

Figure 21    Arwaker, *Divine Addresses*

CORDIS EMOLLITIC
Deus molliuit COR meum

COR, marmor: glaciale, Deus, ceu cera, liqu
Vrere cum tuus hoc cœperit ignis ar.

Figure 22    van Haeften, *Schola Cordis*

My Beloved is mine, and I am his;
he feedeth among the Lillies
Cant. 2. 16.

P. 164.

Figure 23    Arwaker, *Divine Addresses*

Bring my Soul out of prison, that I may
praise thy name. Psal. 142. 9.

P. 204.

Figure 24    Arwaker, *Divine Addresses*

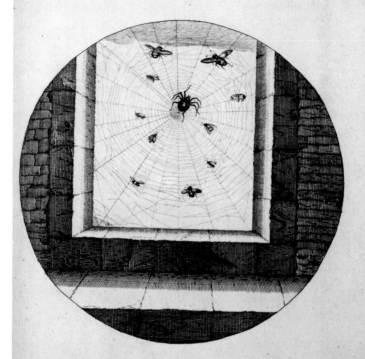

Senec. Agamem.

Corpora morbis | Placet in vulnus
Maiora patent, | Maxima cervix.
Et dum in paſtus | Modicis rebus
Armenta vagos | Longius ævum eſt.
Vilia currunt,

Seneca de Tranq.

Qvi multa agit ſæpe fortunæ poteſta-
tem ſui facit, cogendæ in arctum
res ſunt, vt tela in vanum cadant. An-
guſtanda ſunt patrimonia noſtra, vt mi-
nus ad injurias fortunæ ſimus expoſiti.
Magna armamenta pandentibus multa
ingruant neceſſe eſt.

L　　　　　　　　　　　Wt de

Figure 25　Cats, *Silenus Alcibiadis*

In Taylor's Canticles series (II.115-153) on Canticles 5:10-7:6, most of the poems approach more or less closely to the genre of the emblem poem as they comment upon a series of images and conceits describing the Bridegroom and Bride which Taylor clearly understood to be emblems: The Bridegroom's head of fine gold (Cant. 5:11) is associated with the sun and interpreted as "a Bright Emblem of bright Majesty" (II.118, l. 12). The Bridegroom's hands as golden "Orbs . . . filld with Berill" (Cant. 5:14) provide an "emblem of the Sphere of Grace" (II.122, l. 38). In Canticles 6:7, the Bride's blushing humility, her "Spirituall Beauty [is] . . . Emblemized by the Pomegranate" (II.140, ll. 25-26). The Bride's navel as a round goblet and her belly as a heap of wheat (Cant. 7:2), as they contain or produce water and bread, are "Emblems of Sanctifying Grace most high" (II.149, l. 33).[118] Moreover, Taylor's Canticles series incorporates several passages reminiscent of the Anima-Divine Love sequences. Veen's emblem of Divine Love shedding beams of light from his eyes and face into the breast of Anima is recalled in II.97 (ll. 13-24), as the speaker finds the "ardent flames" from the "Sun-Shine Face" of the Bridegroom necessary to enliven him. Van Haeften's emblem of the flames from Divine Love melting Anima's heart to water-drops [Figure 22] seems suggested in II.119 (ll. 2, 28), in which the Lord's "fiery Eye" fetches "My Heart and Love to thee in Hottest Steams."[119] Taylor's several poems exploiting the Canticles imagery of the soul as garden, and the soul finding Love's arms "Circle thyself about" are reminiscent of the Hugo-Arwaker figure showing Divine Love and Anima seated in a garden crowning each other with coronets of flowers and embracing [Figure 23].[120] Moreover, the playfulness of Taylor's conception of the Bridegroom playing "Bow-peep" with the soul (II.96, l. 50) recalls Hugo's plate of Divine Love hiding and peering out behind a curtain while Anima searches for him.[121]

Numerous other images from Taylor immediately recall emblem plates very familiar in the tradition: The death's-head "With White bare butter Teeth, bare staring bones, / With Empty Eyeholes, Ghostly Lookes" (I.34, ll. 26-27) recalls plates in Wither and Peacham, as well as, of course, images carved on gravestones.[122] The bird-soul "put in / This Wicker Cage (my Corps) to tweedle praise" (I.8, ll. 7-8) recalls the caged bird in Cats' sequences as well as the winged Anima-figure locked in a bird-cage, begging Divine Love for release [Figure 24].[123] The candle held up to the sun ("Lord ting my Candle at thy Burning Rayes," I.16, l. 29) calls to mind emblems of God or Christ lighting an extinguished candle.[124] The speaker as marigold half-frozen when the sun goes down (II.3) recalls the range of plates identified above.[125] The "poore pinnace" sailing through a tempest-tossed sea, guided by

Christ the pole star (II.114, ll. 31-40), has an analogue in Montenay's figure of a man on a ship amid dark and tempestuous seas with God's hand holding forth a lighted candle.[126] Taylor's tropes for the vicious heart—"Dunghill Pit," "Nest of Vipers," "Hive of Hornets," playground for pride and passion—as well as his pleas to Christ to cleanse and cure the heart, recall the van Haeften-Harvey plates showing streams of vanities and follies shooting out of Anima's heart, or the *Vis Amoris* plate in which the Christ-child sweeps vipers and beasts out of the heart with a broom.[127] The heart as sacrifice offered on an altar (II.82) has its analogue in Wither's image of the flaming heart offered on an altar to God; and the heart as harp (II.54; II.102, l. 41; "The Experience") recall the van Haeften-Harvey plates showing Divine Love playing the harp within Anima's heart, or the Christ-child strumming on the harp in the heart in the *Vis Amoris*.[128]

Finally, Taylor has devised several emblem poems of more highly developed formal interest. An early excursus of this kind was his elaborately contrived emblematic and acrostic exercise sent as a love-declaration to his wife-to-be.[129] But the high point of his emblematics occurs in a few occasional poems which present, and comment with conciseness upon, an emblem from the creatures. The famous poem "Upon a Spider Catching a Fly" has a close emblem analogue in Cats' figure of the spider web in which flies peacefully submit to capture but hornets violently tear the web [Figure 25]; in the sacred series the web represents the bonds of the world and the devil, and the motto is *"Pervia Virtuti sed Vilibus Invia,"* permeable to the virtuous but impassible to the vicious.[130] Taylor draws the same significance from the behavior of fly and wasp: though hell's spider spins webs of sin for us, Christ's grace enables some to break the cords. "Huswifery" appears to be without immediate emblem source, but it is conceived and superbly executed in the emblem manner, interpreting two figures, a spinning wheel and a loom, as a complex emblem of regeneration and sanctification—the weaving of the "wedden garment."

The sacred emblem books clearly offered a rich resource to the major seventeenth-century religious lyric poets, who were writing even as this small kind flourished most vigorously. Herbert made the most creative use of these materials, Taylor the most prolific—but Taylor often employed them with the directness and rigidity that betokens the exhaustion of a literary mode. The poets drew upon this resource variously—for imagery, for genre, for ways of visualizing and portraying the Bible and the natural world. More especially, Protestant formulations of emblem theory and Protestant varieties of sacred emblem books contributed significantly to the poetics shaping the dominant strain of religious lyric poetry in seventeenth-century England.

# Art and the Sacred Subject: Sermon Theory, Biblical Personae, and Protestant Poetics

George Herbert was the most articulate of the major seventeenth-century religious poets on the issue of what kind of "art" may be used in presenting religious subject matter, but the question was of obvious importance to other devotional poets as well. Though the poets I am considering here are often assumed to belong to the same "Metaphysical" school, it is clear that their poetic responses to this central question are very different—ranging from the witty and audacious wordplay of Donne, to the disclaimers of art paradoxically associated with elaborately crafted verses in Herbert, to the constant use of biblical epigraphs in Vaughan, to the virtual absence of tropes in Traherne, to the striking colloquial metaphors in Taylor. We can get some insight into the assumptions behind these various poetic stances by examining the contemporary disputes among English Protestants over the uses of art and learning in the framing of sermons and prayers, for in such disputes the theoretical problems attendant upon giving human and public form to matter understood to be sacred in nature were explored at greater length than anywhere else. The issue, constantly addressed in arts of preaching and allied materials, is central to the evolving Protestant poetics which, I am suggesting, links these otherwise very different poets whose religious lyrics span the century.

A related issue engaged by the developing Protestant poetics was that of how the poet can find his own stance and his own poetic voice while treating divinely inspired materials. As we have seen, discussions of the genre, language, and symbolism of scripture intimate and often directly affirm that the biblical poems are the best models for the religious poet, and Protestant meditative theory and Protestant emblematics also directed the poet to biblical sources and materials. But the religious lyric poet must finally consider how to use these models—what attitudes he can take toward his subject, what artistic shaping he can provide, how he is to relate his own poetic voice to the other 'inspired" voices resounding through his materials. One context for considering these questions is provided by the theory which had evolved as to how the experiences, conceptions, and artistry of the biblical poets themselves could find expression in an inspired text. Another is afforded by the example of some predecessors and contemporaries whose lyrics are closely allied to, but finally transcend, biblical paraphrase or imitation; such poems must consider the relation of the biblical poet's persona and voice to that of his modern "imitator," and of the divine voice to both.

## A. Protestant Sermon Theory: Rhetorical Art and Divine Truth

Despite the sermon's obvious differences in form and hortatory mode from the religious lyric poem (which more often adopts the prayer stances—petition, praise, thanksgiving), arguments concerning the relationship of art and truth in the sermon shed considerable light on the poetics of the religious lyric. The religious lyric in general shares with the sermon the problem of rendering divine matter in human terms, and often shares as well a didactic purpose. Moreover, several of the most impressive religious lyrics of the period take as their theme the problems involved in their creation. These poems have an especially close affinity to the *ars praedicandi* and other materials on sermon theory and practice, where analogous questions are explored.

The several studies now available on the contemporary English Protestant sermon indicate that the distinctions in theory and practice are by no means a simple matter of Anglican and Puritan—a witty, ornate, learned, and allusive Anglican style filled with metaphysical conceits, elaborate wordplay, and quotations in foreign tongues, contrasted with an unadorned, unallusive, dialectical Puritan "plain" style. For one thing, Protestant preachers of all persuasions were committed to the careful exposition of scripture in their sermons and, as we have seen, most understood that text to be poetic in many parts, laden with schemes, tropes, and other poetic and rhetorical devices.[1] For another, as the studies of W. F. Mitchell, J. W. Blench, and Horton Davies have shown, the varieties of sermon structures and styles cannot be neatly matched to ecclesiastical parties.[2]

It is possible, however, to identify certain dominant and characteristic stylistic habits or traits with particular seventeenth-century theological postures, as Abraham Wright, a seventeenth-century observer, does in his *Five Sermons, in Five Several Styles.*[3] Of these, the first two are actual sermons typical of their preachers, and the last three are quite believable parodies of recognizable sermon practice. All are artful, though in different ways. The sermon by Lancelot Andrewes displays his word-by-word analysis of the scripture text, his wordplays upon it (often in Latin), his jerkiness and Senecan pointedness of phrase, his metaphysical conceits. Bishop Joseph Hall's sermon illustrates his striking use of biblical and colloquial metaphors, his dramatic scene-painting, his numerous citations of the classics, and his direct and flowing prose. The sermon written in the manner of Thomas Cartwright and Jasper Mayne presents an elaborate treatment of Canticles 2:2 ("As the Lillie among the thorns; so is my love among the daughters") both as a picture and as a similitude: it makes occasional use of authorities and Latin phrases but has much more recourse to colloquial and metaphorical speech. The sermon in the manner of the Presbyterians displays their highly complex scholastic divisions and subdivisions of the text into doctrines, reasons, and uses, with numerous points and subclassifications under each head; their logical, undecorated style; and their habit of persistent scripture quotations. The fifth sermon, in the Independent vein, is a much more personal, colloquial, emotional exhortation to the audience, laced with scripture quotations and with scripture phrases assimilated into the speaker's own language.

From the vantage point of the Restoration, the characteristic "artfulness" of all these modes was denounced by the Anglican establishment preachers as contrary to the norms of a simple, plain style.[4] The metaphysical mode came under attack for punning and quibbling, and for extravagant conceits.[5] The Presbyterian scholastic manner was criticized for its intricate Ramistical divisions and subdivisions and its exclusive concern with "speculative and notional things."[6] The habit of elaborating upon scripture metaphors, common to very many Puritans and Anglicans, was decried as a trifling with Gospel duties and precepts "by childish Metaphors and Allegories."[7] And the biblical diction of the sectaries was scorned as a "whimsical Cant of *Issues, Products, Tendencies, Breathings, Indwellings, Rollings, Recumbencies*, and Scriptures misapplyed."[8] Interestingly enough, after the Restoration it is the Nonconformists who spring to the defense of metaphor, in scripture and in sermons, as the Spirit's way of accommodating theological abstractions to simple understandings. Very evidently, plainness or simplicity is in the ear of the listener, and we need to examine contemporary theoretical statements which seem to set up strict dichotomies between artfulness and simplicity in presenting sacred matter very carefully to understand their precise import, and to estimate their relevance for the Christian poet.

The general issues in the dispute may all be identified in Augustine, whose writings stood (after the Bible itself) as a primary point of reference for all parties. One issue, which reverberated through subsequent debates regarding church ornament, church music, and sermon style, is that of the role of the senses in the service of God. In the *Confessions* Augustine admitted his inability to decide conclusively whether the singing of Psalms—which he found very pleasurable—is a distraction to the senses or a help to devotion.[9] Quoting Augustine on this point Calvin resolved the issue in favor of singing so long as proper priorities are observed: the praises must spring from the heart rather than the voice only, and the melody must be designed to reinforce the text rather than to please the senses.[10] A more fundamental issue, also raised by Augustine, concerns the extent to which preaching or prayer derives from an internal condition of soul which is the work of God's grace, and so beyond considerations of art and method. In his *De Doctrina Christiana* Augustine argues that the primary essential for the preacher must be the true understanding of scripture, which depends upon "charity, 'from a pure heart, and a good conscience, and an unfeigned faith' "—the work of grace in the soul and not of art.[11] Similarly, Calvin in commenting upon Psalm 51:17 ascribed to God rather than to David both the matter of the praise and the purity of heart necessary to produce it.[12] And indeed Protestants generally agreed that worthy sermons and prayers must spring from inner illumination by the Spirit, and from the experience of grace and redemption: whatever the role of art, the artist and his matter must first be formed by God.

But the chief issue concerns the unique character of the sacred matter, and the implications of this for use of the rhetoricians' art. Augustine's *De Doctrina*, which was the starting point for discussion of sermon theory, method, and style throughout the sixteenth and seventeenth centuries, takes a profoundly paradoxical position on this issue. On the one hand, Augustine appears to discredit rhetoric as irrelevant to the presentation of divine matters. The first three of the four books of the *De Doctrina* are concerned not with the rhetorical topics of invention and disposition of matter but with the proper understanding of the scriptures, for this wisdom is the one essential for the preacher: "For one who wishes to speak wisely, therefore, even though he cannot speak eloquently, it is above all necessary to remember the words of Scripture."[13] The true understanding of scripture is not available to the analyses of the grammarians, or logicians, or rhetoricians, though Augustine pays considerable attention to their methods: it attends interpretation directed by the rule of charity—a theological virtue dependent upon grace.[14] Accordingly, when Augustine finally takes up, in the fourth book, such traditional rhetorical questions as how preachers should use the three rhetorical styles (high, middle, and low), he concludes that this matter cannot be referred to any traditional

notion of decorum in suiting style to matter, since everything in the
Christian revelation is of supreme importance and worth.[15]

Mazzeo concludes from all this that Augustine's argument leads
finally to a "rhetoric of silence" wherein the Christian realizes the
uselessness of speech and action and stands silent before the intuition of
Divine truth; and Fish argues the more extreme proposition that the
*De Doctrina* is itself written in such a way as to disabuse the preacher
of confidence in human rhetoric or art, in that it subverts the forms of
art and argument in order to enact the utter dependence upon God
which is the burden of its argument.[16] But this sharp dichotomy be-
tween rhetorical art and divine truth overstates the case, for there is
another element in the Augustinian paradox. Augustine declares that
the preacher, though he may not seek eloquence for its own sake or
seek primarily to please an audience, may and should study rhetoric,
for it would be foolish to hold that "if teachers are made learned by
the Holy Spirit they do not need to be taught by men what they
should say or how they should say it."[17] Moreover, the preacher may
use rhetoric to various purposes in his sermons, notably to teach and
to persuade, and he will use the three styles, or a mixture of them, in
accordance with the needs and nature of his audience.[18] But beyond
all this, the preacher is to be saturated with the words of scripture, and
Augustine finds that text (as he did not in his youth) to be the very
epitome of eloquence—eloquence not deliberately sought but con-
joined with wisdom and truth as an inseparable adjunct. He says of
the biblical writers:

> Not only can nothing seem to me more wise than they are, but also
> nothing can seem more eloquent. . . . There is a kind of eloquence
> fitting for men most worthy of the highest authority and clearly
> inspired by God. Our authors speak with eloquence of this kind, nor
> does any other kind become them. . . . Such things are said that the
> words with which they are said seem not to have been sought by the
> speaker but to have been joined to the things spoken about as if
> spontaneously, like wisdom coming from her house (that is, from the
> breast of the wise man) followed by eloquence as if she were an
> inseparable servant who was not called.[19]

He refers the preacher to the perfect conjunction of wisdom and elo-
quence in the "plain" sermons of the Apostle Paul, and also in the more
figured and ornamented sermons of the prophets, whose words
"poured forth from the divine mind both wisely and eloquently."[20]
Rather than eschewing eloquence and rhetorical art, Augustine seems
rather to expect that, although they are not of the essence of the

preacher's calling, they will in the happiest circumstances accompany the presentation of scriptural truth. Yet the ultimate source of Christian eloquence, even as of Christian wisdom, is God himself, inspiring his human instruments directly and through his Word.

The ambiguity about rhetoric apparent in Augustine characterized many of the Renaissance and seventeenth-century *artes concionandi* influential for Protestant sermon theory. Some of these, notably Erasmus, Melancthon, Hyperius of Marburg, and Bartholomaeus Keckermann,[21] assume the relevance and importance of classical rhetoric to many aspects of the sermon. Accordingly, they assert that the sermon, like the oration, is to move and persuade as well as teach; that the sermon can properly be analyzed in terms of the classical divisions of rhetorical art (invention, disposition, exornation or ornament, pronunciation, and memory); that the sermon has virtually the same parts as a classical oration (exordium, narration, division or proposition, confirmation, confutation, peroration); and that the classical categories of orations—judicial, demonstrative, deliberative—are at least partly valid for sermons. Nevertheless, in discussing the element of invention these theorists had to accommodate the uniqueness of the preacher's subject. They did this most often by means of a discourse on the proper interpretation of scripture, since the preacher's role is not to invent or find matter from the places of logic or rhetoric, but to interpret matter divinely given. This understanding also forced the recognition that sermons do not precisely fit the classical categories. Melancthon repudiated the demonstrative category for preachers, and substituted the didactic sermon for the judicial oration.[22] Hyperius, citing Saint Paul, the prophets, and Christ himself as the great exemplars for the Christian preacher, looked to the various uses of scripture to determine "both what and howe many kindes of divine Sermons there bee"; citing 2 Timothy 3:16, he identified five kinds of sermons—those pertaining to doctrine, to redargution (reproving false belief and error), to correction of vice, to instruction, and to consolation.[23] Keckermann asserted still more vigorously the special character of the sermon, whose categories he defined by the various kinds of scripture texts which might be chosen—didactic, practical (persuading to a good life), or mixed.[24]

The other kind of *ars praedicandi*, especially important for the Puritans, broke much more sharply with the old rhetoric, developing instead a method based directly upon the preacher's special subject matter and role. Seminal for its development was William Perkins' *Arte of Prophecying*, the title itself indicating the association of the preacher's role with that of the prophet rather than the orator: "every

Prophet is partly the voyce of God, to wit, in preaching: and partly the voyce of the people, in the act of praying."[25] This is not, however, a theory of inspiration, but an "Arte" directed almost wholly to the proper interpretation and presentation of the Word of God contained in scripture. Perkins' summary of his method is also a summary of the parts of the sermon:

1. To reade the Text distinctly out of the Canonicall Scriptures.
2. To give the sense and understanding of it being read, by the Scripture it selfe.
3. To collect a few and profitable points of doctrine out of the naturall sense.
4. To apply (if he have the gift) the doctrines rightly collected, to the life and manners of men, in a simple and plaine speech.[26]

The method outlined by Perkins was the basis—with some variation— of subsequent Puritan manuals for preachers: The Westminster Assembly's *Directory for Public Worship* sets forth the basic elements of this system; Richard Bernard's *The Faithfull Shepherd* adopts it but recommends softening its rigors by rhetoric so as to move the congregation more forcefully; William Chappell exaggerates the method so as to make the sermon virtually a Ramist exercise in the logical analysis of a text. John Wilkins' *Ecclesiastes* makes substantial accommodations with the old rhetoric, but still recommends the method of doctrine and use as "that which our gravest Divines by long experience have found most useful."[27]

The issues Augustine had treated with such complexity, concerning the place of divine inspiration, personal holiness, human rhetoric, intrinsic divine eloquence, and biblical stylistic example in the Christian sermon, were discussed endlessly in these sixteenth- and seventeenth-century manuals and in other comments about preaching. It will be useful now to discriminate some characteristic positions regarding style, ornament, and the uses of secular arts and learning in preaching, since these matters bear directly upon the conjunction of divine truth and human art. One common ground is immediately evident: English Protestants of all parties appealed even more directly and centrally than had Augustine to Biblical texture and style as the model for, or at least as a determinant of, the preacher's appropriate art. This appeal does not lead to artlessness or to the abnegation of art in the presentation of sacred subject matter, but rather to the development of an art whose precepts may be derived, and whose stylistic features may be imitated, from the scriptures.

One classic Anglican position on sermon style, which is of little direct importance to the emerging poetics we are tracing because of its broad inclusiveness, defends learning and the arts as *ancillae theologiae*, the handmaidens of theology which may have large scope in presenting sacred subject matter so long as they do not, like Hagar, encroach upon the rights of their mistress, Sarah. This position— supported by biblical references to the Israelites robbing the Egyptians' treasures to adorn God's temple (Exod. 3:22), to Paul's citation of secular writers and poets in his Epistles (Acts 17:23, Titus 1:12) and to the tradition that Moses was learned in all the wisdom of the Egyptians (Acts 7:22)—justified preaching adorned with any amount or kind of learning, art, wit, and eloquence the preacher is capable of, so long only as it is consonant with scripture and does not displace or replace the centrality of its message. Egeon Askew, writing from this viewpoint, argues that the modern preacher may if he wishes go well beyond Paul's example in the matter of eloquence: "A Minister may lawfully, yea must necessarily . . . preach more eloquently than *Paule*, that his eloquence like a cryer or perswader, may allure auditors to the simplicitie of the Gospell."[28]

A second and more interesting theoretical position is that occupied by Donne—unquestionably the most eloquent of the seventeenth-century preachers and usually assimilated to the witty, metaphysical, rhetorical school of Lancelot Andrewes and Thomas Playfere. But Donne's practice differs in important respects from theirs,[29] and his theoretical position is markedly different, for he has little to say about the *ancillae theologiae* as a justification for artful preaching. Instead, he constantly turns to the scripture itself as the epitome of eloquence, and proposes it to the preacher's imitation as the model and sanction for his most exquisite art. This theory, with its interesting ramifications for religious poetry, is as firmly grounded upon the Bible as that of many Puritans, but Donne's conception of "imitation" of the Bible's poetic and rhetorical mode admits of a very creative relationship to that model. Donne formulates very clearly the difference between the world's rhetoric and Christ's as he comments on the simplicity of Christ's language in calling Peter and Andrew (Matt. 4:18-20): "Here . . . there was none of this fire, none of this practise, none of this battery of eloquence, none of this verball violence."[30] Again, though he justifies the use of human traditions and secular ornament in strict moderation, "in som *Auditories*, acquainted with such learnings," yet he warns of abuse: "If your curiosity extort more then convenient ornament, in delivery of the word of God, you may have a good *Oration*, a good *Panegyrique*, a good *Encomiastique*, but not so good a *Sermon*."[31] He expects, though, high art and learning in the matter and style of the sermon: the preacher "shall not present the messages of God rudely, barbarously, extemporally; but with such meditation and preparation as appertains to so great an imployment, from such a King as God, to such a State as his Church."[32] Donne is able to fuse the biblical emphasis with this expectation of art precisely because he takes the scriptures to be the most witty and most eloquent of texts, providing models for the preacher in their art as well as their truth. The Holy Spirit is the perfect rhetorician: "The Holy Ghost is an eloquent Author, a vehement, and an abundant Author, but yet not luxuriant; he is far from a penurious, but as far from a superfluous style too."[33] And the Bible exhibits "not onely the *powerfulnesse* of the matter, but the *sweetnesse* and elegancy" of a perfect piece of rhetoric.[34]

This biblical eloquence is the preacher's proper model: he may and should imitate the Holy Spirit in his flights:

> Religious preaching is a grave exercise, but not a sordid, not a barbarous, not a negligent. There are not so eloquent books in the world, as the Scriptures. . . . Whatsoever hath justly delighted any man in any mans writings, is exceeded in the Scriptures. The style of the Scriptures is a diligent, and an artificial style; and a great part thereof in a musical, in a metrical, in a measured composition, in verse. . . . So the Holy Ghost hath spoken in those Instruments, whom he chose for the penning of the Scriptures, and so he would in those whom he sends for the preaching thereof. . . . Then are we *Musicum carmen in modo*, musick to the soul, in the manner of our preaching, when in delivering points of Divinity we content our selves with that language, and that phrase of speech, which the Holy Ghost hath expressed himself in, in the Scriptures.[35]

That the same standard—the imitation of the eloquence of the Spirit —obtains in the framing of prayer and personal devotion (and presumably in devotional poems) is made evident in Donne's *Devotions upon Emergent Occasions*:

> My *God*, my *God*, Thou art a *direct God*, may I not say a *literall God*. . . . But thou art also . . . a *figurative*, a *metaphoricall God* too: A *God* in whose words there is such a height of *figures*, such *voyages*, such *peregrinations* to fetch remote and precious *metaphors*, such *extentions*, such *spreadings*, such *Curtaines* of *Allegories*, such *third Heavens* of *Hyperboles*, so *harmonious eloquutions* . . . as all *prophane Authors*, seeme of the seed of the *Serpent*, that *creepes*; thou art the *dove*, that *flies*. . . . This hath occasioned thine ancient *servants*, whose delight it was to write after thy *Copie*, to proceede in the same way

in their *expositions* of the *Scriptures*, and in their composing both of *publike liturgies*, and of *private prayers* to thee, to make their access to thee in such a kind of *language*, as thou wast pleased to speake to them, in a *figurative*, in a *Metaphoricall language*; in which manner I am bold to call.[36]

The third and most common position was occupied by a large number of moderate Anglicans and Puritans. Without rejecting modest and circumspect use of secular learning and rhetoric, these men insisted that scripture should provide the preacher's primary model and standard, and, like Donne, they took the scriptures to be unsurpassed in eloquence and power to move and persuade. However, unlike Donne, they found the scripture style characterized not by witty and eloquent figures but by much simpler and more direct rhetorical strategies conveying its powerful message to audiences of all kinds and capacities. It is this graceful style and forceful rhetoric that the preacher ought to adopt, looking especially to the Pauline model of simple but extremely powerful and moving sermon rhetoric, a rhetoric which, as Andrew Willet declared, "useth not any affected eloquence, or elegant style, or entising speach," but which yet is not "base or barbarous," and which "by a pithie and sententious kind of writings, full of arguements, and forcible perswasions, in grave but plaine words, delivreth high mysteries."[37]

George Herbert also articulates this position in his *Priest to the Temple*. Insisting that the country parson for whom he principally writes should be "not witty, or learned, or eloquent, but Holy," he urges the parson to exhibit this holiness in his sermons, through a rhetoric taught by scripture itself. He is to choose "moving and ravishing texts, whereof the Scriptures are full"; he is to imitate the prophets in "turning often, and making many Apostrophes to God"; he is to imitate Saint Paul in "frequent wishes of the peoples good, and joying therein"; and especially for a rural congregation he is to follow scripture precedent in using similes and illustrations drawn from homely things—"a plough, a hatchet, a bushell, leaven, boyes piping and dancing."[38] Daniel Featley, Calvinist, chaplain to the Archbishop of Canterbury (George Abbott) and also a member of the Westminster Assembly, delivered from this centrist position a remarkable stylistic critique of contemporary practice in the framing of prayers. Taking David's Psalms and Paul's Epistles as models, he denounces witty and affected prayers full of wordplay and puns in (we think immediately) the manner of Donne's *Divine Poems*; and he denounces equally those who affect utter plainness:

It would make a prophane man laugh, but a Religious man weepe, to listen and marke how sometimes they court Almightie God with idle complements; sometimes they cast up Prayers with strong lines to heaven, as it were (by force) to pull down a blessing from thence; sometimes they expostulate with *God* in a sawcie, and sometimes pose him in a ridiculous manner. . . . He . . . well deserveth blame who prayeth to *God* that hee may . . . come unto *God*, not *with the soales of his feet, but the feet of his soule*: who layeth open before *God* his . . . *sinnes of an higher straine and deeper staine*; . . . Give me leave to tel these men in their owne language that this is *playing*, not *Praying*; and that in sending up such prayers they burne not *Incense* to *God*, but *incense* him rather. . . . There are a sort of men in direct opposition to these, who affect a kinde of *Rhetoricke* which weedeth out all flowers of *Rhetoricke*. . . . Coursnes to them is strength; dulnes gravity; drinesse judgement; leannesse health: and pack-staffe plainnes . . . *Gospell*. . . . These men in all other things like well of art and wit, where the matter is vile, and base; but in the delivery of heavenly conceptions, utterly abandon them. But they should have considered better, that sharpnesse of wit, and true eloquence are gifts of *God*, and therefore best of all to bee employed in holy things.[39]

Robert Cawdrey, a Nonconformist deprived of his living in 1590, provides a characteristic formulation of this centrist position from the Puritan side. His massive handbook of scripture similies points to the similies and parables of the Bible as teaching the most profitable strategy for preachers:

Christ in whome are hidden all the treasures of wisedome and knowledge . . . spake nothing to the companies of common people, without Parables (which are a kind of Similies). . . . Therefore a Similie is most fit for a Preacher, because it reasoneth from things confessed, and very manifestly, and wonderfully layeth the matter even before the eyes. So that the use of a Similie reacheth very farre: for it is used for ornament, for delight, for plainnesse, & for gravitie.[40]

This emphasis on simile and parable characterizes the Puritan centrists throughout the period. After the Restoration the Nonconformist Robert Ferguson, answering the demands of the new establishment Anglicans for an easy, rational plainness in sermons, developed the implications of this position in great detail in his essay, "Of the Import and Use of Scripture-Metaphors."[41] He also made explicit the paradox inherent in this position—that the highly metaphorical style of scripture is its specific, divinely ordained means to plainness and clarity (and delight) which the preacher should imitate:

> Among other Rhetorical *Tropes* to be found in the Bible, I hardly know any, of which we have more examples than of Metaphors, in which God by similitudes borrowed from known and obvious things, intimates to us the usefullest and sublimest Truths: In such kind of phrases he condescends to lisp those Mysteries to us which would never be so well understood by any other way of expressing them. . . .

> Logical and Metaphysicall Terms are of all others, the most inept to declare them in; nor are there any so accommodated to display and unveil them, as Metaphorical expressions . . . to illustrate them by things sensible and of ocular knowledg.

> The mysteries of Faith require a Rhetorick proper and peculiar to themselves; And as it is only from the Scripture that we can be supplyed with Glorious Images and excellent Idea's of the things themselves which we treat of, so it alone can best furnish us with all Ornaments of Speech and Eloquence as well to beautify as declare them. . . .

> God by his unfolding himself and his Mind to us in several kinds of Metaphorical Terms, hath not only allowed, but sanctified our Use of the like.[42]

Ferguson notes that the Bible sanctions even homely comparisons, and therefore "what some men brand for *Kitchin Metaphors* and *Rascal Similitudes* are cleanly enough."[43] It is worth observing that we have now come full circle from Augustine, who understood the figurative language of scripture not as a means to clarify or accommodate the unutterable divine wisdom, but as a means of forcing the mind beyond human formulations.

A fourth position, occupied by stricter Puritans, called for great plainness in the sermon, since the power of God's word in scripture cannot be enhanced but only hampered by the use of the rhetorical arts. William Perkins' theory, set forth in his classic *Arte of Prophecying* and in several tracts and commentaries, calls for the sermon to be at once plain and marvelously graphic in portraying Christian truth: it "must be plaine, perspicuous, and evident, as if the doctrine were pictured, and painted out before the eyes of men. . . . It is a by-word among us: *It was a very plaine Sermon*. And I say againe, *the plainer*, *the better*."[44] Yet Perkins and his party also believed that the Bible is a most eloquent and often highly figurative text, requiring all the humane arts and sciences for its proper interpretation, and especially the arts of grammar, logic, and rhetoric. Accordingly, Perkins makes a sharp distinction between the preparation of the sermon, which ought to be attended by all such arts, and its presentation, which ought to eschew them all, grounding his argument upon the *locus classicus* for the whole debate, Paul's renunciation of human eloquence before the Corinthians (1 Cor. 2:1-5):

> *Humane wisedome* must be concealed, whether it be in the matter of the sermon, or in the setting forth of the words: because the preaching of the word is the *Testimony of God, and the profession of the knowledge of Christ*, and not of humane skill: and againe, because the hearers ought not to ascribe their faith to the gifts of men, but to the power of Gods word. 1 Cor. 2.1 *When I came unto you brethren, I came not with the eminency of eloquence or of wisdome, declaring unto you the testimonie of God. 2. For I did not decree to know any thing among you but Jesus Christ, and him crucified. 5. That your faith should not consist in the wisedome of men, but in the power of God.*
>
> If any man thinke that by this means barbarisme should be brought into pulpits; hee must understand that the Minister may, yea and must privately use at his libertie the arts, Philosophy, and variety of reading, whilest he is in framing his sermon: but he ought in publike to conceale all these from the people, and not to make the least ostentation. *Artis etiam est celare artem; it is also a point of Art to conceale Art.* . . . Wherefore neither the words of arts, nor Greeke and Latine phrases and quirkes must be intermingled in the sermon. . . . Here also the telling of tales, and all profane and ridiculous speeches must bee omitted.[45]

However, Perkins expects that such plain preaching, concerned to display God's Word unadorned, would achieve the most powerfully moving effect upon the hearers because of the power resident in the Word itself. The preacher becomes the vehicle for that power precisely *as* he avoids any display of rhetoric. This argument Perkins develops from that other important *locus classicus* on preaching, 1 Peter 4:11: "If any man speake, let him speake as the words of God." To do so is to speak "in such a *plainenesse*, and yet such a *powerfulnesse*, as that the capacities of the simplest, may perceive, not man, but God teaching them in that *plainenesse*, and the conscience of the mightiest may feele, not man, but God reprooving them in that *powerfulnes* . . . that he saith, *Certainely God speakes in this man*."[46] According to this theory the preacher is not to imitate scripture rhetoric, as some said, but is rather by his plainness to release the powerful rhetorical effects of the scripture.

The radical sectarian position represented, for example, by William Dell[47] need scarcely concern us here, as its premises involve entire reliance upon the Spirit's illumination in preaching, and thereby lead to the total renunciation of any concern with art and artfulness. But the other prominent theories hold in considerable tension the divine and human activities involved in presenting sacred matter, and point moreover to the scripture as the primary resource for the preacher's art as well as his truth. Such theories promoted a large range of possibilities for the art of the sermon—and, by extension, for the poetics of the religious lyric.

In his *Divine Poems* Donne is concerned with the problem of art and the sacred subject, and with the devotional poet's proper stance, but he does not address such questions directly and he is not very anxious about them. His anxiety is reserved for the more critical matter of his own radical sinfulness and peril of damnation. He usually seems to take for granted the sincerity of his poetic praises—indeed he can affirm that "La Corona" is the product of "my muses white sincerity" (l. 6). Yet he admits a tendency to false or excessive artifice: the speaker of "Holy Sonnet XIX" confesses that on some days, "In prayers, and flattering speaches I court God" (l. 10). And the speaker of "A Litanie" recognizes the possibility of misusing the scripture standard and scripture model: he asks the poets of the Bible to pray "That I by them excuse not my excesse / In seeking secrets, or Poët- iquenesse" (ll. 71-72). Though the danger of misuse is recognized, in general it seems clear that just such a biblical standard authorizes the high flights of wit and poetic exuberance in Donne's theory of divine poetry. His concept, so frequently expressed in the sermons and the *Devotions*, of the soaring wit and surpassing eloquence of the scripture, evidently sanctions for him the intellectual pyrotechnics and witty word-play of his hymns and occasional poems, and the bold conceits of the "Holy Sonnets"—as when the speaker of "Holy Sonnet XIV" so startlingly transforms the biblical metaphor of Christ the bridegroom of the soul into Christ the rapist of the soul. Donne's sermons and *Devotions* contributed to the development of contemporary Protestant theory about the rhetoric and poetics of scripture; though his poems address such issues obliquely, and apparently forgo overt imitation or use of biblical subject matter and language, yet they do imitate what Donne identified as the essence of the biblical style—its wit, exuberance, and soaring eloquence.

In Herbert's poetry, the issue of whether art is appropriate to divine praises, and if so, what kind of art, is central. His position is by no means simple, but it is not contradictory, nor does it abrogate art or the human responsibility, especially the poet's responsibility, to render fit praises. Poem after poem recognizes that the poet's praises (like the preacher's sermon) must emanate from a renewed heart and must be in some sense God's work and not his own: God hews the stony altar of the heart and fits the stones for praise; God must tune the poet's breast as an instrument of praise, must mend him, and must relieve his griefs and miseries before he can praise; God must indeed complete his praises when he cannot.[48] And the poet-speaker must relinquish any claim to his praises as his own work, even as he must to any other spiritual accomplishment.[49]

But this recognition of the divine action in creating the spiritual conditions necessary for praises, and thereby the praises themselves, does not solve the problem of art for the poet any more than did the analogous commonplace for the preacher. In "Jordan (I)" Herbert, like those who renounced human arts in sermons as inappropriate to sacred matter, renounces many of the ornaments of secular poetry— "fictions and false hair"; stock pastoral imagery, riddling allegory. Instead he announces a new ideal of plainness—not as conceived by Perkins but akin to that centrist Protestant recognition of scripture as the model for art as well as truth, always assuming that biblical art is decorous and moving rather than witty and exuberant. To the question posed in "Jordan (I)," "Is there in truth no beautie?" the clearly expected answer is, "Yes, of course there is, they are inextricably linked" —even as Augustine thought. Moreover, the final couplet states explicitly that the new plainness does not mean loss of "rime" (poetic excellence): "Nor let them punish me with losse of rime, / Who plainly say, *My God, My King*"—proving the point by the poem's own fineness and fitness and rhyme. The echo of Psalm 145:1 in the final line (and other such echoes throughout the poems) evokes the standard of biblical eloquence to define the new plainness. "Jordan (II)" clarifies the position. The poet recalls his earlier poetic strategies in which his thoughts "began to burnish, sprout, and swell, / Curling with metaphors a plain intention," and by which he wove himself into the sense. A Friend recommends a new strategy: "*There is in love a sweetnesse readie penn'd*: / Copie out onely that, and save expense"—indicating that God's art (already penned in the scripture, in his heart) is the proper model to be copied, and that it affords its own poetic sweets.

Stanley Fish to the contrary, this plainness is not a renunciation of art but an affirmation of its divine source and its biblical standard. "Easter," a Christian reworking of Psalm 57:7-11, makes the point yet clearer in the role designed for the poetic lute—to "struggle for thy part / With all thy art" (ll. 7-8). Later, without contradiction or backsliding Herbert can affirm, "Wherefore with my utmost art / I will sing thee," in "Praise (II)"; he can indicate his delight in the English language for such marvelous religious puns as that on Son-sun ("The Sonne"); and he can create a wreath of intricate praise to God while praying for the simplicity of life which would enable him to offer a better "crown" ("A Wreath"). Only in the poem "The Forerunners" must he relinquish, reluctantly, his "lovely enchanting language" and baptized metaphors because they will soon be lost by his death. But here the psalm phrase he adopts as his own—*"Thou art [still] my God"* (Psalm 31:14)—testifies that he will lose nothing essential by this inevitable loss, since in death he will retain his abiding relationship to God, the source of beauty and art as well as of truth.

Vaughan approached the issue of art and the sacred subject by relating himself directly to the tradition of Herbert and of biblical poetry; his preface to the complete edition of *Silex Scintillans* (1655) denounces lewd and vain secular verse and praises Herbert as the fountainhead of a new vein of religious poetry, surpassing all his followers because he wrote from deep experiential piety.[50] Though Vaughan's poems seldom treat at length the problem of how to write religious verse, they often affirm that God's grace must enable the speaker to experience the appropriate spiritual emotions (joy, comfort, repentance) so that he may produce his verses. The point is most clearly made in "Anguish," which begins with the psalm tag Herbert uses to conclude "Jordan (I)"— "My God and King"; Vaughan's prayer is for the "art" of true repentance as the prerequisite to the so-difficult "art" of writing true verses:

> O! 'tis an easie thing
>    To write and sing;
> But to write true, unfeigned verse
> Is very hard! O God, disperse
> These weights, and give my spirit leave
> To act as well as to conceive!
>
> (ll. 13-18)

Vaughan proclaims in "H. Scriptures" that he would have the Bible be the standard for his art: "O that I had deep Cut in my hard heart / Each line in thee! Then would I plead in groans / Of my Lords pen-

ning, and by sweetest Art / Return upon himself the *Law*, and *Stones*"
(ll. 9-12). In practice, Vaughan's poems reveal a more direct use of
and appropriation of scripture materials than Herbert's—in terms of
subjects, imagery, use of biblical landscapes, choice of the Mount of
Olives as his Parnassus, and especially in the use of scriptural quota-
tions as headnotes and codas casting new metaphoric significance upon
so many of his poems. In this, Vaughan displays some affinities with those
who would have scripture speak directly in its own terms. His poetic
strategy permits such passages to cast their own light upon his verses,
extending and reinterpreting human art by the divine art.

Traherne's theory of religious lyric enunciates a standard of plain-
ness which is, surprisingly enough, analogous in some ways to that
urged by Perkins, though I do not suggest direct influence. In fact,
Traherne's theory has affinities with both Neoplatonic and stricter
Protestant conceptions of the relation of art to truth, but in the final
analysis it is uniquely his own. Moreover, he applies his standard of
plainness not only to poetic treatments of the sacred matter of scrip-
ture, but also to the whole of God's created universe. For Traherne,
the divine truth shining through God's creatures and God's words
renders them so glorious that they need only to be displayed and seen;
poetic ornament will only mar their splendor. Traherne's prefatory
poem from the manuscript of the *Poems of Felicity* explains the as-
sumptions of this poetics. He offers to present the "naked Truth," in a
"Simple Light, transparent Words, a Strain / That lowly creeps, yet
maketh Mountains plain, / Brings down the highest Mysteries to
sense."[51] The opposition is clearly drawn between the shoddy gilding
and "shadows" of poetic ornament and the true glory of the things
themselves which God has created:

> No curling Metaphors that gild the Sence,
> No Pictures here, nor painted Eloquence;
> No florid Streams of Superficial Gems,
> But real Crowns and Thrones and Diadems!
>
> . . . . . . . . . . . . . . . . .
>
> An easy Stile drawn from a native vein,
> A clearer Stream than that which Poets feign,
> Whose bottom may, how deep so'ere, be seen,
> Is that which I think fit to win Esteem.
>
> (ll. 11-20)

Similarly, in "The Person" he expounds the glories of the unadorned
body in terms that clearly transfer to poetry. Promising to "Glorify
by taking all away," he declares, "The Naked Things / Are most Sub-

lime, and Brightest shew, / When they alone are seen: / . . . When we all Metaphores remove, / For Metaphores conceal, / And only Vapours prove" (ll. 16-26). His poetry endeavors to accomplish this by a style which chiefly names and apostrophizes the various objects of praise, using images and evocative words and relinquishing, though of course not completely, explicit metaphors and tropes. There is strong suggestion in the *Centuries* and the *Thanksgivings* that he found a precedent for this style in the Psalms.[52]

Edward Taylor's position on the issue of art and the sacred subject falls within the large parameters of the centrist position, though his closest affinities are perhaps with Nonconformists such as Robert Ferguson who viewed the art of scripture chiefly in terms of metaphors and tropes and who urged a metaphorical style for the presentation of sacred subject matter. There is, however, one important difference: Taylor found the scripture tropes to be wonderfully magnificent (not, as Ferguson suggested, a device for making divine truth more plain), and he viewed his own metaphors as necessarily humble and inept by contrast. Indeed, he developed two distinct levels of style to represent the distance between God's art and that of the human poet.

Over and over again Taylor asserts that God's praises ought to be rendered in the finest and most eloquent language possible, far surpassing the "Spangled Flowers of sweet-breath'd Eloquence" which the Orator picks from Rhetoric's garden.[53] His divine theme should "raise such waves upon / The Sea of Eloquence, they'd skip thereon"; it deserves to be embellished by a "rich, fine Phansy ripe."[54] The standard of appropriate praise is biblical: "Zions Songs," "King Davids Harp," "sparkling Metaphors, out stilld / From Zion's garden flowers."[55] Especially do the tropes of Canticles provide the touchstone, since they embody the Bridegroom's own praises of the Church his Bride: Christ gilds his Spouse with "Golden words," "sparkling Metaphors," "Silver Metaphors and Tropes."[56] However, the speaker complains constantly of his inability to approach this standard because of his sins, and because of his human ineptitude before such transcendent glories: "I fain would praise thee, Lord, but finde black Sin, / To stain my Tunes, my Virginalls to spoile." "My Metaphors are but dull Tacklings tag'd / With ragged Non-Sense." "In finest Twine of Praise I'm muzzled. / My tazzled Thoughts twirld into Snick-Snarls run." "My Quaintest Metaphors are ragged Stuff, / Making the Sun seem like a Mullipuff."[57]

What he finds is that "My Rhymes do better suite / Mine own Dispraise than tune forth praise to thee,"[58] and this insight provides the ground for his poetics. Reasonably confident of his election, he concludes the great majority of his poems with a promise that when he is in heaven, glorified, he will praise God properly and according to the biblical model of the Psalmist, the Bridegroom of Canticles, and the angelic host. Moreover, he has some confidence that God's grace will make acceptable his poor efforts at praise even now, as his own regeneration proceeds: "Accept this Lisp till I am glorifide."[59] But for now the biblical art is beyond him, and so he contrives blunt, homely figures, tropes of meiosis and antithesis, to display and enact his ineptitude. Taylor thus isolates two languages and styles for religious poetry: the high eloquence and sparkling biblical tropes which ought to be imitated in God's praises but cannot be in this world; and the ragged, colloquial style replete with self-deprecatory tropes and meiotic recasting of God's metaphors, which becomes the vehicle of man's inevitable failures in praise. The model for religious lyric poetry is still biblical, but Taylor finds the model inimitable on earth and uses that fact to validate a new, secular idiom for divine praises.

### B. THE BIBLICAL POETS AND THEIR FOLLOWERS:
IMITATION, INSPIRATION, AND THE PERSONAL VOICE

From every side Protestant poets of the late sixteenth and seventeenth centuries were exhorted to imitate the biblical poets, and especially David. At the source of that stream of advice, as Lily Campbell has shown, was Du Bartas' "L'Uranie" (1574), a short, dream-vision poem in which Urania, now transformed into the Muse of Christian poetry, urged Du Bartas to reclaim for God the noble gift, poetry, which originated in the Bible but was then perverted to idolatrous and immoral uses.[60] She also argued the superiority of biblical subjects over analogous profane or pagan matter, and pointed to the Psalmist as the model *par excellence* for the Christian poet. The crucial stanza in James I's translation of the poem reads:

> Take me for guyde, Lyft up to heaven thy wing
> O *Salust*, Gods immortals honour sing:
> And bending higher Davids Lute in tone
> With courage seke you endles crowne above.[61]

Several poets expressed their wish to imitate the Psalmist: Nicholas Breton desired to be "such a Poet as the Psalmist was"; the frontispiece to King James' translation of the Psalms shows David and James together holding aloft the Book of the Psalms; and Robert Aylett's imitation of Du Bartas' "L'Uranie" has the Muse recommending that Aylett imitate Du Bartas himself and David the sacred Orpheus: "With their divine *Essay's* thy *Muse* acquaint, / Which may be fewel to thy heav'nly fire."[62] The reasons for singling out David the Psalmist as the primary model for Christian poets no doubt include the very great spiritual significance and artistic worth ascribed to the Psalms in contemporary commentary, as well as their use for centuries in Christian liturgy. But in addition, the Psalms were seen to raise with special force and complexity the issues of poetic persona and artistic stance, so that David's example provided the religious lyric poet with some basis for considering problems central to his conception of himself and his role.

The tradition of commentary on the Psalms describes them as incorporating various voices or stances or personations. This was not primarily a matter of authorship. Most Renaissance commentators, like the Fathers before them, attributed most or all of the psalms to David, while recognizing some textual evidence (from the titles) for attributing a few of them to Moses, to Solomon, to Ethan the Ezrahite, to the sons of Corah, to Asaph, and others; yet they dismissed this problem easily with the observation that in any case the Holy Ghost is the author of them all.[63] The issue raised by such commentary is, rather, by what literary means the various voices (David's, Christ's, those of other biblical personages, the Church's, our own) are incorporated within the psalms, and how these various voices and the Spirit's all-pervasive inspiration relate to David's own experience and ideas. In short, to what extent is David perceived as a poet consciously shaping his own poems?

Augustine considered the Psalms to be the song of the entire corporate Church as Body of Christ, contrived not by David but by the Holy Spirit. Various voices are recognized as speaking the various psalms, though all can be assimilated to this one voice, the voice of the whole Church, Head and Body, as Heather Asals has pointed out in her suggestive study of Herbert's debt to Augustine's commentary.[64] Augustine's view is grounded upon a typology in which the type is virtually swallowed up in the antitype:

> Scarce is it possible in the Psalms to find any voices, but those of Christ and the Church, or of Christ only, or of the Church only, which truly in part we also are. And for this cause whenever we recognize our voices, without emotion recognize them we cannot. ... David the king was one man, but not one man he figured; Sometimes to wit he figured the Church of many men consisting, extended even unto the ends of the earth: but sometimes One Man he figured ... The Man Christ Jesus.[65]

Throughout his lengthy commentary Augustine's focus is constantly upon the antitype: the voices are those of Christ, the Church, and ourselves as part of the Church. Some psalms attributed in their titles to David are said to be spoken "in the Person of the very Lord, our Saviour Christ"; in others Augustine explains, "Christ speaks, but in the person of the Church"; and still others, such as Psalm 35, contain both voices: "His Voice then let us hear: now of the Body, now of the Head."[66] Augustine pays scant attention to David's historical experience or to his voice as Psalmist, although on occasion he discusses him as a prophet speaking of or to Christ, or else presents David's sins and repentance as a type of our, and of the Church's, condition: "see ye here our image and the type of the Church." But normally, he treats all these voices as comprehended within Christ's, being part of his Body, the Church: for example, Psalm 43 is said to be of "that *Man* who is extended throughout the whole world, of which the Head is above, the limbs below: . . . We need not then dwell long on pointing out to you who is the speaker here: let each one of us be a member of Christ's Body; and he will be speaker here."[67]

The Protestant exegetes were also interested in the various voices to be heard in the Psalms, but their approach was to focus upon David's own sentiments and experience as ground for his typological "personation" of Christ or of the Church. David was assumed to be in some measure conscious of his role as type and prophet of Christ and the Church (and of us), so that his language and poetic formulations result from his own poetic strategy, even when they have much wider reference. Though Calvin of course insists that "the holy Ghost . . . ruled Davids tung," yet he constantly intimates David's awareness of his role: "That David prophesyed of Christ, herby it appereth of certeintie, bicause he knewe his owne kingdome was but shadowishe." Or again, "David complayneth, in the name of himself and of all the godly."[68] The Geneva Bible also views David as intentionally personating Christ or the Church: "David complained [Psalm 22] because hee was brought into such extremeties that hee was past all hope. . . . And here under his owne person hee setteth forth the figure of Christ, whome he did foresee by the Spirit of prophesie, that he should marveilously, and strangely be dejected, and abased, before his Father shoulde rayse and exalt him againe."[69] Henry Ainsworth singles out four general kinds of personation undertaken by David in the various psalms: (1) David speaks some psalms in his own person, relating his spiritual experiences for the comfort and example of all the godly. (2) Some others he speaks as figure of Christ. (3) Still others he speaks as prophet of Christ. (4) Finally, he delivers certain praises and thanksgivings as spokesman for or in the person of the Church.[70]

Others extended the scope of personation. John Diodati identifies in some psalms God speaking either to his elect or to his enemies, and in others the Psalmist speaking, or causing the Church to speak, either to God in praise or to the faithful in instruction.[71] George Wither adds still more personations from the proper names appearing in the various psalm titles:

> The opinion of the most auncient, both of the Christian Fathers, and *Jewish Rabbines*, is, that *David* composed his *Psalmes* not alway in his owne person, but sometime personated others. And upon examination, you shall find that some are written literally in the person of *Adam*, and his posteritie: some in the person of *Christ*, and his Church: some in the persons before mentioned [Doeg, Solomon, Moses]. . . . *Moses* is thought not to have beene Author of that Psalme, in whose Title his name is remembred: but some thinke it was written by *David*, either personating him; or (which I rather hold) that, *the prayer of Moses the Man of God*, was the Object of our Prophets Meditation, at that time.[72]

Moreover, Protestant exegetes also located our own voices in the Psalms. This proposition is grounded both upon the broad emotional range the psalms comprehend as "anatomies of the soul," and upon our own inclusion in the Body of Christ and thus in the antitypical references. Athanasius' treatise, often reprinted in the period, insists that the Psalms render each man's own emotions and indeed his own voice:

> There every one may see and perceive the motions and affections of his owne hart and soule, both to see whereto he is inclined, and where he is streyned and pinched. . . . Whosoever take this booke in his hande, he reputeth and thinketh all the wordes he readeth (except the wordes of prophecy) to be as his very owne wordes spoken in his owne person . . . first by him conceyved and pronounced . . . as he himselfe felt the same in deede, and therfore, singeth to God those woordes as his very own wordes and petitions.[73]

As we have seen, Luther found in the Psalms the emotional history of all the faithful, and at the same time the particular spiritual autobiography of every particular Christian; and Calvin testified to the validity of such a reading in the particular circumstances of his own life.[74] Acting upon such conceptions, in his meditations on the penitential psalms Theodore Beza conflated his own voice with that of the Psalmist, and paraphrased David's words as applicable to himself, as his own words.[75] John Bate, meditating on Psalm 51, consciously assimilates his own experiences to David's and adapts the Psalmist's words to his needs: "I have cast it [this paraphrase] . . . in mine own plaine language, and paralleling mine with Davids perplexities, applied his plaisters, to my sores."[76] More plainly, Henry Hammond insists that the Psalm texts await our own enacting, to complete their meaning:

> *It is necessary that we say the Psalms with the same spirit with which they were composed, and accommodate them unto our selves in the same manner as if every one of us had composed them . . . not satisfying our selves that they* had their *whole completion* in or by the *Prophet,* but discerning every of us our *own parts* still to be performed and acted over in the *Psalmists* words.[77]

As Joan Webber has demonstrated, Donne regularly identifies his voice with that of the Psalmist in his sermons, so that "almost all his sermons on the Psalms have an urgent immediacy that distinguishes their tone from that of others."[78]

Issues of persona and aesthetic stance were also raised in regard to other biblical poets, but in more limited ways. Jeremiah was assumed to have contrived a series of personae in the Lamentations, usually seen as a lament for King Josiah whose death portends the destruction of Israel. In Calvin's reading, Jeremiah first "assumes the person of one who on seeing something new and unexpected is filled with amazement"; then, at 1:16, he "sustains the person of a woman"; at the beginning of the third chapter he speaks in his own person but for the whole people; in the fifth chapter he "not only speaks in the person of the whole people, but utters also the groans and complaints of each."[79] Protestant discussions of the books of Solomon point out the distinct character and rhetorical stance assumed by him for didactic purposes in each of his three works. It was widely agreed that Proverbs is spoken in "the person of a carefull father [who] counsaileth the young man," as Peter Muffet put it.[80] The persona of the preacher in Ecclesiastes was often taken to be an actual role assumed by Solomon on a single extraordinary occasion, to teach the people by preaching of worldly vanities out of his own life's experiences.[81] On the other hand, because the Song of Songs is so intensely symbolic and prophetic, discussions of Solomon's stance in that work tended to emphasize his situation as instrument of the Holy Ghost: Theodore Beza indeed attributes the very style of Canticles to the Holy Spirit.[82] Nevertheless, Protestant commentators found some scope for Solomon's own art. Dudley Fenner, for example, points to the king's broad knowledge and long practice in making songs as the basis of his poetic language:

> Solomon was indued not onely with a great measure of spirituall understanding, necessarie for the matter, but with the knowledge of the natures of all creatures: whereby so great and heavenlye misteries might be made more easie and plaine to our understanding, when similitudes are aptlie drawne from them, and with the special grace of sounges, which he atteyned by great practice: By all which giftes he was able to frame suche a sounge, as the grace whereof might worke in our hartes a most heavenly melodie.[83]

As a resolution of the possible contradiction, the mode of Solomon's inspiration is often described as a remarkable vision, to which he responded artistically. As Richard Sibbes observes, "Some would have *Solomon* by a *Spirit of Prophecy*, to take here a view of all the time, from his Age to the second comming of Christ: and in this *Song*, as in an abridgement, to set downe the severall *Passages* and *Periods* of the *Church*."[84]

Indeed the Protestant conception of prophetic inspiration, which envisions the prophet as a spectator in a theatre, viewing by divine favor the events he foretells or foreshadows,[85] permitted the prophet-poet considerable artistic freedom in shaping his materials. In his treatise on prophecy John Smith gave currency to the Hebrew idea that the lyric songs of the prophets and the poetic books of Job, David, and Solomon are products of a lower degree of prophetic inspiration than are the writings of Moses and other major prophets which were directly shaped by divine vision or dictate. Although the poet-prophets indeed drew upon their experiences of inspiration, and were enabled with the conjunction or superintendency of the Holy Spirit "to speak excellently . . . *with very elegant language, and admirable similitudes*," their poems are essentially the product of their own art.[86]

Such discussions as these, focusing attention upon multiple voices and personations, divine inspiration and poetic artfulness, have obvious theoretical interest for the major religious lyric poets of this study, who, though not inspired, yet shared in some degree the Biblical poets' problem of giving artistic shape to inspired materials—although at second hand. The poets may also have learned from, and evidently stand in a direct line of development from, certain sixteenth-century English religious lyric poets whose verse is closely related to biblical paraphrase or bears a strong impress of biblical language and symbolism, but who yet found significant scope for the poet's personal voice. These poets engaged the issues of inspiration, imitation, and art in simple but very revealing ways as they sought out and discovered ways to write themselves into or to appropriate God's art.

The Psalms, and especially the Penitential Psalms, invited such treatment. A long tradition of more or less free paraphrases of the Penitential Psalms reaches from Dante's terza rima paraphrase, to Petrarch's almost total transformation of the Psalms into religious meditations adapted to his own circumstances, to George Chapman's highly paraphrastic and ornamented verse descant on Petrarch.[87] Of particular interest here, however, are those paraphrases in which the modern poet subsumes without obliterating the voice and stance of the Psalmist, and in doing so creates strikingly original psalm versions with a complex persona. Some of Luther's hymns are of this kind—grounded upon the Psalms but developed freely in regard to New Testament and contemporary reference, as if Luther had assumed the role of a Christian psalmist presenting his Protestant formulations of the same themes: examples are *Es wollt' uns Gott genädig sein* (from Psalm 67), *Ein' feste Burg* (from Psalm 46), and *Aus tiefer Noth schrei ich zu dir* (an intimately personal descant on the *De Profundis*, Psalm 130).[88] Another early, remarkable example is Wyatt's *Penitential Psalms*, probably composed while he was expecting arrest and trial on charges ranging from treason to immorality, emerging out of the murky political and religious machinations of Henry VIII's court.[89] Wyatt made of the Penitential Psalms a Protestant cycle of spiritual regeneration: he linked them together by means of original poems narrating the course of David's repentance after his sin with Bathsheba; thereby presenting these psalms as specific climactic moments in David's spiritual odyssey. But Wyatt's psalm versions also incorporate long descants upon the speaker's miseries and dangers as he is encompassed by enemies and treacherous friends, merging Wyatt's voice and situation with the Psalmist's. A striking example is Wyatt's 112-line expansion of the ten verses of Psalm 6, lamenting the speaker's trials among his foes and relishing his projected victory over them with a particularity and specificity quite without textual source in the Psalm itself:

> Thus drye I upp among my foes in woe,
> That with my fall do rise and grow with all,
> And me bysett evin now, where I am so,
> With secrett trapps to troble my penaunce.
> Sum do present to my weping yes, lo,
> The chere, the manere, bealte and countenaunce

Off her whose loke, alas, did mak me blynd.
Sum other offer to my remembrans
Those pleasant wordes now bitter to my mynd;

. . . . . . . . . . . . . . . .

I dare them bid: *Avoyd wreches and fle!*
*The lord hath hard the voyce off my complaint;*
*Your engins take no more effect in me.*

. . . . . . . . . . . . . . . .

Shamid be thei all that so ly in whaite
To compas me, by missing of theire pray!
Shame and rebuke redound to suche decayte![90]

Gasciogne's version of the *De Profundis* affords another example of such merging of voices. His lengthy descant renders each verse of the original in an eleven-line stanza, prefacing the whole with a sonnet claiming the psalm as his own outcry in a personal trial. The sonnet narrates an adventure in which the speaker, caught in a violent thunderstorm, at first complains of Jove's wrath thus turned against him, but then determines, "(Although I be wel sowsed in this showre) / To write some verse in honour of hys name."[91] That verse, as his first editor testifies, was "firste this sonet, and afterwardes, the translated Psalme of Deprofundis."[92] Several other psalm paraphrasts also assimilate the Psalmist's voice and stance to their own, intimating that they are in some sense other Davids. Thomas Campion's version of the *De Profundis*, which appears unlabelled among his original "Divine and Moral Songs," follows the structure of the psalm but personalizes and Christianizes the theme. And William Hunnis' versions of the Penitential Psalms present the Christian speaker expatiating throughout upon his own sin and guilt, but appropriating at intervals the words and verses of the Psalmist.[93]

From such works it is an easy step to others which break from the mold of even the freest paraphrase, but which are nevertheless closely modelled upon biblical poems. An impressive example is the *Divine Centurie of Spirituall Sonnets* (1595) by the Protestant poet Barnabe Barnes, evidently conceived by its author as a personal and Christian book of psalms constantly reminiscent of though not directly imitating David's. Barnes defends his haphazard presentation of just such a mix of emotions and modes as the Psalms were thought to contain:

The severall passions of comforte and ghostly combates, albeit they stand in my booke confused, and peradventure therefore may to some readers seeme disordered and straunge, as in their unequall coherence of praises, penitence, and fearefull afflictions, yet upon some especiall occasio⌐s and in earnest true motions of the spirite were they devised.[94]

The pervasive psalm echoes, and especially certain "revised" psalms in sonnet form contribute to the recognition of Barnes' collection as a new book of psalms.[95] In several of these the speaker directly compares his situation or his poems with David's. In Sonnet 66 he desires to claim with David in Psalm 108, "O God, my heart is fixed: I will sing and give praise"—but admits that his own heart is unready. In Sonnet 62 he rejoices that he, like David in Psalm 40, has been given a new song. In Sonnet 92 he promises as David did in Psalm 51 to bring forth psalms out of his repentance. In Sonnet 49 his sentiments and stance are at one with David's in Psalm 102, "Death doe thy worst, but yet (Lord) thine eare give, / Why I with David would not die, but live."[96] His situation as Christian psalmist is further clarified by his incorporation of himself into several biblical metaphors setting forth the various roles of Christ: Christ is a redeemer offering sacrifice and his is an altar-heart (Sonnet 3); Christ is a "gracious Shephearde" and he "was a lost sheepe once" (Sonnet 9); Christ is "Mylde king of Salem," and he is a seeker for peace of conscience (Sonnet 17); Christ is the "Fountaine of life" and he is one who thirsts (Sonnet 22); God is a gracious Master, and he is a servant with a Talent (Sonnet 38).[97]

Alternatively, the Christian poet might seek to define his persona without primary reference to David the Psalmist, but instead through a variety of Biblical metaphors and types. *Sundry Christian Passions* (1597), a sonnet cycle by the Protestant poet Henry Lok which has the Christian pilgrimage as its central metaphor,[98] pioneered strategies which were to be refined and perfected in the seventeenth century. Lok's declared purpose is to "set downe these abrupt passions of my passed afflictions, as witnesses of the impediments most stopping me in my Christian pilgrimage"; he thereby accommodates to this biblical metaphor the personal experiences rendered in his poems, "In which (as in a glasse) may be seene, the state of a regenerate soule, sicke with sinne, sometimes (Ague-like) shivering with cold despaire, straight waies inflamed with fervencie of faith and hope. One while yeelding under the burden of sinne to eternall death, and presently incouraged to runne chearefully forward the appointed course of this his pilgrimage."[99] Though Lok's poems are arranged in the usual haphazard Protestant fashion,[100] the three parts of his book present the classic Protestant paradigm of the way of salvation. The one hundred sonnets of Part I deal with the soul's experience of sin and bondage, and in them the speaker characteristically defines himself by finding Old Testament personages to be correlative types with himself, their experiences recapitulated in his own. He is a new Jonah crying "Fro out the darknesse of this sea of feare, / Where I in whale remaine devourd of sin" (2). He is a new Noah in an ark, "floting on worldes troubled wave" (3); he approaches the mercy gate like David "with brooke and contrite heart" (4); he is an Ishmael, "Of bastard kind, bred up with mothers care, / In wildernesse of world" (20), an Israel fed with manna but longing for the vanities of Egypt (64, 85), a Jacob requiring protection from fleshly Esau (86). The speaker defines himself also in terms of various parabolic or metaphoric New Testament roles: he is an invited wedding guest needing a wedding garment (5); a lame man needing to bathe in Bethesda's pool (7); a sheep watered and fed by a Good Shepherd (9); a servant who has misused his single talent (87). The second set of one hundred sonnets presents the process of regeneration and sanctification as Christian pilgrimage and warfare: the speaker now claims, "I Have begun ô Lord to run the race, / Where flesh and bloud against the world must fight" (6), and again he explores his situation through Old Testament types of himself. He is newly arrived in the land promised of old to Israel (16); he will dance as a David before the homeward-journeying Ark (19); God is leading him as an Israel in the desert by two pillars, his Word and his Providences (80). Several sonnets of this section also address the problem of devising fit praises (3, 19, 40, 41, 42, 43) in language often reminiscent of the psalms of praise, notably Psalms 8, 104, and 148. The one hundred sonnets of Part III are chiefly concerned with the works and praises appropriate to the regenerate state: the governing biblical metaphors for the speaker, recurring in poem after poem, are the fruit-bearing tree and the flourishing seed.

The biblical commentaries and the poems we have been examining focus attention upon the personae of the several poetic books of scripture, upon the problem of inspiration and art, upon the multiple voices and personations in the Book of Psalms, and upon the ways in which later poets may relate to or may assimilate the biblical voices. It seems clear that such theory and example promoted the development of several strategies for the speaker's self-definition, which are of major importance in the poetry of Donne, Herbert, Vaughan, Traherne, and Taylor. Primary among them are the two ways of characterizing the speaker developed at the turn of the century by Barnes and Lok—the poet as Christian psalmist, and the poet as embodiment of certain biblical metaphors and types. These strategies the major seventeenth-century religious lyric poets raised to new aesthetic heights.

Pointing the way to these heights more clearly than any of the works hitherto discussed is the poetic version of the Psalms produced by Sir Philip Sidney and his sister, Mary Herbert, Countess of Pembroke. As contemporary references to them demonstrate, though these psalms were not published for over two centuries, they were well known to the extensive literary and court circles of these great families.[101] At first glance, the Sidney-Pembroke psalms seem not to be part of the development I am tracing because they are true paraphrases, close to their originals and without a clearly-delineated persona whose individual experience merges with that of the Psalmist. Nevertheless, these extremely artful poems, with their intricate and almost infinite varieties of stanzaic forms and metrical patterns, and their fine adjustment of contemporary poetic forms and metaphors to the meaning and tone of particular psalms, do create a new persona for the Psalmist. He is transfigured as an Elizabethan poet, expressing a contemporary religious sensibility with rare and delicate artistry. By thus re-creating the Psalms for the first and only time in the period as good English poems, the Sidney-Pembroke psalter provides a secure bridge to the magnificent original seventeenth-century religious lyric in the biblical and psalmic mode.

Everywhere in these psalms we find portents of things to come. There are dramatic, colloquial opening lines which sound remarkably like Donne, and which Donne must have found instructive:

Tyrant, why swel'st thou thus, (Psalm 52).

Lord, helpe, it is hygh tyme for me to call: (Psalm 12).

My suite is just, just Lord, to my suite hark (Psalm 17).

What? and dòe I behold the lovely mountaines, (Psalm 121).

There are also psalms which look forward to some of Herbert's more contrived poems. Psalm 117—"O Prayse the Lorde all ye heathen: prayse hym all ye nations. / For his mercyful kyndnes is ever more and more towarde us: and the trueth of the Lorde endureth for ever. Prayse the Lorde" [BCP][102]—is rendered by the Countess of Pembroke as an acrostic poem with the first letter of each line spelling out the key text, "Prais the Lord":

P raise him that ay
R emaines the same:
A ll tongues display
I ehovas fame.
S ing all that share

T his earthly ball:
H is mercies are
E xpos'd to all:
L ike as the word
O nce he doth give,
R old in record
D oth tyme outlive.

This is not so far from Herbert's more intricate acrostics on his key text, "Our life is hid with Christ in God," in the poem "Coloss. 3:3." And Herbert's echo poem, "Heaven," has a suggestive precedent in the structure Sidney adopts for Psalm 13:

How long (O Lord) shall I forgotten be?
What? ever?
How long wilt thou thy hidden face from me
Dissever?[103]

Moreover, as J.C.A. Rathmell points out, these psalms often render biblical metaphors in graphic, trenchant, and colloquial terms—qualities associated with metaphysical imagery.[104] In the Geneva version Psalm 139:15 reads, "My bones are not hid from thee, though I was made in a secret place, & facioned beneth in the earth." The Countess gives strikingly vivid and witty elaboration to the somewhat abstract figure:

Thou, how my back was beam-wise laid,
And raftring of my ribbs, dost know:
Know'st ev'ry point
Of bone and joynt,
How to this whole these partes did grow,
In brave embrod'ry faire araid,
Though wrought in shopp both dark and low.
(ll. 50-56)

Again, Psalm 57:1 presents a lovely trope of God's mercy as sheltering wings affording protection against unspecified calamities: "Be mercy-full unto me (O GOD) be mercyfull unto me, for my soule trusteth in thee: and under the shadowe of thy wynges shalbe my refuge, untyll this tyranny [Geneva, these afflictions] be overpast" [BCP]. The Countess boldly and wittily revises the trope, presenting the speaker as a winged creature seeking a "hive" during a clearly-envisaged howling tempest:

> Thy mercie, Lord, Lord now thy mercy show,
> On thee I ly
> To thee I fly
> Hide me, hive me as thine owne,
> Till these blasts be overblown,
> Which now doe fiercely blow.
> (Psalm 57, ll. 1-6)

More remarkable still are the foreshadowings of Herbert evident in line after line of the psalms of affliction:

> Lord, while that thy rage doth bide,
> Do not chide
> Nor in anger chastise me,
> For thy shafts have peirc'd me sore;
> (Psalm 38, ll. 1-4)

> To thee my crying call,
> To thee my calling cry
> I did, O God, addresse,
> And thou didst me attend:
> . . . . . . . . . . . .
> Whole troupes of busy cares,
> Of cares that from thee came,
> Tooke up their restlesse rest
> In sleepie sleeplesse eies:
> . . . . . . . . . . . .
> Are all the conduits dry
> Of his erst flowing grace?
> Could rusty teeth of tyme
> To nought his promise turne?
> Can mercy no more clyme
> And come before his face?
> Must all compassion dy?
> Must nought but anger burne?
> (Psalm 77, ll. 1-4, 17-20, 41-48)

> My wasted eye doth melt away
> Fleeting amaine,
> In streames of pain
> While I my praiers send,
> While I my hands extend,
> To thee, my God, and faile noe day.

> Alas, my Lord, will then be tyme,
>      When men are dead,
>         Thy truth to spread?
> Shall they, whome death hath slaine,
>    To praise thee live againe,
> And from their lowly lodgings clime?
>
> Shall buried mouthes thy mercies tell?
>      Dust and decay
>         Thy truth display?
> And shall thy workes of mark
>    Shine in the dreadfull dark?
> Thy Justice where oblivions dwell?
>                   (Psalm 88, ll. 37-54)

In tone, stance of speaker, rhythmic effects, and deceptively simple formulations of staggering religious paradoxes, such lines as these lead directly to such Herbert poems as "Affliction" (II), (III), and (IV), "Grief," "Deniall," "Longing," "Sighs and Grones," and many others.

Occasionally the verbal and conceptual similarities seem almost to argue imitation. Might the opening question of Psalm 106, "Where are the hymnes, where are the honors due / To our good God, whose goodness knowes no end?" lie behind Herbert's parallel questions about the praises owing to God in "Dulnesse": "Where are my lines then? my approaches? views? / Where are my window-songs?" (ll. 17-18) And might the basic metaphoric development of "Love (III)" have been assisted by the elegant image of an intimate and personal feast in a heavenly banquet hall which Sidney sets forth—without much warrant from the biblical text[105]—in the final stanza of Psalm 23?:

> Thou oil'st my head thou fill'st my cupp:
>      Nay more thou endlesse good,
>         Shalt give me food.
> To thee, I say, ascended up,
>    Where thou, the Lord of all,
>         Dost hold thy hall.
>
>                   (ll. 19-24)

Though critics have recognized the influence of the Sidney-Pembroke psalms upon Herbert,[106] the scope and specific nature of that influence asks much more thorough investigation.

These various poetic experiments from Wyatt to Sidney and his sister obviously invited seventeenth-century religious poets to look to the Psalms and other lyric poetry in the Bible with a new aesthetic consciousness of the possibilities for imitation. Such imitation is related to, but not quite identical with, Protestant typological association based upon historical recapitulations designed by God's providence, since the Christian poet chooses his biblical model and develops the relationships himself. Yet the issue is not quite so clear-cut, for the poet often presents himself as one who seeks, strives, hopes to become a genuine correlative type with one of the biblical poets—as he may, if God so ordains.

Donne's very creative ideas about imitating the magnificent poetry of the scriptures extends to his relationship with the biblical poets: he is bound to no single model, he presents himself as correlative type with various of these poets as occasion dictates, and his stance is not so much that of imitation as of accomplishing a new work in the same spirit. Not surprisingly, he enunciates this principle while praising the Sidney-Pembroke psalms. Donne's poem places the Sidneys virtually on the same plane with David as vehicles of God's Spirit: that Spirit shed upon David enabled him to sing "The highest matter in the noblest forme," and that same Spirit shed again upon the Sidneys led them "In formes of joy and art [to] . . . re-reveale" those Psalms. Moreover, till we come to sing "Extemporall Song" in heaven these Sidnaeian psalms are our best models: "They tell us *why*, and teach us *how* to sing."[107] Donne himself sets forth several poems as "re-revelations" of a more sweeping kind. He has a fairly close verse paraphrase of the Lamentations of Jeremiah (based on the Junius-Tremellius version) but his creative re-revelation of Jeremiah might be said to be the *First Anniversary*, where he assumes the Jeremiah role of lamenting a death which portends the destruction of the whole society. In the *First Anniversary* also the speaker explicitly proposes to thrust himself into the "office" of Moses the Lawgiver by his denunciation of the world, whereas in the *Second Anniversary* he is a new John of Patmos sounding the trumpet for a new creation after the world's destruction.[108] The speaker of the "Holy Sonnets" makes no such overt claims of relation to a biblical poet, yet he seems for all that to associate himself here with the same two figures he claims closest kinship to in the sermons—David in the Penitential Psalms and the anguished Paul testifying to the conflicts within him.[109] This relationship is also closer to "re-revelation" than imitation: Donne presents himself as something like a correlative type, creating works in the same spirit, under the impress of the same emotions.

Herbert's *The Temple* is a medley of voices which derive from and play off against biblical voices. And Herbert's speaker often presents

himself as a New Testament version of (antitype of) various biblical
poets. The teacher-father who advises the "sweet youth" in "The
Church-porch" is a version of the Solomon of Proverbs and the
Preacher of Ecclesiastes. The presenter of the poetic history of the
Church through the ages in "The Church-Militant" encompasses one
dimension of John of Patmos as the commentaries presented him—the
visionary historian of the Church.[110] Several of the poems of "The
Church" are dialogic, incorporating the voice of a "Friend" who acts
upon and with the poet as he seeks his salvation and endeavors to devise
true praises,[111] in a brilliant dramatization of the divine voice relating
itself to the poetic voice. Moreover, Christ speaks the longest of the
lyrics, "The Sacrifice," in his own person, though as a descant upon
verses from the Lamentations of Jeremiah. But especially, by the fre-
quent psalm phrases the speaker invokes to resolve his poetic problems,
by his free paraphrases of Psalms 23 and 104, and by his creative Chris-
tian revision of Psalms 51 and 57 in "The Altar" and "Easter," Herbert
presents "The Church" as a New Covenant psalter, the song-book of
the new temple in the heart, with himself as a Christian David.

"Easter," probably the most complete statement of Herbert's poetics,
is a reworking of Psalm 57:7-11: "My heart is fixed, O God, my heart
is fixed: I will sing, and give praise. / Awake up my glory awake
psalterie and harpe: I my selfe will awake early. / I will praise thee, O
Lord, among the people. . . ." Herbert presents as interlocking elements
in the creation of religious poetry the risen heart (like David's), the
poetic lute which, like David's psaltery and harp, must struggle "With
all thy art" in harmony with the stretched sinews of Christ on the
Cross; and God's Holy Spirit whose "sweet art" must make up our
defects:

> Rise heart; thy Lord is risen. Sing his praise
> > Without delayes,
> Who takes thee by the hand, that thou likewise
> > With him mayst rise:
> That, as his death calcined thee to dust,
> His life may make thee gold, and much more, just.
>
> Awake, my lute, and struggle for thy part
> > With all thy art.
> The crosse taught all wood to resound his name,
> > Who bore the same.
> His stretched sinews taught all strings, what key
> Is best to celebrate this most high day.

Consort both heart and lute, and twist a song
Pleasant and long:
Or, since all musick is but three parts vied
And multiplied,
O let thy blessed Spirit bear a part,
And make up our defects with his sweet art.
(ll. 1-18)

This poetics produces, in Part II of this poem, a simple but exquisite psalm of praise, identifying its chief impulse not in the poet's early awakening (like David), but in Christ's rising: "I Got me flowers to straw thy way; / I got me boughs off many a tree: / But thou wast up by break of day, / And brought'st thy sweets along with thee" (ll. 19-22). Herbert enacts this poetic by occasionally assimilating the Davidic voice into his own poems (as in the Psalm quotations), but chiefly (as in "Easter") by an imaginative echo and transposition of biblical imagery and forms and voices on the strings of his own poetic lute, as he undertakes the role of New Testament Psalmist.

Though Vaughan incorporates three psalm versions among his lyrics (65, 104, 121), he does not relate himself in quasi-typological fashion to David or to any of the other biblical poets. Rather, the speaker defines himself in relation to several biblical metaphors and types, and his poetic voice plays off against the scripture quotations incorporated into his poems as headnotes and postscripts. The poet's voice, responding to, or elaborating upon, or reinterpreted by, such texts is seen to engage them in a kind of dialogue. The effect is again that of a medley of voices, but with the poet squaring his own voice with the terms of that authoritative biblical voice which so often frames his poems.

Moreover, Herbert occupies for Vaughan something like the position that the biblical poets (and especially David) held for Herbert. The preface to *Silex Scintillans* recognizes Herbert as the creator of a new vein of religious poetry, and Vaughan enacts his sense of derivation from Herbert in his poem "The Match" as he takes up the challenge Herbert set forth in his poem "Obedience" for some other poet to "thrust his heart / Into these lines" (ll. 42-43). Herbert is the medium through which Vaughan approaches the biblical poets. He identifies Herbert's poems (and his own) as hagiography—"he that desires to excel in this kinde of *Hagiography*, or holy writing, must strive (by all means) for *perfection* and true *holyness* . . . and then he will be able to write (with *Hierotheous* and holy *Herbert*) A *true Hymn*."[112] He links Herbert (and himself) by the term *Hagiography* with that "third

part" of the Bible so named, which includes the books usually desig-
nated as poetic—the Psalms, Job, Lamentations, the three books of
Solomon.[113] And he reinforces this claim of derivation at one remove
from the biblical poet-prophets by concluding the preface with a
cluster of unidentified verses drawn from Jeremiah, Isaiah, Jonah, and
the Psalms—in effect, taking over these verses as his own declaration
of praise. Throughout the volume Herbert is a constant presence:
Vaughan has appropriated titles, metrical forms, themes, single lines,
and longer passages with little change, so that Herbertian allusions and
echoes are pervasive. It is almost as if Vaughan sees himself as a cor-
relative type with Herbert, discovering his own poetic voice by in-
corporating and responding to Herbert's voice.

Traherne's shorter lyrics are not associated by means of echoes and
allusions with a particular biblical poet, nor do they seem to contain
a medley of voices, although the speaker does define himself typologi-
cally as a recapitulation of innocent Adam and of David who built (in
his Psalms) a "Temple of the Mind."[114] Yet there is clear indication
that Traherne associates his poetics of the unadorned glory of things
with the psalmic model. In the "Third Century" his appropriation of
the voice and persona of David is explicit, extensive, and occurs at the
climactic moment: he incorporates lengthy passages of quotation from
the Psalms into his prose commentary on them so that his voice be-
comes one with the Psalmist's, and he then creates his own ecstatic
prose-poems in the same vein, as continuations or completions of
David's.[115] Moreover, he discovers himself in and through the Psalms,
finding his own experience in David's. And he finds that experience
presented in accordance with his aesthetic ideal: in the Psalms, "Things
which for their Greatness were incredible, were made Evident and
Things Obscure, Plain."[116]

The *Thanksgivings* are a poetic embodiment of this same process:
as the title and form indicate, they are new psalms. Traherne assimi-
lates long unlabeled passages from the Psalms, and models his original
verses so closely upon their rhythms and cadences that it is often not
possible to tell when he has moved from quotation to paraphrase to
imitation, so thoroughly commingled are the voices. Traherne does not,
however, merely paraphrase or imitate the Psalmist, nor does he, like
Herbert, seek to become a New Covenant psalmist recasting David's
entire *œuvre* into his own Christian antitypical terms. Rather, Tra-
herne fuses David's voice (and those of other major prophet-poets
such as Moses, Isaiah, and Jeremiah) with his own, so that the Davidic
voice becomes part of the antitype he himself presents. In "Thanks-
givings for the Body" he points directly to David as his model for the

poetry of sublime plainness, and to the *Thanksgivings* as his attempt to
create "meeter," because Christian, psalms:

> *All Tropes are Clouds; Truth doth it self excel,*
> *Whatever Heights, Hyperboles can tell.*

> O that I were as *David*, the sweet Singer of *Israel!*
> In meeter Psalms to set forth thy Praises.
>
> (ll. 339-342)

For Taylor, the Psalmist and especially the Bridegroom of Canticles
are the superlative models for his own poetic praises, but they are
models for the future conditional, not the present; models for heaven,
not for earth. If his adoption is assured and when he is glorified, Taylor
will "sing / New Psalms on Davids Harpe"; when he is glorified he
promises confidently to produce the psalmic modes and melodies—
hosannas, hallelujahs, "Davids Michtam."[117] For the present, however,
his metaphors are "ragged" and "snick-snarled," his thoughts "taz-
zled."[118] The heavenly future must also be the location for his attempt
to imitate the divine standard for praise set by the Bridegroom of
Canticles in his praises of his Bride, the Church of elect souls: Christ's
"lips do distill / Upon his Spouse such ravishing dews to gust / With
Silver Metaphors and Tropes bedight"; his "Golden words" and
"sparkling Metaphors" adorn the Bride most gloriously.[119] The speaker
longs to participate in the Bride's responsive praises of the Bridegroom,
as recorded in Canticles, but he cannot even approach this standard
with his poor pipe—it must await heavenly tuning:

> Which Rhetorick of thine my Lord descry
>   Such influences from thy Spouses face
> That do upon me run and raise thy Joy
>   Above my narrow Fancy to uncase.
>   But yet demands my praise so high, so much
>   The which my narrow pipe can neer tune such.
> . . . . . . . . . . . . . . . . . . . . . . .
>   I'le with my little pipe thy praises sing.
>   Accept I pray and what for this I borrow,
>   I'le pay thee more when rise on heavens morrow.[120]

Taylor's poems are laced with biblical metaphors, and especially with
the tropes and emblems of Canticles. But the speaker's stance is not that
of imitator so much as exegete and analyst of these figures, explaining
them and relating them to himself in the only ways possible to the
mortal, sinful poet—by commenting on them, by recasting them in the

meiotic, colloquial terms which alone he can command, and by pointing up through deprecatory tropes how thoroughly his own condition contrasts with the glories there described. In Taylor's poems the various voices do not form a medley but a counterpoint. Divine and human rhetoric exist on different planes which will find their conjunction only in heaven—where he will sing David's Psalms and his own psalms with the angels, and where he will be able, as Bride, to respond to the Bridegroom in true imitation of his voice.

# PART III

*The Flowering of the English Religious Lyric*

## CHAPTER 8

# John Donne: Writing after the Copy of a Metaphorical God

Though Donne's sermons contributed vitally to the emerging Protestant poetics, not all of his *Divine Poems* are best explained in its terms. No doubt this fact helps explain why contemporaries referred to Herbert rather than Donne as the wellspring of the new school of English divine poetry. Nevertheless, though the dating of Donne's poems is often uncertain,[1] in general his religious lyrics reflect the Protestant poetics more and more fully, from early work to late.

At first Donne seemed little concerned with the ideas about genre deriving from Protestant poetics. His genres for religious poetry were often derived from secular forms (sonnet, verse letter); or were variations on liturgical forms (litany, hymn); or were ostensibly meditations on major feast days, events of the liturgical cycle, or standard Ignatian themes. But he came to rely increasingly upon the genres important in Protestant devotion and in biblical poetics theory. He praised the Sidney-Countess of Pembroke version of the Psalms as a new revelation of the Holy Spirit virtually equalling David's, and produced a close paraphrase of Lamentations. His *First Anniversary* is a complaint-elegy for a whole people in the Lamentations mode, and also a satire-cum-praise in the mode of the Mosaic hymn in Deuteronomy 32. The *Second Anniversary* is called a hymn, on the biblical poetics ground that it is an exalted praise of God—as revealed through his image in Elizabeth Drury.[2] Donne also wrote three poems of "occasional" meditation upon experience, analyzing significant providential occasions in his own life—"Goodfriday 1613. Riding Westward," "Hymne to Christ," and "Hymne to God my God, in my sicknesse."

A comparable development took place in other areas. Donne's earliest poems—"The Crosse," "Upon the Annunciation and Passion," and the "La Corona" sonnets—treat the great theological mysteries in terms of sacred paradoxes and puns long familiar in the Fathers and the medieval poets, and the same early poems are also linked to traditional meditative and emblematic forms. By contrast the "Holy Sonnets" are characterized by echoes of the Psalms and of the Pauline Epistles as well as by extensive use of prominent biblical metaphors for the sinner's condition. And, though there is little conventional use of typology in Donne's religious verse at any time, the later poems exhibit to a marked degree the Protestant tendency to find biblical events and typological relationships re-enacted within the self. In the "Holy Sonnets" the speaker re-enacts within himself Paul's experience of the predicament of the Christian; in the "Hymne to Christ" the speaker is a new Noah about to encounter a new Flood; in the "Hymne to God my God, in my sicknesse" the speaker's soul becomes the stage for the embodiment of the typological drama of the Old Adam and the New. This character-istic Protestant typological and meditative focus upon the self helps explain Donne's pervasive self-dramatization in these poems, which critics find variously impressive or deplorable.³ Moreover, as we have seen, he manifests some heightening of consciousness about the prob-lems of art and the sacred subject, moving from the comfortable as-sumption that the "La Corona" sequence is a proper fusion of "prayer and praise" devised in an appropriate devotional spirit ("my low devout melancholie"); to a recognition in "A Litanie" of the dangers of "excesse . . . Poëtiquenesse"; to the very self-conscious generic revisions in the "Hymne to God my God, in my sicknesse." He also displays growing concern with biblical personae and models—Jeremiah, Moses, John of Patmos in the *Anniversaries* and, less overtly, David and Paul in the "Holy Sonnets."⁴

We can best comprehend these developments by considering Donne's divine poems in broad generic categories: emblematic poems, poems based upon liturgical forms, poems of complimentary address, biblical paraphrase, poems focusing upon the Protestant drama of regeneration, and occasional meditations. In all these categories many poems, early and late, display in heightened form the Protestant emphasis upon the "application to the self" of all scripture and doctrine.

One group of poems shows the strong impress of Donne's emblematic imagination.⁵ Ostensibly they are traditional meditations in the Catholic manner on religious symbols, or on feast days, or on events in Christ's life. But Donne superimposes upon the meditative matter of these poems an overriding concern with the creation of or the analysis of a controlling emblem. Accordingly, the speaker does not approach his material as a meditator striving to understand and respond emotionally to his subject, but with the emblematist's wit and concern for formal design. Inappropriate expectations arising out of an approach to these poems as meditations accounts for some of the critical dissatisfaction with them.

"The Crosse," perhaps Donne's earliest religious poem,⁶ is a varia-

tion on an emblem poem explaining the significance of and arguing the
spiritual uses of the title emblem, the instrument of Christ's crucifixion.
The poem relates to the controversy in the early seventeenth century
over Puritan pressures to abolish the cross in the churches and the sign
of the cross in baptism, as relics of Popish superstition; James I rejected
those demands at the Hampton Court Conference in 1604, as does
Donne in the lines, "no Pulpit, nor misgrounded law, / Nor scandall
taken, shall this Crosse withdraw" (ll. 9-10). The poem is sometimes
criticized as mere witty display, lacking in religious feeling, but this is
to mistake its genre: it is not intended as a meditation upon the passion
or upon Christ's cross itself, but rather (as with the emblem poems of
Paradin or Peacham) it is an analysis and didactic interpretation of an
abstract symbolic figure. Although the poem is hardly among Donne's
masterpieces, it is much wittier and more artful than most emblem
poems.

Donne's controlling argument, that the cross is and should be omni-
present in our lives, is in two parts. The first proposition is that crosses
cannot in fact be abandoned, since they exist throughout nature:

> Who can deny mee power, and liberty
> To stretch mine armes, and mine owne Crosse to be?
> Swimme, and at every stroake, thou art thy Crosse,
> The Mast and yard make one, where seas do tosse.
> Looke downe, thou spiest out Crosses in small things;
> Looke up, thou seest birds rais'd on crossed wings;
> All the Globes frame, and spheares, is nothing else
> But the Meridians crossing Parallels.
> . . . . . . . . . . . . . . . . . .
> And as thy braine through bony walls doth vent
> By sutures, which a Crosses forme present. . . .
>
> (ll. 17-24, 55-56)

This section of the poem seems directly dependent upon an emblem
plate in Justus Lipsius' *De Cruce* which portrays most of these same
natural crosses—a man praying with arms outstretched; a man swim-
ming with arms extended; the mast of a ship; a cross-shaped handle of a
shovel and a wheelbarrow ("Crosses in small things"); a bird flying
with extended wings; a globe with meridians crossing parallels; a man's
head (presumably with crossed skull sutures).[7] The second proposition
extends and transposes the usual didactic application of the emblem to
derive a new argument on a higher plane—that in the spiritual order we
should supply for ourselves spiritual crosses everywhere, on the analogy
of their omnipresence in the material world. We should bear our crosses

of tribulation and become other Christs crucified; we should cross our
very joy in crosses lest it breed pride; we should cross all our senses in
their craving for pleasure; we should cross our hearts in their undue
dejections and exaltations; and we should cross our brain in its "concu-
piscence of witt." This last observation might well reflect with witty
irony upon the excess this very poem seems to display, in its constant
witty punning on "cross" as noun and verb and in several senses:
"Crosse / Your joy in crosses"; "But most the eye needs crossing";
"crosse thy heart"; "Crosse no man else, but crosse thy selfe in all"
(ll. 41-60). This wit is somewhat tempered by the analytic and didactic
tone characteristic of discrete emblems that present "the creatures" or
material objects as sources of moral and spiritual lessons. Donne's poem
concludes on this note, though very wittily:

> Then doth the Crosse of Christ worke fruitfully
> Within our hearts, when wee love harmlessly
> That Crosses pictures much, and with more care
> That Crosses children, which our Crosses are.
>
> (ll. 61-64)

Another early poem, "Upon the Annunciation and Passion falling
upon one day. 1608," ostensibly celebrates the feast day but actually
develops as a kind of emblem poem.[8] It is not a meditation upon either
or both events celebrated on the day, nor yet upon their Divine Actor.
And though Jonathan Goldberg is right to see typology in the back-
ground,[9] the poem focuses upon conjunctions rather than foreshadow-
ings. It treats the coincidence of these feasts upon a single day as an
emblem of the perfect circularity and unity of the Christian vision,
and to this end introduces the circle emblem immediately: this day
shows Christ "man, so like God made in this, / That of them both a
circle embleme is, / Whose first and last concurre" (ll. 3-4). This
special day, in which opposites are conjoined and united even as they
are in a circle or a globe, is accordingly "Th'Abridgement of Christs
story, which makes one / (As in plaine Maps, the furthest West is
East) / Of the'Angels *Ave*,'and *Consummatum est*" (ll. 20-22). The
circle thus supplies the governing figure for the all-pervasive and ex-
tremely witty paradoxes describing the Church's vision of circularity
and unity on this day:

> Shee sees him nothing twice at once, who'is all;
> Shee sees a Cedar plant it selfe, and fall,
> Her Maker put to making, and the head
> Of life, at once, not yet alive, and dead;

> She sees at once the virgin mother stay
> Reclus'd at home, Publique at Golgotha.
> Sad and rejoyc'd shee's seen at once, and seen
> At almost fiftie, and at scarce fifteene.
>
> (ll. 7-14)

Reflecting upon this emblematic day, the speaker perceives that the circularity and unity pertain not only to Christ's life but to human experience as well—"Death and conception in mankinde is one"—and that they also pertain to God's designing of Creation and Last Judgment as one period (ll. 34, 38). The poem concludes with the speaker's resolve to "uplay" the treasures of this day in gross, so that he may retail them to himself for future meditations.

A much more complex use of the emblem form is to be found in the seven interlinked "La Corona" sonnets, which are set forth as a "crowne of prayer and praise" offered to God.[10] One source of Donne's conception evidently is, as Louis Martz has suggested, the Corona rosary devotions, a special set of six decades with an appendage, devoted to the great events of the Virgin's life; in some versions, for instance that of Sabin Chambers, the subject matter corresponds rather closely to that of the last six sonnets in Donne's sequence. Martz calls attention to several specific precedents for Donne's sequence: the popular English "Corona of our Lord," which adapts the rosary devotions, as Donne does, to Christ; continental and English sequences of linked sonnets called "Coronas" by, e.g., Annibal Caro (1558), Gascoigne (1575), and Chapman (1595); and one Italian sequence combining the devotional and the poetic corona, called *Corona di laudi a Maria Vergine* (1617).[11] Donne's poetic corona of linked sonnets, insofar as it is a sequence of meditations on specific events or mysteries of the Christian faith, has obvious debts to this tradition. But as an exercise explicitly undertaking to fuse two modes of devotion—"*Deigne at my hands this crown of prayer and praise*"—it has biblical analogues which Donne persistently cites as evidencing the circularity and inseparability of prayer and praise. One is the Psalms: Donne observes, for example, that the first and last verses of Psalm 38 are prayers and that thereby "*David* makes up his Circle."[12] Another is the Lord's Prayer, which "being at first begun with glory and acknowledgement of his raigning in heaven, and then shut up in the same manner, with acclamations of power and glory, it is made a circle of praise, and a circle is infinite too, The Prayer, and the Praise is equally infinite."[13] Looking to such models, Donne has created a sequence which is not so much meditation as emblem, a crown of prayer and praise with some resemblance to those emblem figures of olive, bay, and laurel wreaths, representing tributes of praise for notable poetic and military accomplishments and divine reward for Christian perseverance.[14]

In the opening sonnet called "La Corona" this emblematic purpose is immediately announced: Donne relates the crown of prayer and praise he is constructing here for Christ to the crown of glory which he hopes will finally reward his poetry and his life; he also contrasts the crown of worldly honors with that crown of glory, seen as the direct consequence of Christ's crown of thorns:

> But doe not, with a vile crowne of fraile bayes,
> Reward my muses white sincerity,
> But what thy thorny crowne gain'd, that give mee,
> A crowne of Glory, which doth flower alwayes.
>
> (ll. 5-8)

Donne's imagery, opposing the true and false crowns to be won, derives from Isaiah (perhaps, as Helen Gardner suggests, by way of the Advent liturgy): "Woe to the crowne of pride, to the drunkards of Ephraim, whose glorious beauty is a fading flowre . . . / In that day shall the LORD of hosts be for a crowne of glory, and for a diademe of beautie unto the residue of his people" (Isaiah 28:1, 5).[15] The lines allude also to the eternal crowns worn by the white-robed saints in Revelation 4:4, 11, which they cast down before the throne of God in praise.[16]

The emblematic crown created by these sonnets undertakes to, and does, conjoin the two impulses of prayer and praise. The opening sonnet is in the mode of personal prayer to God, begging acceptance of the crown offered, and the reward of another; it modulates to praise at the end, echoing Isaiah 51:4-5, " 'Tis time that heart and voice be lifted high, / *Salvation to all that will is nigh*" (ll. 13-14). The next four sonnets, "Annunciation," "Nativitie," "Temple," "Crucyfying," are in the mode of praise, though praise here does not mean hymnic praise but rather meditative wonder and admiration over the mysteries of redemption. The stylistic embodiment for this admiration and wonder is paradox—brilliantly pointed and witty formulations of the time-honored medieval paradoxes. Christ is he "Which cannot sinne, and yet all sinnes must beare, / Which cannot die, yet cannot chuse but die." The Virgin conceives him who conceived her; she is apostrophized as "Thy Makers maker, and thy Fathers mother"; and she has "*Immensity cloysterd in thy deare wombe.*" The child lying in the manger at the Nativity is he "Which fils all place, yet none holds him"; the child in the Temple is the Word which "but lately could not speake, and loe / It sodenly speakes wonders." During the passion Christ's enemies "prescribe a Fate" to Christ, "Whose creature Fate is, . . . / Measuring selfe-lifes infinity to'a span, / Nay to an inch." Then Christ bears his cross, yet "When it beares him, he must beare more and die."[17]

The turning point in the sequence comes with the reversion to prayer at the end of the fifth sonnet, "Crucyfying": "Now thou art lifted up, draw mee to thee, / And at thy death giving such liberall dole / *Moyst, with one drop of thy blood, my dry soule*" (ll. 12-14). The sixth sonnet, "Resurrection," is wholly in the prayer mode: the speaker does not meditate upon Christ's resurrection but prays for his own resurrection from sin through Christ's blood, and from death at the last day. The final sonnet, "Ascension," weds the impulses of prayer and praise into perfect formal harmony: the octave is praise, extended to the public mode with the speaker exhorting all repentant sinners to "*Salute the last and everlasting day*, / Joy at the uprising of this Sunne, and Sonne." The sestet is again personal prayer to Christ, imaged as in Valeriano's emblems: "O strong Ramme . . . / Mild lambe . . . / Oh, with thine owne blood quench thine owne just wrath."[18] The sequence ends as it began, though now with the recognition, before unexpressed, of the Spirit's necessary role in contriving acceptable prayer and praise:

> And if thy holy Spirit, my Muse did raise,
> *Deigne at my hands this crowne of prayer and praise.*

The poetic devices used in the construction of this corona are subtle rhetorical figures of poetic interlinking and interweaving. Most obviously, the first and last lines of the entire sequence are identical, so that the sequence ends as it begins, as a crown or circle must; also, the last line of each individual sonnet is the first line of the next, so there is no hiatus to interrupt the circle's perfect continuity. And in addition to this, the constant use of ploce, repetition, and antithesis weaves lines and half-lines together—as, "The ends crowne our workes, but thou crown'st our ends, / For, at our end begins our endlesse rest, / This first last end, now zealously possest."[19] The "La Corona" sequence is not, like "The Crosse," an analysis of or a meditation upon an emblem, and neither is it primarily a meditative exercise upon specific mysteries. Rather, Donne here constructs a personal poetic emblem, even as he created his own *impresa* of the anchor-cross, and contrived an emblem *figura* of his own body on his deathbed.[20] "La Corona" creates a poetic crown for Christ out of traditional meditative, liturgical, emblematic, and rhetorical materials.

Two poems adapted from liturgical forms are "A Litanie" and the "Hymne to God the Father." The first is an Anglican version of the

Litany of the Saints—perhaps based upon Cranmer's version of 1544, which removed the long roll-call of individual Saints and retained only the headings of the major classes.[21] The second is in the mode of the congregational hymn or anthem, so impressively developed by Luther and Coverdale. These poems are alike remarkable in that they transpose public forms into private devotions relating directly to the personal situation and experience of the speaker. Yet at the same time, that speaker sees his individual experience as presenting a paradigm of the Christian's situation in the world.

Donne's account of the governing conception of "A Litanie" in his undated letter to Henry Goodyere cites precedents for turning public forms to private uses; he also asserts that his litany attains a true *via media*, honoring the saints in terms befitting a "rectified devotion":

> Since my imprisonment in my bed, I have made a meditation in verse, which I call a Litany. . . . Amongst ancient annals I mean some 800 years, I have met two Letanies in Latin verse, which gave me not the reason of my meditations, for in good faith I thought not upon them then, but they gave me a defence, if any man; to a Lay man, and a private, impute it as a fault, to take such divine and publique names, to his own little thoughts. The first of these was made by *Ratpertus* a Monk of *Suevia*; and the other by *S. Notker* . . . ; they were both but Monks, and the Letanies poor and barbarous enough; yet Pope *Nicolas* the 5, valued their devotion so much, that he canonized both their Poems, and commanded them for publike service in their Churches: mine is for lesser Chappels, which are my friends. . . . That by which it will deserve best acceptation, is, that neither the Roman Church need call it defective, because it abhors not the particular mention of the blessed Triumphers in heaven; nor the Reformed can discreetly accuse it, of attributing more then a rectified devotion ought to doe.[22]

Donne's medieval precedents are not altogether relevant, as he himself recognizes, since they were used as public litanies, not private exercises. Critics have complained that Donne's effort to transpose a public into a private devotion is of its very nature unpromising, and inevitably produced a flawed poem.[23] But there are no laws of aesthetics necessarily condemning such an undertaking, and I think that a sympathetic reading will recognize here not only an ingenious but also a remarkably effective work.

Keeping to the major structural divisions of the Litany of the Saints —the initial invocations to the Trinity; praises of the saints but with Protestant care to avoid the *ora pro nobis* formula or the stance of invocation; petitions for deliverance and for God's hearing (*Libera nos*,

*Domine, Audi nos, Domine*)—Donne analyzes a number of divine or saintly attributes in considerable detail, always applying them to his own circumstances. At the same time, his speaker moves out from an intimately personal posture to present himself as spokesman for, and his experience as typical of, a larger community.

In the first section, addressing the persons of the Trinity individually and collectively, the speaker in quasi-typological fashion proposes himself as a proper subject for the re-enactment of past divine actions. He begs the Father as creator to "re-create" him as a new Adam, out of the red earth to which his sins have reduced him: "My heart is by dejection, clay, / And by selfe-murder, red." He begs the Son, the redeemer, to re-enact the crucifixion within him: "O be thou nail'd unto my heart, / And crucified againe." He begs the Holy Ghost to purge and purify with his flame the sacrilegious temple of mud walls and condensed dust which he has become. And he prays the entire Trinity, with its united and distinguished functions of power, love, and knowledge, to work those effects within him: "Of these let all mee elemented bee, / Of power, to love, to know, you unnumbred three."[24]

The following stanzas (v-xiii) on the Virgin Mary, the angels, and the various categories of saints do not petition them for their prayers, but rather pray God to let them play an important and often precisely appropriate role in the speaker's spiritual life. Mary's office is treated first, but cautiously, and in general rather than personal terms—as if Donne were unsure as to just how a Protestant should formulate the claim upon her assistance: "As her deeds were / Our helpes, so are her prayers" (ll. 43-44). The speaker prays to God regarding the angels, that "mine actions bee / Worthy their sight, though [I am] blinde in how they see" (ll. 53-54). He asks that the patriarchs' desire to see Christ "Be satisfied, and fructifie in mee," who often see less in the "fire" of Grace than they did in the "cloud" of the Law. And he would especially engage the prophets who sounded the heavenly harmony of the two Testaments, and the heavenly poets "which did see / Thy will, and it expresse / In rythmique feet" to pray for him, "That I by them excuse not my excesse / In seeking secrets, or Poëtiquenesse" (ll. 68-72). He prays God also to let the Apostles shape his biblical commentary, "that I goe / Th'old broad way in applying: O decline / Mee, when my comment would make thy word mine" (ll. 79-81). At this point the speaker assumes a more public stance, begging God to permit the other categories of saints to serve "us" in various ways: let the martyrs beg for us the patience neither to seek nor to avoid martyrdom; let the confessors pray that we, like them, may understand our temptations to be a kind of persecution. This sequence ends with two witty counter-examples: the virgins cannot pray that we be preserved as they were in our first integrity, but God can divorce sin in us "And call chast widowhead Virginitie"; and the doctors need to pray for our protection against themselves, that we may not adhere to "what they have mis-done / Or mis-said."

Stanza xiv, introducing the deprecations ("*Libera nos, Domine*"),[25] expresses the idea—implicit in the earlier stanzas—of the conjoined prayers of the saints in heaven and on earth, and wittily prays God's deliverance from trusting in such prayers rather than in God only. Subsequent petitions ask deliverance from excesses or inadequacies in regard to faith or works; they are spoken for the community (us) but obviously couched in terms personally felt. The overriding concern is to find mean ways, evenness in the practice of religion: "From being anxious, or secure / Dead clods of sadnesse, or light squibs of mirth, / . . . From needing danger, to bee good, / . . . From being spies, or to spies pervious, / From thirst, or scorne of fame, deliver us."[26] Finally, the obsecrations beg (by the events of Christ's life) for deliverance from more customary evils—from death, from idolatry and hypocrisy, from evils in church and state, from plague or war or heresy, from all evil in the hour of death and on the eve of Judgment.[27]

The final section, Supplications and Intercessions ("*Audi nos, Domine*"),[28] develops with paradoxical wit all the problems of hearing—of God's hearing us, and of our own "labyrinthine" ears. The speaker begs God to hear himself in us—"Heare us, for till thou heare us, Lord / We know not what to say"; to hear us so "That we may heare"[29] in scripture and nature God's promises and threats; to open his ears so that we may lock ours against sinful speech; to lock his ears against just complaints against us so that we may open ours to profit from them. At length, as the speaker prays to be led to use all God's goods properly, a brilliant emblematic image of God as ear (analogous to that in Hugo and Quarles)[30] together with a conceit of God as the cry which we weakly echo in our own prayers, resolves the problem of ears and hearing:

> That learning, thine Ambassador,
> From thine allegeance wee never tempt,
> That beauty, paradises flower
> For physicke made, from poyson be exempt,
> That wit, borne apt, high good to doe,
> By dwelling lazily
> On Natures nothing, be not nothing too,
> That our affections kill us not, nor dye,
> Heare us, weake ecchoes, O thou eare, and cry.
>
> (ll. 235-243)

The last stanza of the poem declines from this pitch of intensity to a conclusion perhaps over-witty and facile, though not without feeling— a prayer that sin, taken by Christ from us and unable to stick to him, may simply disappear: "As sinne is nothing, let it no where be" (l. 252).

The deceptively simple yet brilliantly witty and withal profoundly moving "Hymne to God the Father" almost defies description. This is not a hymn in the classical or biblical poetics sense of an exalted praise of God; it is more closely related to the anthem or congregational hymn[31]—but with characteristic Donnean personalization. Walton's description of the intense personal emotion Donne felt upon hearing the public performance of this anthem may be partly apocryphal, but it does suggest Donne's special delight in creating poems which are at once public and very private:

> He caus'd it [this Hymne] to be set to a most grave and solemn Tune, and to be often sung to the *Organ* by the *Choristers* of St. *Pauls* Church, in his own hearing, especially at the Evening Service; and at his return from his Customary Devotions in that place, did occasionally say to a friend *The words of this* Hymne *have restored to me the same thoughts of joy that possest my Soul in my sickness when I composed it. And, O the power of Church-musick! that Harmony added to it has raised the Affections of my heart, and quicned my graces of zeal and gratitude;* and I observe, *that I alwayes return from paying this publick duty of* Prayer *and* Praise *to* God, *with an unexpressible tranquillity of mind,* and a willingness *to leave the world.*[32]

The speaker adopts a personal stance throughout, but in the first four lines of each six-line stanza the "I" may be universalized—each member of the congregation could make these interrogations and petitions in his own name, asking God to forgive various generalized categories of sins of which all are guilty. But the pun on done/Donne in the final lines of each stanza personalizes this congregational hymn in an altogether remarkable way—so that it has direct and unique reference to Donne himself, by name. Especially in the final stanza, as the speaker confesses his besetting sin of fear and finds the resolution of his problem in his characteristic sun/Son pun, are we aware of how completely personal the anthem is:

> I have a sinne of feare, that when I have spunne
>      My last thred, I shall perish on the shore;
> Sweare by thy selfe, that at my death thy sonne
>      Shall shine as he shines now, and heretofore;
>           And, having done that, Thou hast done,
>                I have no more.[33]

Yet even here the speaker can have it both ways: only the initiate need recognize that audacious pun on Donne's name, or know of his besetting sin of fear. Donne has contrived a congregational hymn which at one and the same time provides a form of simple devotion for all to sing, and a *tour de force* of wit which is the unique personal expression of its inordinately witty poet.

By common critical consent the most remarkable of Donne's *Divine Poems* are the nineteen "Holy Sonnets," "Goodfriday, 1613. Riding Westward," the "Hymne to Christ," the "Hymne to God my God, in my sicknesse," and a few occasional pieces. These are also the poems most profoundly affected by the Protestant poetics we have been tracing.

The "Holy Sonnets" pose a special problem because of the uncertainty, unresolvable from present knowledge, regarding the sequence in which they were written or were intended to be read. Louis Martz approaches them as discrete poems reflecting, some more and some. less completely, the topics and structure to be found in typical Ignatian meditation—though his discussion indicates that the Ignatian three-part structure (preparation, analysis, colloquy) is present with any completeness only in two or three of them.[34] Helen Gardner, on the basis of persuasive manuscript evidence and somewhat less satisfactory argument from internal evidence, has discriminated a set of six meditations on the Last Things (presumably sent with the dedicatory sonnet "To the E. of D.") and another set of six on the love of God for us and our love for him. These twelve sonnets appear—in the order in which Dame Helen reprints them—in the Group I and Group II manuscripts and in the first edition, 1633. In 1635, four new sonnets were added, interspersed among these; Dame Helen takes them to have been originally intended as a rather loosely organized sequence on the topic of penitence (though the first of them has virtually nothing to do with that matter). The final three are assumed to be separate occasional meditations, written later and available only in the Westmoreland manuscript until their late first printing in 1899.[35] Other readers of the "Holy Sonnets" have suggested other thematic and structural patterns: the Anglican doctrine of contrition, involving a progress from fear to love to contrite sorrow; a penitential exercise deriving from Augustinian devotion as developed by the Franciscans; a spiritual progress in four meditative stages (adapted from Elizabethan love sonnet sequences), leading from religious doubt to assurance; an exploration, lacking sequence and progress, of several dramatic stances from lament to assurance which the speaker adopts in the continuing drama of Christian life.[36]

I suggest that the sonnets are best read in relation to another unifying principle, akin to but transcending such patterns: the Protestant paradigm of salvation in its stark, dramatic, Pauline terms. As meditations these sonnets most closely resemble those regular Protestant exercises of self-analysis which involve a review of the soul's own state and the experiences and evidences of God's actions within it.[37] The paradigm assumes an order which, I suggest, the sonnets reflect, both in Gardner's twelve-sonnet sequence which has some authority from the manuscripts and the first edition, and in the 1635 arrangement made conventional by Grierson. Since Donne left no holographs of these poems, and did not prepare them for publication, and since we cannot even be certain about the dates of composition, it is well-nigh impossible to argue conclusively any questions of sequence. I will discuss the sonnets as they appear in the 1635 ordering, as that seems to be an expansion of the fundamental terms and direction of the twelve-sonnet group; whoever arranged the 1635 sonnets perceived the essential thematic concern of the twelve to be the analysis of states of soul attendant upon Christian regeneration, and inserted the four additional sonnets precisely where they would be thematically most suitable. Obviously, the sonnets may not have been intended as a sequence: Donne may have wished simply to examine various discrete moments in the speaker's spiritual drama. And in some sense, from the Protestant perspective the question of sequence is irrelevant. As the Protestant emblem books and lyric collections make plain,[38] except for a beginning with effectual calling, and an ending with the longing for final glorification, the various states are not so much sequential as concomitant: we may recall Calvin's insistence that God's graces come not singly but together.[39] As topics to be considered in the Protestant meditative exercise of self-examination, such spiritual states as election, calling, conviction of sin, repentance, faith, justification, adoption, may and should be newly experienced and relived at any time, to provide matter for meditative exercise.

My argument is that these poems yield more fully to an analysis of their biblical motifs, their anguished Pauline speaker, their presentation of states of soul attendant upon the Protestant drama of regeneration, than they do to any other meditative scheme. They are permeated with biblical metaphor, psalm allusions, and Pauline echoes—referring not so much to the exact words as to the substance of Romans and Galatians and Corinthians. And the precise theological terms which also resound through these sonnets—"Impute me righteous," "make me new," "adoption"—afford clear evidence of their primary concern with the Protestant paradigm of salvation.

The first poem of the 1635 sequence is one of the interpolated son-
nets. It is easy to see why it is so placed: it is linked thematically (by
the references to creation and to the speaker's psychic condition of
near-despair) to the following poem (the first sonnet in the 1633 se-
quence). It sounds the leitmotifs of the entire series—creation, decay,
death, sin, reparation: "Thou hast made me, And shall thy worke decay?
/ Repaire me now, for now mine end doth haste, / I runne to death"
(ll. 1-3). And it presents graphically the condition of anguish, terror,
helplessness and despair accompanying |the |conviction |of |sin and guilt
which is the first effect of God's calling—the mollifying of hard and
sinful hearts with which the Protestant spiritual drama begins. The
speaker, with echoes of the Psalmist's cry in Psalm 6:6-7—"I am weary
with my groning. . . . / Mine eie is consumed because of griefe"—
expects imminent death from sin's corruption, and is in an agony of
helplessness: "I dare not move my dimme eyes any way, / Despaire
behind, and death before doth cast / Such terrour." The sestet records
a temporary relief through the remembrance of God, but this is under-
cut by the realization that the speaker cannot resist Satan's temptations
"one houre." The only hope—effectual calling—is suggested in the final
couplet, evoking a striking emblem from Georgette de Montenay of
an iron heart drawn irresistibly by an adamant stone held out from
heaven: "Thy Grace may wing me to prevent his art / And thou like
Adamant draw mine iron heart."[40] The second sonnet, "As due by
many titles" (first in the 1633 series) focuses upon the problem of elec-
tion. At the outset the speaker evokes a long series of biblical meta-
phors which establish the various titles by which God could claim
ownership of him, and which might seem to "prove" his election: he
is God's creature, he is bought by Christ's blood, he is son, servant,
sheep, image, and temple of the Holy Spirit. But in the sestet he recog-
nizes that Satan's conquest has undermined these legal titles: he cannot
now be reclaimed unless God will actively fight for him. And he vir-
tually despairs of election. His condition finds definition in the classic
texts in Romans 8:28-30—"All things worke together for good . . .
to them who are the called according to his purpose. / . . . Whom he
did predestinate, them he also called"—in conjunction with the chilling
warning in Matthew 20:16, "Many bee called, but fewe chosen." So
Donne's speaker fears that he may not be among the elect: "thou lov'st
mankind well, yet wilt'not chuse me."

The next three sonnets concern the speaker's grief for sin and efforts
to repent: true repentance is the first outward sign of the working of
God's grace in the soul though, as Perkins points out, even the reprobate
may manifest some of these signs.[41] Donne's speaker has as yet no con-

fidence that his grief is a sign of true repentance. Two of these sonnets (III and V) are new in the 1635 volume. "Sonnet III," "O might those sighes and teares returne againe" is about the condition of fruitless grief: the speaker desires now to "Mourne with some fruit, as I have mourn'd in vaine"—with reference to his former sinful agonies and miseries in his love-idolatries. The speaker longs for the "fruit" of repentance promised in Psalm 126:6, "He that goeth forth and weepeth, bearing precious seed, shall doubtlesse come again with rejoycing; bringing his sheaves with him," but he has no such fruit: "To (poore) me is allow'd / No ease; for, long, yet vehement griefe hath beene / Th'effect and cause, the punishment and sinne." Moreover, he is unable to distinguish essentially between his present and his past griefs, and so does not experience the effect of true sorrow described in 2 Corinthians 7:10—which could almost be the text for this sonnet: "For godly sorrow worketh repentance to salvation not to be repented of, but the sorrow of the world worketh death." In "Sonnet IV" the speaker finds his "blacke Soule" summoned by sickness, death's herald, and, like an exiled traitor or an imprisoned thief, he fears execution far more than present miseries. The essence of his spiritual state is summed up at the beginning of the sestet: "Yet grace, if thou repent, thou canst not lacke; / But who shall give thee that grace to beginne?" God of course must give that prevenient grace and the repentance itself: the speaker proposes to make himself *black* with mourning and *red* with blushing (as he is with sin), but recognizes that it is Christ's blood "which hath this might / That being red, it dyes red soules to white." "Sonnet V," "I am a little world made cunningly," perhaps received its place not only because of the continuation of the motif of grief and repentance, but also from the conception of the "blacke Soule" now threatened with imminent death: "black sinne hath betraid to endlesse night / My worlds both parts, and (oh) both parts must die." The inevitability of this result for his little world is indicated as the lines play off against various texts in Romans (5:12, 6:23): "By one man sinne entred into the world, and death by sin: and so death passed upon all men"; "For the wages of sinne is death." The speaker then envisions that death: he would drown his little world with the tears of his repentance if he could, but he recalls that after Noah worlds are not to be drowned any longer; so he offers hopefully to wash it. But that route of repentance seems not now available: instead he expects and deserves the other punishment established for the great world at the end of time—"But oh it must be burnt"—in punishment of previous burnings by lust and envy. Yet there is still a way to suffer burning which would be restorative and (almost paraphrasing Psalm 69:9)[42] he prays for that:

"burne me ô Lord, with a fiery zeale / Of thee and thy house, which doth in eating heale."

"Sonnet VI," "This is my playes last scene," is something of a turning point: the speaker vividly imagines himself at the moment of death, but not by evoking a deathbed scene in the manner of an Ignatian *compositio loci*. Instead, the speaker calls upon the very familiar biblical metaphors of life as pilgrimage and as athletic race—"here heavens appoint / My pilgrimages last mile; and my race / Idly, yet quickly runne"—and evokes a traditional emblem in the image of a personified, "gluttonous death" unjointing the body.[43] The means for dispelling the shaking fear of God's judgment this vision provokes is specified when the speaker cries out in the couplet, "Impute me righteous": the imputation of Christ's righteousness, forgiving and covering sins with his merits, is the result of justification, and this alone gives assurance of salvation. The speaker's cry indicates that he clearly understands his need and that his faith is now strong enough to formulate it, in terms suggestive of the long discussion in Romans 4:6-24 which begins by referring to the Psalmist's description of "the blessednesse of the man, unto whom God imputeth righteousnesse without works."[44] The speaker hopes, with somewhat strained wit, that this justification might take place for him at the moment of death, for at that time (as not earlier) his soul will leave his body and his body will leave the world, so that if his sins will also (by justification) depart to the hell that bred them he can be said to leave "the world, the flesh, and devill."

"Sonnet VII," "At the round earths imagin'd corners" seems related to the preceding one, as the consideration of the moment of death leads logically to meditation upon the Day of Judgment. There is here some impress of the meditation upon the Last Things, and this sonnet is one of the two or three which exhibit the full Ignatian meditative structure. There is a vivid *compositio loci*: the first line (despite its witty reservation) evokes the scene in Revelation 7:1, "I saw foure Angels standing on the foure corners of the Earth"; and the octave fleshes out the details of the parade of souls arising and seeking their bodies. The dead include the primary categories the speaker considered in Sonnet V while anticipating his own death as microcosm—"All whom the flood did, and fire shall o'erthrow"—as well as other agents of death drawn in part from Revelation 6:8 and Ezekiel 14:21: war, famine, age, agues, tyrannies, despair, law, chance.[45] The sestet provides a sharp *volte* as the speaker prays, "But let them sleepe, Lord, and mee mourne a space." Modifying the conclusion in his previous sonnet, in which he asks God to justify him at the very moment of death, the speaker here observes, " 'Tis late to aske abundance of thy grace, / When wee are there." We might have expected him to say it was too late—but the formulation suggests the growth of the speaker's faith and his recognition that nothing is impossible to God. Now, however, he begs for more time to mourn his sins and asks specifically for the divine gift of true repentance, for that would be a trustworthy sign of his election and justification: "Teach mee how to repent; for that's as good / As if thou'hadst seal'd my pardon, with thy blood."

"Sonnet VIII," "If faithfull soules be alike glorifi'd," is again interpolated, and was evidently placed here in evidence that the speaker has obtained the true repentance he sought. The poem turns on scholastic distinctions of modes of knowing: if the speaker's dead father knows as angels do, he will know his son's repentance to be sincere, but if those sainted souls can be misled by the appearances of grief or feigned devotions, he cannot know this.[46] The speaker however is now confident enough of his repentance—"my mindes white truth"—to appeal directly to God to testify to it: "he knowes best / Thy true griefe, for he put it in my breast." "Sonnet IX," "If poysonous mineralls," enacts the speaker's true repentance and faith: after an almost blasphemous false start in the octave, he suddenly abandons all efforts to mitigate his guilt or to object to the sentence of damnation he deserves, throwing himself without reservation upon Christ's mercy in the earnest hope of justification. The entire sonnet shows the speaker defining himself against Job who maintained his integrity and righteousness before God, implying that God has unjustly dealt with him.[47] By contrast, Donne's speaker admits readily that his sins deserve damnation but, in the octave, he too contends with God about the injustice of the threatened punishment: he protests that his reason unfairly subjects him to punishment not accorded to evils in nature or to vicious animals, and he argues that a God to whom mercy is easy should not show wrath. It is a specious argument, as he recognizes in his outcry, "But who am I, that dare dispute with thee?"—echoing Elihu's rebuke to Job and Paul's rebuke to one who would question God's incomprehensible will: "Therefore hath hee mercie on whom hee will have mercy, and whom he will, he hardeneth / . . . Who art thou that repliest against [disputest with, margin] God? Shall the thing formed say to him that formed it, Why hast thou made me thus?"[48] The speaker finds his only hope in a "heavenly Lethean flood" made up of Christ's "onely worthy blood" and his own tears, to drown the very memory of those sins; in this he defines himself not only against Job, but also against the Psalmist who grounded his plea for God's mercy upon God's remembrance—"according to thy mercie remember thou me."[49] The speaker of this sonnet finds his best hope in God's total forgetting:

"That thou remember them, some claime as debt, / I thinke it mercy, if thou wilt forget." In Calvinist terms, this is precisely what justification means—that God will not see the sinner himself and his own sins, but will remember him only in Christ. This justification, evidenced by his true repentance and faith, brings the speaker a kind of victory over his sins.

That victory leads on to a conquest over death in the "Death be not Proud" sonnet (X), the first of several which focus upon the speaker's manifestation of saving faith—whereby in Perkins' terms he "doth particularly applie unto himselfe those promises which are made in the Gospel."[50] In this sonnet the speaker, confident that he partakes of Christ's conquest over death, is able to face down the fear of death which has haunted him in the foregoing sonnets; moreover, in his tirade against the braggart Death (seemingly "Mighty and dreadfull" but in fact a powerless bully) he even enacts his own imitation of Christ's victory over death. The speaker can afford his condescension ("poore death") because he finds death no longer has power over him—"nor yet canst thou kill mee." And the apocalyptic terrors envisaged in "Sonnet VII" as the instruments of death are here wittily transposed into the unsavory masters of or companions to death: "Thou art slave to Fate, chance, kings, and desperate men, / And dost with poyson, warre, and sicknesse dwell." The whole sonnet, and especially the final lines, show the speaker recapitulating Paul's affirmation of the resurrection as an ultimate victory over death: "In a moment, in the twinckling of an eye . . . the trumpet shall sound, and the dead shall be raised incorruptible, and we shall be changed. / . . . Death is swallowed up in victorie. / O death, where is thy sting? O grave, where is thy victorie?"[51] Donne's speaker proclaims: "One short sleepe past, wee wake eternally, / And death shall be no more, Death thou shalt die."

The next three sonnets are concerned with Christ's crucifixion, as the speaker exhibits his faith by applying the benefits of that crucifixion to himself. He begins by attempting a false application: in "Sonnet XI," "Spit in my face yee Jewes," he imagines himself undertaking the role of the crucified Christ in a surprising reversal of the meditator's usual stance before the crucified one. The speaker seeks to arrogate to himself all the elements of Christ's passion, recognizing that his sins richly deserve them; but his faith reveals, of course, that the gesture is useless: "by my death can not be satisfied / My sinnes." Instead he finds, ironically, that he is one of the crucifiers—"They kill'd once an inglorious man, but I / Crucifie him daily, being now glorified." There is grave danger to the speaker in this recognition: Paul declared

(Heb. 6:6) that those, once enlightened, who fall away, will not again be renewed, "seeing they crucifie to themselves the Sonne of God afresh, and put him to an open shame." The sestet resolves the problem through faith in Christ's infinite mercy. Although the speaker is not strong enough to put on the accoutrements of Christ's passion, Christ, as antitype of Jacob disguised in "vile harsh attire" puts on man's "vile flesh" to make himself "weake enough to suffer woe." "Sonnet XII," "Why are wee by all creatures waited on?" examines the wonderful circumstance that sinful and weak man is served by purer elements, by stronger animals, and by a whole creation untarnished by sin, as a means to understand more fully the wonderful benefits of Christ's crucifixion: "But their Creator, whom sin, nor nature tyed, / For us, his Creatures, and his foes, hath dyed." The last sonnet on this theme, "What if this present were the world's last night?" (XIII), briefly recalls the Apocalypse, but now it is devoid of terror. The speaker now has "in my heart . . . / The picture of Christ crucified," and contemplation of that picture reinforces his faith that the suffering, loving Christ will save him. The sestet plays an almost scandalous variation upon the serious affirmation of faith in the octave: now the speaker begs Christ for reassurance of his mercy, arguing the Platonic connection between Beauty and Goodness which he used to cite in wooing his "profane mistresses"—"This beauteous forme assures a pitious mind." This whimsical wooing of Christ testifies to some confidence in the relationship, but at the same time to the wooer's constant need of reassurance: faith, like repentance, shows its variations and fluctuations over a whole lifetime.

"Sonnet XIV," "Batter my heart, three person'd God," is explicitly about regeneration, "making new." Regeneration, or sanctification, is a process distinct from and yet accompanying justification (the imputing of Christ's merits to the elect), and involves the renovation of the soul by degrees, so that, progressively but never completely, the corruptions of sin are purged from it and the image of God is restored in it.[52] Donne's speaker dramatizes his regeneration in uncompromising Calvinist terms, as solely the effect of God's grace upon his passive and helpless self. The imagery recalls several graphic descriptions and heart emblems representing the softening or mollifying of the heart as the first stage of regeneration:

> Batter my heart, three person'd God; for, you
> As yet but knocke, breathe, shine, and seeke to mend;
> That I may rise, and stand, o'erthrow mee,'and bend
> Your force, to breake, blowe, burn and make me new.[53]

With characteristic dramatic imagination and application of this abstract doctrine to himself, the speaker invites the whole of God's power and force to be directed upon himself in a much more intense form than the biblical norm would seem to require. God usually calls men by knocking—"Behold, I stand at the doore, and knocke: if any man heare my voyce, and open the doore, I will come in to him (Rev. 3:20)"—but the speaker insists that God must break down his door. Or, God customarily gives his spirit to men by breathing upon them— at the creation to give life to Adam, in the upper room to give the Holy Spirit to the Apostles[54]—but this speaker would have God blow upon him more fiercely. Likewise, God's people pray constantly that his face may shine upon them in blessing, but this speaker demands not shining but burning.[55] Mere mending will not suffice to his regeneration: he must be made new by violence. The need for such violence is argued from his present situation, resembling a usurped town or a seduced spouse in the possession of an enemy. The speaker insists that his release must be worked by force, in paradoxical reversal of Christ's customary relationships with the soul—as liberator ("Stand fast therefore in the libertie wherewith Christ hath made us free, and bee not intangled againe with the yoke of bondage") and as Bridegroom:

> Take mee to you, imprison mee, for I
> Except you'enthrall me, never shall be free,
> Nor ever chast, except you ravish mee.[56]

The Calvinist sense of man's utter helplessness in his corruption and total dependence upon God's grace in every aspect of his spiritual life could hardly find more powerful and paradoxical expression than in this declaration that Christ can be liberator of the soul only by becoming its jailer, and can be its Bridegroom only by becoming its ravisher.

The last two sonnets of the 1635 (and 1633) sequences focus upon the further ramifications of justification and regeneration. "Sonnet XV," "Wilt thou love God, as he thee!" invites the soul to meditate upon God's love shown especially in the matter of the speaker's adoption as a son of God. In the Calvinist paradigm adoption is the result of justification: it gives the believer Christian peace of mind and confidence that he is again a child of God, to whom the promise pertains, "And if children, then heires, heires of God, and joynt-heires [co-heires, Rheims] with Christ . . . that wee may be also glorified together (Rom. 8:17)." The speaker exhibits the confidence attendant upon adoption, and reviews all its benefits to himself, attributed variously to the three persons of the Trinity:[57] "the Spirit . . . doth make his Temple in thy brest"; "The Father . . . / Hath deign'd to chuse

thee by adoption, / Coheire to'his glory,'and Sabbaths endlesse rest";
the Son has achieved thy release from bondage, "unbinding" thee from
Satan. The most spectacular evidence and cause of adoption is the In-
carnation: "'Twas much, that man was made like God before, / But,
that God should be made like man, much more."

The final sonnet in both the 1633 and 1635 sequences, "Father, part
of his double interest," takes up the issue of how the regenerate Chris-
tian should serve God, how he should exhibit that "new obedience"
to God's will that was understood to be the effect of regeneration and
adoption[58]—especially in view of the Pauline/Protestant insistence that
none can fulfill the Law laid down by God in the commandments.
The speaker, conscious of the "interest" given him in the kingdom by
his adoption, confronts the knotty issue of how to lay claim to his in-
heritance. Referring to the "two Wills" (the Old and New Testa-
ments) wherein God has set out the terms of that inheritance, and
recognizing that "None doth" fulfill the commandments of the Law,
he appeals to the nature and the effects of the New Covenant: "all-heal-
ing grace and Spirit, / Revive againe what law and letter kill." These
lines echo a medley of Pauline texts: "no man is justified by the Lawe
in the sight of God"; "God / . . . hath made us able ministers of the
New Testament, not of the letter, but of the spirit: for the letter
killeth, but the spirit giveth life."[59] The speaker finds his resolution in
recalling that the New Covenant Law, the summary and epitome of
the Old Law, is simply love of God and neighbor: "Thy lawes abridge-
ment, and thy last command / Is all but love; Oh let that last Will
stand!"[60]

The remaining three sonnets from the Westmoreland manuscript
are more strictly occasional pieces, all of them concerned with one or
another of the exigencies of the regenerate Christian life. "Sonnet
XVII," "Since she whome I lovd, hath payd her last debt," must have
been written after the death of Ann Donne (August 15, 1617). In it
the speaker adopts a Platonic doctrine, viewing his love for his wife
as the means which led him to seek God, "so streames do shew the
head." Now he seeks God's love alone, but is still unsatisfied—"A holy
thirsty dropsy melts mee yett." In the sestet, however, he admits that
he has no grounds for complaint: God has offered all his own love
in exchange for his wife's, and has every reason to be jealous of the
speaker's propensity to give his love to others—not only to holy beings
(angels, saints, his wife) but even to the world, the flesh, and the devil.
The sonnet, especially its conclusion, seems less unified and effective
than is usual with Donne.

"Sonnet XVIII," "Show me deare Christ, thy spouse," might have been conceived as a sequel to the above, moving from the speaker's love of his own spouse to his love of Christ's Spouse, the Church; as Ricks notes, we can read with the emphasis, "Show *me* deare Christ, *thy* spouse."[61] The octave centers upon the problem of identifying that Spouse: one claimant is "richly painted" (Rome); another is "rob'd and tore" (the Reformed Church), and they are variously located "On one, on seaven, or on no hill." Their counterclaims are fraught with paradox: "Sleepes she a thousand, then peepes up one yeare? / Is she selfe truth and errs? now new, now outwore?" The resolution to these baffling paradoxes must rest with Christ's contriving a still more amazing and outrageous paradox. Christ must from Bridegroom turn pander, and so "Betray" his Spouse to the loves of others. And the Spouse, rather than exhibiting the undefiled purity of the Bride of Canticles and of Revelation,[62] must in the necessary promiscuity of her love to many, turn harlot:

> Betray kind husband thy spouse to our sights,
> And let myne amorous soule court thy mild Dove,
> Who is most trew, and pleasing to thee, then
> When she'is embrac'd and open to most men.

Surely no one but Donne would so wittily seem to confuse the Bride with her antithesis in Revelation, the Great Whore of Babylon (Rev. 17:4-18), playing upon the contemporary Protestant term of opprobrium for Rome to point up the essential spiritual qualities God's church must display.

"Sonnet XIX," "Oh, to vex me, contraryes meete in one," could relate to virtually any stage of the Christian saga of regeneration, but it stands as a fitting summary of the vacillations and vicissitudes of the speaker's spiritual life. His changeable vows, his "humorous" contrition, his ague-like fits of devotion, his alterations between courting God in flattering speeches and quaking in "true feare of his rod" describe the varying moods of these sonnets and are a personal version of that perpetual internal warfare Paul describes, between the old man and the new, the body and the spirit. Donne's speaker does not cry as Paul does for deliverance—"Oh wretched man that I am: who shall deliver me from the body of this death?" (Rom. 7:24). Instead, like David the Psalmist, he perceives the special acceptability of a "broken and a contrite heart" and so prefers his agitated emotional state to complacency. His "true feare" may also partake of the quality praised in Job 28:28—"The feare of the Lord, that is wisdome"—affording sound theological basis for his paradoxical conclusion, "Those are my best dayes, when I shake with feare." The wit of these sonnets, though often very daring, is almost always in the service of serious theological analysis and profound emotional responses.

A few of Donne's *Divine Poems* in the genre of the verse letter testify explicitly to Donne's developing engagement with some of the issues important in Protestant poetics. The dedicatory sonnet to Magdalen Herbert, which probably accompanied the "La Corona" sequence,[63] gives early evidence of such engagement, as much by the devices not used as by those employed. There is no sign here of the ubiquitous tears and passionate laments accompanying the Magdalen's dramatic conversion from harlot to penitent which was the topic of so much Counter Reformation art and poetry. Donne's poem is restrained and biblical; it holds the Magdalen forth not as a saint of penitence but as an exponent of the Protestant virtue of "active faith" (l. 3), in that, being made a herald of the Resurrection, she for a time knew more of Christianity than the Church itself. The verse letter "To Mr. Tilman after he had taken orders," probably written after Tilman was ordained priest in March, 1620,[64] is a thoughtful, restrained, and quite effective defense of the ministry as a noble calling; as several critics have noted, Donne's strongly urged complaints against the worldly gentry for their social discrimination against ministers says much more about Donne's own ambivalences in embracing that life than Tilman's.[65] The defense is in distinctly Protestant terms: the speaker assumes that orders have somehow changed Tilman but he does not put his queries about such changes in sacramental terms, nor does he discuss the sacerdotal or even the liturgical functions of a priest. Instead the focus is upon preaching as the essence and the glory of the ministerial office: ministers, like angels, "beare Gods message, and proclaime his lawes" (l. 20).

More directly concerned with the questions of poetics is the verse letter praising the translation of the Psalms by Sir Philip Sidney and the Countess of Pembroke, which must have been written after the Countess's death in 1621, since the speaker puns upon the "translation" of those translators.[66] The issue here, basic to the emerging Protestant poetics, involves the relation of contemporary religious poets (and translators) to the biblical poets, notably David. Donne finds the inspiration and the art of the Sidney-Pembroke psalms to be virtually on a par with the Psalmist's originals: the new psalms are (and Donne intimates that to be successful such works must be) not so much translations as re-revelations of God's Spirit:

> That, as thy blessed Spirit fell upon
> These Psalmes first Author in a cloven tongue;
> (For 'twas a double power by which he sung
> The highest matter in the noblest forme;)
> So thou hast cleft that spirit, to performe
> That worke againe, and shed it, here . . .
> . . . . . . . . . . . . . . . . . . . . .
> The songs are these, which heavens high holy Muse
> Whisper'd to *David, David* to the Jewes:
> And *Davids* Successors, in holy zeale,
> In formes of joy and art doe re-reveale.
>                           (ll. 8-13, 31-34)

These "Sydnean Psalmes" and these new Psalmists (who are also a new Moses and Miriam) are models for contemporary religious poets: "They tell us *why*, and teach us *how* to sing" (l. 22). Donne recognizes that these psalms, with their intricate stanzaic patterns and rhythms, are "chamber" versions, not suitable for congregational singing, yet the standard of art they achieve ought to be realized also in the public liturgy of the English Church, as it is in the Reformed Church abroad. (The much-berated Sternhold-Hopkins Old Version is here contrasted unfavorably with such continental versions as the Maròt-Bèze psalter and the Lutheran psalmody.)[67] The use of the Sidney-Pembroke psalms is to "tune" us for the heavenly hymns we shall some day sing in their company:

> And, till we come th'Extemporall song to sing,
> . . . . . . . . . . . . . . . . . . . . .
> These their sweet learned labours, all the way
> Be as our tuning, that, when hence we part
> We may fall in with them, and sing our part.
>                           (ll. 51, 54-56)

Donne himself undertook a poetic paraphrase of Lamentations, probably sometime after his ordination and perhaps as an outgrowth of his interest in the Sidney psalms;[68] like those psalms it aspires to the realm of art. The paraphrase is fairly close to its original: as the title indicates, it follows the Protestant Latin version by Franciscus Junius and Immanuel Tremellius, though there are also influences from the Vulgate and the Authorized Version, and especially the Geneva Bible.[69] It is also compact: Donne usually renders each verse of the prose chapters (1, 2, 4) in a four-line stanza composed of two iambic pentameter couplets, and he treats the shorter, more lyrical verses of chapters three and five in briefer compass. The compactness, the run-on lines, the strong mid-line caesuras give Donne's paraphrase a kind of taut energy which compares not altogether unfavorably with the Authorized Version. With this work Donne was possibly endeavoring to contribute to the desirable cause he promoted in the verse letter on the Sidney psalms—providing worthy translations of the poetry of the Bible for public uses. His paraphrase is too attentive to speech rhythms and to the dramatic strength of image and argument to be readily singable, though there is a fine contemporary setting by Thomas Ford.[70] Some of the strengths of Donne's translation may be gathered from the opening stanzas:

> How sits this citie, late most populous,
> Thus solitary, and like a widdow thus!
> Amplest of Nations, Queene of Provinces
> She was, who now thus tributary is!
>
> Still in the night shee weepes, and her teares fall
> Downe by her cheekes along, and none of all
> Her lovers comfort her; Perfidiously
> Her friends have dealt, and now are enemie.

But his form accommodates less adequately the lyric verses of chapters 3 and 5. The poignant directness and lyric rhythms of such lines as these in the Authorized Version—"I am the man that hath seene affliction by the rod of his wrath. / He hath led me and brought mee into darknesse, but not into light" (Lam. 3:1-2)—are blunted by Donne's fixed stanza and inversions:

> I am the man which have affliction seene,
> Under the rod of Gods wrath having beene,
> He hath led mee to darknesse, not to light,
> And against mee all day, his hand doth fight.
>
> (ll. 177-180)

The finest flowering of Donne's growing commitment to these Protestant poetic concerns appears in the *Holy Sonnets*, in "Goodfriday, 1613. Riding Westward," in the "Hymne to Christ," and in the "Hymne to God my God, in my sicknesse." These last three poems have close generic affinities to Protestant occasional meditation upon experience. As developed by Joseph Hall, Richard Rogers, and Donne himself in his *Devotions upon Emergent Occasions*, such exercises explore the providential significance of a particular event or experience in the individual's life, usually in relation to a theological or biblical paradigm.[71] Though the poems show the impress of such influences, they are among Donne's most magnificent and most original achievements.

Louis Martz considers "Goodfriday, 1613" to be a classic Ignatian meditation—the extended comparison in the opening lines presenting the preparatory stage; the long central section constituting an intellectual analysis of the crucifixion in terms of its manifold paradoxes; and the final lines containing a heartfelt colloquy or prayer to Christ emerging from the meditative exercise.[72] Modifying this scheme, A. B. Chambers and Donald M. Friedman have usefully highlighted the poem's drama, in the course of which the speaker is led to correct an initial mistake.[73] Chambers finds that mistake in the speaker's erroneous application of the analogy of the spheres with which the poem begins, in that, contradicting the traditional association of the western movement of the spheres with reason and the countermovement with irrationality, he assumes that his western direction is wrong and longs to make an immediate, irrational journey eastward. The rest of the poem corrects the error, as he learns that he does still "see" the crucifixion in memory; that such devotion is the business of a lifetime, not one day only; and that since west and east meet, the movement west will lead him to the east. Friedman finds an even more dramatic development, wherein a "naive" narrator begins with his spheres analogy as a facile excuse for failing to encounter the crucifixion, proceeds to the rather superficial repetition of pious paradoxes about it, but is finally led to an agonized confrontation, growing from the realization of his own inescapable implication in that crucifixion through his sins. Such dramatic emphasis unlocks much of the richness of the poem, but its special quality is perhaps best realized through consideration of the fusion of meditation and drama which Protestant occasional meditation encouraged and which Donne so brilliantly exploits.

The poem's primary subject is the speaker's failure to conduct a traditional "deliberate" Good Friday meditation because of an "emergent occasion" of business or pleasure which takes him away from what should be his devotional center of attention on this day, Jerusalem and Calvary. The somewhat facile opening analogy is not a preparation for a meditation so much as an explanation, by reference to the two distinct forces moving a sphere (its own intelligence and "forraigne motions"), as to why the expected deliberate meditation will not take place: "Hence is't, that I am carried towards the West / This day, when my Soules forme bends toward the East" (ll. 9-10). But the speaker does attempt to come to terms with the occasion of his apparent failure in proper religious devotion, and the poem becomes an occasional meditation on this circumstance. The second section resembles the analytic stage of an Ignatian meditation on the crucifixion in its review of the traditional paradoxes associated with Christ's death: "a Sunne, by rising set, /

And by that setting endlesse day beget"; God dying "that is selfe life"; the hands that tune the spheres pierced with holes. But the speaker's paradoxical situation remains the true focus, for all these meditative paradoxes are controlled by a negative: though he should "see" (i.e., meditate upon) these things on this day, in fact he will not because his own occasions take him elsewhere. As he reviews these paradoxes the speaker responds with growing intensity to Christ and Mary, and to the recognition of his own sin as cause of the crucifixion, but still he does not, cannot, come to terms with the event and is almost glad that his occasions supply some color of an excuse: "Yet dare I'almost be glad, I do not see / That spectacle of too much weight for mee" (ll. 15-16).

The third section, appropriately, is not the colloquy of a meditation on the crucifixion, but the resolution of the problem posed by the occasion—the fact that the speaker has apparently turned his back on Calvary. That resolution does not, I believe, reside in the final identity of West and East: the speaker must finally "turne my face" rather than recognize that his journey has taken him to the right place after all. A first and partial resolution is supplied by memory: "Though these things, as I ride, be from mine eye, / They'are present yet unto my memory, / For that looks towards them" (ll. 33-35)—as indeed we have just seen in the speaker's review of what he should be visualizing and meditating upon. But the more adequate resolution grows out of the very position he has found himself in on this occasion, which he now sees to be providential and instructive for him: it signifies that God must initiate his renovation before he can make the appropriate meditative response. The imagined scene the speaker depicts of Christ looking toward his back and laying on "Corrections" to purge his deformities makes of his particular circumstance an emblem, recalling plates in Hugo and Quarles in which Divine Love lashes Anima across the back as she grinds in a mill.[74] Donne's speaker has created his own emblem on similar lines with himself as central figure, his body turned away from the crucifixion scene but with back bared to Christ on the cross to receive "Corrections":

> . . . thou look'st towards mee,
> O Saviour, as thou hang'st upon the tree;
> I turne my backe to thee, but to receive
> Corrections, till thy mercies bid thee leave.
> O thinke mee worth thine anger, punish mee,
> Burne off my rusts, and my deformity,
> Restore thine Image, so much, by thy grace,
> That thou may'st know mee, and I'll turne my face.
>
> (ll. 35-42)

The "Hymne to Christ, at the Authors last going into Germany" is a deeply felt, and very great poem. The "Hymne" title is appropriate in that the stanzaic regularity and refrain-like close of each stanza are suggestive of the simple congregational hymn or anthem, though there is no record of a setting for it. In essence, however, this poem is an occasional meditation; as the title also indicates, it was composed in 1619 when Donne went to Germany as chaplain to the Earl of Don-caster's diplomatic mission. In the first stanza the speaker invests this occasion with complex emblematic and typological significance:

> In what torne ship soever I embarke,
> That ship shall be my embleme of thy Arke;
> What sea soever swallow mee, that flood
> Shall be to mee an embleme of thy blood;
> Though thou with clouds of anger do disguise
> Thy face; yet through that maske I know those eyes,
>     Which, though they turne away sometimes,
>         They never will despise.
>
>                                     (ll. 1-8)

Donne here adapts a common emblem to his own purposes: his own ship becomes a tempest-tossed, flood-threatened vessel on the storm-wracked sea of life, recalling very similar emblem figures and explica-tions in Montenay and Hulsius.[75] In Donne's poem the Ark reference also has complex typological significance: his speaker imagines himself a new Noah about to experience a new Flood in a new Ark. Moreover, he recognizes himself as antitype of Noah, in that for him the figures will have New Testament significance. His flood will be an emblem of the first Flood's antitype, Christ's blood, and his ship will be (like the Ark's antitype, the Church) a vehicle of spiritual salvation, in that it will promote his personal spiritual growth by separating him from his familiar world. That personal world is not wicked or accursed as was the world from which Noah was saved by the Ark or mankind by the Church; but it is full of distractions from the love of God—fame, wit, other loves, other hopes. By sacrificing that world, divorcing it through this sea voyage, the speaker can center his love on God only, and so be more surely saved. The emblematic sea voyage with its dangers, its relinquishment of the world, and its exclusive search for God also takes on the character of a voyage to death undertaken in the "winter" of life, and finally signifies escape from the storms of life into eternity: "To see God only, I goe out of sight: / And to scape stormy dayes, I chuse / An Everlasting night" (ll. 30-32).

The "Hymne to God my God, in my sicknesse" is perhaps Donne's

most brilliant and most moving religious poem. It has been much
commented on, and much admired, though without full consideration
of the way in which genre theory and typology contribute to its stun-
ning effect. Obviously, it is an occasional meditation upon a personal
and significant event, an illness expected to be terminal—probably that
of 1623 and just possibly Donne's last illness in 1631.[76] The title
"Hymne" is a deliberate misnomer: the poem is neither a congrega-
tional anthem nor yet a lofty hymn of praise, and indeed the argument
of the poem proceeds to redefine its genre by indicating heaven as
the true ambience of the hymn of praise.

To begin with, the imagery of music suggests preparation for the
"Hymne" of the title. The speaker on his supposed deathbed sees
himself about to arrive where he will not only make music in the
heavenly choir but will himself be music—part of the heavenly har-
mony. Therefore he does not sing now: he proposes instead to "tune
the Instrument here at the dore" and this tuning involves not song but
thought, meditation: "And what I must doe then, thinke now before"
(ll. 4-5). Most of the poem is given over to this meditative tuning,
during which the speaker transforms his imagined death scene (as later
he will transform his actual death) into an emblem, a kind of anatomy
lesson with the physicians poring over him like cartographers reading
a map. He likens the circumstances of his illness to the circumstances
of geographical exploration—". . . this is my South-west discoverie /
Per fretum febris, by these streights to die" (ll. 9-10). And this re-
semblance affords some hopeful analogues for his situation: as he is
now a flat map in which the farthest west and east meet, "So death
doth touch the Resurrection" (l. 15); moreover, his own "straits" of
fever remind him that all the traditional locales for Paradise may be
reached only through straits.

At this point he complicates the emblematic allegorical deathbed
scene he has created with typological symbolism. Both Old Testament
type and New Testament antitype are now seen to be embodied in him,
as he finds himself to be the stage for the entire typological drama.
Beginning from the geographical legend that Paradise and Calvary,
Adam's tree and Christ's cross stood on the same site, the speaker dis-
covers that this site is his dying self on his own deathbed, since now in
one moment he suffers the death due to the sin of the first Adam, and
experiences the conquest over death of the Second Adam:

> Looke Lord, and finde both *Adams* met in me;
>     As the first *Adams* sweat surrounds my face,
>     May the last *Adams* blood my soule embrace.
>
> (ll. 23-25)

Indeed, ambiguous pointing actually invites a fusion of the speaker and the Second Adam. In the line, "So, in his purple wrapp'd receive mee Lord" (l. 26), he at once petitions God for his salvation through Christ's blood, and declares confidently his own regal rights. Then the poem achieves its third and final generic identification: it is declared to be a sermon preached to the self on a text set forth formally, and wittily, as the final line of the poem—rather than at the outset, as we would expect of a sermon:

> And as to others soules I preach'd thy word,
>     Be this my Text, my Sermon to mine owne,
>     Therfore that he may raise the Lord throws down.

The speaker has, as it were, only realized as he completed the meditation that it was also a sermon upon a text God had provided, namely, the illness which brought him low but from which his resurrection is assured. This identification plays upon the near-affinity of sermon and meditation in Protestant theory. The poem, then, is an occasional meditation-cum-sermon, which provides the tuning necessary for the singing of true hymns, a genre Donne now identifies with the sublime praises of the choir of saints, and will not attempt to sing on earth.[77]

Donne is the first major English poet in the devotional mode whose lyrics are influenced by a distinctive Protestant poetics. Though he is in some sense a transition figure, in that his earlier poems display liturgical and Counter Reformation influences, the later and finer poems are strongly imbued with characteristic Pauline themes, biblical allusions, Protestant meditative modes, and above all, the characteristic Protestant "application to the self" of typological, meditative, and emblematic patterns. Donne's poetic *œuvre* also displays a growing consciousness and self-consciousness about the uses of biblical models (the Psalms, Lamentations), and about the kind of art appropriate and possible to the religious poet. These concerns find their most complete articulation in Donne's sermons and *Devotions*, which contributed largely to the evolution of a body of Protestant theory on these issues. That theory, which informs many of Donne's poems, is grounded upon the proposition that the divine poet not only may but must imitate God's own method of creation, which, both in nature and in scripture, is supremely witty and artful and self-conscious. The divine poet's model is therefore the Bible, but the nature of that book is such that it stimulates, rather than restricts, his highest flights. The pillars of Donne's biblical, Protestant poetics are: that the scriptures are the most eloquent books in the world, that God is a witty and also "a figurative, a metaphoricall God," and that the religious lyric poet should endeavor to "write after . . . [his] *Copie*."[78]

## CHAPTER 9

# George Herbert: Artful Psalms from the Temple in the Heart

I f we find in Donne's poems a selective and progressive employment of several features important to the new Protestant aesthetics, George Herbert's volume of religious verse, *The Temple*, develops this aesthetics fully and harmoniously, as the very foundation of his poetry. How much Herbert may have been influenced by Donne is impossible to determine, but certainly there would have been some association through Donne's close friendship with Herbert's mother, Magdalen Herbert. And Donne himself testified to the relationship by sending Herbert one of his emblem rings, together with a personal verse letter in Latin.[1] Moreover, the poetics implicit in the sermons of so distinguished a preacher as Donne could hardly have failed to impress his younger contemporary.

But Herbert, not Donne, was the poet praised and imitated by contemporaries as the creator of a new movement and a new model for religious poetry. Vaughan identified Herbert as "The first, that with any effectual success attempted a *diversion* of this foul and overflowing *stream*" of lascivious poetry to sacred uses, and he located himself among the "many pious *Converts*" gained by Herbert's "holy *life* and *verse.*"[2] Richard Crashaw entitled his collection of religious lyrics *Steps to the Temple* in tribute to Herbert; Christopher Harvey conceived his book of lyrics, *The Synagogue*, as a "shadow of *The Temple*"; Robert Herrick's *Noble Numbers* contain many echoes of Herbert; Samuel Speed imitated Herbert closely in several of his *Prison-Pietie* poems; Edward Taylor constantly looked to Herbert's example; his impress is everywhere on the minor religious verse of the period.[3] I suggest that Herbert's art is in large measure founded upon the elements of Protestant poetics we have been considering—biblical genre theory, biblical tropes, Protestant ways with emblem, metaphor, and typology, and Protestant theory regarding the uses of art in religious subjects—and that this poetics affords a necessary corrective to approaches to Herbert through medieval iconography, Salesian meditation, the plain style, or the so-called Augustinian abrogation of art.[4] These approaches, and also the perceptive close readings of several

Herbert poems which Arnold Stein and, more recently, Helen Vendler have given us, have illuminated several aspects of Herbert's art—which is of course finally the product of his unique poetic sensibility.[5] However, we need to recognize how that sensibility responded creatively to several elements in the new Protestant aesthetics in order to take more adequate measure of Herbert's superb art and artfulness.

To begin with, it is clear that the conception of the Christian life rendered in Herbert's prose and poetry conforms in large outline to Protestant-Pauline theology. Herbert's manual for ministers, *A Priest to the Temple, or The Country Parson*, unequivocally asserts the centrality of the scriptures for the religious life of the parson and his congregation: ". . . the chief and top of his knowledge consists in the book of books, the storehouse and magazene of life and comfort, the holy Scriptures. There he sucks, and lives."[6] His only extant theological commentary, the "BRIEFE NOTES relating to the dubious and offensive places in the following CONSIDERATIONS" by Juán de Valdés (Valdesso), a Spanish Catholic biblical scholar and reformer in the Erasmian tradition, registers his delight that ". . . God in the midst of Popery should open the eyes of one to understand and expresse so clearly and excellently the intent of the Gospell in the acceptation of Christs righteousnesse . . . a thing strangely buried, and darkned by the Adversaries, and their great stumbling-block." In one place he paraphrases Valdés approvingly on the matter, against the papists: "He meaneth (I suppose) that a man presume not to merit, that is, to oblige God, or justify himselfe before God, by any acts or exercises of Religion." Nevertheless he finds Valdés too much the papist in his attitude toward scripture. He complains repeatedly that Valdés "slights the Scripture too much," as when he seems to put it on a par with images or pictures of Christ, or speaks of it as "but childrens meat." And he declares that Valdés' "opinion of the Scripture is unsufferable" when he regards it (as Augustine did) as a means which might be dispensed with by those illuminated by the Spirit.[7]

The first poem of *The Temple*, "The Church-porch," is about the externals of the Christian life, the moral virtues and social manners appropriate to a Christian profession. The poem is concerned with the natural order, but it does not treat nature as directly propaedeutic to grace in the scholastic or Hookerian sense. Interestingly enough, several of the topics considered in that poem—the avoidance of covetousness, luxury, drunkenness, gaming, swearing, and especially idleness; the importance of educating children properly, governing one's household, and finding and following a suitable calling; the value of cleanliness,

decency, and order in the person, the household, and in God's house—
are also emphasized in Herbert's *The Country Parson* as traits charac-
terizing the good minister and as qualities he should seek to promote in
his parish. Indeed the catalogue of positive virtues urged in the manual
—"The Countrey Parson is exceeding exact in his Life, being holy, just,
prudent, temperate, bold, grave in all his wayes"—would provide a
useful index for the topics of the poem.[8] Since this is so, we cannot
describe "The Church-porch" simply in terms of the natural and moral
reformation to be undertaken prior to spiritual growth.

Rather, the prescribed behavior is set forth as the interface between
the Church and the world (as the church porch is in architectural
terms). The poem is concerned with the external reformation of life in
its visible manifestations—the turning away from evil promised at
baptism; in Protestant terms, such behavior may or may not be ac-
companied by the action of grace in the heart which alone regenerates.
Herbert's structure builds directly upon that perception: as the "Super-
liminare" engraved above the portal of the Church makes clear, these
are matters of behavior only; the essence of true religion is within "The
Church"—"Thou, whom the former precepts have / Sprinkled and
taught, how to behave / Thy self in church; approach, and taste / The
churches mysticall repast."

The collection of shorter lyrics entitled "The Church" traces the
internal spiritual life of the speaker, who is a particular individual re-
counting personal experience but who also exhibits through that ex-
perience the Protestant-Pauline paradigm of salvation.[9] According to
Izaak Walton's hagiographic biography, Herbert described his book
as "a picture of the many spiritual Conflicts that have past betwixt God
and my Soul, before I could subject mine to the will of Jesus my
Master"; Walton also records that on his deathbed Herbert sent his
manuscript of poems to his good friend Nicholas Ferrar with instructions
to publish it if he thought it would "turn to the advantage of any
dejected poor Soul" and otherwise to burn it.[10] Whether or not these
statements incorporate some Walton embellishments,[11] the assumption
behind them—that a particular spiritual life may epitomize and present
common religious experience—is entirely consonant with Herbert's
recorded views. In *The Country Parson* he urges the minister to preach
to others out of the "Library" of his own life, because, "though the
temptations may be diverse in divers Christians, yet the victory is alike
in all, being by the self-same Spirit. Neither is this true onely in the
military state of a Christian life [the temptations], but even in the
peaceable also; when the servant of God . . . in a quiet sweetnesse seeks
how to please his God."[12] Moreover, the individual-typical speaker of

"The Church" is a Calvinist in theology. In regard to the much-controverted question of whether the Christian can lay claim to anything whatsoever of human merit or of initiative in good actions he is taught in "The Holdfast" that he must absolutely repudiate any such claim:

> I Threatned to observe the strict decree
>> Of my deare God with all my power & might.
>> But I was told by one, it could not be;
> Yet I might trust in God to be my light.
> Then will I trust, said I, in him alone.
>> Nay, ev'n to trust in him, was also his:
>> We must confesse that nothing is our own.
> Then I confesse that he my succour is:
> But to have nought is ours, not to confesse
>> That we have nought. I stood amaz'd at this,
>> Much troubled, till I heard a friend expresse,
> That all things were more ours by being his.
>> What Adam had, and forfeited for all,
>> Christ keepeth now, who cannot fail or fall.

And in "The Water-course" he affirms the Calvinist double predestination, attributing it to the simple dictate of God's will, "Who gives to man, as he sees fit, $\begin{cases} \text{Salvation.} \\ \text{Damnation.''} \end{cases}$ (ll. 9-10).

We do not, however, find in Herbert the agonized outcries by which Donne dramatized the early stages of the process of regeneration—the fears of God's rejection and the terrors of conscience attendant upon the conviction of sin. Rather, though Herbert's speaker often laments his sins and his spiritual barrenness, and often complains of God's withdrawal of favors, he does not agonize about his election. On the "Superliminare" above the portal of entry to the Church is also written, "Nothing but holy, pure, and cleare, / Or that which groneth to be so, / May at his perill further go" (ll. 6-8). He sees himself as one whose groans and longings give presumptive evidence of his own calling to enter the Church. Within "The Church" the first group of poems, beginning with "The Altar" and culminating with the two adjacent poems "Repentance" and "Faith," explores the speaker's conversion in terms of his struggle to understand, accept, and make the appropriate response (repentance and faith) to the fundamental ground of salvation, justification through Christ's sacrifice. The second and much the largest group of poems, from "Prayer (I)" to (perhaps) "The Crosse," presents the alternating afflictions and comforts, temptations and joys, judgments and graces, victories and backslidings, and the emotional states attendant upon these vacillations, which characterize the long, slow process of sanctification in the Protestant paradigm. The final group of poems, from "The Flower" to "Love (III)," presents the mature Christian's attainment of a plateau of joy, confidence, assurance, and anticipation of heaven; in these poems the major conflicts, including his anxieties about his poetic praises, are eased for Herbert's speaker.

The context afforded by Protestant poetics also sheds light upon the vexed question of unity in *The Temple*—the relation of the long prefatory poem, "The Church-porch" and the long epilogue, "The Church Militant," to the central body of lyrics, "The Church," as well as the question of what thematic and structural coherence is manifested in the collection as a whole.[13] The poems were not of course written in their present sequence, and the precise chronology of their composition is not known. "The Church Militant" is presumed to predate the rest of the work; it appears among the sixty-nine (out of one hundred sixty-eight poems of *The Temple*) contained in the Dr. Williams manuscript. The Williams poems, comprising many of those on Church feasts, liturgy, and architecture, were evidently written some time before Herbert's ordination in 1630,[14] and many of them were extensively revised in the later Bodleian manuscript and the 1633 first edition. However, as Amy Charles demonstrates, the poems added to the later collection do not substantially alter, but further develop, the fundamental scheme of the soul's uneven progress already evident in the Williams manuscript.[15] It seems clear from this that the conception of the volume and the basic order of poems carry the poet's authority and have significance. That significance develops in part from the metaphor of Herbert's title, *The Temple*: contemporary Protestant formulations of the temple trope and of the typology of the Old Testament Temple provide the terms for Herbert's unifying motif, the temple in the heart of man.[16]

Herbert critics have pointed to the traditional typological significance of the three parts of the Old Testament Temple—the Porch or Outer Court typifying the external and visible aspect of the Church from which none are excluded, the Holy Place typifying the communion of the invisible Church on earth, and the Holy of Holies, typifying the highest heaven of the saints—and have often tried to fit Herbert's structure to these terms as to a Procrustean bed.[17] It seems obvious that Herbert made some use of these conventional associations in the first two sections of his work, though his application is rather to the Christian individual than to the ecclesiastical body. Joseph Hall provides an analogue for this emphasis: "In every renewed man, the individuall temple of God; the outward parts are allowed common to God and the world; the inwardest and secretest, which is the heart, is reserved onely for the God that made it. . . . Onely the true Christian hath intire and private conversation with the holy One of Israel."[18] This perception was also strikingly rendered by the Protestant emblematist Zacharias Heyns, portraying the risen Christ inhabiting a large human heart with the Old Testament Temple in the background and the motto, "*Templum Christi cor hominis.*"[19]

In Herbert's volume, "The Church-porch" relates to the Porch or Outer Court of the Old Testament Temple. Here the speaker sets forth a series of dry, didactic prescriptions regarding the externals of the Christian life and the behavior fitting a Christian profession which constantly echo classical and Hebraic moral principles. These precepts have a relation both to the Church and to the world, even as a church porch itself does; moreover, Herbert's "Church-porch" as an architectural metaphor has affinities with the entrances both to the Old Testament Temple and to classical temples,[20] since both kinds have contributed directly to the definition of the external moral behavior appropriate to the Christian life, although both are but shadowy types of the Christian temple in the heart. The lyrics of "The Church" define the Christian temple as the inner essence of the Christian experience, the relationship and dialogue between Christ and the individual soul together with the distresses and joys attendant upon that communion.

But the equation does not hold for the third term: Herbert's "Church Militant" cannot be made to relate to the Holy of Holies in the Old Testament Temple, or to its commonly designated antitype, the heavenly kingdom.[21] Indeed, Herbert suggests the soul's movement into that third realm at the end of "The Church," in a series of poems on the last things—"Death," "Dooms-day," "Judgement," "Heaven"— followed by the final, exquisite lyric, "Love (III)," which intimates the soul's gracious reception at the heavenly banquet. This is entirely consonant with the typological terms Herbert has established. At Christ's crucifixion the veil of the Temple separating the Holy of Holies from the Holy Place was rent from top to bottom (Matt. 27:15) so that Christians, exercising the new priesthood of all believers, find no sharp distinction in their spiritual experience between the regenerate life on earth and in heaven, "Having . . . boldnesse to enter into the Holiest by the blood of Jesus, / By a new and living way which hee hath consecrated for us, through the veile, that is to say, His flesh" (Heb. 10:19-20). There is not, then, and ought not to be, an "architectural" counterpoint in Herbert's scheme to the Temple Holy of Holies;

rather, "The Church Militant" shifts from a spatial to a temporal scheme to present a third dimension of the Christian Church on earth—its public, visible form. For "The Church Militant" the significant terms are set forth by the extended opening passage about the Ark—both Noah's Ark and more importantly the Ark of the Covenant—and also by allusions throughout the poem to the fleeing woman of the Apocalypse. All these were recognized types of the Church Militant in its relation to the world, and emphasized as such in contemporary Protestant literature. Robert Cawdrey indicates the basis for this typology in his *Treasurie . . . of Similies*, "As the Arke was carried from place to place, and never rested in one certaine place: So likewise the militant Church here on earth, hath no certaine place, but is posted from piller to post."[22] And Daniel Featley's comment on the images he identifies as "The Embleme of the Church Militant" seems almost a précis of Herbert's poem: "If the Spouse of Christ be a pilgrime, and flieth from place to place, from Citie to Citie, from Kingdome to Kingdom . . . the portable Arke in the Old Testament, and the flying woman in the New, are images of the militant Church in this world."[23] Herbert's "The Church Militant" develops just such a vision of the Church traveling ever westward as Sin dogs her heels, destroying and taking over one by one the civilizations she has established, until at length the Lord comes to judge both the Church and the world.

Herbert's governing conception is that the Old Testament Temple, with its intimations of permanence, has its true antitype only in the hearts of the elect who look forward to individual salvation, but that the wandering Ark is the nearest type for the corporate body of the Church, which has no security here and is (as Augustine also thought) in constant conflict with the world. Herbert's overarching typological symbol, the Temple, is then an appropriate ground of unity for his entire work, foreshadowing in different ways three dimensions of the New Covenant Church. The prefatory poem, "The Church-porch" explores the external behavior proper to the Christian in his interaction with the world. The dominant central section, "The Church" presents the intimate spiritual experience of the regenerate heart. And the epilogue, "The Church Militant" is again concerned with an external dimension, the constant tribulations of the visible church in this world, typified by the wandering Ark which is itself a foreshadowing of the more permanent Temple.[24]

Herbert's conceptual plan for *The Temple* in regard to the genres employed and the stances of the speaker owes something also to the analogy sometimes drawn between the three parts of the Old Testament Temple and the three books of Solomon. Beza compares the Book

of Proverbs to "the utter common court for the people"; he finds that
Ecclesiastes serves as an avenue into the Holy Place—"The Church is as
it were lead to enter into the Holy Place by the *booke of Ecclesiastes,
called the Preacher*"; and he relates Canticles to the movement of the
Church through the Holy Place, bringing it "even to the entery of the
Sanctuary, or Holy of Holies."[25] These equations are reflected in
Herbert's volume: "The Church-porch" is a Christian revision and
fusion of Proverbs and Ecclesiastes (teaching moral precepts pertaining
to external behavior and preparing for entry into the Church); and
"The Church" adumbrates at least some aspects of Canticles, treating
the encounters of Christ and the soul throughout life, and leading the
soul to the point of entry into the Holy of Holies, or Heaven.

As we have seen, many sixteenth- and seventeenth-century exegetes
linked Proverbs and Ecclesiastes closely, as sharing a common didactic
mode and a common subject matter—precepts for moral, political, and
domestic behavior pertaining primarily to the duties of man to man,
though including as well certain sacred duties of piety toward God.[26]
Proverbs, addressed to the young or to new beginners in the Christian
life as if by a father or teacher, were either brief, pithy, pointed sen-
tences enunciating truths or precepts of behavior (maxim, adage,
aphorism), or else "figurative and darke kinde of speeches"[27] (especially
similitude and enigma). Herbert's sustained interest in the first of these
kinds is indicated by his collection and translation of a large number of
*Outlandish Proverbs*, chiefly from French, Italian, and Spanish sources.[28]
In the book of Ecclesiastes Solomon as a preacher set forth moral
commonplaces in the same kinds of figures, but now woven into a
continuous and eloquent poetic sermon on the central topic of moral
philosophy, the highest good or human happiness. Herbert's "The
Church-porch" seems intended as a Christian version of these books.
The speaker adopts the role of father-teacher-preacher setting forth
rules of conduct and behavior in a verse sermon ("A verse may finde
him, who a sermon flies," l. 5) assumed to be delivered as from the
Church Porch to one still outside the Church itself. The audience,
"Thou, whose sweet youth and early hopes inhance / Thy rate and
price, and mark thee for a treasure" (ll. 1-2), is specified (like the
audience of Proverbs) as a typical young beginner in the Christian life
but one giving strong evidence of election. And as "Superliminare"
makes clear, these precepts are understood to bring the youth from the
Common Court to the door of the Holy Place, from the Church Porch
to the Church.

The topics of "The Church-porch" are those associated with Prov-
erbs and Ecclesiastes—precepts of morality and manners. Herbert's

apparently haphazard organization of topics admits of rationalization according to several Christian schemes—the Ten Commandments; the seven deadly sins and their opposing virtues; the four cardinal virtues; duties to self, to neighbor, and to God. In its exploration of these various topics, the sermon also resembles an examination of conscience, usually conducted according to one or another of these formulas.[29] Herbert's governing plan of organization seems to be the last-mentioned one—duties to self, neighbor, and God—with the other patterns complexly related to it, and the whole formulated with special reference to the well-born, socially active youth imagined as audience. Personal moral duties are especially related to the cardinal virtues: upholding temperance, the speaker warns against lust, drunkenness, blasphemy (presented as an abuse of the lips), lies, idleness (involving failures in the duties of one's station in life as magistrate, scholar, estate-holder, father of a family), and finally gluttony. Justice—giving to each his due—is explored in terms of proper thrift in the use of money, that is, avoiding both covetousness and excessive spending on clothes or gaming. Fortitude dictates an appropriate boldness, best evidenced in self-command and the eschewing of duels. Prudence is to be manifested in the proper use of mirth and wit, and a carriage toward the great not marred by pride, servility, or envy. Duties to others are examined in terms of several kinds of relationships: the claims and limitations of friendship; the dictates of civility in discourse; magnanimity in giving and receiving benefits; cleanliness; charity. Duties to God are defined in terms of proper behavior at public sermons and prayers, and proper regard for God's preachers. However, this governing scheme is not easily identifiable; it seems to have been deliberately camouflaged by an apparently haphazard shifting from topic to topic in imitation of the disjunctive form of Proverbs and Ecclesiastes, with their constant shifts in subject matter and their frequent doubling back and repetition of topics.

Like Ecclesiastes, this long stanzaic poem is conceived formally as a loosely ordered poetic sermon, and its precepts are often presented as grounded upon personal experience: "Shall I, to please anothers wine-sprung minde, / Lose all mine own? God hath giv'n me a measure / Short of his canne and bodie" (ll. 37-39); "Were I an *Epicure*, I could bate swearing" (l. 60). Moreover, the rhetorical figures employed are precisely those usually associated with the Book of Proverbs. The stanzas often begin with brief moral imperatives—"Abstain wholly, or wed" (l. 13); "Drink not the third glasse" (l. 25); "Flie idlenesse" (l. 79); "Be thriftie, but not covetous" (l. 151); "Play not for gain, but sport" (l. 193); "Be sweet to all" (l. 211); "Laugh not too much" (l.

229)—and then develop such topics through maxims, aphorisms, similitudes, antitheses and enigmas. Maxims or aphorisms are often found in the couplet conclusion to a stanza: "Stay at the third glasse: if thou lose thy hold, / Then thou are modest, and the wine grows bold" (ll. 41-42); "He pares his apple, that will cleanly feed" (l. 64); "Who breaks his own bond, forfeiteth himself: / What nature made a ship, he makes a shelf" (ll. 119-120); "Who cannot rest till hee good-fellows finde, / He breaks up house, turns out of doores his minde" (ll. 149-150). Antitheses are frequent, though Herbert's stanzaic form precludes the constant use we find in Proverbs: "Some till their ground, but let weeds choke their sonne: / Some mark a partridge, never their childes fashion" (ll. 98-99); "Who fears to do ill, sets himself to task: / Who fears to do well, sure should wear a mask" (ll. 125-126); "Thy clothes being fast, but thy soul loose about thee" (l. 414). Similitude or metaphor is very frequent: "Game is a civil gunpowder, in peace / Blowing up houses with their whole increase" (ll. 203-204); "Man is Gods image; but a poore man is / Christs stamp to boot" (ll. 379-380); "Man is a shop of rules, a well truss'd pack / Whose every parcell under-writes a law" (ll. 141-142); "Christ purg'd his temple; so must thou thy heart" (l. 423); "As gunnes destroy, so may a little sling" (l. 352). And, as in Proverbs, some figures are enigmas, characterized by obscurity and brevity: "God made me one man; love makes me no more, / Till labour come, and make my weaknesse score" (ll. 287-288); "The Jews refused thunder; and we, folly" (l. 449).

"The Church" is in some respects a new version of the Song of Songs, understood in its Protestant signification as an allegorical treatment of the relationship between Christ and every elect soul, rather than in the mystical or ecstatic terms which often characterized Roman Catholic treatments of its central marriage-betrothal situation.[30] So read, Canticles offered Herbert a model for tracing the development of a loving, personal relationship between Christ and the speaker (who incorporates many roles and moods and associations). Herbert, however, transposes the Bridegroom-Bride relationship into an association of loving friends, which also helps to define several other relations between Christ (or the Godhead) and the speaker—of king and subject, lord and servant, Savior and redeemed one, loving father and child. All these relationships are suggested early in the sequence and are explored and transformed as it proceeds. Moreover, Canticles, understood as a collection of love songs or ballads or as an epithalamium with a strong dramatic or dialogic aspect, also provided a model for Herbert's use of motifs and models from love poetry,[31] as well as of various kinds of dialogue.

The opening poems present the beginnings of a love relationship with the principals as yet distant, separated. In "The Altar" the speaker states the fundamental basis of the relationship correctly enough but without much personal warmth, using the lord-servant metaphor—"A broken ALTAR, Lord, thy servant reares"; the speaker's hard heart is the altar which can only be hewed and sanctified by the Lord's power; and the speaker-servant's duty is praise, voluntary or involuntary, resulting from the Lord's action upon him. In "The Sacrifice," the longest poem of the collection, Christ is the speaker, recounting his suffering and grief in irony-laden terms, and indicting mankind for callousness and ingratitude. Christ here woos the soul, confronting it with his love act, his sacrifice, to determine "If stonie hearts will melt with gentle love" (l. 90). The speaker now understands that he has been faced with a love challenge by the author of a new *Ars Amatoria* and his first response (in "The Thanksgiving") is the natural one of attempting to match or even to outdo the lover:

> But how then shall I imitate thee, and
>     Copie thy fair, though bloudie hand?
> Surely I will revenge me on thy love,
>     And trie who shall victorious prove.
> . . . . . . . . . . . . . . . . . .
> Nay, I will read thy book, and never move
>     Till I have found therein thy love,
> Thy art of love, which I'le turn back on thee:
>     O my deare Saviour, Victorie!
>
>                                         (ll. 15-18, 45-48)

Of course he finds to his chagrin that he cannot in any measure imitate or accommodate Christ's passion, and so must perforce accept a love relationship based upon radical inequality, recognizing Christ both as the initiator of the relationship and the enabler of his own response. The speaker's only love victory can be to share in Christ's conquest over him ("The Reprisall"). Working from this new understanding of love, the association between Christ and the speaker develops in terms of a variety of relationships, associated by means of the pervasive love language with the Bridegroom and Bride of Canticles. However, Herbert makes little direct use of that formulation, and when he does, avoids its erotic and mystical connotations. Instead, the love language proclaims God's love as the ground for all the relationships between God and the speaker.

As has been noted above,[32] the speaker's painfully attained realization in these opening poems of the utter inequality which must characterize his love relationship with Christ also functions as a critique of Catholic meditation on the Passion. The speaker is forced to give over his foolish and presumptuous (Catholic) efforts to achieve an imaginative identification with the crucified Christ and to participate in his sacrifice by imitation, turning instead to a proper Protestant concern with the meaning of Christ's sacrifice for his own redemption and his spiritual life. In this interest he explores the relationship which is the theological ground of all the others—Christ as Savior and the speaker as his redeemed. "The Agonie," the poem following immediately upon the challenge-and-response poems just discussed, provides the very definition of love by reference to Christ's role as Savior: "Who knows not Love, let him assay / And taste that juice, which on the crosse a pike / Did set again abroach. . . . / Love is that liquor sweet and most divine, / Which my God feels as bloud; but I, as wine" (ll. 13-15, 17-18).

This Savior-redeemed relation is adumbrated in numerous poems, and it is at times central. In "Easter" the Lord takes the speaker "by the hand" to rise with him (ll. 3-4); in "Grace" the speaker begs for the Savior's "suppling grace" to counter the effects of sin in a hard heart "void of love" (ll. 18-19); in "Even-song" the speaker's opening apostrophe, "Blest be the God of love," grounds that title upon God's gift of his Son and his constant favors; "Prayer (II)" lauds Christ's "unmeasurable love" in taking "our flesh and curse" (ll. 13-15). "Dialogue" harks back to the problem explored in the first love-challenge poems— the infinite distance between the Savior and his redeemed—but now the speaker pridefully attempts to resign completely from the relationship, based as it must be upon his lack of merit: "I disclaim the whole designe" (l. 23). Christ, however, shames the speaker by appealing to his own willing resignation of "*glorie and desert*" to assume the role of Savior (l. 30). Finally, in "The Holdfast" the speaker learns at last, in dialogic exchange with a "friend," that he loses nothing by the total resignation he must make of all claims to merit and even to personal responsibility for his faith and trust, since "all things were more ours by being his. / What Adam had, and forfeited for all, / Christ keepeth now, who cannot fail or fall" (ll. 12-14).

The speaker is related to Christ also as servant to lord, or sometimes subject to king, and the terms of this relationship also are transmuted by love. "Redemption" places the speaker in the relation of a tenant to a "rich Lord," seeking that lord in places of power and wealth to beg for a revision of his lease (a new covenant); then with fine self-irony he discovers his suit already granted as his lord dies amidst "a ragged noise and mirth / Of theeves and murderers" (ll. 12-13). "Afflic-

tion (I)" also brings the speaker to ironic self-realization in terms of
these roles. He entered the service of a king attracted by and expecting
to share in his "glorious houshold stuffe" (l. 9)—his joys and pleasures
—but finds instead groans and sorrows, sickness and disappointment.
He threatens rebellion but then perceives that the greatest loss would
be a loss of the love upon which the relationship is based:

> Well, I will change the service, and go seek
> Some other master out.
> Ah my deare God! though I am clean forgot,
> Let me not love thee, if I love thee not.
>
> (ll. 63-66)

In "Obedience" he undertakes formally, by writing, to convey lord-
ship over himself, but then perceives that he cannot do this by way
of gift or donation; the right is already God's "by way of purchase"
(l. 35). In "Love unknown" he complains vehemently to a "Friend"
about his lord's apparently arbitrary rejection of the various gifts he
offered in testimony of his service, seizing instead upon his heart and
subjecting it to various afflictions. He is advised however that "*your
Master shows to you / More favour than you wot of*," in seeking thus to
make his heart "*new, tender, quick*" (ll. 62-63, 70). In "Artillerie" God,
as "Dread Lord," chides his servant for disobedience to the good mo-
tions sent him, and he responds by begging for some attention to his
own "artillery" of tears and prayers. He concludes, however, that he
must perforce accept God's terms: "Yet if thou shunnest, I am thine: /
I must be so, if I am mine. / There is no articling with thee" (ll. 29-31).
At length in "The Odour. 2 Cor. 2.15" he associates the language of
sweetness and spices reminiscent of Canticles with the terms *Master*
and *Servant*: Exclaiming "How sweetly doth *My Master* sound!" he
finds in these words "an orientall fragrancie" (l. 5), and begs that the
words "*My servant*" might "creep & grow / To some degree of spici-
nesse" to God (ll. 14-15), projecting thereby a developing commerce
in such sweet breathings.

Closely related to the lord-subject or master-servant relation is that
of father and child. In "H. Baptisme (II)" he understands the ideal
spiritual situation to be that of a child—"let me still / Write thee great
God, and me a childe: / Let me be soft and supple to thy will" (ll.
6-8)—though he does not yet invoke God as Father. In the familiar
poem of rebellion, "The Collar," the resolution is attained precisely
through the transmutation of the former relationship into the latter.
The speaker rebels because he perceives himself in servitude, in bond-
age, his collar an emblem of that condition, his life defined by duties

and demands and renunciations dictated by fear. Interrupting these wild rebellious thoughts comes the Lord's call "*Child!*" which reminds the speaker of Paul's assurance that he is not a bond-slave to God but a son, heir to the promises and the kingdom.³³ Recalling that other relationship, he can then accept the master-servant association also: "Me thoughts I heard one calling, *Child!* / And I reply'd, *My Lord*" (ll. 35-36). Later, in "The Crosse" he finds full resolution of his woes and agonies through a most profound understanding of the father-child relationship, identifying his crosses and his filial acceptance of them in in terms of the paradigm established by God's Son, Christ: "these thy contradictions / Are properly a crosse felt by thy Sonne, / With but foure words, my words, *Thy will be done*" (ll. 34-36).

But the primary relation explored through these poems is that of loving friends, not fixed in the Canticles' relation of Bride and Bridegroom but exchanging the roles of lover and beloved; this relation is explored by transmuting and universalizing the love language from Canticles and from contemporary love poetry. In "Good Friday" and "Jesu," Christ is imagined to write upon, or to have his name engraved upon, the speaker's heart in love-emblem fashion. "Love (I)" perceives God as "Immortall Love" and seeks a way to restore to him the love songs now addressed to mortal loves in praise of "a skarf or glove" (l. 13). "Love (II)" petitions God as "Immortall Heat" to kindle true desires in the speaker's heart: "Then shall our hearts pant thee" (l. 6), and send back the fire in true hymns. "Mattens" imagines God as wooer, expending all his art of love upon the speaker—"My God, what is a heart, / That thou shouldst it so eye, and wooe, / Powring upon it all thy art / . . . Teach me thy love to know" (ll. 9-11, 16). Other poems portray the speaker in various conditions common to lovers and to the Bride of Canticles: In "Frailtie" he confesses his fickleness and his attraction to worldly joys, by which he affronts "those joyes, wherewith thou didst endow / And long since wed / My poore soul, ev'n sick of love" (ll. 19-21). In "The Pearl. Matth. 13.45" he feels but overcomes the attraction of other loves (learning, honor, pleasure), depending upon God for a silk-twist (such as Ariadne gave to Theseus) to lead him safely through the world's labyrinth. In "Deniall" he suffers bitterly from apparent rejection: "When my devotions could not pierce / Thy silent eares; / Then was my heart broken, as was my verse: / . . . Therefore my soul lay out of sight, / Untun'd, unstrung" (ll. 1-3, 21-22). In "The Search" he laments the loved one's departure—"Whither, O, whither art thou fled, / My Lord, my Love?"—and, describing his constant sighs and searches, he begs for a reunion. In "Longing" he is a grieving, broken-hearted lover begging for an audience: "With sick and famisht eyes, / With doubling knees and weary bones, / To thee my cries, / To thee my grones, / To thee my sighs, my tears ascend: / . . . Bowels of pitie, heare! / Lord of my soul, love of my minde, / . . . My love, my sweetnesse, heare!" (ll. 1-5, 19-20, 79).

In "Dulnesse" he undertakes a blazon of Christ (who is much fitter than any Petrarchan lady to be the object of his serenades, his "window-songs"):

> Thou art my lovelinesse, my life, my light,
> Beautie alone to me;
> Thy bloudy death and undeserv'd, makes thee
> Pure red and white.
>                                    (ll. 9-12)

But here he aspires to "*Look* onely"—even angels are not fit to love Christ. He does find a way to return love in one of the late poems, "Bitter-sweet"; as his Lord both loves and strikes, so he can answer this duality, "And all my sowre-sweet dayes, / I will lament, and love" (ll. 7-9). In "The Glance," which follows immediately, he proclaims himself able to endure absences by recalling God's first loving glance vouchsafed him—"I felt a sugred strange delight, / Passing all cordials made by any art, / Bedew, embalme, and overrunne my heart" (ll. 5-7); on the strength of that remembered love-glance, he looks forward to the time, "when we shall see / Thy full-ey'd love!" (ll. 19-20). In "Unkindnesse," friendship is designated as the standard for the speaker's evaluation of his responses to Christ's overtures: "But when thy grace / Sues for my heart, I thee displace, / Nor would I use a friend, as I use Thee" (ll. 18-20). And when he weighs by the same standard Christ's sacrifice performed "*Onely to purchase my good-will*" (l. 24), he recognizes that it far surpasses the deed of any friend.

The poem "Clasping of Hands" explores and resolves the paradox of lovers' self-possession through possession of and by each other, by appealing to the quality commonly understood to characterize true friendship, the obliteration of *meum* and *tuum*: "O be mine still! still make me thine! / Or rather make no Thine and Mine!" (ll. 19-20).[34] Finally, in "A Parodie" he is able to transpose a secular Petrarchan love poem into the terms of this special love relationship: the tenor of the secular lament for absence is radically altered by the speaker's parenthetical recognition that Christ is not really, but only apparently, absent from him, and that when he half-believes such lies, "Thou com'st and dost relieve" (l. 30).

In this regard, the dialogic-dramatic character usually ascribed to Canticles, whereby certain passages were ascribed to the Bride and others to the Bridegroom, have an analogue in Herbert's presentation of the love relationship he is tracing. His lyrics present an interplay of voices which combine more intimately as the relationship develops. At the outset the voice of Christ (or of the Godhead) and that of the speaker are quite separate, contained within separate poems. Christ delivers his love-challenge in "The Sacrifice" and in the following poems the speaker attempts, unsuccessfully, to respond to that challenge in his own personal terms, with his individual voice ("The Thanksgiving," "The Agonie"). But then he comes to realize that only when his voice is joined with and responsive to Christ's voice will he be able to love or to praise. At times the divine voice is present directly, as an interlocutor or commentator whose part is quoted verbatim by the speaker, as when, in "Redemption," the tenant-speaker hears and quotes his lord's words establishing the desired New Covenant at his death—"*Your suit is granted*" (l. 14). In "The Bag" he quotes at some length Christ's somewhat bizarre offer of the spear-rent in his side as a mail pouch for petitions to the Father; in "The Pulley" he personates the Creator explaining why he withheld the gift of rest from man; and in "The Crosse" he is recalled from desperation over his griefs and miseries by appropriating Christ's words in accepting his own crosses— "*Thy will be done*" (l. 35). In other poems a "friend" or messenger— or a better self—takes the divine part in directing or rebuking or aiding the speaker, providing thereby an analogue to the catechising which Herbert urged so forcefully as central to the duties of the country parson.[35] In "Artillerie" a seeming shooting star rebukes the speaker for expelling good motions from his heart. In "Jordan (II)" a "friend" provides a directive to the would-be Christian poet struggling to divest his praises of artifice and self-display, to "Copie out" the sweetness love has already penned (ll. 17-18). In "Love unknown" a "Friend" interprets the apparently cruel and arbitrary behavior of the lord toward the speaker and his gifts by pronouncing the interpretive motto for each emblematic episode: "*Your heart was foul, I fear*"; "*Your heart was hard, I fear*"; "*Your heart was dull, I fear*" (ll. 18, 37, 55).

In still other poems, especially those directly concerned with the making of poetry, the speaker often finds the divine voice providing a resolution of his poetic problems through the medium of scripture: a few words of a scripture text are quoted in the poem as a means of relating God's voice and God's art to the poet's own art. In "Jordan (I)" he finds a model for his own plainness in a near-quotation of Psalm 145:1, "*My God, My King*" (l. 15). In "A true Hymne" he tries unsuccessfully to make up a hymn of praise from certain scriptural epithets—"My joy, my life, my crown"[36]—but he cannot get beyond these beginnings; in such a case he can depend upon God to supply the substance of the praises even as he supplies the substance of the love relationship—"As when th'heart sayes (sighing to be approved) / O, *could I love!* and stops: God writeth, *Loved*" (ll. 19-20). And in "The Posie" he adopts as the content of his own posie or motto the phrase, "*Lesse then the least / Of all thy mercies,*" echoing Jacob's words upon returning home a rich man after his exile with Laban.[37]

In a few poems the interaction of the divine and human voices is explored more profoundly. "Deniall" presents a temporary disruption of the relationship: complaining that in God's absence both his heart and verse are broken, the speaker begs for God's return to "cheer and tune my heartlesse breast" (l. 26), and the final lines enact that return through the restoration of rhyme and form to the verses. The poem "Dialogue" exhibits another occasion of apparent collapse of the relationship, as the speaker and Christ engage in a debate in alternating stanzas, the speaker attempting to resign from the divine plan for his salvation grounded as it is upon his utter worthlessness, and Christ pointing to his own resignation of "glorie and desert" in assuming man's guilt. The relationship is restored as the speaker gives over the argument—"Ah! no more: thou break'st my heart" (l. 32). In the penultimate poem of "The Church," "Heaven," Echo supplies authoritative "divine" answers to the speaker's catechism of questions about eternity by repeating the speaker's own words; Echo's admitted origin in the "holy leaves" (of scripture) indicates the basis for the speaker's power to supply the answers to his own questions and to complete his poetic verses through the "divine" echo of his own voice. Here, through dialogic interchange, the human poet and his divine echo collaborate most intimately in the creation of a poem.

Finally, in "Love (III)" the relationship between Christ and the speaker attains full fruition. The speaker is still painfully conscious of his unworthiness and is ready to draw back, but now Christ, identified simply as "Love," assumes the role of perfect host offering a banquet with utmost courtesy to the speaker as an honored guest. He thereby evokes from the guest-speaker a matching courtesy, a willing and graceful acceptance of the host's generosity and his own unworthiness. This banquet of course alludes to the Church's communion banquet and also to the heavenly repast, climaxing the sacramental imagery and motifs developed in several lyrics—"The H. Communion," "The Collar," "Peace," "The Banquet," and many more. But the sacramental motif is not the subsuming theme of the volume; rather it contributes to the complex pattern of relationships between Christ and the soul which we have been tracing, and which are so triumphantly resolved in this final poem. This poem also exhibits a perfect interplay of voices in the Christian poet's praises. We do not find here (as Stanley Fish's version of Herbert's aesthetics might lead us to expect) the Divine Voice subsuming the voice of the human poet and leaving him engaged in silent, ecstatic perception of divine truth. Nor, I think, will most readers find, with Fish, that this exquisite, ritualized colloquy is a rather harsh, brow-beating defeat of the speaker by Christ.[38] Instead, this final poem is also a dialogue with the parts of the two speakers clearly defined, though now intimately blended, in the spirit and tone of courteous exchange appropriate to the occasion, into a poem of the most exquisite harmony and delightfulness. Such divine perfecting of human art is the goal of Herbert's aesthetics and of his speaker's quest as Christian poet.

An even more important generic resource for the lyrics of "The Church" is the Book of Psalms. In fact, Herbert seems to have conceived his book of lyrics as a book of Christian psalms, and his speaker as a new David, a Christian Psalmist. For one thing, Herbert's lyrics clearly exhibit what many patristic commentators and contemporary Protestants understood to be the inner essence of the Psalms, the analysis of the full range of spiritual emotions at their most intense—joy and grief, exaltation and desolation, misery and contentment, sorrow and consolation, fear and hope, rebellion and love of God—representing thereby to man the anatomy of his own soul.[39] Many of Herbert's titles and opening lines indicate his presentation of just such a range of feeling: "Affliction," "Love," "Sighs and Grones," "Miserie," "Dulnesse" ("Why do I languish thus, drooping and dull"), "The Bunch of Grapes" ("Joy, I did lock thee up"), "Longing" ("With sick and famisht eyes"), "The Collar" ("I struck the board, and cry'd, No more"), "The Flower" ("How fresh, O Lord, how sweet and clean / Are thy returns!"), "The Temper (II)" ("It cannot be. Where is that mightie joy, / Which just now took up all my heart?").

In addition, Herbert's lyrics seem to relate themselves to one or another of the three fundamental categories of biblical lyric which commentators found represented in the Book of Psalms—psalms, hymns, and spiritual songs. Psalms were defined by Wither and others as sonnet-like, argumentative, meditative, or prayer-like poems on diverse subjects—a description which encompasses the largest category of Herbert's poems. Hymns were by definition joyful praises of God or thanksgivings to him: in Herbert this category covers the broad range from the elegant simplicity of the hymn portion of "Easter" to the lofty eloquence of "Providence." Spiritual songs were taken to be artful lyric pieces specifically intended for singing: in Herbert there are several song-like poems which were given contemporary musical settings, for instance, "Christmas," "Antiphon (II)," "The Starre," "Vertue," "The Dawning."[40] Also, the numerous lesser kinds which Wither, Willet, Beza, Donne, Gataker, and others found in the Psalms are very fully represented in Herbert. There are some fifteen sonnets (e.g., "Redemption," "The H. Scriptures (I)"); meditations and soliloquies (such as, "Life," "Employment (II)," "The Discharge"); many complaints ("Affliction I-V," "Josephs coat"); laments for tribulations ("Deniall," "Grief," "The Crosse"); prayers for benefits ("The Call," "Grace"); petitions against adversities ("Sighs and Grones"); poems of instruction ("Constancie," "Humilitie," "Charms and Knots"); consolations ("The Flower," "The Forerunners"); rejoicings ("Man," "Church-musick," "Even-song," "Mattens"); praises of God for his glories ("Easter," "Antiphon (I)"); thanksgivings for God's benefits ("Providence," "Praise (II)"); artful acrostic poems ("Coloss. 3:3," and in a related kind, "Paradise," "The Altar," "Easter-wings"); ballads (Herbert's "The 23d Psalme" is in ballad measure); love songs ("A Parodie," "Dulnesse," "Love (I)"); dramatic poems ("Dialogue," "Death"). I do not suggest that Herbert set out to write in each of the lyric kinds contemporary theorists associated with the Psalms, but it seems likely that this theory, together with the example set by the Sidney-Countess of Pembroke psalms, sanctioned and encouraged his incorporation of such a rich variety of forms and kinds in his book of religious lyric. Recognition of this range should counter the critical assumption that Herbert's poems all aspire to the condition of the personal meditation, and the concomitant disposition to rate them according to the complexity with which they render the play of mind and feeling.[41] We ought rather to applaud the rich generic diversity Herbert has achieved in his attempt to provide (even as the Book of Psalms was thought to do) a compendium of religious lyric kinds in his "Church."

Moreover, Herbert's speaker as Christian poet is set forth as a *figura* of the biblical Psalmist. We have noted how readily Protestants from Luther and Calvin to Perkins and Donne presented themselves as correlative types or antitypes to David, recapitulating his spiritual experiences, afflictions, and conflicts in their own lives. We have noted also how constantly David is identified in the sixteenth and seventeenth centuries as the appropriate model for the Christian poet, affording examples of the most magnificent poetic texture and figurative language, but also raising with special force the aesthetic problem of the poet's stance in relation to the divine truth of his subject matter and the necessary divine participation in his poetic creation.[42] Herbert's speaker manifests his role as New Covenant *figura* of David the Psalmist in various ways. His several poems of affliction, complaint, and lamentation recall the Penitential Psalms. And even as David, forbidden to build the Temple of Jerusalem, prepared his Psalms as a songbook for that Temple and as a type of the New Testament Church located in the broken and contrite heart, so Herbert built a *Temple* which is also a volume of lyrics.[43] Moreover, Herbert's pervasive concern with the problem of creating fit praises for God recalls the designation of David's Psalms as *Sephir Tehillim*, the Book of Praises. Also, as the Psalmist was understood to speak sometimes in his own person, at other times to personate the whole company of the faithful, and at still other times to speak for Christ or God himself, so Herbert's speaker renders his personal conflicts in such a way that they represent those of any faithful Christian, and he also often personates the Divine Voice. Finally, as David's Psalms were understood to be of his own penning and yet in another sense wholly inspired by the Spirit, so Herbert wrestles constantly with the paradox of his responsibility to create poems of praise, yet his inability to do so unless God will enable him and participate with him in those praises.

Several poems throughout the collection show Herbert's speaker, in quasi-typological terms, taking on the role of New Covenant psalmist as he appropriates and turns to his own uses the Psalmist's words and forms. The first poem of "The Church," "The Altar," is in some respects a New Testament version of Psalm 51, perhaps the most frequently paraphrased and most fully annotated of all David's psalms (at least by Protestants), and widely recognized as a paradigm for Christian conversion and repentance. Herbert's imagery of the "broken ALTAR . . . / Made of a heart, and cemented with teares" alludes to Psalm 51:17, "The sacrifices of God are a broken spirit: a broken and a contrite heart, O God, thou wilt not despise"—thereby associating the speaker's heart with David's, which is the type of the Christian altar and Church. Moreover, the speaker's prayer that the stones of his heart hewed by God's action may generate praises even without his own volition points up the paradox that in some sense the praises are not his own but God's; David's perception in Psalm 51 that his praises are directly dependent upon the action of God—"O Lord open thou my lips, and my mouth shall shew foorth thy praise" (v. 15)—provides a model for the resolution of that paradox. In "Sion" the speaker again recalls the Psalmist's groans and the praises emerging from his broken and contrite heart (as well as his roles as musician to King Saul and author of the Church's book of prayers and praises). He thereby identifies his own art with the Davidic type of the New

Covenant church in the heart which contrasts so markedly with the gorgeous material splendors of Solomon's physical temple: "All Solomons sea of brasse and world of stone / Is not so deare to thee as one good grone / . . . . The note is sad, yet musick for a King" (ll. 17-18, 24).

The speaker also appropriates the Psalmist's words and forms to confront the problem of praise and to afford models or starting points for his own praises. As we have seen, "Easter" is a New Covenant version of Psalm 57:7-11, involving the interaction of the risen (restored) heart, the struggles of the poetic lute to resound in harmony with Christ's cross, and the corrections and completions afforded by God's Spirit.[44] In this exquisite lyric the Psalmist's emphasis upon his own early awakening is recapitulated and revised by the New Covenant psalmist who recognizes that Christ's rising will ever precede, and be the precondition for, his own spiritual and poetic resurrections. Elsewhere, in "Jordan (I)," the speaker explains his renunciation of the "fictions . . . and false hair" (l. 1) of secular love poetry by echoing a phrase from the Psalms, *My God, My King*.[45] The poem "Providence," in which the speaker presents himself as the world's high priest articulating praises for all creation, is in some portions a very free descant upon several verses of Psalm 104 wherein God's bounty to all living creatures is enumerated and celebrated.[46] Similarly, "Praise (II)" seems closely related to Psalm 116 in its argument of love and praise, and in the speaker's direct and fitting response to God's merciful hearing, sparing, and saving him. As his counterpart to David's promise to offer "the sacrifice of thanksgiving" in the courts of the Lord's house, Herbert's speaker promises his artful praises: "Wherefore with my utmost art / I will sing thee, / And the cream of all my heart / I will bring thee" (ll. 9-12).[47] And in the later, very moving poem "The Forerunners," the poet confronts and then resolves the problem of age and waning poetic powers by repeating as a refrain Psalm 31:14 as his only necessary poetic statement—"Thou art [still] my God"—in final, full understanding that God's power, not his own, is the source of the praises produced by the New Covenant temple built in the heart, even as it is of that Temple itself.

Herbert's "23d Psalme" is his only complete psalm version; it appears near the end of his collection, marking a moment in which Herbert has been able to merge his voice completely with that of the Psalmist. Rendering each of the six psalm verses by one quatrain, and following closely the general argument and imagery of the original, Herbert nonetheless makes the poem wholly his own in diction, tone, and texture. For one thing, he heightens the effect of simplicity and directness by using ballad measure and almost wholly monosyllabic diction. For another, certain formulations unwarranted by the text of the psalm emphasize specifically Herbertian concerns—mutuality ("While he is mine, and I am his, / What can I want or need," ll. 3-4); the question of merit ("And all this not for my desert, / But for his holy name," ll. 11-12); and, most obviously, the poem's concluding focus, not present in the psalm, upon the problem of fit praise:

> Surely thy sweet and wondrous love
>     Shall measure all my dayes;
> And as it never shall remove,
>     So neither shall my praise.
>                              (ll. 21-24)

In "Love (III)" the speaker perfects his role as new psalmist. The dramatic situation rendered in the poem recalls Psalm 23:5, "Thou preparest a table before me, in the presence of mine enemies: thou annointest my head with oyle, my cuppe runneth over," and also Luke 12:37, "The Lord when he commeth . . . shall girde himselfe, and make them to sit downe to meate, and will come foorth and serve them." Though these Old and New Testament texts reverberate profoundly in the poem, Herbert's speaker has here devised his own formulation of the sweetness of divine love and care in terms of the courteous dialogue of host and guest. In so doing, he has moved beyond quotation or paraphrase or imitation of David and even beyond creative variations upon the Psalms, to voice his own intensely personal yet universal, simple yet exquisitely artful, New Covenant psalm of praise.

"The Church Militant" is modeled in some respects upon the Book of Revelation—conceived not as a series of ecstatic prophetic visions but as a poetic treatise on church history, in accordance with the exegetical emphasis of such contemporary Protestant commentators as Henry Bullinger, who described the book as an "ecclesiastical history of the troubles and persecutions of the Church."[48] The central symbol of the Apocalypse was taken to be the Woman clothed with the Sun and fleeing into the Wilderness (Rev. 12), universally identified as a figure of the Church Militant oppressed by her enemies: as Daniel Featley observed, this "embleme" of the Church Militant shows that "The Spouse of Christ . . . [is] a pilgrime, and flieth from place to place, from Citie to Citie, from Kingdome to Kingdome." Moreover, several commentators, notably Paraeus, analyzed the structure of the work as a series of acts presenting "diverse, or rather (as we shall see) the same things touching the Church," separated by choric songs and hymns.[49] Herbert's poem transposes some of these elements into a poetic account of Church history, past and to come. He uses the imagery of Revelation: the Church is the pilgrim-Spouse of Christ, likened to the sun in that she traverses the world in an ever-westward direction. In the course of this journey she establishes various centers of civilization and then is forced to flee from each as Sin takes over in turn the communities she has established. At length both complete the course and arrive at their starting point in the East, where "Judgement may meet them both & search them round" (l. 269). Also, the structure discerned in Revelation of acts separated by choric passages has its analogue in "The Church Militant," in which five episodes or stages in the history of the Church, recounted in heroic couplets, are set off from each other by a repeated lyric refrain combining Psalm verses 139:17 and 89:6, *"How deare to me, O God, thy counsels are! / Who may with thee compare?"*[50] The speaker in this poem adopts the public stance and universal perspective of the church historian (a role the commentators often assigned to John of Patmos)[51] and this persona is at a far remove from the intimate, personal voice speaking the lyrics of "The Church."

In these respects, "The Church Militant" may be seen as Herbert's Book of Revelation, rendering his own all-encompassing account of the providential course laid down for the visible Church throughout history. That generic association, together with the speaker's joyful embracing of this providential course (circular and distressing as it is shown to be within the bounds of earthly history) makes this work a fitting completion for the three-part structure which is Herbert's *Temple.*

Herbert's use of imagery and metaphor also repays scrutiny in terms of artistic precepts and models derived from scripture. His language requires, and has received from such critics as Vendler, Fish, and Stein, a close poem-by-poem analysis to reveal its artful perfection. But one aspect of Herbert's art deserving of much more attention is his elaboration of certain biblical metaphors into pervasive patterns of imagery which unify the volume and further define the Christian speaker. As we have seen, "H. Scriptures (II)" provides a key both to Herbert's understanding of metaphorical patterns in scripture, and to his use of such patterns in his own poetry. The process involves recognizing the subtle connections between disparate texts—"This verse marks that, and both do make a motion / Unto a third, that ten leaves off doth lie:"—and recognizing also how these related texts interpret, and are interpreted by, a Christian's life.[52] This poem indicates that Herbert's fundamental biblical metaphors, activated by biblical allusions and echoes, will not be present in every poem and often not in consecutive poems, but that the patterns will emerge as the images in disparate poems connect with and reflect upon each other. Moreover, as we have seen above, many of Herbert's specific images, and especially the dominant patterns portraying the Christian as God's husbandry and the temple in the heart, are reinforced by visual emblems familiar in contemporary religious emblem books.

One pervasive metaphorical pattern portrays sin (and the grief it causes) as a sickness, afflicting the soul with manifold pains. The speaker complains of such maladies in many poems: "Lord, how I am all ague"; "The growth of flesh is but a blister; / Childhood is health"; "If thou shalt let this venome lurk / And in suggestions fume and work, / My soul will turn to bubbles straight"; "My thoughts are all a case of knives, / Wounding my heart / With scatter'd smart, / . . . Nothing their furie can controll, / While they do wound and pink my soul"; "How shall infection / Presume on thy perfection?"; "My head doth burn, my heart is sick, / While thou dost ever, ever stay"; "My throat, my soul is hoarse; / My heart is wither'd like a ground / Which thou dost curse"; "One ague dwelleth in my bones, / Another in my soul . . . / I am in all a weak, disabled thing."[53] In Herbert's usage the familiar image of God as divine physician is not often a part of this metaphorical pattern, though in several poems God is identified as the source of the cure so badly needed by the soul. In "Affliction (I)" the speaker complains of his physical and spiritual ills with great bitterness: "My flesh began unto my soul in pain, / Sicknesses cleave my bones; / Consuming agues dwell in ev'ry vein, / And tune my breath to grones. / Sorrow was all my soul; I scarce beleeved, / Till grief did tell me roundly, that I lived" (ll. 25-30); moreover, the speaker here accuses God of playing the role of deceiving physician, offering him the "sweetned pill" (l. 47) of academic praises to bind him to the clerical life, and then, lest he achieve contentment, bringing him further sicknesses. In "Repentance" he identifies God's rebuke for sin as the cause of spiritual sickness: "Bitternesse fills our bowels; all our hearts / Pine, and decay, / And drop away, / And carrie with them th'other parts" (ll. 27-30). But he also finds in God the certain cure:

> But thou wilt sinne and grief destroy;
> That so the broken bones may joy,
> And tune together in a well-set song,
> Full of his praises,
> Who dead men raises.
> Fractures well cur'd make us more strong.
>
> (ll. 31-36)

Later, Christ's blood is identified as the balsam "which doth both cleanse and close / All sorts of wounds" afflicting the sinner's heart ("An Offering," ll. 19-21).

Closely associated with this metaphorical pattern is that of God the chastiser, deliberately inflicting torment and anguish upon the guilty soul. Poems developing this metaphor usually conclude that the torment is somehow beneficial. The speaker finds his soul stretched as on a rack when God extends and then seems to withdraw his love: "O rack me not to such a vast extent; / . . . Wilt thou meet arms with man, that thou dost stretch / A crumme of dust from heav'n to hell?" Elsewhere he cries out: "Kill me not ev'ry day, / Thou Lord of life"; or recognizes that "No scrue, nor piercer can / Into a piece of timber work and winde, / As Gods afflictions into man, / When he a torture hath design'd"; or imagines God using his "dart" upon the heart—with allusion to the emblematic darts Divine Love infixed in Anima's heart in several emblems.[54] Two poems focus centrally upon the figure of God the chastiser and tormenter, with the speaker begging to be spared the deserved punishment. In "Sighs and Grones" the speaker begs God not to bruise, scourge, blind, grind, or kill him, or wreak upon him the apocalyptic vengeance: "O do not fill me / With the turn'd viall of thy bitter wrath!" (ll. 19-20), but rather as Savior to reprieve and relieve him. Toward the end of the collection, in "Discipline," the speaker identifies the bow of the God of vengeance described in Exodus with that of the Divine Cupid, thereby arguing that God may achieve the chastisement of the heart through love:

> Then let wrath remove;
> Love will do the deed:
>                 For with love
> Stonie hearts will bleed.
>
> Love is swift of foot;
> Love's a man of warre,
>                 And can shoot,
> And can hit from farre.
>
> Who can scape his bow?
>                 (ll. 17-25)[55]

An even more important metaphorical pattern presents God as gardener and the speaker as plant or tree, expected to flower or to bring forth fruits and be ever responsive to the rains, dews, sunshine, or tempests sent from heaven as well as to the cultivation of the divine gardener. This metaphor-cluster is developed from allusions to God who planted a Garden in Eden with Adam and Eve in it (Gen. 2:8-10);

to Christ who cursed the barren fig tree and declared that his followers should be known by their fruits (Luke 13:6-9, Matt. 7:15-20); and to God as husbandman pruning branches from or grafting branches into the true vine, Christ (John 15:1-8). As we have seen, this metaphor was given visual embodiment in emblems by Camerarius, Wither, Mannich, Peacham, Hulsius, and others.[56] Herbert's speaker in "Employment (I)" begs to be a flower in God's garland, but he fears that he will be "nipt in the bud" by frosts (l. 4). "Employment (II)" contrasts man's cycle of growth, in which the winter of age arrives before fruition, with the orange tree's ideal condition, bearing blossoms and fruits at once:

> Oh that I were an Orenge-tree,
>                     That busie plant!
> Then should I ever laden be,
>                     And never want
> Some fruit for him that dressed me.
>                     (ll. 21-25)

Elsewhere, the speaker sees himself as a dead stock calling for dews of grace from above, or finds that he, "Like a nipt blossome, hung / Discontented." He is sometimes a tree bearing fruit and at other times a "rotten tree."[57] He knows that he was once, but is no more, "a garden in a Paradise," and his sense of barrenness in his vocation is such that he now feels himself "ev'n in Paradise to be a weed."[58]

In the latter half of the collection, several poems use the gardening metaphor centrally and more positively. In "Life" the speaker imagines himself making a posy and watching it quickly wither, deriving therefrom a lesson regarding the sweetness and usefulness even of a short life, for the flower that he himself is: "Since if my sent be good, I care not if / It be as short as yours" (ll. 17-18). "Paradise" presents the speaker as a tree in the paradise of the Church, becoming fruitful through the divine gardener's protection and pruning; the poem is formally an emblem,[59] representing by the artful pruning of the verses (letters are lopped off from the rhyme words in each succeeding line of the triplet stanzas) the necessary pruning of the speaker by God so he may produce better fruit:

> I Blesse thee Lord, because I G R O W
> Among thy trees, which in a  R O W
> To thee both fruit and order  O W.
>
> What open force, or hidden C H A R M
> Can blast my fruit, or bring me H A R M,
> Since the inclosure is thine  A R M?

> Inclose me still for fear I S T A R T.
> Be to me rather sharp and T A R T,
> Then let me want thy hand & A R T.
>
> When thou dost greater judgements S P A R E,
> And with thy knife but prune and P A R E,
> Ev'n fruitfull trees more fruitfull A R E.
>
> Such sharpnes shows the sweetest F R E N D:
> Such cuttings rather heal then R E N D:
> And such beginnings touch their E N D.

"The Flower" might almost serve as an emblem poem beneath the Wither emblem depicting flowers alternately scorched by the sun of afflictions and temptations and revived by the rain and dew of God's grace.[60] The speaker sees himself as a flower experiencing the return of spring showers after winter frosts: he can hardly believe that "my shrivel'd heart / Could have recover'd greennesse" or remember "That I am he / On whom thy tempests fell all night" (ll. 8-9, 41-42). He longs for Paradise "where no flower can wither," but rejoices that "now in age I bud again, / . . . I once more smell the dew and rain, / And relish versing" (ll. 23, 36, 38-39). The poem's conclusion makes the flower-gardener metaphor fully explicit and brings the metaphorical pattern to happy resolution:

> These are thy wonders, Lord of love,
> To make us see we are but flowers that glide:
> Which when we once can finde and prove,
> Thou hast a garden for us, where to bide.
>
> (ll. 43-46)

Herbert's dominant metaphor is that of the temple in the heart of man, developed from a variety of texts which identify the Christian as the temple of the Holy Spirit, as a lively stone in God's temple, or as God's building (1 Cor. 3:9, 16; 1 Pet. 2:5), and which contrast Solomon's Old Testament Temple with this new temple not made with hands (Acts 7:47-48). Assimilated to the metaphorical pattern are other texts presenting the heart as synecdoche for the Christian himself and so as the site of this temple: the Psalmist's claim that the Lord desires "a broken and a contrite heart" rather than burnt offerings (Psalm 51:16-17), God's promise to write the Law not in stone tablets but in the fleshy tables of the heart (Jer. 31:33), God's promise to take away our stony hearts and give us new hearts of flesh (Ezek. 36:26). As we have seen, the School of the Heart emblem books drew upon the same range of biblical imagery, and Herbert's poems often recall such visual representations. Herbert's sequence presents a version of this metaphorical pattern akin to that in several of the Protestant heart emblems and most notably in the heart-book of Cramer; in these emblems the hands of God work externally and powerfully upon the heart to soften, cure, shape, and build it into a fitting temple or dwelling place.[61] Herbert begins to develop the pattern in these terms in "The Altar," which presents the speaker's heart as antitype of the Old Testament altars of unhewn stone, in that it must be shaped by God's hand, not man's, into a fitting altar of praise. Like David's heart this heart-altar is broken and contrite, but it is still a "hard heart" made of stones. In "Nature" the heart is seen to be stony, requiring the engraving of God's law upon it, or better still, the substitution of the promised new heart of flesh:

> O smooth my rugged heart, and there
> Engrave thy rev'rend Law and fear;
> Or make a new one, since the old
>                          Is saplesse grown,
>                 And a much fitter stone
> To hide my dust, then thee to hold.
>                                    (ll. 13-18)

"The Church-floore" begins the construction within the heart—"Blest be the *Architect*, whose art / Could build so strong in a weak heart" (ll. 19-20)—and "Sion" directly contrasts Solomon's glorious but inferior Temple at Jerusalem with this new temple now building: "And now thy Architecture meets with sinne; / For all thy frame and fabrick is within. / There thou art struggling with a peevish heart" (ll. 11-13). Other poems point to specific actions of God upon the heart: the speaker is amazed that God treats the heart as if it were "Silver, or gold, or precious stone / . . . Powring upon it all thy art"; the name "Jesu" is "deeply carved" in the heart but the letters are scattered since the heart is broken; the heart is "cut" by the crossed ropes of contradiction and frustration.[62] "Love unknown" develops an emblem-book sequence (strongly reminiscent of certain plates in Cramer and Mannich) in which a "Lord" acts arbitrarily and apparently strangely toward the speaker's heart, casting it first into a font where it is bathed with blood from a rock, then into a huge blazing furnace labelled "AFFLICTION," and finally onto a bed of thorns to cure (respectively) its foulness, hardness, dullness.[63] Later poems emphasize especially God's soothing and curative actions upon the heart: in "An Offering" a balsam or blood from heaven cleanses and cures its "many holes" (l. 4), and in "The Glance" the speaker feels "a sugred strange delight, / Passing all cordials made by any art, / Bedew, embalme, and overrunne my heart" (ll. 5-7).

Less prominent than the formulation just traced are two other ways of imaging the divine action on the heart which have affinities to the Jesuit Heart Books of Haeften, Bivero and the *Vis Amoris*; Herbert's occasional use of these formulations softens somewhat the emotional effect of the Protestant version of the metaphor, with its overwhelming emphasis upon God's activity and man's helplessness. In a few poems, Herbert presents the heart as an active character. Sometimes the speaker engages by dispute or remonstrance with its recalcitrance: he urges his "greedie heart" to be content, to "sit down" and "Grasp not at much." Again, he complains that it is a "Busie, enquiring heart," which is seen to "prie, / And turn, and leer" in its seeking after the future. Elsewhere the heart, as synecdoche for the speaker, undertakes various pious actions: it prays and "lies all the yeare" at Christ's feet; weeping for Christ's absence it picks up crumbs of hope, and knocks at Christ's door desiring his return.[64] The effect of this is to show the heart galvanized to some activity though not to much accomplishment—an altogether different effect from that achieved in Haeften' emblems of Anima and Divine Love together accomplishing all the stages in the purification of the heart. Some other Herbert poems recall Jesuit emblems of the Divine Cupid or the Dove inhabiting the heart, but in these poems the Christ figure is more like the adult, resurrected Christ of Heyns' emblem, occupying a heart presented as antitype of the Old Testament Temple.[65] In Herbert's poems Christ's occupancy of the heart is uneasy and incomplete: he is constantly disturbed by "loud complaints and puling fears," and he is restricted to "some one corner of a feeble heart," pinched and straitened by Sin and Satan.[66] Also, the Spirit's residency is not a present fact but a future hope: in "Whitsunday" the speaker prays that the Spirit may come to "spread thy golden wings in me; / Hatching my tender heart" (ll. 2-3). The effect is to suggest that the divine occupancy is just beginning, since the temple of the heart is still under construction.

Herbert also makes constant use of the biblical symbolic mode, typology, to characterize the speaker and to explore the nature of the spiritual life. This symbolism is important not only to *The Temple* as a whole (as we have seen), but also to the argument of many individual lyrics. Herbert's use of typology is characteristically Protestant in its focus upon the individual Christian as referent for the types, but the emphasis is uniquely his own. He characteristically presents within the compass of a single poem the speaker's progress from an identification with and recapitulation of various Old Testament types, to a comprehension within himself of the Christic fulfillment of those types.[67] The first poem in "The Church" sets forth the terms for this progress from type to antitype with reference to the various aspects most important to the speaker's self-definition—as a Christian everyman, as priest, and as poet. The emblematic poem "The Altar" presents the speaker's heart as recapitulation of that altar of unhewn stones divinely prescribed in the Old Testament ("thou shalt not build it of hewen stone: for if thou lift up thy toole upon it, thou hast polluted it," Exod. 20:25):

> A broken A L T A R, Lord, thy servant reares,
> Made of a heart, and cemented with teares:
>    Whose parts are as thy hand did frame;
>    No workmans tool hath touch'd the same.
>          A  H E A R T  alone
>          Is   such   a   stone,
>          As  n o t h i n g  but
>          Thy pow'r doth cut.
>          Wherefore each part
>          Of my hard heart
>          Meets in this frame,
>          To praise thy Name:
>    That, if I chance to hold my peace,
>    These stones to praise thee may not cease.
> O let thy blessed S A C R I F I C E be mine,
> And  sanctifie  this  A L T A R  to be  thine.

But since the new altar is not simply stone, but a heart, it is also the antitype to the Old Testament altar—pointed to in that medley of biblical texts promising the exchange of a heart of flesh for the stony heart (Ezek. 11:19); or a new covenant inscribed in the heart, "I will put my law in their inward parts, and write it in their hearts" (Jer. 31:33); or a new dwelling place for God not in houses built by men's hands but with the man "that is poore and of a contrite spirit" (Isa. 66:1-2). The fundamental situation of the speaker as Christian everyman is thus posed in typological terms in this first poem: the need for his Old Testament stony altar-heart to be hewn by God's power and wholly transformed into its New Testament antitype, a heart of flesh, a temple not built with hands.

The speaker's progress from type to antitype is perhaps most clearly traced in "The Bunch of Grapes," which also affords the most explicit statement of Herbert's conception of typology as God's symbolism. As Rosemond Tuve has noted, the poem depends for its mean-

ing upon our recognition of the traditional typological relationship
between the grapes hanging from the pole carried by the spies and
Christ on the cross, the true vine pressed in the winepress of the Pas-
sion (Isa. 63:3) to become the wine of the New Covenant.[68] What is
most significant and characteristic, however, is the location of the en-
tire typological relationship in the heart of the speaker. The poem is
about the speaker's loss of spiritual joy and contentment; as he explores
that loss he first sees himself recapitulating the wanderings of the Israel-
ites in the desert, as a correlative type with them:

> For as the Jews of old by Gods command
> Travell'd, and saw no town;
> So now each Christian hath his journeys spann'd:
> Their storie pennes and sets us down.
> A single deed is small renown.
> Gods works are wide, and let in future times;
> His ancient justice overflows our crimes.
>
> (ll. 8-14)

Unlike the Israelites, however, he is given no cluster of grapes, no
tangible earnest or assurance of the Promised Land. The resolution
comes as the speaker recognizes the antitype, Christ's redemptive sacri-
fice, as a yet more basic part of his spiritual experience: "But can he
want the grape, who hath the wine?" (l. 22). Tracing a progress within
himself from type to antitype, he can finally affirm that this earnest
of Christ's sacrifice affords him a less tangible but far more certain
and all-embracing guarantee of spiritual joy. More complexly, "Josephs
coat" traces the same typological paradigm within the speaker.

Joseph's coat of many colors (gift of his loving father but cause of
his sufferings and imprisonment) is the type of the humanity of Christ,
of which he was denuded at the crucifixion.[69] The speaker, rendering
in song his many griefs and sorrows—"Wounded I sing, tormented I
endite"—seems to possess a "Joseph's coat" of many colors in the
variety of joys and pains in his life. He is brought to this condition be-
cause God has given to anguish "One of Joyes coats" (the flesh of
Christ), and thereby has provided "relief / To linger in me" (ll. 11-
12). Accordingly, he is himself a new Joseph, possessed of a new coat
of many colors, in that he can now see his variegated life of joys and
sorrows as evidence of his Father's special love: "I live to shew his
power, who once did bring / My *joyes* to *weep*, and now my *griefs*
to *sing*" (ll. 13-14).

The emphasis in "The Altar" upon the speaker's desire to praise, and
his prayer that the stones of his heart might themselves send forth

praises if his intended praises fail, point also to the speaker's role as priest: as New Covenant priest he has special responsibility to offer the sacrifice of praise, which is the antitype of the Old Testament bloody sacrifice. Subsequent poems also explore in typological terms this aspect of the speaker's self-definition as priest. "The Collar" at first presents him in fierce rebellion, regarding his clerical collar as an emblem of slavery, and complaining especially that the eucharistic elements afford him no sense of joy and fruition: "Sure there was wine / Before my sighs did drie it: there was corn / Before my tears did drown it" (ll. 10-12). His problem is that he experiences the spiritual life entirely in terms of duties, obligations, and Old Testament legal servitude. This problem is resolved as the Lord's call, "*Child!*" reminds him that his New Covenant status (Gal. 4:3-7) is not that of a bondslave, but that of a child and son, heir to the promises and the kingdom. The same pattern obtains in "Aaron," but in this poem the New Covenant resolution is more fully possessed. The speaker begins by recognizing his need as priest to clothe himself with Aaron's Old Testament priestly garments and ornaments, yet his utter inability to put on the holiness they symbolize—and demand. He then comes to understand that this responsibility is now not his, that Christ is now his head, breast, music, dress. At length, he perceives that as a priest of the New Covenant he is himself (through Christ) the antitype and fulfillment of the Old Testament Aaron:

> So holy in my head,
> Perfect and light in my deare breast,
> My doctrine tun'd by Christ, (who is not dead,
> But lives in me while I do rest)
> Come people; Aaron's drest.
>
> (ll. 21-25)

The focus on praise in "The Altar" also inaugurates the theme of the special responsibility of the Christian poet to find fit ways to praise, relating that theme also to the typological paradigm of the Old Testament altar of stone, and New Covenant temple in the heart. The Jordan poems continue this motif. In "Jordan (I)," the title invokes the typological relationship of the Israelites' crossing Jordan into the Promised Land to Christian baptism, to announce the baptism of the speaker's verse to the service of God; the poem proclaims his renunciation of "old" poetic styles for a new, plain, devotional and biblical mode. "Jordan (II)" explores the matter more profoundly, and in more personal terms. The speaker finds that he himself began by adhering to a "law of works" in poetry, seeking out "quaint words, and trim invention" (l. 3) and curling his plain intention with metaphors, on the assumption that such embellishments are appropriate to divine praise. But he then discovers that such "works" have no merit, because of his corruption—"so did I weave myself into the sense" (l. 14). Finally he recognizes that worthy praises, like the renovation of the heart, must be essentially God's doing, and adopts a proper New Covenant poetic—to copy out the sweetness that is *"in love . . . [al]-readie penn'd"* (l. 17), i.e., in God's Word. He has hereby crossed Jordan again and situated his verse more securely in the Promised Land. "Sion" brings this motif to a kind of resolution: the speaker now fully understands that Solomon's Temple with its glorious embellishments was not the mode of praise God most desires: "All Solomons sea of brasse and world of stone / Is not so deare to thee as one good grone" (ll. 17-18). Such "grones," which find their type in the Psalmist and their antitype in the speaker, are now perceived as the true New Covenant mode of praise, and the truest music. In these hymns, produced by the humble and contrite heart, "the note is sad, yet musick for a King" (l. 24).[70]

Again, "Love (III)" brings these typological themes to their period. The stone altar has become a banquet table of intimate communion, and the communion table is itself type of the heavenly feast, when God "shall girde himselfe, and make them sit downe to meate, and will come foorth and serve them" (Luke 12:37). The speaker as Christian everyman thus experiences the complete transformation of his stony heart, the speaker as priest participates in the sacrament of thanksgiving, and the speaker as poet has created an exquisite hymn of New Covenant praises, based now not on groans but upon perfected joys.

From all this it is evident that these diverse, artful, and exquisitely crafted poems are founded upon a far more sophisticated poetics than is sometimes inferred from those Herbertian lines which seem to renounce art as inappropriate to religious subject matter, to embrace "plainness," and to affirm utter dependence upon God. Rather, such passages ask interpretation in terms of various biblical contexts, even as contemporary sermon theory defined sermonic art according to a scriptural standard. As we have seen, Herbert constructs a biblical frame of reference for his poems: they receive generic definition by reference to certain poetic books of the Bible, they utilize dominant biblical metaphors as unifying image patterns, and they employ typological symbolism in characteristically Protestant ways to explore the spiritual development of the speaker and to serve as an organizing principle of the entire volume. The art Herbert eschews involves the conventional poetic devices and ornament of secular poetry; and the plainness he embraces is consonant with that "sweet art" embodied in the scriptures.

Moreover, Herbert explores the role of the Christian poet by setting his speaker in quasi-typological relation to the great biblical poets, so that his poems become in some respects responses to and creative versions of their works. At various times his speaker assumes a persona like that of the Solomon of Proverbs and Ecclesiastes, the Beloved in Canticles, the prophet-historian of Revelation, and especially the Psalmist. And even as the biblical poets were perceived to create their own poems but withal to serve as agents for the Holy Spirit who is the primary author of everything in the scriptures, so Herbert recognized and dramatized the divine agency by incorporating the Divine Voice in several of his poems, and showing it in dialogic tension with that of the human speaker. Like so many of his predecessors and contemporaries in the creation of Christian poetry, Herbert in the lyrics of "The Church" modeled himself most directly upon David the Psalmist, manifesting in himself David's spiritual agonies and states of soul, and echoing and reworking Davidic themes, images, and entire psalms in his own verses. But his poetry constitutes an impressive new achievement in this kind, in that it moves beyond an imitative and derivative to a genuinely creative conception and use of biblical poetics. Herbert undertakes nothing less than the task of becoming a Christian psalmist, transposing (as he indicates in "Easter") the elements of biblical art upon a Christian lute resounding in harmony with Christ's cross. The undertaking results in the creation of religious lyrics of surpassing beauty, biblically-derived yet original, simple yet of great variety and complexity, "plain" yet exhibiting "Utmost art."

## CHAPTER 10

# Henry Vaughan: Pleading in Groans of My Lord's Penning

According to Vaughan's own testimony, George Herbert's example was largely responsible for making him a religious man and a religious poet. In his book of meditations, *Mount of Olives* (1652), Vaughan quotes or commends several of Herbert's poems.[1] In a preface added in 1655 to *Silex Scintillans* he praises Herbert as the first reformer effectively to convert lyric poetry from lewd to sacred uses, he identifies Herbert as a primary model for "this kinde of *Hagiography*, or holy writing," and he proclaims himself one of the many "pious *Converts*" gained by Herbert's "holy *life* and *verse*."[2] Vaughan also appropriated the subtitle of *The Temple*, "*Sacred Poems and Private Ejaculations*," as the subtitle of his own volume, and his poem "The Match" makes a formal declaration of partnership with Herbert in the dedication of self and verse to God.

The poems themselves, as Vaughan's editors and critics have demonstrated,[3] give overwhelming evidence of discipleship. Some twenty-six have titles appropriated from *The Temple*;[4] several ("Praise," "Trinity-Sunday," "Rules *and* Lessons," and "Easter-day") owe their metrical form to Herbert;[5] many begin with an exact or nearly exact quotation of a line from Herbert ("The Passion," "The Resolve," "The Palm-tree," "The Morning-watch," "Unprofitablenes," "Praise," "Easter-day," "The Holy Communion," "Begging [I]," "Admission," "The Tempest"); a few (notably "The Storm," "Easter-day," "Son-Dayes") are very close throughout to Herbert originals;[6] and echoes, allusions, and quotations from Herbert are pervasive, especially in Part I. Moreover, Vaughan is manifestly indebted to Herbert for precedents in using some elements of Protestant poetics. Yet for all this, *Silex Scintillans* is a brilliantly original volume, in which Protestant poetic theories and methods, as well as borrowings from Herbert, are shaped by Vaughan's unique religious and poetic sensibility. As Joan Bennett has cogently observed, "Herbert may have made Vaughan a poet, but he did not make him in his own image."[7]

The two parts of *Silex Scintillans* are composed of discrete poems,[8]

but like *The Temple* the volume as a whole has impressive unity. How-
ever, that unity does not derive (as Herbert's does) from the metaphor
of the title. That metaphor—the flashing flint—is exhibited visually in
the emblem Vaughan prefaced to the 1650 edition and later dropped;
it shows the speaker's heart as a flinty rock from which God's weap-
onry strikes fire, resulting, according to the accompanying Latin em-
blem poem, in the heart's broken fragments flashing spiritual and poetic
fire. This figure and others based upon Herbert's synecdoche of the
stony heart[9] recur occasionally in later poems: in the first "Dedication"
the speaker describes his calling through the figure of Christ's blood
falling upon his heart and making it bud;[10] in "Repentance" he per-
ceives the stones of the landscape to be "much softer than my heart"
(l. 36); in "Misery" he prays anew for God to "Open my rockie heart,
and fil / It with obedience to thy wil" (ll. 101-102); in "The Tempest"
he calls for repetition of God's attack to "grind this flint to dust" (ll.
58-60); and in the concluding poem of Part I, "Begging [I]," he calls
anew for the exercise of God's "Art / To reduce a stubborn heart"
(ll. 13-14). But the elimination of the emblem and emblem poem
from the 1655 volume, and the avoidance of most such imagery in
Part II, indicate Vaughan's recognition that this Herbertian motif is
only a minor theme for him—even though his title identifies the
poems themselves as flashes struck off from that flint, his heart. For
Vaughan the controlling metaphor is the Christian pilgrimage.

Both Herbert and Vaughan trace the Protestant paradigm of salva-
tion in their respective volumes, but in doing so reveal some striking
differences in religious sensibility. Though Vaughan has a few liturgi-
cal or ecclesiastical poems (four on the Holy Communion, nine on
feast-days, a few on related topics),[11] and though he agonized about
the plight of the church under the Puritans ("The Brittish Church,"
"The Men of War") his religious imagination is not stimulated by the
things of the Church, as Herbert's is. Although Herbert focuses
sharply upon personal (rather than corporate) religious experience, he
often portrays that experience by means of ecclesiastical imagery: it is a
temple that is built in the heart. By contrast, the ecclesiastical ordi-
nances and ceremonies seem to be something Vaughan's speaker en-
counters, along with much else, on his Christian pilgrimage through
life, but his imagination is chiefly affected by the encounters with
God's Word and works. Louis Martz's comment that for Vaughan
"it is as though the earthly church had vanished, and men were left to
walk alone with God,"[12] may be something of an overstatement, but it
conveys the dominant impression of these poems. Herbert places his
temple in the Christian heart, whereas Vaughan places his Christian

pilgrim in the "temple" of Nature, searching out the way to God in company with the natural creatures and the personages of biblical history.[13]

In addition, Vaughan's speaker seldom experiences the direct encounters and developing relationship with God or Christ so important to Herbert. The few cases of divine interpolation in the thought or discourse of Vaughan's speaker are usually remembered generalities rather than dramatic events: in "Repentance" he recalls that "a friend / Came oft from far, and whisper'd, *No*" (ll. 15-16) when he was tempted to scorn God's laws and promises, and something similar is recounted in "Faith" and "Misery."[14] Vaughan's one genuinely dramatic dialogue between God and the speaker is "Retirement," in which God interrupts the speaker in his sinful course, decries his rebellion at length, and urges upon him a continual *memento mori*: "Up then, and keep / Within those doors, (my doors) dost hear? *I will*" (ll. 54-55). Whereas Herbert found in Christ a man, a friend, a person to meet in a relationship, Vaughan looked to Christ primarily as a mediator, the only means of knowing God and restoring man to union with him. Vaughan's speaker finds vestiges of the Divine everywhere but he does not engage with a person; he is, rather, consumed with longing for a relationship yet to come.

Part I of *Silex Scintillans* presents the earlier stages of the speaker's experience as Christian pilgrim: these include his keen awareness of the Fall and the resultant total depravity of man; his concomitant sense of the progressive decay of religion in the world since the early ages and in man since early childhood; his experience of God's calling, election, and of the beginnings of regeneration; his abiding consciousness of death and of the obscurity of human vision; and his many vicissitudes as he strives toward greater life and light. "Regeneration" (after the prefatory verses the poem which begins Part I) appropriately establishes the theological terms, the biblical frame from Canticles, the motifs, the tone, and the mixture of allegorical and typological modes characteristic of the first section of the volume. As its title indicates, the poem presents in rather precise theological detail the speaker's account of his regeneration,[15] the starting point of the Christian life, under the allegory of a fictional journey. He explains that, as "A Ward, and still in bonds," he went walking one day upon a primrose path in a false spring, but then perceived that his interior climate was wintry, that the spring was "Meere stage, and show," and that he was a pilgrim in a monstrous, mountainous landscape enduring freezing rains. Climbing to the mountain top he found a pair of scales (a conspicuously emblematic scene recalling plates from Cramer, Mannich, and many

others)[16] and discovered that the "late paines" of his hard climb were
far outweighed by the "smoake, and pleasures" of his sins and follies.
At this some cried "*Away*" and he fled to the "faire, fresh field" that is
Jacob's Bed, where he entered a lovely springtime grove with azure
sky, shining sun, garlands of flowers, spicy air, a murmuring fountain
with a cistern full of stones (some lively and some heavy and still), a
bank of flowers with some buds open and some closed, and a rushing
wind proclaiming its intention to blow "*Where I please.*"

The basis for the imagery and development of the poem derives
from conventional Protestant exegesis of the allegory of Canticles
2:10-12, "Rise up, my Love, my faire one, and come away. / For loe,
the winter is past, the raine is over, and gone. / The flowers appeare
on the earth, the time of the singing of birds is come, and the voice of
the turtle is heard in our land." George Gifford's sermon upon this
passage explains much of Vaughan's allegory:

> The allegorie . . . is taken from the times of the yeare. . . . And that
> is, what the state of all the elect was before their calling: and then
> what it is after they be called of the Lord and regenerate. Before
> they be called, their hearts bee even like the earth in winter, under
> the colde frost and stormes of sinne: for there can no sweete thing
> grow up, there is an utter barrennes. After that the Lord hath
> called them, and that they bee regenerate, there is an heavenly
> warmth of his spirit, and the sweete dew of his graces, and then the
> sweete flowers appeare, then the holesome fruites doe bud forth:
> then is there peace and joy in the Holy Ghost, even heavenly melo-
> die, which is represented heere by the singing of the birds.[17]

Other exegetes understood the winter season to apply specifically to
"the menaces and showring threats of the Law" as John Robotham put
it, and the subsequent spring to the Gospel Covenant;[18] this meaning is
adumbrated in "Regeneration" by the speaker's situation as a ward, and
by the balance scales on the mountain top (Sinai, evidently) which
reveal graphically the ineffectuality of the speaker's works, so that he
is warned away from this mountain even as was another pilgrim by a
character named Evangelist in another *Pilgrim's Progress.* The voice
(the effectual calling) leads him to Jacob's Bed, Bethel, the garden of
the Church[19] watered by the living fountain which is Christ and his
Word. Here the speaker finds that grace alone makes some flowers
bloom and some stones lively (in 1 Peter 2:5 the faithful are termed
"lively stones"), and he must come to terms with the harsh fact of
predestination and the unfathomable will of God controlling election
and reprobation when he hears the rushing wind (the Spirit) reveal

that it blows *"Where I please."* His final cry is a plea to be numbered among the elect who, dead to sin and regenerate in Christ, will escape spiritual death: "Lord, then said I, *On me one breath,* / *And let me dye before my death!"*[20] The postscript, drawn from Canticles 4:16, leads into the matter of the subsequent poems, the progress toward sanctification: it was glossed by Protestants as a reference to the soul's need for both the north winds of affliction and the refreshing south winds of God's grace to produce the fruits of sanctification.

Continuing the theme of death and new life, a sequence of three poems immediately following "Regeneration"—"Death," "Resurrection and Immortality," "Day of Judgement"—anticipate (with trepidation) the ultimate death and rebirth. In another mode, several poems assumed to be occasioned by the death of Vaughan's brother William in 1648 work through grief for that death to affirmation of the new life which the deceased now enjoys and the speaker expects.[21] Other poems highlight specific stages or episodes in the speaker's spiritual life: "The Call" summons the self to repentance; "The Match" dedicates life and verse to God; "Repentance" is a formal confession of sin and recognition that the guilt of it is borne by Christ; "Faith" affirms the replacement of Old Testament types and shadows by the simple declaration *"I do believe"*; and several markedly Herbertian poems explore the struggles, vicissitudes, and spiritual emotions of the Christian life—"Distraction," "Misery," "The Mutinie," "The Relapse," "Disorder *and* Frailty." But the speaker's spiritual experience in Part I is chiefly characterized by his painful awareness of the veils, clouds, and darkness which shroud mortal existence, and his longing to escape to life and light through recovery of the purer days of childhood and of the patriarchal ages, through release of the soul in death, or through the apocalyptic renewal of all flesh. In "Corruption," for example, the glimmers of Edenic brightness and the awareness of angelic presences which still obtained in the first ages are contrasted with the darkness we now endure: "thy Curtains are Close-drawn; Thy bow / Looks dim too in the Cloud, / Sin triumphs still, and man is sunk below / The Center, and his shrowd; / All's in deep sleep, and night; Thick darknes lyes / And hatcheth o'r thy people" (ll. 33-38). The final poem of Part I, "Begging [I]" asks for consummation of these spiritual beginnings: "Perfect what thou hast begun, / Let no night put out this Sun" (ll. 3-4).

The topics, tone, and poetic strategies of Part II indicate a marked advance in the speaker's spiritual life. But though they have sometimes been so interpreted, even the more rhapsodic of these poems cannot properly be termed mystical: they render the speaker's longing for transcendence but they do not claim to have attained to mystical union or communion.[22] Rather, they celebrate the state which Calvinists termed assurance—the settled condition of the mature, experienced Christian well advanced in the path of sanctification, whose eyes and desires are firmly fixed upon heavenly things. In these poems the speaker desires more intensely than before, but yet anticipates with more assurance and calmness, his soul's impending liberation in death. His controlling vision, however, is apocalyptic, looking beyond the soul's incorporeal life in heaven to the re-creation of nature, the making of all things new. Again the opening poem, "Ascension-day," affords an epitome of the whole. The speaker finds Christ's ascension typologically recapitulated in his own spiritual experience, raising him to a new plateau of spiritual assurance above the turmoils of Part I:

> Thy glorious, bright Ascension (though remov'd
> So many Ages from me) is so prov'd
> And by thy Spirit seal'd to me, that I
> Feel me a sharer in thy victory.
>   I soar and rise
>   Up to the skies,
>     Leaving the world their day,
>   And in my flight,
>   For the true light
>     Go seeking all the way.
>
>                                     (ll. 5-14)

He shares first in the experience of Christ's resurrection and the forty-day sojourn on earth, during which the earth seems restored to its Edenic condition—"All now as fresh as *Eden*, and as fine" (l. 38). Finally, he sees the ascension as type of the Second Coming, echoing John's plea to Christ at the end of the Book of Revelation to "Come quickly."[23]

The poems immediately following "Ascension-day" extend these themes. "Ascension-Hymn" especially celebrates Christ's Second Coming, at which he will "rebuild man" and "Make clay ascend more quick then light" (ll. 40, 42). In the next poem the speaker envisions the one he mourns in bliss—"I see them walking in an Air of glory"—and pleads for his own release.[24] There are still poems of tribulation and temptation ("The Proffer," "Joy," "The Timber," "Abel's blood," "The Men of War") but the temptations or afflictions now come from outside (Cromwell's army, the temptations of high position) and the sorrows and groans have primary reference to old guilts rather than present inconstancies. The new assurance is everywhere: in "Trinity-Sunday" the speaker finds in himself the *"Anty-types"* of those natural emblems of the Trinity—Spirit, Water, Blood—in that he was "Elected, bought, and seal'd for free"; he also finds evidence in himself of the spiritual "Seed growing secretly." The book concludes with a sequence of poems relating to Last Things which carry no trace of the former fears and anxieties about death and Judgment. The sequence begins and ends with striking visions of the Apocalypse—"The day of Judgment," "L'Envoy"—and the poems enclosed by these visions ("Psalm 65," "The Throne," "Death," "The Feast," "The Obsequies," "The Water-fall," "Quickness," "The Wreath," "The Queer," "The Book," "To the Holy Bible") are all exemplars, here given final formulation, of poetic modes and motifs central to the volume. By this structure Vaughan catches up these modes and motifs into the Apocalypse, which is to bring about the renewal of all creation.

Though Vaughan does not, like Herbert, relate his volume of lyrics in generic terms to certain poetic books of the Bible, his numerous epigraphs, postscripts, quotations, and allusions from Canticles establish a biblical frame for the spiritual experience the poems explore. As we have noted earlier, though the Song of Songs in Catholic tradition was usually interpreted as a treatment of the contemplative life or of the mystical experience, Protestants read it as an allegory of the Church's historical situation or of the typical Christian life.[25] The latter allegory was seen to begin with the effective calling and the start of regeneration—"Draw me, we will run after thee" (Cant. 1:4); it then presents the uneven course of spiritual failures and triumphs which mark the process of sanctification; and it concludes with the state of intensified longing for the Second Coming: "Make haste, my beloved, and be thou like to a roe, or to a young Hart upon the mountaines of spices" (Cant. 8:14).[26] This *schema* conforms rather closely to that traced in *Silex Scintillans*: Vaughan's speaker, as elect Christian, presents his own experience as in some sense a specific historical embodiment of the allegory of Canticles, and at times he assumes the voice of the Bride.

As we have just seen, the Canticles imagery in the poem "Regeneration"—the garden, flowers, spices, fountain, rushing wind—presents the speaker's effectual calling, the beginning of his regeneration. In "Religion" the speaker laments the corruption and poisoning of the once-pure spring of religion and prays for its purification, setting forth the ideal of its purity in an appended epigraph: *"My sister, my spouse is as a garden Inclosed, as a Spring shut up, and a fountain sealed up"*

(Cant. 4:12). The speaker of "The Brittish Church" assumes the voice of the Bride-Church throughout; the final lines in a direct quotation of Canticles 8:14 implore the Bridegroom's swift return at the Second Coming to save his ravaged Spouse; and the concluding quotation, "*O Rosa Campi! O lilium Convallium! quomodò nunc facta es pabulum Aprorum!*" fuses Canticles 2:1 and Psalm 80:13 to represent graphically the sufferings of the English Church under the Puritans.[27] Canticles imagery is also prominent in the communion poems: in "The Holy Communion" the speaker employs the epithets from Canticles 2:1 with reference to Christ rather than the Church; in "The Feast" he identifies (briefly) with the Bride—"O what high joys / The Turtles voice / And songs I hear!" (ll. 49-51); in "Dressing" he explores his need of purgation with reference to the purity demanded by the Bridegroom as he feeds "among the Lillies" (ll. 1-2, Cant. 2:16). This last motif is wittily reversed in "Cock-crowing," as the speaker begs for the removal in eternity of his veil of mortality and corruption but also pleads for the indulgence of the Bridegroom's continued presence despite his own earthly impurity—"O take it off! or till it flee, / Though with no Lilie, stay with me!" (ll. 47-48). The speaker of "The World" is led to apprehend more fully his privilege as Bride. Surprised that his marvelous vision of eternity "Like a great *Ring* of pure and endless Light" is ignored by most worldlings, he hears a whispered explanation, "*This Ring the Bride-groome did for none provide / But for his Bride*" (ll. 2, 59-60). In "Fair and yong light" the speaker imagines his own association with the Bridegroom on those "everlasting spicy mountains" (l. 50) of Canticles 8:14. In "The Night" the speaker, paraphrasing Canticles 5:2, briefly takes on the Bride's persona: "When my Lords head is fill'd with dew, and all / His locks are wet with the clear drops of night; / His still, soft call; / His knocking time" (ll. 32-35).[28] The Canticles passage was usually glossed as presenting the soul's awakening from the somnolence produced by worldly concerns when Christ calls and sheds upon her the dew of grace won in the night of his earthly life and passion. The speaker finds this allegory re-enacted in him as he turns from "this worlds ill-guiding light" (l. 47) to receive Christ's call and visitation in the night.

A second biblical frame is created by quotations, epigraphs, postscripts, and echoes from the Book of Revelation, supplemented by other references to the Second Coming or to the end of time. Prepared for by the Ascension/Second Coming typology of "Ascension-day," this frame pertains especially to Part II of *Silex*;[29] it affords a typological perspective, so that the speaker's present experience becomes a type of his perfected life at the Apocalypse. Consonant with this typology, the poems often move from an immediate experience and then attain a glimpse of the apocalyptic moment. In "Ascension-day" the speaker's sense of spiritual advancement through identification with Christ's ascension foreshadows the completion of his sanctification at the Judgment. The speaker of "The Seed growing secretly" finds evidence of his own secret growth nurtured by grace, and he looks forward to the harvest: "Keep clean, bear fruit, earn life and watch / Till the white winged Reapers come!" (ll. 47-48). The speaker of "The Rainbow" perceives in that symbol of God's covenant not to destroy the world with rain an adumbration of the world's final destruction by fire: "Yet I know well, and so our sins require, / Thou dost but Court cold rain, till *Rain* turns *Fire*" (ll. 41-42). In "Palm-Sunday" the speaker's re-enactment (echoing Herbert's "Easter") of the praise appropriate to the day—"I'le get me up before the Sun, / I'le cut me boughs off many a tree" (ll. 35-36)—foreshadows the antitype of his praise in the New Jerusalem (Rev. 7:9),[30] where he hopes for "But one *green Branch* and a *white robe*" (l. 46).

This framework also permits the speaker to identify himself and the contemporary English royalists with the suffering saints portrayed in Revelation, and at times he assumes their voice. In "Abels blood" he associates the suffering English saints with those "souls behinde the altar" of Revelation 6:9-10, who "with one strong, incessant cry / Inquire *How Long*? of the most high. / Almighty Judge!" (ll. 20-23);[31] he prays, however, that his countrymen's blood will not call for vengeance as Abel's did, but for forgiveness and peace in association with Christ, the antitype of Abel. "The Men of War" begins with a near quotation of Revelation 13:10 describing "the patience and the faith of the Saints,"[32] and then proceeds to apply the verse to the suffering royalists: "For in this bright, insructing verse / Thy Saints are not the Conquerors; / But patient, meek, and overcome" (ll. 17-19). At the Judgment, "when *thy Throne is set*, and all / These *Conquerors* before it fall," he begs to be found among those who forgo violence, "Who by no blood (here) overcame / But the blood of the *blessed Lamb*" (ll. 47-48, 51-52).

In the final group of poems the speaker often imagines himself among the triumphant saints. "Tears," couched in Revelation imagery throughout, describes Christ bringing "His white and holy train, / Unto those clear and living *Springs*, / Where comes no *stain*!" (ll. 2-4), and the speaker begs that he may drink after them. In "The day of Judgement [II]" he calls impatiently for that day's arrival, to vindicate the saints:

> O come, arise, shine, do not stay
> > Dearly lov'd day!
> The fields are long since white, and I
> With earnest groans for freedom cry,
>
> . . . . . . . . . . . . . . . . .
>
> > > let not man say
> *Thy arm doth sleep*; but write this day
> Thy judging one.
>
> > > > (ll. 11-14, 43-45)

In this context Vaughan's paraphrase of Psalm 65, which follows immediately, takes on intimations not present in the original of the millennial renewal of all the earth. In "The Throne," with headnote reference to Revelation 20:11,[33] the speaker imagines himself before "The great and white throne / . . . Of my dread Lord" (ll. 3-4), making his final submission, *"Thy will be done!"* And in "The Wreath" his earthly poetic "twin'd wreath of *grief* and *praise*" offered to Christ[34] becomes an earnest of the wreath he will receive "Where cloudless Quires sing without tears, / Sing thy just praise, and see thy face" (ll. 9, 18-19). Finally, in "L'Envoy" he imagines the Second Coming with burning immediacy:

> O the new worlds new, quickning Sun!
> Ever the same, and never done!
>
> . . . . . . . . . . . . . . . . .
>
> > Arise, arise!
> And like old cloaths fold up these skies,
> This long worn veyl: then shine and spread
> Thy own bright self over each head,
> And through thy creatures pierce and pass
> Till all becomes thy cloudless glass.
>
> > > > (ll. 1-2, 7-12)

But he then draws back, adopting again the posture of the patient and faithful saint willing to wait upon earth till the number of the elect is completed—"Till all be ready, that the train / May fully fit thy glorious reign" (ll. 27-28).

The ordering metaphor of *Silex Scintillans* is the Christian pilgrimage, developed by means of a variety of images, brief allegories, and typological references throughout the volume.[35] As we have seen, the first poem of the volume, "Regeneration" presents an allegory of pilgrimage, a fictional account of two misconceived journeys (down the primrose path, up Mount Sinai) followed by a blessed journey to the garden of the Church, within which the speaker undertakes a further ambulatory exploration, commenting upon its flowers, spices, fountains, stones.[36] This wandering about, observing, and commenting upon landscapes and happenings characterizes many poems in the volume. In some, e.g., "The Pursuit" and "Man," the speaker sees himself straying restlessly, his path lost; in "The Resolve" he warns his soul to return from such wanderings to the true path: "To mind / One path, and stray / Into another, or to none, / Cannot be love; / . . . there is / An ancient way / All strewed with flowres, and happiness / And fresh as *May*; / There turn, and turn no more" (ll. 3-6, 21-25). In "The Retreate" the speaker longs to undertake a reverse pilgrimage, so as to "travell back" to his "Angell-infancy":[37]

> But (ah!) my soul with too much stay
> Is drunk, and staggers in the way.
> Some men a forward motion love,
> But I by backward steps would move,
> And when this dust falls to the urn
> In that state I came return.
>
> (ll. 27-32)

In "Peace" the speaker attempts to stir up his soul to a journey by describing the goal in allegorical, almost fairy-tale terms: "My Soul, there is a Countrie / far beyond the stars, / . . . If thou canst get but thither, / There growes the flowre of peace" (ll. 1-2, 13-14). The speaker of "The Pilgrimage" sees himself benighted on his journey, longing for home and requiring (like Elijah) sustenance for his passage: "So strengthen me, Lord, all the way, / That I may travel to thy Mount" (ll. 27-28).

So pervasive is the pilgrim metaphor in the volume that poems on quite different subjects are assimilated to it by means of the characteristic imagery. In a meditation on a dead tree, "The Timber," the speaker likens the tree to the true pilgrim dead to the world, walking "A narrow, private way" (l. 34), yet still stirred by grief for past sins. In a poem on "The Shepheards" he speculates as to whether their special privilege of learning first about Christ's birth was granted them as descendants of the great Old Testament patriarch-pilgrims—"those first and blessed swains / Were pilgrims on those plains" (ll. 9-10). After the angels' departure the shepherds themselves take up a pilgrim posture: "All towards *Bethlem* walk / To see their souls great shepheard, who was come / To bring all straglers home" (ll. 44-46). Elsewhere, "Righteousness" is described as the "Fair, solitary path! Whose blessed shades / The old, white Prophets planted first and

drest: / Leaving for us . . . / A shelter all the way, and bowers to rest"
(ll. 1-4). Finally, "I walkt the other day (to spend my hour)" links the
speaker's continual meditative activity to his pilgrimage: we see him
walking about in an emblematic landscape en route to heaven, medi-
tating as he goes on the objects and circumstances that offer them-
selves to view.

The pilgrimage motif in these poems is also developed through
typology: the speaker often sees himself as a pilgrim in a quasi-biblical
landscape, recapitulating the wanderings of the Old Testament patri-
archs. "White Sunday" articulates the basis for such a strategy in
terms of correlative typology:

> Besides, thy method with thy own,
> Thy own dear people pens our times,
> Our stories are in theirs set down
> And penalties spread to our Crimes.
>
> (ll. 29-32)

Like Donne and Herbert, though with different emphasis, Vaughan
sometimes makes the speaker the locus of both Old Testament and
New Testament experience. In "The Law, and the Gospel" he describes
the journey of God's people from Mount Sinai to Mount Sion, and
the advantages accruing to the latter state, but he then asks that both
type and antitype be embodied in himself: "O plant in me thy *Gospel*,
and thy *Law*, / Both *Faith*, and *Awe*" (ll. 27-28).

Often, the speaker-pilgrim expresses the spiritual advantages of the
New Covenant, whereby he fulfills the types *forma perfectior*. So, in
"Mans fall, and Recovery" he recapitulates the history of the race—
exiled from the "Everlasting hills," sojourning two thousand years in
the wilderness, convicted of sin and guilt by the Law, but at length
saved by Christ's blood:

> This makes me span
> My fathers journeys, and in one faire step
> O're all their pilgrimage, and labours leap,
> For God (made man,)
> Reduc'd th'Extent of works of faith; so made
> Of their *Red Sea*, a *Spring*; I wash, they wade.
>
> (ll. 27-32)

Yet there is some ambiguity about his typological stance, since the
progressive decay and corruption of religion from the time of the
patriarchs[38] places him in important respects beneath them; also, in
contrast to Herbert's speaker, he does not often press his claim (through

Christ) to a privileged role as antitype. Rather, as one continually expecting and longing for the Second Coming, he usually finds himself on much the same plane of experience with those first awaiting the Messiah—a correlative type with them. He does, however, expect to share in the antitypical fulfillment of all the promises and the types at the end of time.

One favorite type for the speaker is Israel wandering in the desert. In the opening lines of "The Mutinie"—"Weary of this same Clay, and straw"—he sees himself recapitulating the situation of Israel enslaved at the brick-kilns of Egypt, and later he too is wandering in the wilderness. He re-enacts also the Israelites' murmurs against God, especially since he seems not to be experiencing the New Testament privileges he supposedly ought to enjoy; he knows God has "a shorter Cut / To bring me home, than through a wildernes, / A Sea, or Sands and Serpents" (ll. 29-31), yet he still wanders like Israel of old. The conclusion affirms his willingness, despite all this, to follow whatever path God has devised for him, and the epigraph promises the "*hidden* Manna" and the "white stone" (Rev. 2:17) of apocalyptic fulfillment. In "Joy of my life!" he is on pilgrimage to the New Jerusalem and finds himself guided, as Israel was, by a pillar of fire:

> Gods Saints are shining lights: who stays
>      Here long must passe
> O're dark hills, swift streames, and steep ways
>      As smooth as glasse;
> . . . . . . . . . . . . . . .
> They are (indeed,) our Pillar-fires
>      Seen as we go,
> They are that Cities shining spires
>      We travell too.
>                          (ll. 17-20, 25-28)

Again, the speaker often identifies himself with Ishmael, the first-born of Abraham by the bondmaid Hagar, who was cast out with his mother into the desert so that he might not inherit with Isaac, the chosen seed, and who was saved from dying of thirst when an angel directed his mother to a spring. Though medieval exegetes regarded Ishmael as a type of the reprobate or the heretic,[39] Vaughan seems rather to call upon Luther's interpretation of the story, in which Ishmael is a type of the gentiles who were to became heirs of the promise, and God's providential act in preserving him is a foreshadowing of that grace.[40] Vaughan's speaker finds himself recapitulating the situation of the weeping, thirst-wracked Ishmael: he prays that on his way through the desert his bottle may be filled with the tears of his repentance ("The Timber"); he complains of God's coldness to his cries, whereas of old "thou didst hear the *weeping Lad!*" ("Begging [II]," l. 12); he finds in Ishmael's rescue a type of the care he receives from God ("Providence," ll. 1-6); and in "The Seed growing secretly" he cries out as a new Ishmael for the dew of grace from heaven—"O fill his bottle! thy childe weeps!" (l. 16).

Alternatively, the speaker is often in the situation of Jacob, who set forth for Laban's country "on foot, in poore estate," as Henry Ainsworth explains, with only his staff in his hand.[41] In "The Pilgrimage" he finds himself lodged like Jacob in some nameless place but dreaming of heaven; in "Religion" and "The Search" he finds himself at Jacob's well but he desires instead its antitype, Christ, the fountain of living waters offered to the Samaritan woman (John 4:1-4). In "Regeneration" the speaker's allegorical journey is intersected by one typological episode: he reposes in the "faire, fresh field" (l. 27) of Bethel where Jacob slept on a stone and dreamed of a ladder reaching to heaven, and where he later annointed the stone as an altar to God; here the speaker discovers the antitype—the Garden of the Church. In "Jacobs Pillow, and Pillar" the speaker finds the comfort afforded by Jacob's simple stone pillow far surpassed by the antitype he enjoys.

The speaker also discovers certain New Testament types of his Christian pilgrimage. In "Palm-Sunday" he initiates a not wholly felicitous identification with the "harmless, yong and happy Ass, / . . . Ordain'd, and made to bear his Maker" to Jerusalem on that day (ll. 28, 31). In "The Ass" the speaker recapitulates the situation of that beast, "in this busie street / Of flesh and blood, where two ways meet" (ll. 1-2), and he begs to recapitulate as well its humility and relation to Christ:

> Let me thy Ass be onely wise
> To carry, not search mysteries;
> Who carries thee, is by thee lead,
> Who argues, follows his own head.
>                     (ll. 21-24)[42]

In "Tears" he assumes the persona of the Ass, begging that when the glorious saints have drunk of the living stream, God may "Bid thy poor Ass . . . / Drink after them" (ll. 11-12). In "The Night" the speaker identifies with that "Most blest believer" Nicodemus, who sought and found the divine light in Christ by night. The speaker in some degree recapitulates this experience, since he also finds the night to be a time of visitation and illumination for him, but he looks forward to the fulfillment of the Nicodemus type *forma perfectior*, when he will at last dwell in the "deep, but dazling darkness" that God is.

The metaphorical and typological pilgrimage rendered in these poems takes place in a unique landscape, the creation of which is one of Vaughan's most remarkable poetic achievements. It is sometimes the real Welsh countryside (as in the opening lines of "The Showre" or "The Water-fall"), sometimes emblematic (the scales on the mountain in "Regeneration"), often biblical (the groves in "Religion" where the pilgrim-speaker retraces the wanderings of the patriarchs, complaining that he does not, like them, see angels or hear God). Characteristically, the landscape is a fusion of all these elements, as in "The Search":

> 'Tis now cleare day: I see a Rose
> Bud in the bright East, and disclose
> The Pilgrim-Sunne; all night have I
> Spent in a roving Extasie
> To find my Saviour; I have been
> As far as *Bethlem*, and have seen
> His Inne, and Cradle.
>
> (ll. 1-7)[43]

The effect of such fusion is to suggest that Vaughan's speaker—an Anglican royalist poet in strife-torn, seventeenth-century Britain—is also a Christian Everyman whose spiritual journey takes place in an inner landscape where biblical history, moral universals, and contemporary reality interpenetrate.

The pilgrimage is further characterized by other biblical metaphors whose prominence will by now be evident. It is a pilgrimage in a land of veils, clouds, mists, darkness, of "days, which are at best but dull and hoary, / Meer glimering and decays."[44] But it is directed toward a place of clear vision, light, and glory, of "mighty, and eternall light / Where no rude shade, or night / Shall dare approach us," a place where "One everlasting *Saboth* there shall runne / Without *Succession*, and without a *Sunne*."[45] But the metaphor is treated complexly, for in this world the day is often a time of spiritual decline while the night is a time of divine illumination ("The Morning-watch," "The Night"). Also, though the speaker longs for cloudless light, he recognizes in "The Night" that God paradoxically unites light and dark—"There is in God (some say) / A deep, but dazling darkness" (ll. 49-50).

Again, the pilgrimage is from a land of death and bondage to one of life and liberty, a polarity made explicit in "The Ass":

                              break or untye
           These bonds, this sad captivity,
           This leaden state, which men miscal
           Being and life, but is dead thrall.

           ·  ·  ·  ·  ·  ·  ·  ·  ·  ·  ·  ·  ·  ·  ·  ·

           O let him by his *Lord* be led,
           To living springs, and there be fed
           Where light, joy, health and perfect peace
           Shut out all pain and each disease;
           Where death and frailty are forgotten,
           And bones rejoyce, which once were broken!
                              (ll. 53-56, 59-64)

Elsewhere, the polarity is between false life and true, as in "Quick-
ness": "False life! a foil and no more, when / Wilt thou be gone? / . . .
Thou art a toylsom Mole, or less / A moving mist / But life is, what
none can express, / *A quickness, which my God hath kist*" (ll. 1-2,
17-20). Vaughan's rendering of life and growth under the imagery of
quickness and greenness relates to another biblical metaphor of some
importance in the poems, the Christian as seed or plant fostered by
God's husbandry ("Unprofitablenes," "Disorder *and* frailty," "Idle
Verse," "Love, and Discipline," "The Seed growing secretly," "I walkt
the other day"). Paradoxically, the movement from deadness (or false
life) to true life is through Death—Christ's death and ours: "Dear,
beauteous death! The Jewel of the Just."[46]
     Vaughan's poems trace, then, the familiar Protestant-Pauline par-
adigm of regeneration and the spiritual life; and they do so by ex-
ploiting in distinctive ways the familiar biblical metaphors and typo-
logical strategies. Recognition that he stands upon the firm common
ground of the English Protestant tradition in theology and poetics
should force revision of pervasive critical notions about Vaughan the
mystic, Vaughan the Cambridge Platonist, or Vaughan the creator of
an eccentric private imagery.[47]
     *Silex Scintillans* does not approach *The Temple* in the range of
kinds and forms of verse; the poems are in couplets, in quatrains, and in
variously patterned stanzas in which lines of uneven length are linked
in regular rhyme schemes. Neither does Vaughan find his chief model
for religious lyric kinds where Herbert did, in the Book of Psalms.
*The Temple* itself provides Vaughan with some generic exemplars. He
has a few brief allegories which recount fictional incidents in Herbert-
like tones of naïveté and simplicity—"The Ornament," "Peace," "The
Garland." There are a few "definition" poems reminiscent of Herbert's

"Prayer (I)" or "The Quidditie"—Vaughan's "Righteousness," "Quickness," "Son-dayes." Vaughan also attempts a few near-hieroglyphs, much less intricate and witty than Herbert's—"Love-sick," "Trinity-Sunday," "The Wreath." "Rules and Lessons" presents a series of Christian proverbs whose sententious style and stanzaic form are obviously modeled upon "The Church-porch."[48] There are three dialogue poems between Body and Soul ("Death," "Resurrection and Immortality," and "The Evening-watch") which are, from one point of view, meditations on death as an avenue to eternal life but which also develop some little dramatic tension between the interlocutors. Finally, although Vaughan made no real effort as Herbert did to subsume the Davidic voice, he has three Psalm versions, two of which (Psalms 121 and 104) are rather close paraphrases and the last (Psalm 65) a free transformation of the original.

Vaughan has very few hymns, either congregational anthems or exalted praises and thanksgivings.[49] The two poems so labeled are metrically regular, with singable lines and stanzas: "Easter Hymn" with its familiar, colloquial diction, is more nearly in the congregational mode while "Ascension-Hymn" rises to the exalted tone and focus on God's greatness expected in the higher hymnic kind. Other hymn-like poems are "Praise" (an imitation of Herbert's "Easter") and "The Morning-watch," both of which have the two-part structure and shift in metrical form found at times in Herbert's hymns. But whereas Herbert's hymnic works (e.g., "Easter") often begin with a meditative analysis and conclude with a lyric hymn resulting from it, these poems begin with ecstatic hymnic praise and then shift to meditation or petition, as awareness of human limitation intrudes upon the speaker's consciousness. The most successful of Vaughan's hymns and one of his finest poems is the magnificent "Morning-watch," a hymn of personal praise sung in harmony with all nature. The hymnic part is:

> O Joyes! Infinite sweetnes! with what flowres,
> And shoots of glory, my soul breakes, and buds!
>> All the long houres
>> Of night, and Rest
>> Through the still shrouds
>> Of sleep, and Clouds,
>> This Dew fell on my Breast;
>> O how it *Blouds*
> And *Spirits* all my Earth! heark! In what Rings,
> And *Hymning Circulations* the quick world
>> Awakes, and sings;

The rising winds,
And falling springs,·
Birds, beasts, all things
Adore him in their kinds,
Thus all is hurl'd
In sacred *Hymnes*, and *Order*, the great *Chime*
And *Symphony* of nature.

(ll. 1-18)

Then comes a definition of prayer which virtually conflates it with hymn—"Prayer is / The world in tune, / A spirit-voyce, / And vocall joyes / Whose *Eccho is* heav'ns blisse" (ll. 18-22)—and finally a petition for the return of such graces. The shift appears to intimate the impossibility of unalloyed praise on earth.

Two of Vaughan's psalm translations are hymnic: his version of Psalm 104 is a close rendering of David's eloquent hymn celebrating all God's works,[50] but the version of Psalm 65 transforms that rather eclectic work into a unified, exalted, and rhythmic hymn. Vaughan was evidently led to such recasting by the view he expressed to a contemporary versifier of the Psalms, that the Psalmist's religious emotions were at times inadequately controlled by art.[51] Vaughan's version is spoken as by one welcomed to the Lord's house and joining with the saints in appropriate praises. Coming as it does in the sequence of poems on the *eschaton*, this reworked psalm indicates the speaker's final achievement of sustained praise—deriving from the Church's common store (the Psalter) and in consort with that of the saints, but yet individual. It appears that for Vaughan, as also for Donne though for quite different reasons, the hymnic mode is truly realized only in God's eternal dwelling-place:

*Sions* true, glorious God! on thee
Praise waits in all humility.

· · · · · · · · · · · · · · · ·

Happy is he! whom thou wilt choose
To serve thee in thy blessed house!
Who in thy holy Temple dwells,
And fill'd with joy, thy goodness tells!

· · · · · · · · · · · · · · · ·

The fruitful flocks fill every Dale,
And purling Corn doth cloath the Vale;
They shout for joy, and joyntly sing,
*Glory to the eternal King!*

(ll. 1-2, 9-12, 45-58)

By far the largest number of Vaughan's poems are meditations, in most of the kinds urged and exemplified in the contemporary Protestant treatises, and in Vaughan's own meditative work, *The Mount of Olives*.[52] Early in Part I, Vaughan's speaker undertakes, and discovers the fallacies of, two faulty modes of meditation; the poems in question provide a critique of modes which readers have sometimes wrongly attributed to Vaughan himself.[53] We recall that both Donne in "Goodfriday, 1613. Riding Westward" and Herbert in the opening poems of "The Church" present speakers who embark upon conventional Catholic meditations on the Passion, and then painfully come to realize that they must recast the exercise in more appropriate Protestant terms.[54] Vaughan's "The Search" also describes an exercise in the Catholic manner, starting with the senses and focusing upon the events of Christ's life and death: the speaker declares, "all night have I / Spent in a roving Extasie / To find my Saviour" (ll. 3-5), and he then relates attempt after attempt to manage a proper composition of place, to find Christ by placing himself in the various locales and circumstances in which he lived and taught and suffered. Failing this, the speaker considers a monastic retreat to the wilderness in imitation of Christ, promising himself rich spiritual delights: "What pleasures should my Journey crown, / What silent paths, what shades, and Cells, / Faire, virgin-flowers, and hallow'd *Wells* / I should rove in, and rest my head / Where my deare Lord did often tread, / Sugring all dangers with successe" (ll. 68-73). But he is then told that this concentration on "the skinne, and shell of things" is caused "By meer Despair / of wings," and he is directed to a sounder course: "Search well another world; who studies this, / Travels in Clouds, seeks *Manna*, where none is" (ll. 81, 86-87, 95-96). The directive is explicated by a coda from Acts 17:27-28, through which the speaker is instructed to consider heaven where Christ is now ascended, and the world of his own soul; specifically, the epigraph urges upon him the Protestant meditative and hortatory emphasis upon the meaning of Christ's redemptive acts for his own spiritual life: "*he be not far off from every one of us, for in him we live, and move, and have our being.*"

The speaker makes another false attempt, as the title itself signifies, in "Vanity of Spirit." Here his method is something like that in Bonaventure's *Itinerarium Mentis in Deum*, the ascent to God through the ladder of created things, which, as Louis Martz points out, is related to a more general Augustinian meditative mode evoking intuitions of the divine through an interior illumination grounded in memory.[55] Martz associates Vaughan with this meditative method, citing "Vanity of Spirit" in evidence, but the poem is really an enactment of its failure, by reason of the ravages wrought in the soul by original sin. The speaker is seeking knowledge of the Creator and of the mystery of good and evil: "Who gave the Clouds so brave a bow, / Who bent the spheres, and circled in / Corruption with this glorious Ring" (ll. 4-6). He questions the creatures with a thoroughness and tenacity which parodies the Bonaventuran method and amounts to a ravaging of nature: "I summon'd nature: peirc'd through all her store, / Broke up some seales, which none had touch'd before, / Her wombe, her bosome, and her head / Where all her secrets lay a bed / I rifled quite, and having past / Through all the Creatures, came at last / To search my selfe" (ll. 9-15). Unsuccessful with the creatures (which, even when properly examined, can only display *vestigia Dei*, not answer such questions as the speaker has set), he looks within himself to find the *imago Dei* which Augustine and Bonaventure located in the faculties of the soul. But though he finds some mysterious traces and echoes, the speaker discovers, with Calvin, that the *imago Dei* is almost wholly dismembered by the Fall:[56] his breast is strewn "With Hyergliphicks quite dismembred, / And broken letters scarce remembred" (ll. 23-24). At this point he despairs of any approach to God in this world, given the "*veyls*" of nature and his own "*Ecclips'd Eye*," and can only seek death: "*I'le disapparell, and to buy / But one half glaunce, most gladly dye*" (ll. 30, 33-34). Calvin and the Protestant meditators drew a very different conclusion from the same evidence: while fallen man cannot rise to God through nature itself, if he reads the Book of Nature by the light of the scriptures it can reveal much about God and his attributes.[57] The speaker in this poem left out the essential element, scripture, and so his meditative exercise is vanity.

"*Isaacs* Marriage" follows "The Search," and is almost certainly intended as an example of proper meditation—in several modes at once. One key to this intention is the fact that Vaughan's text here, Genesis 24:63, was a *locus classicus* for meditative practice, cited in all the Protestant manuals. The Authorized Version renders the text, "And Isaac went out, to meditate in the field, at the eventide: and he lifted up his eyes, and saw, and behold, the camels were comming." Vaughan's decision to use the term "pray" instead of "meditate" in his epigraph quotation of this verse serves again to underscore his tendency to conflate the two exercises.[58] Rather remarkably, the poem serves as a paradigm for the several meditative kinds important in *Silex*. It is a meditation on a biblical event—and is conducted so as to draw out that event's moral and spiritual meanings for us. It is an occasional meditation upon a particular marriage (there are to be several poem-meditations in Vaughan's volume upon a particular death). It is a meditation upon experience—Isaac's courtship, and our courtships, and God's ways with Isaac. It is a meditation upon a biblical text, displaying in the Protestant way the speaker-meditator's engagement with that text and its meanings for him and us. Moreover, it incorporates a brief nature-meditation on Lahai-roi's well, in which a cyclical round of emanations resulting in showers which produce perfumes is set forth as an emblem of Isaac's prayers. The speaker's mixture of meditative modes in this paradigmatic meditative poem at once prepares for his later use of these several kinds, and for his frequent mixture of them.

Vaughan's few meditations upon biblical events are carried on in terms of the understandings gained in "The Search": the focus is upon the significance of the event for the speaker's spiritual life. In "The Passion" the speaker rather awkwardly explores the paradox that Christ's sufferings produce his good—"thy *Death*, my *Life*" (l. 56). The speaker of "Christs Nativity" urges himself to awake and sing in consort with nature, recognizing his own earthly clay as the locus for the true incarnation—"And let once more by mystick birth / The Lord of life be borne in Earth" (ll. 29-30). "The Shepheards" are seen primarily as exemplars, in their humility and contentment, for all Christian pilgrims. The speaker in "Easter-day" calls upon himself to come forth from his darkened state—"Awake, awake, / And in his Resurrection partake" (ll. 5-6). And in "White Sunday" the speaker describes the darkness of his own times, calling for the fiery tongues again. In "Jesus weeping [I]" he asks for Christ's tears shed over Jerusalem to be poured out on us; and in "Jesus weeping [II]" he takes upon himself a weeping role in response to Christ's grief, but finds that weeping to be a source of joy: "A grief so bright / . . . Shall send me (*Swan-like*) singing home" (ll. 50, 53). The final exercise in this meditative mode is "The Obsequies," included in the sequence on Last Things: it is a meditation upon Christ's death, but the subject is really the effect of such meditation upon the speaker's soul—"Thy death may keep my soul alive" (l. 32). In *The Mount of Olives* Vaughan linked meditative themes such as these with preparations for and thanksgiving after the sacrament,[59] and *Silex* also contains a few rather conventional communion poems—"Dressing," "The Holy Communion," "The Sap."[60] A poem in the final sequence, "The Feast" concludes this motif, relating the sacrament to the marriage feast of the Lamb and to a consideration of "what in the next world to eat" (l. 78).

The most Herbertian of Vaughan's poems are several meditations upon experience, probing God's dealings with the soul and its responses. Most of them occur in Part I; many are soliloquies to God or the self; some are moving, though they cannot compete with Herbert's sustained representations and sensitive analyses of the spiritual emotions. The arresting opening lines (echoing or modeled upon lines from Herbert) often epitomize the spiritual state to be analyzed, as is the case with "Distraction"—"O knit me, that am crumbled dust!"[61] "The Relapse" records an experience of divine rescue—"My God, how gracious art thou! I had slipt / Almost to hell, / And on the verge of that dark, dreadful pit / Did hear them yell" (ll. 1-4). "Unprofit-ablenes" (a close imitation of Herbert's "The Flower") records a fresh accession of grace after deprivation, "How rich, O Lord! how fresh thy visits are." "Admission," beginning with a quotation from Her-bert, "How shril are silent tears?" analyzes the experience of prayer and of the divine response to it.[62] Poems of this kind in Part II are some-times efforts to deal with specific temptations ("The Proffer," "Joy"); or they are records of special favors—God's "glance of love" ("The Favour"), or the recovery of lost assurance of election ("The Agree-ment"). This mode finds its culmination in the final sequence with "The Queer," which delightedly raises queries about a newly-gained, secret assurance of election and adoption, bringing a joy "Which wears heaven, like a bridal ring, / And tramples on doubts and despair" (ll. 3-4).

A number of Vaughan's poems are meditations on death.[63] A few are "deliberate," often linking the topic to a biblical text in an epigraph headnote or footnote. The Body-Soul dialogue in "Death [I]" explores the imagery of Job 10:21-22, "*the land of darknesse, and the shadow of death*"; the Soul-Body dialogue in "The Evening-watch" analyzes sleep as an emblem of death. In "The Check" the spirit teaches the flesh to heed the universal language of death taught by all creatures, and so to redeem the time. "Buriall" is cast as a prayer to God to pre-serve body and dust in the resurrection; it is a personal enactment of the epigraph text from Romans 8:23, "*our selves also, which have the first fruits of the spirit . . . grone within ourselves, waiting for the adoption, to wit, the redemption of our body.*"

More interesting is a sequence of "occasional" meditations, probably on the death of Henry's brother William; these poems are untitled; they are dispersed throughout the volume but linked together as a sequence by the same typographical symbol. In their progression from pain and grief to joyful celebration of the lost one's place among the saints, these poems display in little the speaker's larger spiritual progress. In the first poem, "Thou that know'st for whom I mourn," the griev-ing speaker recognizes God's use of this particular death to call him from his sins; in "Come, come, what doe I here?" his chief desire is to sleep in death with the deceased; in "Joy of my life!" he becomes aware of the guidance the dead person's soul provides him in the earthly pilgrimage—"Gods Saints are shining lights" (l. 17). In "Silence, and stealth of dayes!" he attempts to "track" the departed spirit but fails—yet is able by the "*Pearle*" of the Gospel to "Find Heaven, and thee" (l. 32) while yet on earth. In "Sure, there's a tye of Bodyes!" he finds he shares in the common human disposition to forget the dead, but he determines to be his own death's-head and carry on such meditation. In "I walkt the other day" he finds in the sleep and expected rebirth of a flower root an analogue for the dead person, and then makes the prayerful application, "shew me his life again / At whose dumbe urn / Thus all the year I mourn" (ll. 61-63). In Part II, immediately following the Ascension poems, comes "They are all gone into the world of light!" in which the speaker envisions the one he mourns among the saints, "walking in an Air of glory" (l. 9). "As time one day by me did pass" contrasts the dead one's hopeful posture in the grave expecting resurrection, with the speaker's dismay "that I have out-liv'd / My life" (ll. 39-40). In the final poem of the series, "Fair and yong light!" he eagerly seeks release through death from the bondage of sin, praying that his spirit may inhabit the garden of Canticles. The poem "Death [II]" in the poetic sequence on Last Things[64] brings this meditative topic and mode to its period: here an assured speaker calmly admonishes a personified Death that Christ in dying has thoroughly searched and lighted Death's "dark land" and that God's dead saints are yet alive—"though fled from you, their spirits hive" (l. 30).

Some of the finest and most distinctive of Vaughan's poems are meditations on the creatures. Taking his lesson from "Vanity of Spirit" the speaker reads the creatures in the light of the Word, and often with reference to biblical texts which explore them metaphorically or suggest their didactic or symbolic meaning. Vaughan's poetic subjects in this mode are common topics in treatises of occasional or creature meditation, and many of them are familiar emblems as well, circulated widely in the emblem books.[65] Recognition of such analogues casts some light upon the vexed question of Vaughan's Hermeticism.[66] It seems clear that some of Vaughan's arresting vocabulary derives its special imagistic force from the Hermetic writings—such terms as *beam, balm, balsam, essence, glance, grain, hatch, influence, ray, magnetism, sympathy, tie* sometimes have Hermetic force—but their function is inevitably to reinforce Christian concepts. Also, Vaughan uses the Hermetic concept of the magnetic attraction between a heavenly planet and the earthly body which carries its "seed" in "Cock-crowing" and "The Starre," though in both instances as analogues to a Christian perception about the link between God and the soul. Vaughan's contact with Hermetic writings (perhaps through his twin brother Thomas)[67] had its chief effects in heightening his sense of the wonder and mystery of God's creation, of the sentience and quickness of all things, and of the excellence of the creatures who maintain their constancy to God while fallen man vacillates. But he does not see them as more than *vestigia Dei*, symbols or emblems by which to know something about the transcendent God, as *The Mount of Olives* and several poems make clear. Moreover, Vaughan's constant use of biblical texts as keys to the reading of nature's signs, together with his Christian sense of the substantial reality of God's creation, align him more closely with Protestant meditative theory than with such contemporary Platonists as Peter Sterry, who calls upon the spiritual man to read the world as a "Type of God" and its creatures as signs of him, at the same time recognizing their insubstantiality as "meer images."[68]

In the Protestant manuals, "creature" is a broadly inclusive term, and may refer to the handiwork of man as well as of God. Vaughan's poem "The Lampe" is of this kind:[69] its analogues and its chief themes are to be found in numerous examples of occasional meditation upon a lamp or lantern illuminating the darkness, and in emblems such as those in Quarles' *Hieroglyphics*, in which a burning candle is the emblem of man's life. Ostensibly beginning from a real occasion—"'Tis dead night round about"—the speaker compares a lamp he sees lighting the darkness to his (man's) spiritual life, and interprets the lamp's elements and qualities as an allegory of human virtues. At length, with Quarles and Farley, he indicates wherein the analogy fails: "Only, one point escapes thee; that thy Oile / Is still out with thy flame, and so both faile; / But whensoe're I'm out, both shalbe in, / And where thou mad'st an end, there I'le begin" (ll. 23-26).[70] The concluding epigraph from Mark 13:33 provides a biblical basis and wider resonance for these lessons.[71]

Several poems on the natural creatures emphasize, as Calvin did, the difficulty fallen man, or the speaker, has in learning Nature's lessons or following its example. "The Constellation" reads the stars in the familiar Protestant way as manifestations of and exemplars to man of *"Obedience, Order, Light"* (l. 29), lamenting the contrasting chaotic disorder in men's lives and in the war-torn nation. "Man" contrasts "the stedfastness and state / Of some mean things which here below reside" (ll. 1-2)—birds, bees, flowers—with man's continual restlessness and disorder. In "Midnight" the speaker observes the "Emanations, / Quick vibrations / And bright stirs" of the stars (ll. 11-13) and contrasts these with his own cold affections, praying that God might kindle the blood and water in his breast to a similar "firie-liquid light" (l. 18).[72] In "The Showre" the speaker observes the phenomenon of the title to be caused by the exhalation of a stagnant lake which, "Too grosse for heaven, . . .

fall'st in teares, and weep'st for thy mistake"; the analogue to his own stagnancy is close, but he hopes to improve on the lesson, softening his hard heart with tears, so that "My God would give a Sun-shine after raine" (ll. 5-6, 18). "The Storm" begins with application of the title emblem—"I see the use:" drawing a contrast between tempests incited in the sea by storms and those bred, paradoxically, in his breast by fair weather (sinful ease), the speaker deduces that in his case storms would be salutary. "The Tempest" is the most complex poem of this didactic sort. The speaker proposes to derive instruction from "This late, long heat" (l. 3) followed by rain, and sets his lesson forth in a little allegory of the earth sighing to heaven for her dry breasts and withered flowers and so inviting rain (ll. 5-16). But the speaker finds man inattentive to these "lectures for his eie, and ear" (l. 20) which the Creator hid in the creature; although "All things here shew him heaven" (l. 25), man grovels below. Accordingly, the speaker's case requires resolution in terms of the volume's title emblem: "If I must / Be broke again, for flints will give no fire / Without a steel . . . / grind this flint to dust" (ll. 57-60).

More impressive are the several poems, chiefly from Part II, which view the creatures as true images or divinely ordered symbols of God's truth or of man's life. "The Palm-tree" is based upon an emblem going back to Alciati—the palm tree growing more vigorously under burdens;[73] in Vaughan's poem the emblem signifies fallen man's growth and aspiration for heaven despite the weights of sin and death, and (through allusions to Revelation 7:9 and 13:10) it symbolizes both the suffering saints and their heavenly triumph to come. "The Bird" is almost a nature poem in which the speaker describes his delight in the bird-song which rejoices the day after nighttime storms, but he suggests also the *significatio* of the bird as purveyor of true praise to God and as image of God's providence in life's storms.[74] "The Timber" takes a dead tree, still responsive to winds and storms, as image of the Christian's lot in life, dead to the world yet still afflicted by grief and pain for sin. In "The Rain-bow" the speaker's meditative problem is to discover what meaning the rainbow, the biblical symbol of God's covenant with man to destroy the world no more by flood, now has when seen in his own sky. Surprised to find it "Still yong and fine" given the world's sad decline and man's covenant-breaking, the speaker sees it as a comet, augur of the Last Judgment and the impending destruction of the world by fire: "Thou dost but Court cold rain, till *Rain* turns *Fire*" (l. 42).

Most successful as poems are those in which the speaker-meditator portrays himself in the act of seeking for, discovering, and probing deeply into the profoundly symbolic significance of certain of the creatures. "Resurrection and Immortality," the third poem in the volume, enacts by means of a Soul-Body dialogue the difficulties of such inquiry. From the silkworm, a conventional emblem and natural symbol of resurrection,[75] Body derives only a general analogy to its own case, grounded upon God's evenhandedness: "Shall I then thinke such providence will be / Lesse friend to me?" (ll. 15-16). Soul berates Body for such timidity and insists upon a genuinely symbolic reading, informed by a broad vision of nature's constant transformations of matter into more refined forms, and by the epigraphs from Hebrews 10:20 and Daniel 12:13 which begin and end the poem—contexts which adumbrate not only Body's restoration but also its transformation and glorification. The penultimate poem of Part I, "I walkt the other day (to spend my hour) / Into a field," is a meditation on the same theme, but here achieved without misstep. In the opening lines the speaker puts himself into the posture of the biblical meditator Isaac who "went out to meditate in the field"; he misses a "gallant flowre" found here before, but discovers that its root ("warm Recluse") lies below the soil, awaiting and expecting its rebirth "most fair and young"; at length he understands the symbolism and its relevance to the one he mourns.

In "Cock-crowing" the speaker again explores the meaning of a natural symbol ordained by God: "Father of lights! what Sunnie seed, / What glance of day hast thou confin'd / Into this bird?" (ll. 1-3).[76] The "Sunnie seed," the source of the magnetic attraction between the sun and its bird, causes it to long for and to herald the sun's appearance. The speaker reads this Hermetic symbol in Christion terms: the relationship between the bird and the natural sun images that between the soul (God's seed in man), and God, and the speaker prays that the ramifications of this symbolism may be fully realized in himself: "Seeing thy seed abides in me, / Dwell thou in it, and I in thee" (ll. 23-24). The hindrance to this is the veil of the flesh which stands between the speaker on earth and Christ in heaven. The speaker's longing to pierce the veil is intense, but his witty, final allusion to Canticles testifies to his Christian (rather than Platonic) awareness that God can dwell even in sinful flesh:

> O take it off! make no delay,
> But brush me with thy light, that I
> May shine unto a perfect day,
> And warme me at thy glorious Eye!
> O take it off! or till it flee,
> Though with no Lilie, stay with me!
> (ll. 43-48)

The final nature meditation is included in the sequence on Last Things: it explores a fitting natural symbol of man's passage to death/ life, "The Water-fall."[77] At first the murmuring, hesitating falling water seems to image mankind's fear of death: "this steep place . . . / The common pass / Where, clear as glass, / All must descend" (ll. 6-9). However the speaker, noting the circularity of the water's flow and its restoration to the stream of light from whence it came, speaks assurance to his soul that it will return to the stream of light which was its origin, and to his "frail flesh" that God will restore all he takes from it. He considers then the sacramental significance of this "useful Element and clear" (l. 23)—the baptismal cleansing which first consigned him to those "Fountains of life, where the Lamb goes" (l. 26). At this point he reaffirms the need to interpret nature's symbols through revelation from the Spirit who created them and invested them with meaning:

> What sublime truths, and wholesome themes,
> Lodge in thy mystical, deep streams!
> Such as dull man can never finde
> Unless that Spirit lead his minde,
> Which first upon thy face did move,
> And hatch'd all with his quickning love.
>
> (ll. 27-32)

Now, he observes that the circling rings sent out from the falling water break upon the banks and disappear, giving some intimation of man's passage to an estate which cannot be imaged in nature:

> O my invisible estate,
> My glorious liberty, still late!
> Thou art the Channel my soul seeks,
> Not this with Cataracts and Creeks.
>
> (ll. 37-40)

Meditations on the creatures are now no longer useful, and the speaker bids farewell to a favorite mode.

Finally, several poems are of that classic Protestant kind, meditations upon a biblical text. We have seen that biblical texts are an integral part of most of the poems in this volume, woven into their texture through allusion or quotation, or cited or quoted in headnote or endnote to create a frame for the poem. But the poems in question here are centrally concerned with the analysis of a biblical text and the application of it so as to illuminate personal experience, in the spirit of

Vaughan's description of the "H. Scriptures" as "The Key that opens to all Mysteries, / The *Word* in Characters, God in the *Voice*" (ll. 7-8). Often these poems incorporate nature emblems also,[78] for the speaker's disposition is to draw together closely God's two books of revelation.

Though "The Dawning" does not cite a biblical text by chapter and verse, its first lines point to the parable of the wise and foolish virgins awaiting the Bridegroom (Matt. 25:1-13), and Christ's concluding admonition, "Watch therefore, for ye know neither the day nor the hour wherein the Son of Man cometh." The speaker begins his poem by responding to this verse—"Ah! what time wilt thou come? when shall that crie / The *Bridegroome's Comming*! fil the sky?"—and proceeds to imagine the scene occurring at various times. A nature emblem—"this restless, vocall *Spring*" which "All day, and night doth run, and sing" —teaches him his own proper posture, that he should not calculate times but should be at every hour "drest and on my way, / Watching the Break of thy great day" (ll. 33-34, 47-48). "The World," often misread as a poem of mystical vision, is essentially a meditation on the text quoted in the epigraph at the end, 1 John 2:16-17, which opposes the transitory nature of "*All that is in the world, the lust of the flesh, the lust of the Eys, and the pride of life*" to the eternity of him "*that doth the will of God.*" The speaker visualizes this text in emblems: Eternity as a "great *Ring* of pure and endless light" (l. 2); the lust of the flesh as a "doting Lover" with his lute, his gloves and love knots, his gaze fixed upon a flower (ll. 8-15); the pride of life as a "darksome States-man hung with weights and woe" (l. 16); the lust of the eyes as a "fearfull miser on a heap of rust" (l. 31) hugging his gold.[79] "The Seed growing secretly" refers in title and headnote to Mark 4:26-29, comparing the kingdom of heaven to a man sowing seed which grows "he knoweth not how / . . . But when the fruite is brought foorth, immediately he putteth in the sickle, because the harvest is come." This text supplies the pattern for the speaker's spiritual experiences—his cries for the "dew" of grace, his awareness of "secret *Greenness*! nurst below / Tempests and windes, and winter-nights," and his preparation for the harvest: "Keep clean, bear fruit, earn life and watch / Till the white winged Reapers come" (ll. 25-26, 47-48). In "The Stone" the speaker desires to do some wickedness but fears to, lest all Nature cry out against him. The text cited in the headnote—Joshua 24:27, in which Joshua designates a stone as a "witnesse unto us, for it hath heard all the words of the LORD which hee spake unto us"—provides the basis for the poem's title, situation, and resolution, as well as for the speaker's striking description of nature's sentience:

>        That busie commerce kept between
>        God and his Creatures, though unseen.
>
>        They hear, see, speak,
>        And into loud discoveries break,
>        As loud as blood.
>                                    (ll. 20-24)

If Hermetic, this vision of nature nonetheless finds its sanction in a biblical text.

In the best of these poems the speaker encounters his biblical text dramatically, striving to come to terms with its complex implications for himself. "And do they so?" is perhaps the most striking example in Part I; its epigraph, a Latin rendering of Romans 8:19, stands in lieu of a title. The poem develops in terms of this text and the verses immediately following:

> For the earnest expectation of the creature, waiteth for the manifestation of the sonnes of God.
> . . . . . . . . . . . . . . . . . . . . . . . . . . .
> Because the creature it selfe also shall be delivered from the bondage of corruption, into the glorious libertie of the children of God.
> For wee know that the whole creation groaneth, and travaileth in paine together untill now.
> And not only they, but our selves also which have the first fruites of the spirit, even we our selves groane within our selves, waiting for the adoption, to wit, the redemption of our body (Rom. 8:19, 21-23).

The speaker at first responds to the text with amazement, since its assertion of the creatures' sentience seems to discredit conventional wisdom:

>        And do they so? have they a Sense
>              Of ought but Influence?
>        Can they their heads lift, and expect,
>              And grone too? why th'Elect
>        Can do no more: my volumes sed
>              They were all dull, and dead,
>        They judg'd them senslesse, and their state
>              Wholly Inanimate.
>        Go, go; Seal up thy looks,
>              And burn thy books.
>                                    (ll. 1-10)

The perception that the whole creation is in common plight, groaning for liberty, leads the speaker to that familiar *topos* in Protestant creature meditation, the contrast between the creatures' steadfastness to God and man's giddiness. His prayer for release is grounded first upon the special privilege the biblical text promises to the elect, the enjoyment of the first fruits: "thy bloud is mine, / And my soul should be thine" (ll. 35-36). But then, with fine poetic appropriateness, he presents himself metaphorically before God as one of the creatures: "Sure, thou wilt joy to see / Thy sheep with thee" (ll. 39-40).

Perhaps the most complex, and the finest, of Vaughan's poems is "The Night."[80] The text is John 3:2—"[Nicodemus] . . . came to Jesus by night"—and the poem is the speaker's effort to understand and somehow appropriate that nighttime experience. The speaker sees Nicodemus' apprehension of light in darkness as doubly paradoxical: despite the veil of Christ's humanity he "saw such light / As made him know his God by night"; and, "in that land of darknesse and blinde eyes" he "Did at mid-night speak with the Sun" (ll. 5-6, 8, 12). Moreover, Nicodemus found Christ not in the Temple, but in the place the speaker himself so often looks, in the "temple" of Nature—"his own living works did my Lord hold" (l. 21). The speaker, reflecting, finds that the night is also a time of visitation for him, when he hears the Bridegroom's call to the Bride and has some intimations of spiritual ascent; such spiritual vision at night opposes the common daylight afforded by "this worlds ill-guiding light" (l. 47). Finally and paradoxically he identifies God with darkness as well as light—"a deep but dazling darkness"—and imagines himself fulfilling, as antitype, Nicodemus' experience by relating to both terms of the divine paradox— "O for that night! where I in him / Might live invisible and dim" (ll. 53-54). This complex revaluation of light and darkness is not a treatment of mystical encounter (though it anticipates in imagination that ultimate union). Instead, despite its Platonic imagery, this poem shows the speaker coming to terms with the clouds, veils, and darkness he has so often decried, providing a basis for the patient resignation that accompanies the intensified longing for the end in Part II of *Silex*. Here is the final repudiation of the rash Platonist of "Vanity of Spirit," as this speaker recognizes (through Nicodemus) that now and in eternity he can at night *"have commerce with the light."*[81]

In the penultimate position in *Silex Scintillans* are two poems in which the speaker links together, and bids farewell to, the two "Books" which have provided the substance of his meditations. In the poem "The Book" he considers the creatures—grass, trees, beasts—which have provided the paper, wood cover, and leather binding of his aged book, the Bible, subject of the poem immediately following. The Book of the Creatures is here treated as the physical embodiment of the Book of the Scriptures, and the poet concludes with a prayer for his own apocalyptic renewal along with all the creatures:

> O knowing, glorious spirit! when
> Thou shalt restore trees, beasts and men,
> When thou shalt make all new again,
> Destroying onely death and pain,
> Give him amongst thy works a place,
> Who in them lov'd and sought thy face!
>
> (ll. 25-30)

The following poem, "To the Holy Bible," recognizes and bids farewell to the Book, "lifes guide," which, "having brought me home, didst there / Shew me that pearl I sought elsewhere" (ll. 1, 25-26).

Unlike Herbert, Vaughan does not present his speaker working out in poem after poem a highly complex poetics of the religious lyric,[82] but in the Preface to Silex and in several poems he points to some aspects of the poetics governing the volume. The Preface voices the Protestant concern—reaching back to Coverdale and Du Bartas—to renounce lascivious fictions and idle words, and to exchange "*vain and vitious subjects,* for *divine Themes* and *Celestial praise.*"[83] This concern finds poetic formulation in "Idle Verse" as the speaker banishes the "queint folies, sugred sin" of his youthful love poetry—"The idle talk of feav'rish souls / Sick with a scarf, or glove" (ll. 1, 15-16)—and embraces his present wintry season. The evil potentialities of the art renounced are exhibited in "The Daughter of *Herodias*"—a figure for "Vain, sinful Art" who "made grave *Musique* like wilde *wit /* Erre in loose airs beyond her bounds" (ll. 1-4).

Another element in Vaughan's poetics is the Herbertian recognition that God's grace alone produces the spiritual emotions and conditions necessary to write profound and artful religious poetry: in the Preface Vaughan contrasts pedestrian writers of religious verse who do not write from personal experience with a poet such as Herbert who strives for "*perfection* and true *holyness*" and thereby experiences "heavenly *refreshments,*" having "*a door . . . opened to him in heaven*" (Rev. 4:1).[84] In this vein the speaker in "Chearfulness" delights in an experience of God's presence—"Lord, with what courage, and delight / I doe each thing / When thy least breath sustaines my wing!" (ll. 1-3)—and he sees that if such transformations were sustained he could easily produce hymns: "And to thy praise / A Consort raise / Of *Hallelujahs* here below" (ll. 22-24). "Praise," closely imitating Herbert,[85] is itself a hymn resulting from grace and spiritual joy:

> King of Comforts! King of life!
>     Thou hast cheer'd me,
> And when fears, and doubts were rife,
>     Thou hast cleer'd me!
> . . . . . . . . . . . . .
> Wherefore with my utmost strength
>     I will praise thee.
>
>                 (ll. 1-4, 9-10)

Then, characteristically changing modes, the speaker prays that his poetic praise-offering may be received—"Let him (though poor,) / Strow at thy door / That one poor Blossome" (ll. 54-56).

His more usual experience, however, is of the effort to produce poetry (by God's grace) out of the groans of affliction and repentance. Apostrophizing the "God of Harmony, and Love" the speaker of "Church-Service" seeks to link the "Interceding, spirituall grones" of the Dove with his own "Musick . . . —My sighes, and grones" (ll. 4, 20, 23-24). In "Joy" the speaker eschews mirth—"Be dumb course measures, jar no more; to me / There is no discord, but your harmony. / False, jugling sounds";—and takes groans and grief as his appropriate poetic tone: "Thou hast / Another mirth . . . overcast / With clouds and rain" (ll. 1-3, 13-15). And in "Anguish," which begins with the psalm tag Herbert appropriated in "Jordan (I)"—"My God and King"—the poet prays for the "art" of true repentance which is the prerequisite to the so-difficult art of writing true verse. He illustrates the difficulty, as Herbert often did, by "breaking" the poetic pattern: but whereas Herbert usually begins in poetic disorder and at length resolves the poem into true rhyme and metrical order (e.g., "Deniall," "The Collar") Vaughan exhibits here a final aesthetic disruption arising from unresolved spiritual crisis:

> O! 'tis an easie thing
>     To write and sing;
> But to write true, unfeigned verse
> Is very hard! O God, disperse
> These weights, and give my spirit leave
> To act as well as to conceive!
>
> O my God, hear my cry;
>     Or let me dye!—
>
>                 (ll. 13-20).[86]

In "St. Mary Magdalen" Vaughan embodies in that figure—a counterpoint to Herodias—the qualities of true art arising from repentance. Mary has cast aside her former artful care to have everything about her "sumptuous, rare and neat," but her "Cheap, mighty Art" of love and repentance has brought true beauty—pure, innocent, lively-fair, "like a childes, spotless and fresh" (ll. 14, 49, 70). Again, like Herbert and even more explicitly, Vaughan points to the scriptures as the guide to appropriate spiritual emotions and as the model for their poetic formulation. Apostrophizing the scriptures he declares, "O that I had deep Cut in my hard heart / Each line in thee! Then would I plead in groans / Of my Lords penning, and by sweetest Art / Return upon himself the *Law*, and *Stones*."[87] Vaughan did not find a specific biblical "type" or model for himself as poet, as Herbert did in David the Psalmist, though there is some suggestion in his prefatory declaration of intention to excel in "*Hagiography*, or holy writing" that he places himself generally in the line of those poet-prophets who composed the third section of the Bible called the Hagiographia— among them David, Solomon, Job, Jeremiah, Daniel.[88] That relation is further emphasized by his assimilation, without citation or any separation from his own text, of a long series of biblical verses at the end of his preface—chiefly from Jeremiah, Isaiah, and the Psalms.

As Herbert's poetic river was Jordan, so Vaughan's poetic mountain is the Mount of Olives. Vaughan's first poem with this title distinguishes his "Sweete, sacred hill" from other hills (The Cotswolds and Coopers Hill) associated with civil affairs and accomplishments, and identifies it as peculiarly the hill for poets because of Christ's activities there:

> Their Lord with thee had most to doe;
> He wept once, walkt whole nights on thee,
> And from thence (his suff'rings ended,)
>> Unto glorie
>> Was attended.

> (ll. 20-24)

These activities—weeping, walking-meditating, and ascending—are the concerns of Vaughan's speaker. And Vaughan's choice of the same title for his book of prayers and meditations as for these lyrics about religious poetry identifies the religious lyric with meditation and prayer. In "Mount of Olives [II]" the speaker places himself on that hill, enjoying a sustained experience of beauty and joy arising from the divine glance which causes him to flourish anew as poet: "I shine and shelter underneath thy wing / Where sick with love I strive thy name to sing, / Thy glorious name!" (ll. 23-25).

Vaughan is a finer poet in his total *œuvre* than he is sometimes taken to be: though he has written some banal verse, and some diffuse poems, he is much more than the creator of a handful of successful poems and several striking passages.[89] The volume as a whole is carefully unified— through the dominant metaphor of the Christian pilgrimage; the progression from regeneration to the plateau of assurance in the speaker's spiritual life; the controlling biblical frames from Canticles and the Book of Revelation; the exploration of a wide variety of Protestant meditative kinds; the remarkable landscape fusing naturalistic, emblematic, and biblical elements; the pervasive texture created from biblical metaphoric polarities of darkness-light, and death-life. And the whole volume is climaxed by an apocalyptic sequence of poems, which sets the various progressions and meditative modes in the perspective of the Second Coming. The speaker is also artfully conceived: individualized as to time and place (he is a seventeenth-century royalist Anglican British poet), he also incorporates the paradigmatic emotions, the soul-body dichotomies, and the classic spiritual experiences of the perennial Christian pilgrim; at times also he takes on the voices of the Bride of Canticles, the patient Palm Sunday ass, and the suffering and then triumphant saints of the Book of Revelation.

The nineteen sacred poems published in *Thalia Rediviva* (1678) are appropriately subtitled "Pious Thoughts and Ejaculations."[90] This collection cannot claim, like *Silex Scintillans*, a unity arising from dominant motifs and the portrayal of a speaker's spiritual progress.[91] Nor do these poems, most of them in octosyllabic couplets, exhibit the stanzaic variety of the *Silex* poems, or use biblical epigraphs and codas to present a medley of voices. Yet these poems do display the fundamental elements of Vaughan's Protestant poetics. Pilgrimage is again the central metaphor: the speaker recalls the "Fair, shining *Mountains* of my pilgrimage" ("Looking back," l. 1), and he also envisions the incarnate Christ as pilgrim: "He travels to be born, and then / Is born to travel more agen" ("The Nativity," ll. 3-4). Nature and the creatures are again objects for meditation and praise—"Fresh *fields* and *woods*! the Earth's fair *face*, / God's *foot-stool*, and mans *dwelling-place*" ("Retirement," ll. 1-2). The speaker again defines himself by association with Old Testament types of the pilgrim—"Give me my *staff* then . . . / With this *poor stick* I'le pass the *Foord* / As *Jacob* did" ("The World," ll. 78-83); he identifies also with humble creature-pilgrims—now with "The Bee" as before with "The Ass." And again Herbertian allusions proliferate: the opening lines of "To his Books" recall the series of epithets in "Prayer (I)"; the apostrophe to the sun as "weak *shiner*" in "The Recovery" recalls Herbert's address to the same "willing shiner" in "Christmas"; and in "To Christian Religion" (ll. 9-14) a direct reference to Herbert as "Seer" introduces a six-line summary of "The Church Militant." Indeed, the sacred poems of the *Thalia* volume not only resemble but deliberately invite retrospection to the *Silex* poems. The first lyric, "To his Books," and the second, "Looking back," identify the speaker's library and his former experiences as a store of knowledge available to present meditation, and the collection as a whole, by pervasive echoes of lines, images, rhythms, and patterns in *Silex Scintillans*, points to that volume as holding the quintessence of Vaughan's knowledge and experience as Christian poet.[92]

Many of Vaughan's poems are demonstrably more carefully constructed and more tightly unified than is often recognized, if we consider their biblical texts, their particular meditative modes, and the kinds of spiritual experience they intend to explore. To take the full measure of Vaughan's achievement we should understand that the elements of the Protestant poetics—biblical models and language, typology, emblems, meditation—are of the very substance of his poetry, though very differently deployed than in Herbert. Above all, we should observe Vaughan's use of biblical language. Vaughan does not look to the completion of his verse by God in Herbert's way, but he does create an individual poetic style which is an intricate texture of biblical allusion, echo, quotation, and paraphrase rendered in personal, experiential terms: the speaker does indeed "plead in groans / Of my Lords penning." Remarkably, the result is an original, and often strikingly effective, poetic idiom.

# Thomas Traherne: Naked Truth, Transparent Words, and the Renunciation of Metaphor

Traherne included extracts from Donne's sermons in his *Church's Year-Book*, as well as the whole of Herbert's poem, "To all Angels and Saints."[1] Moreover, Traherne's poems, rediscovered in 1896 after falling into oblivion for more than two centuries, were first ascribed to Vaughan.[2] Yet despite these links, both Traherne's theology and his art appear to set him apart from the major strain of seventeenth-century Protestant poetry and poetics.

His most striking departure from the Protestant consensus is his ecstatic celebration of infant innocence, which all but denies original sin as an hereditary taint, ascribing its effects chiefly to corruption by the world as the infant matures.[3] His Neoplatonic conception of man's dignity and unlimited spiritual potential (often echoing Pico, Hermes Trismegistus, Theophilus Gale, and the Cambridge Platonists)[4] is grounded upon the conviction that man's will is free and that he may always choose to live within the spiritual rather than the mundane order. Also Neoplatonic (and some feel, mystical)[5] is Traherne's celebration of vision as the means whereby Christians may experience even now the bliss of eternity. In all this, Traherne seems to abandon the fundamental Protestant paradigm of the spiritual life with its Pauline classifications and its metaphors of struggle and pilgrimage. He seems also to avoid the Protestant emphasis upon providential history, which tends to assimilate individual Christian lives to typological patterns. Instead, as Stanley Stewart has noted, Traherne's pervasive imagery of circularity breaks through linear time categories, associating infant innocence and regenerate vision with the sanctity and bliss enjoyed in the heavenly kingdom.[6]

Traherne's poetry is also quite different from that of Donne, Herbert, and Vaughan. Except for *The Thanksgivings* it hardly qualifies as devotional poetry: instead of prayers or hymnic praises to God or meditations upon scripture, the creatures, or the sinful self, Traherne's lyrics are chiefly analyses and celebrations of the speaker's glorious condition, privileges, and joys. In addition, Traherne's distrust of language and figures seems much more radical than the doubts and hesitations voiced by other Protestant religious lyrists about poetic ornament. His poetics disparages metaphor as obscuring naked truth, and, although his poetry does not wholly eliminate tropes, the language is often curiously flat, with little development or exploitation of figures.

Yet for all this, the fundamental elements of the Protestant poetics shape Traherne's poetry, and contribute largely to its often considerable power. It is usually valued below his prose, especially the dense, profound, tonally complex, and often strikingly beautiful *Centuries of Meditation*. At the same time, studies of Traherne's markedly original thought tend to treat both modes together, as interchangeable vehicles of expression.[7] By contrast, my concern with religious lyric requires attention to Traherne's poems in their own terms—to see what kind of poetic statement they make, by what poetic means, and how successfully. Stanley Stewart has in part redressed the customary depreciation of Traherne's poetry promoted by new critical preferences for densely metaphorical, as opposed to more abstract, poetic language. But there is need to study Traherne's use and adaptation of the concepts and concerns of Protestant poetics in his various poems, with special attention to the rather different poetic methods employed in his three poetic sequences.

Traherne has a few miscellaneous lyrics and epitaphs among the entries in an early university notebook. There are also a few poems interspersed among the prose passages in his several books of meditation, philosophy, and devotion, which are best read in these contexts. The eight rather somber poems in *Christian Ethicks*[8]—ranging in length and kind from a two-line epigrammatic couplet to a thirteen-stanza lyric—underline the special nobility, and the difficulty, of living as if in heaven while yet in the fallen world. The first poem inserted in the chapter on "Courage" sets this tone:

> For Man to Act as if his Soul did see
> The very Brightness of Eternity;
> For Man to Act as if his Love did burn
> Above the Spheres, even while its in its *Urne*;
> For Man to Act even in the Wilderness,
> As if he did those Sovereign Joys possess,
> Which do at once confirm, stir up, enflame,
> And perfect Angels; having not the same!
> It doth increase the Value of his Deeds,
> In this a Man a Seraphim exceeds.
>
> (ll. 1-10)[9]

Each of the six sections of Traherne's *Meditations on the Six Days of the Creation* concludes with a poem celebrating and often apostrophizing the specific works of God produced on the given day; like the meditations themselves these poems are often derivative, the first two recalling and echoing Du Bartas.[10] *The Church's Year-Book* includes three hymns: one a version of the famous *Veni Creator Spiritus*; one adapted with significant alterations from a lyric by Peter Damian; the third—"An Hymne upon St Bartholomews Day"—an original hymn in characteristically ecstatic tones celebrating Traherne's spirit as a "TEMPLE OF ETERNITIE," possessing an "Inward Omnipresence" like to God's.[11]

More remarkable are the seven poems from the *Centuries of Meditation*, all, interestingly enough, from the overtly autobiographical portion, "The Third Century." Two of these, "On News" and the poem later entitled "The Approach," are also included in Traherne's poetic sequences. Another, beginning "In Salem dwelt a Glorious King," celebrates David as a poet-philosopher—and clearly a model for Traherne—whose role as psalmist is at once superior to, and inclusive of, all his other offices and functions:

> He was a Prophet, and foresaw
> Things extant in the World to com:
> He was a Judg, and ruled by a Law
>     That then the Hony Comb
> Was Sweeter far: He was a Sage,
> And all His People could Advise;
> An Oracle, whose evry Page
> Contain in vers the Greatest Mysteries
> But most He then Enjoyd Himself, when he
> Did as a Poet prais the Dietie.
>
> A Shepherd, Soldier, and Divine,
> A Judge, a Courtier, and a King,
> Priest, Angel, Prophet, Oracle did shine
>     At once; when He did sing.
> Philosopher and Poet too
> Did in his Melodie appear.[12]

Much more interesting are the two manuscript collections of Traherne's lyrics. Scholars are generally agreed that the poems in the Dobell manuscript are an ordered sequence, set forth in Thomas Traherne's own hand.[13] As John Wallace, Anne Ridler, and Stanley Stewart have argued, the poems in Philip Traherne's manuscript—entitled *"Divine Reflections* On The Native Objects of *An Infant-Ey"*

—also seem to constitute a loosely-ordered sequence, if we excise those Dobell manuscript poems which Philip apparently incorporated as he revised and prepared his brother's poems for publication.[14] In the sequence thus isolated—perhaps taken by Philip from a manuscript now lost[15]—the speaker as exemplary persona traces the course of his spiritual autobiography. His point of view is that of a mature Christian seeking to understand his present spiritual state by reflection upon the innocence and bliss of his infancy and the stages through which he has passed from that time to the present. These poetic meditations upon spiritual experience past and present are addressed primarily to the self, but yet the poetic record of his own progress also takes on a didactic and hortatory dimension in that it is presented "to the Critical Peruser" as an exemplary lesson in how to seek felicity and how to enjoy "thy Highest Bliss."[16]

The prefatory poem to this sequence, "The Author to the Critical Peruser" is Traherne's most extended statement about poetics; its relevance extends beyond the poems in this sequence but it is peculiarly appropriate to them. The poet proposes to display the "naked Truth" and "inward Beauties" by means of "transparent Words" and a lowly strain that "Brings down the highest Mysteries to sense" (ll. 1-5). Like the Neoplatonist he is, but also like those Protestants (Perkins and his followers) who would have the truth and power of God's Word shine through and act through the preacher's unadorned words,[17] Traherne is primarily concerned that the true glories of God's works, especially the human body and soul, be truly seen and admired—as they are not by those poets "Who Cloaths admire, not the Man," or by those who slight God's works to magnify their own (ll. 38, 43). He would show God's wondrous creation without the tawdry glitter of florid poetic ornament or strained metaphysical conceits or feigned mythological marvels:

> No curling Metaphors that gild the Sence,
> Nor Pictures here, nor painted Eloquence;
> No florid Streams of Superficial Gems,
> But real Crowns and Thrones and Diadems!
>
> . . . . . . . . . . . . . . . . . .
>
> An easy Stile drawn from a native vein,
> A clearer Stream than that which Poets feign,
> Whose bottom may, how deep so'ere, be seen,
> Is that which I think fit to win Esteem:
> Els we could speak *Zamzummim* words, and tell
> A Tale in tongues that sound like *Babel-Hell*;

In Meteors speak, in blazing Prodigies,
Things that amaze, but will not make us wise.
. . . . . . . . . . . . . . . .
To make us Kings indeed! Not verbal Ones,
But reall Kings, exalted unto Thrones;
And more than Golden Thrones! 'Tis this I do,
Letting Poëtick Strains and Shadows go.

(ll. 11-36)

In large part Traherne's poetry follows this program. There is much naming of beauties or joys or glories (often in long, incantatory lists whose terms re-echo in poem after poem) as if such naming will call forth the essence of the thing: e.g., "His Talk was to be all of Prais, / Thanksgiving, Rapture, Holy-days; / For nothing els did with his State agree: / Being full of Wonder and Felicity."[18] Though rhetorical and poetic tropes are often used they are simple, not conceited, strained, or luxuriant. Verbal schemes relying upon repetitions of words or sounds or syntax are common, creating patterns which intensify the emotion conveyed:

How desolate!
Ah! how forlorn, how sadly did I stand
When in the field my woful State
I felt! Not all the Land,
Not all the Skies
Tho Heven shin'd before mine Eys.
Could Comfort yield in any Field to me,
Nor could my Mind Contentment find or see.

(ll. 1-8)

As in these lines from "Solitude," verbal schemes are often nicely adjusted to rather intricate stanzaic patterns and rhyme schemes. Traherne's inventiveness in this realm is quite surprising: hardly any two poems of this sequence have the same stanza and rhyme pattern, and the variations of line lengths within often very long stanzas at times approximate free verse, save that the patterns once set are maintained throughout a given poem. Anne Ridler attributes this variety to Traherne's failure to find a stanza with which he could be comfortable,[19] and surely he does lack the fine metrical sense of a superb lyrist like Herbert. But it would seem also that in this stanzaic variety Traherne has undertaken to supply a formal complexity which he denies to himself in diction and imagery.

Traherne's avowed poetic program for celebrating God's divinest work, man's body and soul, gave rise in this "Infant-Ey" sequence to a sharp focus upon the speaker himself; the poems trace his own experiences in discovering the way to felicity, his own "Progress of the Soul." But, as we have seen, such location of and exploration of the paradigm of salvation within the speaker is a primary characteristic of Protestant poetics, linking Traherne closely with Donne, Herbert, and Vaughan. Moreover, it is precisely Traherne's probing of his own psyche that adds tension and tonal range to poems whose language sometimes approaches flatness or too great abstraction: we respond to the intensity of the speaker's evocation of remembered childhood bliss, the joys afforded by spiritual vision, the special insights attending particular experiences. An example is the account of his childhood perception of a city:

> The City, fill'd with Peeple, near me stood;
>     A Fabrick like a Court divine,
>     Of many Mansions bright and fair;
>         Wherin I could repair
> To Blessings that were Common, Great and Good:
>         Yet all did shine
>         As burnisht and as new
> As if before none ever did them view:
>         They seem'd to me
> Environ'd with Eternity.[20]

In addition, the paradigm of the spiritual life exhibited in the speaker's experience, though profoundly transformed by Traherne's original theology, conforms in broad terms to the classic Protestant paradigm: initial innocence, a fall into sin and grief, a process of regeneration and restoration, and then a process of spiritual growth involving an expanding awareness of the privileges of adoption. It also exhibits the influences of certain Protestant meditative modes. Traherne's sequence is, broadly, a meditation upon spiritual experience focused primarily upon this last phase: the speaker traces his spiritual development from "Things to Thoughts," exploring thereby what it means to be, by creation and then by restoration, God's image, child, and heir, possessor of all things. The influence of Baxterian heavenly meditation is also apparent in these poems—with the significant difference that Traherne finds in present experience, when transmuted by spiritual understanding, not only the adumbration but the substance of heavenly bliss.[21] The speaker's development is plotted also in terms of typology, with characteristic Protestant emphasis upon the individual Christian as antitype. The speaker sees his infant innocence as a recapitulation of Adam's state; associates his new birth after his fall from innocence with the celebration of Christ's birth; and finally undertakes by his right thoughts about God and man to replicate David's "Temple in the Mind."

The first poem, "An Infant-Ey," identifies the speaker's own infancy with the state of Edenic innocence, characterized by true spiritual perception such that every object is seen in "an hev'nly Light," and thereby reveals "Felicity":

> The *East* was once my Joy; and so the Skies
> And Stars at first I thought; the West was mine:
> Then Praises from the Mountains did arise
>     As well as Vapors: Evry Vine
> Did bear me Fruit:the Fields my Gardens were;
> My larger Store-house all the Hemisphere.
>
> (ll. 31-36)

The next poem, "The Return," indicates that this meditative review of the first state is undertaken to promote spiritual growth: "To Infancy, O Lord, again I com, / That I my Manhood may improv"; the speaker will "fly / . . . to the Womb, / That I may yet New-born becom" (ll. 1-2, 9-12). The next several poems ("News," "Felicity," "Adam," "The World") explore the special qualities of that time and that vision: simplicity, felicity, joy and thankfulness for all God's works, delight in and entire possession of all the beauties of earth and sky and the human self. The mature speaker both remembers his infant-Adamic perception of the world's goodness and claims that this goodness has been restored to him through Christ: "all God's Works divine / Are Glorious still, and Mine. / Sin spoil'd them; but my Savior's precious Blood / Sprinkled I see / On them to be, / Making them all both safe and good."[22] He asserts an exact equation between his infancy and Eden: "As *Eve* / I did believ / My self in *Eden* set, / . . . All Bliss / Consists in this, / To do as *Adam* did; / And not to know those superficial Joys / Which were from him in *Eden* hid."[23] But as an underburden in some of these poems and a dominant theme in the next group ("The Apostacy," "Solitude," "Poverty," "Dissatisfaction"), he treats his own Fall from this Eden by succumbing to the world's false valuation of and desire for man-made riches and baubles—Traherne's version of the way in which every man is infected by original sin. The results are grief, solitude, loss of contentment, complaints of poverty, loss of communion with the creatures and with God, loss of and overwhelming desire to regain felicity.

The turning point leading to restoration is typically Protestant, and is identical with that recorded in "The Third Century": the discovery of a long-desired "Book from Heaven" which teaches the speaker anew, in conceptual terms, what he sensed instinctively as an infant— his own glorious nature, value, and powers. The short poem "The Bible" renders the speaker's wondering delight in this new knowledge:

That! That! There I was told
That I *the Son of God* was made,
*His Image.* O Divine! And that fine Gold,
With all the Joys that here do fade,
Are but a Toy, compared to the Bliss
Which Hev'nly, God-like, and Eternal is.
That We on earth are Kings;
And, tho we're cloth'd with mortal Skin,
Are Inward Cherubins; hav Angels Wings;
Affections, Thoughts, and Minds within,
Can soar throu all the Coasts of Hev'n and Earth;
And shall be sated with Celestial Mirth.

The following poems manifest the effects of the speaker's restoration, and point to Christ as its cause. In "Christendom" the speaker recalls how that unfamiliar term triggered his childish imaginations of an idyllic city, whose glories he finds now materialized in the Christian cities he knows. "On Christmas-Day" associates his own rebirth with Christ's birth and the rebirth of nature; "Bells" celebrates the purification of his own "Mettal" so that he also may ring God's praises; "Churches" records his new-found delight in the edifices and communal ceremonies of God's praise and service.

The next several poems explore the speaker's progress from "Things to Thoughts"—from the infant's instinctive delight in and possession of all God's works to the man's intellectual comprehension of his nature and privileges. This last is Traherne's version of the regenerate condition and the privileges of adoption, in which state earthly and heavenly blessedness seem almost to coalesce. "Misapprehension" locates the source of human woes in the failure to understand rightly that the world is our treasure; "The Odour" and "Admiration" are exercises in the proper valuation of the glories of man's body and mind; "Right Apprehension" completes this little sequence with the affirmation that giving "things their tru Esteem" (l. 1) calls for a thoughtful understanding which "improves" infant perceptions:

What Newness once suggested to,
Now clearer Reason doth improv, my View:

By Novelty my Soul was taught
At first; but now Reality my Thought
                Inspires; and I
                With clarity
        Both ways instructed am; by Sense
Experience, Reason and Intelligence.
                                    (ll. 33-40)

The next poems identify further sources of and grounds for such
right thoughts and apprehensions. "The Evidence" points to the Bible
as confirming the speaker's ideas of his blessedness and title to all things.
So also particular episodes from "unexperienc'd Infancy," such as a
fanciful misinterpretation of shadows appearing in a pool of water,
can now be read as a true emblem of heavenly existence ("Shadows
in the Water"). From such experiences, the speaker concludes (in the
poem "Sight") that the infant has both sensory and spiritual vision,
intuiting spiritual realities the adult will understand in intellectual
terms. In "Walking" the speaker finds his evidences of spiritual favors
and adoption in a conventional meditation upon the creatures, now
become matter of thought rather than sight: "To *walk* abroad is, not
with Eys, / But Thoughts, the Fields to see and prize" (ll. 1-2); the
child's instinctive enjoyment "tumbling among Grass and Leaves"
now gives way to the "Sight / Which perfect Manhood may delight"
(ll. 43-47). "Dreams" finds in the dream experience of a world within,
which the child takes to be as real as that without, a further evidence of
the power of thought to give things their true reality. "The Inference"
draws precisely this conclusion: "Well-guided *Thoughts* within pos-
sess / The Treasures of all Blessedness / *Things* are indifferent; nor giv
/ Joy of themselves, nor griev" (ll. 1-4). In Part II of this poem the
speaker associates himself typologically with David, who built a
"Temple in his Mind" (the Psalms) more glorious than any physical
temple:

        *David* a Temple in his Mind conceiv'd;
        And that Intention was so well receiv'd
        By God, that all the Sacred Palaces
        That ever were did less His Glory pleas.
        . . . . . . . . . . . . . . . . .
        How glorious, how divine, how great, how good
        May we becom! How like the Deity
        In managing our Thoughts aright! A Piety
        More grateful to our God than building Walls
        Of Churches. . . .

                                    (ll. 1-4, 26-30)

The temple metaphor and the reference to Psalm 51 again link Traherne with Herbert and Vaughan. But whereas Herbert locates his Davidic temple in the heart, and Vaughan in the created world, Traherne locates it in the mind of the regenerate man who possesses true thoughts and conceptions of God, the self, the world, and of felicity.

At this point, several transformations of a typological kind seem to have occurred: infant instincts are fulfilled in the mature speaker's thoughts; infant delight in the creatures of nature is fulfilled in the mature speaker's meditations upon them; the many Christian churches (themselves the antitype of the one Temple of Solomon in that they afford such manifold opportunities for God's praise and service) find their antitype in the temple in the mind; and "The City" has become for the mature speaker the place which actualizes all the glories the infant associated imaginatively with the term, "Christendom," and which is thereby both the embodiment and the type of the New Jerusalem.[24] The final group of poems, at times almost dithyrambic in tone, displays the speaker's longing for and expectation of greater delights to come, which he now sees as antitypes of those he presently enjoys. His limitless desires are unsatisfied by any goods of this world or of many worlds ("Insatiableness"); and his unbounded, wide-ranging imagination which peoples eternity anticipates the time when we shall "with content / All in their places see, / As doth the Glorious Deity."[25] Concluding this group, the hymn "Hosanna" seems almost to locate that antitype in the speaker, as he again lays claim to the present possession and enjoyment of "All"—transcendent as well as natural goods. He reigns "With God enthron'd" (l. 55).

The final poem, "The Review, I," like Wordsworth's "Intimations" ode, queries whether or not the mature state represents a progress from infancy's bliss. The burden of the last half or more of the sequence is that there is a progress, that transcendent thoughts attain to a higher felicity than the instinctive delights perceived and enjoyed by the infant senses. But that note was sounded hesitantly at best, in view of the bliss and joy so constantly associated with the infant state. The ambiguity is now faced directly by the speaker:

> Did I grow, or did I stay?
> Did I prosper or decay?
>    When I so
> From *Things* to *Thoughts* did go?
> Did I flourish or diminish,
> When I so in *Thoughts* did finish
> What I had in *Things* begun.
>
>            (ll. 1-7)

The problem is that thoughts are both glorious and treacherous: they can "create a Paradise" but they also destroyed one. Part II of this poem provides some resolution in metaphor: the entire childhood experience is a "sphere" of joys, thoughts, and affections, which can serve (as in this meditative re-view) as a continuing source of benefits, a stimulus to see again "in better sort" the things then seen.

This final poem completes the development of two familiar biblical metaphors upon which Traherne calls persistently and complexly throughout the sequence. One is the metaphor of the Christian as child: the speaker engages himself to a kind of reverse pilgrimage (Matt. 18:3), to become again a little child to enter the kingdom of heaven, and he seeks to apprehend fully the privileges God's children enjoy by their adoption (Rom. 8:15-17) as "heires of God, and joynt-heires with Christ."[26] In developing this metaphor, however, Traherne ignores the Pauline view of the Christian child as a ward who can enter into the full enjoyment of his inheritance only in heaven (Gal. 4:1-6), and instead insists that his full privileges by the original creation have now been restored by Christ so that he can even now enjoy an eternity and infinity of blessedness. The other metaphor associates the innocent and regenerate states with light and vision, as in the several biblical passages identifying Christians as "children of light" (Ephes. 5:8, 2 Cor. 4:6, 1 Thess. 5:5).[27] Traherne's formulations focus upon light as perception, apprehension, vision—and again he ignores the Pauline qualification, "For now we see through a glasse, darkely; but then face to face" (1 Cor. 13:12). Instead he finds that the divine light characteristic of innocent infancy is fully restored and perhaps intensified in the mature Christian.

Both these metaphors coalesce in the central, unifying emblem or symbol of the sequence, the "Infant-Ey." The figure occurs in the title (which of course may not be authorial) given to the sequence in Philip Traherne's manuscript, "Divine Reflections On The Native Objects of An Infant-Ey." The initial poem of the sequence is titled "An Infant-Ey," and there is hardly a poem in which this figure is not somehow invoked. In the infant and in Adam it was an "Angel's Ey"; after the apostasy of the Fall it becomes a "blemisht" eye, a "blind" eye or an "Idle Ey."[28] As Stanley Stewart's fine study suggests, the spherical contours of the "Infant-Ey" relate it to those other spheres, the world and the universe, which with all their objects can be reflected in, and thereby included in, the eye. It takes on an emblematic quality and becomes a singularly impressive and precise poetic figure for a vision which encloses and encompasses all things. In the poem of that name, the "Infant-Ey" is at first likened to the Sun's orb, dispensing light:

A simple Light from all Contagion free,
A Beam that's purely Spiritual, an Ey
That's altogether Virgin, Things doth see
    Ev'n like unto the Deity:
That is, it shineth in an hevenly Sence,
And round about (unmov'd) its Light dispense.

(ll. 1-6)

In "News," perhaps not properly a part of this sequence,[29] the infant
eye includes all things but does not understand its own greatness:

But little did the Infant dream
That all the Treasures of the World were by,
And that himself was so the Cream
And Crown of all which round about did ly.
            Yet thus it was! The Gem,
                The Diadem,
            The Ring enclosing all
            That stood upon this Earthen Ball;
                The hev'nly Ey,
            Much wider than the Sky,
            Wherin they All included were;
            The Lov, the Soul, that was the King
            Made to possess them, did appear
                A very little Thing.

(ll. 43-56)

"Felicity" describes the infant seeking beyond the skies for felicity,
where he sees (taught by "Dame Nature") the image, the "very face"
of the endless space within his own soul. But it remains for the man to
understand what the infant only senses, that felicity is the mind and
eye of God, a "Sphere of Lov" above all other spheres, which includes
and thereby exalts the speaker. In "Sight" the speaker recalls the ex-
perience of the infant—"Mine Infant-Ey / Abov the Sky / Discerning
endless Space" (ll. 1-3)—as ground for discovering in himself two
sights, three orbs. Two are sensory and "Of narrow Bound," but the
other is boundless, "for the Ball / Was Spirit'all" (ll. 17, 20-21). For
the infant the spiritual eye is "A Looking-Glass / Of signal Worth"
(ll. 50-51) presenting all objects in their true excellence and discerning
the infinite space within the soul. But it is for the man to know the
further uses of that eye—"it can pry / Into the End / To which things
tend, / . . . The very Ground and Caus / Of sacred Laws, / All Ages
too, Thoughts, Counsels, and Designs" (ll. 63-71). Finally, the poem

"Consummation" transfers the imagery of boundless spherical inclusiveness associated with the Infant-Eye to the domain of thought:

> The Thoughts of Men appear
> Freely to mov within a Sphere
> Of endless Reach; and run,
> Tho in the Soul, beyond the Sun.
> The Ground on which they acted be
> Is unobserv'd Infinity.
>
> (ll. 1-6)

By his treatment of this controlling figure, Traherne does not so much blur or undermine the sense of temporal development or progress as transpose such development from linear to spherical terms. The progress is finally in terms of the nature, the means, and the locus of vision: from intuition to knowledge, from things to thoughts, from the infant eye to the adult mind. The final poem, "The Review, II," indicates that the spiritual pilgrimage is not a linear movement from Eden to the New Jerusalem, but a matter of ever-widening spheres whose expansion is forwarded by meditation upon the things seen and the ways of seeing in infancy: "My Childhood is a Sphere / Wherin ten thousand hev'nly Joys appear" (ll. 31-32). Such returns to beginnings give the speaker's life the character of "a Circle of Delights; / A hidden Sphere of obvious Benefits" (ll. 9-10). Yet the end is not the beginning: from such reviews the adult learns to see the childhood things "In better sort," and his present sphere of existence opens out to a further expansion, encompassing but at the same time foreshadowing apocalyptic fulfillment: it is itself "An Earnest that the Actions of the Just / Shall still revive, and flourish in the Dust" (ll. 11-12).

As has been suggested, most of the poems of this sequence may be loosely characterized as meditations upon the speaker's spiritual state. Yet they are not meditations in the traditional Ignatian, Augustinian, or even in the general Protestant sense, for they are directed wholly to the understanding and do not culminate in an exercise to move the affections or in a colloquy with God or with the self. They are rather like verse essays exploring a topic or a personal experience: often beginning from a precept or from a recollection of infant innocence and its privileges, the poems characteristically explore the speaker's claim to and experience of restored felicity, vision and possession of all things. In form, these poems resemble those Protestant occasional meditations which had close affinities with the Baconian familiar essay.[30]

Although Traherne did not experiment with lyric genres as he did with stanza forms, at critical junctures he introduced into the sequence poems of other kinds. A series of three poems—"Shadows in the Water," "On Leaping over the Moon," and an untitled poem "To the same purpos;"—combine the emblem genre with the occasional meditation upon a specific providential episode. These poems turn a remembered childhood incident into an emblem which the mature speaker proceeds to read for its spiritual significance. In their concreteness and complexity, these are among Traherne's most successful poems.

Stanley Stewart's excellent and exhaustive critical reading of "Shadows in the Water" makes a full account of it unnecessary here.[31] The speaker retells an episode in which as an "unexperienc'd" infant he made a "sweet Mistake" in supposing that the shadows he views in a puddle of water constitute another cosmos. "Water Peeple" mysteriously drowned beneath the water are crowned "with another Hev'n"; they walk about and enjoy another sun; their feet even touch and press against his own. The interest and complexity of the poem arise in part from the skill with which the mature speaker at once recaptures and renders the naive responses of the child to this phenomenon and also transforms the whole episode into an emblem yielding "afterward" new depths of spiritual understanding:

> Mistake tho false, intending tru;
> A *Seeming* somewhat more than *View*;
>> That doth instruct the Mind
>> In Things that ly behind,
> And many Secrets to us show
> Which afterwards we com to know.
>
>> (ll. 3-8)

The lesson of the emblem is rendered through the speaker's wondering speculation about the significance of the episode even as he relives the child's initial wonderment at the experience itself. As Stewart perceptively notes, the episode reverses the Narcissus myth: the speaker recalls seeing reflections of his companions as well as himself, and his sense of discovering a whole new world inhabited by "yet unknown Friends" (l. 56), with lofty skies surrounding it and perhaps "lofty Hevens" hurled round those skies. He speculates as to whether the images seen in the water (and perhaps himself and his companions) may be but "the Representatives / Of other Peopl's distant Lives" (ll. 71-72). The incident of course intimates to the mature speaker the continuity of our existence in another world which promises as yet unknown joys, as the final stanzas indicate:

O ye that stand upon the Brink,
Whom I so near me, throu the Chink,
With Wonder see: What Faces there,
Whose Feet, whose Bodies, do ye wear?
    I my Companions see
    In You, another Me.
They seemed Others, but are We;
Our second Selvs those Shadows be.

Look how far off those lower Skies
Extend themselvs! scarce with mine Eys
I can them reach. O ye my Friends,
What *Secret* borders on those Ends?
    Are lofty Hevens hurl'd
    'Bout your inferior World?
Are ye the Representatives
Of other Peopl's distant Lives?

Of all the Play-mates which I knew
That here I do the Image view
In other Selvs; what can it mean?
But that below the purling Stream
    Som unknown Joys there be
    Laid up in Store for me;
To which I shall, when that thin Skin
Is broken, be admitted in.
              (ll. 57-80)

The next poem, "On Leaping over the Moon," is of the same kind: the speaker reports a nocturnal childhood experience (this time one reported by his brother) of leaping over a stream of water in which the moon is reflected. He terms this incident "A much more strange and wondrous Sight" (l. 8) than his own experience, viewing the leap as an amazing, Icarus-like flight without wings, risking a fall "Not from, but from abov, the Sky" (l. 30). Part of the wonder and significance of the experience lies in the fact that it happened to a brother (the speaker's natural brother, but also his brother man) and is thereby universalized: "Nor could the World exhibit such another, / So Great a Sight, but in a Brother" (ll. 9-10). This experience is again made into an emblem by the mature speaker: the image of a body poised between the sky above and the sky beneath (reflected in the water) affords the perception that while yet on earth we are even now above and within the skies, in heaven: "On hev'nly Ground within the Skies we walk, /

And in this middle Center talk: / Did we but wisely mov / On Earth in Hev'n above, / We then should be / Exalted high / Abov the Sky" (ll. 51-57). In the final lines the *significatio* is set forth explicitly: "Thus did he yield me in the shady Night / A wondrous and instructiv Light, / Which taught me that under our Feet there is / As o'er our Heads, a Place of Bliss" (ll. 67-70). Immediately following, an untitled poem also based upon the brother's experience records his "mistaken" apprehension that the moon, seen the night before in another place, has followed him home. The *significatio* for the mature speaker is that all God's benefits serve all men, and serve each individually, as if meant only for him.

Another group of three consecutive poems is uniquely concerned with God's praise. "On Christmas-Day" approaches the celebratory ode or hymn. Despite its borrowings—verbal echoes of Herbert's "Christmas" and "Easter," pervasive suggestions of Herrick's "Corinna" in the imagery of the green boughs decking streets and houses in seeming transformation of winter into spring, perhaps an allusion to Crashaw's "Weeper" in the breakfasting cherubim—the poem is effective. The speaker first undertakes to awaken his sluggish soul to join in the praises all creatures offer on this day—"Thy Lute, thy Harp, or els thy Heart-strings take" (l. 17). He hopes also to participate in the city's transformation from winter to spring: "Let pleasant Branches still be seen / Adorning thee, both quick and green; / . . . Be laden all the Year with Fruits; / Inserted into Him, / For ever spring" (ll. 31-36). He then joins with the bells, the churches, and the whole Christian community in the exercises of praise: "The whole Assembly sings; / The Minster rings" (ll. 119-120). "Bells" develops from one aspect of this hymn—the praises rung by the bells. But this poem is an occasional meditation or emblem rather than a hymn: the bells are first analyzed in terms of their quality of sound, their nature (refined from clay), and their function of praise; then, in Part II, the speaker applies the emblem to himself: "Thou must ascend; taught by the Toll / In what fit place thou mayst adore; / Refin'd by fire, thou shalt a Bell / Of Prais becom, in Mettal pure" (ll. 36-39). "Churches" also develops from the Christmas hymn, focusing upon those places fitted for praise. Part I is an emblem of sorts, analyzing the delight the speaker takes in the various parts and aspects of physical churches—"Those Stately Structures which on Earth I view" (l. 1). Part II contrasts the single Old Testament Temple with the multitude of New Testament churches which facilitate and multiply opportunities for praise.

Another hymn-like poem, exalted in language and tone, is "Hosanna," the penultimate poem of the sequence. It is properly a thanksgiving for the benefits the speaker enjoys—which are all the goods of the earth and all the transcendent delights of heaven. Yet, curiously, the celebration is rather of the self than of God: the rejoicing is for the infinite felicity the speaker experiences as he himself is "enthron'd" with God, and even the praises directed to God are seen to be in some sense for the speaker in that they are his greatest source of joy. This is not egomania or blasphemy however: it is clear that the singular privileges of Traherne's speaker are gifts of God, who made man in his image and endows him with all good. Yet as a hymn the poem cannot but surprise; technically a thanksgiving to God, it celebrates the speaker himself:

> Transcendent Objects doth my God provide,
> In such convenient Order all contriv'd,
>     That All things in their proper place
>         My Soul doth best embrace,
>     Extends its Arms beyond the Seas,
>     Abov the Hevens its self can pleas,
>         With God enthron'd may reign:
>             Like sprightly Streams
>         My Thoughts on Things remain;
>             Or els like vital Beams
> They reach to, shine on, quicken Things, and make
> Them truly Usefull; while I *All* partake.
>
> For Me the World created was by Lov;
> For Me the Skies, the Seas, the Sun, do mov;
>     The Earth for Me doth stable stand;
>         For Me each fruitful Land
>     For Me the very Angels God made *His*
>     And *my* Companions in Bliss:
>         His Laws command all Men
>             That they lov Me,
>         Under a Penalty
>             Severe, in case they miss:
> His Laws require His Creatures all to prais
> His Name, and when they do't be most my Joys.
>                                           (ll. 49-72)

The thirty-seven autograph Dobell poems, as John B. Wallace has noticed, constitute a unified meditative sequence.[32] But despite such suggestive titles as "The Preparative" and "The Approach," the sequence does not conform very closely to the three- (or five-) stage

Ignatian model Wallace proposes, nor yet to the loosely structured, digressive, incremental Augustinian model suggested by Martz.[33] We find rather a "deliberate" meditation upon a topic—Traherne's favorite topic, man's felicity—which proceeds by analysis of and affective response to two main subtopics, infant felicity and the felicity of the regenerate Christian. This structure distinguishes this body of poems from the "Infant-Ey" sequence, which is primarily a meditation upon spiritual experience considered in developmental, autobiographical terms.

As with the "Infant-Ey" poems, the initial poems in this sequence treat the child's blest condition. But the speaker's stance is not nostalgic: he undertakes to "becom a Child again" through meditative exercise, in order to promote his further spiritual growth.[34] It is again clear that the mature Christian's felicity, because grounded in understanding, may be superior even to that of the child, and it is also clear that the felicity of child and man flows from God's grace. As he makes plain in "The Approach," the mature speaker has undergone a classic conversion experience and knows himself to be regenerate, transformed by grace:

> O Lord I wonder at thy Love,
> Which did my Infancy so Early move:
> But more at that which did forbear,
> And move so long, tho Sleighted many a yeer:
> But most of all, at last that Thou
> Thyself shouldst me convert I scarce know how.
>
> Thy Gracious Motions oft in vain
> Assaulted me: My Heart did Hard remain
> Long time: I sent my God away,
> Grievd much that he could not impart his Joy.
> I careless was, nor did regard
> The End for which he all these Thoughts prepard.
>
> But now with New and Open Eys,
> I see beneath as if above the Skies;
> And as I Backward look again,
> See all his Thoughts and mine most Clear and Plain.
> He did Approach, he me did Woo
> I wonder that my God this thing would doe.
>
> (ll. 13-30)

"The Person" voices a poetics for this sequence akin to that proclaimed for the "Infant-Ey" poems in "The Author to the Critical Peruser." One structural difference is that "The Person" does not introduce the

Dobell sequence, but rather begins the stage of meditation devoted to the mature speaker's felicity achieved through thought; appropriately, the poem sets forth principles for proper poetic celebration of the divine goods (here the human body) which the speaker now understands in their true glory. Again, these principles involve stripping away poetic ornament in order to reveal God's glorious workmanship:

> Ile make you Bright.
> Mistake me not, I do not mean to bring
> New Robes, but to Display the Thing:
> Nor Paint, nor Cloath, nor Crown, nor add a Ray,
> But Glorify by taking all away.
> . . . . . . . . . . . . . . . . . .
> Their Worth they then do best reveal,
> When we all Metaphores remove,
> For Metaphores conceal,
> And only Vapours prove.
> They best are Blazond when we see
> The Anatomie,
> Survey the Skin, cut up the Flesh, the Veins
> Unfold: The Glory there remains.
> The Muscles, Fibres, Arteries and Bones
> Are better far then Crowns and precious Stones.
>
> (ll. 12-32)

Fortunately, Traherne does not remove all metaphors from this sequence, but, as in the "Infant-Ey" poems, he relies chiefly upon biblical tropes. Moreover, these lines point to a poetic strategy, used much more extensively here than in the other sequence, of naming and listing objects and qualities, as if by such naming to evoke their essence. In "Eden" the speaker lists the qualities pertaining to that state—"Joy, Pleasure, Beauty, Kindness, Glory, Lov, / Sleep, Day, Life, Light, / Peace, Melody" (ll. 15-17). "The Circulation" produces other lists— of things that must receive before they can give forth, "A Sigh, a Word, a Groan, / A Colour, or a Glimps of Light, / The Sparcle of a Precious Stone, / A virtue, or a Smell; a lovly Sight, / A Fruit, a Beam, an Influence, a Tear" (ll. 32-36). The poem "Desire" lists delights ("Trees Waters Days and Shining Beams / Fruits, Flowers, Bowers, Shady Groves and Springs," ll. 35-36), and also lists the faculties, moved by desires, which mediate heavenly joys ("Sence, feeling, Taste, Complacency and Sight," l. 60). The speaker's intense feeling as he relives, analyzes, probes, recounts, and celebrates his own spiritual experience contributes largely to the effectiveness of the Dobell poems, even as to the "Infant-Ey" sequence. But the Dobell speaker, who is undertaking a formal meditation upon the topic of felicity, rather than a meditation specifically upon his own experience, adopts a wider range of expressive modes and produces a richer poetic texture. He is sometimes hortatory—preaching, or drawing lessons for, or exhorting his own soul or an audience: "Spue out thy filth, thy flesh abjure; / Let not Contingents thee defile"; or, "He seeks for ours as we do seek for his, / Nay O my Soul, ours is far more His Bliss / Then his is ours."[35] He is sometimes epigrammatic, setting forth in maxim and *sententia* the wisdom gleaned from his experience: "That Custom is a Second Nature, we / Most Plainly find by Natures Purity"; or, "A quiet Silent Person may possess / All that is Great or High in Blessedness."[36]

More remarkably, he sounds at times an ecstatic note virtually absent from the "Infant-Ey" sequence, when his train of meditations gives way to a breathless series of exclamations which attempt a mimesis of the inexpressible wonder he feels. With the possible exception of the poem "Love," these raptures can be called mystical only in a very qualified sense. They do not proclaim or explore an experience of union or communion with the deity (though the speaker's participation in the divine attributes and joys as image of God is understood to be the ground of his feeling). Yet instead of intimating some kind of self-transcendence, these poems apostrophize the wondrous self. In four poems this tone is prominent, though by no means all-pervasive. "The Rapture" addresses the Infant Self: "Sweet Infancy! / O fire of Heaven! O Sacred Light! / How Fair and Bright! / How Great am I, / Whom all the World doth magnifie!" (ll. 1-5). "Thoughts. I" and the second part of "Thoughts. II" define and celebrate their subject by means of a tissue of apostrophes: "Ye brisk Divine and Living Things, / Ye great Exemplars, and ye Heavenly Springs. . . ." "Ye Engines of Felicitie; / Ye Wondrous Fabricks of his Hands. . . ." "Ye Representatives, and Springs / Of Inward Pleasure! / Ye Joys! Ye Ends of Outward Treasure! / Ye Inward, and ye Living Things." "Ye hidden Nectars, which my GOD doth drink, / Ye Heavenly Streams, ye Beams Divine, / On which the Angels think, / . . . Ye Images of Joy that in me Dwell. . . ."[37] The poem "My Spirit" rises in its final stanza to what may be the highest pitch of exaltation reached in this sequence, as the speaker stands amazed before the glories of his own spirit, glories which he intuited in infancy and can now comprehend and articulate:

>           O Wondrous Self! O Sphere of Light,
>                 O Sphere of Joy most fair;
>           O Act, O Power infinit;
>           O Subtile, and unbounded Air!
>                 O Living Orb of Sight!
>           Thou which within me art, yet Me! Thou Ey,
>           And Temple of his Whole Infinitie!
>           O what a World art Thou! a World within!
>                                   (ll. 103-110)

The first stanza of "Love" describes something more closely approaching mystical feelings as usually understood—"The true Mysterious Depths of Blessedness" (l. 38), as the poem later terms it. But here also the apostrophes are not directed to God, nor indeed to God as the essence and origin of Love (though that is implied), but rather to the quality itself as the means by which the speaker is joined with God:

>           O Nectar! O Delicious Stream!
>           O ravishing and only Pleasure! Where
>                 Shall such another Theme
>           Inspire my Tongue with Joys, or pleas mine Ear!
>                 Abridgement of Delights!
>                 And Queen of Sights!
>           O Mine of Rarities! O Kingdom Wide!
>           O more! O Caus of all! O Glorious Bride!
>           O God! O Bride of God! O King!
>           O Soul and Crown of evry Thing!
>                                   (ll. 1-10)

Although the poetic texture is richer, fewer lyric kinds are represented in the Dobell than in the "Infant-Ey" sequence. There are no hymns (though one or two stanzas in "The Estate" and "Desire" rise to hymnic praise). There are no prayers, except for the final lines of "Thoughts. IV." And there are no meditations on specific personal experiences become emblems, in the manner of "Shadows in the Water." Nor is there such a prodigal variety of stanzaic forms as in the "Infant-Ey" sequence but, rather, some meaningful recurrence of verse forms keyed to particular meditative styles. There are several long poems in heroic couplets often employing and usually beginning with epigrammatic maxims or axioms which associate them with the biblical genre of Proverbs. These poems—"Dumnesse," "Silence," "Nature," "Thoughts. III," "Thoughts. IV"—tend to be logical, ordered analyses of rather complex arguments or abstract concepts. A larger number of

poems are in regular lyric stanzas. Those in four- or five-line stanzas—
"The Instruction," "Ease," "Another," "The Rapture"—are simple
songs or lessons, lyric expressions of a single impulse or emotion. Sev-
eral others in regular stanzas of six, seven, or eight lines—"The Saluta-
tion," "The Vision," "Amendment"—are rather more elaborate in tone
and argument. The rest, in long, intricately patterned stanzas with ir-
regular line-lengths and highly complex rhyme schemes, are dithy-
rambic, ode-like: "The Preparative," "My Spirit," "Fullnesse," "The
Anticipation," "The Recovery," "Love," "Thoughts. I," "Thoughts.
II," "Desire," "Goodnesse." Traherne, it seems, has distinguished his
basic meditative kinds by developing a formal analogy to the old
rhetorical scheme of low, middle, and high styles.

His meditative sequence on man's felicity is ordered in three stages,
each of which has two parts. The first stage, as Wallace has noted,[38]
is a kind of preparation: the speaker recalls the experience of his in-
nocent infant state and then derives from that experience a program
and method for meditation. In the first four poems, the speaker recalls
the infant felicity he once knew, as a basis for understanding the true
human condition. But only the opening poem, "The Salutation," under-
takes to render the infant's response directly, with the speaker per-
sonating the child in the moment of discovering and rejoicing in his
limbs and senses and the world around him: "Welcom ye Treasures
which I now receiv. / . . . Into this Eden so Divine and fair, / So Wide
and Bright, I com his Son and Heir" (ll. 12, 35-36). Yet even in this
poem the naïve response is filtered through the mature speaker's mind,
as the diction of stanza four with its reference to "Organized Joynts,
and Azure Veins" indicates, providing thereby a double perspective
on the experience. The next poems, in the past tense, are clearly the
mature speaker's recollections. "Wonder" records his response to the
shining glory of all the creation and his sense that the world and its
people are all his own: "How like an Angel come I down! / How
Bright are all Things here! / When first among his Works I did appear"
(ll. 1-3). "Eden" defined that bliss as a "learned and a Happy Igno-
rance" (l. 1) of all the vanities and errors and baubles of men, so that
like Adam he saw only "The Glorious Wonders of the DEITIE" (l.
49). "Innocence" identifies the chief bliss of that time as the absence
of sin and guilt; skirting the question of whether evil comes through
custom rather than nature, or whether God "by Miracle" removed the
guilt of his original sin early, the speaker claims only that he did in
fact recapitulate the Adamic innocence: "I was an Adam there, / A
little Adam in a Sphere" (ll. 51-52). As Wallace notes, these poems
present something like a traditional meditative composition of place—

with the significant difference that the normative scheme and pattern of perfection is taken from his own life rather than Christ's, in a radical extension of that application to the self so characteristic of Protestant meditation, typology, and sermons. The speaker concludes this initial phase with a formal resolution to undertake a species of reverse pilgrimage: "I must becom a Child again."

The next poems consider the means to that end, meditation, and again infancy provides the model. In "The Preparative" the speaker recalls his soul's earliest moment of consciousness, when it was as yet unaware of its bodily habitation, and still enjoyed unlimited vision of all things as "A Living Endless Ey, / Far wider then the Skie" (ll. 12-13). This conception of his soul as "A Meditating Inward Ey" (l. 27) dictates a meditative program of withdrawing from the world and the flesh so as to become again a serene and pure mind—"My Soul retire, / Get free, and so thou shalt even all Admire" (ll. 69-70). "The Vision" concludes this preparatory stage by identifying the purpose of the flight-meditation: "Flight is but the Preparative: The Sight / Is Deep and Infinit" (ll. 1-2). The speaker's goal is to learn to see the fountain of bliss, God, and more especially to recognize himself as the end or purpose of that bliss, and the recipient of all God's treasures.

The first meditative topic, infant felicity, is explored in two parts, the first of which, beginning with "The Rapture" and concluding with "Silence," analyzes the kind of seeing characteristic of infancy. Reversing the Ignatian method, Traherne's meditations often begin with a stirring of the affections, and then proceed to analysis. In "The Rapture" the speaker, even as he retains his adult consciousness, personates the infant marveling at his own greatness and querying its source, even as Adam might have done:

> O how Divine
> Am I! To all this Sacred Wealth,
> This Life and Health,
> Who raisd? Who mine
> Did make the same? What Hand Divine!
> (ll. 16-20)

Then, in the analytic mode, "The Improvement" forcefully and logically argues the proposition, "Tis more to recollect, then make"—that is, God's wisdom, power, and love are better displayed in the speaker's re-collection of all things as his own possessions, than they were in the initial creation. He recalls also that his "Infant Sence" perceived God's attributes by instinct and effect, rather than (as now) by understanding (ll. 67-70). In "The Approach" he marvels at God's initial advances—

"He in our Childhood with us walks, / And with our Thoughts Mysteriously he talks" (ll. 7-8)—but wonders still more at God's assaulting, wooing, and converting his adult heart, so that he now sees "with New and Open Eys" (l. 25). The next two poems present the wordless, speechless condition of the child as guide to the meditator, for the child's dumbness and deafness enabled him "with Cleerer Eys / To see all Creatures full of Deities; / Especialy Ones self" ("Dumnesse," ll. 39-41).

The shift to the second aspect of this topic, the kind of felicity won through the infant vision, is indicated by another rhapsody stirring the affections. "My Spirit" celebrates the speaker's amazed, ecstatic recognition of the infant seer-self as literally Godlike—simple, a "perfect Act" of seeing (l. 26), his mind encompassing all places and things. Subsequent poems, from "The Apprehension," to "The Design," analyze this condition and its applicability to the speaker now. In "The Apprehension" he perceives that this intuition constituted "my whole felicitie" (l. 7), and in "Fullnesse" he recognizes in that awareness the "Fountain" or "Spring" of present bliss and understanding (l. 15). In "Nature" the speaker finds that nature's instantaneous teachings about the beauties of earth and sky reveal God's love to be the fountain and himself to be the recipient of all created good—a perception which understanding may preserve. "Ease" (in simple four-line stanzas contrasting sharply with the complex argument just concluded) expands lyrically upon the theme, "How easily doth Nature teach the Soul" (l. 1). "Speed" testifies again to the instantaneousness of the infant's perception of the glories of creation, of his possession of all things, and of his own divine state. Finally, "The Designe" relates these insights to the *topos*, "Truth the daughter of Eternity," personifying that truth which was made lovely to him in infancy.

The second meditative topic looks beyond infant experience as model and guide, to consider the felicity proper to the adult Christian. This topic is also explored in two parts, but in this case the progression is from the nature of the felicity to the faculty by which it is attained. The first part, beginning with "The Person" and ending with "Love," analyzes the mature Christian's felicity in terms of his place in the divine economy, as the end of all God's works and desires and the source of all the praises and thanksgivings returned to God. "The Person" celebrates the body and all its functions, senses, and powers—not the infant or the Adamic body but the body the speaker now possesses and prizes. The speaker proposes now to add to what he at first perceived intuitively of the body's glory by creating "A richer Blazon . . . then first I found" (ll. 2-3); this poetic blazon will be radically unmetaphorical, with all ornament removed so as to display the body's naked beauty. The poem ends with a catalogue of the body's glorious parts—"My Tongue, my Eys, / My Cheeks, my Lips, my Ears, my Hands, my Feet"—as "Themes" and "Organs" of divine praise (ll. 60-64). In "The Estate" the mature speaker claims all the splendors of the world as his estate, possessed and enjoyed by means of the body's faculties and senses; the poem rises to a high pitch of emotion by the mimesis of the speaker's excited voice counting over all his wealth:

> We plough the very Skies, as well
> As Earth, the Spacious Seas
> Are ours; the Stars all Gems excell.
> The air was made to pleas
> The Souls of Men; Devouring fire
> Doth feed and Quicken Mans Desire.
> The Sun it self doth in its Glory Shine,
> And Gold and Silver out of very Mire,
> And Pearls and Rubies out of Earth refine,
> While Herbs and Flowers aspire
> To touch and make our feet Divine.
>
> (ll. 57-67)

The next group of poems is more abstract, exploring in ever more complex terms the interconnections among God, the world, and man, which constitute the basis for man's felicity and enable his praises. By a series of analogues from the natural order—the sponge must take up water before expressing it, the wine jug must receive wine before pouring it forth, the tenant must receive land before he can raise corn or pay rent—"The Circulation" argues the proposition that man must receive gifts and blessedness before he can give praise: "He must a King, before a Priest becom" (l. 22). Receiving is a matter of seeing rightly the gifts which are always there: "*Tis Blindness Makes us Dumb. / Had we but those Celestial Eys, / . . . we should overflow / With Praises*" (ll. 25-28). God seems at first to be exempt from this law of circulation, being the spring and ocean of all goods, but "Amendment" and "The Demonstration" revise this perception, affirming the greater value all things take on in God's eyes as they are enjoyed by, and evoke praises from, men. At the outset of "The Anticipation" the speaker is struck with amazement—"My Contemplation Dazles in the End / Of all I comprehend / And soars abov all Heights" (ll. 1-3)—arising from the recognition of God as the ground of the whole circulation, the fountain, means, and end, a being with infinite desires and wants and joys. "The Recovery" urges man's profound responsibility for promoting God's felicity by his own "Gratitude, Thanksgiving, Prais" (l. 55), and especially by offering "One Voluntary Act of Love":

> For God enjoyd is all his End.
> Himself he then doth Comprehend.
> When He is Blessed, Magnified,
> Extold, Exalted, Praisd, and Glorified
> Honord, Esteemd, Belovd, Enjoyd,
> Admired, Sanctified, Obeyd,
> That is receivd. For He
> Doth place his Whole Felicitie
> In that, who is despised and defied
> Undeified almost if once denied.
>
> (ll. 11-20)

This section culminates in "Love," an ecstatic paean itself providing that voluntary act of love. The Poem conveys feeling and experience approaching if not attaining to mystical rapture. Beginning in a high rhetorical strain, the speaker seeks for analogues for God's gifts and God's love in Jove's golden rain showered on Danaë, and Jove's elevation of Ganymede to his own banquet table. These are virtually the only mythological allusions in Traherne's lyrics, and even here the speaker soon gives over his recourse to the usual resources of poetic eloquence. Only a simple list of sanctioned biblical metaphors can adequately suggest the love binding God and man:

> But these (tho great) are all
> Too short and small,
> Too Weak and feeble Pictures to Express
> The true Mysterious Depths of Blessedness.
> I am his Image, and his Friend.
> His Son, Bride, Glory, Temple, End.
>
> (ll. 35-40)

The second part of this topic explores the faculties by which the speaker as a mature Christian knows his glorious condition: the infant's *eye* was an organ of intuitive vision, to which the adult speaker's *thoughts* are the counterpart. "Thoughts. I" is a long series of apostrophes describing and analyzing thoughts: they are "brisk Divine and Living Things," "Engines of Felicitie," a means to possess all joys (ll. 1-6, 13). Their special quality is their omnipresence and eternity;

ranging through space and time, they make past and future joys
present, and in this they surpass even the Infant Eye, being the
"Sweetest, last, and most Substantial Treasures" (l. 20). "Thoughts. II"
identifies a thought as the quintessence and fruit of all God's works and
also the highest work of man, the temple of praise built by David.
"Thoughts. III" urges the divinity of thought:

> Thoughts are the Things wherwith even God is Crownd,
> And as the Soul without thems useless found,
> So are all other Creatures too. A Thought
> Is even the very Cream of all he wrought.
>
> . . . . . . . . . . . . . . . . . . . . . . .
>
> A Thought can Cloathe it self with all the Treasures
> Of GOD, and be the Greatest of his Pleasures.
> It all his Laws, and Glorious Works, and Ways,
> And Attributs, and Counsels; all his Praise
> It can conceiv, and Imitate, and give:
> It is the only Being that doth live.
>
> (ll. 15-18, 49-54)

"Desire" begins as a thanksgiving to God for the "restlesse longing
Heavenly Avarice" (l. 8) which led the speaker to find an unknown
paradise above the skies. "Thoughts. IV" argues that, since thoughts
may at any time be present at God's throne and see "The New Jeru-
salem, the Palaces, / The Thrones and feasts, the Regions of the
Skie, / The Joys and Treasures of the DEITIE" (ll. 10-12), they are
then the means by which "we in heav'n may be / Even here on Earth
did we but rightly see" (ll. 35-36). Through thoughts, God's omni-
presence enters us, setting us above with the Seraphim. Thoughts, then,
are Traherne's means for locating in the individual speaker (even as
Donne locates in Elizabeth Drury) both infant innocence and heavenly
glory; the speaker's thoughts recapitulate the one and foreshadow the
other, making both present. As Richard Jordan notes, Traherne holds
that the Christian living his life in the world lives at the same time in
eternity.[39] The conclusion to this poem (which might seem to be an
apt conclusion to the sequence) is a brief prayer to God for grace to
live in accordance with the terms just defined:

> O give me Grace to see thy face, and be
> A constant Mirror of Eternitie.
> Let my pure Soul, transformed to a Thought,
> Attend upon thy Throne, and as it ought
> Spend all its Time in feeding on thy Lov,

> And never from thy Sacred presence mov.
> So shall my Conversation ever be
> In Heaven, and I O Lord my GOD with Thee!
> (ll. 95-102)

But this is not the end. Having discovered himself to be closely conjoined with God in the circulations of thought, the speaker, in the final poem ("Goodnesse") joins with others in further circulations. Like God he finds his chief bliss in "The Bliss of other Men" (l. 1), and like God he basks in the beams reflected from other men's faces. Moreover, he finds his own full fruition in other men's harvests—"The Soft and Swelling Grapes that on their Vines" ripen (l. 49), and the praises produced by the "Swelling Grapes" of their lips:

> Their Lips are soft and Swelling Grapes, their Tongues
> A Quire of Blessed and Harmonious Songs.
> Their Bosoms fraught with Love
> Are Heaven all Heavens above
> And being Images of GOD, they are
> The Highest Joys his Goodness did prepare.
> (ll. 65-70)

Traherne is characteristically Protestant in this return from contemplation to action, from right principles to active charity, from heavenly bliss to life in the world. To be sure, the world for Traherne is no vale of tears and sin but is itself enclosed within eternity for those whose right principles enable them so to view it. Yet Traherne's Christian elect must confront a challenge not altogether unlike that confronting the more traditionally conceived Protestant *miles Christianus* or *peregrinatus*: he must in a fallen world replete with sin and misery win through to, and hold fast to, spiritual vision—those "good thoughts" which alone reveal to man his true condition of felicity.

The dominant tropes in this as in the "Infant-Ey" sequence are light, sphere, and temple: they are first associated with the child's felicity and then, in altered terms, with the man's. The dominant symbol or synecdoche for the child and his special intuitive vision is (as before) the eye. The presentation of the speaker as child, and as disembodied eye, is often reminiscent in a general way of emblem plates and books, though the poems do not conform very closely to the details of specific emblems.[40]

In these metaphorical terms, the child is first aware of a light conveying to him "a World of true Delight"; he enjoys "The anchient Light of Eden," and was "A little Adam in a Sphere." And even before he became aware of his own senses and of the world they conveyed to him, he was aware of his soul as "an Inward *Sphere of Light*, / Or an Interminable Orb of *Sight* / . . . all Sight, or Ey."[41] God's wisdom, power, and goodness reflected in his works delight the child's eye which is "The Sphere / Of all Things," yet the mature speaker intimates his possession of an "eye" which can see farther than the child's: "But Oh! the vigor of mine Infant Sence / Drives me too far: I had not yet the Eye / The Apprehension, or Intelligence / Of Things so very Great Divine and High."[42] Speechless, dwelling within a "World of Light," the child's eyes bring the spiritual meaning of the universe into the "Temple" of his mind, in which ceremony the earth serves as priest:

> Before which time a Pulpit in my Mind,
> A Temple, and a Teacher I did find,
> With a large Text to comment on. No Ear,
> But Eys them selvs were all the Hearers there.
> And evry Stone, and Evry Star a Tongue,
> And evry Gale of Wind a Curious Song.
> The Heavens were an Orakle, and spake
> *Divinity:* The Earth did undertake
> The office of a Priest; and I being Dum
> (Nothing besides was dum;) All things did com
> With Voices and Instructions.[43]

In "Silence" the speaker sees the infant spirit as a sphere encompassing both God and the world: "The World was more in me, then I in it. / The King of Glory in my Soul did sit. / . . . For so my Spirit was an Endless Sphere" (ll. 81-82, 85). Expanding on that last image, "My Spirit" ecstatically celebrates the child's soul as "all Ey, all Act, all Sight" like the Deity, imaging and so embodying all things as "A Strange Mysterious Sphere," "A Strange Extended Orb of Joy," which is, like God, center and circumference of everything (ll. 29, 76, 86). Modulating to the present tense in an apostrophe to that child-soul which is at once sphere, eye and temple, he intimates that the soul's nature and capacities remain unchanged in the mature speaker:

> O Wondrous Self! O Sphere of Light,
> 　　O Sphere of Joy most fair;
> O Act, O Power infinit;
> O Subtile, and unbounded Air!
> 　　　O Living Orb of Sight!
> Thou which within me art, yet Me! Thou Ey,

And Temple of his Whole Infinitie!
O what a World art Thou! a World within!
All Things appear,
All Objects are
Alive in thee! Supersubstancial, Rare
Abov them selvs, and nigh of Kin
To those pure Things we find
In his Great Mind.
(ll. 103-116)

In the section concerned with adult felicity the key metaphors—
light, sphere and temple—are associated with thought (rather than
with the eye) as the quintessence of the human spirit. In "The Circula-
tion" the soul's participation in a cosmic spherical process is indicated:
the source of the soul's bliss is the reflection of the "fair Ideas" from
the sky in the "Spotless Mirror" of the mind (ll. 1, 3), and the soul
cooperates in the eternal circulation of gifts and praises exchanged
between God and Man, whereby both are at once fountain, stream,
and end of all things. Vision is now a matter of gaining the "Celestial
Eys" to recognize these circulations and contribute the praises which
make up man's part—"*Tis Blindness Makes us Dum*" (ll. 24, 25). But
as "The Demonstration" shows and its title implies, celestial eyes are a
function more of thought than of sight: eyes are susceptible to "Miste,"
and the highest things—such as these principles of circulation—are
"only capable of being *Known*" (ll. 2, 3). Such knowledge however
finally dissolves in light—"My Contemplation Dazles in the End / Of
all I comprehend" ("The Anticipation," ll. 1, 2). The "Thoughts"
poems assume and argue the dominance of thought over sight. In
"Thoughts. I" thoughts are identified as "Engines of Felicitie" seated
in the spirit: serving as a mirror to reflect all things, they thereby
contain them and so endow the soul "with Life and Sight," whereby it
comprehends eternity, time, and space (ll. 6, 50). Thoughts, though
unseen, are thus, paradoxically, supreme. In "Thoughts. II" a thought is
identified as the quintessence and fruit of all God's works and also the
ultimate human creation: "That Temple David did intend, / Was but
a Thought, and yet it did transcend / King Solomons" (ll. 25-27). As
such it is a world (sphere) which far surpasses the world created by
God: "It is a Spiritual World within. / A Living World, and nearer far
of Kin / To God, then that which first he made" (ll. 43-45). "Thoughts.
III" represents thoughts (when good) as the offspring of God, spheres
which bear "the Image of their father's face" (l. 31); as the greatest,

most transcendent, and most divine of beings they make the soul infinite and omnipresent as God is:

> The Best of Thoughts is yet a thing unknown,
> But when tis Perfect it is like his Own:
> Intelligible, Endless, yet a Sphere
> Substantial too: In which all Things appear.
> All Worlds, all Excellences, Sences, Graces,
> Joys, Pleasures, Creatures, and the Angels Faces.
>
> (ll. 67-72)

Finally, "Thoughts. IV" presents God's eternity as a "true Light" enclosing us, and God's omnipresence as an "Endless Sphere, / Wherin all Worlds as his Delights appear" (ll. 41, 29-30), identifying thought as the vehicle for living even now in God's eternity and omnipresence. Moreover, as the soul by thought dwells above with God, so God by his eternity and omnipresence dwells in the "pure Soul, transformed to a Thought" (l. 97):

> It enters in, and doth a Temple find,
> Or make a Living one within the Mind.
> That while Gods Omnipresence in us lies,
> His Treasures might be all before our Eys:
> For Minds and Souls intent upon them here,
> Do with the Seraphims abov appear:
> And are like Spheres of Bliss, by Lov and Sight,
> By Joy, Thanksgiving, Prais, made infinite.
>
> (ll. 87-94)

The final spheres the speaker enjoys and possesses are seemingly more commonplace but even more wonderful—the "grapes" of other men's harvests and other men's lips employed in praises ("Goodnesse").

As their title suggests, Traherne's *Thanksgivings* are in the hymnic mode.[44] We have seen that the two meditative sequences contain little in the mode of prayer or praise: the Dobell sequence calls for and argues the necessity for man's praises in the total divine economy, but does not actually produce them. The apostrophes and celebrations in both of these sequences are directed to the glorious self. But Traherne's *Thanksgivings* is a book of divine praises and thanksgivings, modeled upon and indeed incorporating large segments from the Book of Psalms.[45] Such assimilation is akin to Traherne's characteristic inclusion of lengthy extracts from other men's writings in his *Church's Year-Book* and *Meditations on the Six Days of the Creation*,[46] but his purpose and aesthetic accomplishment here are very different. The *Thanksgivings* is an achieved poetic work, not a collection of extracts nor a series of meditations upon biblical texts: in them various biblical voices, and especially David's, are fused with Traherne's own. Traherne does not merely paraphrase or imitate the Psalmist, nor does he, like Herbert, seek to become a New Covenant psalmist, recasting the Psalmist's role in his own antitypical terms. Rather, he assimilates the Psalmist's voice to his own, so that the Davidic type becomes part of the antitype he himself presents. This strategy has produced poems which are set forth as hymns of thanksgiving, closely modeled upon the rhythms and cadences of the psalms and the prophetic books. However, Traherne's hymns are not lyrical; they are indeed hardly poetry in the usual sense. Rather, they are long prose-poems or free-verse rhapsodies, in a mixture of styles but in an overall tone of sublime exaltation. Curiously enough, the poetics defined in these praises is not unlike that set forth in the other sequences, but here the Psalmist is claimed as the model for Traherne's consistently-held ideal of sublime plainness:

> *All Tropes are Clouds; Truth doth it self excel,*
> *Whatever Heights, Hyperboles can tell.*

> O that I were as *David*, the sweet Singer of Israel!
> In meeter Psalms to set forth thy Praises.[47]

Though the *Thanksgivings* contain extracts from and allusions to some other biblical books, for all but the last of them the Psalms provide the pervasive ground tone. "Thanksgivings for the Body" is probably the most complex, conjoining the greatest variety of modes of discourse. The poem begins with a verbatim extract from Psalm 103:1-5, introducing the pattern of long, free-verse lines of sonorous praise: "Bless the Lord, O my Soul: and all that is within me bless his holy name. . . ." A short passage in the poet's own "psalmic" but more personal voice follows, proclaiming his intention to praise: "O Lord who are clothed with Majesty, / My desire is, to praise thee. / With the holy Angels and Archangels / To glorifie thee" (ll. 10-13). Another extract (Psalm 139:14-18) follows, ringing out again the Psalmist's lofty praises: "I will praise thee, for I am fearfully and wonderfully made, marvellous are thy works . . ." (ll. 20-21). Then, for a long passage, the speaker's analytic voice takes over, making large use of syntactical parallelism, repetitive schemes, and Ramistical outlines to divine, enumerate, list, and categorize the elements and aspects of the body he praises. The following passage is typical of this mode:

O blessed be thy glorious Name!
That thou has made it,
A Treasury of Wonders,
Fit for its several Ages;
For Dissections,
For Sculptures in Brass,
For Draughts in Anatomy,
For the Contemplation of the Sages.
Whose inward parts,
Enshrined in thy Libraries,

Are { 
The Amazement of the Learned,
The Admiration of Kings and Queens,
The Joy of Angels;
The Organs of my Soul.
The Wonder of Cherubims.

(ll. 59-73)

Or this, in a more schematic and cryptic vein of analysis:

Even for our earthly bodies, hast thou created all things.

All things { 
Visible.
Material.
Sensible.

Animals,
Vegetables,
Minerals,
Bodies celestial,
Bodies terrestrial,
The four Elements,
Volatile Spirits,
Trees, Herbs, and Flowers,
The Influences of Heaven,
Clouds, Vapors, Wind,
Dew, Rain, Hail, and Snow,
Light and Darkness, Night and Day,
The Seasons of the Year.

(ll. 242-258)

This analytic mode is punctuated throughout by allusions to and extracts from the psalms of praise, and (occasionally) from other biblical books. Such passages are sometimes quoted verbatim, but are more often adapted so as to blend unobtrusively with the syntax and rhythms of the speaker's voice. The poem also has two extended passages of personal meditation[48] in a smooth and elegant middle style (iambic pentameter couplets) which falls somewhere between the plain (curt) style of the analytic sections and the rhapsodic psalmic passages. The final lines of the work are virtually a melange of psalm extracts, culminating with extracts from Canticles (4:9-11, 6:12-13, 8:2, 8:1) which present in the love exchanges of the Bride and Bridegroom the highest pitch of exaltation of the body and the senses. The work concludes with a prose prayer petitioning and thanking God for the power to praise him.

The remaining Thanksgivings—"for the Soul," "for the Glory of God's Works," "for the Blessedness of God's Ways," "for the Blessedness of his LAWS," "for the Beauty of his Providence," "for the Wisdom of his WORD," "for God's Attributes"—are somewhat simpler in structure in that they have nothing resembling the couplet passages included in the "Thanksgivings for the Body," and only the "Thanksgivings for the Soul" ends (like the former poem) with a prose prayer. Otherwise, they exhibit the same mix of modes—psalm extracts, rhapsodic passages imitative of the Psalms, schematic analytic passages, brief biblical allusions and quotations chiefly but not exclusively from the Psalms—all assimilated without identification or distinction into the poet's complex voice.[49] The subjects of praise dictate the manner of development and the choice of biblical material. In "Thanksgivings for the Soul" Traherne invokes his favorite eye and temple tropes for the soul:

> For the Glory of my Soul:
> Which out of Nothing thou has builded,
>    To be a Temple unto God.
> A living Temple of thine Omnipresence.
>    An understanding Eye.
> A Temple of Eternity.
>    A Temple of thy Wisdom, Blessedness, and Glory.
>                                 (ll. 16-22)

The "Thanksgivings for the Glory of God's Works" draws most heavily upon the psalms praising the creatures, including man—Psalm 8, 65, 103, 104, and the Mosaic blessings in Deuteronomy 33:13-16. The "Thanksgivings for . . . his LAWS" is a kind of descant upon extracts and passages from that long, artful celebration of the Law, Psalm 119.

The final poem, "A Thanksgiving and Prayer for the NATION," is cast, as its title signifies, in a more complex mode. With this poem, the *Thanksgivings*, like the meditative sequences, conclude by reaching out to other men, as the speaker defines his role in relation to others. As he has been a psalmist incorporating the stance and voice of David in giving praises to God, so now he becomes a prophet adopting and adapting the words and manner of the major prophets in speaking to God, about and for God's people:

> O Lord spare thy people;
>> Spare thy people, O my God!
> Those Jewels in thy Cabinet, those Persons on thy Stage,
> that fill the World with wonderful Actions.
>
> Make me a $\begin{cases} Moses, \\ Nehemiah, \\ Ezra, David \end{cases}$ to thee & them.

> (ll. 47-53)

The biblical extracts in this work are from the major prophets—Moses (Deut. 9), Isaiah, Jeremiah, David's psalms of meditation, and especially Lamentations. Indeed, at one juncture, Traherne not only echoes particular passages in Lamentations but takes on the persona, developed in chapters one and two of that book, of the city as bereaved widow weeping for her desolation and that of her children:

> Tread not underfoot thy mighty men,
>> In the midst of me,
>>> Crush not my young men.
> Carry not my Virgins away Captive O Lord.
> They respect not the persons of Priests or Elders.
> Let not the breath of our Nostrils be taken in their pits;
>> Nor our Princes suffer the reproach of Servants. Nor our
> Fathers be abused; nor our Bodies lie as Dung upon the Ground;
> nor our Wives be ravished; nor our Children slain in the top of
> every Street.
> . . . . . . . . . . . . . . . . . . . . . . . . . . .
>
> In the days of her affliction, all the pleasant things that my
> people had of old, would come into mind;
>> Increase my Melancholy,
> And shew me the filth of her skirts in those.

> (ll. 153-176)

Traherne's three verse sequences are conceptually fascinating, as daring attempts to link together intricate philosophical argument and rhapsodic emotional response; moreover, they show conscious experimentation in a variety of genres and styles and verse forms. With Traherne, the Protestant poetics of the religious lyric develops in one clearly defined direction out from the center occupied by Herbert and Vaughan. Traherne is as conscious a theorist as Herbert about the poet's responsibility to praise God and about the issue of appropriate plainness for the religious lyric; he also experiments as readily, though in different ways, with biblical models and genres and with the appropriation of biblical personae as quasi-typological figures for himself as poet. Moreover, his poetic sequences derive their special power from that personal testimony and self-probing which is the dominant characteristic of the Protestant line: in Traherne's poems this power inheres in a complex persona who registers urgently and vibrantly a wide spectrum of spiritual emotions and experiences.

But Traherne's religious lyrics are less successful as poems than those of Donne, Herbert and Vaughan—in part perhaps because his version of the Protestant aesthetic involved approaching language as a transparent medium pointing to essences rather than as a densely and complexly suggestive poetic matrix. Accordingly, he draws upon biblical models and genres and personae, biblical metaphors and typological symbolism in rather direct and conceptual ways, whereas the other poets discussed here were able to use these elements as stimuli for their own creative responses and as a treasury of language, symbolism, and association which could give a special charge to their own words. To say this is to recognize that although Traherne's achievement in the religious lyric is considerable, his mind and sensibility are those of a philosopher even more than of a poet, and that he has moved the religious lyric and its poetics some distance in the direction of philosophical abstraction.

## CHAPTER 12

# Edward Taylor: Lisps of Praise and Strategies for Self-Dispraise

That Edward Taylor's literary debts to Herbert are both profound and pervasive is a critical commonplace. Taylor's editor Donald Stanford declares that *The Temple* was probably the greatest single poetic influence on Taylor, and Louis Martz observes that "like Henry Vaughan, Edward Taylor appears to have a mind saturated with Herbert's poetry."[1] There are several more or less obvious allusions and echoes: Herbert's phrase, "crumme of dust" from "The Temper (I)" occurs five times in Taylor's "Prologue," and the opening lines, "Lord, Can a Crumb of Dust the Earth outweigh, / Outmatch all mountains, nay the Chrystall Sky?" especially recall the Herbert poem.[2] Taylor's refrain "Was ever Heart like mine?" from *Preparatory Meditations* (I.40) seems to echo Herbert's refrain from "The Sacrifice," "Was ever grief like mine?"[3] The few titled poems in Taylor's meditative sequences—"The Experience," "The Return," and "The Reflexion" —recall Herbert's titles, and Taylor's stanza form throughout is that of Herbert's "The Church-porch." As Martz notes, several of Taylor's apostrophes to the self or to God might almost be mistaken for lines from Herbert: "My Dear, Deare, Lord I do thee Saviour Call"; "Lord speake it home to me, say these are mine"; "Oh! that I ever felt what I profess"; "What rocky heart is mine?"; "Dull, Dull indeed! What shall it e're be thus?"[4] Again, Taylor's analysis of the manifold properties of the Rose of Sharon (I.4) and his witty figure of the Church as Rose seated at the banquet table ("The Reflexion") strongly recall very similar metaphoric procedures in Herbert's "The Rose" and "Church-rents and Schisms."[5] Moreover, Taylor's poems, like Herbert's, often explore his own uncomfortable situation as a Christian poet who owes God worthy praise he cannot provide, because his human limitations and fallen condition preclude any fitting treatment of God's infinite and unimaginable perfections.

By such echoes and allusions Taylor claims some relation to Herbert and his kind of poetry, inviting a comparison which usually leads to critical judgments about Taylor's insufficiencies, Puritan rigidities, or poetic ineptitudes. But the interesting question is what to make of such resemblances, given the obvious differences in diction, in the uses of poetic figures, in metrical smoothness, in poetic craftsmanship. Is Taylor a belated American Metaphysical, using bold conceits, colloquial language, and daring paradoxes, although in a more naïve, uneven, and sometimes poetically inept manner?[6] Is he indeed a practitioner of what Karl Keller calls a "wilderness baroque," utilizing the elements of metaphysical wit—conceit, catechresis, radical metaphor, pun, dramatic exaggeration—as a way of expressing his passionate joy and delight in the beauty of Christ and the things of God?[7] Or does he exhibit a specifically Puritan poetics, differing radically from that of Donne, Herbert, and Vaughan, and characterized by meiosis, repudiation of art, and an emblematic rather than a genuinely symbolic or sacramental conception of language and nature?[8]

This Metaphysical-Puritan dichotomy pointed up by the critics is, I think, a false one for Taylor, who stands in the line of Donne, Herbert, Vaughan, and Traherne as a Protestant poet practicing a Protestant poetics. In her stimulating and suggestive essay, Kathleen Blake has begun to assimilate Taylor to such a tradition, grounding her argument in the Calvinist doctrine of the sacrament shared by the English Protestant poets as well as Taylor.[9] In contradistinction to that metamorphosis of physical into spiritual reality which is formulated in the Catholic doctrine of transubstantiation and which may lead to religious and poetic stances expressive of mysticism or of sheer carnality, Blake finds a special reliance upon metaphor at the core of Protestant poetics, metaphor being the verbal communicator across the ever-present gap between earthly and heavenly reality. Taylor does indeed incorporate all the familiar elements shaping the seventeenth-century Protestant religious lyric in England—Protestant meditative modes, biblical genre theory, biblical metaphor and typology, Protestant emblem methods, Protestant concerns about artful language—though of course he employs these common elements in a quite distinctive fashion. Taylor's Puritanism brought him to the New World, and pointed him in new poetic directions, but for all that it did not finally lead him to a new poetic country.

Though all the poets here studied (except Traherne) are Calvinists on the essential doctrinal points, and none is a crypto-Catholic in regard to the sacrament, some theological emphases do help shape Taylor's particular version of the Protestant poetics. As a covenanted member, and leader, of a Puritan gathered church of "visible saints" in Westfield, Connecticut, Taylor held a rigorous and unambiguous conception of the five points of the Synod of Dort—total depravity, unmerited election, limited atonement, irresistible grace, and perseverance of the saints. Interpretation of these doctrines with Puritan rigor produced in Taylor an intense consciousness of the immense gulf between God and man, to be bridged only and entirely by God's grace and in no smallest degree by anything in nature or in the responses of the elect.[10] The clearest poetic statement of these theological emphases is probably to be found in Meditation I.36, as Taylor recognizes and queries the reason for his heart's continued vileness:

> But Did I say, I wonder, Lord, to spie
>     Thy Selfe so kind; and I so vile yet thine?
> I eate my Word: and wonder more that I
>     No viler am, though all ore vile to shine.
>     As full of Sin I am, as Egge of meate.
>     Yet finde thy golden Rod my Sin to treate.
>
> Nay did I say, I wonder t'see thy Store
>     Of kindnesses, yet me thus vile with all?
> I now Unsay my Say: I wonder more
>     Thou dash me not to pieces with thy maule,
>     But in the bed, Lord, of thy goodness lies
>     The Reason of't, which makes my Wonders rise.
>
>     .   .   .   .   .   .   .   .   .   .   .   .   .   .   .   .   .
>
> I scarce know what t'make of myselfe. Wherefore
> I crave a Pardon, Lord, for thou hast Store.
>                                    (ll. 19-30, 35-36)

Again, the title affixed to Taylor's meditative lyrics, written over a period of forty years—*Preparatory Meditations before my Approach to the Lords Supper. Chiefly upon the Doctrin preached upon the Day of administration*—testifies to the absolute centrality of the Lord's Supper to Taylor's imaginative life, even as his long dispute with Solomon Stoddard opposing any liberalization of requirements for admission to the Supper does to its centrality in his theology.[11] As his *Treatise Concerning the Lord's Supper* makes clear, the sacrament is important to Taylor as the seal of the covenant, the divine gift offered only to the elect whom God has called, regenerated, and clothed with the "wedden garment" of sanctification. According to Taylor's *Treatise*, sacrament days should provoke meditations on God's overwhelming benefits to us and on our own total unworthiness, but also upon the evidences of election and regeneration produced by his grace; the sacrament also lays upon us the obligation to render the tribute of praise. Precisely these themes are treated in poem after poem, and the sacramental focus probably accounts for the rather surprising tone sounded in many of them. The speaker is curiously serene: he writes as one sufficiently assured of election and regeneration to have decided to approach the sacrament, and this assurance dispels a good deal of the tension which might be expected to accompany his profound awareness of personal worthlessness, the unfathomable distance between himself and God, and the failures of his art. Though he laments these conditions he can do nothing to remedy them and so does not actively grapple with his psyche or his art as do Donne, Herbert, Vaughan, and even Traherne; rather, his poetry deliberately enacts failure, as a means to glorify God. Any adequate response to God on his part, in life or in art, must await the glorification God will bestow upon him in the life to come.[12] But as an aspect of his assurance he has some confidence that his poetic attempts can be accepted in lieu of achievement, and so prays God to "Accept this Lisp till I am glorifide."[13]

The sacrament is also the seal of full membership in the gathered church of elect saints, and this fact also had an effect upon Taylor's imaginative life. Like Herbert and to some extent Vaughan, Taylor wrote sequences of lyrics which present a record of life within the Church—the ever-changing spiritual emotions, tribulations, and experiences attendant upon such a life. But his portrayal of the experience of entering the Church differs from theirs, as does his conception of the Church itself. In Herbert's first poem, "The Church-porch," the promising young man is "lessoned" by a preacher in the externals of the Christian life and thereby brought to the portal of entry into the Church proper, the realm of the inner, sanctified spirit. In Vaughan's first poem, "Regeneration," the speaker is led away from fruitless moral efforts (climbing Mount Sinai) into the garden of the Church where he finds some Christians responsive to grace (the marigolds and the lively stones) but others unresponsive—the unregenerate.[14] Both these versions of entry into the Church postulate a clear separation but not a cataclysmic divide between nature and grace, moral goodness and the life in grace, since the visible Church contains souls in both states, and there seems to be no clear way to identify them in this world. For Taylor the situation is otherwise, as is evident in his long dialogic poem—really a kind of morality play—*God's Determinations*.[15] The action centers upon the difficulties experienced by the various classes of the elect, those who come early and rather easily to Christ and those who resist his call, in believing that they have a part in the promise. Satan's temptations, Christ's consolations, and the good advice and counsel of those already in Church fellowship as visible saints all bear hard upon the late-comers, and the chariot of the Church, sent forth from God to gather up the elect, pursues them throughout the poem. The final short lyrics celebrate the situation of the elect soul—as Bride; as flower planted in Christ's garden (which contains some buds and some blooming flowers but none unresponsive); and as member of the choir of saints "Encoacht for Heaven," joyously and sweetly singing praises produced in them by grace rather than art.[16] Herbert also insists that praises must be a response to grace, but with the significant difference that for Herbert, grace lays upon the Christian poet's lute the responsibility to "struggle for thy part / With all thy art" ("Easter," ll. 7-8) whereas for Taylor the elect remain wholly inadequate to the task of artful praise in their lifetime.

In addition to his two numbered sequences of *Preparatory Meditations*, Taylor also wrote a few miscellaneous lyrics.[17] Some of these are among his finest poems, displaying greater diversity in stanzaic form, greater economy, acuteness, and precision of language and imagery, and a more varied and more intense palette of tones and emotions than do most of the *Preparatory Meditations*. These poems utilize the metaphoric, emblematic, and meditative techniques common to the tradition and characteristic of Taylor, but with a sharp focus upon a particular image or emblem, a given occasion, or a strong emotion.

"[When] Let by rain" is an occasional meditation upon a providential experience: meeting with a sudden rainstorm, the speaker applies his vacillations about going forth or staying home to his own spiritual state: "Ye Flippering Soule, / Why dost between the Nippers dwell? / Not stay, nor goe" (ll. 1-3). He instances bottled soured wine, and fireballs in a blacksmith's shop, as figures for the threat of dangerous explosions from frustrated spirits enclosed in a confining place. By these analogies he recognizes his spiritual danger—the catastrophe threatened by "One sorry fret" within the "Temple" of the soul—and he prays to escape it: "Lord forbid the same" (ll. 25-30). "Upon the Sweeping Flood Aug: 13.14. 1683" interprets a torrential storm upon that date as heaven's response to unspecified sins of carnal love in which the speaker has part. His first reading of the occasion underscores heaven's sorrow: since the sinners did not weep, tears "ran down the skies darke Cheek" (l. 6) to drown the love. His second reading emphasizes heaven's revulsion by the use of base imagery: the sin acts as physic causing the heavens to purge and vomit, shedding "Their Excrements upon our lofty heads" (l. 12).

Especially remarkable and complex are certain emblem-like poems. "Upon a Spider Catching a Fly" is reminiscent of several emblem plates,[18] though the poem is more intricate and less overtly didactic than the usual emblem poem. The speaker addresses a spider with a fly in his web, evidently just captured and immediately killed, and he recalls a similar scene (another emblem plate?) in which the spider gently stroked a captured wasp lest he "in a froppish, waspish heate" (l. 18) should tear the web. He then interprets the emblems: Hell's spider spins nets "To tangle Adams race" but God affords grace to some "to breake the Cord" (ll. 36, 43). "Upon a Wasp Child with Cold" is also emblem-like, though I have not found close emblem analogues. The *pictura* presents a wasp blasted by the north wind, but holding up all her limbs and head to the sun and exercising all her faculties, until she is finally able to fly away; the application is to the nimble spirit containing sparks of rationality and divinity which control its actions. The poet recognizes this divinely ordered emblem in nature as a "schoolmaster" and a ladder leading him to God (ll. 34, 42). Somewhat reminiscent of several Herbert poems, and also of Vaughan's initial emblem poem on the flashing flint, Taylor's "The Ebb and Flow" effectively explores the speaker's spiritual experience by contrasting two "emblems" for his heart. Just after regeneration it was a tinderbox within which his affections often caught sparks of heavenly fire and flamed forth; now it is a trim censer seldom feeling the sparks from God's "Holy flint and Steel." The speaker's fear that his fire might be an *ignis fatuus* is resolved by the realization that when the Spirit blows away the ashes in the censer, "then thy fire doth glow" (l. 18).

"Huswifery" is perhaps Taylor's best-known poem. Structured as an emblem poem interpreting two figures—a spinning wheel and a loom —it presents the key equations by means of three parallel petitions. The speaker first begs to be made Christ's spinning wheel, with the holy Word his distaff, his affections the flyers, his soul the holy spool, his conversation the reel. Then he urges the Lord to make him a loom on which the Holy Spirit winds quills and the Lord weaves the web, beating it in the "Fulling Mills" of his ordinances (l. 10) and dyeing it in heavenly colors. Finally, he begs God to clothe him with the web so woven—"Understanding, Will, / Affections, Judgement, Conscience, Memory / My Words, and Actions" (ll. 13-15). This is a complex emblem of regeneration and sanctification, presenting God's use and control of all the speaker's faculties so as to make from him and place upon him "Holy robes for glory"—the "wedden garment," which is so pervasive as concept and image in Taylor.

Taylor wrote two formal elegies—on his wife Elizabeth, and, in a higher style befitting an occasion of public grief, on the distinguished Connecticut pastor, Samuel Hooker.[19] But a much more impressive poem in the elegiac mode is the poignant "Upon Wedlock, and Death of Children," a retrospective account of the birth of four children and the death of two. The controlling metaphor presents the speaker as a plant set within a love-knot in God's garden, his stock bearing flowers which are then cropped. The metaphor is generally sustained in the description of the first loss: Christ in glory desired a choice flower which the speaker resigned to him. But it does not accommodate the desperate grief occasioned by the agonizing illness preceding the death of the second child: "But oh! the tortures, Vomit, screechings, groans, / And six weeks Fever would pierce hearts like stones" (ll. 35-36). The conclusion takes up the original pastoral metaphor with a calm resignation that ignores rather than resolves the challenge posed by this outcry: "I joy, may I sweet Flowers for Glory breed, / Whether thou getst them green, or lets them seed" (ll. 41-42).

"A Fig for thee Oh! Death" also invites discussion here as a "defiance of death" poem in the tradition of Donne's famous sonnet. As in Donne's poem, Taylor's speaker challenges a personified Death, pictured according to familiar emblem or gravestone iconography:[20]

> Thou King of Terrours with thy Gastly Eyes
> With Butter teeth, bare bones Grim looks likewise.
> And Grizzly Hide, and clawing Tallons, fell,
> . . . . . . . . . . . . . . . . . . . .
> Thou'rt not so frightfull now to me. . . .
>
> (ll. 1-3, 11)

Admitting the power of Death with his "Poundrill" to dash "My Flesh and bones to bits" (ll. 9-10), he takes comfort that by this means his nut or kernel soul escapes the body, which he willingly surrenders to Death's dungeon and mill. At length he expects that the dust will rise "Christalized" (a pun?), that "Soule and body . . . as two true Lovers" will "hug and kiss each other," and rise glorious (ll. 44, 47-48). The conclusion intensifies the challenge to Death, urging him in the spirit of Herbert's "Time"[21] to come more quickly:

> Why camst thou then so slowly? Mend thy pace.
> Thy Slowness me detains from Christ's bright face.
> Although thy terrours rise to th'highst degree,
> I still am where I was, a Fig for thee.
>
> (ll. 53-56)

Taylor's two sequences of *Preparatory Meditations* (some 217 poems, a few of them in two versions) display little variety in genre or form. All are written in the same stanza form (a six-line iambic pentameter stanza rhymed *ababcc*) and most are between thirty and seventy lines in length. These poems owe little to theories regarding the biblical lyric genres, or to the poetic books of the Bible themselves. Though Taylor occasionally alludes to instruments or tunes mentioned in the Book of Psalms in petitioning Christ or the Holy Spirit to play upon him as passive instrument, he wrote no Psalm paraphrases,[22] or New Covenant psalms in creative imitation of David as did Herbert and Traherne, and he based only a handful of his meditations upon psalm texts. Moreover, though Taylor placed the Book of Canticles under contribution for texts and allusions far more often than any other source, he seldom drew upon it for generic models. In fact, as their title indicates, the two sequences are meditations, and specifically, sacramental meditations. They are also, as is indicated by the biblical text headings supplied to almost all of the poems, conceived as Protestant "deliberate meditations" upon biblical texts, and are thereby closely aligned to sermons.[23] Present evidence hardly warrants the certitude with which Norman Grabo has described Taylor's habits of composition—that the poems were written for the regular monthly sacrament days, after the sermon for the day was composed and before it was preached.[24] But it is clear from Taylor's *Christographia* sequence (where we have both sermon and poem for fourteen such occasions) that there are close relations in imagery and theme between sermon and poem, and that, except in one striking instance, the biblical text used as point of departure and title is the same for both.[25] Yet in this sequence the poems do not epitomize or recapitulate or reformulate the argument or doctrine of the sermon: rather, as we would expect from Protestant meditative theory, the poetic meditations undertake an "application to the self" of whatever aspect of text or argument or doctrine is seen to address the speaker's own condition most forcefully.[26] And since these are poems, they focus most often upon an image, trope, epithet, or other term offered by the biblical text, analyzing or commenting upon or expanding that term in relation to the underlying theological idea it points to, and probing the speaker's responses to its implications.

A few poems depart from the formula for sacramental-deliberate meditation, and cautiously claim another generic identity. The first poem of the first series bears no biblical text and is entitled simply "Meditation"—evidence that it is not related to a sermon and was composed specifically as an introduction to the poems. Its subject is Christ's love—apostrophized and celebrated for its manifestations in the incarnation and the passion, and at length petitioned to overflow and inflame the speaker's heart. The poem entitled "The Experience" is unique in these sequences in that it is a meditation upon a personal spiritual experience—a particular joy felt by the speaker on the last sacrament day. It is strongly reminiscent of several Herbert poems, notably "The Temper (II)."[27] The speaker, as so often in Herbert, longs to recapture an evanescent awareness of God's closeness: "Oh! that I alwayes breath'd in such an aire, / As I suckt in, feeding on sweet Content!" (ll. 1-2). Considerable emotional tension arises from Taylor's desire to recapture the lost sense of joy, content, fullness, and closeness to Christ: the memory of the "Flame which thou didst on me Cast" (l. 13) occasions some pain for its loss, but it also provides consolation, leading the speaker to claim confidently, by reason of the incarnation, a throne higher than that of the angels: "Give place, ye Angells Bright. / Ye further from the Godhead stande than I. / My Nature is your Lord; and doth Unite / Better than Yours unto the Deity" (ll. 19-22). "The Return," which follows immediately, is Taylor's only attempt to write a hymn-anthem—evidently, the praise "The Experience" has called forth. Its several stanzas celebrate Christ's love and gracious favors to the speaker, each of them ending with some version of the refrain, "Oh! that thou Wast on Earth below with mee / Or that I was in Heaven above with thee" (ll. 5-6).[28] However, the speaker relates this and any other earthly praises he produces to the Lord's playing upon him as instrument, reserving his own active praises for heaven:

> Be thou Musician, Lord, Let me be made
>     The well tun'de Instrument thou dost assume.
> And let thy Glory be my Musick plaide.
>     Then let thy Spirit keepe my Strings in tune,
>     Whilst thou art here on Earth below with mee
>     Till I sing Praise in Heaven above with thee.
>                                                    (ll. 49-54)

Though Taylor's poems are in large measure discrete exercises, as the circumstances of their composition would seem to dictate, the First Series of *Preparatory Meditations* (1-49) may have been conceived in terms of, or at any event accommodated to, the meditative program suggested in his *Treatise Concerning the Lord's Supper*. That program calls for a train of meditations focusing upon the sacrament as epitome of the covenant of redemption, and considering the following topics: the glory and beauty of the Bridegroom; the happiness and preferment of the Bride; the Bridegroom's purchase of his Bride with all his estate; the Bridegroom's suffering, death, conquest over death, and ascent to heaven; the benefits and gifts bestowed upon the Bride; the contract celebrated in the "wedden feast" of the sacrament.[29] The poems do in fact seem to follow such a pattern, whose completion is indicated by the fact that Taylor begins a new sequence after number 49. The dominant theme of this first sequence, Christ's love, is sounded by the initial poem, and the next four poems show the speaker personally experiencing and responding to that love. Meditations 4-13 celebrate through consideration of appropriate biblical texts (often from Canticles) the beauty, excellence, and glory of the Bridegroom and the sacramental feast. Meditations 14-22 focus on Christ's mediatorial role (his offices, his passion, his exaltation and enthronement in heaven). Meditations 23-40 develop the benefits the soul enjoys through the Covenant of Grace (it is espoused by Christ; it enjoys forgiveness of sins and fullness of grace; it is adopted by God, made a new creature, made heir to all things present and to come). The last poems (41-49) present the heavenly kingdom as the final benefit of the Covenant—the throne the elect will occupy, the various crowns they will wear, their white robes, their participation in the joys of the Lord—but suggest also the foretastes of that joy in the prospect, and in the consciousness of God's love and grace here.

The second series of *Preparatory Meditations*, in very general terms and perhaps through inadvertent assimilation of the classic Protestant paradigm, reflects the speaker's spiritual growth and development. He begins by approaching Christ through Old Testament types of the Covenant (1-30); proceeds to the direct apprehension and description of Christ the Redeemer in his many aspects (31-56); explores in several short, disparate sequences his doubt-plagued efforts to claim the major benefits of the New Covenant (57-114); undertakes in the Canticles sequence (115-153) a long and probing examination of his participation in Christ's spousal relation to his Church; and concludes with an occasional and partial assumption of the persona of the Bride (154-165). In its broadest terms, this scheme resembles the pattern William Epperson has discerned in Taylor's poems,[30] but I do not find the conformation he suggests to the classic paradigm of Catholic mysticism. As with the other collections of Protestant religious lyrics examined here, Taylor's sequence avoids presenting the spiritual life as a steady progress through fixed stages, and portrays instead, through recurring themes, problems, and vacillations, a continuing spiritual struggle which does not end in this life. In "Meditation II.156," Taylor does seem to reach (as do Herbert and Vaughan) something like a plateau of assurance, displaying thereafter a greater delight in and confidence in the relation with the Bridegroom. But even in the last poems that relation is portrayed as very tentative and partial.

Indeed, even this general intimation of spiritual progress is under-mined by the fact that virtually every poem in Taylor's two medita-tive sequences enacts in little the essential spiritual dilemma as he per-ceived it—a dilemma he cannot resolve on earth. On the one hand, God's glory and love and benefits to the speaker are beyond all meas-ure in their greatness and magnificence. On the other hand, his vileness and utter insignificance prevent his sharing in, or approaching, or com-prehending, or in any way responding properly in his life or in his verse to that goodness and greatness. He is utterly dependent upon God's approaches—in the types, in Christ, in the emblems and sacra-ments and ordinances and other manifestations of grace—for the pre-paration of the "wedden garment" of sanctification required of the Bride. Whatever the topic, then, the issue in all the poems is always the same: has the speaker the right to apply to himself the spiritual promises and goods described? He poses that question to himself again and again, in terms seldom agonized but almost always tentative, con-ditional, petitionary: he finds grounds for assurance, and indeed for great wonder and joy, in contemplating the honors and privileges ac-corded the elect by God; but there is no settling the matter and moving on to some higher state of sanctity or mystical union. The question must be, and is, confronted every time he considers any topic relating to the spiritual life.

This central issue dictates the structure of almost all the meditations. Most are designed according to a simple, contrastive scheme or, per-haps more properly, according to a logic of thesis, antithesis, and resolution. Perhaps most often, the speaker begins by celebrating the greatness, glory, and benefits of the Lord. He then portrays his own vileness and unworthiness to receive such benefits, and the impossi-bility of rendering proper praise for them. At length he petitions for God's gracious acceptance of him and his praises, despite his vileness—while often looking forward to his transformation in heaven from vileness to glory. Alternatively, the speaker may begin with his own vileness, then contrast the divine goodness and magnificence, and pro-ceed to the same resolution. Like the stanzaic pattern of these poems, this structural design recurs with monotonous regularity.

Taylor calls upon a much wider range of biblical metaphors and figures, and uses them more constantly, than do the other poets here studied. His poems often focus upon a particular biblical trope or fig-ure for Christ, developing it through association with clusters of related or contrasting images or figures—sometimes biblical, sometimes em-blematic, often homely and colloquial, sometimes deliberately base—in order to exhibit the gulf between the speaker and his God. This way with biblical metaphor differs significantly from that of the other poets. Though Taylor recurs often to familiar ranges of imagery—the descriptions of Bridegroom and Bride from Canticles and the sacramental metaphors of Christ as bread and as vine or wine—he usually does not, like Donne, unify individual poems in terms of a single striking image or metaphor. Nor does he, like Herbert and Vaughan, attempt to unify a collection of lyrics by appropriating and developing creatively in his own terms a few dominant biblical metaphors. Nor, like Traherne, does he undertake to forego tropes in order to reveal the naked truth behind the verbal sign or name. He is in some ways closest to Donne in his joyous response to the figurative richness of the Spirit as biblical poet, and indeed he expresses great admiration for the metaphorical texture of scripture in Sermon IX of the *Christographia*:

> All Languages admit of Metaphoricall forms of Speech, and the Spirit of God abounds in this manner of Speech in the Scripture and did foreshew that Christ Should abound in this Sort of Speech Ps. 78.2. Matt. 13.35, and this Sort of Speech . . . was . . . a neate Rhetoricall, and Wise manner of Speaking. Hence saith Gods Spirit in the Psalmist Ps. 49.3.4: I will open my mouth in Wisdom: the meditation of my heart shall be of understanding. I will encline mine eare to a Parable and open my dark Saying upon my harp. Hence then this form of Speech is a truth Speaking form, Convaying the thoughts of the heart of the Speaker unto the hearers in Such words as are apt to do it metaphorically and wisely.[31]

But whereas Donne finds in the Spirit's metaphors a warrant for his own imitation of such poetic richness, Taylor announces in poem after poem that he cannot in this life engage in such competition. He can only appropriate, analyze, comment upon, and thereby enrich his text with large numbers of biblical figures, praising God in his own terms. Often he sets these biblical figures over against others which are colloquial, homely, or base, as if such as these are the only creation possible from his vile and worthless creaturely self.

Many poems are developed through analysis of or commentary upon a principal metaphor or term pertaining to Christ or his salvific, mediatorial role, usually taken from or suggested by the poem's biblical text heading. Key tropes governing a succession of such poems identify Christ as an ointment, the Rose of Sharon, the lily of the valley, the living bread, a feast of fat things, the sun of wisdom, the Spouse, an advocate with the Father, the tree of life, the head of his body, the sun of righteousness with healing in his wings. Other text headings highlight more abstract theological terms, which also admit of and receive metaphorical development: Christ is high priest, great prophet, king of kings, his visage is marred in the passion; he is exalted in his resurrection, ascension, and enthronement in heaven; he is all fullness; he is the Love which gives his life for his friend; he gives life to his elect in the Sacrament.

One primary method of developing such figures and terms is analytic or associative: the speaker works out the implications and aspects and ramifications of the figure, or moves from it by rather free association to other figures and concepts. In such poems the speaker is essentially a commentator or paraphraser, elaborating upon the key figures and terms by means of related figures of a similar kind, or through plain-style exposition—and always with application to himself. One of Taylor's most successful poems of this kind is Meditation I.4, "Cant. 2. 1. I am the Rose of Sharon." This metaphor for Christ, and the properties associated with it, are developed with a unity he does not often achieve. The poem begins with a brief and loosely drawn allegor- ical presentation of his own state—he has locked up "a Sparke of Love" which the "gawdy World" solicits, but his love, choosing a "Pilgrims life," courts the rose of Sharon. The speaker petitions in a series of apostrophes that this rose's properties be made his own: he would lodge in "this sweet Rosy Bower"; he would have the "Blood Red Pretious Syrup of this Rose" purge his soul; he would have this "Rosy Oyle" serve as a balm for his wounded conscience; he would have the "Shugar of Roses made of Sharon's Rose" cure his consump- tive, dwindling soul; he would have his soul swim and his "Conscience bibble" in rose water distilled from this rose. Then, lamenting that this rose "must Pluckt, stampt, squeezed bee, / . . . To make a Physick sweet, sure, safe for mee" (ll. 50-52), he punningly rejoices that "this mangled Rose rose up again" and prays to it as "Rose of Heaven" that he may lodge in its leaves. The concluding stanza rather effectively draws the strains together, recurring also to the vague allegory of the opening lines:

> My Dear-Sweet Lord, shall I thy Glory meet
>    Lodg'd in a Rose, that out a sweet Breath breaths.
> What is my way to Glory made thus sweet,
>    Strewd all along with Sharons Rosy Leaves.
> I'le walk this Rosy Path: World fawn, or frown
> And Sharons Rose shall be my Rose, and Crown.
>                   (ll. 61-66)[32]

Of the same kind are Meditations I.38 and I.39, on the trope in 1 John 2:1, "An Advocate with the Father." The first of these poems works out a complete but somewhat mechanical elaboration of the terms: the speaker is to be tried in God's court of justice; angels are sergeants who will lay before the judge his deeds "both White, and Black" (l. 8); Christ is the advocate who never loses a plea, who pleads without a fee, and who pays the fine for his clients. The second poem uses the figures more effectively. After a graphic description of the speaker's pitiable condition—"My Sin! my Sin, My God, these Cursed Dregs, / Green, Yellow, Blew streakt Poyson hellish, ranck" (ll. 1-2)—he finds his only hope in the advocate. Admitting that "I have no plea mine Advocate to give" (l. 25), he takes comfort that the advocate will draw his arguments "Out of his Flesh and Blood" and that this "Dear bought Plea" will win his client life. As fee he promises his faith, repentance, and obedient service.

Another and perhaps more common mode of development is by meiosis[33]—a recasting of God's metaphors in homely, colloquial terms. By this means the poet represents the immense gulf between himself and God's glory and greatness, and enacts the utter impossibility of proper description and worthy praise. He uses this method most often in connection with the sacrament, describing the indescribable feast with kitchen metaphors. Meditation I.8 on John 6:51, "I am the Living Bread," begins with a somewhat extraneous image of the bread of life tracing a golden path from heaven to his door, but then introduces the dominant imagery of bread-famine-cookery through a quasi-allegorical description of fallen man as a starved bird—reminiscent of several bird-in-cage emblem plates:[34]

> When that this Bird of Paradise put in
>    This Wicker Cage (my Corps) to tweedle praise
> Had peckt the Fruite forbad: and so did fling
>    Away its Food; and lost its golden dayes;
>    It fell into Celestiall Famine sore:
>    And never could attain a morsell more.
>
>                 (ll. 7-12)

Unable to find soul's food here—the creatures' fields have none, angels have none, and the "Worlds White Loafe is done"—the bird-soul is fed by the bread of life, which metaphor Taylor literalizes in graphic and rather shocking ways. God is a baker who takes "The Purest Wheate in Heaven, his deare-dear Son"; who "Grinds, and kneads [him] up into this Bread of Life"; and then bakes and sends that bread forth as "Heavens Sugar Cake" (ll. 21-22, 30). The kitchen metaphors are pervasive also in a loosely knit sequence of eucharistic poems in Taylor's second sequence. Meditation II.71, "I Cor. 5. 8. Let us keep the Feast, not with old Leven," begins, "Oh! What a Cookroom's here?" and proceeds to describe Heaven's "Cookery" almost as if supplying a recipe for a banquet,

> Where Pastie past is Godhead, filld at least
>     With Venison, of Paschall Lamb the best.
>     All spic'd and Plumb'd with Grace and disht up right
>     Upon Gods Table Plate Divinely bright.
>
> (ll. 15-18)

Forcing his metaphor to its limit, he begs God to "load my trencher with thy Paschall Lamb. / . . . And let my Faith on thy rost mutton feed" (ll. 32, 35). In II.81 he draws out the repellent and almost cannibalistic implications of his figures in order to denounce the doctrine of transubstantiation and insist upon the spiritual understanding of the metaphor:

> What feed on Humane Flesh and Blood? Strang mess!
>     Nature exclaims. What Barbarousness is here?
>
> .  .  .  .  .  .  .  .  .  .  .  .  .  .  .  .  .  .  .  .  .
>
> This Sense of this blesst Phrase is nonsense thus.
>     Some other Sense makes this a metaphor.
> This feeding signifies, that Faith in us
>     Feeds on this fare, Disht in this Pottinger.
>
> (ll. 13-14, 19-22)

But having cleared this point, he is then free to work his kitchen metaphors hard: Christ's works "knead in / The Pasty Past, (his Flesh and Blood) most fine / Into Rich Fare, made with the rowling pin / His Deity did use." He is "My Souls Plumb Cake" (II.81, ll. 25-28, 56). Or again, he is "Soule Sweet Bread . . . in Gods Back house, made / On Heavens high Dresser Boarde and throughly bakd: / On Zions Gridiron, sapt in'ts dripping trade" (II.82, ll. 31-33).[35]

A more radical technique, and perhaps the most common, is metaphoric antithesis. In poems using this technique the speaker sets over against biblical metaphors embodying God's glory and God's promises deprecatory images and figures for himself most often chosen from the base vocabulary of scatology and disease. He is, in a series of poems, a dirt ball, a muddy sewer, a dung-hill, a pouch of passion, a lump of loathsomeness, a bag of botches, a sink of nastiness; he is candied over with leprosy, pickled in gall, wrapped in slime.[36] The contrast between God's greatness and his own nothingness is often pointed through precisely drawn antithetical figures: he is a "Crumb of Dust" beside God's glory; he is "Dead Dust" wondrously made to eat "Living Bread"; his soul has an ague thirst assuaged by the red wine of Christ's blood; he is a sluggish servant "More blockish than a block" while his Lord is glorious; he is a "Leaden Oritor" given the "Golden Theame" of Christ's love to sing; his "Clay ball" will be dressed in God's "White robes"; Christ's love is the apple of the Tree of Life while he is a "Wormhol'de thing"; Christ's head contains profoundest wisdom and his contains "addle brains."[37]

In a variation on this method the speaker sometimes sets up his metaphoric antitheses within the same field of imagery so that, finally, the metaphors argue a relationship between himself and Christ as well as a contrast. In this vein he presents his heart as a "poore Eggeshell" or box to hold the precious ointment that Christ is; he wishes to be (in several poems) the valley of which Christ is the lily, or a flowerpot to hold Christ the flower; he would be a vessel to catch Christ's blood, and his "Pipkin" or "Acorn Cup" overflows with Christ's fullness; he is a prisoner in a darksome, noisome pit without water but sails forth on the Red Sea of covenant blood.[38] In Meditation I.29 on John 20:17, "My Father, and Your Father, to my God, and Your God," the speaker is (in the central metaphor) a "Withred Twig" to be grafted into the "rich Tree / The Tree of Life" which is Christ (ll. 7-9). Building upon that metaphoric contrast which is also a relationship, the speaker also claims a host of other bonds to Christ—"I am thy Patient, Pupill, Servant, and / Thy Sister, Mother, Doove, Spouse, Son and Heire. / Thou art my Priest, Physician, Prophet, King, / Lord, Brother, Bridegroom, Father, Ev'ry thing" (ll. 21-24). At length, in the words of the biblical text heading, he claims all Christ's family as his own—"Thy Father's mine, thy God my God, and I / With Saints, and Angells draw Affinity" (ll. 29-30)—and punningly prays "That I may grace thy gracefull Family" (l. 39).

Meditation I.37, "1 Cor. 3. 23. You are Christ's" uses several very effective metaphoric antitheses. The first stanza sets up a paradox: how can the speaker be so nearly related to Christ as the text indicates, and yet find his soul so "blotcht"? The biblical metaphors of relation contrast sharply with those denoting his actual sinful state:

> Shall I thy Vine branch be, yet grapes none beare?
>     Grafft in thy Olive stand: and fatness lack?
> A Shackeroon, a Ragnell, yet an Heire?
>     Thy spouse, yet, oh! my Wedden Ring thus slack?
>     Should Angel-Feathers plume my Cap, I should
>     Be swash? but oh! my Heart hereat grows Cold.

What is my Title but an empty Claim?
   Am I a fading Flower within thy Knot?
A Rattle, or a gilded Box, a Flame
   Of Painted Fire, a glorious Weedy Spot?
                        (ll. 7-16)

Following these witty yet poignant queries the speaker presses to be accorded the proper accompaniments of his promised condition as vine-branch, child, heir, and Spouse, but he only finds further antitheses as he observes how imperfectly those metaphors accommodate him:

Am I hop't on thy knees, yet not at ease?
   Sunke in thy bosom, yet thy Heart not meet?
Lodgd in thine Arms? yet all things little please?
   Sung sweetly, yet finde not this singing sweet?
   Set at thy Table, yet scarce tast a Dish
   Delicious? Hugd, yet seldom gain a Kiss?
                       (ll. 31-36)

The final stanza retains tonal complexity, avoiding the pat resolution which is all too often a feature of Taylor's poems. Continuing to press the inquiry—"Why? Lord, why thus? Shall I in Question Call / All my Relation to thyselfe?"—he petitions at least to be included within another, less personal, metaphoric field: "Then ope the sluce: let some thing spoute on me. / Then I shall in a better temper bee" (ll. 37-38, 41-42).

Meditation I.40 on 1 John 2:2, "He is a Propitiation for our Sin," is almost wholly given over to the description of the speaker's sorry state, by means of a torrent of base and loathsome metaphors. The query, "Was ever Heart like mine?" runs like a refrain through several stanzas, and the answers to the query depict the heart as

A Sty of Filth, a Trough of Washing-Swill
A Dunghill Pit, a Puddle of mere Slime.
A Nest of Vipers, Hive of Hornets; Stings.
A Bag of Poyson, Civit-Box of Sins.
                      (ll. 3-6)

It is also Satan's bowling alley where he plays at nine-pins, his palace garden, and his butcher's stall. In that heart "Pride, Passion, . . . / Ath'ism, and Blasphemy, pot, pipe it, dance / Play Barlybreaks, and at last Couple in Hell" (ll. 20-21). In that heart grace is shuffled away, "Repentance's Chalkt up Noddy" (l. 29), sins bite like badgers, and the Spirit scarce stirs. After all this the speaker cries out helplessly, "I know not what to do: What shall I doe?" (l. 44)—and barely escapes the despair of thinking his sin greater than God's grace. Finally, he holds over against all this the biblical text pronouncing Christ's name the propitiation for sins, and he finds a contrasting but still colloquial metaphor to embody the process of that regeneration: "Lord . . . soake my soule in Zions Bucking tub / With Holy Soap, and Nitre, and rich Lye. / From all Defilement me cleanse, wash and rub" (ll. 55-58).

In Taylor's ways with metaphor there is a sense of exuberance, daring, and outrageousness more nearly resembling Donne than any other poet we have considered. But the springs of this curious excess are radically opposed in the two poets. Donne finds his creative freedom in the challenge to imitate the inexhaustible poetic richness of the Spirit; Taylor finds his in recognizing the utter impossibility of such an undertaking, which allows him to invent a new idiom, a meiotic, secular language of non-praise which is nevertheless devoted to the glory of God. As Karl Keller observes,[39] Taylor exhibits constant delight in language, as is perhaps most clearly evident in his persistent wordplays and puns (another point of contact with Donne): the speaker would be Christ's gold, minted by him, and thereby an Angel (I.6); Christ the Rose of Sharon rose up again in his resurrection (I.4); Christ is Almighty and the speaker a "mightless" mite (II.48). Taylor also plays on words through the devices of ploce and traductio—as in the forms of *love* in Meditation I.12:

> My *Lovely* One, I fain would *love* thee much
> > But all my *Love* is none at all I see,
> Oh! let thy Beauty give a glorious tuch
> > Upon my *Heart*, and melt to *Love* all mee.
> > Lord melt me all up into *Love* for thee
> > Whose *Loveliness* excells what *love* can bee.
> > > (ll. 43-48)[40]

But Keller's argument that this delight in language springs from Taylor's all-pervasive spiritual joy and delight demands some qualification, for though Taylor did not doubt his election he was often dismayed by his inevitable failures in spiritual attainment and in praise. The delight arises rather from his discovery of an area, however humble, in which he could exercise his creativity freely, in God's honor.

Types are strewn about in Taylor's poems as prodigally as biblical metaphors. His approach to typology is generally conservative and inclusive, relating a large number of personal and ritual Old Testament types to their antitype, the incarnate Christ. In Sermon IX of the

*Christographia* series, Taylor states, with reference to Calvin's engraving metaphor, his orthodox Calvinist understanding of the types as foreshadowing and presenting Christ:

> He is the Object of all the Old Testament Prophesies, and Metaphoricall Descriptions of the Messiah. He was variously foretold in the Old Testament even from Adam to the latter end of Malachy. . . . As he is foretold in the Type, God doth as it were pensill out in fair Colours and [ingrave] and portray Christ and his Natures and Properties. . . . He is the Truth of all the Prophesies, and Types of the Old Testament. . . . The types, and Ceremonies were shadows of Good things to come, but the body is of Christ. Col. 2. 17.[41]

In Taylor's poetic sequence on the types (II.1-30), the biblical text titles are almost always from the New Testament, focusing attention sharply upon Christ the antitype, and the speaker's wished-for association with him. In summary form, the sequence incorporates almost the entire range of Old Testament typology as schematized in Samuel Mather's compendium.[42] The opening poem (II.1) points to this range: the speaker's frozen heart, dull spirits, and deep stains are set in opposition to "The glory of the world slickt up in types" (l. 13)—all which glory meets in and is excelled by Christ. The first group of poems (II.1-II.13 and also II.30) deals with the so-called personal types— Adam, Noah, Abraham's seed, Isaac, Jacob, Joseph, Moses, Joshua, Samson, David, Solomon, Jonah. The next group (II.14-II.27) deals with Israelite offices and rituals as types (prophetic types, kingly types, priestly types, Nazarites; altars, tabernacles, festivals, sacrifices, ceremonies). Number 29 deals with one "typical" object, Noah's ark. The typology of events such as the Exodus and the Covenant, and the typology of the Church as antitype of the garden of Canticles serve as subjects of later poems.

Karl Keller has noted that Taylor attempts in various witty ways to include himself in the typological process; in this, as we have seen, he stands in the mainstream of Protestant typological exegesis.[43] Taylor found his justification for extending typological reference to the individual Christian precisely where others did, in the notion that the types also refer to Christ's mystical body, his members: "Tho' they may Speake out particular things that are not to be founde in Christ personally considered, yet they are in Christ Mystically Considered."[44] But from the plethora of types he includes, it is clear that Taylor does not, like Herbert, Vaughan, and Traherne, identify himself imaginatively with some one or some few particular Old Testament types such as David the Psalmist or Jacob the pilgrim. He locates himself in the course of typological history by insistent and constant identification with Christ the antitype.

Taylor's typological poems begin, characteristically, with a depiction of his own sinfulness, worthlessness, and inability to praise. He then develops, sometimes very briefly and sometimes in elaborate detail, the ways in which a particular type adumbrates some aspect of Christ's redemptive mission. Very occasionally he associates himself with that type after the manner of correlative typology, but most often he at once claims relation to Christ, the antitype of all the types, through whom he often asserts something of an antitypical role for himself— seeking a better Canaan, finding a new Ark in the Church, and enjoying the garden of the Church, the antitype of Solomon's garden and Isaiah's vineyard. He relates himself to Christ the antitype primarily through the vehicle of language, writing himself into the typological equation by assigning himself a humble, ancillary role in Christ's antitypical redemptive act. In II.2, celebrating Christ as "First Born of Every Creature" (Col. 1:15), he begs inclusion in the familial relationship implied: "Make mee thy Babe, and him my Elder Brother" (l. 37). In II.4, which treats a classic text in typological theory—(Gal. 4:24) comparing Hagar and Sarah, the bondmaid and the free woman—he prays to embody the antitype rather than the type: "Blesst Lord, let not the Bondmaids type / Take place in mee. But thy blesst Promised Seed" (ll. 25-26). As Jacob sought and found a spouse, he prays to be the Spouse found by Christ (II.6). As Aaron caught the sacrificial blood in his vessel, so his soul will be the "Vessel" to catch Christ's blood (II.23, ll. 37-38). He needs to wash in Christ's blood, the "Choice Fountain" whose type was the purificatory washings of the Old Testament (II.26, l. 31). He must be "Arkd in Christ" the antitype of Noah's Ark (II.29, l. 32).

The poem on Joseph (II.7, on Psalm 105:17, "He sent a man before them, even Joseph, who was sold etc.") is a particularly effective example of this method. The speaker begins by lamenting his flat and dull spirits, his dim ink and blunt pencil, and therein contrasts himself with both the type and the more glorious antitype: "Is Josephs glorious shine a Type of thee? / How bright art thou?" (ll. 7-8). He then recounts the typological parallels as one finds them in Mather: Joseph was betrayed, cast into a pit, sold by his brothers, endured temptation, was cast into jail, was restored to power and glory, and effected the salvation of his starving people with bread—all which have antitypes in Christ, whose glorious image is "pensild out" in Joseph's (l. 35). At this point, characteristically, the speaker writes himself into the relation: his dull skin requires the "brightsome Colours" of Joseph's coat but more especially of Christ's blood and glory.[45]

The poems on Exodus motifs often present the speaker in a somewhat more direct relation to the typological equation—initially as a correlative type with Israel in bondage and wandering in the desert, but then as the antitype fulfilling those types. The first poem of the brief Exodus series (II.58-II.61) makes the basis for this relation quite explicit, by extending the typological reference beyond the physical Christ to his members:

> But Isra'ls coming out of Egypt thus,
>      Is such a Coppy that doth well Descry
> Not onely Christ in person unto us.
>      But Spirituall Christ, and Egypt Spiritually.
>      Egyptian Bondage whence gates Israel shows
>      The Spirituall bondage whence Christs children goe.
>                                        (ll. 31-36)

On this understanding the speaker presents himself as antitype of Israel: he escapes from Goshen, passes through the Red Sea of God's wrath tamed by Christ's cross, endures a wilderness state, finds Christ to be his pillar of the cloud leading him through the wilderness to Canaan; he also finds the manna to be his bread of life, washes himself in the water from the rock (Christ), and is cured by the brazen serpent (Christ) of the bite of the fiery serpent.[46]

Taylor's ways of inserting himself into the typological equation are entirely consonant with that focus on the self characteristic of the Protestant exegetes and poets. What is unusual, however, is his elaboration of the metaphorical and emblematic aspects of various properties associated with the typological personages or the ceremonial types. Such elaboration does not undermine the historicity of the types or their centrality in these poems, as several critics have argued,[47] but it does make for a mixture of modes. Taylor finds warrant for such a mixture in the Bible's presentation of the same Christ under diverse modes—in types, in allegories, and in straightforward description:

They [the Old Testament faithful] had Christ dispensed in Promises and Types, as a Mediator to Come. We have him dispensed in a Cleare, and Manifest way as Come already. But the different manner of dispensing of the Messiah, doth not produce, a Different Christ, nor a different Faith on Christ. Sometimes the Church sets forth Christ as an Obscure person standing behinde the Wall, peeping in at the Window, and making a flowrish thro' the lattice as Can. 2.9. Sometimes she setts him out in orientall Colours and in most Allegoricall accomplishments as Cant. 5.10-16. Yet this differing way of Setting him out, makes not any Personall Difference. Its the same Person, and Beloved in the one description, as is described in the other.[48]

An effective example of such mixture of modes is Meditation II.24, on John 1:14, "Tabernacled amongst us." The type is the Old Testament tabernacle, presenting the Godhead "Cabbin'd in a Myrtle bowre, / A Palm branch tent" (ll.14-15); this type easily lends itself to metaphoric exfoliation into tents, boxes, canopies, cabins, and tenements. But the antitype, the incarnation, much exceeds the type in wonder, and provides another sort of "tenement" for God—one which involves the speaker with Christ in metaphoric exchanges of tabernacles and rent arrangements, and thereby involves him directly in the typological relationship:

> But yet the Wonder grows: and groweth much,
>   For thou wilt Tabernacles change with mee.
> Not onely Nature, but my person tuch.
>   Thou wilst mee thy, and thee, my tent to bee.
>   Thou wilt, if I my heart will to thee rent,
>   My Tabernacle make thy Tenament.
>
> Thou'lt tent in mee, I dwell in thee shall here.
>   For housing thou wilt pay mee rent in bliss:
> And I shall pay thee rent of Reverent fear
>   For Quarters in thy house. Rent mutuall is.
>   Thy Tenant and thy Teniment I bee.
>   Thou Landlord art and Tenant too to mee.
>                                   (ll. 43-54)

Taylor's poems are also replete with emblems. As we have seen, he obviously regards certain objects in nature and certain biblical metaphors as divinely instituted emblems, invested by God with spiritual significance conveyed by the visual details of physical appearance and circumstances.[49] This is especially true of Canticles' images, many of which Taylor explicitly designates and interprets as emblems. Moreover, as Norman Grabo has acutely observed,[50] Taylor's poetry is everywhere indebted to the emblem manner in its detailed visualization of an analytic approach to metaphor and symbol. To recognize this is not, however, to agree with Alan Howard that the "richly figured surface" of Taylor's poetry simply disappears, that we must view it

"as if it did not exist at all."[51] Though emblems and emblematic imagery
are organized by a logical rather than a naturalistic scheme, they are
not devoid of sensuous affect: indeed they are intensely visual, and we
take the impact of that quality. Grabo has the right of it when he de-
scribes the effect of Taylor's poems as "rich and ornate; but like stained
glass or medieval illuminations . . . strangely two-dimensional."[52] He
has the right of it also in calling attention to the plethora of other
sensations to which we respond: tactile sensations of snarled and ragged
cloth; the reeking of incense, flowers, pillars of perfume; twangs and
tweedles; kinesthetic sensations of wallowing, submersion, or bouncing
like a tennis ball. Taylor's poems work according to a metaphoric/em-
blematic logic of their own, but they hardly reduce to doctrinal
abstraction.

With Taylor as with Herbert, the issue of how to praise God in
poetry is paramount. As we have seen, Taylor enacts through meta-
phoric procedures of meiosis and antithesis his poetic assumptions
about the impossibility of rendering true praise, but he also addresses
the issue of praise directly throughout his poems. Standing astonished
before the manifestation of God's love in the sacrament, or before his
wisdom, or his glory, Taylor characteristically exclaims, "How shall I
praise thee then? My blottings Jar / And wrack my Rhymes to pieces
in thy praise" (I.10, ll. 31-32). Or again, "My Phancys in a Maze, my
thoughts agast, / Words in an Extasy; my Telltale Tongue / Is tongue-
tide, and my Lips are padlockt fast / To see thy Kingly Glory" (I.17,
ll. 13-16). Meditation I.22 develops more fully the speaker's paradoxical
dilemma of finding the service of praise at once absolutely necessary
and utterly impossible:

> When thy Bright Beams, my Lord, do strike mine Eye,
>     Methinkes I then could truely Chide out right
> My Hide bound Soule that stands so niggardly
>     That scarce a thought gets glorified by't.
>     My Quaintest Metaphors are ragged Stuff,
>     Making the Sun seem like a Mullipuff.
>
> Its my desire, thou shouldst be glorifi'de:
>     But when thy Glory shines before mine eye,
> I pardon Crave, lest my desire be Pride.
>     Or bed thy Glory in a Cloudy Sky.
> .   .   .   .   .   .   .   .   .   .   .   .   .   .   .   .   .   .   .
>     Whether I speake, or speechless stand, I spy,
>     I faile thy Glory: therefore pardon Cry.

But this I finde; My Rhymes do better suite
  Mine own Dispraise than tune forth praise to thee.
Yet being Chid, whether Consonant, or Mute,
  I force my Tongue to tattle, as you see.
                                    (ll. 1-10, 17-22)

Elsewhere he laments, "In finest Twine of Praise I'm muzzled. / My
tazzled Thoughts twirld into Snick-Snarls run" (I.32, ll. 9-10).

To this dilemma he offers two kinds of resolutions—in the sub-
junctive mood and the future tense. He prays, on the one hand, that
God will so restore his faculties that they will produce praises made
acceptable by grace. The issue here is sanctification, not art: because
his heart and faculties are as yet imperfectly restored, more appropriate
praises must wait upon the advancement of that process. In "The
Experience" he prays that his heart might become "thy Golden
Harp . . . / Well tun'd by Glorious Grace" (ll. 25-26), and he promises
better praise if the experience of "sweet content" and nearness to Christ
in the Sacrament is repeated. In "The Return" he begs Christ to play
upon him as instrument and petitions the Spirit to "keepe my Strings
in tune, / . . . Till I sing Praise in Heaven above with thee" (ll. 52-54).
In I.27 he promises that when God's fullness dwells in his heart, "I
then shall sweetly tune thy Praise" (l. 47). In I.41 he begs Christ to
produce in him the love and the skill "To tend thy Lord in all ad-
miring Style" until he is able "to pay in glory what I owe" (ll. 38, 48).
In these terms, he alludes at times to the Davidic instruments and
tunes—but he is rather an instrument upon which the Spirit plays than
an artful imitator of David. In I.18 he prays to be made such an instru-
ment—his breast the virginals, his affections the strings, his panting
heart the stops and falls on which the Spirit plays its psalm, "ALTA-
SCHATH MICHTAM, in Seraphick Tune" (l. 48).

But though more loving praise may be made possible by further
sanctification of the heart, this resolution does not meet the problem
of the woeful inadequacy of all human art in the praise of God. When
art is in any way the issue, Taylor moves to a second resolution—a
prayer that God will accept his feeble and inept attempts as tokens of
his faith and duty, usually promising to provide fit and appropriate
praise when he is translated to the only realm where that is possible—
heavenly glory. The models of praise occasionally mentioned—David
the Psalmist, the angels—can be properly imitated only in heaven:
"Were I an Angell bright, and borrow could / King Davids Harp, I
would them play on gold" (I.32, ll. 5-6). Here he can only tattle a

"slippery Verse," and beg that it be accepted as his best effort: "I'le bring unto thine Altar th'best of all / My Flock affords. I have no better Story. / I'le at thy Glory my dark Candle light: / Not to descry the Sun, but use by night" (I.21, ll. 20-24). In I.34 he again declares the impossibility of praise, but hopes for acceptance of his poor effort on the strength of a domestic analogue:

> My tongue Wants Words to tell my thoughts, my Minde
>       Wants thoughts to Comprehend thy Worth, alas!
> . . . . . . . . . . . . . . . . . . . . . .
> But seeing Non-Sense very Pleasant is
>       To Parents, flowing from the Lisping Child,
> I Conjue to thee, hoping thou in this
>       Will finde some hearty Praise of mine Enfoild.
>                                         (ll. 3-4, 7-10)

He will pay the debt due, with true art, in glory: "My Tunes shall dance then on these Rayes and Caper / Unto thy Praise. When Glory lights my Taper" (II.76, ll. 41-42); "And when my Clay ball's in thy White robes dresst / My tune perfume thy praise shall with the best" (I.46, ll. 53-54). When he wears the promised crown of glory, he will sing fit praises after the angels' model:

> When thou shalt Crown me with these Crowns I'l bend
>       My Shallow Crown to crown with Songs thy Name.
> Angels shall set the tune, I'le it attend:
>       Thy Glory'st be the burden of the same.
>       Till then I cannot sing, my tongue is tide.
>       Accept this Lisp till I am glorifide.
>                                         (I.43, ll. 37-42)

Interestingly enough, he anticipates a change of genre in the heavenly praises: they will be in the high style, heroics, sounded on trumpet as well as strings. In glory, he will be ". . . the Golden Trumpet of thy Praise" (I.24, l. 42); and his verse will ". . . run on Heroick golden Feet" (I.21, l. 5).

Taylor is especially concerned in his typological series (II.1-30) with the problem of rendering appropriate praise. Somewhat surprisingly, he presents himself there in quasi-typological relation to David. The poem about David (II.12, on Ezekiel 37:24, "David my Servant shall be their King") voices his special attraction to David as type of Christ and as singer of Christ's story. Lamenting his own dullness despite Christ's "Rich, Quick'ning" promises and sparkling colors (ll. 1-3), he finds himself attracted by David's typical brightness:

> David in all his gallantry now comes,
>     Bringing to tende thy Shrine, his Royall Glory,
> Rich Prowess, Prudence, Victories, Sweet Songs,
>     And Piety to Pensill out thy Story;
> To draw my Heart to thee in this brave shine
> Of typick Beams, most warm. But still I pine.
>                                             (ll. 13-18)

He prays that this beauty may affect him and that Christ may refine him until he too shines and his own strings are "loaded with thy Praise" (l. 34). The Davidic allusions (often to the tunes and the instruments mentioned in the Psalms) intimate two kinds of relationship to David. As in the lines just quoted, several poems suggest that the speaker might become a correlative type with the Psalmist in singing praises if and when the process of sanctification is further advanced in him. This is a matter of grace, not of art—of Christ moving him to render the praises due and making those praises "sweet" by the grace accorded him. When he more fully experiences the privileges of his adoption he will "hang my love then on his [Christ's] heart, and sing / New Psalms on Davids Harpe to thee and him" (II.2, ll. 41-42). Or again, God's grace in his heart will build there "Wonders Chappell where thy Praise / Shall be the Psalms sung forth in gracious layes" (II.3, ll. 35-36). However, whenever the issue relates to artful or even adequate praises produced by the poet's imitation of or competition with David, the scene shifts to heaven. He begs that "thy bright Angells catch my tune, and sing't. / That Equalls Davids Michtam which is in't" (II.18, ll. 65-66). And he promises his own Davidic psalms on the appropriate tunes and instruments in glory: "With Angells soon / My Mictams shall thy Hallalujahs tune" (II.8, ll. 41-42); "In Angells Quires I'le then my Michtams sing, / Upon my Jonath Elem Rechokim" (II.30, ll. 77-78).

The poetic sequence on the words of sacramental institution (II.102-111) also forces the issue of praise, because the sacrament requires the response of praise and thanksgiving. In the earlier poems of the sequence Taylor articulates the problem in familiar terms, praying that God will accept his feeble efforts until, sanctified or in glory, he can do better. But Meditation II.110, on Matthew 26:30, "When they had sung an Hymn," complicates the issue, for the text has reference to a hymn sung directly after the Lord's Supper—creating a precedent for, and indeed a requirement of, immediate praise. As Taylor has shared the feast he must make a similar response—and he does, with the sweeping declaration that "this rich banquet makes me thus a Poet" (l. 24).

But though the joy of the feast prepares the guests to sing "Hallelujahs in sweet musicks dress," and the feast itself supplies rich matter, Taylor must petition both for the instruments and the musician, neither of which he can supply. He begs that his heart may be a pipe filled with the Holy Ghost, that he himself may be a golden trumpet, and that Christ will play his own praises on these instruments. He also prays that his sanctification be completed: when his soul is made a cittern whose wires are his cleansed affections and whose strings are tuned "most Just" by Christ, he can meet the requirement of praise—"Ile close thy Supper then with Hymns, most sweet" (ll. 52-53).

The fourteen poems (II.42-56) which parallel the sermons Taylor conceived and bound together under the title *Christographia*, invite special attention as a unified series. The special interest of these poems derives not only from the sermon links, which invite important inferences about Taylor's understanding of the specific domain of the meditative lyric, but also from the superior quality of several of these poems and their diverse poetic strategies. By their title, the *Christographia* sermons claim to present the emblem or portrait of Christ, incorporating, according to the subtitle of the sermon volume, the following aspects: "Christs Person, Natures, the Personall Union of the Natures, Qualifications, and Operations." Each of the poems concerns itself with the particular aspect of Christ which is central to the parallel sermon—Christ's human body, his divinity, the Word made flesh, his wisdom, his fullness, his life, his almightiness, his grace, his truth, his fullness in the Church, his power as priest, his power as prophet and king, his mediatorial power joining all these offices, and finally, his glorious works. But in the poems the procedure is appropriately metaphorical rather than logical: the poems develop the various aspects of Christ not by doctrinal argument but through tropes, epithets, or terms rich in connotation and significance.

In virtually every case the metaphors associated with a specific aspect of Christ are sharply contrasted with tropes pointing up the human speaker's antithesis to Christ in the quality noted, and the resolution begs for the speaker's salvation through, or for his participation in, that quality. The focus is on Christ, but also on the speaker as he applies one or another aspect of Christ closely to his own situation. And since the speaker is a poet, the problem of writing verses looms very large indeed in this series. Having undertaken to depict Christ graphically, to draw his picture, Taylor must confront his human inadequacy and fallenness in virtually every poem. Responding to this pressure, he links even more closely than elsewhere the salvation which he prays to find in Christ and the acceptable praises that will flow from it. Again,

this salvation will not make the praises artful or in any degree adequate
to the task of depicting Christ, but they will be "sweet" because per-
fumed by grace and played by Christ himself on the instrument
(Taylor) which Christ will tune.

The speaker forcefully declares his utter incapacity to his task in
Meditation II.43, on the text from Romans 9:15, "God blessed forever."
The topic is Christ's divinity, and the speaker expatiates upon the utter
absurdity of all his words before the "shining Majesty" of Christ's
divine nature. His organs of speech are "trancifide," and "Speeches
Bloomery" cannot find words "from the Ore / Of Reasons mine" (ll.
2, 4, 6-7). Thoughts, speech, and writing are alike disgraced: "Words
Mentall are syllabicated thoughts: / Words Orall but thoughts Whiffld
in the Winde. / Words Writ, are incky, Goose quill-slabbred
draughts, / . . . Words are befould, Thoughts filthy fumes that smoake"
(ll. 13-15, 19). Of necessity then must his "muddy Words . . . dark thy
Deity, / And cloude thy Sun-Shine" (ll. 23-24). But he comes to terms
with the problem by eschewing the attempt to praise or define the
deity, assigning his words a more humble task:

> Yet spare mee, Lord, to use this hurden ware.
>     I have no finer Stuff to use, and I
> Will use it now my Creed but to declare,
>     And not thy Glorious Selfe to beautify.
>                               (ll. 25-28)

The remainder of the poem conforms precisely to this program: it is
a plain-style analysis of various doctrinal abstractions concerning the
Divine Nature. The final stanza returns to the issue of praise, declaring
that if God will elect and accept him and tune his soul his praises will
also be acceptable, "buskt up in Songs perfum'de" by grace (l. 52).

A similar strategy prevails in several other poems of the series.
Meditation II.44, on the text from John 1:14, "The word was made
Flesh," begins by contrasting the "Spangled Flowers of sweet-breathd
Eloquence" plucked from rhetoric's gardens for the use of secular
orators, with the lack of appropriate language to treat a theme that
utterly transcends human reason: "Shall bits of Brains be candid thus
for eares? / My Theme claims Sugar Candid far more cleare" (ll. 25-
26). The speaker retreats to the plain style of doctrinal statement to
treat the *Theathrophy* or union of the two natures, but then rises to
exclaim in wonder at this honor to human nature. At length he prays
that Christ's print be stamped on his heart, and that Christ himself will
produce the praises: "If thou wilt blow this Oaten Straw of mine, /
The sweetest piped praises shall be thine" (ll. 53-54).

Perhaps the wittiest and most remarkable of the series is II.48, on two words from Revelation 1:8, "The Almighty." Here the principal terms are "might" and "mite," homophones which are at the same time antitheses, and which afford large opportunity for pun and word-play and paradox as Taylor points up the opposition between Christ's might and his own mite, and at the same time suggests the union of the two through the identity of sound. The poem begins with the simple contrast between human might matched with right (the source of strength in earthly sovereigns) and Christ's Almightiness; he then introduces the speaker as the absolute antithesis to any such might— "But what am I, poor Mite, all mightless thing!" (l. 13). Nevertheless, and paradoxically, this mite lays claim to some might in serving the Almighty Christ who accepts widows' mites: it would spend "its mitie Strength for thee / Of Mightless might, of feeble stronge delight" (ll. 20-21). And in so doing, this mite mocks earthly or hellish might and power: "Their Might's a little mite, Powers powerless fall" (l. 27). Upheld by the Almighty, he abandons trust in his own might, but yet trusts because his mite is so upheld. The final stanza rings still more changes on the paradoxical union, achieved so wittily through pun and incessant wordplay, which has bridged the antithesis of Christ and the speaker, might and mite:

> If thy Almightiness, and all my Mite
>     United be in sacred Marriage knot,
> My Mite is thine: Mine thine Almighty Might.
>     Then thine Almightiness my Mite hath got.
> My Quill makes thine Almightiness a String
> Of Pearls to grace the tune my Mite doth sing.
>                                          (ll. 37-42)

Later poems in this sequence look forward to future and more per-fect praises as the effects of Christ's offices procure the speaker's fur-ther sanctification and, ultimately, his glorification. He longs for, and looks forward to, purgation of his dullness by the coal that purged Isaiah's lips, hoping to become "a Golden Trumpet . . . / All full of Grace" (II.52, ll. 31-32); he begs that his rusty and untuned heart-harp may be tuned by grace "to tune thee praise" (II.54, l. 54). In the final poem, on Christ's works, he brings this issue to some resolu-tion as he looks to derive his own "fruits" (works, poems) from Christ's glorious works of grace which "Out vie both works of nature and of Art" (II.56, l. 44).

Taylor's meditations on Canticles texts invite consideration as a group: they comprise sixty-six poems in all, almost one-third of his production in this kind. Moreover, as the first and last few poems in Taylor's total *œuvre* are based on Canticles, and the longest unified sequence (II.115-153) is on consecutive verses from Canticles 5:10 to 7:6, that biblical work may fairly be said to encompass and dominate Taylor's poems. The metaphors and images of Canticles—the spousal relationship of Bridegroom and Bride, the physical beauty of the spouses, the gardens of nuts and spices, the luxuriant feasts, the jewels, perfumes, flowers, colors, and textures—are the very substance of these poems. This pervasive imagery, together with the traditional medieval explication of Canticles as an allegory of mystical experience and love-union with Christ, has led some critics to postulate a strong strain of mysticism and ecstatic religious experience in Taylor.[53] However, though Taylor revels in the Canticles' language and always refers the Canticles texts in some way to his own spiritual life, only very occasionally does he identify his religious experience with the love experiences recounted by the Spouse—and when he does so the experiences described are hardly mystical. He does not, as if he were a Puritan Crashaw or St. Teresa, take on the persona of the Spouse as sexual-spiritual lover.

On the other hand, Taylor's treatment of Canticles departs from the usual Protestant conception of it as an allegorical narrative of the history of the Church and the process of regeneration. His approach is exegetical, directed to the language of the particular biblical verses which serve as headings to his poems. Yet the assumptions of the familiar Protestant allegorical narrative lie behind almost all these poems. For Taylor, the Bridegroom is of course Christ and the Spouse is, most often, the Church as the entire company of the elect: "thy Spouse . . . doth consist of all / Gods blesst Elect regenerate within / The tract of time from first to last" (II.136, ll. 31-33). At times Taylor relates himself to the spousal metaphor by begging association with and incorporation within the Spouse; at other times he does so by exploring whether the Bridegroom's words to the Spouse apply in the particular sense to himself as elect soul. He reads the other primary metaphor of Canticles, the Garden, in terms of the same conventional allegorical symbolism: "This Garden, Lord, [is] thy Church"; "The Garden too's the Soule, of thy Redeem'd" (II.83, ll. 19, 25). The speaker's stance in such poems is to seek plantation and cultivation within the garden-Church (to be a flowerbed, vine, or lily in the garden), and sometimes to ask that the garden be planted and tilled within him. In most of these poems, Taylor probes intensively the metaphors and emblems of Canticles to produce praises for the Bridegroom and Spouse, and to clarify the theological basis of the speaker's relation to both. The few poems in which the speaker relates his own experience of Christ's love to that of the Spouse, or takes on her persona to describe such experiences are not mystical in any precise sense, but display the spiritual affections often treated at length in the Protestant allegory of Canticles.[54]

Some twenty poems on Canticles texts precede the consecutive Canticles sequence. Several of these (I.2, I.3, I.4, "The Reflexion," I.5) set forth key metaphors or emblems for Christ the Bridegroom—sweet-smelling ointment, rose of Sharon, lily of the valley—which serve both to praise Christ and to extend to the speaker the properties these tropes signify (grace, cure, relationship). Meditation I.3, on a phrase from Canticles 1:3, "Thy Good Ointment," illustrates a frequent formula. The poem begins with praises of the Lord's sweetness as the quality adumbrated by the metaphor of the text: "How sweet a Lord is mine? . . . / A Box of Ointments, broke; sweetness most sweet. / A surge of spices: Odours Common Wealth, / A Pillar of Perfume: a steaming Reech / Of Aromatick Clouds" (ll. 1, 7-10). We might at first suppose that the speaker takes on here the persona of the Canticles Bride enjoying the Bridegroom in these sensory terms, but in fact, the speaker complains of his failure to experience the sweet perfume of the Canticles metaphor, and queries whether he has been "denos'de" (l. 19), or has lost his smell, or smells too much of the world's sweets. "The Reflexion" expands upon the "Rose of Sharon" metaphor, with the speaker again complaining that the sweets and properties of that Rose are so seldom enjoyed by him. One time in the past he had a visionary experience which brought him the sweets the Rose metaphor promises, but he reads this memory as a glorious emblem evincing a theological point rather than as a love experience:

> Once at thy Feast, I saw thee Pearl-like stand
> 'Tween Heaven, and Earth where Heavens bright
> glory all
> In streams fell on thee, as a floodgate and,
> Like Sun Beams through thee on the World to Fall.
> Oh! sugar sweet then! my Deare sweet Lord, I see
> Saints Heavens-lost Happiness restor'd by thee.
> (ll. 25-30)

Several poems on Canticles 6:11, "I went down into the Garden of Nuts, to see the fruits" (II.63-65), invite analysis of the metaphors and emblems in terms of the Church as nut garden. The nuts signify "meate, and med'cine" (II.63, l. 43), and the pomegranates and vines are elect souls whom the speaker hopes to join. The speaker prays to be set in the garden of the Church, and to have a garden of fruits in his heart (II.62-65). Another group of poems (II.83-85) on Canticles 5:1, "I am come into my Garden; I have gatherd my Myrrh with my Spice; I have eate my Hony, etc." interprets all these images as emblems of the graces fixed by Christ in the Church and in the souls of his elect—the myrrh of repentance, and such fruits as patience, humility, faith, hope, and love. Meditation II.79 on the text, "My Beloved is mine and I am his" (Cant. 2:16) might seem to afford an opportunity to expatiate on the love union, but instead this poem explores analytically and through many witty turns the paradox of mutual propriety. It ends with a prayer that the spouses may be beds for each others' loves, but the erotic potential of that figure is largely dispelled by the logical analysis which has preceded it. Meditation II.96, "Cant. 1. 2. Let him kiss me with the Kisse of his mouth," is a complaint that the speaker does not receive the evidences of love described by the Spouse. His consolation to himself is twofold: the Bridegroom's love may be present without external evidences; and also, the fruition of love is for heaven, not earth:

> But listen, Soule, here seest thou not a Cheate.
>     Earth is not heaven: Faith not Vision. No.
> To see the Love of Christ on thee Compleate
>     Would make heavens Rivers of joy, earth overflow.
>     This is the Vale of tears, not mount of joyes.
>     Some Crystal drops while here may well suffice.
>                                                    (ll. 43-48)

The sequence (II.115-153) on Canticles 5:10 to 7:6 is more unified in theme and structure than is usually recognized. The first poem, on the words "My Beloved," introduces the speaker querying whether he may speake the Spouse's words as his own: "What art thou mine? Am I espoused to thee?" But he does not appropriate her words or her persona directly; rather, her love is the model—"Thy Spouse, the best of Loving Ones: Her Love, the Best of Love" (ll. 38-39)—against which he measures his own inadequate response to the love and loveliness of the Bridegroom. The next poem, focusing on the Spouse's description of the Bridegroom as "White, and Ruddy" (Cant. 5:10) celebrates Christ as epitome of (Petrarchan) beauty and prays that this beauty may incite his love. The next several poems treat the descriptive images and metaphors offered by the biblical verses as further elaborations of the great beauty of the Bridegroom and usually as emblems denoting particular qualities of Christ and aspects of his redemptive role. He is a king, "The Chiefest among ten thousand" (II.117); his head of gold transforms all his members and their faculties to gold

(II.118); his cheeks are as a bed of spices and sweet flowers (II.120); his lips are lilies dropping the sweet-smelling myrrh of grace and doctrine (II.121); his hands are golden orbs emblematic of the sphere of grace (II.122); his marble legs are supports for his body the Church (II.123 B); his countenance is like Mount Lebanon whereon grow cedars to build spiritual temples (II.125). Meditation II.127, on the text "He is altogether lovely" (Cant. 5:16), draws the abstract conclusion from these emblematic particulars: "Thou altogether Lovely art, all Bright. / Thy Loveliness attracts all Love to thee" (ll. 25-26).

In the next five poems (II.128-132) on Canticles 6:1-6:3—"Whither is thy Beloved gone, Oh! thou Fairest among Women?" "My Beloved is gone down into his Garden, to the Beds of Spices"; "He feeds among the Lillies"—the speaker identifies himself with the Daughters of Jerusalem addressing this query to the Spouse (the Church). He recognizes that this query will elicit the response "to his garden which I am," and he prays to enter into that garden by "Graces garden doore" (II.129, ll. 6, 26). Within the garden, the spices will perfume with grace the "beds of Saints," the "Elect Lillies" the Bridegroom comes to gather, and the speaker prays to be among them: "Set me a Lilly in, thy Bed of Spices."[55] Meditation 133, on Canticles 6:2 (Taylor treats the verse out of order, to bring this section to a fitting close), presents the speaker adopting the voice and stance of the Spouse-Church, elaborating upon the title text, "I am my beloved and my beloved is mine." The Spouse-Church here addresses the Daughters of Jerusalem (with whom the speaker has previously identified himself), warning them not to think "To steale from me my Souls beloved" (l. 3); she points out that the Spouse is no single person but "an agrigate," and therefore invites the Daughters to "be members made of mee," so that all shall be united: "He'l be your Bridegroom, you his Spouse shall be. / Thus you in me enjoynd shall be made bright" (ll. 27, 29-31).

This invitation to the speaker to establish his relationship to the Spouse-Church, as well as to the Bridegroom, leads into the next sequence of poems (II.134-153), which explores the chief metaphors for the Spouse afforded by Canticles 6:4-7:6. These metaphors also are usually treated as emblems, displaying the glorious beauty and representing the spiritual and salvific qualities of the Church from which the speaker would benefit or in which he would share as a member of the Bride. She is "Terrible as an Army with banners" armed at all points under her captain (II.135); her hair is curled as a flock of goats; her teeth are like a flock of sheep, importing true faith and meditation (II.137, 138); her temples shine with the pomegranate of humility and

spiritual beauty, and he would have his own temples to shine thus
(II.139, 140). She is the Garden of Nuts, and he also desires to bear
fruits and nuts (II.144); her feet are beautiful with shoes, and he begs
that his may be also as they walk the ways of faith and repentance
(II.148); her navel is a goblet of spiritual liquor and her belly a heap
of wheat, emblems of the sacrament and the sanctifying grace it brings
(II.149); her breasts are like two roes to suckle Christ's babes, and he
prays that these "nibbles" be placed in his mouth (II.150, l. 13).
Throughout, his prayer is, "Make me a member of thy Beautious
Bride, / I then shall wear thy lovely Spouses shine (II.151, ll. 55-56);
and as he finds himself conformed to her, he will be enabled to "sing
the Bridall Melodies out best" (l. 60). Toward the end of this section
he can occasionally assume the Spouse's persona and stance. In II.146,
he takes the words "Return, oh Shulamite, return return" as ad-
dressed to himself and available for consolation during periods of the
Lord's seeming absence, experiences which he describes in the familiar
terms associated with the soul's spiritual development in the Protestant
allegory of Canticles:

> When as thy Love doth Touch my Heart down tost
>     It tremblingly runs, seeking thee its all,
> And as a Child when it his nurse hath lost
>     Runs seeking her, and after her doth Call.
>     So when thou hidst from me, I seek and sigh.
>     Thou saist return return Oh Shulamite.
>
> (ll. 7-12)

In this Canticles sequence, Taylor alters somewhat his characteristic
approach to metaphor and to the problem of praise. The contrastive
method—setting God's metaphors against his own homely ones—is no
longer much in evidence. Nor does he often enact by deliberate meiosis
his inability to praise—though in one place he petitions to be one of the
hairs of Christ's spouse, curled by the Spirit's crisping pins (II.137,
ll. 51-54). However, he still proclaims his utter inability to frame
worthy praises, and even sees his usual problem complicated (like
Herbert's in "The Forerunners")[56] by his Muse's age: "Her Spirits
shiver doe, her Phancy's Laws / Are much transgresst. She sits so
Crampt with cold. / Old age indeed hath finde her, that she's grown /
Num'd, and her Musicks Daughters sing Ahone" (II.122, ll. 8-12).
Moreover, now he must not only devise appropriate praises for God,
but also express his own more intense love:

> My sweet-sweet Lord who is it, that e're can
> Define thyselfe, or Mine affections strong
> Unto thyselfe with inke? Who is the man
> That ever did, or can these riches Sum?
> Thy Sweetness no description can define
> Nor Pen and Inke can my hearts Love out line.
>                                      (II.130, ll. 1-6)

But the pressures of decorum in handling the Canticles texts, and Taylor's thematic concern here to establish his own relationship to Bridegroom and Spouse in terms of analogy, precludes much use of the meiotic or contrastive strategies for dealing with this problem. Instead, the speaker now presents himself as a commentator, in plain or "homely" style, upon the Spirit's glorious text: "Fain I would brighten bright thy glory, but / Do feare my Muse will thy bright glory smoot. / Thy Spirits Pensill hath thy Glory told / And I do stut, commenting on the Same."[57]

But in addition to such plain-style commentary, exposition, and interpretation of the images, metaphors, and emblems supplied by his text, he comments also (and primarily) by means of imagistic and metaphoric amplification, seeking analogues for the Spirit's splendid figures. This strategy flows naturally from his recognition that the Book of Canticles, and specifically the Bridegroom's praises of the Bride, offer the highest, indeed the divine, model for praise: "Oh! what a Speech is this" (II.145, l. 19); "What Golden words drop from thy gracious lips, / Adorning of thy Speech with Holy paint" (II.138, ll. 13-14). He does not attempt creative imitation of these praises, and his amplifications are also bound to fail, since the model is inimitable, dazzling and blinding the poet even as it attracts him. Meditation II.152 poses sharply the problem set for the human poet by the divine poet:

> My Deare Deare Lord! my Soul is damp Untun'd.
> My strings are fallen and their screw pins slipt.
> When I should play thy praise each grace perfumd
> My strings made fit with graces wax most slick.
> My notes that tune thy praise should, pleasantly,
> Will onely make an harish symphony.
>
> Thou gildest ore with sparkling Metaphors
> The Object thy Eternall Love fell on
> Which makes her glory shine 'bove brightest stars.
>                                      (ll. 1-9)

The final poem in the Canticles sequence (II.153 on Canticles 7:6, "How Fair and how pleasant art thou, O love, for delight?") is wholly concerned with the way in which the poet now sees his task. At this point he simply abandons the sequence, and with it the impossible *paragone* the divine poet has forced upon him by his all-delightful poetry. The problems of poetics he now confronts cannot be met even partially by his former meiotic, antithetic strategies, and so must be resolved in heaven:

> My Glorious Lord thy work upon my hand
> > A work so greate and doth so Ample grow
> Too larg to be by my Souls limits spand.
> > Lord let me to thy Angell Palace goe
> > To borrow thence Angelick Organs bright
> > To play thy praises with these pipes aright.
>
> You Holy Angells lend yee mee your Skill.
> > Your Organs set and fill them up well stuft
> With Christs rich praises whose lips do distill
> > Upon his Spouse such ravishing dews to gust
> > With Silver Metaphors and Tropes bedight.
> > How fair, how pleasant art, Love, for delight?
>
> Which Rhetorick of thine my Lord descry
> > Such influences from thy Spouses face
> That do upon me run and raise thy Joy
> > Above my narrow Fancy to uncase.
> > But yet demands my praise so high, so much
> > The which my narrow pipe can neer tune such.
>
> Hence I come to your doors bright Starrs on high
> > And beg you to imply your pipes herein.
> Winde musick makes the Sweetest Melody.
> > I'le with my little pipe thy praises sing.
> > Accept I pray and what for this I borrow,
> > I'le pay thee more when rise on heavens morrow.

The last poems in the Second Series (154-165) include several on Canticles texts, chiefly from Canticles 2:1-5. Though a number of these are unfinished (because of Taylor's age and sickness) there seems to be some advance in the confidence and the frequency with which he associates himself with the Spouse, and adopts her voice. He seems in these poems to reach something like the "plateau of assurance" also evident in the latter portions of *The Temple* and *Silex Scintillans*, in which a higher stage of the spiritual life, marked by greater confidence and peace, is attained. Meditation 156, on Canticles 5:1, "Eate oh Friendes and drink yea drink abundantly oh Beloved," begins with the speaker's incredulous response to these words, which he takes to be addressed to himself: "Callst thou me Friend? What Rhetorick is this? / It is a piece of heavenly Blandishments" (ll. 1-2). But after exclaiming over the impossibility of his befriending Christ, he recognizes that Christ has indeed become to him "A Friend, yea the best friend that heaven hath" (l. 19), and he concludes with a firm acceptance of the relationship, culminating in praises which almost for the first time are *not* conditional and engaged to the future: "Thou drinkst a Cup to me of't spiced wine / And bidst mee pledge thee and I pledge will. / My heart top full of these sweet dainties comes / Runs over with thy prais in sweetest songs" (ll. 27-30). He sees himself invited to the Bridegroom's banqueting house, and he now claims to enjoy the relationship he had so long requested, of being valley to Christ's lily: "I am thy Vally where thy lilly grows / Thou my White and Red blest lilly fresh" (II.160, ll. 19-20).

Most interesting, perhaps, is the lovely poem on Canticles 2:3, "His fruit was sweet to my Tast" (II.163).[58] The term "sweet" is the focus of the poem, and the speaker unhesitatingly assumes the Bride's voice in amplifying the key term: Christ is "all sweet from top to bottom all"; he is sweet in all the stages of his life—"Sweet in the Virgin wombe and horses Manger"; he is all sweet metaphors and emblems— "My Love, my Lilly, my Rose and Crown / My brightest Glory, and my Hony sweet" (ll. 1, 14, 19-20); he is sweet in all his functions— mediatorial actions, righteousness, holiness. The metaphors pour forth thick and fast to explicate this sweetness:

> A Cabbinet of Holiness, Civit box
>     Of Heavenly Aromatick, still much more,
> A treasury of Spicery, rich knots,
>     Of Choicest Merigolds, a house of Store
>     Of never failing dainties to my tast
>     Delighting holy Palates, such thou hast.
>
> A sugar Mill, an Hony Hive most rich
>     Of all Celestial viands, golden box
> Top full of Saving Grace, a Mint house which
>     Is full of Angells, and a cloud that drops
>     Down better fare than ever Artist could,
>     More pleasant than the finest liquid Gold.
>                                        (ll. 43-54)

Then, recurring to the larger context of the verse—"I sat under his shadow with greate delight and his fruit was sweet to my taste"— the speaker without qualification expresses his own experience of this sweetness in the Bride's words:

> While I sat longing in this Shadow here
>     To tast the fruite this Apple tree all ripe
> How sweet these Sweetings bee. Oh! sweet good Cheere
>     How am I filld with sweet most sweet delight.
>     The fruite, while I was in its shady place
>     Was and to mee is now sweet to my tast.
>
> (ll. 61-66)

With Edward Taylor an era in the writing of religious lyric poetry ended, an era which began in England with Wyatt and Coverdale and reached its apogee with Donne and Herbert. The poets I have concentrated upon did not constitute a distinct school or write in a common style; rather, despite their variousness and individuality they developed and shared what was in large part a common poetics. This poetics derived its major impetus from Protestant conceptions of the Christian life, of the language and poetic genres of scripture, and of the role of art in religious expression. Furthermore, it drew upon a common body of materials (biblical tropes, typological symbolism, divine emblems, biblical lyric models, Protestant meditation, and Protestant sermon theory). Though certain emphases in Taylor's Puritan theology kept him from assuming (as others did) that he could produce worthy divine praises on the basis of this Protestant poetics, he was able to release a new vein of creativity in himself by using the familiar materials and paradigms of that poetics as a counterpoint to his own deliberately homely style.

After Taylor Protestant poetics was radically undermined by an attenuation of faith in dogmatic Christianity and in its sacred Book, which had served in so many ways as poetic model and resource. Some lesser poets whose concerns and achievements were rather devotional than artistic continued to write in these terms, and biblical imagery and typological reference remain generally important in later literature.[59] But major poets seeking to give lyric expression to religious impulses looked elsewhere for the grounds of a religious aesthetics— in universal religious principles, in romantic pantheism, in personal moral imperatives, in private mythologies, in ecclesiastical ritual, in existential *angst*. However, for sixteenth- and seventeenth-century English poets, and especially for Donne, Herbert, Vaughan, Traherne, and Taylor, the Protestant poetics here described provided a powerful stimulus to the imagination by promoting a profound creative response to the written word of scripture and inviting a searching scrutiny of the human heart. The consequence was a body of religious lyric unrivaled in our literature.

# Afterword

This analysis of the aesthetics governing a major strain of religious lyric poetry from Donne to Taylor intends to set up some landmarks in a vast terrain, much of which requires further exploration. For one thing, we ought to discover how far other religious lyrics of the period participate in the Protestant poetics here described. How well do these terms accommodate Herrick's *Noble Numbers?* Or the few but impressive religious lyrics of Ben Jonson, Andrew Marvell, or even Abraham Cowley? Or the vast quantity of minor devotional verse by Protestant poets such as Robert Aylett, Nicholas Breton, William Drummond of Hawthornden, Mildmay Fane, Phineas Fletcher, Fulke Greville, John Hall, Christopher Harvey, Francis Quarles, John Quarles, Joshua Sylvester, and George Wither?[1]

Also, though the basic contrasts are obvious enough, we might examine more precisely just how Tridentine aesthetics relates to this Protestant poetics. The question can be explored with reference to Crashaw and such earlier recusant poets as Robert Southwell, William Alabaster, and Henry Constable,[2] whose primary emphasis is upon the senses, the liturgy, and the lives of Christ, the Virgin, and various saints. The contrasts and possible points of connection might be especially illuminated by attention to Crashaw's use of emblem materials and his often startling epigrams on biblical texts. The comparison might also be usefully extended to other national literatures in the period, most notably the French religious lyric.[3]

Again, what of Milton? His psalm paraphrases belong to the tradition here described, and several lyrics (e.g., "On the Morning of Christ's Nativity," "The Passion," "Upon the Circumcision," Sonnets VII, XVIII, and XIX) mix elements derived from Protestant poetics with other generic resources. Yet probably the most fruitful study of Milton in these terms would focus upon *Paradise Lost*—upon the ways in which the prayers, praises, and songs of Adam and Eve and the angelic choir draw upon biblical models and resources in the Psalms, Canticles, and the Book of Revelation.

Finally, there are questions for literary historians pertaining to influence and continuity. I have suggested that Edward Taylor represents the end of an era, the exhaustion of the particular configuration of elements constituting a Protestant poetics of the religious lyric. Yet literary movements are not so neatly circumscribed as this judgment indicates, and some aspects of the Protestant poetics obviously survive, transformed, in later poetry. Poets of the eighteenth-century religious sublime, as David Morris has shown, often employ the biblical diction characteristic of poets in the previous century, but without their personal intensity. And though the Romantic poets exchanged the diction and imagery of the Bible for that of nature, M. H. Abrams has indicated how much they owe to the Christian psycho-biography which flourished in the seventeenth century.[4]

Study of these and related literary questions will, I trust, be encouraged by this account of the period in which a Protestant poetics of the religious lyric came to full fruition in England and America. As we have seen, this poetics gave rise to a brilliant and various body of major poems designed to explore and exhibit the truth—and beauty —to be found in the language of scripture and in the experience of living the Christian life.

# Notes

## CHAPTER 1

1 See, e.g., Steadman, *The Lamb and the Elephant: Ideal Imitation and the Context of Renaissance Allegory* (San Marino, 1974); Murrin, *The Veil of Allegory: Some Notes Toward a Theory of Allegorical Rhetoric in the English Renaissance* (Chicago and London, 1969); Allen, *Mysteriously Meant: The Rediscovery of Pagan Symbolism and Allegorical Interpretation in the Renaissance* (Baltimore and London, 1970); Heninger, *Touches of Sweet Harmony: Pythagorean Cosmology and Renaissance Poetics* (San Marino, 1974). See also Sir Philip Sidney, *The Defence of Poesie* (London, 1595).

2 All quotation of and references to Herbert's poetry and prose are to the edition by F. E. Hutchinson, *The Works of George Herbert* (Oxford, 1941; rev. ed., 1945), hereafter cited as Hutchinson.

3 See Abrams, *Natural Supernaturalism: Tradition and Revolution in Romantic Literature* (New York, 1971); Fletcher, *The Prophetic Moment: An Essay on Spenser* (Chicago and London, 1971); Wittreich, ed., *Milton and the Line of Vision* (Madison, 1975), especially the essays by Kathleen Williams, S. K. Heninger, and Joseph Wittreich; Kerrigan, *The Prophetic Milton* (Charlottesville, 1974); Frye, *Fearful Symmetry: A Study of William Blake* (Princeton, 1947); Roston, *Prophet and Poet: The Bible and the Growth of Romanticism* (London, 1965).

4 See Frye, *Anatomy of Criticism* (New York, 1966; 1st ed., Princeton, 1957), esp. pp. 131-162, 325-326.

5 For arguments locating the full flowering of a biblical aesthetics in the eighteenth and early nineteenth centuries, see David B. Morris, *The Religious Sublime: Christian Poetry and Critical Tradition in 18th-Century England* (Lexington, 1972); and Roston, *Prophet and Poet*.

6 Martz, *The Poetry of Meditation: A Study in English Religious Literature of the Seventeenth Century* (New Haven, 1962); Martz, *The Paradise Within: Studies in Vaughan, Traherne, and Milton* (New Haven, 1964); Grant, *The Transformation of Sin: Studies in Donne, Herbert, Vaughan, and Traherne* (Montreal and London, 1974).

7 Ross, *Poetry and Dogma: The Transfiguration of Eucharistic Symbols in Seventeenth-Century English Poetry* (New Brunswick, 1954).

8 Augustine, *De Doctrina Christiana*, trans. D. W. Robertson, Jr. (Indianapolis and New York, 1958).

9 Mazzeo, "St. Augustine's Rhetoric of Silence: Truth vs. Eloquence and Things vs. Signs," *Renaissance and Seventeenth-Century Studies* (New York and London, 1964), pp. 1-28, esp. p. 19.

10 Summers, *George Herbert, His Religion and Art* (London and Cambridge, Mass., 1954), pp. 73-79; Stein, *George Herbert's Lyrics* (Baltimore, 1968), pp. xiii-xxix; Fish, *Self-Consuming Artifacts: The Experience of Seventeenth-Century Literature* (Berkeley, 1972), esp. pp. 21-77, 156-223.

11 Curtius, *European Literature and the Latin Middle Ages*, trans. Willard R. Trask (New York, 1953; 1st ed., Princeton, 1953), pp. 39-48, 72-75, 203-246, 446-467, 547-558.

12 Sedulius, *Opus Paschale*, ed. Johannes Huemer, "Corpus Scriptorum Ecclesiasticorum Latinorum" (Vienna, 1885), X, 176-177; Leigh, *Annotations on Five Poetical Books of the Old Testament* (London, 1657), sig. A 6.

13 Jerome, "Prologus Galeatus," "Hieronymus Paulino," "In Psalterium," in *Biblia Sacra*, [Vulgate] (Venice, [1616]), sigs. +4 - +6$_v$, ++$_v$.

14 Isidore, *Etymologiarum*, I.xxxix.9-18, *Pat. Lat.*, LXXXII, 118-120.

15 Cassiodorus, "De Schematibus et Tropis, Necnon et quibusdam locis rhetoricis s. scripturae," *Pat. Lat.*, LXX, 1269-1280; *Expositio in Psalterium*, *Pat. Lat.*, LXX, 9-1056; Bede, *De Schematis et Tropis Sacrae Scripturae Liber*, *Pat. Lat.*, XC, 175-186.

16 Charlemagne to Abbot Baugulf, cited in Curtius, *European Literature and the Latin Middle Ages*, p. 48; "Le Familiari, x.4," in *Petrarch, the First Modern Scholar and Man of Letters*, trans. James Harvey Robinson (New York, 1898), pp. 261-264.

17 Augustine, *De Doctrina Christiana*, II.x, Robertson, p. 43.

18 Aquinas, *Summa Theologica*, I. Q.1, Art. 10, *Basic Writings*, ed. Anton C. Pegis, 2 vols. (New York, 1945), I, 16-17.

19 "Epistola X, to Can Grande della Scala," *Epistolae, the Letters of Dante*, ed. Paget Toynbee (Oxford, 1966), p. 199.

20 Campbell, *Divine Poetry and Drama in Sixteenth-Century England* (Cambridge and Berkeley, 1959).

21 Du Bartas, "L'Uranie," *La Muse Chrestiene* (Bordeaux, 1574), republished in revised form in *Les Œuvres* (Paris, 1579); see Campbell, *Divine Poetry and Drama*, pp. 74-92; Hallett Smith, "English Metrical Psalms in the Sixteenth Century and their Literary Significance," *HLQ*, 9 (1946), 249-271.

22 King James I, "The Uranie, or Heavenly Muse," *The Essayes of a Prentise, in the Divine art of poesie* (Edinburgh, 1584), sigs. D-G; Joshua Sylvester, trans., "Urania," in "Fragments and Other Small Workes of Bartas," *Devine Weekes and Workes . . .* , 2 vols. (London, 1605), II, 528-542, republished in 1608, 1611, 1613, 1621, 1641, etc. See, e.g., Antoine La Pujade, "La Muse Chrestienne," in *Les Œuvres Chrestiennes*, Part II (Paris, 1604), fols. 63-66; Robert Southwell, *Saint Peters Complaynt* (London, 1595), sigs. A2-A3; Sir John Stradling, *Divine Poems in Severall Classes* (London, 1625), pp. 74-86; J[oseph] F[letcher], *Christs Bloodie Sweat* (London, 1613), sig. [A 3]; Robert Aylett, "Urania, or the Heavenly Muse," *Divine, and Moral Speculations, in metrical numbers, upon various subjects* (London, 1654), pp. 89-97.

23 Baroway, "The Bible as Poetry in the English Renaissance: An Introduction," *JEGP*, 32 (1933), 447-480; "The Hebrew Hexameter: A Study

in Renaissance Sources and Interpretation," *ELH*, 2 (1935), 66-91; "'The Lyre of David': A Further Study in Renaissance Interpretation of Biblical Form," *ELH*, 8 (1941), 119-142; "The Accentual Theory of Hebrew Prosody," *ELH*, 17 (1950), 115-135.

24 Murray Roston, *Biblical Drama in England from the Middle Ages to the Present Day* (Evanston, 1968); Harold Fisch, *Jerusalem and Albion: The Hebraic Factor in Seventeenth-Century Literature* (New York, 1964).

25 Jason Rosenblatt, "Structural Unity and Temporal Concordance: The War in Heaven in *Paradise Lost*," *PMLA*, 87 (1972), 31-41; Rosenblatt, "The Mosaic Voice in *Paradise Lost*," *Milton Studies*, 7 (1975), 207-232; Michael Fixler, "The Apocalypse within *Paradise Lost*," in Thomas Kranidas, ed., *New Essays on* Paradise Lost (Berkeley, 1969), pp. 131-178; Leland Ryken, *The Apocalyptic Vision in* Paradise Lost (Ithaca and London, 1970); Kerrigan, *The Prophetic Milton*; Austin C. Dobbins, *Milton and the Book of Revelation: The Heavenly Cycle* (University, Alabama, 1975); Wittreich, "'A Poet Amongst Poets': Milton and the Tradition of Prophecy," in *Milton and the Line of Vision*, pp. 97-142; Burton O. Kurth, *Milton and Christian Heroism: Biblical Epic Themes and Forms in Seventeenth-Century England* (Berkeley, 1959); Lewalski, *Milton's Brief Epic: The Genre, Meaning, and Art of* Paradise Regained (Providence and London, 1966); Lewalski, "*Samson Agonistes* and the 'Tragedy' of the Apocalypse," *PMLA*, 85 (1970), 1050-1061.

26 Milton, *Complete Prose Works*, Vol. I, 1624-1642, ed. Don M. Wolfe (New Haven, 1953), pp. 812-816. Similar arguments are set forth in *PR*, IV.331-350 and in the "Preface" to *Samson Agonistes*.

27 See Summers, *George Herbert*; C. A. Patrides, "Introduction," *The English Poems of George Herbert* (London, 1974); E. C. Pettet, *Of Paradise and Light: A Study of Vaughan's* Silex Scintillans (Cambridge, 1960); Stanley Stewart, *The Expanded Voice: The Art of Thomas Traherne* (San Marino, 1970); Coburn Freer, *Music for a King: George Herbert's Style and the Metrical Psalms* (Baltimore, 1972); Heather Asals, "The Voice of George Herbert's 'The Church,'" *ELH*, 36 (1969), 511-528; Maren-Sofie Rostvig, "Structure as Prophecy: the influence of biblical exegesis upon theories of literary structure," in Alastair Fowler, ed., *Silent Poetry: Essays in Numerological Analysis* (London, 1970), pp. 32-72; Edward Gosselin, *The King's Progress to Jerusalem: Some Interpretations of David During the Reformation Period and Their Patristic and Medieval Background* (Los Angeles, 1976).

28 Donne, *Devotions upon Emergent Occasions* (1624); Vaughan, *The Mount of Olives: or, Solitary Devotions* (1652); Traherne, *Meditations upon the Six Days of Creation*, *Centuries of Meditation*, and *The Church's Year-Book* (wr. c. 1669-1674); Edward Taylor, *Preparatory Meditations before my Approach to the Lords Supper* (wr. 1682-1725).

29 Mario Praz, *Studies in Seventeenth-Century Imagery*, 2nd ed. (Rome, 1964); Rosemary Freeman, *English Emblem Books* (London, 1948); Summers, *George Herbert*; Rosalie Colie, "*My Ecchoing Song*": *Andrew Marvell's Poetry of Criticism* (Princeton, 1970).

30 This is not of course to deny that specific poems may be greatly illuminated by studying them in relation to the liturgy of specific feasts or seasons—as in Rosemond Tuve's fine study of Herbert's "The Sacrifice" with particular reference to the *Improperia* (Reproaches) of Good Friday, in *A Reading of George Herbert* (Chicago, 1952), pp. 19-99; or Helen Gardner's discussion of Donne's "La Corona" sonnets in relation to the Advent liturgy in her edition, *John Donne: The Divine Poems* (Oxford, 1952), pp. 57-59. Nor is it to deny some pervasive liturgical influence upon the structure and development of Herbert's *The Temple*. For a suggestive treatment of influences from the entire Christmastide liturgy upon the imagery and motifs of some poems and poetic sequences in Donne, Herbert, and Vaughan, see A. B. Chambers, "Christmas: The Liturgy of the Church and English Verse of the Renaissance," *Literary Monographs*, vol. 6, ed. Eric Rothstein and J. A. Wittreich, Jr. (Madison, 1975), pp. 109-151.

31 *The Booke of common-praier* ([London], 1559), sigs. A_v-[C vi_v]. See John E. Booty, ed., *The Book of Common Prayer, 1559* (Charlottesville, 1976), pp. 14-47. The Preface and Calendar of readings were issued with the first edition of the Prayerbook in 1549.

32 See the discussion in Booty, *Book of Common Prayer*, pp. 372-382.

33 Marvell's poems in this vein include "On a Drop of Dew," "The Coronet," "Eyes and Tears," "Bermudas," "A Dialogue between the Resolved Soul and Created Pleasure," and "Clorinda and Damon." I have discussed these poems in "Marvell as Religious Poet," in *Approaches to Marvell: The York Tercentenary Lectures*, ed. C. A. Patrides (London, 1978). See also Annabel Patterson, "*Bermudas* and *The Coronet*: Marvell's Protestant Poetics," *ELH*, 44 (1977), 478-499. Milton's relation to this lyric tradition is too complex to admit of treatment here, as his poems so constantly mix genres and their conventions. See, e.g., the discussion of Milton's use of psalmic materials in *Samson Agonistes* in Mary Ann Radzinowicz, *Toward Samson Agonistes: The Growth of Milton's Mind* (Princeton, 1978).

34 Martz, *Poetry of Meditation*; Mary P. Ramsey, *Les Doctrines Médiévales chez Donne*, 2nd ed. (Oxford, 1924); Patrick Grant, *The Transformation of Sin*; Dennis Quinn, "Donne's Christian Eloquence," *ELH*, 27 (1960), 276-297; Tuve, *A Reading of George Herbert*.

35 McAdoo, *The Spirit of Anglicanism: A Survey of Anglican Theological Method in the Seventeenth Century* (London, 1965), p. 5. See also Charles D. Cremeans, *The Reception of Calvinistic Thought in England* (Urbana, 1949).

36 Pettit, *The Heart Prepared: Grace and Conversion in Puritan Spiritual Life* (New Haven and London, 1966), p. 5, n. 5.

37 George and George, *The Protestant Mind of the English Reformation, 1570-1640* (Princeton, 1961), p. 69, and see n. 110.

38 Lewalski, *Donne's* Anniversaries *and the Poetry of Praise* (Princeton, 1973).

39 Halewood, *The Poetry of Grace: Reformation Themes and Structures in English Seventeenth-Century Poetry* (New Haven and London, 1970).

40 Luther, Lectures on Romans, trans. Wilhelm Pauck, "Library of

Christian Classics" (London, 1961); Luther, *A Methodicall Preface prefixed before . . . Romans*, trans. W. W. (London, [1590?]); *A Commentarie of . . . Martin Luther upon . . . Galathians*, trans.? (London, 1575); Calvin, *A Commentarie . . . upon the Epistle to the Galathians*, trans., R. V[aux?] ([London], 1581); Perkins, *The Arte of Prophecying. Or, A Treatise Concerning the Sacred and Onely True Manner and Methode of Preaching*, trans. Thomas Tuke, *Workes*, 3 vols. (London, 1612-1613), II, 650-651. See John S. Coolidge, The Pauline Renaissance in England: Puritanism and the Bible (Oxford, 1970).

41 Draxe, *The Earnest of our Inheritance* (London, 1613), p. 1.

42 *The Holy Bible* (London, 1611). Except where otherwise indicated, bible texts are quoted from this first edition of the Authorized (King James) Version [AV].

43 Aquinas, *Summa Theologica*, I, Q. 95, Art. I; *S.T.*, I-II, Q. 82, Art. 4; Q. 83, Art. 4; Q. 85, Arts. 1-6; Q. 86, Arts. 1-2, *Basic Works*, I, 911; II, 677-678, 684-685, 694-707.

44 Calvin, *Institutes*, I.xv.4, II.i.9, ed. John T. McNeill, 2 vols., "Library of Christian Classics" (London, 1960), I, 190, 253.

45 Donne, *Sermons*, ed. G. F. Potter and Evelyn Simpson, 10 vols. (Berkeley, 1953-1962), I, 155; VI, 116-117. See also I, 292-293.

46 Thomas Rogers, *The Faith, Doctrine, and religion, professed and protected in the Realme of England . . . Expressed in 39 Articles* (Cambridge, 1607), p. 47. Donne possessed a copy of Rogers' commentary on the Articles, containing Donne's own signature and motto. See Geoffrey Keynes, *A Bibliography of Dr. John Donne, Dean of Saint Paul's*, 4th ed. (Oxford, 1973), p. 275.

47 Donne, *Sermons*, II, 170; IX, 119. See William R. Mueller, *John Donne: Preacher* (Princeton, 1962), pp. 178-194.

48 Perkins, *A Golden Chaine: Or, The Description of Theologie, Workes*, I, 24.

49 Perkins, *An Exposition of the Symbole or Creed of the Apostles, Workes*, I, 284.

50 Perkins, *A Golden Chaine, Workes*, I, 78.

51 See Pettit, *The Heart Prepared*, pp. 48-124.

52 Calvin, *Institutes*, III.xi.11, McNeill, I, 739.

53 Luther, *Commentarie . . . upon . . . Galathians*, fols. 107-108ᵥ.

54 Ames, *The Marrow of Sacred Divinity*, trans. [John St. Nicholas?] (London, 1642), pp. 136-138; first Latin edition, *Medulla S. S. Theologiae* (Amsterdam, 1623).

55 Luther, *Lectures on Genesis*, ed. Jaroslav Pelikan, *Workes*, vol. 1- (St. Louis, 1958-    ), I, 64-65.

56 Calvin, *Institutes*, III.iii.9, McNeill, I, 601.

57 Perkins, *The Whole Treatise of the Cases of Conscience, Workes*, II, 16-18.

58 Hooker, *A Learned Discourse of Justification, Workes, and how the foundation of faith is overthrowne* (Oxford, 1612), pp. 4-7.

59 *Ibid.*, pp. 8, 26, 11.

60 Donne, *Sermons*, VII, 158-159; V, 316.

61 New, *Anglican and Puritan: The Basis of Their Opposition, 1558-1640* (Stanford, 1964), pp. 5-29. New uses the term "Anglican" to label those Englishmen who may be contrasted with the Puritans not only in regard to Church polity but also in terms of the doctrinal emphases discussed here. I have avoided the term as an anachronism—suggesting much more polarization in doctrinal matters than obtains before Laud, and strictly appropriate only after the Restoration. In the earlier part of the century, as New himself states, both factions are included within a doctrinal consensus best defined as Reformed Protestantism or Calvinism.

62 Donne, *Sermons*, I, 271-272.

63 *Ibid.*, III, 366.

64 Perkins, *A Golden Chaine, Workes*, I, 78-79.

65 Cited in Pettit, *Heart Prepared*, p. 68.

66 Perkins, *A Treatise tending unto a Declaration, whether a man be in the Estate of Damnation, or in the Estate of Grace, Workes*, I, 364; *Two Treatises*: I. *Of the nature and practise of repentance*. II. *Of the combat of the flesh and spirit, Workes*, I, 455.

67 Calvin, *Institutes*, III.iii.16, McNeill, I, 609.

68 Perkins, *The Estate of Damnation, or . . . Grace*, pp. 365-366.

69 Rogers, *Seven Treatises Containing such Direction as is Gathered out of the Holie Scriptures . . . called the practice of Christianitie* (London, 1603), pp. 68-71.

70 Perkins, *The Estate of Damnation, or . . . Grace*, pp. 368-370.

71 Rogers, "The Second Treatise, Shewing at Large what the Life of the True Beleever is," *Seven Treatises*, pp. 72-211.

72 "Preface," sigs. [A 5-B 4ᵥ]; Culverwell, "To the Christian Reader," sigs. A 3ᵥ-A 4.

73 Rogers, *Seven Treatises*, p. 44.

74 *Ibid.*, pp. 90-91, 140.

75 *Ibid.*, p. 59. See Herbert, "Praise (I)," "The Temper (I)," "Church-musick"; Vaughan, "Praise," "Chearfulness," "The Morning-watch"; Traherne, *Thanksgivings*; Taylor, "The Experience," "The Return."

76 Rogers, *Seven Treatises*, p. 44.

77 *Ibid.*, pp. 280, 120-124.

78 *Ibid.*, pp. 118-120, 259-278.

79 *Ibid.*, pp. 280, 114-118.

80 Perkins, *The Estate of Damnation, or . . . Grace*, pp. 371-373.

81 *Ibid.*, pp. 374-377.

82 All references to the texts of Donne's *Divine Poems* are to Helen Gardner's edition (see n. 30), hereafter cited as Gardner. For reasons explained in chap. 8, I retain as Gardner does not the order of the "Holy Sonnets" from the 1635 edition. See "Holy Sonnets" VI and XIV in that conventional numbering.

83 All references to the texts of Vaughan's poems are to L. C. Martin, *The Works of Henry Vaughan*, 2nd ed. (Oxford, 1957), hereafter cited as Martin.

84 All references to the texts of Traherne's poems are to the editions by H. M. Margoliouth, *Thomas Traherne: Centuries, Poems and Thanksgivings*, 2 vols. (Oxford, 1958), and Anne Ridler, ed., *Thomas Traherne: Poems, Centuries and Three Thanksgivings* (London, 1966), hereafter cited as Margoliouth, and Ridler.

85 All references to the texts of Taylor's poems are to the edition by Donald E. Stanford, *The Poems of Edward Taylor* (New Haven, 1960), hereafter cited as Stanford.

## CHAPTER 2

1 For the theory of the classical hymn in the Renaissance see O. B. Hardison, Jr., *The Enduring Monument: A Study of the Idea of Praise in Renaissance Literary Theory and Practice* (Chapel Hill, 1962), esp. pp. 95-102; Philip Rollinson, "The Renaissance of the Literary Hymn," *Renaissance Papers, 1968* (Durham, 1969), pp. 11-20; Rollinson, "A Generic View of Spenser's *Four Hymns*," *SP*, 68 (1971), 292-304; Rollinson, "Milton's Nativity Poem and the Decorum of Genre," *"Eyes Fast Fixt": Current Perspectives in Milton Methodology*, ed. Albert C. Labriola and Michael Lieb, *Milton Studies*, 7 (1975), 165-188. See also Julius-Caesar Scaliger, *Poetices libri septem*, I.xliv-xlv ([Lyons], 1561), pp. 47-49; Sidney, *Defence*, sigs. B 3ᵥ-B 4, Cᵥ-C 2.

2 René Wellek and Austin Warren, *Theory of Literature*, 3rd ed. (New York, 1956), pp. 226-237.

3 *Dictionary of the Bible*, ed. James Hastings, rev. ed., F. C. Grant and H. H. Rowley (Edinburgh, 1963), p. 103.

4 Gregory Nazianzen, *Carmina*, "Poemata Dogmatica XII," ll. 16-18, *Pat. Graec.*, XXXVII, 473; Cyril of Jerusalem, "Catechesis IV.xxxv," *Pat. Graec.*, XXXIII, 499; Miles Coverdale, *Biblia: The Byble: that is the holy Scrypture of the Olde and New Testament* (London, 1535); Immanuel Tremellius and Franciscus Junius, *Biblia Sacra* (London, 1593), sig. [A aa]. Jerome saw the Hagiographia as comprising nine books, but he found particular poetic quality in the Psalms, the Song of Songs, and Job. See "Prologus Galeatus," "Hieronymus Paulino," "In Psalterium," *Biblia Sacra*, sigs. +4 - +6ᵥ, ++ᵥ.

5 For discussion of this tradition see Lewalski, *Milton's Brief Epic*, pp. 10-28.

6 *The thyrde parte of the Byble conteyning these bokes: The Psalter. The Proverbes. Ecclesiastes. Cantica Canticorum* [London, 1550]. Similarly, the Douay Bible designates the parts of the Old Testament as Legal, Historical, Sapiential, and Prophetical, assimilating Job to the historical part and leaving the Psalms, Proverbs, Ecclesiastes, Canticles, Wisdom, and Ecclesiasticus as the Sapiential third part (*The Holie Bible faithfully translated . . . by the English College of Doway*, 2 vols. [Douai, 1609-1610]), I, sigs. ++2 - ++2ᵥ.

7 Luther's earliest hymns appeared in: *Etlich cristlich lider Lobgesang un Psalm* (Wittenburg, 1524); *Eyn Enchiridion odor Handbuchlein* (Erfurt,

1524); *Geystliche Gesangk Buchleyn* (Wittenburg, 1524); *Geistliche Lieder* (Wittenburg, 1529). For a good résumé and discussion of Luther's hymnody see John Julian, *A Dictionary of Hymnology*, rev. ed. (London, 1925), pp. 414-416, 703-704.

8 See the collection in *Geistliche Lieder* (Leipzig, 1545), a fully revised text containing 35 Luther hymns.

9 Cited in L. W. Bacon and N. H. Allen, *The Hymns of Martin Luther* (New York, 1883), p. xxi. For some consideration of Luther as hymn writer and "literary critic" of various books of the Bible see H. G. Haile, "Luther and Literacy," *PMLA*, 91 (1976), pp. 816-828.

10 *Goostly Psalmes and Spirituall Songes*, in *Remains of Miles Coverdale*, ed. George Pearson (Parker Society, Cambridge, 1846), pp. 533-588. Only one copy of Coverdale's first edition is extant, at Queens College, Oxford. For discussion of the debt to Luther see Julian, *Dictionary of Hymnology*, pp. 442-443, 916.

11 *Goostly Psalmes, Remains*, p. 537.

12 *Ibid.*, p. 539.

13 Hall, *The Courte of Virtue* (London, 1565), sig. B 6.

14 John Hall also produced such a collection, in ballad measure—*Certayne Chapters of the proverbes of Salomon drawen into metre* [London, 1550]—containing, in addition to Proverbs, portions of Ecclesiastes, Sapientia, Ecclesiasticus, and Psalms 34, 54, and 144. The volume was erroneously ascribed to Thomas Sternhold.

15 See the Sternhold-Hopkins Psalter, *The Whole Booke of Psalmes . . . by T. Starnhold  J. Hopkins  & others* (London, 1562); [Parker], *The Whole Psalter translated into English Metre* (London, [1567]); and Ravenscroft's revised edition of Sternhold-Hopkins, *The Whole Booke of Psalmes: with the Hymnes Evangelicall, and Songs Spirituall* (London, 1621).

16 Drayton, *The Harmonie of the Church* (London, 1591), sig. [A 3].

17 Sandys, *A Paraphrase upon the Divine Poems* (London, 1638). Some others are: Henry Dod, *All the Psalmes of David: With certeine Songs and Canticles of Moses, Debora, etc.* ([London], 1620); Samuel Slater, *Epithalamium, or Solomons Song: Together with the Songs of Moses, etc.* (London, 1653).

18 Sandys, *Paraphrase*, sig. \*\*\*; one such writer, Sidney Godolphin, accounts for Sandys' surprising exclusion of the Song of Songs on the ground that it might have proved too pleasing to our senses in Sandys' "perfumed" verse, sigs. \*\*$_v$-\*\*2.

19 *The Psalms, Hymns, and Spiritual Songs of the Old and New Testament*, 5th ed. (London, 1680); the first edition, of Psalms only, was *The Whole Booke of Psalmes* ([Cambridge, Mass.], 1640).

20 Wither, *The Hymnes and Songs of the Church* (London, 1623), sigs. A 2-A 2$_v$; an earlier version was *The Songs of the Old Testament* (London, 1621).

21 Wither, *Hymnes and Songs of the Church*, p. 7.

22 Boyd, *The Psalmes of David in Meeter* (Glasgow, 1648); *The Songs of the Old and New Testament* (Glasgow, 1648).

23 Sidney, *Defence*, sigs. C$_v$-C2. See also [Puttenham], *The Arte of English Poesie* (London, 1589), p. 230.

24 Donne, *Sermons*, IV, 179-180.

25 Rollock, *Lectures upon the Epistle of Paul to the Colossians* (London, 1603), pp. 337-338.

26 See, e.g., *The Dutch Annotations upon the whole Bible*, trans. Theodore Haak (London, 1657), pt. 3, sig. Rr 3; Paul Bayne, *An Entire Commentary upon the Whole Epistle of . . . the Apostle Paul to the Ephesians* (London, 1643).·

27 *The Bible: That is, The Holy Scriptures* [Geneva-Tomson version] (London, 1590), pt. 3, fol. 90.

28 Rogers, *A Strange Vineyard in Palaestina: in an Exposition of Isaiahs Parabolical Song of the Beloved* (London, 1623), pp. 8-9.

29 [Puttenham], *Arte of English Poesie*, pp. 21-23; Quintilian, *Institutio Oratoria*, III.vi.3-28; Menander, *Peri Epideiktikon*, in *Rhetores Graeci*, ed. Leonardi Spengel (Leipzig, 1856), III, 333-340; Scaliger, *Poetices libri septem*, I.xliv-1, III.cxii-cxiv, pp. 47-52, 162-163.

30 Hallett Smith, "English Metrical Psalms," pp. 249-271; Lily Campbell, *Divine Poetry and Drama*, pp. 9-54; Coburn Freer, *Music for a King*, pp. 1-115. A useful study of the analogous development of religious poetry in France, and the impact of the Psalms upon it, is Terence Cave's *Devotional Poetry in France c. 1570-1613* (Cambridge, 1969). See also Carl Calendar, "Metrical Translations of the Psalms in France and England: 1530-1650," Diss., Oregon, 1972; and Frances Yates, *The French Academies of the Sixteenth Century* (London, 1947).

31 E.g., Thomas Wyatt, *Certayne psalmes . . . called thee vii. penytentiall Psalmes* [London], 1549; Surrey (Psalms 8, 55, 73, and 88), *Poems of Henry Howard, Earl of Surrey*, ed. F. M. Padelford (Seattle, 1928), pp. 108-114; William Hunnis, *Seven Sobs of a Sorrowfull Soule for Sinne* [penitential psalms] ([London], 1583); Joseph Hall, *Some Fewe of Davids Psalms Metaphrased* [first nine psalms] (London, 1607); John Davies of Hereford, "The Dolefull Dove: or, *Davids* 7. Penitentiall Psalmes," in *The Muses Sacrifice, or Divine Meditations* (London, 1612); Sir Edwin Sandys, *Sacred Hymns. Consisting of fifti select psalms of David* ([London], 1615); George Buchanan, *An Assay, or Buchanan his Paraphrase of the first twentie Psalms of David* (London, 1627); Francis Bacon, *Translation of Certaine Psalmes into English Verse* [Psalms 1, 12, 90, 104, 126, 137, 147, 149—dedicated to George Herbert] (London, 1625); Milton, Psalms 114, 136, 80-88, 1-8, in Merritt Y. Hughes, ed., *John Milton: Complete Poetry and Major Prose* (New York, 1957), pp. 3-4, 149-158, 162-167. Subsequent references to Milton's poetry will be to this edition.

32 Noted by Freer, *Music for a King*, pp. 14-15.

33 Crowley, *The Psalter of David newely translated into Englysh metre* ([London], 1549); Sternhold-Hopkins, etc., *The Whole Booke of Psalmes*;

and see Freer, *Music for a King*, p. 11; Parker, *The Whole Psalter*; James I [and William Alexander], *The Psalmes of King David, Translated by King James* ([London], 1631); Ravenscroft, *The Whole Booke of Psalmes*; Sandys, *Paraphrase upon the Psalmes* [London], 1636; George Wither, *The Psalmes of David Translated into Lyrick-Verse* (The Netherlands, 1632); H[enry] K[ing], *The Psalmes of David, from the New Translation of the Bible Turned to Meter* (London, 1651); Clement Marot and Theodore de Bèze, *Les Pseaumes mis en Rime Françoise*, with *La Bible* ([Geneva], 1562 —the first complete Marot-Bèze Psalter); J.C.A. Rathmell, ed., *The Psalms of Sir Philip Sidney and The Countess of Pembroke* (Garden City, 1963). For discussion of the composition, dating, and manuscript circulation of the work see William A. Ringler, Jr., ed., *The Poems of Sir Philip Sidney* (Oxford, 1962), pp. 500-516; *Whole Booke of Psalmes* [Bay Psalm Book].

34 *The Whole Booke of Psalmes*, T.P.

35 *The Whole Book of Psalmes* (Cambridge, 1647), T.P.

36 Wither, *A Preparation to the Psalter* (London, 1619), pp. 3, 7.

37 Josephus, *Antiquities of the Jews*, VII.xii.3, in *Josephus*, ed. H. St. J. Thackeray, 8 vols. (Loeb: London, 1926-1943), V, 522; Eusebius, *Preparatio Evangelica*, XI.v, *Pat. Graec.*, XXI, 854. Both are excerpted and quoted in the prefatory matter of Archbishop Parker's *Psalter*, sigs. F iii_v-F iiii_v. See also Jerome, "Hieronymus Paulino," *Biblia Sacra*, sig. [+6]: "David Simonides noster. Pindarus & Alcaeus Flaccus quoque Catullus, atque Serenus"; and Jerome, "Prefatio in librum II Chronicorum Eusebii," *Pat. Graec.*, XIX, 313-314: "Denique quid Psalterio canorius, quod in morem nostri Flacci, et Graeci Pindari, nunc iambo currit, nunc Alcaico personat, nunc Sapphico tumet, nunc semipede ingreditur?"

38 Gomarus, *Davidis Lyra: seu nova Hebraea S. Scripturae Ars Poetica* (Lyons, 1637); Lodge, *A Defence of Poetry, Music, and Stage-Plays*, ed. David Laing (London, 1855), p. 10; Churchyard, "A Praise of Poetrie" (London, 1595), rpt. with *A Musicall Consort of Heavenly Harmonie* (London, 1817), p. 35; Hammond, *A Paraphrase and Annotations upon the Books of the Psalms* (London, 1659), p. 2.

39 Sidney, *Defence*, sig. B 4; Ainsworth, *Annotations upon the Five Bookes of Moses, the Booke of the Psalmes, and the Song of Songs* (London, 1637), *Psalmes*, pp. [194-195]; Wither, *Preparation to the Psalter*, pp. 58-63. For studies of Renaissance theories of the Hebrew meters, see the several articles by Baroway cited in chap. 1, n. 23, above.

40 *The Holie Bible* [Douay], II, 5-6.

41 "Athanasius in Psalmos," Parker, *Psalter*, sig. B iv_v.

42 "Basilius in Psalmos," Parker, *Psalter*, sigs. E ii, E iii.

43 Martin Luther, *A Manual of the Book of Psalms*, trans. Henry Cole (London, 1837), p. 5; *Biblia Sacra*, sigs. Aaa 2-Aaa 3_v; *Dutch Annotations*, sig. Iiii 2_v.

44 "Basilius in Psalmos," Parker, *Psalter*, sig. E ii_v.

45 "Athanasius in Psalmos," Parker, *Psalter*, sig. [B iv_v].

46 Luther, *Manual*, pp. 5-7.

47 Calvin, *The Psalmes of David and others*, trans. [Arthur Golding] (London, 1571), sig. [*6ᵥ].

48 [John Bate], *The Psalme of Mercy: Or, A Meditation upon the 51. Psalme* (London, 1625), sig. A 4.

49 Donne, *Sermons*, V, 299.

50 *Annotations upon all the Books of the Old and New Testament . . . By the Joynt-Labour of Certain Learned Divines* (London, 1645), sig. XX 2.

51 In Parker, *Psalter*, sigs. C iiᵥ-D iv.

52 Luther, *Manual*, pp. 13-14; Beza, *The Psalmes of David*, trans. Anthonie Gilbie (London, 1581), p. [A 7].

53 Diodati, *Pious and Learned Annotations upon the Holy Bible*, 2nd ed. (London, 1648), pt. I, p. 321.

54 Luther, *Manual*, pp. 9-10.

55 Parker, *Psalter*, sig. [VV iv].

56 See Rathmell, ed., *Psalms of . . . Sidney*, "Introduction," pp. xi-xxxii.

57 Ainsworth, *Annotations upon . . . Psalmes*, p. 5.

58 Wither, *Preparation to the Psalter*, p. 54.

59 Strigelius, *A Proceeding in the Harmonie of King Davids Harpe*, trans. Richard Robinson (London, [1595-1596]), sig. A 2ᵥ; Beza, *Christian Meditations upon eight Psalmes of the Prophet David*, trans. I. S. [John Stubs] (London, 1582). The tradition that the Psalms, or some of them, are meditations, was handed down by, e.g., Thomas Aquinas' commentary on the Psalms, *Commentarii in soliloquia sive hymnos Davidicos* [Lyons, 1520], sig. a iiᵥ; and by the preface to the Book of Psalms in *The Holy Byble* [Bishops'] (London, 1585), pt. 1, fol. [267ᵥ], which reprints the comment of Basil the Great, "Some intituleth it, *liber contemplationum, sive soliloquiorum*: A booke of contemplations or secrete meditations, whereby the godly speaketh solitarily and alone to almightie God."

60 Hammond, *Annotations upon . . . Psalms*, p. 510.

61 Beza, *Psalmes of David*, pp. 304-305; for another view of these psalms as specifically ceremonial, see Luther, *A Commentarie upon the Fifteene Psalmes, called Psalmi Graduum, that is, Psalmes of Degrees*, trans. Henry Bull (London, 1615).

62 Gataker, "Davids Instructor," in *Certaine Sermons, First Preached, and after Published at Several Times* (London, 1637).

63 *Dutch Annotations*, pt. 1, sig. Oooo.

64 Donne, *Sermons*, V, 288.

65 Wither, *Preparation to the Psalter*, p. 77.

66 Wither, *Psalmes of David*, sig. A 6ᵥ.

67 Quarles, *Divine Fancies: Digested into Epigrammes, Meditations, and Observations* (London, 1632), Bk. IV, no. 39, p. 176.

68 Donne, *Sermons*, II, 49-50.

69 *Ibid.*, V, 315; IV, 123.

70 *Ibid.*, VI, 293; V, 270. See also II, 50 ff., 144 ff.; V, 327-328, 364 ff.; VI, 39 ff.

71 *Ibid.*, II, 144.

72 *Ibid.*, IX, 251-252, 350.

73 *Ibid.*, II, 72-78; VIII, 193.

74 *Ibid.*, V, 289.

75 *Ibid.*, V, 364.

76 *Ibid.*, V, 270-271.

77 *Ibid.*, IX, 350.

78 The Junius-Tremellius Bible does, however, present the Psalms in five books, according to the Hebrew divisions: 1-41, 42-72, 73-89, 90-106, 107-150, *Biblia Sacra*, pt. 3, fols. 16-53. See also, e.g., Richard Bernard, *David's Musick . . . unfolded* (London, 1616), p. 2; and Wither's summary, *Preparation to the Psalter*, pp. 44-53.

79 Wither, *Preparation to the Psalter*, pp. 48, 50-53.

80 Augustine, *Expositions on the Book of Psalms*, trans. J. Tweed, et al., 6 vols. (Oxford, 1847-1857), VI, 453.

81 Parker, *Psalter*, pp. 146, 280, 424.

82 Wither, *Preparation to the Psalter*, p. 47.

83 Gardner, pp. 33-35.

84 William Baldwin, *The Canticles or Balades of Salomon, phraselyke declared in Englysh metres* ([London], 1549); Jud Smith, *A misticall devise of the spirituall and godly love between Christ the Spouse, and the Church or Congregation* [5th and 6th chapters] (London, 1575); Dudley Fenner, *The Song of Songs* (Middleburgh, 1587); Gervase Markham, *The Poem of Poems: or, Sions Muse* (London, [1596]); Michael Drayton, "The most excellent Song which was Salomons," *The Harmonie of the Church* ([London, 1591]); Robert Aylett, *The Song of Songs Which Was Solomons*, in *Divine, and Moral Speculations in Metrical Numbers* (London, 1643); George Wither, "The Song of Songs," in *Hymnes and Songs of the Church*; Henry Ainsworth, *Solomons Song of Songs. In English metre* (London, 1623); Francis Quarles, *Sions Sonets. Sung by Solomon the King, and periphras'd by Francis Quarles* (London, 1625). For a brief discussion of the sixteenth-century metrical versions of Solomon see Campbell, *Divine Poetry and Drama*, pp. 55-66.

85 Proverbs, by, e.g., Philip Melancthon, *Proverbia Salomonis iuxta Hebraicam veritatem* (Nurenburg, 1534); [John Hall], *Certayne Chapters of the proverbes of Salomon*, chaps. 1-11; Hall, *Courte of Virtue* (chap. 30); Wither, "Song of King Lemuel, Prov. 31:10," *Songs of the Old Testament*, p. 35, reprinted in *Hymnes and Songs of the Church*, pp. 9-10; Anon., "A most excellent new dittie, wherein is shewed the saage sayings, and wise sentences of Salomon," noted in Campbell, *Divine Poetry and Drama*, p. 63. Ecclesiastes, by, e.g., Surrey, "Ecclesiastes 1-5," *Poems*, pp. 100-108; Hall, *Certayne Chapters of the proverbes* (Eccles. 1-3); Henry Lok, *Ecclesiastes, Otherwise Called the Preacher. Containing Salomons Sermons or Commentaries . . . upon the 49. Psalme of David . . . paraphrastically dilated in English Poesie* (London, 1597); George Sandys, "A Paraphrase upon Ecclesiastes," *Paraphrase upon the Divine Poems*; Francis Quarles, *Solomons Recantation, entituled Ecclesiastes, Paraphrased* (London, 1645).

86 Origen, *The Song of Songs. Commentary and Homilies*, trans. R. P. Lawson (London, 1957), p. 41.

87 *Ibid.*, p. 53.

88 *Holie Bible* [Douay], II, 333-334.

89 Henoch Clapham, *Three Partes of Salomon his Song of Songs, expounded* (London, 1603), p. 4.

90 Hall, *Salomons Divine Arts* (London, 1609); Rogers, *A Golden Chaine . . . also, The Pretious Pearles of King Salomon* (London, 1587).

91 Beza, *Sermons upon the Three First Chapters of the Canticle of Canticles*, trans. John Harmar (Oxford, 1587), p. 12; see also, [William Gouge], *An Exposition of the Song of Solomon: called Canticles* (London, 1615), pp. 1-2.

92 Perkins, *Arte of Prophecying*, p. 648.

93 *Biblia Sacra*, pt. 3, fol. 53ᵥ; *English Annotations*, sig. DDDᵥ.

94 E.g., *Biblia Sacra* [Junius-Tremellius], pt. 3, fol. 53ᵥ; *Holie Bible* [Douay], II, 268; T[homas] W[ilcox], *A Short, yet Sound Commentarie: written on . . . The Proverbs of Salomon* (London, 1589), p. 1; *Dutch Annotations*, sig. [Aaaaa 4]; Diodati, *Annotations*, pt. 1, p. 387.

95 This tradition is traced in detail by Cornelius à Lapide, *Commentaria in Proverbia Salomonis* (Antwerp, 1740; 1st ed., Paris, 1637), pp. 1-2.

96 *Holy Byble* [Bishops'], prefatory matter, sig. ¶¶ᵥ; *The Bible* [Geneva] (Geneva, 1560), pt. 1, fol. 267.

97 Miles Mosse, *Scotlands Welcome. A Sermon Preached at Needham* (London, 1603), p. 6.

98 *The Bible* [Geneva], pt. 1, fol. 267; *Biblia Sacra*, pt. 3, fol. 53ᵥ; "Sententiae, verba, sive dicta graviter & paucis concinnata, quae in omnium animis haerere, & in ore versari debent"; Trapp, *A Commentary or Exposition upon These following Books of holy Scripture; Proverbs of Solomon, Ecclesiastes, the Song of Songs, etc.*, in *Annotations upon the Whole Bible*, III (London, 1660), p. 1.

99 Pellican, *In Job, Psalterium, Proverbia, Ecclesiasten, & Cantica Salomonis . . . Commentarii* (Zurich, 1581): "Proverbia vel similitudines quae Graecis parabolae dicuntur."

100 Wilcox, *Short, yet sound Commentarie*, p. 1.

101 Donne, *Sermons*, VII, 315.

102 *Holie Bible* [Douay], II, 268.

103 Cleaver, *A Briefe Explanation of the Whole Booke of the Proverbs of Salomon* (London, 1615), pp. 1-2.

104 *The Bible* [Geneva], pt. 1, fols. 267, 270; *Dutch Annotations*, sig. [Aaaaa 4]; Diodati, *Annotations*, pt. 1, p. 387; Matthew Henry, *An Exposition of the Five Poetical Books of the Old Testament* (London, 1710), sig. Eeeᵥ.

105 Cleaver, *Briefe Explanation*, pp. 152-153.

106 Wither, *Hymnes and Songs of the Church*, pp. 9-10.

107 Melancthon, *Proverbia Salomonis*.

108 Lapide, *Commentaria in Proverbia Salomonis*, pp. 2-3, 217.

109 Bacon, *De dignitate et augmentis scientiarum libros ix* (London, 1623), p. 388; *Of the Advancement and Proficience of Learning, or the Partitions of Sciences IX bookes*, trans. Gilbert Wats (Oxford, 1640), p. 371. See also pp. 107-108, 371-397, and Bacon, *Of the Proficience and Advancement of Learning, Divine and Humane* (London, 1605), I, 30; II, 18ᵥ-19, 89.

110 See, e.g., Origen, *Song of Songs, Commentary*, p. 41. Jerome, "Hieronymus Paulino," *Biblia Sacra* [Vulgate], sig. [+6]: "Solomon . . . mores corregis [in Proverbs], naturam docet [in Ecclesiastes] Ecclesiam jungit, & Christum sanctarumque nuptiarum dulce canit epithalamium [in Canticles]."

111 John Serranus, *A Godlie and Learned Commentarie upon . . . Ecclesiastes*, trans. John Stockwood (London, 1585), sig. PP ii,ᵥ; Donne, *Sermons*, III, 48; Granger, *A Familiar Exposition or Commentarie on Ecclesiastes* (London, 1621), sig. A 7-A 7ᵥ.

112 *The Holie Bible* [Douay], II, 317; *Biblia Sacra* [Junius-Tremellius], pt. 3, fol. 65; Lapide, *Commentarius in Ecclesiasten, Canticum Canticorum et Librum Sapientiae* (Antwerp, 1725), p. 5 (*Ecclesiastes*, 1st ed., 1639). Patrick, *A Paraphrase upon the Book of Ecclesiastes* (London, 1710), pp. viii-ix.

113 *The Bible* [Geneva-Tomson], pt. 2, fol. 37ᵥ.

114 [Martin Luther], *An Exposition of Salomons Booke, called Ecclesiastes or the Preacher* (London, 1573), pp. 5-6.

115 Beza, *Ecclesiastes, or the Preacher. Solomons Sermon made to the people* (Cambridge, [1593?]), sig. A 2.

116 Serranus, *Commentarie*, p. 1.

117 *Dutch Annotations*, pt. 1, sig. Iiiiᵥ.

118 Donne, *Sermons*, IX, 279.

119 Surrey, "Ecclesiastes i-v," *Poems*, pp. 100-108; Lok, *Ecclesiastes*.

120 Luther, *Exposition of . . . Ecclesiastes*, p. 10ᵥ.

121 Donne, *Sermons*, III, 51, 48.

122 Lok, *Ecclesiastes*, pp. 1, 116; Luther, *Exposition of . . . Ecclesiastes*, sig. B iiᵥ-B iii.

123 In the Roman Catholic tradition the Spouse was also identified as the Virgin. The Douay Bible (II, 335) traces patristic warrant for "three sortes of spouses"—the Church as the "*General Spouse*," every particular holy soul as the "special spouse," and "his singular spouse, his most blessed and most immaculate Virgin Mother." Lapide, *Commentarius in . . . Canticum Canticorum*, explicates every part of the Song in these three senses.

124 Augustine, *City of God*, XVII.xx, *The Works of Aurelius Augustine*, ed. Marcus Dods (Edinburgh, 1871-1876), II, 212.

125 *The Bible* [Geneva], pt. 2, fol. 40ᵥ.

126 Origen, *Song of Songs*, pp. 51, 98.

127 Beza, *Sermons upon . . . Canticles*, sig. [¶ 4]; Lapide, *Commentarius in . . . Canticum Canticorum*, sig. ** 2ᵥ.

128 *Dutch Annotations*, pt. 1, sig. Mmmmm; see also *Biblia Sacra* [Junius-

Tremellius], pt. 3, fol. 70; *English Annotations*, sig. FFF v$_v$.

129 *The Most Sacred Bible* [Taverner's edition] (London, 1539), p. CCXIX.

130 *Holie Bible* [Douay], II, 335.

131 See, e.g., Origen, *Song of Songs*, p. 247. Cf. 243-244, 252-253; *Holie Bible* [Douay], II, 335-337; Bernard of Clairvaux, *Cantica Canticorum: Eighty-six Sermons on the Song of Solomon*, trans. Samuel J. Eales (London, 1895), pp. 12-17, 347-354.

132 Fenner, *Song of Songs*, sigs. B 2$_v$-B 3.

133 Clapham, *Salomon his Song of Songs*, p. 2. See also pp. 1, 91, 141.

134 Wither, *Preparation to the Psalter*, p. 96.

135 *Biblia Sacra* [Junius-Tremellius], "Argument," pt. 3, fol. 70.

136 [William Gouge], *An Exposition of the Song of Solomon: called Canticles* (London, 1615), p. 2. Chap. 8 is interpreted as a historical survey, presenting specific references to the Incarnation, the calling of the Gentiles, and the conversion of the Jews at the last day.

137 Sibbes, *Bowels Opened: Or, A Discovery of the Neare and Deare Love, Union and Communion betwixt Christ, and the Church, and consequently betwixt Him and every beleeving Soule* (London, 1641), pp. 4-5.

138 Origen, *Songs of Songs*, pp. 47, 76, 77, 268; 240-248.

139 Bernard, *Cantica Canticorum*, pp. 317, 523-524.

140 De Sales, *The Mystical Explanation of the Canticle of Canticles*, trans. H. B. Mackey (London, 1908, first pub. 1643), sig. xvii, pp. 36, 1-40.

141 *Holie Bible* [Douay], II, 334.

. 142 Gyffard [Gifford], *Fifteene Sermons, upon the Song of Salomon* (London, 1598).

143 Dove, *The Conversion of Salomon* (London, 1613).

144 Robotham, *An Exposition on the whole booke of Solomons Song* (London, 1651), esp. pp. 711 ff.

145 Watters, "With Bodilie Eyes: A Study of Puritan Iconography, 1670-1810," Diss. Brown 1979, pp. 40-83.

146 Brightman, *A Commentary on the Canticles or Song of Solomon . . .*, in *The Workes of . . . Thos. Brightman* (London, 1644); Cotton, *A Brief Exposition of . . . Canticles* (London, 1642).

147 Jerome, "Hieronymus Paulino," *Biblia Sacra*, sig. +6; Slater, *Epithalamium, or Solomons Song* (London, 1653), sig. A 3$_v$; Robotham, *Solomons Song*, p. 7; Donne, *Sermons*, IX, 132; Dove, *Conversion of Salomon*, p. 13.

148 Hall, *An Open and Plaine Paraphrase upon the Song of Songs, which is Salomons* (London, 1609), sig. N 2-N 2$_v$; Henry, *An Exposition of the Five Poetical Books of the Old Testament* (London, 1710), sig. iv.

149 Baldwin, *The Canticles or Balades of Salomon, phraselyke declared in English Metres* ([London], 1549), sigs. A iv, A ii; Thomas Matthew, *The Byble* ([London], 1537), sig. Ccxlv$_v$. See also *Most Sacred Bible* [Taverner's edition].

150 Dove, *Conversion of Salomon*, pp. 8-13.

151 Clapham, *Salomon his Song of Songs*, p. 5.

152 Origen, "First Homily," *The Song of Songs*, p. 268.

153 *Holie Bible* [Douay], II, 334; *The Byble* [Matthew], sigs. Ccxlv$_v$-Ccxlvii; Beza, *Sermons upon the Three First Chapters of the Canticle of Canticles*, p. 8; Paraeus, *A Commentary upon the Divine Revelation of . . . John*, trans. Elias Arnold (Amsterdam, 1644), p. 20.

154 Lapide, *Commentarius . . . in Canticum Canticorum*, sig. \*\*4-\*\*4$_v$; Milton, *Reason of Church Government, Prose Works*, I, 815.

155 [Markham], *The Poem of Poems. Or, Sions Muse, Contayning the divine Song of King Salomon, divided into eight Eclogues* (London [1596]).

156 *Ibid.*, sigs. B, I.

157 Origen, *Song of Songs*, pp. 46-50; Diodati, *Annotations*, pt. 1, p. 435; *English Annotations*, sig. FFF v$_v$.

158 Beza, *Sermons on . . . Canticles*, sig. ¶ 2$_v$; Gouge, *An Exposition of the Song of Salomon* (London, 1615), sig. A 3$_v$; Aylett, *The Song of Songs*, p. [96].

159 Lapide, *Commentarius in . . . Canticum Canticorum*, sigs. \*\*4 AA; Patrick, *The Song of Salomon Paraphrased* (London, 1710), p. 38.

160 Cotton, *Exposition of . . . Canticles*, p. 9.

161 For this theory see, e.g., *Biblia Sacra* [Junius-Tremellius], pt. 4, fols. 65$_v$-66; Calvin, *Commentaries on the Book of the Prophet Jeremiah and the Lamentations*, trans. John Owen, 5 vols. (Edinburgh, 1850), V, 299; Heinrich Bullinger, *Jeremias . . . Accessit his brevis Threnorum explicatio* (Zurich, 1575), sig. Bb 4; John Hull, *An Exposition upon a Part of the Lamentations of Jeremie* (London, 1618), pp. 11-12; Wither, *Hymnes and Songs of the Church*, pp. 7, 22.

162 For this view see, e.g., Calvin, *Commentaries on the Four Last Bookes of Moses*, trans. Charles W. Bingham, 4 vols. (Edinburgh, 1852-1855), IV, 355; *Biblia Sacra* [Junius-Tremellius], pt. 1, fol. 173$_v$; pt. 4, fol. 10; Rogers, *Strange Vineyard*, pp. 5, 6, 9.

163 See Lewalski, *Donne's Anniversaries and the Poetry of Praise*, pp. 219-263.

164 For this theory see, e.g., Rogers, *Strange Vineyard*, p. 8; Wither, *Preparation to the Psalter*, pp. 54, 71-75; Diodati, *Annotations*, pt. 2, pp. 451, 476; Thomas Brightman, *A Revelation of the Apocalyps: Containing an Exposition of the whole Book of the Revelation*, in *Workes* (London, 1644), pp. 65, 254; Heinrich Bullinger, *A Hundred Sermons upon the Apocalips* (London, 1561), pp. 172, 177, 474, 559-562; George Gifford, *Sermons upon the Whole Book of the Revelation* (London, 1599), pp. 232-234, 365, 370.


CHAPTER 3

1 Donne, *Devotions upon Emergent Occasions*, ed. Anthony Raspa (Montreal and London, 1975), "Expostulation 19," p. 99.

2 Ross, *Poetry and Dogma*, p. 61. See above, chap. 1, p. 5.

3 Davies, *The Worship of the English Puritans* (London, 1948), p. 270.

4 Augustine, *De Doctrina*, I.i-ii, Robertson, pp. 7-9.

5 *Ibid.*, I.ii, xii, Robertson, pp. 9, 13. See Fish, *Self-Consuming Artifacts*, pp. 21-43.

6 Augustine, *De Trinitate*, *Works*, ed. Dods, VII, esp. pp. 424-429; *De Doctrina*, I.xxxvi-xl, Robertson, pp. 30-33.

7 *De Doctrina*, III.xxix, Robertson, pp. 102-103.

8 *Ibid.*, III.xxix, Robertson, pp. 103-104.

9 Mazzeo, "St. Augustine's Rhetoric of Silence," pp. 10-11.

10 *De Doctrina*, II.vi, Robertson, p. 38.

11 *Ibid.*, III.x, I.xxxix, Robertson, pp. 88, 32.

12 *Ibid.*, III.xxvii, Robertson, pp. 101-102.

13 Mazzeo, "St. Augustine's Rhetoric of Silence," pp. 19, 24. See Fish, *Self-Consuming Artifacts*, pp. 21-43.

14 Aquinas, *Summa Theologica*, I, Q.1, Art. 10, *Basic Writings*, I, 16-17. See also *Quodlibitales Questiones* [Paris, 1516], VII, Q.6, Arts. 14-16, fols. 93v-94.

15 *Summa Theologica*, I, Q.1, Art. 10, *Basic Writings*, I, 16-17.

16 *Ibid.*, p. 17.

17 See Madsen, *From Shadowy Types to Truth: Studies in Milton's Symbolism* (New Haven and London, 1968), pp. 22-26.

18 Aquinas, *Scriptum Super Primum Magistri Sententiae* [Peter Lombard], Prolog., Q.1, Art. 5, ad. 3 ([Venice], 1503), fol. 5v: "Ad tertium dicendum, quod poetica scientia est de his quae propter defectum veritatis non possunt a ratione capi; unde oportet quod quasi quibusdam simultudinibus ratio seducatur: theologia autem est de his quae sunt supra rationem; et ideo modus symbolicus utrique communis est, cum neutra rationi proportionetur"; *Summa Theologica*, I, Q.1, Art. 9, *Basic Writings*, I, 15.

19 *Summa Theologica*, I, Q.1, Art. 9, *Basic Writings*, I, 15-16.

20 J. S. Preus, *From Shadow to Promise: Old Testament Interpretation from Augustine to the Young Luther* (Cambridge, Mass., 1969); H. Jackson Forstman, *Word and Spirit: Calvin's Doctrine of Biblical Authority* (Stanford, 1962); R. S. Wallace, *Calvin's Doctrine of the Word and Sacrament* (London, 1953); U. Milo Kaufmann, The Pilgrim's Progress *and Traditions in Puritan Meditation* (New Haven and London, 1966); Madsen, *From Shadowy Types to Truth*; Lewalski, *Donne's* Anniversaries *and the Poetry of Praise*, chaps. 3-5; Lewalski, "Typological Symbolism and the 'Progress of the Soul' in Seventeenth-Century Literature," in *Literary Uses of Typology from the Late Middle Ages to the Present*, ed. Earl Miner (Princeton, 1977), pp. 79-114.

21 *Institutes*, IV.xvii.20-21, McNeill, II, 1383-1386.

22 *Ibid.*, IV.xvii.11, McNeill, II, 1371.

23 *Ibid.*, IV.xvii.10, McNeill, II, 1370-1371.

24 Wiclif, *The true Copye of a Prolog written about two C. yeres paste* (London, 1550), pp. [94-95].

25 Erasmus, *Ecclesiastae, Sive de Ratione Concionandi* (Basle, 1535), Book III.

26 [Luther], *Exposition of . . . Ecclesiastes*, p. 8ᵥ.

27 William Tyndale, "Prologue to . . . Exodus," *The Whole Workes . . .* (London, 1573), p. 7.

28 Bernard, *The Faithfull Shepherd*, 2nd ed. (London, 1621), p. 41.

29 *Ibid.*, pp. 47-48.

30 Weemse, *The Christian Synagogue*, 4th ed., in *Workes*, 4 vols. (London, 1632-1637), I, 278-288.

31 Perkins, *Arte of Prophecying*, *Workes*, II, 650.

32 *Ibid.*, p. 656.

33 Perkins, *The Golden Chaine*, *Workes*, I, 72.

34 Sidney, *Defence of Poesie*, sig. [B 4].

35 Wither, *Preparation to the Psalter*, pp. 71, 75.

36 Cassiodorus, "De Schematibus et Tropis," *Pat. Lat.*, LXX, 1269-1280; *Expositio in Psalterium*, *Pat. Lat.*, LXX, 9-1056.

37 Bede, "De Schematis," *Pat. Lat.*, XC, 175-186.

38 Melancthon, *Institutiones Rhetoricae* (Haguenau, [1521]).

39 Peacham, *The Garden of Eloquence* (London, 1577), sig. A iii.

40 Matthias Flacius [Illyricus], *Clavis Scripturae*, 2 pts. (Basle, 1617), I, 176.

41 *Ibid.*, II, Tract 1, 64-83; Tract 5, 450-524.

42 Glass, *Philologiae sacrae, qua totius sacrosanctae Veteris et Novi Testimenti Scripturae . . . Libri Quinque*, 3rd. ed. (Frankfurt, 1653; 1st ed., Jena, 1623).

43 *Ibid.*, pp. 1045-1480.

44 Lukin, *Introduction to the Holy Scripture* (London, 1669), sig. [A 8-A 8ᵥ].

45 *Ibid.*, pp. 101-102.

46 Hall, *Centuria Sacra* (London, 1654); *Rhetorica Sacra: Or, a Synopsis of the most materiall Tropes and Figures contained in the sacred Scriptures* (London, 1654), sig. L 3-L 3ᵥ.

47 Smith, *The Mysterie of Rhetorique Unvail'd* (London, 1656), T.P.

48 *Ibid.*, sigs. [A 5-A 6].

49 Keach, *Tropologia* (London, 1682).

50 Zehner, *Adagia Sacra, sive Proverbia Scripturae* (Leipzig, 1601).

51 Cawdrey, *A Treasurie or Store-House of Similies* (London, 1600).

52 *Ibid.*, sigs. A 2ᵥ, A 3ᵥ. A related work, providing a very long alphabetized list of metaphorical terms, and the scripture places from which they are drawn—e.g., *Advocatus-Christus, Clientes-Christiani* (1 John 2:1)—is the *Artifex Evangelicus: Sive Similtudinum ac Symbolorum Sylva* (Cologne, 1640), by the Jesuit Maximilianus Sandaeus. See also Sandaeus, *Symbolica. Ex omni antiquitate sacra, ac profana . . .* (Mainz, 1626).

53 Donne, *Sermons*, II, 170-171.

54 *Ibid.*, I, 236.

55 *Ibid.*, I, 210; II, 55.

56 *Ibid.*, VII, 77, 53.

57 *Ibid.*, VII, 65.

58 Donne, *Devotions upon Emergent Occasions*, p. 99.

59 Donne, *Sermons*, VI, 62.

60 *Ibid.*, VII, 316.

61 *Ibid.*, IX, 226.

62 *Ibid.*, II, 130.

63 A modern treatment of the subject which identifies a number of biblical images and metaphors, though without special period emphasis, is Stephen J. Brown, *Image and Truth: Studies of the Imagery of the Bible* (Rome, 1955).

64 See Perkins, *A Commentarie or Exposition upon . . . Galatians, Workes*, II, 298; and William Whitaker, *Disputatio de Sacra Scriptura* (Cambridge, 1588), p. 300, trans., William Fitzgerald, *A Disputation on Sacred Scripture*, "Parker Society" (Cambridge, 1849), p. 404, for discussion of "accommodated" allegories, grounded upon scripture tropes and applied to the audience.

65 Kaufmann, *Traditions in Puritan Meditation*, pp. 3-60, 151-165. This attention to metaphor is not only a feature of Puritan "heavenly meditations" on the afterlife, as Kaufmann suggests, but is a constant feature of Puritan sermons.

66 Perkins, *The Estate of Damnation, or . . . Grace, Workes*, I, 365-366.

67 Adams, "Physicke from Heaven," *Workes* (London, 1629), p. 271.

68 Schleiner, *The Imagery of John Donne's Sermons* (Providence, 1970), pp. 68-85. See discussion in Lewalski, *Donne's* Anniversaries *and the Poetry of Praise*, pp. 96-102.

69 Sibbes, "The Dead-Man," in *Beames of Divine Light* (London, 1639), pp. 145-146, 155-156.

70 Donne, *Sermons*, X, 233, 234, et passim. See also *Devotions*, "Prayer 18," p. 96.

71 See, e.g., Rollock, *Lectures upon . . . Colossians*, p. 248.

72 Goodwin, *A Childe of Light Walking in Darknesse: or A Treatise Shewing the Causes, by which, the Cases, wherein, The Ends, for which God leaves his children to distresse of conscience* (London, 1636), pp. 30-31.

73 *Ibid.*, pp. 2, 30.

74 *The Bible* [Geneva-Tomson], pt. 3, fol. 78v.

75 *Paradise Lost*, III, 1-55; Herbert, "Submission," l. 20.

76 Cowper, *Heaven Opened. Wherein the Counsaile of God Concerning mans Salvation is . . . manifested* (London, 1611), pp. 50-52.

77 Willet, *Hexapla . . . upon the most Divine Epistle . . . to the Romans* (London, 1611), 365-371.

78 See, e.g., Richard Baxter, *A Christian Directory: or, A Summ of Practical Theologie* (London, 1673), pp. 105-128; John Downame, *The Christian Warfare* (London, 1608).

79 Hieron, "The Good Fight," *Sermons* (London, 1624), pp. 224-225.

80 Some literary and iconographic uses of the metaphor have been studied by Samuel C. Chew, *The Pilgrimage of Life* (New Haven, 1962); J. Paul Hunter, *The Reluctant Pilgrim: Defoe's Emblematic Method and Quest for Form in Robinson Crusoe* (Baltimore, 1966); George H. Williams, *Wilderness and Paradise in Christian Thought* (New York, [1962]). For discussion of a Tudor Protestant revision of Langland as a manifestation of an emerging Protestant poetics, see John N. King, "Robert Crowley's Editions of *Piers Plowman*: A Tudor Apocalypse," *MP*, 73 (1976), 342-352.

81 Cowper, *Heaven Opened*, pp. 44-48. See also Samuel Hieron, *The Christians Journall . . .*, *Workes*, esp. pp. 11-13, 28; [Anon.], *The Pilgrimage of Man, Wandering in a Wildernes of Woe* (London, 1606).

82 Taylor, *The Pilgrims Profession: Or A Sermon Preached at the Funerall of Mrs. Mary Gunter* (London, 1622), pp. 103-105.

83 Diodati, *Annotations*, pt. 2, p. 48.

84 Baxter, *The Saints Everlasting Rest*, pt. 4 (London, 1650), pp. 631-632; cf. Adams, "The Way Home," *Workes*, pp. 848-849.

85 Calvin, *A Commentarie on the Whole Epistle to the Hebrewes*, trans. C. Cotton (London, 1605), p. 294.

86 Ainsworth, *The Communion of Saintes. A treatise of the fellowship that the faithful have with God, and his Angels, and one with an other; in this present life* (Amsterdam, 1607), pp. 285-288, 292-295.

87 Cowper, *Heaven Opened*, pp. 330-331.

88 Andrewes, *XCVI Sermons* (London, 1629), pp. 279-280.

89 Stanley Stewart has studied the metaphor in relation to Canticles in *The Enclosed Garden* (Madison, 1966).

90 Hieron, "The Spirituall Tillage," *Sermons*, pp. 394-397; see also Thomas Taylor, *The Parable of the Sower and the Seed* (London, 1621), pp. 19, 385.

91 John Bunyan, *The Barren Fig-Tree; Or, The Doom and Downfal of the Fruitless Professor* (London, 1688), pp. 19, 23-26, 35; see also Thomas Goodwin, *The Tryall of a Christians Growth* (London, 1641), pp. 14-15.

92 See above, chapter 2, pp. 62-64. See also Abrams, *Natural Supernaturalism*, pp. 37-46, for discussion of various Old Testament texts developing the metaphor of a marriage between God and his chosen people, Israel, and of exegesis presenting Canticles as a kind of prothalamium prefiguring the apocalyptic epithalamium in the Book of Revelation.

93 Donne, *Sermons*, VII, 87.

94 Sibbes, *Bowels Opened*, p. 130; see also Gifford, *Sermons upon the Song of Salomon*, pp. 79-80; Robotham, *Solomons Song*, pp. 345, 503-504, 521.

95 Donne, *Sermons*, VII, 302.

96 Adams, "The Temple," *Workes*, pp. 981, 987; see also Andrewes, *XCVI Sermons*, pp. 483, 492.

97 Featley, "The Arke under the Curtaines," *Clavis Mystica: A Key*

*Opening Divers Difficult and Mysterious Texts of Holy Scripture* (London, 1636), pp. 582-583.

98 Weemse, *The Portraiture of the Image of God in Man, Workes*, I, 21.

99 Perkins, *The Estate of Damnation, or . . . Grace, Workes*, I, 375.

100 Calvin, *Institutes*, II.iii.6, 9, McNeill, I, 297, 301, 312.

101 Perkins, *A Golden Chaine, Workes*, I, 78-80.

102 Hall, *Contemplations upon the Principall Passages of the holy Storie, Works*, 3 vols. (London, 1628-1634), II, 1221-1222.

103 Donne, *Sermons*, IX, 175-176.

104 "Sighs and Grones," ll. 8, 13-16, 19-20. Cf. Luke 16:1-13, Exod. 10:21-23, Gen. 3:7, Rev. 16:1-17.

105 See, e.g., "Religion," "The Search," "*Isaacs* Marriage," "The Brittish Church," "Mount of Olives," "The Retreate," "Corruption." Cf. Rev. 14:14-18.

106 See, e.g., "Death. *A Dialogue*," "Resurrection and Immortality," "Midnight," "Silence, and stealth of dayes!," "I walkt the other day," "Ascension-day," "Quickness."

107 "The Night," ll. 49-50.

108 "The Author to the Critical Peruser," ll. 11-12, 36, 1-2.

109 "Thanksgivings for the Wisdom of his WORD," ll. 252-254.

110 "The Author to the Critical Peruser," l. 14.

111 See, e.g., "Wonder," ll. 33-36, 41-44.

112 "Love," ll. 39-40.

113 "Innocence," ll. 4, 51-53, 60.

114 "The Salutation," ll. 29-36.

115 "An Infant-Ey," l. 4.

116 *Preparatory Meditations*, II.138, "Cant. 6.6," ll. 13-14.

117 *Ibid.*, II.14, II.27, II.67[B].

118 See, e.g., I.38, I.41.

119 See, e.g., I.14, I.15, I.36, I.40.

120 See, e.g., II.114, II.7, I.16 (l. 29).

121 See, e.g., I.4, I.5, "The Reflexion," II.115-II.153.

122 See, e.g., I.5, II.64, II.65, II.83-II.85, II.129-II.132, II.144.

123 See, e.g., I.29, I.33, I.37, II.3, II.4.

## CHAPTER 4

1 For some discussion of Reformation theology in relation to typology see, e.g., Preus, *From Shadow to Promise*; Wallace, *Calvin's Doctrine of the Word and Sacrament*; Victor Harris, "Allegory to Analogy in the Interpretation of Scriptures," *PQ*, 45 (1966), 1-23; Sacvan Bercovitch, "Typology in Puritan New England: The Williams-Cotton Controversy Reassessed," *AQ*, 19 (1967), 166-191. For some discussion of the literary uses of typology in the period, see, e.g., Tuve, *George Herbert*; William G. Madsen, *Shadowy Types to Truth*; Richard D. Jordan, *The Temple of Eternity: Thomas*

*Traherne's Philosophy of Time* (Port Washington, and London, 1972); J. A. Mazzeo, "Cromwell as Davidic King," in *Renaissance and Seventeenth-Century Studies*, ed. Mazzeo, pp. 183-208; Steven Zwicker, *Dryden's Political Poetry: The Typology of King and Nation* (Providence, 1972); Lewalski, *Milton's Brief Epic*; Lewalski, *Donne's Anniversaries and the Poetry of Praise*. See also the several essays on typology, *Literary Uses of Typology*, ed. Miner. For a useful bibliography of materials bearing upon typological exegesis and its literary applications in all periods but with particular emphasis on Renaissance and seventeenth-century developments, see Sacvan Bercovitch, "Annotated Bibliography," in *Typology and Early American Literature*, ed. Bercovitch (Amherst, 1972), pp. 245-337; first published in briefer form in *EAL*, 5 (1970), pp. 1-76.

2 Auerbach, *Mimesis*, trans. Willard Trask (Princeton, 1953); Auerbach, " 'Figura,' " in *Scenes from the Drama of European Literature* (New York, 1959), pp. 11-76. On this distinction see also H. Flanders Dunbar, *Symbolism in Medieval Thought and its Consummation in the Divine Comedy* (New Haven, 1929), and A. C. Charity, *Events and their Afterlife: the Dialectics of Christian Typology in the Bible and in Dante* (Cambridge, 1966).

3 There is a good discussion of this terminology in Thomas M. Davis, "The Exegetical Traditions of Puritan Typology," *EAL*, 5 (1970), 11-50; rpt. in *Typology and Early American Literature*, ed. Bercovitch, pp. 11-45.

4 Jean Daniélou, *Origen*, trans. Walter Mitchell (New York, 1955), pp. 161-162. See also Daniélou, *From Shadows to Reality: Studies in the Biblical Typology of the Fathers*, trans. Wulstan Hibbard (London, 1960).

5 *The Writings of Origen*, ANCL, Vols. X, XXIII (Edinburgh, 1894), esp. *De Principiis*, IV.i, ANCL, X, 294-342; *Contra Celsum*, IV.xliv-xlix, ANCL, XXIII, 200-216.

6 See above, chap. 3, pp. 73-75.

7 Augustine, *De Doctrina*, II.x, Robertson, p. 43. In another tract, *De utilitate credendi*, iii, Augustine designates four "senses" of scripture, the first three of which constitute the full literal meaning: historical, indicating what historical action is conveyed; etiological, explaining "for what cause anything has been done or said"; and analogical, adjusting the meaning of the particular passage to the broader "intent" of the whole scripture. The fourth sense he terms the "allegorical," in which a passage is "to be understood in a figure" (*Pat. Lat.*, XLII, 68-69).

8 *City of God*, XV-XVII, XXII.xxx, *Works*, ed. Dods, II, 49-216, 540-545.

9 *Confessions*, XIII, *Works*, ed. Dods, XIV, 351-394; *Expositions on . . . Psalms*, I, 375; III, 160.

10 *Confessions*, XIII.xxiv, *Works*, ed. Dods, XIV, 383.

11 *De Spiritu et littera*, *Works*, ed. Dods, IV, 157-232, esp. pp. 161, 184-185.

12 See Preus, *From Shadow to Promise*, pp. 16-21, 45; Froehlich, "The State of Biblical Hermeneutics at the Beginning of the Fifteenth Century," in *Literary Uses of Typololgy*, ed. Miner, pp. 20-48.

13 Cassian, *Conlations*, xiv.8, *Pat. Lat.*, XLIX, 962-965. See H. de Lubac, *Exégèse Médiévale: Les Quatres Senses de l'Ecriture* (Paris, 1959), pp. 187 ff.; Beryl Smalley, *The Study of the Bible in the Middle Ages* (Oxford, 1941), p. 15.

14 Hugh, [*De Sacramentis*], *On the Sacraments of the Christian Faith*, trans. Roy J. Deferrari (Cambridge, Mass., 1951), p. 5. See Smalley, pp. 58-80.

15 Aquinas, *Summa Theologica*, I, Q.1, Art. 10, *Basic Writings*, I, 16-17.

16 *Ibid.*, p. 17.

17 See, e.g., Aquinas, "Ad Galathas," IV, Lectio vii, *Super Epistolas Pauli Commentaria* ([Paris], 1526), fols. cxlv-cxlvi; "Quodlibet VII," Q.6, Arts. 14-16, *Quodlibetales Questiones*, fols. 93ᵥ-96; *Summa Theologica*, I, Q.1, Art. 10, *Basic Writings*, I, 16-17.

18 I am indebted for some of these formulations to an unpublished lecture by F. E. Cranz, "Some Historical Structures of Reading and of Allegory," which he kindly made available to me.

19 *Summa Theologica*, I, Q.1, Art. 10, *Basic Writings*, I, 17.

20 "Quodlibet VII," Q.6, Art. 16, ad. 3, Responsio, *Quodlibetales Questiones*, fol. 96: "Sicut enim homo potest adhibere ad aliquid significandum aliquas voces vel aliquas similitudines fictas, ita Deus adhibet ad significationem aliquorum ipsum cursum rerum suae providentiae subjectarum."

21 Dante, *Convivio*, trans. W. W. Jackson (Oxford, 1909), p. 34.

22 Dante, "Letter to Can Grande," *Epistolae*, pp. 199-200.

23 Tyndale, "Prologue into . . . Leviticus," *Workes*, p. 15.

24 Luther, *Table Talk*, *Works*, ed. Pelikan, LIV, 46; *A Commentarie . . . upon . . . Galathians*, fol. 210ᵥ. See also *Lectures on Genesis*, *Works*, I, 231-235.

25 See *Lectures on Genesis*, *Works*, I-VIII; *Selected Psalms* [Commentary], *Works*, ed. Pelikan, XII-XIV; "Preface to the Old Testament," *Works*, XXXV, pp. 235-354. Luther's terminology about typology is inconsistent. In the early lectures on Genesis, he uses *typos*, *schema* and *figura* as generally synonymous; in later writings he ordinarily uses the terms *figura* and *typos*—quite often together as if to give the significance of *typos* to the Latin term. But he can also use terms for picture, example, and image in contexts that convey a typological meaning.

26 Cf. Luther, *Lectures on Romans* (Rom. 10:6), ed. Pauck, p. 288:

Moses writes these words [Who shall ascend into heaven?] in Deut. 30:12, and he does not have the meaning in mind they have here, but his abundant spiritual insight enables the apostle to bring out their inner significance. It is as if he wanted to give us an impressive proof of the fact that the whole Scripture, if one contemplates it inwardly, deals everywhere with Christ, even though in so far as it is a sign and a shadow, it may outwardly sound differently. That is why he says: "*Christ is the end of the law*" (Rom. 10:4); in other words: every word in the Bible points to Christ. That this is really so, he proves by showing that this word here, which seems to have nothing whatsoever to do with Christ, nevertheless signifies Christ.

See also Luther's "Preface to the Old Testament" (1523), *Works*, ed. Pelikan, XXXV, 247: "If you would interpret [the Old Testament] well and confidently, set Christ before you, for he is the man to whom it all applies, every bit of it."

27 See Preus, *Shadow to Promise*, pp. 153-175, 200-225.

28 Pauck, "Introduction," *Lectures on Romans*, p. xxxiii.

29 Preus, *Shadow to Promise*, p. 185.

30 Commentary on "Psalm 113.1" [114:1], *Dictata super Psalterium, Martin Luthers Werke: Kritische Gesamtausgabe*, ed. J. C-F Knaake, et al., vols. 1- (Weimar, 1883-  ), IV, 261-262.

31 *Dictata super Psalterium*, III, 374.

32 See, e.g., Calvin's Commentary on Ezek. 17:22, Isa. 52:8, 10; Psalm 41:10, and 118:25, Sermon on Matt. 2:23, cited and discussed in Wallace, pp. 45-53; and *Institutes*, II.16.6, McNeill, I, 510.

33 Madsen, *From Shadowy Types to Truth*, p. 29. Calvin in fact finds only a few Psalms, e.g., Psalm 110, which seem to him to have *only* Christological reference. See Calvin, *Psalmes*, pt. 2, fol. 132ᵥ.

34 Calvin, *Psalmes*, pt. 1, fols. 82, 81, 77ᵥ.

35 Calvin, *Institutes*, II.ix.3, McNeill, I, 426. See also *The Institution of Christian Religion*, trans. John Dawes (London, 1561).

36 Calvin, *Commentarie on . . . Hebrewes*, pp. 200-201.

37 Whitaker, *Disputatio de Sacra Scriptura* (Cambridge, 1588).

38 See Charles K. Cannon, "William Whitaker's *Disputatio de Sacra Scriptura*: A Sixteenth-Century Theory of Allegory," *HLQ*, 25 (1961-1962), 129-138.

39 Whitaker, *Disputation*, trans. Fitzgerald, pp. 405-408.

40 Perkins, *A Commentarie or Exposition upon the Five First Chapters of the Epistle to the Galatians* (Cambridge, 1604), p. 346.

41 Weemse, *Christian Synagogue, Workes*, I, 229-230.

42 Weemse, *Exercitations Divine: Containing diverse Questions and Solutions for the right understanding of the Scriptures*, in *Workes*, IV, 182.

43 See, e.g., Lukin, *Introduction to . . . Holy Scripture*, pp. 114-124.

44 For elaboration of these points see Madsen, *Shadowy Types to Truth*, pp. 35-48, and George L. Scheper, "Reformation Attitudes toward Allegory and the Song of Songs," *PMLA*, 89 (1974), 551-562.

45 James Durham, *Clavis Cantici: Or, an Exposition of the Song of Solomon* (Edinburgh, 1668), pp. 10-11, 22-23. See above, chap. 2, pp. 59-64.

46 Diodati, *Annotations*, pt. 2, p. 20.

47 Whitaker, *Disputation*, p. 404. See also Luther, *Lectures on Genesis, Works*, ed. Pelikan, I, 233-234; Perkins, *Arte of Prophecying, Workes*, II, 651, 660.

48 Madsen, *Shadowy Types to Truth*, p. 38.

49 Guild, *Moses unveiled; or, those figures which served unto the patterne*

*and shaddow of heavenly things, pointing out the Messiah Christ Jesus*
(London, 1620); Taylor, *Christ Revealed: Or The Old Testament Explained*
(London, 1635), revised and reissued as *Moses and Aaron, Or the Types and
Shadows of our Saviour in the Old Testament. Opened and Explained* (London, 1653); Vertue, *Christ and the Church: Or Parallels* (London, 1659);
Keach, *Tropologia: A Key to open Scripture Metaphors . . . Together with
Types of the Old Testament* (London, 1681); Mather, *The Figures or
Types of the Old Testament* (Dublin, 1683).

50 Mather, *Figures or Types*, p. 163.

51 Keach, "Moses's Vail Removed: Or Types of the Old Testament Explained," in *Tropologia*.

52 Mather, *Figures and Types*, p. 162. See pp. 74-77.

53 *Ibid.*, pp. 71-72.

54 Augustine, *De Spiritu et littera*; Hugh, *On the Sacraments of the Christian Faith*; Peter Lombard, *Sententiarum Libri Quatuor*, IV.i.1-5, *Pat. Lat.*,
CXCII, 839-840; Aquinas, *Summa Theologica*, I-II, Q.107, *Basic Writings*,
II, 957-966.

55 *The New Testament . . . by the English College at . . . Rheims*
(Antwerp, 1600), p. 627.

56 See, e.g., Aquinas, *Summa Theologica*, I-II. Q.107, Art. 1, *Basic Works*,
II, 959.

57 Luther, "Dictata super Psalterium," *Werke*, IV, 251, cited in Preus,
*From Shadow to Promise*, pp. 209-210.

58 *Institutes*, II.x.2, McNeill, I, 429-430.

59 Calvin, *Psalmes*, pt. 1, fol. 198.

60 Calvin, *A Commentarie upon S. Paules Epistles to the Corinthians*,
trans. Thomas Tymme (London, 1577), fols. 112-112ᵥ, 117; cf. *The Bible*
[Geneva-Tomson], pt. 3, fol. 73ᵥ. The Rheims New Testament, annotating
the same text, flatly denounced the new Protestant emphasis: "It is an impudent forgerie of the Calvinists, to write upon this place, that the Jewes
received no lesse the truth and substance of Christ and his benefites in their
figures or Sacraments, then we do in ours: and that they and we al eate and
drinke of the self same meate and drinke: the Apostle saying only, that they
among them selves did al feede of one bread, & drinke of one rocke; which
was a figure of Christ" (p. 446).

61 Calvin, *Commentarie on . . . Hebrewes*, p. 201.

62 *Holy Byble* [Bishops'], pt. 2, fol. 118ᵥ; Diodati, *Annotations*, pt. 2,
p. [379]; Taylor, *Christ Revealed*, p. 4.

63 Jemmat, "The Epistle Dedicatorie," *Christ Revealed*, sig. A2ᵥ.

64 Mather, *Figures and Types*, pp. 5, 10, 70.

65 Murray Roston terms this phenomenon "postfiguration," in *Biblical
Drama in England*, pp. 69-78, but I shall use and argue for a terminology
closer to contemporary usage.

66 See, e.g., Henry Bullinger, *A Hundred Sermons upon the Apocalypse*
(London, 1573), sig. Aiiiᵥ; Brightman, *Revelation of the Apocalypse*,

*Workes*, pp. 194, 332; Brightman, *A Commentary on the Canticles, Workes*; Joseph Mede, *Clavis Apocalyptica* (Cambridge, 1627); Mede, *Daniels Weekes* (London, 1643); John Cotton, *A Brief Exposition of . . . Canticles . . . Lively describing the Estate of the Church in all the Ages thereof, both Jewish and Christian, to this day*; see also Michael Fixler, *Milton and the Kingdoms of God* (Evanston, 1964), pp. 13-45.

67 See Haller, *The Rise of Puritanism* (New York, 1938); and Haller, *Foxe's 'Book of Martyrs' and the Elect Nation* (London, 1963); Zwicker, *Dryden's Political Poetry*; Bercovitch, "Typology in Puritan New England," 166-191; Lamont, *Godly Rule: Politics and Religion, 1603-60* (London, 1969), p. 23.

68 William Perkins, *A Clowd of Faithfull Witnesses, Leading to the Heavenly Canaan, Workes*, III, pp. 42-43.

69 Mather, *Figures and Types*, pp. 194, 203-204.

70 Bercovitch, "Typology in Puritan New England," pp. 179-181.

71 See the discussion of this point and the justification of the term "correlative typology" in Lewalski, "*Samson Agonistes* and the 'Tragedy' of the Apocalypse," pp. 1054-1057.

72 Adams, "Englands Sicknesse," *Workes*, p. 302.

73 See, e.g., William Leigh's funeral sermon for Elizabeth, *Queene Elizabeth, Paralleld in her Princely virtues, with David, Josua, and Hezekiah* (London, 1612); Joshua Sylvester, *Lachrymae Lachrymarum* ([London, 1612]); John Williams' funeral sermon for King James, *Great Britains Solomon* (London, 1625); Paul Knell, *Israel and England Paralleled* (London, 1648); Thomas Westfeild, *Englands Face in Israels Glas: or the sinnes, mercies, judgments of both nations* (London, 1655); John White, *The Parallel between David, Christ, and K. Charls* (London, 1661). See theoretical discussion in Lewalski, *Donne's* Anniversaries *and the Poetry of Praise*, pp. 15-29; Lewalski, "*Samson Agonistes* and the 'Tragedy' of the Apocalypse," pp. 1053-1055; Zwicker, *Dryden's Political Poetry*, pp. 3-26.

74 See, e.g., Thomas Taylor, *The Famine of the Word* (London, 1653); Milton, *Readie and Easy Way*, rev. ed., in *Complete Poetry and Major Prose*, ed. Hughes, 898-899.

75 See Cotton Mather, *Magnalia Christi Americana*, ed. Thomas Robbins (Hartford, 1853), I, 43, 48, 166, cited in Bercovitch, "Typology in Puritan New England," pp. 184, 185 n. 40.

76 *Summa Theologica*, I, Q.1, Art. 10, *Basic Works*, I, 17.

77 Preus, *Shadow to Promise*, pp. 233-234.

78 Cited in Preus, *Shadow to Promise*, pp. 220-221.

79 Calvin, *Psalmes*, pt. 1, fol. 164$_v$.

80 Calvin, Commentary on Gen. 37:18-19, cited in Wallace, p. 47.

81 Calvin, *Psalmes*, sigs. *[vii$_v$], **i.

82 *Ibid.*, p. 31.

83 See Daniélou, *From Shadows to Reality*, pp. 153-226.

84 Perkins, *Clowd of Faithfull Witnesses, Workes*, III, "Epistle Dedicatorie," p. 200.

85 Cowper, *The Triumph of a Christian* (London, 1608), pp. 39, 63-64, 105.

86 See, e.g., Thomas Adams, "The Temple," *Workes*, pp. 980-981; Andrew Willet, *Hexapla in Exodum: that is, a Sixfold Commentary upon the Second Book of Moses Called Exodus* (London, 1608), p. 629; Featley, "The Arke under the Curtaines" (1613), *Clavis Mystica*, p. 576.

87 Adams, "The Temple," *Workes*, pp. 987-988.

88 Hall, *Contemplations, Works*, II, 1220-1222.

89 Perkins, *Clowd of Faithfull Witnesses*, p. 76.

90 Hammond, *Annotations upon . . . Psalms*, sig. c $2_v$.

91 Donne, *Sermons*, II, 97.

92 *Ibid.*, I, 287-288.

93 *Ibid.*, III, 313.

94 *Ibid.*, X, 141-142.

95 *Ibid.*, VII, 51.

96 *Ibid.*, II, 75, 99.

97 *Ibid.*, VII, 356.

98 *Ibid.*, VII, 403; I have argued elsewhere the influence of this exegetical practice upon Donne's *Anniversaries* and his poetry of praise and compliment; see *Donne's* Anniversaries *and the Poetry of Praise*, esp. chaps. 2, 4-8.

99 This is Joan Webber's formulation in *Contrary Music: The Prose Style of John Donne* (Madison, 1963), p. 124.

100 Donne, *Sermons*, I, 235.

101 *Ibid.*, IV, 182-183.

102 See above, pp. 117-118.

103 Donne, *Sermons*, III, 241, 255; cf. VIII, 96.

104 *Devotions upon Emergent Occasions*. See argument in Lewalski, *Donne's* Anniversaries *and the Poetry of Praise*, pp. 96-102, 159-160.

105 In a miscellaneous notebook edited by Perry Miller, *Images or Shadows of Divine Things* (New Haven, 1948). Another Edwards manuscript, based upon a series of sermons delivered in 1739, *A History of the Work of Redemption* (New York, 1841), sets forth a conservative, biblical doctrine of typology.

106 In "Images or Shadows of Divine Things: The Typology of Jonathan Edwards," *EAL*, V (1970), 141-181, Lowance challenges Perry Miller's view that Edwards merely extends the concept of typology, intending chiefly to reform the Puritan use of tropes by conforming them to the more rigorous system of typology.

107 See numbers 35, 50, 52, Edwards, *Images or Shadows*, pp. 50, 58, 59.

108 Jonathan Edwards, "Types of the Messiah," or "Miscellany 1069," *The Works of President Edwards* (Edinburgh, 1847), IX, 401. Cited in Lowance, pp. 150-151.

109 See, e.g., numbers 7, 26, 45, 55, 58, 64, 185, Edwards, *Images or Shadows*, pp. 44, 49, 56, 60, 61-63, 67, 125. See also no. 156: "The book of Scripture is the interpreter of the book of nature two ways, vis., by declaring to us those spiritual mysteries that are indeed signified and

typified in the constitution of the natural world; and secondly, in actually making application of the signs and types in the book of nature as representations of those spiritual mysteries in many instances."

110 See Lewalski, *Donne's Anniversaries and the Poetry of Praise*, pp. 169-173.

111 Ira Clark calls attention to a similar movement in several Herbert poems, noting the speaker's discovery "that he himself is a contemporary neotype of Christ akin to Old Testament types of Christ," " 'Lord, in thee the *Beauty* lies in the *Discovery*': 'Love Unknown' and Reading Herbert," *ELH*, 39 (1972), 560-584. Clark invents the term "neotype" to describe what he sees as a special use of typology in Herbert; because he approaches the typological tradition as a unified one, he does not consider Herbert's relation to contemporary Protestant (as distinct from medieval and Counter Reformation) typology, with its involvement of the individual Christian directly in the typological equation.

112 See Jordan, *The Temple of Eternity*, pp. 58-73.

113 See *Preparatory Meditations*, II, 7, 22, 4.

114 See *Preparatory Meditations*, II, 82, 5, 23, 59.

115 See *Preparatory Meditations*, II, 10, 29, 63. For discussion of some of these methods see Robert E. Reiter, "Poetry and Typology: Edward Taylor's Preparatory Meditations, Second Series, Numbers 1-30," and Karl Keller, " 'The World slickt up in Types': Edward Taylor as a Version of Emerson," in *EAL*, 5 (1970), 111-123, 124-140.

116 For discussion of some of these later uses, and the transformations involved, see the essays by Paul J. Korshin, Karl Keller, George P. Landow, and Theodore Ziolkowski in *Literary Uses of Typology*, ed. Miner.


CHAPTER 5

1 See Martz, *Poetry of Meditation*, pp. 1-2..

2 Martz, *Poetry of Meditation*, pp. 25-26, 145-149, 249-259; *The Paradise Within*, pp. 17-31, 54-57.

3 See Albert Hyma, *The Christian Renaissance: A History of the "Devotio Moderna,"* 2nd ed. (Hamden, 1965). There is a link between the writings of Johan Wessel Gansfort, a prominent figure in the *Devotio Moderna* movement, and the influential Protestant *Arte of Divine Meditation* (London, 1607; 1st ed., 1606) by Joseph Hall, in that Hall's system of meditative analysis was derived from Gansfort by way of Joannes Mauburnus.

4 Rogers, trans., *Of the Imitation of Christ. Three, both for wisedome, and godlines, most excellent bookes, made 170 yeeres since by one Thomas of Kempis . . . now newlie corrected* (London, 1617; 1st ed., 1580). Rogers replaced the eucharistic fourth book of the *Imitatio* with Thomas à Kempis' *Soliloquium Animae. The sole-talke of the Soule.* See also Rogers, trans., *A Pretious Booke of Heavenlie Meditations; called, A private talke of the Soule with God* (London, 1612; 1st ed., 1581), published with two other

pseudo-Augustinian works. These books went through many editions. Bunny, trans., *A Booke of Christian Exercise, Appertaining to Resolution . . . by R. P.[arsons]* (London, 1585).

5 Parsons, *The Christian Directory, Guiding Men to Eternal Salvation* ([Douai?], 1607), Preface, [sig. *ᵥ].

6 Grabo, "The Art of Puritan Devotion," *Seventeenth-Century News*, 26 (1968), 7-9. See especially Abraham Fleming, *The Diamond of Devotion, cut and squared into six severall points* (London, 1608); Daniel Featley, *Ancilla Pietatis, or, The Hand-Maid to Private Devotion*, 3rd ed. (London, 1628); Henry Bull, ed., *Christian Prayers and Holy Meditations* (1566, 1570), "Parker Society" (Cambridge, 1842). See also Helen C. White's bibliography of such works in *English Devotional Literature (Prose) 1600-1640*, University of Wisconsin Studies in Language and Literature, 29 (Madison, 1931), pp. 271-291. The proliferation of such works requires that the polemical assertions of Parsons and others to the effect that contemporary Protestants borrowed Roman works because they could not produce their own be greeted with some skepticism (Parsons, *Directory*, sig. *ᵥ). See Martz, *Poetry of Meditation*, pp. 4-13. The English Protestants did indeed begin with such borrowings (heavily revised) but soon moved beyond them. Their original treatises were not "methodical" in the Jesuit way, because they sought, quite deliberately, not to make them so.

7 Kaufmann, *Traditions in Puritan Meditation*, pp. 126-133; Lewalski, *Donne's Anniversaries and the Poetry of Praise*, pp. 73-107.

8 Cf. Halewood, *Poetry of Grace*, pp. 71-87.

9 Rogers, "Of Meditation, the second private helpe," *Seven Treatises*, pp. 235-259.

10 Rogers, *Seven Treatises*, sig. [A 6-A 6ᵥ]. See Loarte, *The Exercise of a Christian Life* [trans. Stephen Brinkley] ([Rheims?], 1584); Parsons, *A Christian Directorie* ([Rouen], 1585).

11 T. Rogers, trans., *Imitation of Christ*, sig. A 9.

12 Greenham, "Grave Counsels and Godlie Observations," *Workes*, ed. H. Hammond, 3rd ed. (London, 1601), p. 23; Culverwel, *Time Well Spent in Sacred Meditations, Divine Observations, Heavenly Exhortations* (London, 1634), p. 217; Gataker, *The Spirituall Watch, or Christs Generall Watch-Word. A Meditation on Mark 13:37* (London, 1619), p. 100. A comparable biblical focus is also observed in French Protestant devotional manuals and poetry by Terence Cave, *Devotional Poetry in France*, pp. 38-77.

13 See, e.g., Rogers, *Seven Treatises*, p. 235; Hall, *Arte of Divine Meditation*, pp. 57, 62-63; Isaac Ambrose, *Prima, Media, and Ultima, The First, Middle, and Last Things* (London, 1659), "Media," p. 217.

14 Haller, *Rise of Puritanism*, p. 151.

15 Tyndale, "Prologue . . . shewing the use of the Scripture," *Workes*, p. 4. Jewel, "A Learned and Godly Sermon," trans. R. V., *Workes* (London, 1611), pp. 37, 47.

16 Donne, *Sermons*, III, 367; cf. *Sermons*, II, 159.

17 Kaufmann, *Traditions in Puritan Meditation*, pp. 49-55.

18 Ambrose, *Prima, Media, and Ultima*; Edmund Calamy, *The Art of Divine Meditation* (London, 1680).

19 Hall, *Arte*, pp. 6-7.

20 *Ibid.*, p. 20.

21 *Ibid.*, pp. 10-11.

22 Boyle, *Occasional Reflections upon Several Subjects. Whereto is premis'd A Discourse about such kind of Thoughts* (London, 1665), pp. 4, 13-14.

23 Ambrose, *Prima, Media, and Ultima*, "Media," pp. 216-217. See also Lewis Bayly, *The Practise of Pietie* (London, 1616), pp. 477-478; Richard Rogers, *Seven Treatises*, p. 235.

24 A blurring of the distinction between prayer and meditation was probably encouraged by the alternative translation of the Hebrew word *soach* in the description of Isaac in the fields (Gen. 24:63) as either *to pray* or *to meditate*. See Calvin, *Commentaries on the First Book of Moses Called Genesis*, 4 vols. (Grand Rapids, 1948), II, 28. The Geneva Bible reads "Ishak went out to pray in the field"; the AV reads, "to meditate." The mix of kinds was also encouraged by Saint Bernard's often-cited dictum that meditation is a preparative to prayer and prayer is the end of meditation; and also by the example of the popular pseudo-Augustinian *Manuale*, in which reflections on spiritual topics are intermixed with short apostrophes to God and to the soul. See, e.g., Thomas Rogers, ed., *S. Augustines Manuel: Containing Speciall and picked Meditations, and godlie Prayers* (London, 1581), esp. preface, sig. a 3. This book, in Rogers' version and others, went through several editions in the sixteenth and seventeenth centuries.

25 Bull, *Christian Prayers and Holy Meditations*; Bayly, *Practise of Pietie*; Alliston, *The Exercise of true Spiritual devotion. Consisting of holy Meditation and Prayers* (London, 1610).

26 Bacon, *Essayes. Religious Meditations. Places of perswasion and disswasion* (London, 1597); *Essaies. Religious Meditations . . .* (London, 1598).

27 Hall, *Meditations and Vowes, Divine and Morall* (London, 1605), dedicated to Sir Robert and Lady Drury; *Holy Observations* (London, 1607).

28 Hall, *Occasionall Meditations* (London, 1633). This second edition was revised and expanded to include forty-nine meditations in addition to the ninety-one included in the first edition (London, 1630).

29 Ambrose, *Prima, Media, and Ultima*, "Media," pp. 219-221.

30 Boyle, *Occasional Reflections*, sigs. A 8-a 8, p. 24.

31 See, e.g., Perkins, *Arte of Prophecying, Workes*, II, pp. 646-673; Richard Bernard, *Faithfull Shepherd*, pp. 272-327. See also below, chap. 7.

32 Bernard, *Faithfull Shepherd*, pp. 24, 332.

33 Donne, *Sermons*, II, 49; VI, 347-348.

34 Greenham, "Grave Counsels," *Workes*, p. 22. This near-conflation of sermon and meditation is also indicated by the titles of several sermons: e.g., Thomas Gataker, *David's Remembrancer. A Meditation on Psalm 13:1* (London, 1623); Gataker, *True Contentment in the Gaine of Godliness . . . A Meditation on 1 Timoth 6.6* (London, 1620); Gataker, *A Mariage*

*Praier, or Succinct Meditations: Delivered in a Sermon* (London, 1624); and many others.

35 Hall, *Arte*, pp. 88, 89-94, 150.

36 Ambrose, *Prima, Media, and Ultima*, "Media," pp. 222-223.

37 Calamy, *Art of Divine Meditation*, pp. 189-190.

38 Baxter, *Saints Everlasting Rest*, pt. 4, pp. 749-751. James Ussher, Archbishop of Armagh, also made direct and explicit use of the sermon as structural model for the meditation in his direction that the meditator, after prayer to God for help, first choose his text, and then draw his doctrines, reasons, and uses from it, as in "Ordinary Preaching," *A Method for Meditation* (London, 1651), pp. 54-56.

39 Recognition of this enduring Protestant tradition forces modification of Martz' claim that Baxter's was the "first Puritan treatise on the art of methodical meditation" (*Poetry of Meditation*, p. 154), and that Baxter forged the link between the sermon and the meditation in order to render meditative practice more acceptable to Protestants (p. 174).

40 Baxter, *Christian Directory*, pp. 307-308.

41 Rogers, *Seven Treatises*, p. 236.

42 Greenham, "Grave Counsels," *Workes*, p. 22.

43 Goodwin, *The Vanity of Thoughts Discovered: With their Danger and Cure* (London, 1637), pp. 120-122; see also Culverwel. *Time well spent*, pp. 214-217.

44 Hieron, "The Preachers Plea," *Sermons*, p. 550; cf. Hall. *Arte*. pp. 58-59.

45 Ussher, *Method for Meditation*, pp. 49, 15-16.

46 Calamy, *Art of Divine Meditation*, p. 31.

47 Donne, *Sermons*, VII, 327-329.

48 Rogers, *Seven Treatises*, p. 236.

49 *Ibid.*, p. 246. See pp. 247-259.

50 Baxter, *Christian Directory*, p. 300.

51 Hall, *Arte*, pp. 71-73.

52 E. Brooks Holifield, *The Covenant Sealed: The Development of Puritan Sacramental Theology in Old and New England, 1570-1720* (New Haven and London, 1974), calls attention to the increasing value accorded to the use of the senses and the imagination in the sacramental theology of the later Puritans.

53 Sutton, *Godly Meditations upon the most holy Sacrament of the Lords Supper* (London, 1613), pp. 255-265.

54 Hildersam, *The Doctrine of Communicating worthily in the Lords Supper*, 9th ed. (London, 1636), pp. 98-99.

55 E.g., Richard Vines, *A Treatise of the Right Institution, Administration, and Receiving of the Sacrament of the Lords Supper* (London, 1657), p. 167.

56 Calamy, *Art of Divine Meditation*, p. 1.

57 Sibbes, *The Fountaine Opened: Or, The Mysterie of Godlinesse*, in *Light From Heaven* (London, 1638), pp. 197-198.

58 Culverwel, *Time Well Spent*, pp. 214-215.

59 Taylor, *The Practice of Repentance* (London, 1629), p. 299.

60 Thomas Gataker, *Spirituall Watch*, pp. 77-79.

61 Ambrose, *Prima, Media, and Ultima*, "Media," pp. 61, 86-87.

62 *Ibid.*, "Media," p. 70.

63 Ussher, *Method for Meditation*, p. 15.

64 Hildersam, *Doctrine of Communicating Worthily*, p. 95.

65 William Bradshaw, *A Preparation to the Receiving of Christs Body and Bloud* (London, 1634), p. 82ᵥ; see also Richard Sibbes, *Divine Meditations and Holy Contemplations* (London, 1638), sig. A 5-A 5ᵥ.

66 See Norman Pettit, *The Heart Prepared*, for a full discussion of this kind of meditation, and the theology upon which it is based.

67 Hooker, *The Application of Redemption* (London, 1656), pp. 208, 214, 217.

68 *Ibid.*, p. 266.

69 Sibbes, *The Soules Conflict with it selfe, and Victorie over it selfe by Faith* (London, 1635), p. 673. See also Baxter, *Christian Directory*, p. 302.

70 J[ohn] B[artlet], *The Practical Christian* (London, 1670), pp. 69-70.

71 Ambrose, *Prima, Media, and Ultima*, "Media," pp. 164-181.

72 *Ibid.*, "Media," pp. 176-177, 182-189. See also Sibbes, *Divine Meditations*.

73 See, e.g., Bayly, *Practise of Pietie*; Richard Rogers, William Perkins, et al., *A Garden of Spirituall Flowers* (London, 1616). For discussion of the *topos* of sin as sickness historically and as a field of imagery in Donne, see Schleiner, *Imagery of John Donne's Sermons*, pp. 68-85. See above, chap. 3, pp. 87-88.

74 Hall, *Occasionall Meditations*, pp. 254-255.

75 Boyle, *Occasional Reflections*, pp. 187-240.

76 Rogers, *Seven Treatises*, pp. 256-257.

77 Hall, *Occasionall Meditations*, pp. 193-195.

78 See, e.g., Calamy, *Art of Divine Meditation*, pp. 36-37.

79 See, e.g., *The Bestiary: A Book of Beasts* (12th century), ed. and trans. T. H. White (New York, 1954); Bonaventure, *Itinerarium Mentis in Deum.* (Paris, 1505?); trans. "Father James," *The Franciscan Vision* (London, 1937). See also Robert Bellarmine, *A Most Learned and pious treatise, framing a Ladder, Whereby our Mindes may ascend to God by the stepps of his Creatures (De Ascensione Mentis in Deum)*, trans. T. B. (Douay, 1616).

80 For some discussion of ways of reading and meditating upon nature in the seventeenth century, see Kitty W. Scoular (Datta), *Natural Magic: Studies in the Presentation of Nature in English Poetry from Spenser to Marvell* (Oxford, 1965); Martz, *The Paradise Within*; Perry Miller, *The New England Mind: The Seventeenth Century* (1939; rpt. Boston, 1968); Jeannie de Brun Duffy, "Henry Vaughan and Thomas Traherne and the Protestant Tradition of Meditation upon the Book of Creatures," Diss. Brown 1973; Ellen Goodman, "The Design of Milton's World: Nature and the Fall in Christian Genesis Commentary and *Paradise Lost*," Diss. Brown

1976. Anne Williams, "The Background of Wordsworth's Theodicy of the Landscape," Diss. Cornell 1973.

81 Hall, *Arte*, pp. 16-17.

82 Hall, *Occasionall Meditations*, pp. 331, 38-39, 89-90, 128-130, 226-229.

83 Boyle, *Occasional Reflections*, pp. 19, 79.

84 Spurstow, *The Spiritual Chymist: or, Six Decads of Divine Meditations on Several Subjects* (London, 1666), pp. 6, 18-19, 60.

85 Symson, *Heptameron, The Seven Dayes: That is, Meditations and Prayers, upon the Works of the Lord's Creation* (St. Andrews, 1621), pp. 73, 78.

86 Calvin, *Institutes*, I.v.1, 9, McNeill, I, 52-53, 62.

87 *Ibid.*, I.v.11, 14, McNeill, I, 63-68.

88 *Ibid.*, I.vi.1, McNeill, I, 70.

89 *Ibid.*, I.xiv.20-21, McNeill, I, 179-180.

90 Topsell, *The Historie of Foure-Footed Beastes . . . Collected out of . . . Conrad Gesner* (London, 1607), sig. A 4.

91 Taylor, *Meditations from the Creatures. As it was preached in Aldermanbury*, 2nd ed. (London, 1629), pp. 10-23.

92 Baxter, *Christian Directory*, p. 301.

93 G[odfrey] G[oodman], *The Creatures praysing God: or, the Religion of dumbe creatures* (London, 1622).

94 See Martz, *Poetry of Meditation*, pp. 153-175; Martz, "Foreword," *Poems of Edward Taylor*, ed. Stanford, pp. xiii-xxxvii; Kaufmann, *Traditions in Puritan Meditation*, pp. 133-150.

95 Baxter, *Saints Everlasting Rest*, pt. 4, p. 678. See also pp. 670-673.

96 Hall, *Arte*, p. 84.

97 Hall, *The Great Misterie of Godliness, Laid forth by way of affectuous and feeling Meditation* (London, 1652), p. 85; see also Sibbes, *Light from Heaven*, p. 197.

98 Baxter, *Saints Everlasting Rest*, pt. 4, p. 690.

99 Sibbes, *The Soules Conflict*, pp. 256-257.

100 Baxter, *Saints Everlasting Rest*, pt. 4, p. 759.

101 Sibbes, *A Glance of Heaven, or, A Pretious Taste of a glorious Feast* (London, 1638), pp. 16-17.

102 Baxter, *Saints Everlasting Rest*, pt. 4, pp. 762-763, 765, 768.

103 Sibbes, *Soules Conflict*, pp. 259-260.

104 Hall, *The Invisible World, Discovered to spiritual eyes, and Reduced to usefull Meditation* (London, 1652), pp. 223-225, 355-356.

105 By, e.g., Louis Martz, *The Poetry of Meditation*, pp. 138-140; Thomas F. Van Laan, "John Donne's *Devotions* and the Jesuit Spiritual Exercises," *SP*, 60 (1903), 191-202; Anthony Raspa, ed., *Devotions upon Emergent Occasions*, pp. xix-xl.

106 In his attractive new edition Raspa marshals the evidence for this date (pp. xiii-xix); see also R. C. Bald, *John Donne: A Life* (Oxford, 1970), pp. 450-455.

107 See the discussion of this fusion in my *Donne's* Anniversaries *and the Poetry of Praise*, pp. 96-101.

108 Mueller, "The Exegesis of Experience: Dean Donne's *Devotions upon Emergent Occasions*," *JEGP*, 67 (1968), 1-19.

109 As Raspa notes, "Introduction," pp. xxxv.

110 Raspa has shown the importance for the *Devotions*, and for Donne's thought generally, of the three "Books" of divine revelation identified in Donne's *Essays in Divinity*—the book of the creatures, the scripture, and the register of the elect, or Book of Life, described in Revelation 5. See *Devotions*, "Introduction," pp. xxvi-xxxi, and Raspa, "Theology and Poetry in Donne's *Conclave*," *ELH*, 32 (1965), 478-489.

111 *Devotions*, ed. Raspa, p. 40.

112 Martz, *Poetry of Meditation*, pp. 107-112.

113 The first sixteen of these poems are titled "Divine Meditations" in some manuscripts, though we do not know whether by authorial warrant. See the detailed description of the manuscript versions of the "Holy Sonnets" in Gardner's edition of the *Divine Poems*, pp. xxxvii-lv; lxxxi-xcvi.

114 Herbert, *A Priest to the Temple, or, The Country Parson* (1652), Hutchinson, p. 255. Stanley Fish, *The Living Temple: George Herbert and Catechizing* (Berkeley, 1978), finds such self-catechizing to be the key to *The Temple*'s structure and the essence of its poetic movement.

115 *Priest to the Temple*, p. 255. See also p. 278: "For the temptations with which a good man is beset, and the ways which he used to overcome them, being told to another, whether in private conference, or in the Church, are a Sermon."

116 Bell, " 'Setting Foot into Divinity': George Herbert and the English Reformation," *MLQ*, 38 (1977), 219-241. Bell argues that these poems, which appear in Herbert's first collection, the Dr. Williams manuscript, register a repudiation of the more Catholic methods evident in Herbert's Latin sequence, *Passio Discerpta*. For a different interpretation of Herbert's development, based upon speculation that the Dr. Williams English poems were written early in Herbert's career, see Amy M. Charles, *A Life of George Herbert* (Ithaca and London, 1977), pp. 81-94.

117 Vaughan, *Mount of Olives*, Martin, p. 140.

118 "Rules *and* Lessons," ll. 87, 115-116, 121-122.

119 *Mount of Olives*, Martin, pp. 176-177.

120 Bodleian MS Eng. th. e. 51. This is Traherne's most clerical work, evidently written in 1670, as Carol L. Marks (Sicherman) has pointed out ("Traherne's *Church's Year-Book*," *PBSA*, 60 [1966] 31-72). There may be a lost first part, on the period from Advent to Good Friday. The source closest in conception is Edward Sparke's *Scintillula Altaris* (London, 1652), but the eclectic manner, as we have seen, is very common in the Protestant manuals. See Marks, "*Church's Year-Book*," for a full account of the borrowings.

121 The *Meditations* were first published in *A Collection of Meditations and Devotions* (London, 1717), a collection ascribed by the editor to

Traherne's friend, Susanna Hopton. See Lynn Sauls, "Traherne's Debt to Puente's *Meditations*," *PQ*, 50 (1971), 161-174; and Luis de la Puente, *Meditations upon the Mysteries of our Holie Faith*, trans. John Heigham (St. Omer, 1619), II, 708-766.

122 The Osborn Manuscript, Beinecke Library, Yale University. See James M. Osborn, "A New Traherne Manuscript," *TLS*, Oct. 8, 1964, p. 928.

123 The *First Century* begins with no. 81, the *Fourth* ends with no. 68, the *Second* and *Third* are complete. The marked attention here to some controversial topics (absent from the published *Centuries*)—e.g., The Church, the importance of good works, Arminianism—together with the fragmentary nature of the work, may argue for an early date of composition, perhaps shortly after the Restoration, as Martz thinks (*The Paradise Within*, pp. 209-210).

124 Margoliouth dates the work about 1670. He also argues (I, 297) that the *Centuries* attain a sense of completion with V.10 such that, despite the title and the prior intention, the work could hardly have been continued.

125 *Centuries*, I.3: "Is it not a Great Thing, that you should be Heir of the World? . . . It is my Design therfore in such a Plain maner to unfold it, that my Friendship may appear, in making you Possessor of the Whole World" (Margoliouth, I, 3-4).

126 Martz, *The Paradise Within*, pp. 35-102; Gerald H. Cox, III, "Traherne's *Centuries*: A Platonic Devotion of 'Divine Philosophy,'" *MP*, 69 (1971), 10-24.

127 *Centuries*, I.8, 10, Margoliouth, I, 5-6.

128 *Ibid.*, III.1, 6, Margoliouth, I, 110, 114.

129 *Ibid.*, III.71-94, Margoliouth, I, 153-165.

130 *Ibid.*, V.10, Margoliouth, I, 232.

131 Philip Traherne prepared a volume of Thomas Traherne's poetry for publication (though it was not in fact published until 1910) under the title *Poems of Felicity* (B.M. Burney MS 392). Anne Ridler, in her edition of Traherne, separates the Dobell from the *Felicity* poems, thereby providing a text which may approximate that of the missing manuscript sequence.

132 See, e.g., "The Inference, I," "The City," "Insatiableness," "Consummation."

133 Wallace, "Thomas Traherne and the Structure of Meditation," *ELH*, 25 (1958), 79-89.

134 The title was supplied by Taylor though it is not clear just when he so labelled his manuscript.

135 See Norman S. Grabo's "Introduction" to his edition of *Edward Taylor's Christographia* sermons and poems (New Haven, 1962) for the argument that the poems were regularly composed after the sacrament-day sermons and on the doctrine rather than the text of the sermons. Louis Martz, in his "Foreword" to the Stanford edition of Taylor's *Poems* (p. xxvi), assumes just this relationship: "The sermon prepares the ground, the doctrine, for the Meditation; while the act of Meditation in turn prepares the

preacher to receive and administer the sacrament, and to deliver his sermon on that day with 'the bloud and spirits of Affection.' " Robert M. Benton, "Edward Taylor's Use of His Text," *AL*, 39 (1967), 31-41, assumes that the preparatory meditations reflect Taylor's "regular habit of meditation" before a monthly administration of the Supper. Thomas M. Davis, "Edward Taylor's 'Occasional Meditations,' " *EAL*, 5 (1971), 17-29, by a careful analysis of the intervals between the poems (almost all dated) for the years 1685-1698, argues from the irregularity of the intervals that the poems cannot have been rigidly tied to sacrament-day sermons.

136 The *Christographia* poems are nos. 42-56 of the "Second Series." A newly discovered manuscript of Taylor sermons at the University of Nebraska has sermons corresponding to poems II.1-7, 9-18, 20-27, 29, 58-61, 71; study of these sermons and the associated poems should afford further insights into the relation between sermon and poetic meditation in Taylor.

137 Edward Taylor, *Treatise Concerning the Lord's Supper*, ed. Norman S. Grabo (East Lansing, 1965), a sequence of eight sermons setting forth Taylor's doctrine of the right administration and reception of the sacrament.

138 Taylor, *Treatise*, pp. 201-203.

139 *Ibid.*, p. 203.

140 *Ibid.*, pp. 203-214.

141 *Ibid.*, p. 185.

142 Charles W. Mignon, "A Principle of Order in Edward Taylor's *Preparatory Meditations*," *EAL*, 4 (1969-1970), 110-116, finds a tripartite scheme of self-examination, contemplation of doctrine, and application in most of the poems. Martz in his "Foreword" to the Stanford edition (pp. xxiii-xxxvii) finds the poems reflecting an Ignatian tripartite structure, colored by Baxter's emphasis upon soliloquy and the use of the senses for imagining heavenly things. Martz's argument is substantially repeated in Michael D. Reed, "Edward Taylor's Poetry: Puritan Structure and Form," *AL*, 46 (1974), 304-312. But the fit between any of these schemes and the bulk of Taylor's poems is not very close. See also Norman Grabo, "Introduction," *Christographia*, p. xxxv; William J. Scheick, "Tending the Lord in All Admiring Style: Edward Taylor's *Preparatory Meditations*," *Language and Style*, 4 (1971), 163-187, rpt. in *The Will and the Word: The Poetry of Edward Taylor* (Athens, Ga., 1974), pp. 117-149.

143 Some indication of such accommodation is found in the fact that Taylor began a new numbered series after no. 49, and that he inserted two unnumbered poems into the sequence between no. 3 and no. 4, "The Experience" and "The Return."

## CHAPTER 6

1 Mario Praz, *Seventeenth-Century Imagery*; W. S. Heckscher, "Emblem, Emblembuch," in *Reallexikon zur deutschen Kunstgeschichte* (Stuttgart, 1959); Arthur Henkel and Albrecht Schöne, *Emblemata. Handbuch*

*zur sinnbildkunst des XVI und XVII Jahrhunderts* (Stuttgart, 1967). See also Rosemary Freeman, *English Emblem Books*; R. J. Clements, *Picta Poesis: Literary and Humanistic Theory in Renaissance Emblem Books* (Rome, 1960); Liselotte Dieckmann, *Hieroglyphics: The History of a Literary Symbol* (St. Louis, 1970); Giuliano Pellegrini, "Introduzione alla Letteratura degli Emblemi," *Rivista di Letterature Moderne e Comparate*, 29 (1976), 5-98; Josef Lederer, "John Donne and the Emblematic Practice," *RES*, 22 (1946), 182-200; Joseph Summers, *George Herbert*; Rosalie Colie, *"My Ecchoing Song"*; and Alan B. Howard, "The World as Emblem: Language and Vision in the Poetry of Edward Taylor," *AL*, 44 (1972), pp. 359-384.

2 This side of the emblem heritage is ably reviewed by Liselotte Dieckmann in *Hieroglyphics*.

3 Horapollo, Ἱερογλυφικά (Venice, 1505), Latin trans., Augsburg, 1515. Horapollo (Horus Apollo) was thought to be an Egyptian of the second or fourth century A.D. A Greek manuscript of the collection ascribed to him was discovered in 1419.

4 Colonna, *Hypnerotomachia* (n.p., 1499); Valeriano, *Hieroglyphica sive de Sacris Ægyptiorum literis commentarii* (Basle, 1556).

5 Ficino, *Opera Omnia* (Basle, 1576), II, 1901: "Imitantes Ægyptii ipsam universi naturam, fabricamque deorum, ipsi quoque mixticarum reconditarumque nationum imagines quasdam in symbolis conficiendis ostendunt, quem admodum & natura rationes occultas in apparentibus informis, quasi symbolis exprimit, & dii veritatem idearum per manifestas imagines explicant." Neoplatonic iconography of the cosmos as presented in S. K. Heninger, *The Cosmographical Glass: Renaissance Diagrams of the Universe* (San Marino, 1977), exemplifies these ideas in another mode.

6 Ficino, II, 1768, cited in E. H. Gombrich, *Symbolic Images: Studies in the Art of the Renaissance* (New York, 1972), pp. 158-159. See also Dieckmann, *Hieroglyphics*, pp. 34-47.

7 Alciati, *Emblematum liber* ([Augsburg], 1531); Mignault, "Syntagma de symbolis: Stemmatum et schematum ratione, quae insignia seu arma gentilitia vulgò nominantur: Déque Emblematis," in Alciati, *Emblemata. Cum Claudius Minois ad eadem Commentariis* (Lyons, 1600), pp. 1-15.

8 Praz, *Seventeenth-Century Imagery*, pp. 22-25.

9 Bargagli, *Delle Imprese* (Siena, 1578; with 2nd and 3rd part, Venice, 1594), pp. 3-5; Tesauro, *Il Cannocchiale Aristotelico* (Turin, 1670; 1st ed., 1654), p. 636. Tesauro subsequently argued that both *Imprese* and Emblems are symbolic metaphors, with one signification to the sense, another to the mind; that both are composed of a body (picture and motto) and soul (significance); and that both are in the form of a metaphor of proportion rendered through a poetic argument (pp. 636-641).

10 G. C. Capaccio, *Delle Imprese* (Naples, 1592), pp. 2ᵥ-3:

Per ciò che l'Emblema haurà solamente da pascer la vista, e l'Impresa l'Intelletto; Quello alla sola moralità attende; e questa al concetto delle cose rimira; quello tanto è più vago, quanto è più ornato di figure, &

ancor che dell'essenza dell'Emblema non siano, bisogna che altre Imagini o grandi, o picciole, o Gotteschi, o Arabeschi, o altri simili l'adornino, e questa tal'hor semplice e nuda, a cui principale ornamento faccia un Cartoccio, all'occhio con più leggiadria aggradisce. In somma, hà l'Emblema il suo titolo, quasi sentenza, spirito dell'Icona, e l'Impresa contiene il motto che dona solamente spirito al figurante, che col secreto concetto produsse fuori la figura.

11 *Ibid.*, p. 3.

12 Tasso, *Della realta & perfettione delle Imprese* (Bergamo, 1612), p. 294: "Conciosia che ne l'Impresa prenda suo essere da semplice Motto; ne l'Emblema sia tale per la inscrittione. Perche contengasi questo moralità, & risguardi l'universale, & sarà Emblema tanto seza inscrittione, quanto con essa: & esso stesso, quasi ripentito, il dice poco sotto. Et l'Impresa, se ben haurà Motto, ma non tale, che nulla dica senza la Figura, Impresa non sarà."

13 Fraunce, *Insignium Armorum, Emblematum, Hieroglyphicorum, et Symbolorum, quae ab Italis Imprese nominantur, explicatio* (London, 1588), sig. N 3: "In emblemate vox figuram exponit, quod in symbolo vitiam vel maximum esse solet, in quo, non vox figuram, nec figura vocem: sed figura cum voce, animi notionem explicat. Emblema ita constituitur, ut generalis sit illius praeceptio & doctrina: symbolum autem proprium est, & ad unius alicuius hominis institutum indicandum, accommodatum."

14 H. A. [Henry Hawkins], *Partheneia Sacra. Or the Mysterious and Delicious Garden of the Sacred Parthenes* ([Rouen], 1633), p. 3.

15 Estienne, *L'art de faire les devises* (Paris, 1645); *The Art of Making Devices*, trans. Thomas Blount (London, 1646).

16 Giovio, *Dialogo dell'Imprese* (Rome, 1555), pp. 8-9, trans. Daniel, *The Worthy Tract of Paulus Jovius, contayning a Discourse of rare inventions* (London, 1585), sig. B iii,. In his preface to the reader, Daniel offers even more rigid rules for the *impresa*, e.g., that the motto have no more than three words.

17 Bargagli, *Delle Imprese*, p. 5; cited in Estienne, *Art of Making Devices*, p. 10.

18 Giovio, trans. Daniel, sig. B iii,-B iiii. Mignault, "De Symbolis," *Emblemata*, pp. 1-15; Estienne, *Art of Making Devices*, pp. 29-30.

19 Whitney, *A Choice of Emblemes* (Leyden, 1586), sig. **4; Peacham, *Minerva Britanna, or a Garden of Heroical Devices* (London, 1612), sig. A 3ᵥ.

20 Puttenham, *Arte of English Poesie*, sigs. i-iii [after p. 84].

21 Georgette de Montenay, *Emblemes, ou Devises Chrestiennes* (Lyons, 1571).

22 Whitney, *Choice of Emblemes*, sig. **3ᵥ.

23 Also, the Jesuit center at Antwerp became a flourishing center of emblem-book production. See Praz, *Sevententh-Century Imagery*, pp. 134-368.

24 Montenay, *Emblemes*, sig. A 4ᵥ.

25 I am indebted to Carl J. Rasmussen for calling my attention to Van

der Noot. In "'Quietnesse of Minde': *A Theatre for Worldlings* as a Protestant Poetics" (forthcoming in *Spenser Studies*), he argues that *A Theatre* invites the reader to learn by evaluating the responses of the several speakers or personae—Petrarch, Du Bellay, John of Patmos—to the emblematic scenes depicted and described. The Dutch version of Van der Noot's *Theatre* is *Het Theatre oft Toon-Neel* (London, 1568), followed in the same year by a French edition, *Le Theatre* (London, 1568). The English edition is entitled, *A Theatre wherein be represented as wel the miseries & calamities that follow the voluptuous Worldlings, As also the great joyes and plesures which the faithfull do enjoy* (London, 1569). Spenser's translations were published again, without plates—the Du Bellay much revised and in complete form, the Petrarch transformed from twelve-line epigrams to sonnets—in Spenser's *Complaints* (London, 1591).

26 *A Theatre*, fol. 12ᵥ.

27 See above, chap. 5, pp. 162-165.

28 Estienne, *Art of Making Devices*, p. 2.

29 Quarles, *Emblemes* (London, 1635), sig. A 3.

30 *Ibid.*

31 Willet, *Sacrorum Emblematum Centuria Una . . . in tres classes distributa, quarum prima emblemata typica, sive Allegorica: altera historica, sive re gesta: Tertia Physica, a rerum natura sumpta continet* (Cambridge, [1592]), T.P.

32 Hall, "The Imprese of God. In two sermons preacht at the court, in the yeeres 1611-1612," in *A Recollection of . . . Treatises* (London, 1620-1621), pp. 430-432.

33 Calvin, *Institutes*, IV.xiv.18, McNeill, II, 1294.

34 *Ibid.*, IV.xiv.4-6, McNeill, II, 1328.

35 Mede, *The Key of the Revelation*, trans. Richard More (London, 1643), sig. [b 2ᵥ], a translation of Mede's *Clavis Apocalyptica* (Cambridge, 1627).

36 *Ibid.*, sig. bᵥ.

37 The mix of kinds and the moralizing tendency are evident in the expanded edition of Alciati, *Emblemata . . . Acceserunt nova aliquot ab autore emblemata, suis quoque eiconibus insignita* (Lyons, 1550); they are full-blown in Mignault's edition of 1600, which orders the plates thematically in the manner of a commonplace book, and often attaches moral significance to emblems initially quite innocent of such meaning.

38 Camerarius, *Symbolorum et Emblematum Centuriae Tres . . . Accessit Noviter Centuria* ([Nuremburg], 1605); first *Century* published, 1590; Paradin, *Devises Heroiques* (Lyons, 1557), trans. P. S., *The Heroicall Devises of M. Claudius Paradin* (London, 1591); Ripa, *Iconologia, o vero Descrittione delle Virtù, Vitii, Affetti Passioni humane, Corpi Celesti, mondo e sue parti* (Padua, 1611; 1st ed., Rome, 1593). See also Jean Baudoin, *Iconologie, ou, explication nouvelle de plusieurs images, emblemes, et autres figures . . . Tirée des rescherches & des figures de C. Ripa, moralisées* (Paris, 1644); Jacobus Typotius, *Symbola Divina & Humana, Ponti-*

*ficum, Imperium, Regum* (Prague, 1601); Theodore Beza, *Icones . . . quibus adiectae sunt nonnullae picturae quas Emblemata vocant* (Geneva, 1580).

39 Whitney, *A Choice of Emblemes, and Other Devices, for the most part gathered out of sundrie writers, Englished and Moralized.*

40 Peacham, *Minerva Britanna*, sig. A 3ᵥ.

41 Jacob Cats, *Silenus Alcibiadis, Sive Proteus* (Middleburgh, 1618).

42 Heyns, *Emblemata Moralia* (Rotterdam, 1625); see also Daniel Cramer, *Emblemata Moralia Nova* (Frankfurt, 1630).

43 George Wither, *A Collection of Emblemes, Ancient and Moderne: Quickened With Metricall Illustrations, both Morall and Divine: And disposed into Lotteries, That Instruction, and Good Counsell, may bee furthered by an Honest and Pleasant Recreation* (London, 1635). Wither's "Lotteries" were a parlor game in which players would spin hands on wheels to discover which emblems they would be directed to as especially suited to their own vices, virtues, and spiritual qualities. The emblems in the four books are discrete, save that the entire collection ends with a "crown" emblem, representing the fitting conclusion to the moral and spiritual struggles of life. For Wither's source of emblems see Gabriel Rollenhagen, *Nucleus Emblematum Selectissimorum* ([Arnheim, 1611]); and *Selectorum Emblematum Centuria Secunda* ([Arnheim], 1613).

44 Camerarius, I, 49, fol. 51; Zacharias Heyns, *Emblemata, Emblemes Chrestienes et Morales* (Rotterdam, 1625), sig. D 2; B[artholomaeus] H[ulsius], *Emblemata Sacra*, no. 19 ([Amsterdam?], 1631), p. 11.

45 Montenay, *Emblemes*. See also, in this kind, Stephen Bateman, *A Christall glasse of christian reformation* (London, 1569); Willet, *Sacrorum Emblematum Centuria Una*; Thomas Jenner, *The Soules Solace, or Thirtie and One Spirituall Emblems* ([London], 1612).

46 Mannich, *Sacra Emblemata LXXVI* (Nuremburg, 1624).

47 Farley, *Lychnocausia sive Moralia Facum Emblemata. Lights Moral Emblems* (London, 1638); Quarles, *Hieroglyphikes of the Life of Man* (London, 1638); Saltmarsh, *Holy Discoveries and Flames* (London, 1640).

48 [Phillippe de Mallery], *Typus Mundi in quo eius Calamitates et Pericula nec non Divini, humanique Amoris Antipathia* (Antwerp, 1627).

49 Van Veen [Vaenius], *Amoris Divini Emblemata* (Antwerp, 1615). Veen's earlier book of love emblems, *Amorum Emblemata* (Antwerp, 1608), displays the power and exploits of Eros.

50 See Hoyer, *Flammulae Amoris* (Antwerp, 1629); and J[ohn] H[all], *Emblems with elegant Figures* [or] *Sparkles of Divine Love* (London, 1658)—a selection from Hoyer's plates.

51 Van Haeften [Haeftenus], *Regia Via Crucis* (Antwerp, 1635).

52 Hugo, *Pia Desideria* (Antwerp, 1624).

53 Almost half a century later, Edmund Arwaker provided an English translation of Hugo (*Pia Desideria: or, Divine Addresses*, London, 1686), though his Protestant sensibilities led him to delete all the classical fictions,

saints' lives, and martyrologies Hugo had interspersed in his commentaries, replacing some with biblical stories.

54 Quarles, *Emblemes*. Reissued in 1639, 1643, 1658, 1660, 1663, 1676, 1684, and in numerous eighteenth- and nineteenth-century editions.

55 Van Haeften [Haeftenus], *Schola Cordis* (Antwerp, 1629).

56 Harvey, *Schola Cordis, or, The Heart of it selfe, gone away from God; brought back againe to him; and instructed by him* (London, 1647). Harvey is also the author of a sequel to Herbert's *The Temple*, called *The Christian Synagogue* (London, 1648).

57 [Jean Messager], *Vis Amoris Jesu in Hominum corda singularis* (Paris, 1624). The same series (executed by Martin Baes with a few additions and in somewhat different order) is used in Etienne Luzvic and Etienne Binet, *Le cœur devot, Throsne royal de Jesus Pacifique Salomon* (Douai, 1627), and also in the English version of H. A. [Henry Hawkins], *The Devout Hart or Royal Throne of the Pacifical Salomon* (n.p., 1634). See the introduction by K. J. Höltgen to the Scolar Press facsimile (1975) of Hawkins' *Devout Hart*. A related kind of heart book is the "Appendix" to Pedro Bivero's *Sacrum Oratorium Piarum Imaginum Immaculatae Mariae et Animae Creatae* (Antwerp, 1634), which presents David as the type of the penitent sinner, with texts from his 51st Psalm accompanying plates displaying God's action within the heart.

58 See, e.g., Wither, *Emblemes*, I.43, II.15, II.29, pp. 43, 77, 91; Mannich, *Sacra Emblemata*, fols. 12, 13, 15, 17, 19, 36, 37, 46, 47, 51, 72, 77, 84.

59 Cramer, *Emblemata Sacra. Hoc est Decades Quinque Emblematum ex Sacra Scriptura* (Frankfurt, 1624).

60 The Jesuit heart book, Francisco Pona's *Cardiomorphoseos sive Ex Corde Desumpta Emblemata Sacra* (Verona, 1645), seems at first glance to contradict this generalization: the heart is portrayed alone, without an Anima figure, and is sometimes acted upon from without. But in such cases the actor is most often the Infant Divine Love, not the strong arm of God. And when various entities or shapes appear within the heart (a skull, eyes, flowers, flames) the suggestion is usually of the heart's own dispositions and transformations rather than of overpowering divine grace.

61 Richard Crashaw, *Carmen Deo Nostro, Te Decet Hymnus* (Paris, 1652).

62 See Crashaw's *"Adoro Te," "Sancta Maria Dolorum"* (a version of the *Stabat Mater*) *"O Gloriosa Domina," "In the Glorious Assumption of Our Blessed Lady."* Cf. Henry Hawkins, *Partheneia Sacra*.

63 Camerarius, *Centuriae*, I.99, fol. 101; Paradin, *Devises Heroiques*, pp. 248-251; Wither, *Emblemes*, IV.50, p.258.

64 Herbert, "A Wreath"; Vaughan, "The Wreath"; Taylor, I.43, I.44, I.45.

65 Donne, "A Litanie," l. 243; Herbert, "Prayer I," l. 5; "Deniall," ll. 1-2; "Prayer II," l. 3; "The Search," ll. 17-20.

66 Hugo, *Pia Desideria*, no. 17, opposite p. 134; Quarles, IV.2, p. 188. See

Herbert, "The Pearl," ll. 38-40; Vaughan, "Retirement," ll. 19-22; Taylor, II.113, l. 5.

67 Hugo, *Pia Desideria*, no. 39, opposite p. 342. The emblem is reproduced in Quarles, V.9, p. 275, and is a sacred version of the moral emblem on the hindrance of poverty to wit (Whitney, *Choice of Emblemes*, p. 152, and Wither, *Emblemes*, III.42, p. 176). Cf. Vaughan, "Ascension-day," ll. 9-10; Taylor, I.20, ll. 37, 41; Herbert, "Home," ll. 61-65.

68 Camerarius, I.55, fol. 57; Wither, II.42, p. 104; III.6, p. 140.

69 Herbert, "Vanitie (I)," l. 25. Vaughan, "The Showre," ll. 17-18; "The Sap." Taylor, II.131, l. 27; II.47.

70 Wither, II.45, p. 107; Peacham, *Minerva Britanna*, p. 12; Vaughan, "Regeneration," ll. 65-72; Taylor, *Gods Determinations*, "The Glory of and Grace in the Church set out," pp. 456-457.

71 Wither, II.8, p. 70; Mannich, fol. 15.

72 Herbert, "The Flower," ll. 9-10, 41-42. See also "Affliction (V)," ll. 20-24. Vaughan, "Unprofitableness"; "Mount of Olives [II]," l. 22; "Affliction," ll. 13-15; "Love and Discipline," ll. 17-18.

73 Montenay, *Emblemes*, p. 50; Heyns, *Emblemata Moralia*, p. 21; Peacham, *Minerva Britanna*, p. 192; Hulsius, *Emblemata Sacra*, no. 17, p. 57.

74 Taylor, II.144, l. 12.

75 See Appendix G in Helen Gardner's edition of Donne's *Divine Poems* for a thorough discussion of the date of this poem, and an argument for emending the title used in the first edition (1650). The Latin poem, with English translation, appears on pp. 52-53 in Gardner. See Walton, "The Life of Dr. John Donne," in *Lives* (London, 1670), p. 56.

76 Paradin, *Devises Heroiques*, pp. 9, 10, 107.

77 Walton, "Life of Donne," p. 56.

78 *Ibid.*, p. 75.

79 Gardner, p. 53. See frontispiece for *Deaths Duell*, reproduced in *Sermons*, ed. Potter and Simpson, X, T.P.

80 Lipsius, *De Cruce Libri Tres* (Antwerp, 1593), I.x, p. 21.

81 Valeriano, *Hieroglyphica*, fols. 286$_v$-289; Beza, *Icones*, Emblema I, sig. Kk iii$_v$; Donne, "Upon the Annunciation and Passion falling upon one day. 1608," l. 4.

82 Donne, "A Hymne to Christ, at the Authors last going into Germany," ll. 1-2; Hulsius, *Emblemata Sacra*, no. 19, p. 65.

83 Valeriano, *Hieroglyphica*, fols. 74$_v$-77$_v$; cf. Hulsius, *Emblemata Sacra*, nos. 26 and 27, pp. 88-93. Donne, "La Corona," "Ascension," ll. 9-10.

84 Montenay, *Emblemes*, p. 5; Donne, "Holy Sonnet I," l. 14.

85 Cramer, *Emblemata Sacra*, nos. 1, 4, pp. 17, 29; Mannich, *Sacra Emblemata*, fol. 12. Karl Josef Höltgen, "Eine Emblemfolge in Donne's *Holy Sonnet XIV*," *Archiv fur das Studium der Neueren Sprachen und Literaturen*, 200 (1963), 347-352, has pointed to a number of emblematic analogues for this poem, and to its pervasive emblematic manner, recognizing however that the most suggestive "heart" emblems postdate the poem.

86 Valeriano, *Hieroglyphica*, fols. 171, 6, 95-96; Camerarius, II.10, II.73, III.47, fols. 12, 75, 47.

87 Colie, *The Resources of Kind: Genre-Theory in the Renaissance* (Berkeley, 1973), p. 53.

88 See Hugo, *Pia Desideria*, no. 14, opposite p. 106; Quarles, *Emblemes*, III.14, p. 176; Camerarius, I.100, fol. 102; Paradin, *Devises Heroiques*, p. 258.

89 Summers, *George Herbert*, pp. 123-146.

90 Herbert, "Sion," ll. 1-13; Heyns, *Emblemes Chrestienes*, sig. C 2.

91 Herbert, "The Sinner," l. 5; van Haeften, *Schola Cordis*, II.2, p. [96].

92 Herbert, "The Familie," l. 3; "Decay," ll. 11-14; *Vis Amoris*, nos. 4, 5.

93 Herbert, "Whitsunday," ll. 1-3; van Haeften, *Schola Cordis*, III.12, p. [414].

94 *Vis Amoris*, nos. 13, 14. See also "Deniall" and "A true Hymne."

95 Wither, *Emblemes*, II.15, p. 77; Cramer, *Emblemata Sacra*, no. 1, p. 17.

96 Cramer, *Emblemata Sacra*, no. 23, p. 103; Cramer's motto, not directly relevant to Herbert's poem, is "*Praedestinor.*"

97 Cramer, *Emblemata Sacra*, no. 21, p. 97; Mannich, *Sacra Emblemata*, fol. 10.

98 Herbert, "Longing," l. 82; "Discipline," ll. 22-24; Cramer, *Emblemata Sacra*, no. 47, p. 201.

99 Herbert, "An Offering," ll. 19-22; Cramer, *Emblemata Sacra*, no. 12, p. 61; no. 41, p. 177.

100 See van Haeften, "*Cordis Mundatio*," "*Cordis Probatio*," *Schola Cordis*, II.14, II.18, pp. [216], [266].

101 Montenay, *Emblemes*, p. 81; Cramer, *Emblemata Sacra*, nos. 24, 22, pp. 109, 101.

102 Vaughan, "Regeneration," ll. 19-24; Cramer, *Emblemata Sacra*, no. 18, p. 85.

103 Vaughan, "H. Scriptures," ll. 9-10; van Haeften, *Schola Cordis*, III.3, p. [328]; Harvey, *Schola Cordis*, no. 26, p. 104.

104 Camerarius, I.49, fol. 51; Wither, *Emblemes*, IV.1, p. 209; Paradin, *Devises Heroiques*, p. 41; Heyns, *Emblemes Chrestienes*, sig. D 2; Hulsius, *Emblemata Sacra*, no. 4, p. 11.

105 "Sure, there's a tye of Bodyes!" ll. 7-8; "Regeneration," ll. 65-68.

106 Cats, *Silenus Alcibiadis*, III.51, p. 105.

107 Quarles, *Hieroglyphikes*, VIII, pp. 30-33; Farley, *Lychnocausia*, 58, sigs. I 2ᵥ-I 3.

108 Alciati (1531), p. 19; Wither, *Emblemes*, I.28, p. 28.

109 Camerarius, I.100, fol. 102; Paradin, *Devises Heroiques*, p. 258.

110 See, e.g., Quarles, *Emblemes*, I.9, p. 36; Peacham, *Minerva Britanna*, p. 127.

111 Wither, *Emblemes*, III.22, p. 156; Traherne, "Love," ll. 31-34.

112 Traherne, "Misapprehension," ll. 53-65; Heyns, *Emblemata Moralia*, p. 29.

113 Saltmarsh, *Holy Discoveries and Flames*; Horapollo, *De sacris notis et sculpturis libri duo* (Paris, 1551), p. 45. Wither, *Emblemes*, I.43, p. 43.

114 See Traherne, "The Preparative," l. 12; "Sight," ll. 1-2; "My Spirit," ll. 103, 107; "News," ll. 51-53.

115 Hugo, *Pia Desideria*, no. 22, opposite p. 182; Arwaker, *Divine Addresses*, p. 120. Figures 21, 23, 24 are from the London, 1690, edition of Arwaker. Traherne, "The Approach," ll. 7-8.

116 Edward Taylor gathered fourteen sermons which explore in a sequential manner the nature and offices of Christ into a separate manuscript under this title. Clearly, he conceived of them as a unified sequence, drawing such a "portrait." See Grabo, ed., *Edward Taylor's Christographia*.

117 *Ibid.*, pp. 443-444.

118 A number of these references have been located by Thomas E. Johnston, Jr., "Edward Taylor: An American Emblematist," *EAL*, 3 (1968-1969), 186-198.

119 Van Haeften, *Schola Cordis*, II.13, p. [206]; Veen, *Amoris Divini Emblemata*, pp. 18-19; Hugo, *Pia Desideria*, no. 35, opposite p. 304.

120 Taylor, II.129, II.130, II.131, II.132; Hugo, *Pia Desideria*, no. 33, opposite p. 284; Arwaker, *Divine Addresses*, p. 184.

121 Hugo, *Pia Desideria*, no. 42, opposite p. 369; Quarles, *Emblemes*, V.12, p. 288. Cf. also Taylor's image in the same poem of "sins bowling alley," with *Typus Mundi*, p. 105.

122 Wither, *Emblemes*, I.21, p. 21; Peacham, *Minerva Britanna*, p. 8.

123 Cats, *Silenus Alcibiadis*, I.13, p. 27; II.13, p. 29; III.13, p. 29. Hugo, *Pia Desideria*, no. 40, opposite p. 350; Arwaker, *Divine Addresses*, p. 230. Quarles, *Emblemes*, V.10, p. 262 [280].

124 Quarles, *Hieroglyphikes*, II, 6-9; Montenay, *Emblemes*, p. 57.

125 See above, n. 104.

126 Montenay, *Emblemes*, p. 11.

127 Taylor, I.40, I.43, I.49; van Haeften, *Schola Cordis*, II.2, p. [97]; Harvey, *Schola Cordis*, no. 5, p. 20; *Vis Amoris*, no. 5.

128 Wither, *Emblemes*, II.15, p. 77; van Haeften, *Schola Cordis*, III.11, p. [402]; *Vis Amoris*, no. 14.

129 See, e.g., the reproduction of this curious hieroglyphic and the discussion of it in Karl Keller, *The Example of Edward Taylor* (Amherst, 1975), pp. 167-168.

130 Cats, *Silenus Alcibiadis*, III.39, p. 81.


CHAPTER 7

1 See above, chap. 3, pp. 77-104.

2 W. Fraser Mitchell, *English Pulpit Oratory from Andrewes to Tillotson* (London, 1932); J. W. Blench, *Preaching in England in the Late Fifteenth and Sixteenth Centuries: A Study of English Sermons 1450-c. 1600* (Oxford, 1964); Horton Davies, *Worship and Theology in England from Cranmer to Hooker, 1534-1603* (Princeton, 1970); Davies, *Worship and*

*Theology in England from Andrewes to Baxter and Fox, 1603-1690* (Princeton, 1975).

3 Abraham Wright, *Five Sermons, in Five Several Styles; or Waies of Preaching* (London, 1656).

4 See Richard F. Jones, "The Attack on Pulpit Eloquence in the Restoration: An Episode in the Development of the Neo-Classical Standard for Prose," *The Seventeenth Century: Studies in the History of English Thought and Literature from Bacon to Pope* (Stanford, 1951), pp. 111-142. Cf. Mitchell, *English Pulpit Oratory*, pp. 347-379.

5 See John Eachard, *The Grounds and Occasions of the Contempt of the Clergy* (London, 1670), p. 52; Herbert Croft, *The Naked Truth* ([London], 1675), p. 25; Joseph Glanvill, *A Seasonable Defence of Preaching: And the Plain Way of It* (London, 1678), p. 109.

6 John Evelyn, *Memoirs* (19th September, 1655), ed. William Bray (London, 1870), p. 245.

7 Samuel Parker, *A Discourse of Ecclesiastical Politie* (London, 1670), pp. 74-75.

8 Robert South, "The Scribe Instructed" (preached July 29, 1660), in Irène Simon, ed., *Three Restoration Divines*, 2 vols. (Paris, 1967, 1976) II.1, p. 246.

9 Augustine, *Confessions*, X, xxxiii, *Works*, ed. Dods, XIV, 272-273. See the translation by William Watts (London, 1631), pp. 674-677, a Protestant version intended in part as an answer and corrective to the earlier Roman Catholic translation of Tobie Matthew, which was published in 1620 at St. Omer.

10 Calvin, *Institutes*, III.xx.31-32, McNeill, II, 894-896. It is easy to overstate the role played by the suspicion of the senses in seventeenth-century Calvinist-Puritan aesthetics, as I believe U. Milo Kaufman does (*Traditions in Puritan Meditation*, pp. 55-60) in his emphasis upon Ramist logic and *logos* in Puritan sermons. This emphasis, though important, was by no means universal, and was often associated with imaginative and extensive use of metaphor.

11 Augustine, *De Doctrina*, I.xl, Robertson, p. 33.

12 Calvin, *Psalmes*, pt. 1, fol. 206: "He prayeth that his lippes may be opened, which importeth as much as that matter of prayse should be ministered unto him. I knowe, that this place is woont to be expounded in this wyse, as though David should wish his tung to be directed by Gods spirit, so as he myght be meete to setfoorthe his prayses: and truly, except GOD minister wordes unto us, wee shall bee utterly dumb. But David ment another thing, namely, that now he is after a sort dumb, untill he be called too thanksgiving by obteyning forgyvenesse."

13 Augustine, *De Doctrina*, IV.vii, viii, Robertson, p. 122.

14 *Ibid.*, I.xii, xxxvi-xxxix, Robertson, pp. 13-14, 30-33.

15 *Ibid.*, IV.xviii-xix, Robertson, pp. 143-146.

16 See Mazzeo, "St. Augustine's Rhetoric of Silence," pp. 10-11; Fish, *Self-Consuming Artifacts*, pp. 37-41.

17 Augustine, *De Doctrina*, IV.xvi, Robertson, p. 141.

18 *Ibid.*, IV.xxii-xxvi, Robertson, pp. 158-164.

19 *Ibid.*, IV.vi, Robertson, pp. 123-124.

20 *Ibid.*, IV.vii, Robertson, pp. 125, 132.

21 Erasmus, *Ecclesiastae sive de ratione concionandi libri quatuor* (Basle, 1535); Philip Melancthon, *De Rhetorica libri tres* (Haguenau, 1521); Andreas Gerardus [Hyperius], *De formandis concionibus sacris . . . libri ii* (Basle, 1573), trans. John Ludham, *The Practis of preaching, otherwise called the Pathway to the Pulpet* (London, 1577); Bartholomaeus Keckermann, *Rhetoricae Ecclesiasticae, sive Artes formandi et habendi conciones sacras libri duo* (Hanover, 1606).

22 Melancthon, *De Rhetorica*, esp. sigs. G 4ᵥ-H 1ᵥ; see also his tract on the sermon, "De Officiis Concionatoris," appended to *Ratio Brevis et Docta, Piaque, Sacrarum tractandorum Concionum, vulgo Modus Praedicandi adpellata* (Zurich[?], 1535); reprinted with several other *artes concionandi* by Joannes Reuchlin, Joannes Hepinus, and an anonymous writer, *De Arte concionandi formulae* (London, 1570). See also Erasmus, *Ecclesiastae*, I, pp. 1-6, 39; II, pp. 112, 121.

23 Hyperius, *Practis of Preaching*, p. 18.

24 Keckermann, *Rhetoricae Ecclesiasticae*.

25 Perkins, *Workes*, II, 646; the tract was first published in 1592.

26 *Ibid.*, p. 673.

27 See, e.g., *A Directory for the Publique Worship of God, Through the Three Kingdoms* (London, 1644); Bernard, *The Faithfull Shepherd*, pp. 32-33, 297-305, 349-350; Chappell, *Methodus Concionandi* (London, 1648), trans. *The Preacher, or the Art and Method of Preaching* (London, 1656); Wilkins, *Ecclesiastes, or, A Discourse concerning the Gift of Preaching as it fals under the rules of Art* (London, 1646), pp. 4, 13, 71.

28 Askew, *Brotherly Reconcilement* (London, 1605), pp. 269-270. The tract contains a lengthy appendix, "An Apologie, of the use of Fathers, and Secular learning in Sermons," pp. 257-353. See esp. pp. 259-270, 352-353.

29 See Mitchell, *English Pulpit Oratory*, pp. 186-194.

30 Donne, *Sermons*, II.282.

31 *Ibid.*, X, 147-148.

32 *Ibid.*, II, 166-167.

33 *Ibid.*, V, 287.

34 *Ibid.*, VIII, 270-273.

35 *Ibid.*, II, 170-171.

36 Donne, *Devotions*, ed. Raspa, pp. 99-100.

37 Willet, *Hexapla . . . upon . . . Romans*, p. 8.

38 Hutchinson, pp. 233-234, 257.

39 Featley, *Ancilla Pietatis*, pp. 20-23.

40 Cawdrey, *Treasurie . . . of Similies*, sig. [A 4-A 4ᵥ].

41 Ferguson, *The Interest of Reason in Religion; With the Import and Use of Scripture-Metaphors* (London, 1675).

42 *Ibid.*, pp. 281-282, 322-325, 294, 367.

43 *Ibid.*, p. 373.

44 Perkins, *A Commentarie . . . upon . . . Galatians, Workes*, II, 222.

45 Perkins, *Arte of Prophecying, Workes*, II, 670-671.

46 Perkins, *Of the Calling of the Ministerie, Two Treatises, Workes*, III, 430.

47 Dell, *The Tryal of Spirits both in Teachers and Hearers* (London, 1653), p. 27; see also in the same publication his "Plain and necessary Confutation of divers Errors delivered by Mr. Sydrach Simpson."

48 See "The Altar," "The Temper (I)," "Praise (I)," "Dulnesse," "Repentance," "Employment (I)," "The Flower," "Josephs coat," "Deniall," "The Method," "A true Hymne."

49 See "The Thanksgiving" and, especially, "The Holdfast."

50 Martin, p. 392.

51 Traherne, "The Author to the Critical Peruser," ll. 1-5.

52 See below, pp. 248-249, and n. 116.

53 *Preparatory Meditations*, II.44, ll. 1-2.

54 II.53, ll. 5-6; II.74, l. 1.

55 I.32, l. 6; II.35, ll. 14-15.

56 II.138, l. 13; II.152, l. 7; II.153, l. 11.

57 II.6, ll. 1-2; II.36, ll. 31-32; I.32, ll. 9-10; I.22, ll. 5-6.

58 I.22, ll. 19-20.

59 I.43, l. 42.

60 Campbell, *Divine Poetry and Drama*, pp. 74-92. See chap. 1, pp. 8-9 and nn. 21, 22.

61 James I, "Uranie," sig. D iii,v.

62 Breton, *An Excellent Poeme, upon the longing of a Blessed Heart* (London, 1601), sig. C 2; *The Psalms of King David. Translated by King James* [Oxford, 1631]; Robert Aylett, "Urania, Or the Heavenly Muse," *Divine, and Moral Speculations*, pp. 89-97, esp. p. 93. See also Antoine La Pujade, *La Muse Chrestienne*, in *Les Oeuvres Chrestiennes*, Part II, fols. 63-66; Sir John Stradling, *Divine Poems*, pp. 74-86; J[oseph] F[letcher], *Christs Bloodie Sweat*, sig. [A 3].

63 See, e.g., the résumé of the opinions of the various patristic and later exegetes on the authorship question in Wither, *Preparation to the Psalter*, pp. 27-34.

64 Asals, "The Voice of George Herbert's 'The Church,'" *ELH*, 36 (1969), 511-528.

65 Augustine, *Expositions on . . . Psalms*, III, 160.

66 *Ibid.*, I, 6; I, 170; I, 375.

67 *Ibid.*, I, 139; II, 385, 199.

68 Calvin, *Psalmes*, pt. 1, fols. 22v, 3-3v, 30v.

69 *The Bible* [Geneva-Tomson], pt. 2, fol. 5.

70 Ainsworth, *Annotations upon . . . Psalmes*, p. 3.

71 Diodati, *Annotations*, pt. 1, p. 321.

72 Wither, *Preparation to the Psalter*, p. 54. See also pp. 31-32.

73 In Parker, *Psalter*, sigs. C i-C ii.

74 Luther, *Manual*, pp. 10-11; Calvin, *Psalmes*, pt. 1, fols. * viiv, 164v. See above, chap. 2, pp. 42-43, chap. 4, pp. 132-134.

75 Beza, *Christian Meditations upon eight Psalmes of the Prophet David*, trans. I.S. [John Stubs] (London, [1582]).

76 [Bate], *The Psalme of Mercy*.

77 Hammond, *Annotations upon . . . Psalms*, sig. C 2ᵥ.

78 Webber, *Contrary Music*, p. 167. See Donne, *Sermons*, II, 49-50; V, 299.

79 Calvin, *Commentaries on . . . Jeremiah and . . . Lamentations*, V, 301, 332, 389, 494. See also John Udall, *Commentarie upon . . . Lamentations* (London, 1637), esp. pp. 1, 92; and Donne, *Sermons*, X, 192-212, for a similar argument.

80 Muffet, *A Commentarie upon the Whole Booke of the Proverbs of Solomon* (London, 1596). See also R[obert] A[llen], *An Alphabet of Holy Proverbs of King Salomon* (London, 1596)—a commonplace book arranging Solomon's maxims alphabetically according to topics, especially addressed to Solomon's supposed audience, children; Samson Price, *The Two Twins of Birth and Death* (London, 1624); *The Bible* [Geneva], pt. 1, fol. 267.

81 See above, chap. 2, pp. 57-59.

82 Beza, *Sermons upon . . . Canticles*, p. 4; see also Wilcox, *An Exposition upon the Booke of the Canticles* (London, 1624), p. 2; Fenner, *The Song of Songs* (Middleburgh, 1587), sig. B 2ᵥ.

83 Fenner, *Song of Songs*, sig. B 2ᵥ.

84 Sibbes, *Bowels Opened*, p. 4; see also Diodati, *Annotations*, pt. 1, pp. 435-436; Simon Patrick, *The Song of Solomon Paraphrased. With Annotations* (London, 1685), p. iii.

85 See, e.g., John Smith, "Of Prophecy," in *Select Discourses* (London, 1660), pp. 178-181. See also Kerrigan, *The Prophetic Milton*, pp. 83-118; and see John Hull, *An Exposition upon . . . Lamentations*, p. 2.

86 Smith, "Of Prophecy," pp. 229-239.

87 *I Sette Salmi Penitenziali di Dante Alighieri e di Francesco Petrarca* (Firenze, 1827); "Petrarchs Seven Penitentiall Psalms" (1612), in *The Poems of George Chapman*, ed. Phyllis B. Bartlett (New York, 1941), pp. 204-220.

88 See chap. 2, n. 7.

89 Kenneth Muir, ed., *Collected Poems of Sir Thomas Wyatt* (London, 1963), pp. 203-226. See introduction for dating (c. 1540) and discussion of the circumstances of Wyatt's arrest, trial, and subsequent release, and the charges against him, which included rumors of scandal involving Anne Boleyn. For the influence of Luther and Tyndale on the paraphrase of the Penitential Psalms and for their distinctively "reformed" character, see Harold A. Mason, *Humanism and Poetry in the Early Tudor Period* (London, 1959), pp. 206-221; and Mason, *Editing Wyatt* (Cambridge, 1972), pp. 178-192.

90 Wyatt, *Poems*, ll. 80-108, pp. 207-208. Compare Psalm 6:7-10:

> 7. Mine eie is consumed because of griefe; it waxeth olde because of all mine enemies.

8. Depart from me, all yee workers of iniquitie: for the LORD hath heard the voice of my weeping.

9. The LORD hath heard my supplication; the LORD will receive my prayer.

10. Let all mine enemies be ashamed and sore vexed: let them returne and be ashamed suddainly.

91 "Gascoignes De Profundis," in *The Whole Woorkes of George Gascoigne Esquyre* (London, 1587), pp. 25-28.

92 [Gascoigne], *A Hundreth sundrie Flowres bounde up in one small Poesie* (London, [1573]), p. 373. This edition contains the sonnet only, not the psalm.

93 Campion, *Two Books of Airs. The First, containing Divine and Moral Songs: the Second, Light Conceits of Lovers,* in *Poetical Works,* ed. Percival Vivian (London, [1907]), p. 46; William Hunnis, *Seven Sobs.*

94 Barnabe Barnes, *A Divine Centurie of Spirituall Sonnets* (London, 1595), in *The Poems of Barnabe Barnes,* ed. Alexander Grosart (London, 1875), [sig. A 3ᵥ].

95 See, e.g., Sonnet 35 (Psalm 68), Sonnet 46 (Psalm 148), Sonnet 62 (Psalm 40), Sonnet 73 (Psalm 46), Sonnet 92 (Psalm 51), and Sonnet 49 (Psalm 102).

96 Barnes, *Divine Centurie,* pp. 189, 192, 207, 185.

97 Two of Barnes' sonnets (28 and 32), almost wholly comprised of epithets, are suggestive for the technique of Herbert's "Prayer (I)."

98 Published with his *Ecclesiastes.* The separate title-page introducing the *Christian Passions* reads, *Sundry Christian Passions, Contained in two hundred Sonnets . . . The first consisting chiefly of Meditations, Humiliations, and Prayers. The second of Comfort, Joy, and Thankesgiving.* The appended third century of sonnets, "Sundry Affectionate Sonets of a Feeling Conscience" is clearly intended as part of the thematic sequence. See edition and critical discussion by James Scanlon, "*Sundry Christian Passions*: A Critical Edition by James J. Scanlon," Diss. Brown 1970.

99 *Sundry Christian Passions,* sig. I viii.

100 *Ibid.,* sig. I viiiᵥ. He argues indeed that the poems' "disorder doth best fit the nature of mankind," and that they are placed "as they were by God ministred unto my mind to set downe by sundrie Accidents."

101 See the bibliographical and historical introduction in Rathmell, *Psalms of . . . Sidney and the Countess,* the only modern edition of the entire work to appear since the first publication in 1823. My quotations are from the Rathmell edition.

102 Psalm texts are cited from the Geneva Bible [1560] or the Prayer Book *Psalter or Psalmes of David* (London, 1570) [BCP], whichever is closer. As Rathmell points out (p. xix), "it is clear that Sidney and his sister carefully compared versions of the psalms found in the Prayer Book psalter and the two current versions of the Bible, the Geneva Bible of 1560 and the Bishops' Bible of 1568," as well as the psalm commentaries of Calvin and Beza in English translation. See G. F. Waller, " 'This Matching of Con-

traries': Calvinism and Courtly Philosophy in the Sidney Psalms," *ES*, 55 (1974), 22-31.

103 Cf. Herbert, "Heaven," ll. 1-4:

> O who will show me those delights on high?
> *Echo.*                    I.
> Thou Echo, thou are mortall, all men know.
> *Echo.*                    No.

104 Rathmell, "Introduction," pp. xx-xxi.

105 Cf. Psalm 23:5-6:

> Thou shalt prepare a table before me, agaynst them that trouble me: thou hast annoynted my head with oyle, and my cup shalbe full.
>
> But thy lovyng Kyndnesse and mercye shal folow me all the dayes of my lyfe: and I wyll dwell in the house of the Lorde for ever.

106 See Martz, *Poetry of Meditation*, p. 273, and Rathmell, pp. xviii-xix. Martz's observation that these psalms provide "the closest approximation to the poetry of Herbert's *Temple* that can be found anywhere in preceding English poetry" is the appropriate starting point for such investigation.

107 "Upon the translation of the Psalmes by Sir Philip Sydney, and the Countesse of Pembroke his Sister," 11, 34, 22.

108 See Lewalski, *Donne's* Anniversaries, pp. 236-240, 275-279.

109 Donne, *Sermons*, II, 49.

110 See below, chap. 9, pp. 304-305.

111 See, e.g., "The Sacrifice," "Antiphon (II)," "The Quip," "Dialogue," "Peace," "Love unknown," "The Method," "Artillerie," "The Bag," "The Collar," "Heaven," "Love (III)."

112 Martin, p. 392.

113 See above, chap. 2, p. 32.

114 See above, chap. 4, p. 143. See also Elizabeth Jefferis Bartlett, " 'All Soul and Life, and Ey most bright' ": A *Persona* Study of the Writings of Thomas Traherne," Ph.D. Diss. Brown 1976.

115 *Centuries*, III, 71-100. The final entries, 96-100, are his own New Testament completions of the psalm sequence.

116 *Centuries*, III, 66, Margoliouth, I, 149.

117 *Preparatory Meditations*, II.2, 41-42; II.18, 65-66; II.8, 41-42; I.15, 59-60.

118 See above, pp. 230-231.

119 II.153, 9-11; II.138, 13-14; II.152, l. 7.

120 II.153, 13-24.

## CHAPTER 8

1 See discussion on dating in Gardner, pp. xv-lv.

2 See above, chap. 2, pp. 49, 70. Also see discussion of these identifications for the *Anniversaries* in Raymond B. Waddington, *The Mind's Empire: Myth and Form in George Chapman's Narrative Poems* (Baltimore, 1974),

pp. 11-17. Robert Bozanich ("Donne and Ecclesiastes," *PMLA*, 90 [1975], 270-276) has argued the generic association of the *First Anniversary* with Ecclesiastes.

3 This self-dramatization and persistent focus on the self has been noted, somewhat pejoratively, by T. S. Eliot, "Lancelot Andrewes," *Selected Essays* (New York, 1950), p. 302; Douglas Bush, *English Literature in the Earlier Seventeenth Century, 1600-1660* (Oxford, 1945; rev. ed. 1962), pp. 140-141; J. B. Leishman, *The Monarch of Wit* (London, 1962), pp. 264-265; Frank Kermode, *John Donne* (London, 1957), p. 39; Wilbur Sanders, *John Donne's Poetry* (Cambridge, Eng., 1971), pp. 111-138. Some others have recognized Donne's use of the self to religious ends, e.g., Donald M. Friedman, "Memory and the Art of Salvation in Donne's Good Friday Poem," *ELR*, 3 (1973), pp. 418-442; and John N. Wall, Jr., "Donne's Wit of Redemption: The Drama of Prayer in the *Holy Sonnets*," *SP*, 73 (1976), 189-203. For discussion of the issue in relation to traditions of anthropomorphism, see William Kerrigan, "The Fearful Accommodations of John Donne," *ELR*, 4 (1974), 337-363.

4 See above, chap. 7, p. 245.

5 Josef Lederer ("John Donne and the Emblematic Practice," *RES*, 22 [1946], 182-200) has identified several possible emblem sources for Donnean passages in the secular as well as the religious poetry. I am concerned here with emblem influence on a broader scale, giving shape and definition to an entire poem.

6 Gardner's suggestion, p. xxi. No precise date can be assigned to this work.

7 See above, chap. 6, p. 202, and n. 80.

8 Lederer, "Donne and the Emblematic Practice," pp. 189-190, points to several emblems relating to specific lines, e.g., the cedar of Lebanon as an emblem of high birth. But he does not discuss the poem itself as a species of emblem poem.

9 Goldberg ("Donne's Journey East: Aspects of a Seventeenth-Century Trope," *SP*, 68 [1971], 470-483) notes that traditional typological foreshadowing lies behind the association of the Annunciation and the Passion, seen to be joined by the rhythm of expectation.

10 Gardner (pp. 55-56) dates this sequence about July 1607, on the strength of a dated prose letter to Magdalen Herbert which purported to accompany some "*Holy Hymns* and *Sonnets*" that were probably, though not certainly, these. See also H. W. Garrod, "Donne and Mrs. Herbert," *RES*, 21 (1945), for discussion of the date of the letter.

11 Martz, *Poetry of Meditation*, pp. 105-112.

12 Donne, *Sermons*, II, 50. Cf. V, 270.

13 *Ibid.*, V, 271.

14 See above, chap. 6, p. 197.

15 Gardner, pp. 57-58. For consistency, and to avoid the implication that Donne had reference to some particular English version of the Bible in writing these poems, I have quoted throughout from the Authorized Version (1611), even though many of Donne's *Divine Poems* almost certainly pre-

date it. Besides having some acquaintance with the Hebrew and Greek orig-
inals, Donne knew intimately the Vulgate and Junius-Tremellius Latin ver-
sions (the last of which was his avowed text for the "Lamentations of
Jeremy"), as well as the Bishops', Douay-Rheims, and Geneva versions.

16 As Annabel Patterson has pointed out to me, the various crown images
conjoined in the opening sonnet are also suggestively conjoined in Donne's
sermon on James I (alluding to a passage in Tertullian's *De Corona*). Donne
is explicating the various "crowns" of Solomon (Christ) referred to in
Cant. 3:11:

> *Behold King Salomon crowned*, etc. . . . The Crown wherewith his
> Father crowned his *Humane nature*, was the glory given to that, in his
> *Ascension.* . . . The *Crown wherewith his Mother crowned him* . . . was
> his *passion*, his *Crown of thornes*; for so *Tertullian*, and divers others take
> this Crown of his, from her, to be his *Crown of thorns: Woe to the
> Crown of pride, whose beauty is a fading flower*, says the Prophet; But
> blessed be this Crown of Humiliation, whose flower cannot fade." (*Ser-
> mons*, VI, 287)

17 "Annunciation," ll. 3-4, 12; "Nativitie," l. 10; "Temple," ll. 5-6; "Crucy-
fying," ll. 7-11.

18 Ll. 9-12. See above, chap. 6, p. 202 and n. 83.

19 "La Corona," ll. 9-11.

20 See above, chap. 6, pp. 200-201.

21 See Gardner, p. 83.

22 Donne, *Letters to Severall Persons of Honour* (London, 1651), pp.
32-34.

23 See Gardner, pp. xxvii-xxviii.

24 Stanzas i-iv.

25 Stanzas xiv-xvii.

26 Ll. 127-128, 136, 152-153.

27 Stanzas xviii-xxii.

28 Stanzas xxii-xxviii.

29 Ll. 218, 203-204, 216.

30 See above, chap. 6, p. 198 and nn. 52, 54. Cf. Figure 1.

31 See above, chap. 2, pp. 38-39.

32 Walton, *Life of Donne*, p. 55.

33 Ll. 13-18. I give the 1633 reading, "sonne . . . he," though there is a
good deal of manuscript authority for "Sunne . . . it."

34 Martz, *Poetry of Meditation*, pp. 43-53. The tripartite structure of
these sonnets has been challenged by Stanley Archer, "Meditation and the
Structure of Donne's 'Holy Sonnets,'" *ELH*, 28 (1961), 137-147.

35 See Gardner, pp. xxxvii-lv. She assigns to 1609 the composition of the
twelve sonnets published in 1633, and speculates that the four added in 1635
were probably composed not long after. The three from the Westmoreland
manuscript seem to be unrelated to these, and one of them at least (XVII)
postdates Ann Donne's death in 1617. H.J.C. Grierson, *The Poems of John*

*Donne*, 2 vols. (Oxford, 1912)—long the standard edition—made conventional the numbering of the sonnets according to the 1635 edition; Gardner reorders these as follows: II, IV, VI, VII, IX, X; XI, XII, XIII, XIV, XV, XVI; I, V, III, VIII; XVII, XVIII, XIX. I discuss the poems in the 1635 sequence, using that numbering, but I use Gardner's texts of the poems. (The E. of D. is probably Richard, Earl of Dorset.)

36 The arguments, respectively, of Douglas L. Peterson, "John Donne's *Holy Sonnets* and the Anglican Doctrine of Contrition," *SP*, 56 (1959), 504-518; Grant, *Transformation of Sin*, pp. 56-65, and "Augustinian Spirituality and the *Holy Sonnets* of John Donne," *ELH*, 38 (1971), 542-561; Don M. Ricks, "The Westmoreland Manuscript and the Order of Donne's 'Holy Sonnets,'" *SP*, 63 (1966), 187-195; Wall, "Donne's Wit of Redemption," 189-203. Ricks' reading is based upon the somewhat different order of the poems in the Westmoreland manuscript.

37 See above, chap. 5, pp. 158-162.

38 See above, chap. 6, pp. 192-196, and chap. 7, pp. 238-240.

39 See discussion of this point in Calvin, *Institutes*, III.xi.6, McNeill, I, 732.

40 Montenay, *Emblemes*, p. 5; see Figure 6.

41 Perkins, "The Whole Treatise of the Cases of Conscience," *Workes*, II, pp. 13-15; see above, chap. 1, pp. 21-22.

42 "For the zeale of thine house hath eaten mee up." Cf. John 2:17.

43 See Heb. 11:13, "they were strangers and pilgrims on the earth"; 1 Cor. 9:24, "Know yee not that they which runne in a race, runne all, but one receiveth the price [sic]? So runne, that yee may obtaine." See above, chap. 3, pp. 93-94; chap. 6, n. 122.

44 See Rom. 4:6: "David also describeth the blessednesse of the man, unto whom God imputeth righteousnesse without works." Paul's reference is to Psalm 32:2: "Blessed is the man unto whom the LORD imputeth not iniquitie: and in whose spirit there is no guile." See above, chap. 1, pp. 16-18.

45 Rev. 6:8, "And I looked, and behold, a pale horse: and his name that sate on him was Death, and hell followed with him: and power was given unto them, over the fourth part of the earth, to kill with sword, and with hunger, and with death [pestilence], and with the beastes of the earth"; Ezek. 14:21, "I send my foure sore judgements upon Jerusalem; the sword, and the famine, and the noisome beast, and the pestilence."

46 For discussion of angelic and human modes of knowing see Aquinas, *Summa Theologica*, I, Qq. liv-lvii, *Basic Writings*, I, 509-548.

47 See, e.g., Job 13:15, "Though hee slay mee, yet will I trust in him: but I will maintaine mine owne wayes before him"; Job 31:6, 35, "Let me bee weighed in an even ballance, that God may know mine integritie / . . . My desire is, that the Almightie would answere me."

48 Rom. 9:18, 20; see also Job 33:13.

49 In Psalm 25:7 David pleads to God to forget his sins but to remember him: "Remember not the sinnes of my youth, nor my transgressions: according to thy mercie remember thou me, for thy goodnesse sake, O

LORD." In a sermon on Psalm 6:1, Donne interpreted this stance of David: "As much as David stands in feare of this Judge, he must intreat this Judge, to remember his sinnes: Remember them, O Lord, for els they will not fall into my pardon; but remember them in mercy, and not in anger; for so they will not fall into my pardon neither." *Sermons*, V, 320-321.

50 Perkins, *A Golden Chaine, Workes*, I, 80.

51 1 Cor. 15:52, 53-55.

52 See above, chap. 1, pp. 18-19.

53 See above, chap. 1, pp. 21-22; chap. 6, pp. 193-196, and Figure 11.

54 Gen. 2:7; John 20:22.

55 See, e.g., Num. 6:25; Psalms 31:16, 67:1, and esp. 80:3, 7, 19: "Turne us againe, O God: and cause thy face to shine, and wee shall bee saved."

56 Gal. 5:1; Cant., passim.

57 See above, chap. 1, pp. 17-18.

58 See above, chap. 1, pp. 23-24.

59 Gal. 3:11; 2 Cor. 3:5-6.

60 He alludes to such texts as "love is the fulfilling of the Law" (Rom. 13:10); "Thou shalt love the Lord thy God with all thy heart, and with all thy soule, and with all thy minde. / This is the first and great Commandement. / And the second is like unto it, Thou shalt love thy neighbour as thy selfe. / On these two Commandements hang all the Law and the Prophets" (Matt. 22:37-40).

61 Ricks, "Westmoreland Manuscript," p. 194.

62 Cf. Cant. 5:2, "Open to me, my sister, my love, my dove, my unde-filed"; and Rev. 19:8, "And to her [the Bride] was granted, that she should bee arayed in fine linnen, cleane and white: for the fine linnen is the righteousnesse of Saints."

63 Gardner, pp. 55-56, develops the argument that the poems sent to Mrs. Herbert are the "La Corona" poems, in part on the ground that the sonnet terms them "Hymns" to Christ, which the "Corona" poems, as praise, can fairly be called.

64 See Bald, *John Donne*, pp. 302-304, for discussion of date. Conceivably, the *terminus a quo* could be December 1618, when Tilman was ordained deacon.

65 See Bald, *John Donne*, p. 304; Gardner, Appendix D, pp. 127-132.

66 See Gardner, p. 102.

67 See above, chap. 2, pp. 39-40.

68 Gardner speculates (pp. 103-104) that the undertaking may have been stimulated by the distress of the German Protestants after the defeat of the Elector Palatine in 1620, when the Catholic League overran Bohemia and handed the territories over to the Emperor Maximilian. Certainly Donne was thinking of Lamentations at this period: he chose a text from that book for his Fifth of November sermon in 1622, in which he celebrated the near escape of England from the biblical calamities, in that England's Josiah (King James) was spared, and England was not taken captive by the Roman Babylon (*Sermons*, IV, 235-263).

69 The title is, "The Lamentations of Jeremy, for the most part according to Tremelius." Grierson (II, 245) and Gardner (p. 104) have noted some debts to the Vulgate and the AV, but John J. Pollock has demonstrated that the major influence (after Junius-Tremellius) was the Geneva Bible ("Donne's 'Lamentations of Jeremy' and the Geneva Bible," *ES*, 55 [1974], 513-515).

70 Reprinted in John Shawcross's edition, *The Complete Poetry of John Donne* (New York, 1967), p. 372, from MS 736, f. 21a at Christ Church, Oxford.

71 See above, chap. 5, pp. 151-152, 168-169.

72 Martz, *Poetry of Meditation*, pp. 53-56.

73 Chambers, " 'Goodfriday, 1613. Riding Westward': The Poem and the Tradition," *ELH*, 28 (1961), 31-53; Friedman, "Memory and the Art of Salvation in Donne's Good Friday Poem," pp. 418-442.

74 Hugo, *Pia Desideria*, no. 4, opposite p. 28; Quarles, *Emblemes*, III.6, p. 136.

75 Montenay, *Emblemes*, p. 11; Hulsius, *Emblemata Sacra*, no. 19, p. 65.

76 For discussion of dating see Gardner, Appendix E, pp. 132-135. The earlier date was entered by Sir Julius Caesar on a manuscript copy of the "Hymne" which he received; Walton is the source of the deathbed dating (*Life of Donne*, p. 60).

77 See above, chap. 2, pp. 38-39. See also the similar conclusion to the poem on the Sidney-Pembroke Psalms. It is noteworthy that among the various genres of religious poetry Donne attempts he nowhere undertakes the high hymnic mode.

78 *Devotions*, "Expostulation 19," ed. Raspa, pp. 99-100. See above, chap. 7, pp. 220-222. And see *Sermons*, VII, 60-61; IV, 98-99.


CHAPTER 9

1 See above, chap. 6, pp. 200-201.

2 Vaughan, "The Authors Preface To the following Hymns," prefaced to *Silex Scintillans* (1655), Martin, p. 391.

3 Crashaw, *Steps to the Temple. Sacred Poems* (London, 1646, 1648). Harvey, *The Synagogue, or, The Shadow of the Temple. Sacred Poems and Private Ejaculations. In Imitation of Mr. George Herbert* (London, 1640). Samuel Speed, *Prison-Pietie: Or, Meditations Divine and Moral* (London, 1677). Herrick, *His Noble Numbers: Or, His Pious Pieces* (London, 1647), with *Hesperides* (London, 1648); poems especially reminiscent of Herbert include "God's Part"; "To God," N-25 and N-48; "Upon Time"; "Another, to God"; "Another New-yeere's Gift"; "On Heaven"; "The Widdowes teares"; "His Saviours words, going to the Crosse." On Taylor and Herbert see, e.g., Louis L. Martz, "Foreword" and Stanford's annotations in *Poems of Edward Taylor*, ed. Stanford. See also Kathleen Blake, "Edward Taylor's Protestant Poetic: Nontransubstantiating Metaphor," *AL*, 43 (1971), 14-24.

4 See Rosemond Tuve, *A Reading of George Herbert*, for a most suggestive, though too exclusively medieval, description of Herbert's use of typology and iconography; Martz, *Poetry of Meditation*, pp. 249-287, for the Salesian meditative context; Arnold Stein, *George Herbert's Lyrics*, pp. xiii-xliv, 1-44, for discussion of the debt of Herbert's plain style to Augustinian and Baconian influences. An extended argument for Herbert's Augustinian sense of language, culminating in a "rhetoric of silence," is developed by Mark Taylor, *The Soul in Paraphrase: George Herbert's Poetics* (The Hague, 1974), and more radically by Stanley Fish, *Self-Consuming Artifacts*, pp. 1-77, 156-223.

5 Stein, *Herbert's Lyrics*; Vendler, *The Poetry of George Herbert* (Cambridge, Mass., and London, 1975). For a penetrating analysis of Vendler's "Romantic" critical assumptions and their limitations, see the review article by Richard Strier, " 'Humanizing' Herbert," *MP*, 74 (1976), 78-88.

6 *The Country Parson* was first published in Herbert's *Remains* (1652); see Hutchinson, p. 228.

7 The "Briefe Notes" were solicited by Herbert's friend Nicholas Ferrar of Little Gidding, and published with his English translation of Valdés' *Considerations* in 1637. See Hutchinson, pp. 304-320. Ilona Bell's article, "George Herbert and the English Reformation," studies some of these theological issues.

8 *Country Parson*, Hutchinson, p. 227. See especially pp. 227-228, 235-247, 267-288. The poem and the manual also have some conformity with matters usually treated in Part II of contemporary theological manuals, concerned with "observance" or "works"; Part I is normally concerned with faith. See, e.g., William Ames, *The Marrow of Sacred Divinity*. For a discussion of the considerable emphasis even in some Calvinist theologians (Richard Sibbes and John Preston among others) upon "preparation" for grace, in part by turning from evil and reformation of life, see Pettit, *The Heart Prepared*, pp. 66-73.

9 See above, chap. 1, pp. 13-24. A counterposition to that which I argue here asserts that "The Church" contains several speakers all subsumed into the one voice of the Church, which includes the Head (Christ) and all the members of his mystical Body. See Asals, "The Voice of George Herbert's 'The Church.' "

10 Isaak Walton, "The Life of Mr. George Herbert," *Lives*, p. 74.

11 J. Max Patrick, "Critical Problems in Editing George Herbert's *The Temple*," *The Editor as Critic and the Critic as Editor* (Clark Library, Los Angeles, 1973), pp. 6-14, discounts the story as an example of Walton's frequent fictionalizing, as documented in David Novarr, *The Making of Walton's Lives* (Ithaca, 1958). However, Joseph Summers (*George Herbert*, p. 84), takes the story as essentially true. And it is worth noting that the story is substantiated in its general outlines by the résumé of the event in John Ferrar's contemporary life of his brother Nicholas, published in *The Ferrar Papers*, ed. B. Blackstone (Cambridge, 1938), p. 59. That ac-

count indicates clearly that it was the manuscript of the poems (not, as Patrick speculates, that of *The Country Parson*) which was delivered to Nicholas Ferrar, "appointing him to be the midwife, to bring that piece into the World, If he so thought good of it, else to [burn it]."

12 *Country Parson*, Hutchinson, pp. 278-279.

13 On this question see especially Summers, pp. 73-94; Martz, *Poetry of Meditation*, pp. 249-287; John David Walker, "The Architectonics of George Herbert's *The Temple*," *ELH*, 29 (1962), 289-305; Annabel Endicott (Patterson), "The Structure of George Herbert's *Temple*: A Reconsideration," *UTQ*, 34 (1965), 226-237; Valerie Carnes, "The Unity of George Herbert's *The Temple*: A Reconsideration," *ELH*, 35 (1968), 505-526; Fredson Bowers, "Herbert's Sequential Imagery: 'The Temper,'" *MP*, 59 (1962), 202-213; Lee Ann Johnson, "The Relationship of 'The Church Militant' to *The Temple*," *SP*, 68 (1971), 200-206; Elizabeth Stambler, "The Unity of Herbert's 'Temple,'" *Cross-Currents*, 10 (1960), 251-266.

14 On the dating of "The Church Militant" see Hutchinson, p. 543, and Summers, *George Herbert*, p. 217, n. 28. On the Williams manuscript see Amy Charles, "The Williams Manuscript and *The Temple*," *Renaissance Papers* (1971), pp. 59-77. See also Hutchinson, pp. xxxii-xxxix, lii-lvi.

15 The added poems constitute essentially the second half of "The Church," though new ones are also interspersed among the Williams poems in the first part. Herbert gives further evidence of strengthening his design by eliminating or redistributing the final four poems from the Williams manuscript, so as to end the volume of lyrics with "Love (III)." The poem "Perseverence" which concludes the Williams collection is eliminated entirely; it asserts rather bleakly the speaker's final inability to know for certain whether he is of the elect, whether his poems might save others though he himself is damned. He happily determined to conclude the later collection on a note of triumphant affirmation.

16 See above, chapter 3, pp. 100-101, and nn. 95-97, for discussion of the Temple trope. Although the title cannot be proved to be Herbert's, the Temple motif is so central as to leave little room for doubt.

17 See especially Walker, "Architectonics of . . . *The Temple*," pp. 289-305.

18 Hall, *Contemplations*, *Works*, II, 1221.

19 Heyns, *Emblemata Chrestienes*, sig. C 2; see above, chap. 6, p. 204, and Figure 8.

20 On the classical allusions and materials see Mary Ellen Rickey, *Utmost Art: Complexity in the Verse of George Herbert* (Lexington, 1966), pp. 1-58.

21 As Annabel Endicott (Patterson) cogently argues in "Structure of George Herbert's *Temple*," pp. 226-237.

22 Cawdrey, *Treasurie . . . of Similies*, pp. 93-94.

23 Featley, "The Embleme of the Church Militant: A Sermon Preached in Mercers Chapell," *Clavis Mystica*, p. 301.

24 I have argued this point regarding the typological relation of the three parts of *The Temple* in "Typology and Poetry: A Consideration of Herbert, Vaughan, and Marvell," in *Illustrious Evidence: Approaches to English Literature in the Early Seventeenth Century*, ed. Earl Miner (Berkeley, 1975), pp. 51-53.

25 Beza, *Sermons upon . . . Canticles*, p. 12.

26 See discussion above, chap. 2, pp. 55-59. See also Carole Kessner, "Entering 'The Church-porch': Herbert and Wisdom Poetry," *George Herbert Journal*, 1 (1977), 10-25, which documents the influence of the Wisdom Books and especially Ecclesiasticus.

27 T[homas] W[ilcox], *Commentarie . . . on . . . Proverbes*, p. 1.

28 Though there is some question as to how many of the more than 1000 proverbs in the collection first published in 1640 under the title *Outlandish Proverbs* were collected by Herbert, scholars agree that he contributed a large proportion of them. See Hutchinson, pp. 568-573.

29 For a discussion of "The Church-porch" in terms of these moral topics, see Clark Chalifour, "Genre and Didactic Purpose in George Herbert's *The Temple*," Diss. Brown 1970, pp. 6-57.

30 See above, chap. 2, pp. 62-64.

31 The topic of Herbert's use of or parody of the devices and conventions of love poetry has been often addressed: cf. Martz, *Poetry of Meditation*, pp. 259-273; George Watson, "The Fabric of Herbert's *Temple*," *JWCI*, 26 (1963), 365-368; Rosemary Freeman, "Parody as a Literary Form: George Herbert and Wilfred Owen," *EIC*, 13 (1963), 307-322; Rosemond Tuve, "George Herbert and *Caritas*," *JWCI*, 22 (1959), 301-331; Tuve, "Sacred 'Parody' of Love Poetry, and Herbert," *S Ren*, 8 (1961), 249-90; Chalifour, "Genre and Didactic Purpose," pp. 109-155. I suggest that Canticles provides the framework for Herbert's use and transformation of the love-poetry devices.

32 See above, chap. 5, p. 171, and n. 116.

33 See Rom. 8:14-17, and see above, chap. 3, pp. 94-95.

34 This language, I suggest, relates specifically to the exploration of the Platonic "loving friends" relationship; it is not, as Fish implies (*Self-Consuming Artifacts*, p. 173), yet one more testimony of the speaker's self-abnegation.

35 See Hutchinson, pp. 255-57: "The Countrey Parson values Catechizing highly: for . . . in Catechizing there is an humblenesse very sutable to Christian regeneration, which exceedingly delights him as by way of exercise upon himself, and by way of preaching to himself, for the advancing of his own mortification; for in preaching to others, he forgets not himself . . . at Sermons, and Prayers, men may sleep or wander; but when one is asked a question, he must discover what he is." Stanley Fish, *The Living Temple*, argues that the process of catechizing—often associated with 'Temple-building' in the seventeenth century—is central to Herbert's conception and poetic method in *The Temple*.

36 Cf. Psalm 43:4, "Then will I goe unto the Altar of God, unto God my exceeding joy"; Rev. 2:10, "Bee thou faithfull unto death, and I will give thee a crowne of life"; Phil. 4:1, "My brethren, dearely beloved and longed for, my joy and crowne"; John 14:6, "I am the Way, the Trueth, and the Life."

37 See Gen. 32:10: "I am not worthy of the least of all the mercies, and of all the trueth, which thou hast shewed unto thy servant; for with my staffe I passed over this Jordan, and now I am become two bands."

38 Fish, *The Living Temple*, p. 131-136.

39 See chap. 2, pp. 42-45; also see chap. 1, pp. 20-24, for discussion of the Protestant paradigm of salvation, especially the emotional states and vacillations attendant upon the middle stage of the Christian life, and the plateau of confidence and assurance attained by the old experienced Christian as a foretaste of his heavenly condition.

40 See chap. 2, pp. 45-49, for discussion of the lyric kinds in the Psalms. And see Louise Gittings Schleiner, "Herbert's 'Divine and Moral Songs': Song-Text Features in *The Temple* and Their Importance for Herbert's Poetic Idiom," Diss. Brown 1973, pp. 129-214.

41 The basic assumption of Helen Vendler's *Poetry of George Herbert*.

42 See above, chap. 4, pp. 133-136; chap. 7, pp. 230-250.

43 In a letter to Arthur Woodnoth, Herbert observed, "David built the Temple as much as Solomon because he desired it, & prepared for it" (Hutchinson, p. 381).

44 See above, chap. 7, pp. 246-247. In *The Country Parson* Herbert also paraphrases this Psalm as a starting point for his own praise-prayer before the sermon: "Blessed be the God of Heaven and Earth! who onely doth wondrous things. Awake therefore, my Lute, and my Viol! awake all my powers to glorifie thee! We praise thee! we blesse thee! we magnifie thee for ever!" (Hutchinson, p. 289).

45 Psalm 145:1: "I will extoll thee, my God, O King: and I will blesse thy name for ever and ever."

46 See esp. verses 10-18, 27-28.

47 See Psalm 116, esp. verses 12, 17-19:

What shall I render unto the LORD: for all his benefits towards mee?

. . . . . . . . . . . . . . . . . . . . . . . . . . . . . . . .

I will offer to thee the sacrifice of thankes-giving: and will call upon the Name of the LORD.
I will pay my vowes unto the LORD: now in the presence of all his people:
In the Courts of the LORDS house, in the middes of thee, O Jerusalem.

48 Bullinger, *Sermons upon the Apocalips*, sig. A iii; Thomas Brightman (*Revelation of the Apocalyps*, p. 194) declared that Revelation describes "all the dangers and extremities which the Church is to undergo through the whole race thereof upon the earth" until the Last Judgment.

49 Featley, "The Embleme of the Church Militant," *Clavis Mystica*, p. 301; Paraeus, *Commentary upon the Divine Revelation of the Apostle and Evangelist John*, trans. Elias Arnold (Amsterdam, 1644), p. 20.

50 "Howe deare are thy counsayles unto me, O God: O howe great is the summe of them," Psalm 139:17. "For who is he among the cloudes, that shalbe compared unto the Lorde?" Psalm 89:6 [BCP]

51 For discussion of this point see Lewalski, "*Samson Agonistes* and the 'Tragedy' of the Apocalypse," *PMLA*, 85 (1970), 1050-1062.

52 Ll. 5-6. See above, chap. 3, pp. 105-106.

53 "The Sinner," l. 1; "H. Baptisme (II)," ll. 14-15; "Nature," ll. 7-9; "Affliction (IV)," ll. 7-9, 11-12; "Miserie," ll. 35-36; "Home," ll. 1-2; "Longing," ll. 7-9; "The Crosse," ll. 13-14, 17.

54 "The Temper (I)," ll. 9, 13-14; "Affliction (II)," ll. 1-2; "Confession," ll. 7-10; "The Temper (II)," l. 3, and "Longing," l. 82. Cf. van Haeften, *Schola Cordis*, III.14, p. [436]; Harvey, no. 33, p. 132. See also (for "Confession") the van Haeften emblem II.12, p. [196], of a giant screw pressing the heart.

55 Cf. Cramer, *Emblemata Sacra*, no. 47, "Vulneror," p. 201, for an emblem of God as "Man of War" shooting his arrows into the heart "from farre."

56 See above, chap. 6, pp. 199-200.

57 "Grace"; "Deniall," ll. 24-25; "Man," l. 8; "Obedience," l. 22.

58 "Miserie," l. 70; "The Crosse," l. 30.

59 See Hulsius' emblem (Figure 5 above, *Emblemata Sacra*, no. 17, p. 57) of God's hand pruning branches from a tree.

60 Wither, *Emblemes*, II.viii, p. 70; and Mannich, fol. 15. See above, chap. 6, p. 199, and Figure 4.

61 See discussion above, chap. 6, pp. 195-196, 204-206.

62 "Mattens," ll. 6, 11; "Jesu"; "The Crosse."

63 See chap. 6, p. 206. Ira Clark demonstrates that the emblems of the poem also invite a typological reading ("'Love Unknown' and Reading Herbert"); see chap. 4, p. 141, and n. 111.

64 "The Size," ll. 1, 37-38; "The Discharge," ll. 1-3; "Longing," l. 81; "The Glimpse."

65 See above, chap. 6, p. 204, and Figure 8.

66 "The Familie," l. 3; "Decay," ll. 12-15.

67 See chap. 4, pp. 141-142. The argument of the following pages was in part developed in my article, "Typological Symbolism and the 'Progress of the Soul'" in *Literary Uses of Typology*, ed. Miner, pp. 89-92. Note that Donne treats sequentially in the *Anniversary* poems the movement from innocence to regeneration, from Nature to Grace, and that his *Devotions upon Emergent Occasions* treats in adjacent sections ("Meditations" and "Expostulations") the movement from sickness of body to an analogous sickness of soul; by contrast, Herbert normally compresses such a movement within the compass of the individual poem.

68 Tuve, *A Reading of George Herbert*, pp. 113-117.

69 See Tuve, *A Reading of George Herbert*, pp. 175-180, for the conventional medieval typology of Joseph's coat of many colors.

70 See the suggestive discussion of "Sion" in Taylor, *Soul in Paraphrase*, pp. 29-41.

## CHAPTER 10

1 Vaughan quotes from "The Church-porch," ll. 421-426, and reprints the whole of "Life." He also refers to Herbert as a "most glorious true *Saint* and a *Seer*," and recommends his "incomparable prophetick Poems, and particularly these, *Church-musick, Church-rents, and schisms, The Church militant*" (Martin, p. 186).

2 "The Authors Preface To the following Hymns," Martin, pp. 392, 391.

3 See Martin, pp. 727-751, *passim*; Pettet, *Of Paradise and Light*, pp. 51-70; Summers, *George Herbert*, p. 189.

4 These poems are: "Death," "The Search," "The Brittish Church," "The Call," "Content," "The Storm," "Peace," "H. Scriptures," "Son-dayes," "Repentance," "Faith," "The Dawning," "Praise," "The Holy Communion," "Affliction," "The Pilgrimage," "The World," "Misery," "Man," "White Sunday," "The Starre," "Trinity-Sunday," "The Jews," "Providence," "St. Mary Magdalen," "The Wreath."

5 These have the same metrical forms as, respectively, Herbert's "Praise (II)," "Trinity Sunday," "The Church-porch," and "The Dawning."

6 Cf. Herbert's "The Storm," "The Dawning," "Prayer (I)," "Sunday."

7 Bennett, *Four Metaphysical Poets: Donne, Herbert, Vaughan, Crashaw,* 2nd ed. (Cambridge, 1953), p. 85.

8 Part I was published in 1650, with emblem, Latin emblem poem, and a fourteen-line poem, "The Dedication." Part II was added in 1655 (*Silex Scintillans: Sacred Poems and private Ejaculations. The Second Edition, In two Books* [London, 1655]). The emblem and emblem poem were dropped in this edition; a new prose preface, a second dedicatory poem, and the short prefatory epigram, "Vain Wits and eyes" were added. Also added on the title page was an epigraph from Job 35:10-11, "Where is God my Maker, who giveth Songs in the night? / Who teacheth us more then the beasts of the earth, and maketh us wiser then the fowls of heaven?"

9 See above, chap. 9, pp. 309-312.

10       Some drops of thy all-quickning blood
           Fell on my heart; those made it bud
           And put forth thus, though Lord, before
           The ground was curst, and void of store.
           Indeed I had some here to hire
           Which long resisted thy desire,
           That ston'd thy servants. . . . (ll. 5-11)

In the second dedicatory poem, making the point that the poems originate from God, not himself, the speaker continues his emblem metaphor: "If the Sun rise on rocks, is't right, / To call it their inherent light?" (ll. 19-20).

11 "Dressing," "The Holy Communion," "The Sap," "The Feast," "Christs Nativity," "Easter-day," "Easter Hymn," "Ascension-day," "Ascension-Hymn," "White Sunday," "Trinity-Sunday," "Palm-Sunday," "Church-Service," "Son-dayes."

12 Martz, *Paradise Within*, p. 13.

13 Cf. Goodman, *The Creatures praysing God*, pp. 22-23: "behold the magnificence of their Temple, which is the materiall world, the naturall Temple of God, a Temple made by God for himselfe, and by himselfe consecrated to his owne use, where the heavens are the roofe, and earth is the footstoole . . . : here all the Creatures dayly attend, and are ever conversant in this Temple."

14 "Faith," ll. 41-44: "So that I need no more, but say / *I do believe*, / And my most loving Lord straitway / Doth answer, *Live*"; "Misery," ll. 29-31: "If thou steal in amidst the mirth / And kindly tel me, *I am Earth*, / I shut thee out."

15 The poem has been explicated in these general terms by Ross Garner, *Henry Vaughan: Experience and the Tradition* (Chicago, 1959), pp. 47-62; and Halewood, *Poetry of Grace*, pp. 127-133. By contrast, Martz reads it as personal meditation in *The Paradise Within*, pp. 8-12, and R. A. Durr as an account of mystical experience, in *On the Mystical Poetry of Henry Vaughan* (Cambridge, Mass., 1962), pp. 82-99. I have set forth the substance of the reading which follows in "Typology and Poetry: A Consideration of Herbert, Vaughan, and Marvell," in *Illustrious Evidence*, ed. Miner, pp. 59-61.

16 Cf. Cramer, *Emblemata Sacra*, no. 18, p. 85; Mannich, *Sacra Emblemata*, fol. 37.

17 Gifford, *Sermons upon the Song of Salomon*, pp. 79-80.

18 Robotham, *Solomons Song*, p. 345. See above, chap. 2, pp. 63-64, chap. 3, pp. 95-96.

19 See Henry Ainsworth, *Annotations, Genesis*, p. 107. For Vaughan's ecclesiastical reading of Bethel, see "Jacobs Pillow, and Pillar," ll. 1-2, 31-40.

20 See Rom. 6:3-11.

21 Though William is not identified by name in the poems, there is considerable critical agreement that he is the subject of these elegiac poems. See, e.g., Pettet, *Of Paradise and Light*, p. 16; Martin, p. 731, n. to p. 416, "Thou that know'st"; French Fogle, *The Complete Poems of Henry Vaughan* (Garden City, 1964), p. 165.

22 The case for Vaughan's mysticism is argued by Durr, *Mystical Poetry of Henry Vaughan*; Robert Ellrodt, *L'Inspiration Personnelle et L'Esprit du Temps chez Les Poètes Métaphysiques Anglais*, Tome II, Première Partie, Livre iv (Paris, 1960); and especially by Itrat-Husain, *The Mystical Element in the Metaphysical Poets of the Seventeenth Century* (Edinburgh and London, 1948; rpt. 1966). The counter argument is cogently developed by E. L. Marilla, "The Mysticism of Henry Vaughan: Some

Observations," *RES*, n.s. 18 (1967), 164-166; Frank Kermode, "The Private Imagery of Henry Vaughan," *RES*, n.s. 1 (1950), 206-225; and especially in James D. Simmonds, *Masques of God: Form and Theme in the Poetry of Henry Vaughan* (Pittsburgh, 1972), pp. 3-41.

23 This common typological association is grounded upon the statement of the angels at the Ascension, Acts 1:11, "This same Jesus, which is taken up from you into heaven, shall so come, in like maner."

24 "They are all gone into the world of light!" l. 9.

25 See above, chap. 2, pp. 60-64.

26 See, e.g., Sibbes, *Bowels Opened*; Henry Ainsworth, *Solomons Song of Songs*; Gifford, *Fifteene Sermons*; Robotham, *Salomons Song*; Dove, *The Conversion of Solomon*.

27 "O rose of the field! O lily of the valleys! how art thou now become the food of wild boars." Cf. Cant. 2:1, "I am the rose of Sharon, and the lillie of the valleys"; and Psalm 80:13, "The boare out of the wood doth waste it: and the wild beast of the field doth devoure it."

28 Cant. 5:2 reads: "I sleepe, but my heart waketh: it is the voyce of my beloved that knocketh, saying, Open to me, my sister, my love, my dove, my undefiled: for my head is filled with dewe, and my lockes with the drops of the night."

29 Such allusions are not absent from Part I, of course: see, e.g., "One everlasting *Saboth* there shall runne / Without *Succession*, and without a *Sunne*" ("Resurrection and Immortality," ll. 69-70); "Ah! what time wilt thou come? when shall that crie / The *Bridegroome's Comming*! fil the sky?" ("The Dawning," ll. 1-2); "But hark! what trumpets that? what Angel cries / *Arise! Thrust in thy sickle*" ("Corruption," ll. 39-40).

30 "After this I beheld, and lo, a great multitude, which no man could number, of all nations, and kindreds, and people, and tongues, stood before the throne, and before the Lamb, clothed with white robes, and palmes in their hands."

31 "I saw under the altar, the soules of them that were slaine for the word of God, and for the testimony which they held: / And they cried with a lowd voice, saying, How long, O Lord, holy and true, dost thou not judge and avenge our blood on them that dwell on the earth?"

32 "Hee that leadeth into captivitie shall goe into captivitie: He that killeth with the sword, must be killed with the sword. Here is the patience and the faith of the Saints." Vaughan's verse paraphrase (ll. 1-8) reads:

> If any have an ear
> Saith holy *John, then let him hear.*
> He that into Captivity
> Leads others, shall a Captive be.
> Who with the sword doth others kill,
> A sword shall his blood likewise spill.
> Here is the patience of the Saints,
> And the true faith, which never faints.

See also the partial paraphrase in "The Palm-tree"; "Here is the patience of the Saints: this Tree / Is water'd by their tears . . . / Here is their faith too" (ll. 21-22, 25).

33 Rev. 20:11-12 is relevant: "And I saw a great white throne, and him that sate on it, from whose face the earth and the heaven fled away, . . . / And I sawe the dead, small and great, stand before God: and the books were opened: and another booke was opened, which is the booke of life: and the dead were judged out of those things which were written in the books, according to their works."

34 Cf. Donne, "La Corona," I, ll. 1-2: "Deign at my hands this crown of prayer and praise, / Weav'd in my low devout melancholie."

35 This argument is in part developed in my essay, "Typological Symbolism and the 'Progress of the Soul' in Seventeenth-Century Literature," in *Literary Uses of Typology*, ed. Miner, pp. 79-114. For the pilgrimage metaphor see above, chap. 3, pp. 93-94.

36 The pilgrim stance and activity accounts for what Halewood sees as discursiveness, an "allegorical overplus" (*Poetry of Grace*, p. 131). In fact Vaughan is allegorizing not a theological scheme but an experience, and to this the wandering, perceiving, questioning are wholly apt.

37 He hopes to reach "that plaine" from which can be seen the "shady City of Palme trees"—Jericho, shown to Moses in the vision of the Promised Land from Mount Pisgah, and so a type of Heaven. Cf. the more pedestrian poem, "Childe-hood," which also identifies that state with the pilgrim's path, "For sure that is the *narrow way*" (l. 44).

38 See especially "Religion," "Corruption."

39 See commentary on Gen. 21:12 in the Douay Bible (I, 74) and on Gal. 4:22-26 in the *Glossa Ordinaria, Pat. Lat.*, CXIV, 580-581.

40 Luther, *Works*, ed. Pelikan, IV, 42-43: "even though Ishmael is cast out of the house and the church of Abraham . . . I do not doubt that Ishmael and many of his descendents were converted to the true church of Abraham. For the expulsion does not mean that Ishmael should be utterly excluded from the kingdom of God. No, the purpose is to let him know that the kingdom of God is not owed to him by reason of a natural right but comes out of pure grace. . . . Later on he came into the inheritance as a guest, as Paul says about the Gentiles in the Epistle to the Ephesians [2:11-12]." See also annotations on Galatians 4:22-31 in the Geneva-Tomson Bible, pt. 3, fols. 83ᵥ-84.

41 See the commentary on Gen. 28:2-22 and 32:10, in Ainsworth, *Annotations, Genesis*, pp. 105-107, 120; see also Thomas Playfere, *The Whole Sermons* (London, 1623), pp. 112-113; Thomas Gataker, "Jacobs Thankfulnes to God, for Gods Goodnes to Jacob: A Meditation on Genesis 32:10," *Certaine Sermons* (London, 1637), p. 297.

42 Cf. Mark 11:4: "And they . . . found the colt tied by the doore without, in a place where two wayes met." In *The Mount of Olives*, Vaughan indicates the basis for this identification: "Now again I meet thee on the

Asse, made infinitely happy by so glorious a rider. . . . Sure, it was his simplicity and ordinary contempt with man, that made him so acceptable in thy sight" (Martin, p. 162).

43 See also "Mans fall, and Recovery": "Farewell you Everlasting hills! I'm Cast / Here under Clouds . . ." (ll. 1-2); cf. "Corruption," "The Retreate," and many more.

44 "They are all gone into the world of light!" ll. 11-12.

45 "Resurrection and Immortality," ll. 63-65, 69-70. The final allusion is to Rev. 22:5: "And there shalbe no night there, and they need no candle, neither light of the Sunne, for the Lorde God giveth them light: and they shall reigne for ever and ever."

46 See above, chap. 3, pp. 97-99, and for emblem analogues, chap. 6, pp. 199-200.

47 See above, n. 22. Kermode's essay, "The Private Imagery of Henry Vaughan," gives full recognition to the sources of Vaughan's distinctive image clusters in biblical, Herbertian, and sometimes Hermetic materials, but he does not attend sufficiently to the pervasive biblical image patterns throughout *Silex Scintillans* which largely control Vaughan's "private" imagery. Florence Sandler ("The Ascents of the Spirit: Henry Vaughan on the Atonement," *JEGP*, 73 [1974], 209-226) argues that Vaughan's Anglican piety was "relatively untouched by the doctrines of Luther and Calvin" (p. 214); that his theology is Neoplatonic and Johannine rather than Pauline; and that his most basic affinities are with Ralph Cudworth, the Cambridge Platonist, and Thomas Traherne.

48 Vaughan's shorter collection of maxims is ordered more simply than Herbert's; it follows the course of a Christian's day, regarded as epitome of the course of a Christian life.

49 See above, chap. 2, pp. 36-39, for classical/biblical poetics conception of the hymn.

50 Commentators customarily identified this as a hymn of thanksgiving: see Beza, *Psalmes of David*, p. 243; Ravenscroft, *Whole Booke of Psalmes*, sig. A 4v.

51 See "To Mr. M. L. *upon his reduction of the* Psalms *into Method*" (Martin, p. 628).

> SIR,
> You have oblig'd the *Patriarch*. And tis known
> He is your Debtor now, though for his own.
> What he wrote is a *Medley*. We can see
> Confusion trespass on his Piety.
> Misfortunes did not only Strike at him;
> They charged further, and oppress'd his pen.
> For he wrote as his *Crosses* came, and went
> By no safe *Rule*, but by his *Punishment*.
> His *quill* mov'd by the *Rod*; his witts and he
> Did know no *Method*, but their *Misery*.

You brought his *Psalms* now into *Tune*. Nay, all
His measures thus are more than musical.
Your *Method* and his *Aires* are justly sweet,
And (what's *Church-musick* right) like *Anthems* meet.
You did so much in this, that I believe
He gave the *Matter*, you the *form* did give. (ll. 1-17)

52 See discussion above, chap. 5, pp. 171-172. Most of the Protestant kinds were discussed or exemplified in Vaughan's manual. "Heavenly" meditation, as recommended by Baxter and Sibbes, was represented in a treatise Vaughan translated and appended to his manual, perhaps to render it more nearly complete: "Man in Glory: or, a Discourse of the blessed state of the Saints in the New Jerusalem. Written in Latin by the most Reverend and holy Father Anselmus Archbishop of Cãnterbury," in the reign of William Rufus (1087-1100), Martin, p. 191.

53 See Martz, *Poetry of Meditation*, pp. 86-90, for discussion of "The Search" as "a highly original variation on the whole procedure of meditating on the life of Christ, from Nativity to Crucifixion" (p. 86).

54 See above, chap. 5, 170-171.

55 Martz, *Poetry of Meditation*, pp. 150-152; *Paradise Within*, pp. 17-31, 54-57. Cf. Bonaventure, *Itinerarium* (1259), trans. Father James, *The Franciscan Vision* (London, 1937); and Robert Bellarmine, *De ascensione mentis in Deum per scalas rerum creatarum* (1615), trans. T.B., *A Most Learned and Pious Treatise . . . framing a Ladder, wherby our Mindes may Ascend to God.* (Douai, 1616). See discussion of the latter tract in Ruth Wallerstein, *Studies in Seventeenth-Century Poetic* (Madison, 1965), pp. 213-215. As Martz recognizes, the Augustinian/Bonaventuran method depends upon "a recognition of the incalculable value of the Image which lies beyond and beneath all deformity" (*Poetry of Meditation*, p. 152), but it is just this image which the speaker finds virtually destroyed in himself, exactly as Calvin described.

56 Calvin, *Institutes*, I.v.9-15, McNeill, I, 61-69. Cf. "Vanity of Spirit," ll. 27-28: "but this neer done, / The little light I had was gone." See the discussion of the differences between the conception of the *imago Dei* in Catholic and Protestant theory, in Lewalski, *Donne's Anniversaries and the Poetry of Praise*, chapter 4; and see above, chap. 5, pp. 163-164.

57 Calvin, *Institutes*, I.vi.1, McNeill, I, 69-70: "God . . . sets forth to all without exception his presence, portrayed in his creatures. . . . [But] Just as old or bleary-eyed men and those with weak vision, if you thrust before them a most beautiful volume, even if they recognize it to be some sort of writing, yet can scarcely construe two words, but with the aid of spectacles will begin to read distinctly; so Scripture, gathering up the otherwise confused knowledge of God in our minds, having dispersed our dullness, clearly shews us the true God." See also *Institutes*, I.v.10, McNeill, I, 63: "We must therefore admit in God's individual works—but especially in them as a whole—that God's powers are actually represented as in a painting."

58 As did other Protestants: Calvin notes that the Hebrew term *soach* may mean either *meditate* or *pray* (*Commentaries on the First Book of Moses Called Genesis*, II, 28). See above, chap. 5, pp. 152-154.

59 In *Mount of Olives* the focus is also upon the significance of such events for the meditator: "Meditate with thy self what miracles of mercy he hath done for thee. Consider how he left his Fathers bosome to be lodged in a manger, and laid by his robes of glory . . . that he might cloath thee with Immortality. Call to minde his wearisome journeys. . . . Consider againe (if thou canst) of what unmeasureable love was he possessed, who . . . did by his last Testament give himself with all the merits of his life and death to be wholly thine, and instead of them took upon him all thy trans-gressions, bore all thine iniquities" (Martin, pp. 157-158). After receiving the Sacrament, he proposes meditations upon Christ's "birth, life, doctrine and passion, his death and buriall, resurrection and ascension, and his second coming to judgement." His approach to these topics is also personal: he advises the reader, "Instead of printed Meditations . . . to read over all these following parcels of Scripture, *John* 6.22. *to the end*, *John* 17. *Rom.* 8. 2 *Cor.* 5. *Ephes.* 1. & 4. *Heb.* 10. 1 *Pet.* 1. *Rev.* 5" (Martin, pp. 164-165). These scriptures all focus upon doctrine and application to the self, rather than event.

60 "Dressing" testifies to a distinctively Protestant sacramental theology: "Whatever thou dost bid, let faith make good, / Bread for thy body, and wine for thy blood" (ll. 23-24).

61 *Mount of Olives* proposes a number of short "Ejaculations," in the manner of the arresting opening lines of some Vaughan poems, to meet such various "incident occasions" and experiences as these: "When the Clock strikes," "Upon some suddaine fear," "Upon any disorderly thoughts," "Upon any occasions of sadnesse," "Upon any Diffidence," "When thou art weary of the cares and vanities of this world" (Martin, pp. 153-155).

62 See also, in this mode, "The Resolve," "Retirement," "Disorder *and* frailty."

63 This is the meditative topic given most attention in *Mount of Olives*; a segment of the tract subtitled "Man in Darkness, or, A Discourse of Death" is primarily concerned to promote and exemplify such meditation: "the businesse of a *Pilgrim* is to *seek his Countrey*. But the *land* of *darknesse* lies in our way, and how few are they that study this *region*, that like holy *Macarius* walk into the wildernesse, and discourse with the skull of a dead man?" (Martin, p. 169). ". . . happy is that religious liver, who is ever medi-tating upon the houre of death before it comes" (Martin, p. 173). He records examples of occasional meditations and meditations upon the creatures di-rected to this topic, declaring, "There is no *object* we can look upon, but will do us the kindnesse to put us in minde of our mortality, if we would be so wise as to make use of it" (Martin, p. 174).

64 This poem, in imagery and themes, seems a direct counterpoint to the earlier poem in the volume, also entitled "Death."

65 See above, chap. 5, pp. 162-165, for the meditative tradition, and chap. 6,

pp. 207-208, for emblem analogues. Significantly, many of the subjects in such poems as "the Starre," "The Ass," "Cock-crowing," "I walkt the other day," "The Bird" find analogues in *Mount of Olives*. See Martin, pp. 161, 162, 176-177, 187.

66 For discussion of this topic, see, e.g., Elizabeth Holmes, *Henry Vaughan and the Hermetic Philosophy* (Oxford, 1932; rpt. 1962); Wilson O. Clough, "Henry Vaughan and the Hermetic Philosophy," *PMLA*, 48 (1933), 1108-1130; Patrick Grant, "Hermetic Philosophy and the Nature of Man in Vaughan's *Silex Scintillans*," *JEGP*, 67 (1968), 406-422; Alan W. Rudrum, "The Influence of Alchemy in the Poems of Henry Vaughan," *PQ*, 49 (1970), 469-480; and "Vaughan's 'The Night': Some Hermetic Notes," *MLR*, 64 (1969), 11-19; and "Henry Vaughan's 'The Book': A Hermetic Poem," *AUMLA*, 16 (1961), 161-166. I am in substantial agreement with Garner in *Vaughan: Experience and the Tradition*, and Simmonds, *Masques of God*, in rejecting the centrality of Hermeticism to Vaughan's thought.

67 Thomas was the leading exponent of Hermeticism in Britain, and the author of several Hermetic works, among them *Anthroposophia Theomagica*, *Magia Adamica*, *Euphrates*, in *Works*, ed. A. E. Waite (London, 1919). Henry Vaughan himself translated two Hermetical works by Henry Nollius, related to medicine: *Hermetical Physick: or, The Right Way to preserve, and to restore Health* (London, 1655), and *The Chymists Key to shut, and to open: or, The true doctrine of Corruption and Generation* (London, 1657).

68 See *Mount of Olives*, Martin, pp. 176-177; "Rules and Lessons," ll. 95-96; "I walkt the other day," ll. 50-54; "The Starre," ll. 9-10. Cf. Peter Sterry, *The Rise, Race and Royalty of the Kingdom of God in the Soul of Man* (London, 1683), pp. 2-7.

69 Also "Content," a meditation upon clothes.

70 See above, chap. 5, pp. 151-152, and chap. 6, pp. 207-208, n. 107.

71 The epigraph is, "*Watch you therefore, for you know not when the master of the house commeth, at Even, or at mid-night, or at the Cock-crowing, or in the morning.*"

72 The epigraph from Matt. 3:11 glosses this prayer: "I indeed baptize you with water unto repentance, but he that commeth after me, is mightier than I, . . . he shall baptize you with the holy Ghost, and with fire."

73 See above, chap. 6, p. 208, n. 108.

74 Cf. G[oodman], *The Creatures praysing God*, pp. 12-13, 24-26; Vaughan, *Mount of Olives*, Martin, p. 176.

75 See above, chap. 6, p. 207, n. 106.

76 For background on this symbol, see Don Cameron Allen, "Vaughan's 'Cock-Crowing' and the Tradition," *ELH*, 21 (1954), 94-106; rpt. in *Image and Meaning: Metaphoric Traditions in Renaissance Poetry*, rev. ed. (Baltimore, 1968), pp. 226-241.

77 For discussion of the poem as a "dramatized exegesis of a particular symbol" charged with multiple levels of meaning, see Michael Murrin, *The Veil of Allegory*, pp. 135-141.

78 I am indebted to David Watters for this observation, developed especially in relation to "*Isaacs* Marriage."

79 See above, chap. 6, p. 208, n. 110.

80 The poem has been much explicated. See, e.g., Pettet, *Of Paradise and Light*, chap. 8, pp. 138-154; M.E.A. Bradford, "Henry Vaughan's 'The Night': A Consideration of Metaphor and Meditation," *ArlQ*, 1 (1968), 209-222; R. A. Durr, "Vaughan's 'The Night,'" *JEGP*, 59 (1960), 34-40; S. Sandbank, "Henry Vaughan's Apology for Darkness," *SEL*, 7 (1967), 141-152; Bain T. Stewart, "Hermetic Symbolism in Henry Vaughan's 'The Night,'" *PQ*, 29 (1950), 417-422.

81 The whole poem seems to answer that despairing question in "Vanity of Spirit"; "(*for at night / Who can have commerce with the light?*)," ll. 31-32.

82 For discussion of some broader aspects of his poetics, and its Jonsonian sources, see Simmonds, *Masques of God*, pp. 22-41.

83 Martin, p. 391.

84 *Ibid.*, pp. 391-392.

85 Cf. Herbert, "Praise (II)."

86 Herbert's "Grief" is the probable source for this strategy, though Herbert uses it infrequently.

87 "H. Scriptures," ll. 9-12.

88 See discussion of the Hagiographia, chap. 2, p. 32.

89 See discussion of Vaughan's art in Simmonds, *Masques of God*, pp. 42-64.

90 In Martin, pp. 659-675.

91 Chambers, "Christmas," pp. 134-139, argues persuasively that several of these poems are informed by image patterns and motifs from the Christmas-tide liturgy. Yet these elements, even if derived from that source, are common Christian terms, and in most of these poems are so subordinated to other themes that any case for a unified "Christmas" sequence would be hard to sustain.

92 For example: ll. 7-14 of "Looking back" recall several lines of "The Morning-watch"; "Retirement" recalls "Religion," "Mount of Olives [I]," "The Shepheards," and several other poems; "The World" has close thematic affinities with the more familiar *Silex* poem of the same name. The opening lines of "The Revival"—"Unfold, unfold! take in his light, / Who makes thy Cares more short than night"—recalls "L'Envoy," ll. 8-10: "Arise, arise! / And like old Cloaths fold up these skies, / This long worn veyl." And the final lines of "The Request"—"This is the portion thy Child begs, / Not that of rust, and rags and dregs"—echoes the end of "The Water-fall": "Thou art the Channel my soul seeks, / Not this with Cataracts and Creeks."

CHAPTER 11

1 This work, untitled in the manuscript (Bodleian Ms. Eng. th. e. 51), was labeled *The Church's Year-Book* by Margoliouth, to call attention to its liturgical organization and wholesale borrowings from religious writers past and present. Dobell's title, *The Book of Private Devotions*, is also apt, for the work is a compilation intended for private "Meditations and Devotions," as the headings to several of its sections indicate. The borrowings from Donne include a brief quotation on the flyleaf from his Easter sermon of 1630 (*Sermons*, IX, 189) and from a Pentecost sermon probably preached the same year (IX, 240-241, 245). See *CYB*, fols. ii$_v$, 51$_v$, 57-57$_v$. Herbert's hymn is included with the materials for All Saints Day (fol. 112). For a full discussion of these and other debts see Carol L. Marks (Sicherman), "Traherne's *Church's Year-Book*," *PSBA*, 60 (1966), 31-72. There are also notable reminiscences of Herbert's Temple/Church metaphor in the introductory prayer to this compilation (fol. 1) and especially to Herbert's "Antiphon (II)" in Traherne's recommendation to the reader to place himself "in the Body of His Church among ye Saints Militant . . . Who Eccho to ye Angels in all their Grateful praises."

2 See Margoliouth, I, xii. The attribution to Vaughan by A. B. Grosart was challenged by Bertram Dobell, whose remarkable literary detective work proved the poems to be Traherne's. A full account appears in Dobell's 1903 edition of the *Poems*. Except where noted, quotations from Traherne's poems and *Centuries* are from Margoliouth's edition.

3 See *Centuries of Meditation*, III.8: "I clearly find how Docible our Nature is in natural Things, were it rightly entreated. And that our Misery proceedeth ten thousand times more from the outward Bondage of Opinion and Custom, then from any inward corruption or Depravation of Nature: And that it is not our Parents Loyns, so much as our Parents lives, that Enthrals and Blinds us. Yet is all our Corruption Derived from Adam: inasmuch as all the Evil Examples and inclinations of the World arise from His Sin," Margoliouth, I, 115. Cf. "Wonder," "Innocence," "Apostacy."

4 The strong Neoplatonic strain in Traherne's thought is evident to any careful reader, and some of its sources are identified in his *Commonplace Book* (Bod. Ms. Eng. Poet. C. 42) which contains long extracts from John Everard's translation of Hermes Trismegistus' *The Divine Pymander* (1657), from Theophilus Gale's *The Court of the Gentiles* (1670), and from several treatises by Alexander Jackson. Others are indicated in his so-called *Ficino Notebook* (BM Ms. Burney 126) which includes long extracts from Ficino's *Epitomes* of Plato's *Dialogues* (especially those concerned with ethical and political matters), Ficino's "Argument" to *Hermes Trismegistus*, and an unidentified Latin *Life of Socrates*. For full discussion of these manuscripts see the following articles by Carol L. Marks (Sicherman): "Traherne's *Ficino Notebook*," *PBSA*, 63 (1969), 73-81; "Thomas Traherne and Cambridge Platonism," *PMLA*, 81 (1966), 521-534; and "Thomas Traherne and Hermes Trismegistus," *RN*, 19 (1966), 118-131.

5 See, e.g., A. L. Clements, *The Mystical Poetry of Thomas Traherne* (Cambridge, Mass., 1969); and A. J. Sherrington, *Mystical Symbolism in the Poetry of Thomas Traherne* (St. Lucia, Australia, 1970).

6 Stewart, *The Expanded Voice*, pp. 159-161.

7 See, e.g., Martz, *The Paradise Within*, pp. 35-102, which is almost wholly concerned with *The Centuries*, and the acute and penetrating study of Traherne's thought in Richard Jordan's *Temple of Eternity*, which cites the poetry and prose interchangeably, but gives major emphasis to the *Centuries*.

8 Published in 1675, this treatise on ethics, or more properly on Christian virtue, was the only systematic treatise on the subject published in English for the layman during the thirty years after the Restoration. It shows affinities with the writings of Henry More, Peter Sterry, and others of the Cambridge Platonists, and its foundation is Traherne's conception of human potential and of the importance of action to embody and communicate goodness to others. Many passages in the newly discovered manuscript of "Select Meditations" show the same focus. See Carol L. Marks (Sicherman) and George R. Guffey, eds., *Christian Ethicks* (Ithaca, 1968).

9 *Christian Ethicks*, p. 165.

10 Margoliouth (II, 399-401) points out debts to Sylvester's *Du Bartas* (1621). See above, chap. 5, pp. 173-174.

11 The Damian hymn was adapted from the version which appeared in the pseudo-Augustinian devotional manual, *The Meditations, Soliloquia, and Manuall of the Glorious Doctour, S. Augustine*, trans. [John Floyd] (Paris, 1631), pp. 93-98. For the "St. Bartholomew" Hymn, see Margoliouth, II, 202-203.

12 "On News" (no. 26 of the "Third Century") appears as "News" in the "Infant-Ey" sequence; "The Approach" (no. 4) appears in the Dobell sequence and also in Philip Traherne's compilation, *Poems of Felicity*. The "Salem" poem is no. 69 of the "Third Century" (Margoliouth, I, 150-153, ll. 31-46).

13 A strong case for the unity of the Dobell poems is put forth by John M. Wallace, in "Thomas Traherne and the Structure of Meditation," *ELH*, 25 (1958), 79-89.

14 Philip evidently worked from two manuscripts. On the pages of the Dobell manuscript he inserted titles and page numbers from another manuscript, as a directive for a composite publication. As Margoliouth (II, 360) and Anne Ridler (in her edition of *Traherne*, p. 777) point out, Traherne wrote "An Infant-Ey. p. 1" after the poem "Innocence" in Dobell, so that poem must have been the first poem of the missing manuscript book. Wallace speculates that this second manuscript book contained a unified devotional sequence paralleling Dobell ("Structure of Meditation," p. 89), and Stewart argues persuasively for this hypothesis (*Expanded Voice*, p. 156, and n. 16, p. 226).

15 Philip Traherne's hybrid sequence *Poems of Felicity* takes groups of poems, usually in order, from Dobell, interspersing the other poems, also

in groups, among them. The directives written in the Dobell manuscript conform partly but not perfectly to the order of the *Poems of Felicity*, indicating some changes in Philip Traherne's plans as he proceeded. But the evidence points to the existence of a second manuscript of poems by Thomas Traherne, arranged in something like the order we have in the *Poems of Felicity* with the Dobell poems excised. Both Margoliouth and Anne Ridler print these poems in this order, except for the prefatory poem, "The Author to the Critical Peruser." I cite and quote from Margoliouth's edition for this group of poems.

16 "The Author to the Critical Peruser," l. 10.

17 See above, chap. 7, pp. 224-226.

18 "Adam," ll. 7-10.

19 Ridler, p. xviii.

20 "The City," ll. 11-20. The city may be Traherne's native Hereford.

21 See above, chap. 5, pp. 165-168.

22 "The World," ll. 11-16.

23 "The Apostacy," ll. 19-21, 37-41.

24 See the poems "Walking," "Churches," "The Inference," "Christendom," "The City."

25 "Consummation," ll. 50-52.

26 See above, chap. 1, pp. 17-18, chap. 3, pp. 94-95.

27 See above, chap. 3, pp. 89-90.

28 "Adam," l. 27, "The Apostacy," l. 58, "Walking," l. 13, "Consummation," l. 38.

29 It first appeared in *Centuries of Meditation* and may have been taken by Philip from that source directly rather than from the manuscript that supplied most of these poems. There are some significant verbal changes in the two versions—the effects of Philip's emendations.

30 See above, chap. 5, pp. 151-152.

31 See the discussion in Stewart, *Expanded Voice*, pp. 145-155.

32 See Wallace, "Structure of Meditation," pp. 79-89. These poems are printed together and in proper order in Ridler's edition, which I have used and quoted from in discussing this sequence. Margoliouth, concerned to display Philip's alterations, organizes his edition on comparative principles, printing together (where they exist) versions of the same poem in Dobell and the *Poems of Felicity*.

33 See Martz, *Paradise Within*, pp. 43-54. Martz's argument has particular reference to the prose *Centuries*.

34 See, e.g., "Innocence," l. 60: "I must becom a Child again."

35 "The Instruction," ll. 1-2; "Another," ll. 1-3.

36 "Nature," ll. 1-2; "Silence," ll. 1-2.

37 "Thoughts.I," ll. 1-2, 6-7, 51-54; "Thoughts.II," pt. 2, ll. 1-5.

38 Wallace, "Structure of Meditation," pp. 80-83.

39 Jordan, *Temple of Eternity*, pp. 28-29, 106.

40 See above, chap. 6, pp. 208-209.

41 "Innocence," ll. 47, 50, 52; "The Preparative," ll. 15-16, 36.

42 "The Improvement," ll. 23-24, 67-70.

43 "Dumnesse," ll. 57-67.

44 First published under the title, *A Serious and Pathetical Contemplation of the Mercies of God, in several most Devout and Sublime Thanksgivings for the same* (London, 1699). The work was published by the Reverend George Hicks, with an unsigned preface which Hicks asserted was written by the gentleman from whom he had the manuscript, but he may well have had both from Traherne's friend Susanna Hopton. The title was probably not Traherne's. The frontispiece portrays King David with his Psalter at the center, surrounded by the saints in heaven and the faithful on earth praising God, a picture which, whatever its provenance, locates the book accurately in the psalmic tradition.

45 Traherne quotes, or adapts, his psalm passages and other biblical passages from the AV.

46 See above, chap. 5, pp. 173-174.

47 "Thanksgivings for the Body," ll. 339-342.

48 Ll. 319-340, 430-465.

49 The few marginal notations supplied in the text identify only a small fraction of the biblical materials used, and were probably added rather at random by the editor.

## CHAPTER 12

1 Stanford, "Edward Taylor," in Everett Emerson, ed., *Major Writers of Early American Literature* (Madison, 1972), pp. 62-63; Martz, "Foreword," *Poems of Edward Taylor*, ed. Stanford, p. xiv.

2 Cf. "The Temper (I)," ll. 13-14, "Wilt thou meet arms with man, that thou dost stretch / A crumme of dust from heav'n to hell?"

3 Taylor's *Preparatory Meditations* are cited in my text by series, number, and line number. The line quoted from Taylor is not strictly a refrain, as it recurs only five times in the eleven stanzas, and in varying positions (ll. 2, 7, 19, 30, 43), but its unvarying repetition serves some of the functions of a refrain.

4 Martz cites these and several other examples ("Foreword," Stanford, p. xiv). Despite all these allusions and echoes, Herbert is not mentioned by name in any of the Taylor manuscripts, and *The Temple* is not known to have been in Taylor's library.

5 Compare "Brave rose, (alas!) where art thou! In the chair / Where thou didst lately so triumph and shine . . ." ("Church-rents and schisms," ll. 1-2) with "Dost thou sit Rose at Table Head" ("The Reflexion," l. 33).

6 See, e.g., Austin Warren, "Edward Taylor's Poetry: Colonial Baroque," *Kenyon Review*, 3 (1941), pp. 355-371; W. C. Brown, "Edward Taylor: An American 'Metaphysical,'" *AL*, 16 (1944), pp. 186-197; Herbert Blau, "Heaven's Sugar Cake: Theology and Imagery in the Poetry of Edward Taylor," *NEQ*, 26 (1953), 337-360.

7 Karl Keller, *Example of Edward Taylor*, pp. 163-188.

8 See, e.g., Roy Harvey Pearce, "Edward Taylor: The Poet as Puritan," *NEQ*, 23 (1950), pp. 31-46; Charles W. Mignon, "Edward Taylor's *Preparatory Meditations*: A Decorum of Imperfection," *PMLA*, 83 (1968), 1423-1428; Howard, "The World as Emblem," p. 384; Reed, "Edward Taylor's Poetry," p. 309-310. Mignon's discussion of Taylor's poetic strategies is illuminating, though his argument that Herbert and Taylor practice a very different poetics rooted in their respective "Anglican" and "Puritan" views of the relation between art and grace is, I think, misleading.

9 Kathleen Blake, "Edward Taylor's Protestant Poetic: Nontransubstantiating Metaphor," *AL*, 43 (1971), 1-24.

10 See above, chap. 1, pp. 13-20. See esp. New, *Anglican and Puritan*.

11 For a résumé of the dispute with Stoddard and its significance, see Grabo, "Introduction" to Taylor's *Treatise Concerning the Lord's Supper*," pp. ix-xlvii.

12 William J. Scheick (*The Will and the Word*) argues that Taylor thought poetic excellence would result from the regenerate will and the Spirit's aid (pp. 117-144), and Michael Reed ("Edward Taylor's Poetry," pp. 304-312) drew the corollary that Taylor's testimonies to his poetic ineptitude indicate his doubts as to his election. In my judgment Taylor does not make this equation: for him, regeneration is indeed necessary to acceptable praise, praise which God will himself produce and find sweet, but artful praise consonant with the divine subject is always beyond the human artist. Taylor never supposes that bad poetry is a sign of unregeneracy, though because he is elect he longs to be able to produce the worthy praises Christ deserves from him.

13 *Preparatory Meditations*, I.43, l. 42.

14 See above, chaps. 9 and 10, pp. 284-285/319-321.

15 *God's Determinations touching his Elect: and the Elects Combat in their Conversion, and Coming up to God in Christ together with the Comfortable Effects thereof*, in Stanford, pp. 385-458.

16 "The Joy of Church Fellowship rightly attended," l. 4.

17 Stanford's edition includes the two series of *Preparatory Meditations* and *Gods Determinations* complete, along with eleven miscellaneous poems. Texts of other miscellaneous poems are published in Stanford, "The Earliest Poems of Edward Taylor," *AL*, 32 (1960), 136-151. Taylor's very long and largely derivative "Metrical History of Christianity" has not been published in its entirety; the MS. is in the Redwood Library, Newport, R.I.

18 See above, chap. 6, p. 212.

19 Though Taylor attempts the high style in the Hooker elegy, he punctuates it, characteristically, with several colloquial figures and puns, the most outrageous being wordplays on Hooker's name as the embodiment of his gospel office as fisher of men:

> Shall angling cease? And no more fish be took
> That thou callst home thy Hooker with his Hook?
> Lord, spare the flock: uphold the fold from falling.
> Send out another Hooker of this Calling. (ll. 195-198)

20 See above, chap. 6, n. 122.

21 Cf. especially the opening lines of the Herbert poem: "Meeting with Time, Slack thing, said I, / Thy sithe is dull; whet it for shame."

22 Taylor's single psalm quotation of any length (from Psalm 24:7) occurs in a description of angelic song on the occasion of Christ's ascension (I.20, ll. 27-30):

> Sing Praise, sing Praise, sing Praise, sing Praises out,
> Unto our King sing praise seraphickwise.
> Lift up your Heads ye lasting Doore they sing
> And let the King of Glory Enter in.

23 See above, chap. 5, pp. 152-154.

24 Grabo, "Introduction," *Christographia*, pp. xi-xliv. For a counter-argument see Davis, "Edward Taylor's Occasional Meditations," pp. 17-29. And see the discussion above, chap. 5, p. 176, and n. 135.

25 The significant change occurs in II.47. The companion sermon (VI) takes as text Col. 1:19: "For it pleased the Father, that in him should all fulness dwell"; the poem takes the text heading from John 5:26, "The Son hath life in himselfe." The change highlights the concern of the poems with a key trope or term (in this case the term "life" is not explicit in the sermon text though it is dealt with in the sermon as an aspect of "fulness"). But since Taylor obviously thinks of the poems as elaborating key figures and terms, he chooses a text that will supply a significant term. The other changes— in the order of a few words or phrases—do not seem very significant, though sometimes they throw the dominant figure or trope into greater prominence.

26 The newly discovered Nebraska sermons will afford a further test of the way in which the parallel poetic meditations are conceived. See above, chap. 5, p. 136, and n. 136.

27 Cf. "The Temper (II)," ll. 1-2: "It cannot be. Where is that mightie joy / Which just now took up all my heart?"

28 As Norman S. Grabo points out (*Edward Taylor* [New York, 1961], pp. 139-142), Taylor makes use of some rather intricate devices of verbal repetition based upon ploce and polyptoton. Only one other time (in II.95) does he use a refrain-like structure, very reminiscent of Donne's punning refrain in the "Hymne to God the Father" in its fundamental idea. Stanzas 5, 6, and 7 begin with the phrase "But thats not all"; and the seventh stanza concludes the series with the words, "that's but all." These stanzas would have an enhanced lyric quality were they detached from the longer meditation in which they are embedded.

29 Taylor, *Treatise*, p. 185. See discussion above, chap. 5, pp. 176-177.

30 William R. Epperson, "The Meditative Structure of Edward Taylor's 'Preparatory Meditations,'" Diss. Kansas 1965.

31 *Christographia*, ed. Grabo, p. 273.

32 The poem invites comparison with Herbert's "A Rose," in which also a frame allegory of temptation by the world encloses (as answer to the

temptation) an analysis of the rose's properties. Herbert's rose, however, is itself the emblem of worldly pleasure and beauty, not the rose of Sharon.

33 For a suggestive discussion of Taylor's techniques of meiosis and ineffective amplification as signs of a fallen rhetoric, see Mignon, "Taylor's *Preparatory Meditations*: A Decorum of Imperfection," pp. 1423-1428.

34 See above, chap. 6, p. 211.

35 Interestingly enough, in the sequence on the words of institution of the Sacrament (II.102-II.111) this technique is not much in evidence; more prominent is a plain-style explication of and commentary on the terms.

36 Karl Keller (*Edward Taylor*, pp. 191-211) has discussed in great detail Taylor's imagery of filth and disease. But the imagery is not so pervasively excremental as Keller's discussion suggests, nor is its counterpoint specifically erotic—though these elements contribute to the larger antithesis Taylor's imagery defines. Keller rightly calls attention to the pervasiveness of scatological and related imagery among the reformers from Luther forward, to describe the loathsome state of fallen man.

37 "Prologue"; I.9, l. 32; I.10; I.24, l. 14; I.26, ll. 7-8; I.46, l. 53; II.33, l. 15; II.37, l. 6

38 I.2, l. 27; I.5; I.7; I.28, ll. 9, 21; II.50; II.69; II.78.

39 Keller, *Example of Edward Taylor*, pp. 163-188.

40 My emphasis.

41 *Christographia*, ed. Grabo, pp. 269, 276-277.

42 Samuel Mather, *Figures or Types of the Old Testament*. For discussion of the centrality of Mather's compendium in colonial America see Mason I. Lowance, Jr., "Introduction" to the reprint of Mather's second (1705) edition (New York and London, 1969), pp. v-xxv. Also see Robert E. Reiter, "Poetry and Doctrine in Edward Taylor's *Preparatory Meditations*, Series II, 1-30," in *Typology and Early American Literature*, ed. Bercovitch, pp. 163-174.

43 Keller, " 'The World Slickt Up in Types,' " in *Typology and Early American Literature*, ed. Bercovitch, pp. 175-190; see above, chap. 4, pp. 131-136.

44 Taylor, *Christographia*, p. 277.

45 Cf. Herbert's treatment of this theme in "Josephs coat," with the same emphasis upon the application of type and antitype to the speaker's emotional state.

46 See also II.22 on 1 Cor. 5:7: "Christ our Passover is sacrificed for us."

47 See, e.g., Ursula Brumm, *American Thought and Religious Typology*, trans. J. Hoaglund (New Brunswick, 1970), pp. 56-85; Keller "Taylor as a Version of Emerson," *Typology and Early American Literature*, ed. Bercovitch, pp. 175-190.

48 *Christographia*, p. 287.

49 See above, chap. 6, pp. 209-212.

50 Grabo, *Edward Taylor*, pp. 154-159.

51 Howard, "The World as Emblem," p. 384.

52 Grabo, *Edward Taylor*, p. 159.

53 See, e.g., Stanford, "Edward Taylor," in *Major Writers of Early American Literature*, ed. Emerson.

54 See above, chap. 2, pp. 62-64. See also Karen E. Rowe, "Sacred or Profane?: Edward Taylor's Meditations on Canticles," *MP*, 72 (1974-75), 123-138, for a thoroughly documented demonstration that Taylor's poems on Canticles texts stand squarely in the tradition of Puritan exegesis of that allegorical book.

55 II.130, ll. 26, 29; II.131, l. 38.

56 See above, chap. 7, p. 228.

57 II.141, l. 14; II.123[B], ll. 11-14.

58 This is the last completed poem; those following are fragmentary.

59 See the essays in Miner, ed., *Literary Uses of Typology*.


## Afterword

1 Aylett, *Divine and Moral Speculations*; Breton, *An Excellent Poeme, upon the longing of a Blessed Heart* (London, 1601); Breton, *A Solomne Passion of the Soules Love* (London, 1623); Drummond, *Flowres of Sion* (London, 1623); Fane, *Otia Sacra* (London, 1648); Greville (Lord Brooke), Sonnets 85-109 of *Caelica*, in *Certaine Learned and Elegant Workes* (London, 1633); John Hall, *The Second Booke of Divine Poems*, with *Poems* (Cambridge, 1646); Harvey, *The Synagogue, or, The Shadow of the Temple*; Francis Quarles, *Divine Fancies*; John Quarles, "Divine Meditations," with *Fons Lachrymarum* (London, 1648); Sylvester, *Panthea: or Divine Wishes and Meditations* (London, 1630); Wither, *Hymns and Songs of the Church*.

2 Crashaw, *Steps to the Temple* (London, 1646; 1648); Crashaw, *Carmen Deo Nostro*; Southwell, *Mœoniæ. Or, Certaine excellent Poems and Spirituall Hymnes* (London, 1595); Southwell, *S. Peters Complaynt*; Alabaster, *Sonnets*, ed. G. M. Story and Helen Gardner (Oxford, 1959); Constable, *Poems*, ed. Joan Grundy (Liverpool, 1960). See also the collection, *Recusant Poets*, ed. Louise Imogen Guiney (London and New York, 1938).

3 Such a comparison would build upon and extend Terence C. Cave's very suggestive study, *Devotional Poetry in France, 1570-1613*.

4 Morris, *The Religious Sublime*; Abrams, *Natural Supernaturalism*.

# Index

Most works are indexed under their authors or probable authors; short titles are used for many works. References to notes are given in parentheses following the page on which the note appears.

*Library of Congress Cataloging in Publication Data*

Lewalski, Barbara Kiefer, 1931-
    Protestant poetics and the seventeenth-century
religious lyric.

    Includes bibliographical references and index.
    1.   English poetry—17th century—History and
criticism.   2.   Christian poetry, English—History and
criticism.   3.   Protestantism in literature.
4.   Reformation—England.   I.   Title.
PR545.R4L48      821'.4'0931      78-70305
ISBN 0-691-06395-8
ISBN 0-691-01415-9 (pbk.)